New Voyages to Carolina

New Voyages to Carolina
Reinterpreting North Carolina History

EDITED BY Larry E. Tise and Jeffrey J. Crow

The University of North Carolina Press   Chapel Hill

This book was published with the assistance of the Blythe Family Fund of the University of North Carolina Press and grants from Martin H. Brinkley and James W. Clark Jr. / North Caroliniana Society and William S. Price Jr.

© 2017 The University of North Carolina Press
All rights reserved
Manufactured in the United States of America
Set in Miller by Tseng Information Systems, Inc.
The University of North Carolina Press has been a member of the Green Press Initiative since 2003.

Cover illustration: A manuscript field map of the Carolina coast sketched by Christoph von Graffenreid (1661–1743), founder of New Bern, in 1710. Reproduced with permission from Burgerbibliothek Bern Mss. Mül.466.ma.

Library of Congress Cataloging-in-Publication Data
Names: Crow, Jeffrey J., author, editor. | Tise, Larry E., author, editor.
Title: New voyages to Carolina : reinterpreting North Carolina history / edited by Larry E. Tise and Jeffrey J. Crow.
Description: Chapel Hill : The University of North Carolina Press, [2017] | Includes bibliographical references and index.
Identifiers: LCCN 2017013225| ISBN 9781469634586 (cloth : alk. paper) | ISBN 9781469634593 (pbk : alk. paper) | ISBN 9781469634609 (ebook)
Subjects: LCSH: North Carolina—Historiography. | North Carolina—History.
Classification: LCC F253.2 .N49 2017 | DDC 975.6—dc23
LC record available at https://lccn.loc.gov/2017013225

Contents

Preface, ix

Introduction, 1
   Larry E. Tise and Jeffrey J. Crow

An Uncompromising Environment: North Carolina's "Land of Water" Coastal System, 14
   Stanley R. Riggs and Dorothea V. Ames

Voyages to Carolina: Europeans in the Indians' Old World, 41
   Michael Leroy Oberg and David Moore

Intercolonial Conflict and Cooperation during the Tuscarora War, 60
   Stephen Feeley

The Conundrum of Unfree Labor, 85
   Bradford J. Wood and Larry E. Tise

Land Tenure as Regulator Grievance and Revolutionary Tool, 110
   Carole Watterson Troxler

Evangelical Geographies of North Carolina, 144
   Charles F. Irons

Money in the Bank: African American Women, Finance, and Freedom in New Bern, North Carolina, 1868–1874, 166
   Karin Zipf

Educational Capital and Human Flourishing: North Carolina's Public Schools and Universities, 1865–2015, 194
   Glenda Elizabeth Gilmore

Linthead Stomp: Carolina Cotton Mill Hands and the Modern Origins of Hillbilly Music, 217
   Patrick Huber

Tar Heel Politics in the Twentieth Century: The Rise and Fall of the Progressive Plutocracy, 241
   Karl E. Campbell

Defying *Brown*, Defying Pearsall: African Americans and the Struggle for Public School Integration in North Carolina, 1954–1971, 269
  Jerry Gershenhorn

It's Easier to Pick a Yankee Dollar than a Pound of Cotton: Tourism and North Carolina History, 290
  Richard D. Starnes

Chasing Smokestacks: Lessons and Legacies, 316
  James C. Cobb

Failing to Excite: The Dixie Dynamo in the Global Economy, 332
  Peter A. Coclanis

A New Description of North Carolina, 354
  Larry E. Tise and Jeffrey J. Crow

About the Editors and Contributors, 391

Index, 395

Figures and Tables

FIGURES

1.1 A generalized geologic map of the North Carolina Coastal Plain, 17

1.2 Maps showing the location of the ocean shoreline at different time points, 21

1.3 Images showing the impact of hurricanes on the North Carolina coast, 23

1.4 Historic maps of the Roanoke Island coastal area, 28

1.5 Aerial photographs of the Nags Head village, 1932 and 1999, 32

1.6 Images showing the changing coastline of South Nags Head, 34

1.7 Topographic map of North Carolina's "Land of Water," 36

2.1 Indian towns visited by Juan Pardo's second expedition in 1567–68, 43

3.1 Map of South Carolina military campaigns against the Tuscaroras, 1711–15, 62

4.1 U.S. Census map, 1860, showing percentage of slave inhabitants in every county in the South, 96

5.1 Plan of the camp and Battle of Alamance culminating the War of the Regulation, 1771, 112

6.1 Map of ethnic settlement patterns in North Carolina, c. 1800, 155

6.2 Map of various churches in North Carolina, c. 1800, 155

7.1 Headquarters of Vincent Collyer, superintendent of the poor, in New Bern, 1862, 169

7.2 Recorded complexions of female depositors to Freedman's Savings and Trust, New Bern branch, 1869–1874, 173

7.3 Recorded gender and marital status of depositors to Freedman's Savings and Trust, New Bern branch, 182

7.4 Recorded marital status and occupations of nonwhite female depositors to Freedman's Savings and Trust, New Bern branch, 184

7.5 Recorded occupations of nonwhite female depositors from the countryside to Freedman's Savings and Trust, New Bern branch, 186

8.1 Idealized campus for a community Rosenwald school, 1924, 205

8.2 Drawings of one- and two-teacher Rosenwald schools, 1924, 205

8.3 Architectural drawing of the east and west elevations, Simon G. Atkins High School, 1929, 210

8.4 Architectural drawing of the basement plan, Simon G. Atkins High School, 1929, 211

9.1 Charlie Poole and the North Carolina Ramblers, 1927, 223

10.1 Groundbreaking for the Hanes Research Laboratory, Research Triangle Park, 1960, 257

11.1 Political cartoon about the Pearsall Plan, c. 1956, 273

12.1 President Franklin D. Roosevelt en route to the opening performance of *The Lost Colony*, 1937, 299

13.1 Political cartoon of "Hodges Raiders," c. late 1950s, 320

14.1 Map of manufacturing-plant closings in North Carolina, 2003–4, 342

15.1 William Churton map of the Granville District, 1768, 368

15.2 Collier Cobb map of North Carolina, 1880, 378

TABLES

1.1 Drainage history of North Carolina's Coastal Plain pocosins: Three centuries of swampland development, 30

7.1 Recorded gender of depositors to Freedman's Savings and Trust Company, New Bern branch, 167

7.2 Recorded occupations of nonwhite female depositors to Freedman's Savings and Trust Company, New Bern branch, 180

7.3 Recorded occupations of nonwhite female New Bern residents who were depositors to Freedman's Savings and Trust Company, New Bern branch, 1869–1874, 181

9.1 North Carolina mill hands who made hillbilly music recordings, by hometown, 1925–1942, 220

Preface

The inception of the book began in 2010 as a valedictory testimony of three historians who had served as directors of the then Division of Archives and History in the North Carolina Department of Cultural Resources for nearly four decades: Larry E. Tise (1975–81), William S. Price Jr. (1981–95), and Jeffrey J. Crow (1995–2012). Over the years they had collaborated on numerous conferences and symposiums charting North Carolina's vast history. In 1979 Crow and Tise coedited essays from one of those conferences titled *Writing North Carolina History* (University of North Carolina Press). That book provided the first comprehensive view of North Carolina's historical literature. In the intervening years, however, the growth and expansion of works on the state's history have gone far beyond the benchmark established in 1979. The three colleagues believed it was time for a new assessment that reflected the diverse studies appearing annually in books, journals, and increasingly on the Internet.

One symposium could not encompass the broad new historical literature that has appeared since the 1970s. The three collaborators determined to hold four conferences across the state to attract as many participants as possible. With a small planning grant from the North Carolina Humanities Council, the three collaborators invited six other scholars of North Carolina history to meet in the fall of 2010 and to help identify principal themes and subjects for consideration.

The historical community in North Carolina and across the nation responded enthusiastically to the plans for the conferences. Many historians living and working outside the state had used North Carolina's extraordinary research facilities to research and write books, articles, and essays that focused on North Carolina's experience as the locus for their explorations. Despite limited budgets, six state universities stepped forward to host and underwrite the conferences. The inaugural conference, titled "The First North Carolina," took place at East Carolina University in February 2012. The second conference, titled "The Old North State," was held on the campuses of the University of North Carolina at Chapel Hill and North Carolina Central University in October 2012. The University of North Carolina at Asheville and Western Carolina University jointly hosted the third conference, titled "The Cultural Roots of North Carolina," which met in Asheville in November 2012. The fourth and final conference, "The Tar Heel State," received a warm welcome from the University of North Carolina at Greensboro in February–March 2013. In the end, forty-five scholars made presentations at the four conferences. In addition, the Historical Society of North Carolina, the North Carolina Literary and Historical Association, and the then Office of Archives and History in the North Carolina Department of Cultural Resources provided critical financial and logistical support for the conferences.

From the beginning the three organizers planned to produce a book that would grow out of the numerous presentations. But the organizers were also determined that the eventual book would in no way have the characteristics of published proceedings. Rather, they hoped to identify topics and themes that emerged from conference deliberations that might become components of a new narrative of North Carolina's history. Fortunately the conferences were filled with persuasive presentations and lively discussions, proving that the North Carolina story was ripe for a thorough retelling.

Narrowing the many stimulating ideas that the conferences produced and organizing them into a manageable set of essays proved challenging. All who attended the conferences recognized that the vibrant scholarship of the past four decades offered an opportunity to rethink North Carolina history, to develop new themes and tropes, to depart from past verities, and to chart an outline for a new narrative history. As with most history written before the 1970s, North Carolina history texts and story lines reflected a Eurocentric point of view, with an emphasis on white men, politics, and wars. The conferences showed that North Carolina's past has been shaped heavily by its unique environment and geography, its rich mixture of native and immigrant cultures, its formative role in establishing an industrial base in the New South, and its contradictory images as either a conservative or a "progressive" state.

In deciding which presenters to invite to submit essays, the three organizers considered several critical questions. Which presentations addressed fundamental issues that help to define the trajectory of North Carolina history? Which presentations offered new interpretations or new information encompassing entire periods that were missing from earlier histories? Which presentations brought forth important topics, themes, or perspectives that overturned previous assumptions and arguments? The organizers had a rich bounty from which to choose. After the organizers extended invitations, sixteen scholars ultimately submitted fourteen essays. In two instances, the organizers asked two scholars to collaborate because their topics and interpretations harmonized so closely. Crow and Tise assumed the editorship of this volume.

The resulting essays offer chronological coverage fairly well—from prehistory to the global economy of the twenty-first century. Of course, not every topic that received consideration in the four conferences could be included in the book. Nor could such landmarks as the American Revolution, the sectional crisis, the Civil War, and woman's suffrage, to name a few, appear in discrete essays. Yet taken as a whole, the essays offer an impressive survey of the state's history in both scope and depth. Above all, they indicate new ways to think about North Carolina's past, ways that inevitably should emerge in a new narrative history.

The editors owe a debt of gratitude to many people who made the four conferences and this volume possible. In particular we would like to thank Dean Alan White of the Thomas Harriot College of Arts and Sciences at East Carolina University; Harry L. Watson and Robert G. Anthony Jr. of the University of North Carolina at Chapel Hill; Freddie Parker of North Carolina Central University; Richard D. Starnes of Western Carolina University; Dan Pierce of the University of North Carolina at Asheville; and Charles C. Bolton of the University of North Carolina at Greensboro. In the Department of Cultural Resources Michael E. Hill was always a source of dependable help and assistance. To David Perry (now retired) and Mark Simpson-Vos of the University of North Carolina Press we extend our thanks for believing in this project over a long period of gestation. Although one of our original organizers and one of our closest colleagues, Bill Price, decided to rest on his laurels after we finished our conferences and selected the topics for the essays contained in this book, we are grateful for the many good questions he asked in the beginning and for pointing out a number of dangerous shoals as we set out on this voyage. After the book was accepted for publication, Bill also generously provided a subvention to reduce the costs of production for the University of North Carolina Press. Additionally, the North Caroliniana Society contributed a second subvention to support the book's publication. In particular we wish to thank the society's president, James W. Clark Jr., and secretary-treasurer Martin H. Brinkley for their unstinting support.

In our quest for compelling illustrations, we had the invaluable assistance of colleagues, archivists, and librarians. Catherine Bishir and Michael Southern, who wrote a three-volume architectural history of North Carolina, alerted us to the existence of rare architectural drawings of a Rosenwald school in Winston-Salem. In the Special Collections of the North Carolina State University Libraries, Jennifer Baker helped us find and reproduce those fragile, oversize drawings. At the North Carolina State Archives we had the expert assistance of archivists Kim Andersen, Ian Dunn, Vann Evans,

Donna Kelly, and Allison Thurman. At the North Carolina Collection at the University of North Carolina at Chapel Hill, Jason Tomberlin and Matthew Turi supplied two key illustrations. To all we offer our sincere thanks.

Two further special groups of people are due especial recognition. To the many historians and audiences who participated in our four conferences—making them living and breathing events—we thank them for their lively participation and penetrating questions. To our families we offer heartfelt appreciation for support of our long quest to preserve, interpret, and share North Carolina's history. We could not have made the journey without you.

Larry E. Tise
Jeffrey J. Crow
September 2016

New Voyages to Carolina

INTRODUCTION

Larry E. Tise and Jeffrey J. Crow

In 1709 John Lawson—naturalist, surveyor general, and explorer—published *A New Voyage to Carolina* (London). Lawson's book provided a meticulous account of his 550-mile, 57-day journey through the backcountry of what would eventually become the states of both South Carolina and North Carolina. Beginning in the port city of Charles Town in December 1700, Lawson and nine other adventurers traveled northwestward toward present-day Charlotte, North Carolina. From there he explored the Piedmont basins of the Catawba and Yadkin Rivers before turning eastward toward present-day Bath, arriving there late in February 1701. Along the way Lawson recorded with remarkable detail the flora, fauna, topography, and Native Americans he encountered. His book became a classic, unsurpassed in its depiction of the Carolina landscape before European settlers ventured forth from the coastal areas to occupy territories that had been Indian homelands for thousands of years.

This collection of essays takes its title from Lawson's legendary work. The essays are elaborations of approximately one-fourth of the total number of presentations made at four conferences held on five university campuses across North Carolina. In our judgment, these particular authors offered perspectives that showed promise for articulating important elements of a new narrative of North Carolina history. As editors we did not establish a template for the resulting essays but encouraged the authors to expand their perspectives in the manner that seemed most appropriate to the themes they were developing. Thus, the essays presented here are those that seemed most fertile in establishing discrete and innovative approaches to North Carolina history.

Our principal aim was to identify topics in North Carolina history that had shown major advances in research and writing in the past twenty-five years but had not penetrated North Carolina's basic historical narrative. The determining guideline for inclusion among the resulting essays was not that a particular essay best filled in all topics or periods of North Carolina's past but, rather, that it laid out a scheme for understanding some fundamental aspect of North Carolina history.

We deliberately spread our nets wide in seeking scholars, including the interdisciplinary perspectives of geologists and archaeologists. We noticed that many scholars have used North Carolina as a locus for investigating regional and national topics without reference to how such new research might fit into a broader interpretation of the state's history. We challenged the scholars to pursue their respective topics with an eye toward how they might encourage other historians to rethink North Carolina's past, and we sought fresh ideas, not a refutation or an incremental refocusing on past ideas. Consequently, readers will find in this collection great diversity and a disparity in methodology, style, and focus.

When we launched this enterprise, the idea of producing a book of historiographical essays, such as we did in *Writing North Carolina History* four decades ago, was not our intent.[1] The earlier work was one primarily of interest to other scholars. It provided broad chronological coverage of the state's history and surveyed the state's vast historical literature. *Writing North Carolina History* generated new research, but it did not stimulate new story lines for the North Carolina narrative. With this volume we hope to spark discussion and debate on what should be the key elements in devising a provocative and lively narrative of North Carolina history. Traditional guideposts such as wars, historic periods, political movements, and economic crises are largely absent in this volume. Instead these essays examine topics that have engaged historians in recent decades and pose new questions about African Americans, Indians, women, the impact of North Carolina's unusual environment, and its powerful legacies—cultural, economic, and political. The volume should be used alongside existing North Carolina texts, not necessarily supplant them. Our hope is that historians, academics, and history teachers will use these essays to inspire a new era of thinking about the state's past.

■ The historical literature on North Carolina is extensive. Its roots can be traced to the early nineteenth century when the state's first historians gloried in the conquest of European settlement and cherished the distinctive role of North Carolina in the founding of the nation. The framework for narrative histories of the state, however, emerged in the post–Civil War era. That framework, which reached its apogee before the Second World War, has remained largely static for more than a century. Highly detailed and lengthy multivolume histories by such historians as Samuel A. Ashe; Robert D. W. Connor, William K. Boyd, and J. G. de Roulhac Hamilton; and Archibald

Henderson dominated the first half of the twentieth century. These works focused heavily on the great men of agriculture, business, industry, and law who transformed North Carolina into a thriving industrial economy by the first decades of the twentieth century.[2] They also exhibited certain biases. Topics such as race, slavery, sectional conflict, and political insurgency did not receive sympathetic treatment, if at all. Women and Indians played minor roles. Hamilton's unbridled prejudice against blacks, Republicans, and Reconstruction can still astonish, and Connor plainly endorsed the white supremacy campaigns that led to Democratic hegemony at the turn of the twentieth century.

By the middle of the twentieth century a new style of history writing emerged, one that concentrated on political chronology as the framework for telling the state's history. Three admired historians of political narrative laid out North Carolina's story in a manner that remained the norm until the last decade of the twentieth century. Hugh T. Lefler and Albert Ray Newsome's *North Carolina: The History of a Southern State*, first published in 1954 and followed by newer editions in 1963 and 1973, endures as a staple of North Carolina historiography.[3] The prolific William S. Powell followed with *North Carolina through Four Centuries* in 1989.[4] After more than a quarter century it remains the chief narrative history of the state. All of these works showed in-depth research and an appreciation of North Carolina's unique characteristics. Just as many other histories of that time, they concentrated on chronology, politics, institutions, wars, great white men, and a Whiggish interpretation that viewed history as a march of progress.

Since the 1970s the historical landscape has changed considerably. New generations of historians have addressed subjects too long ignored or neglected. In the last decade both Milton Ready and William A. Link have written nuanced histories of North Carolina, aimed at the college textbook market, that reflect modern historians' interpretations. Yet, while a new paradigm has emerged, a synthesis on the scale of Lefler and Newsome or Powell remains to be written. Historians have begun to look at race, class, and gender as new tools for deconstructing the past. Where once white, male privilege was assumed, historians now ask more skeptical, incisive questions. Old assumptions about the European age of exploration, colonial penetration of the backcountry, conditions of servitude for whites, blacks, and children, and the changing status of women have all received revisionist attention. Intense interest in the Populist-Republican fusion experiment in the 1890s, a biracial political coalition, has yet to wane. Twentieth-century North Carolina history, once considered a wasteland, is more vital than ever.[5]

The new paradigm emphasizes social history, class conflict, gender-based studies, the African American experience (including civil rights), economic development, and working-class struggles. Modern historians do not eschew political history—they place it in broader contexts of region, nation, culture, and changing demographics. They also ask hard questions about the political penchants of North Carolinians and the meaning of such ideas as progressivism in a state with persistent strains of both populism and conservative values. For example, the Great Migration of blacks from their southern homeland to the Northeast, Midwest, and West between the First World War and the 1960s has reversed, with more blacks moving to the South than leaving it. The economic rise of the Sunbelt after the Second World War has brought millions of Northerners to the South and changed electoral dynamics. The social makeup of North Carolina has changed probably more in the last 40 years than in the previous 140 years. North Carolina has one of the fastest-growing Hispanic populations in the nation. The modern histories reflect those changes as historians examine new topics that earlier generations could not have conceived or else ignored.[6]

■ The essays in this collection broadly correspond to one or more of the themes addressed by the four conferences: explorations and exploitations; North Carolina's character as molded by social, political, and religious forces; North Carolina's political economy and reputation as the most progressive southern state; and North Carolina's rich cultural legacy. No one essay or collection of essays can provide comprehensive coverage of such broad subjects, but these essays open new avenues for exploring such questions and offer new directions for interpreting the state's history.

Careful readers will note persistent themes that link the essays. Those themes reflect a collective combination of values, ideas, and shared verities. Readers may find that continuities, rather than disjunctions, characterize the arc of North Carolina's history. Land, habitation, and immigration, for example, reveal patterns that appear and reappear in the essays. Europeans were but the latest addition to the peoples who had long existed on the soil that became North Carolina. Native Indians had lived on the land for thousands of years. The land, of course, became contested territory. Europeans built their settlements on the same sites as preexisting Indian villages. They followed the same paths and byways that had long supported a lively Indian culture. In time war, disease, and removal greatly reduced the Indian population, as whites occupied coastal regions and then poured into the backcountry. Control of the land shifted with changing political regimes—from lords proprietors to royal governors to a revolutionary government. An age-old question then emerged: with home rule, who would rule at home? As the Revolution played out, it became clear that the colonial elite, not the Regulators who opposed them, would control the destiny of the new state and nation.

With immigration came a diverse population. Despite a national program of forced removal, Indians never entirely disappeared. North Carolina still possesses the largest Indian population east of the Mississippi River. Eighteenth-century North Carolina resembled a patchwork quilt of ethnicities: English, Scots, Scots-Irish, Germans, Swiss, and Africans. North Carolina's racial and ethnic makeup remained remarkably unchanged until the dramatic growth of a Hispanic population in the late twentieth century.

All came seeking economic opportunity, except for Africans who arrived in chains. Despite its seeming isolation and provincialism, North Carolina has always been part of a global economy. Even prehistoric Indians traded with tribes east of the Mississippi River and on the shores of the Great Lakes. Europeans coveted animal skins and plant cultures, which in time gave way to commercial crops such as naval stores, tobacco, and cotton. Industry arose when North Carolina's nonnavigable rivers were converted into interlocking chains of hydroelectric-generating dams and stations. By using its rivers to produce cheap electricity and its surplus farm populations to supply low-cost labor, North Carolina was able to attract the capital to make the state a competitive player in textile manufacturing and in the fabrication of wood and aluminum products.

To work the land and run the machinery North Carolina depended on cheap labor. Small planters, indentures, and then Indian and African slavery defined the colony's earliest labor system. But concentrated landholdings, sharecropping, tenancy, and nonunion workers emerged from the economic crisis of the Civil War. Plantation culture took root in the industrial village. Much as slaveholders, mill owners supervised not just the workers' labor but also their housing, stores, churches, and recreation. Changes in the global economy in the twenty-first century have undermined this nexus of industry, forcing North Carolina to seek new ways of deploying its ample natural, human, and technical resources.

Politics and citizenship offer other persistent themes in this volume. North Carolina has always nurtured a dissenting tradition, dating back to the absentee governance of the original lords proprietors. Antislavery Quakers and pacifist Moravians, Regulators, loyalists, insurgent slaves, unionists, populists, and civil rights demonstrators have challenged the political establishment generation after generation. Likewise, tension has existed between persisting antipathies toward government (first articulated by the iconic curmudgeon Nathaniel Macon) and the advocates of a proactive government (exemplified by the paragon of public works Archibald DeBow Murphey). More often than not, North Carolina government has come to the aid of planters and businessmen with the construction of the North Carolina Railroad, internal improvements in canals, rivers, and harbors, lucrative tax incentives, and the untrammeled exploitation of the environment, such as the timber industry both in the mountains and along the coast.

That tension continues to today, as does the issue of what constitutes citizenship and who can vote. Efforts to limit voting date back to the earliest colonial days. First property and gender restricted voting rights and then, after 1835, race. That year the constitutional convention disfranchised free blacks and effectively all people of color, including Indians. Throughout North Carolina's history, a long habit of paternalism has circumscribed women's rights and underpinned the state's political culture. Slaveholders dominated antebellum politics and maintained a high barrier based on property to limit common whites from voting for state senators. After a brief experiment in democracy during Reconstruction with the admission of male African Americans to the electorate, a reinvigorated white elite centralized power in their hands and in time disfranchised blacks all over again in 1900. Even the debate on woman's suffrage in 1920 focused on a lingering white fear of enfranchising black women. Rulers want a safe and predictable electorate, and before the Second Reconstruction of the 1960s that meant a white man's government.

Patterns of diversity also characterize North Carolina's cultural life. Geography, race, region, and religion have influenced the state's culture in conspicuous ways. Hillbilly music sprang up among textile workers in the Piedmont, whereas folk music in Appalachia reflected Celtic traditions brought from the Old World. Menhaden fishermen on the coast sang work songs based on African time signatures. North Carolina's literary traditions likewise show a wide range of styles and subjects, from symphonic dramas about the story of Raleigh's Lost Colony to the novels and short stories that seek to depict the "real" people and their home places in the high country.

North Carolina's rich religious tradition defined cultural norms in other ways. Quakers, Baptists, Presbyterians, Moravians, and Methodists, far from provincial, maintained national, even international ties with coreligionists. Catholicism and Judaism, virtually unknown in the antebellum era, have grown sizably in the latter part of the twentieth century, especially with migrations from Latin America and the North. Religions also helped fill an educational void. State support for primary education has always been parsimonious. Education has been limited and mostly segregated except for a brief period in the 1970s and 1980s. Various denominations established colleges to train teachers and preachers. Even the University of North Carolina had significant Presbyterian influences in its earliest years.

Finally, readers will want to consider what engenders North Carolina's identity and spirit. Despite ending in failure, is the Lost Colony North Carolina's genesis story? It represented both a dynastic effort to extend a European empire to the New World and a cultural invasion that threatened Native Americans' way of life. How did those inherent conflicts become part of North Carolina's genesis story, too long overlooked and misunderstood? What other colony can claim John White's drawings, Thomas Harriot's scientific studies of the New World, and John Lawson's unsurpassed portrayal of a colony on the threshold of explosive growth and change? Therein, perhaps, lie North Carolina's identity and spirit.

■ Turning to the first three essays, one can see a radical new departure in interpreting North Carolina's colonial beginnings. The traditional narrative presents a triumphalist vision of English attempts to plant a permanent settlement on the Outer Banks in the 1580s. The Lost Colony symbolizes the fragile hold Europeans had on the New World. Largely ignored have been the Spanish who explored the backcountry nearly a half century earlier. Native Americans, portrayed as either noble or treacherous, likewise appear passive in older accounts. The influence of geography and the environment similarly receives minimal attention.

Stanley R. Riggs and Dorothea V. Ames present a geologic and environmental examination of North Carolina's "Land of Water." When the first English explorers arrived in the 1580s, they had no notion of the dynamic environment that they encountered. Much of coastal North Carolina is subject to the rhythms of wind and water, periodically flooding lowlands as far west as one hundred miles. The Outer Banks in particular has changed dramatically over the millennia, with inlets opening and closing, and will continue to do so as climate change causes the oceans to rise and long-known configurations of barrier islands and estuary coasts to melt away. The work of Riggs and Ames shows just how tenuous settlement was for colonizers who hugged the coast.

Of course, geography and the environment were not the only reasons that European settlement proceeded so slowly in North Carolina before the eighteenth century. Native Americans initially impeded westward movement. Indeed, as Michael Leroy Oberg and David Moore demonstrate, the first European explorers survived only at the sufferance of the Indians among whom they settled. First at Fort San Juan in the foothills of the Blue Ridge Mountains in the 1560s and then at Roanoke Island in the 1580s, Native

Americans extended hospitality to the Spanish and English, respectively, as long as it suited the hosts' purposes. When the Europeans became too demanding, aggressive, and violent, the outraged Indians destroyed the settlements. Similarly, the Tuscarora Indians of the inner coastal plain blocked colonial expansion to the west for more than fifty years. The Tuscaroras controlled trade between European settlers along the coast and Native American tribes farther inland. When European encroachments on Indian lands, the enslavement of Indians, and dishonest trade practices threatened the Tuscaroras' hegemony, they struck. The Tuscarora War (1711–13), Stephen Feeley argues, involved more than just one colony. North Carolina bore the brunt of the war, but the conflict revealed different policies and strategies for dealing with Indians among colonies from South Carolina to New York. The war also marked the demise of Indian strength east of the Appalachian mountain chain.

The development of the social and economic institutions in North Carolina before the Civil War in many respects followed that of other southern colonies and states. Yet North Carolina acquired certain distinctive characteristics, too. From its earliest colonial days North Carolina exhibited a strong antiauthoritarian temper. Despite weak religious institutions in the eighteenth century, evangelical religion came to dominate the spiritual life of North Carolinians by the mid-nineteenth century. And though slavery eventually became rooted in the economic and social life of the state, its growth at first proved slow and unsteady.

Bradford J. Wood and Larry E. Tise tackle the conundrum of how a poor colony and impecunious state came to adopt systems of unfree labor. Labor shortages plagued the early settlers, who turned to bound labor, Indian slavery, and eventually African slavery to meet their workforce needs. First indentured servitude and then bond slavery prevailed during North Carolina's first two hundred years despite a small planter class, inadequate capital, a sketchy transportation system, and a sizable antislavery community made up of Quakers and obstreperous yeoman farmers. Nonetheless, on the eve of the Civil War fully 72 percent of North Carolinians owned no slaves. Wood and Tise attempt to explain how first indentured servitude and then slavery became so engrained.

Those obstreperous yeoman farmers are the subject of Carole Watterson Troxler's essay on the War of the Regulation (1766–71). Frustrated by unjust and corrupt government at the provincial and local levels, rebellious farmers known as Regulators posed the largest and most violent threat to colonial authority in pre-Revolutionary America. Troxler digs deep into the legal and land records to reveal tensions between acquisitive landholders and men of means and struggling yeomen intent on making a livelihood for their families and establishing a New Canaan for their community. The Regulation revealed class tensions, sectional conflict, and a millennial belief in a fairer, more just, and sanctified society. Troxler shows how a "land grab" added to the Regulators' list of grievances. Along the way she explores the always tenuous links between the Regulation and the Revolution.

That the Regulator uprising had a religious dimension is reinforced by Charles F. Irons's survey of North Carolina's evangelical geographies. By the turn of the nineteenth century evangelical churches such as Baptists, Methodists, and Presbyterians dominated the state's religious landscape. A large and strong Protestant presence would persist late into the twentieth century. Irons establishes how those churches—both black and white—became the preferred churchly forms of worship even after the Civil War divided the races on Sunday mornings. The churches' influence extended to schools, higher education, the press, and even politics. Irons shows how that influence started and expanded.

The post–Civil War era brought revolutionary changes to North Carolina's society, economy, and politics. The greatest change, of course, was the emancipation of more than 300,000 enslaved African Americans. Freed people redefined labor arrangements, social relations, and political institutions. Karin Zipf carefully examines the records of the Freedman's bank in New Bern to offer new perspectives on African American women during Reconstruction. The bank records, Zipf argues, reveal heretofore hidden insights into family structure, work patterns, legal and extralegal ownership of property, and the network of relationships that succored black women. To a surprising degree African American women took control of their property, their labor, and their newly won freedom. Zipf's findings expand upon and revise the growing literature on African American women making the transition from slavery to freedom.

Glenda Elizabeth Gilmore offers a longitudinal study that discusses both public and higher education as a form of developing human capital for the century between the first Reconstruction following the Civil War and a second Reconstruction during the 1960s following the Supreme Court decision in *Brown v. Board of Education*. Much of North Carolina's reputation as a progressive southern state rests on its schools and universities. In Gilmore's essay education becomes an index for measuring how limiting or capacious that progressivism was. As the renowned historian C. Vann Woodward reminds us, progressivism was for "whites only."[7] Gilmore documents the appalling conditions of segregated black schools—from grade schools to universities—that in no way provided separate but equal education. In fact, she argues, the drive to equalize black schools in North Carolina had the surprising effect of improving education for all races. After the hard-won victories of the civil rights movement in the 1950s and 1960s, Gilmore questions whether North Carolina's reputation for progressivism can endure in the twentieth-first century.

The rise of the textile industry after the Civil War became an economic and social movement. Struggling white farmers, displaced by the grinding poverty brought on by sharecropping and tenancy, found employment in the cotton mills for themselves and their families. It was in those dusty, noisy mills of the Piedmont, Patrick Huber shows, that hillbilly music arose. Music provided a form of protest and a creative outlet for the mill hands, who worked long hours for meager wages. The most talented singers, musicians, and songwriters eventually took their sound to radio stations, particularly WBT in Charlotte. In time hillbilly music would generate other styles and sounds that would go nationwide on the Grand Ole Opry stage in Nashville and the Sun Studio in Memphis. Huber's essay provides a unique look at labor history with music as its cultural expression.

North Carolina's status as the most progressive southern state, the subject of several essays in this collection, has generated considerable controversy for a generation or more. Karl E. Campbell takes head-on the state's reputation for progressivism with an original interpretation of the state's political culture in the twentieth century. Campbell demonstrates that North Carolina's so-called progressive plutocracy, as posited by political scientist V. O. Key Jr. in 1949, held sway for more than fifty years. North Carolina's brand of business progressivism assured industrialists, manufacturers, businessmen, large agriculturalists, and bankers that under one-party rule they would enjoy good roads, cheap nonunion labor, segregated schools, and moderate but necessary taxation to generate prosperity for themselves and their class. The civil rights movement of the 1950s and 1960s began to break down that consensus and to inaugurate a political realignment that continues to unfold in the twenty-first century. Campbell uses Key's theory of party realignment to test old assumptions about the origins of North Carolina's political parties.

Jerry Gershenhorn returns to the question of education in an essay that examines North Carolina's response to the 1954 *Brown v. Board of Education* decision to desegregate public schools. If North Carolina was so progressive, why did it delay the integration of its schools for more than a decade? The state's segregationists used a reactionary Pearsall Plan to forestall any meaningful integration. The push to integrate the schools, Gershenhorn contends, came from courageous African American parents and students. In the end it took busing in the 1970s to break down an obstinate system of inequality and discrimination. As Gershenhorn shows, progressivism wore a thin veneer in North Carolina.

What gives North Carolinians their inimitable identity? Articulating the state's culturally distinct traditions is fraught with difficulties. NASCAR, moonshine, barbecue, pottery traditions, literature, visual arts, music (gospel, blues, bluegrass, hillbilly, and jazz)—North Carolina has much to celebrate. Richard D. Starnes takes up the challenge with an innovative look at how commerce and heritage have worked hand in hand. North Carolina's beautiful landscape from the mountains to the sea began luring visitors as early as the mid-nineteenth century. The state's rich legacy in arts and crafts and many historic sites attracted visitors as much as sandy shores, verdant mountains, and pine-lined fairways. As Starnes demonstrates, North Carolina government officials and businessmen alike chased that "Yankee dollar" wherever they could find it. Tourism became the second largest industry in the state. But Starnes also raises troublesome questions about what is authentic and what is artificial in North Carolina's tourism domain.

If tourism now makes a huge imprint on North Carolina's economy, what has become of the state's traditional industries—textiles, tobacco, and furniture? The answers, according to James C. Cobb and Peter A. Coclanis, are not encouraging. In two essays that strikingly complement each other, they reveal that the economic foundations of a progressive plutocracy masked fundamental problems that continue to plague twenty-first century Tar Heels. Cobb follows the trail of smokestacks across North Carolina that promised factory jobs for an agrarian state but failed to generate enduring prosperity. North Carolina's strategy for attracting industry—a dispersed network of factories in rural areas, cheap, unskilled labor, tax incentives, and hostility to unions—dissolved in the last quarter of the twentieth century. The state's holy trinity of industries fled overseas. Coclanis picks up the trail in Asia and Latin America where the Tar Heel jobs absconded. He is not optimistic that North Carolina can recover economically without a massive investment in training a new skilled labor force that can compete globally. To be sure, globalization is not the only reason for North Carolina's economic difficulties in the opening decades of the twenty-first century. The emergence of banking in Charlotte and the growth of such industries as biotech, telecommunications, and computer engineering have provided exciting new possibilities. But they largely are confined to robust urban complexes with large universities in the Research Triangle (Raleigh, Durham, Chapel Hill), the Triad (Greensboro, Winston-Salem, High Point), and Metrolina (Charlotte-Mecklenburg). The growing inequality between rural and urban areas is having a profound effect on everything—schools, roads, and stubborn pockets of unemployment and poverty. Cobb and Coclanis offer a sober analysis of North Carolina's current economic potential and the many pitfalls that need to be avoided as the state redefines its relationship to the global economy.

The voyages undertaken in this collection lead to many destinations. The essays do not propose a single course to navigate toward a new narrative. Instead they sail past old ports and seek new landings from many different routes. We invite other voyagers to embark with us as we explore new worlds that reveal the diverse geography of North Carolina's past. We have been plying these waters ourselves for several years. We thus propose at the end the outlines of a new North Carolina narrative that will set forth at least our take on where these diverse and protean essays might lead us to a fuller and richer understanding of North Carolina's complicated history.

NOTES

1. Jeffrey J. Crow and Larry E. Tise, eds., *Writing North Carolina History* (Chapel Hill: University of North Carolina Press, 1979).

2. Samuel A. Ashe, *History of North Carolina*, 2 vols. (Greensboro, N.C.: Charles L. Van Noppen, 1908–25); Robert D. W. Connor, William K. Boyd, and J. G. de Roulhac Hamilton, *History of North Carolina*, 3 vols. (New York: Lewis, 1919); Archibald Henderson, *North Carolina: The Old State and the New*, 2 vols. (Chicago: Lewis, 1941).

3. Hugh T. Lefler and Albert Ray Newsome, *North Carolina: The History of a Southern State*, 3rd ed. (Chapel Hill: University of North Carolina Press, 1973).

4. William S. Powell, *North Carolina through Four Centuries* (Chapel Hill: University of North Carolina Press, 1989).

5. Milton Ready, *The Tar Heel State: A History of North Carolina* (Columbia: University of South Carolina Press, 2005); William A. Link, *North Carolina: Change and Tradition in a Southern State* (Wheeling, Ill.: Harlan Davidson, 2009); H. G. Jones, "North Carolina, 1946–1976: Where Historians Fear to Tread," in Crow and Tise, *Writing North Carolina History*.

6. The historical literature of the past forty years is too broad and too deep to cite many individual titles. A few representative examples include Paul D. Escott, *Many Excellent People: Power and Privilege in North Carolina, 1850–1900* (Chapel Hill: University of North Carolina Press, 1985); Jacqueline Dowd Hall, James L. Leloudis, Robert R. Korstad, Mary Murphy, Lu Ann Jones, and Christopher Day, *Like a Family: The Making of a Southern Cotton Mill World* (Chapel Hill: University of North Carolina Press, 1987); Jeffrey J. Crow, Paul D. Escott, and Flora J. Hatley, *A History of African Americans in North Carolina*, 2nd rev. ed. (Raleigh, N.C.: Department of Cultural Resources, Office of Archives and History, 2011); William H. Chafe, *Civilities and Civil Rights: Greensboro, North Carolina, and the Black Struggle for Freedom* (New York: Oxford University Press, 1980); Glenda Elizabeth Gilmore, *Gender and Jim Crow: Women and the Politics of White Supremacy, 1896–1920* (Chapel Hill: University of North Carolina Press, 1996); David S. Cecelski and Timothy Tyson, eds., *Democracy Betrayed: The Wilmington Race Riot of 1898 and Its Legacy* (Chapel Hill: University of North Carolina Press, 1998); Sarah Caroline Thuesen, *Greater than Equal: African American Struggles for Schools and Citizenship in North Carolina, 1919–1965* (Chapel

Hill: University of North Carolina Press, 2013); and Tom Eamon, *The Making of a Southern Democracy: North Carolina Politics from Kerr Scott to Pat McCrory* (Chapel Hill: University of North Carolina Press, 2014).

7. C. Vann Woodward, *Origins of the New South, 1877–1913* (Baton Rouge: Louisiana State University, 1971), 369.

AN UNCOMPROMISING ENVIRONMENT
NORTH CAROLINA'S "LAND OF WATER" COASTAL SYSTEM

Stanley R. Riggs and Dorothea V. Ames

INTRODUCTION

Geology is the study of our planet's history, the dynamic processes and sequential development of our planet from its ancient beginnings through the present and into the future. The earth environment inherited by the human species when it developed was dictated by a long history of these earth processes. To fully comprehend the complex interdependencies of the earth's processes, interactions, and responses and the human environment and cultural development requires large-scale, interdisciplinary approaches that integrate numerous specialty fields of study. To accomplish this understanding we must integrate human history with many other disciplines, including geologic history, with the physical and chemical dynamics that control and maintain the biological ecosystem response, as well as location and abundance of fundamental resources, including water, energy, minerals, and soils; the archaeological record that grades into and documents the human history of ancient people and civilizations; and the fields of evolution, religion, economics, politics, and health.

The geographic character of coastal North Carolina, along with the associated ocean dynamics, is truly distinctive, as displayed on any map of North America or the North Atlantic Ocean. The North Carolina Coastal Plain and Continental Margin provinces represent the long-term products resulting from a continuous series of unique coastal systems that have existed since the initial formation of the Atlantic Ocean. They represent over a two-hundred-million-year history of dramatic change. Prior to that time, the supercontinent called Pangaea—the ancient combined landmass consisting of North and South America, Europe, and Africa—began to split down the middle, it opened a long and narrow Atlantic Ocean. This was the beginning of a coastal system in eastern North Carolina that built a new land area seaward through time into the expanding North Atlantic Ocean as we know it today. The geologic record of marine sediments that make up the Coastal

Plain and Continental Margin demonstrates major shifts in ocean dynamics and climatic conditions that evolved from lake basins and tropical coral reefs to the wildly fluctuating climates and deposits of the ice ages. This history of change within the North Carolina coastal system and adjacent landscapes dictated the region's cultural heritage, still severely impacts our modern civilization, and will continue its influence as the earth and its peoples evolve together into the future.

Where the western boundary of the vast Atlantic Ocean intersects the irregular topography of the North Carolina landmass, a broad and shallow coastal system occurs. North Carolina's coastal system is dominated by and a product of energetic storms that build, maintain, and drive its evolution. In this complex network of diverse geomorphic features and ecosystems, change is the only constant. The coastal system consists of approximately 325 miles of unique barrier islands with around twenty-four inlets, approximately 3,500 square miles of shallow-water inland seas or estuaries, approximately 10,000 miles of estuarine shorelines, and associated sediment bank, marsh, and swamp-forest ecosystems.[1]

The upland Coastal Plain topography was sculpted by previous coastal systems as the level of the Atlantic Ocean rose and fell, causing the coastal system to migrate back and forth across the Coastal Plain and Continental Margin during the last couple million years. These ongoing processes of climate change (fluctuations in sea level, storms, floods, droughts, and ocean dynamics) dictate whether the ocean levels rise or fall, coastal waters flood or drain the river valleys, shorelines erode or build, ecosystems evolve or migrate, and barrier islands transgress or regress. The water-based processes of the coastal system move through time and space and sculpt the associated landforms within the provinces of North Carolina's Coastal Plain and Continental Margin. The historical evolution of the ancient to modern coastal system has been extensively analyzed and mapped, so now the evolutionary changes can be projected into the short-term future with a certain level of confidence.

North Carolina's coastal system began to play a key role in human affairs when Native Americans arrived in the Coastal Plain about thirteen millennia ago. Its importance was magnified with the beginning of European settlement in the sixteenth century. Human history within North Carolina's coastal system has, in part, been dictated by the earth's history, which in turn determines the geologic framework and ongoing dynamic processes of climate change (sea-level fluctuations, storms, floods, and drought). Evidence indicates that the first Native Americans within the North Carolina Coastal Plain arrived during the time anthropologists call the Paleo-Indian

Period (from about 13,000 to 10,000 years ago).[2] These hunter-gatherers were nomadic peoples who adapted to severe climatic conditions as the earth transitioned from the cold climate of the last ice age into the warmer climate of today's interglacial episode. Archaeological evidence of Native American habitation sites is preserved on braid bars (large sand and gravel bars) within the braided river valleys that were products of the cold, dry, and stormy climate that existed during the last glacial maximum and continued through the Paleo-Indian Period. Since the beginning of the Archaic Period (~10,000 to 3,200 years ago) and through the Woodland Period (from ~3,200 years ago until early European settlement during the 1600s), the climate slowly warmed and became wetter, and the Native Americans grew more abundant, diverse, and widespread over the landscape. Archaeological sites within the coastal system suggest that Native Americans were major inhabitants of the coastal mainland, with temporary encampments on the coastal barriers throughout the Woodland Period.

European settlement began in coastal North Carolina in 1584 and has since dominated the growth and development of North Carolina's coastal system.[3] Because the wild and swampy nature of North Carolina's "Land of Water" landscape was dominated by the Native Americans, European settlement was initially restricted to a few small and scattered villages. Severe alteration and engineering of the coastal system landscape did not begin until the European settlers displaced the existing Native American population during the Tuscarora Indian War (1711–13). Then European expansion into previous wilderness, along with minor areas of subsistence farming, began and has increased exponentially into the twenty-first century.

This essay presents a new history of North Carolina's "Land of Water" coastal system, beginning with a brief summary of its geologic framework and natural dynamic processes of change.[4] The recent arrival of humans is then superimposed on that stage. The wild and beautiful coastal system of North Carolina has always had a magical draw for human occupation, which most recently has become an essential component, forever increasing economic growth and development. However, continued expansion in a dynamic coastal system dominated by high-energy storms and change has set growth and development on a collision course with natural processes. This essay suggests an alternative vision for integrating scientific and cultural history into a new paradigm for the North Carolina Land of Water and for adapting to the ongoing processes of change.[5] It is essential that North Carolina build a viable coastal economy that is compatible with the natural system dynamics and maintains a healthy system of natural resources.

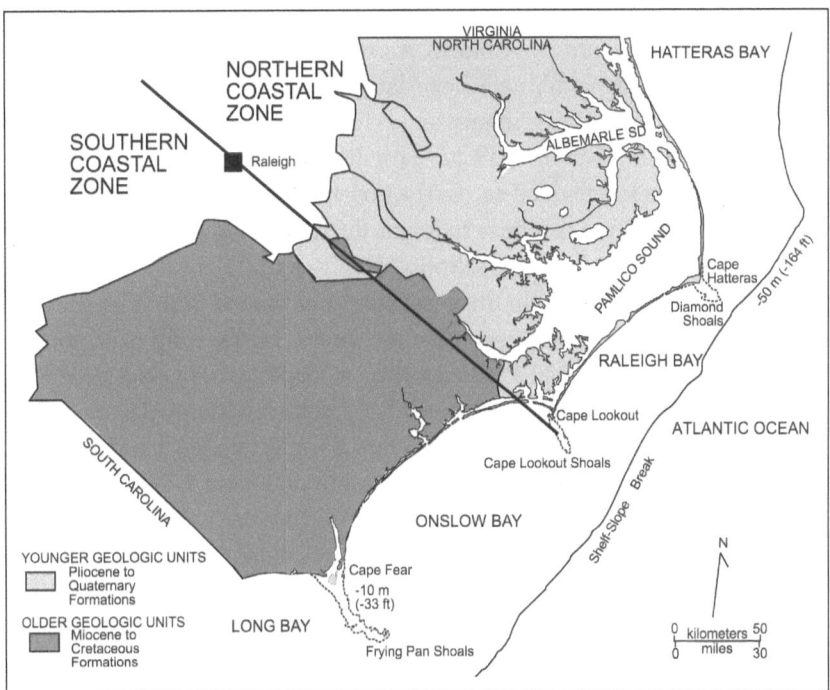

FIGURE 1.1. This generalized geologic map of the North Carolina Coastal Plain shows the two coastal zones, separated by the black line drawn between Raleigh and Cape Lookout. It also shows the four coastal bays formed by the three capes and cape-shoal features, and the outer edge of the continental shelf where the seafloor begins to descend into the deep sea. Along the northwest edge of the Coastal Plain is the contact or fall line, where the land rises up onto the Piedmont Province.

NORTH CAROLINA'S EARTH HISTORY

Setting the Stage

The North Carolina Coastal Plain is bordered on the ocean side by its drowned partner, the submarine Continental Margin, and on the inland side by the fall line that separates the Coastal Plain from the Piedmont and Appalachian provinces (fig. 1.1). The Piedmont and Appalachians are ancient landforms (older than 250 million years) that have substantial elevation above modern sea level and are composed primarily of ancient metamorphosed sediments and crystalline granitic and basaltic rock types.[6] They were produced by mountain-building processes that took place about 490 to 250 million years ago, forming the ancient supercontinent Pangaea, which existed for about fifty million years. The opening of the modern Atlantic Ocean began about 200 million years ago and continues today, separating the European and African continents from North America and South America. As the ocean expanded, the combined ocean-land interactions formed the Coastal Plain and Continental Margin provinces (fig. 1.1). Throughout the history of the Atlantic Ocean, water levels have oscillated like an accordion, and the ocean has alternately flooded across the Coastal Plain and retreated onto the Continental Margin in response to major fluctuations in global climate and physical changes within North Carolina's landscape.

Major differences occur in the geography and time of formation for each of North Carolina's three geographic provinces. In traveling from today's Smoky Mountain National Park eastward to Cape Hatteras National Seashore, geologic time passes from the oldest landforms and rocks, measured in billions to hundreds of millions of years, to the youngest landforms and sediments, where geologic time is measured in millennia to years and days. A dramatic range in land elevation also occurs, from thousands of feet above sea level to only feet to inches above the ever-changing levels of the modern ocean. The processes of change also range greatly, from erosion rates within the Appalachian and Piedmont provinces, measured in inches to feet per millions of years to erosion rates within the coastal system that generally occur in feet to miles per century. Thus, the coastal system is extremely different from the rest of North Carolina in time scales of formation, geologic framework and topography, and ecosystems and processes of change. The unique geologic environment of coastal North Carolina directly affected the settlement of Native Americans and the growth of post-European settlement and it continues to shape the state's history today and will do so into the future.

History of the Coastal Plain and Continental Margin

North Carolina's coastal system initially formed at the time the Atlantic Ocean began to develop. Historically that coastal system migrated westward across what is now the modern Coastal Plain and retreated eastward across the adjacent Continental Margin numerous times. These dramatic fluctuations in sea level over the past 200 million years were caused by major changes in the global climate and were responsible for systematically building North Carolina's Coastal Plain and Continental Margin.[7] This history of changing sea level led to the accumulation of a wedge of marine sediments that today thickens from zero eastward from the fall line and Piedmont, with its much older crystalline rocks, to over 10,000 feet at Cape Hatteras and 40,000 feet off the east side of the Continental Margin (fig 1.1). These marine sediments include ancient coral reef deposits (~200 million years ago), riverine delta deposits that contain fossil trees and dinosaur bones (~144 to 65 million years ago), fossiliferous limestone aquifers (~65 to 28 million years ago), valuable phosphate deposits (~28 to 5.3 million years ago), shallow marine, shell-rich mudstones (~5.3 to 2.6 million years ago), and the coastal sediments of our barrier islands and estuaries that formed during the Quaternary Period (~2.6 million years ago) and continue today.

The North Carolina Coastal Plain begins at the fall line, where the upper Coastal Plain has general elevations of a few hundred feet above present sea level.[8] The ramped topographic surface slopes gently eastward to the low elevations of the modern coastal system that dominate the lower Coastal Plain, referred to as the North Carolina Land of Water.[9] The North Carolina coastal system can be further divided into two distinct zones that are very different in their geometry and geologic processes by a line drawn from Raleigh to Cape Lookout. Short, stubby barrier islands that hug a relatively steep mainland shoreline characterize the southern coastal zone, resulting in narrow back-barrier estuaries connected to the ocean by many shallow inlets. The very low slope of the land surface in the northern coastal zone results in long barrier islands. These barrier islands form a "sand dam" on the seaward side of a broad expanse of drowned-river estuaries of the Albemarle and Pamlico Sounds and their associated flooded tributary drainage systems. The northern coastal system consists of the Inner Banks and Outer Banks that connect with the ocean through a few major inlets and project seaward to form Cape Hatteras and Cape Lookout.

The North Carolina barrier island system and its adjoining Continental Margin can be further divided into four coastal bays, each with its own distinctive underlying geologic framework, physical and chemical dynamics, and biologic components. Capes and their associated cape shoals—shallow sand bodies that extend into the ocean perpendicular to the coast for about ten miles (Diamond Shoals off Cape Hatteras), fifteen miles (Cape Lookout Shoals off Cape Lookout), and thirty miles (Frying Pan Shoals off Cape Fear)—define the embayments. These extensive shoal systems, which have taken many mariners to their demise, give the North Carolina coast today the dubious sailing honor of being known as the "Graveyard of the Atlantic."

QUATERNARY ICE AGES AND NORTH CAROLINA'S COASTAL SYSTEM

Sea-Level Fluctuations

The last period of geologic time, the Quaternary (~2.6 million years ago to the present), is known as the Ice Ages.[10] This is a period of severe global climate fluctuations that alternate between "hot-house" and "icebox" conditions. These global oscillations of warm and cold climates led to the alternating interglacial and glacial episodes characterized by high sea levels and low sea levels, respectively. During warm climatic episodes, the earth's tropical and temperate zones expand poleward, causing most global precipitation to occur as rainfall that flows back into the oceans, maintaining higher sea levels, much as is the case today. The earth is presently in the modern interglacial episode that has existed for the past 10,000 years. However, during cold climates, precipitation over the expanded polar and boreal regions occurs as snow and accumulates, forming vast continental and mountain glaciers. These continental ice sheets are often one to two miles thick and cover the northern two-thirds of North America, Greenland, northern Europe and northern Asia, as well as Antarctica. The water to form these vast glaciers is derived from the oceans and accumulates on land as snow-ice when the climate is cold enough, lowering global sea levels.

The last glacial maximum occurred between 25,000 and 18,000 years ago, with the North American ice sheet covering most of Canada and the northern United States southward to the Missouri and Ohio Rivers.[11] This glaciation formed the Great Lakes, Cape Cod, Long Island, and the great "breadbasket soils" of the midwestern United States. North Carolina had a boreal zone climate that was semiarid and very stormy, with large braided (multichanneled and sediment-rich) river valleys and abundant dune fields. Vegetation was scattered and dominated by spruce and fir trees and inhabited by a population of large mammals, such as wooly mammoths, mastodons, rhinoceros, tigers, and bison. Global sea level was substantially lower during the last glacial maximum. Consequently, sea level in North Carolina was about 410 feet below the present ocean level (fig. 1.2). This placed the coastal system off the edge of the continental shelf and seaward about sixty miles east of Wilmington and Morehead City, about forty miles east of Nags Head, and fifteen miles east of Cape Hatteras.[12] Thus, the Coastal Plain was about double its present size, with rivers flowing across the present Continental Margin. If the climate were to warm and all existing ice on Greenland and Antarctica were to melt, the rise in sea level in North Carolina would place the shoreline somewhere near the western edge of the Coastal Plain, along the fall line and Interstate 95. No science suggests that this will happen anytime in the near future, but the shoreline has been there in the geologic past.

Between 18,000 and 10,000 years ago the climate was warming, the glacial ice mass was retreating poleward, meltwaters were flowing back into the ocean, and sea level was rising.[13] During this transition period, rising sea level moved the coastal system upward and landward onto the continental

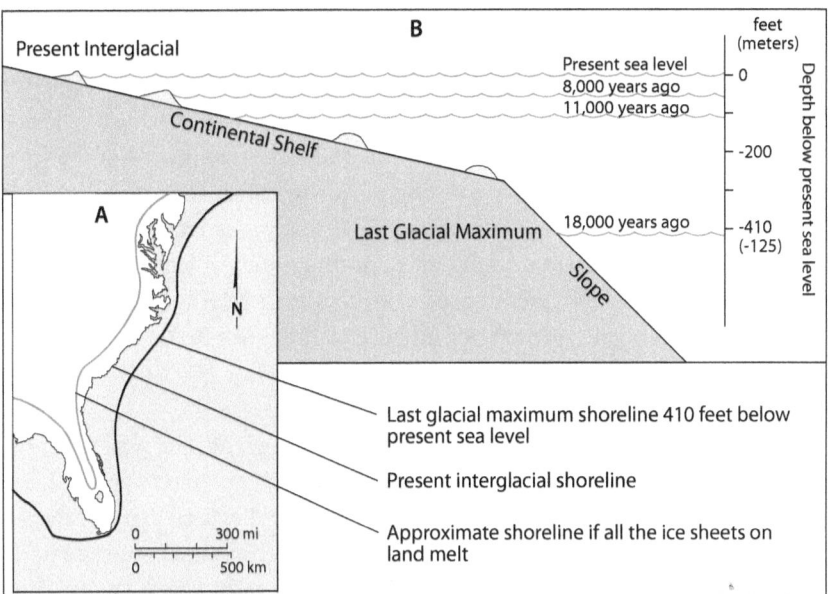

FIGURE 1.2. Panel A (*lower left*): Location of the ocean shoreline at three different stages of climate: the cold climate of the last glacial maximum (~18,000 years ago), today, and sometime in the future if the climate warms sufficiently for all glacial ice in Greenland and Antarctica to melt. This future shoreline would be approximately at the western edge of the Coastal Plain. Panel B (*upper right*): Schematic cross-section of the continental shelf and upper slope showing the location of the ocean shoreline at four different time periods: 1) 18,000 years ago during the last glacial maximum when sea level was about 410 feet below present; 2) 11,000 years ago at about 100 feet below present sea level; 3) 8,000 years ago at about 50 feet below present sea level; and 4) present sea level.

shelf. By about 10,000 years ago the modern North Carolina estuaries began to form as rising sea level flooded up the river valleys. By 3,000 years ago, portions of the modern barrier islands began to form near where they exist today. Since then, the estuaries have continued to expand and flood vast portions of those land areas with lower elevations. The barrier islands continue to erode on the front side and migrate upward and landward. Some of the sand-poor barriers have collapsed into inlets and shallow shoals in response to major storm events and reformed into subaerial barriers; frequently they have reformed within the last five hundred years.

Scientists measure sea-level change of the world's oceans at different scales during the Quaternary.[14] Sea-level changes are plotted for the past 125,000 years since the last interglacial episode, the past 18,000 years since the last glacial maximum, and the past 10,000 years since start of the present interglacial episode when North Carolina's modern coastal system began to form.[15]

Both the amount and resolution of data for each of these sea-level curves become more complete and have better accuracy as the present day is approached. Types of data used to determine the historical record of sea level for the past include isotopic age dating of salt-marsh accretion, tide-gauge measurements, drowned in situ stumps of freshwater trees, the geologic record of change in coastal sediment deposition and erosion, and the historical record of flooded human coastal structures (e.g., wharfs, foundations of buildings, maritime shipwrecks, and archaeological sites).

Storm Dynamics

Since coastal systems form at the intersection of the land, sea, and air, if sea level is rising the coastal system will migrate upward and landward with the interface (fig. 1.2). Sea-level rise by itself is a fairly slow and gentle process, like filling a bathtub. However, frequent coastal storms superimposed upon rising sea level contain the energy to do the work of building and moving coastal systems. These storms are the drivers of change that erode shorelines, move barrier islands, and cause ecosystems to migrate.[16] For many millennia before the first English explorers landed on Roanoke Island in 1584, extratropical storms, tropical storms, and hurricanes played substantial roles in the processes of changing and rearranging the natural coastal system, and impacting the lives of native peoples living within the coastal system.

Two kinds of storms are dominant within the North Carolina coastal system.[17] Tropical cyclones range from the common tropical depressions to tropical storms and the less frequent hurricanes; they occur primarily in summer and fall. Extratropical storms include nor'easters and sou'westers and occur primarily in fall through spring and summer, respectively. Records of North Carolina's tropical cyclones began to be kept in the early 1850s.[18] Since then many hundreds of tropical depressions, tropical storms, and hurricanes have passed into the North Carolina coastal system. Figure 1.3A shows a direct hit by Hurricane Isabel in 2003, and figure 1.3B shows the number of tropical storms and hurricanes that occurred within a two-hundred-mile zone of Cape Lookout between 1853 and 2010. Of these 252 tropical storms, 93 were category 1 through 5 hurricanes that represent an average of about six hurricanes per decade. In addition, North Carolina gets up to thirty extratropical coastal storms per year. The geometry of North Carolina's coastline, together with its proximity to the confluence of the warm-water Gulf Stream and cold-water Labrador Current off Cape Hatteras, makes the North Carolina

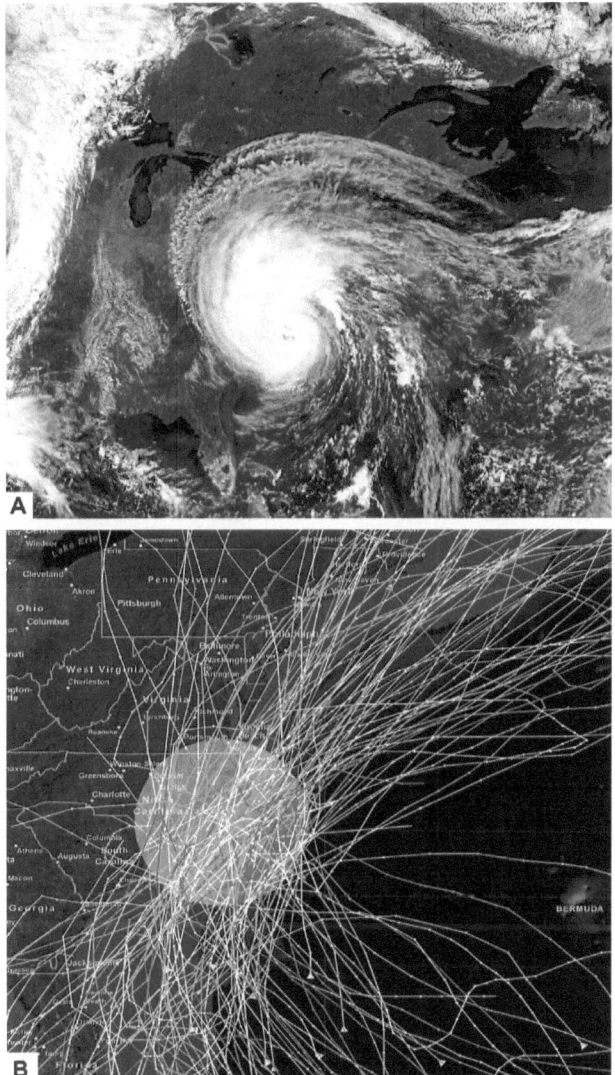

FIGURE 1.3. (*A*) Satellite image of Hurricane Isabel obtained on September 18, 2003, as it approached the North Carolina coast in the vicinity of North Core Banks and Ocracoke Inlet. Isabel was a category 5 hurricane while at sea but slowed and diminished in intensity as it approached North Carolina. It came ashore as a category 2 storm with about a six- to eight-foot storm surge and winds at one hundred miles per hour. The storm opened Isabel Inlet adjacent to Hatteras Village and came very close to opening additional inlets on Hatteras Island between Avon and Buxton and the northeast segment of Ocracoke Island. Image is from NASA's SeaWiFS Project, 2003. (*B*) Storm tracks of all tropical storms and hurricanes that occurred between 1853 and 2010 within a two-hundred-mile radius of Cape Lookout (circle). During this period about 252 tropical systems impacted coastal North Carolina, of which 93 were hurricanes. Data from the U.S. National Hurricane Center, 2013.

coast a highly storm-driven system (fig. 1.3). Extensive coastal development in the twentieth century on a storm-dependent coastal system has created a "perfect storm" of conflict, with immense long-term consequences for the coastal-based economy.

The consequences of any one storm or set of storms are highly variable and generally unpredictable.[19] The impact upon the coastal system depends on the storm type, size, strength, duration, and amount of precipitation. Additional variables include the forward speed of the storm, height of the storm surge, storm track relative to the orientation of the coast, state of the astronomical tides, geometry of the adjacent continental shelf, and the frequency and pattern of subsequent storms. Coastal shorelines and their geomorphic features (e.g., barrier islands and associated wetlands) are directly built by and maintained by the region's storm dynamics and are essential for the coastal system migration in response to regional changes in sea level and tectonics. The coastal system is not the fragile component; rather, it is the human structures built at or near sea level and on dynamic and mobile barrier islands that are out of equilibrium with the natural dynamics and represent the fragile components.

HUMAN HISTORY IN COASTAL NORTH CAROLINA

Environmental Controls

The history of human development in coastal North Carolina is unlike that of many other human endeavors, due to the high energy and dynamic character of the coastal system. The evolutionary formation of the modern North Carolina coastal system has taken place during the latter part of the Quaternary Period (since ~125,000 years ago) and continues today as a major work in progress.[20] Change within the coastal system happens at rates that defy the conventional human experience, economic development patterns, and legal jurisprudence that dominate more stable and inland terrains such as the Piedmont and Appalachian provinces.

While Native Americans probably began to inhabit North Carolina about 13,000 years ago,[21] there is today a limited record of their occupancy of the coastal zone. Even an archaeological record of the first European settlement on northern Roanoke Island, 1584–87, has been largely obliterated by shoreline recession.[22] The processes of change continue to take their toll today as every nor'easter and hurricane places its mark upon the shifting sands of time. If the rapid rates of coastal evolution of the past millennia, centuries, and decades continue, no great remnants from our present coastal civilization will survive in their present form generations from now.

Geologists are generally perceived as dealing with millions or billions of years of earth history. To be sure, when considering the origin of the Appalachians, Piedmont, Coastal Plain, and Atlantic Ocean, geologists do think in terms of millions and billions of years. However, when considering modern earth processes such as earthquakes, volcanic eruptions, riverine floods, hurricanes, and sea-level rise, the time scales shift to hours, days, years, decades, and centuries. Thus, in considering high-energy coastal systems, geologic time is synonymous with the time experienced during a trip to the beach, a uniquely powerful storm or series of storms, an individual life-span, or even a few generations of family summers at the beach. At these scales, geologic time is human time.

Native American Occupation

The transition period from the last glacial maximum to the present interglacial episode was a time of massive climatic changes as the earth shifted from "ice house" to "hot house" conditions.[23] A limited archaeological record suggests that the arrival of humans in the North Carolina Coastal Plain occurred contemporaneously with development of the warmer interglacial climate. The existing archaeological records for both the Paleo-Indian and Archaic Periods tend to be associated with the major river valleys within the upper and central portions of the Coastal Plain. Any preexisting sites within the lower Coastal Plain (North Carolina's coastal zone) would have been eroded as the rising sea level flooded across the Continental Margin and up the riverine valleys, producing our modern drowned-river estuarine system.[24]

The only Paleo-Indian cultural remains consist of scattered remnants of tools and projectile points that have been eroded and reworked from in situ sites. Recent research, however, has located numerous in situ Archaic Period sites along the major riverine floodplains of the upper and central Coastal Plain.[25] These sites generally occur on top of the various river terraces (paleo-braidplains) that formed during the transition period following the last glacial maximum. The Archaic deposits are commonly overlain by deposits of Woodland cultural remains that occur along terrace boundaries where paleo-dune fields were periodically reactivated, burying and preserving new settlements. The multiple occupations of these sites occurred during times of relative surface stability followed by episodes of climatic fluctuations (storms, floods, or droughts) and burial by wind-blown deposits.

The hunter-gatherer communities increased in abundance and/or preservation throughout the Woodland period. These sites are still intimately tied to the trunk river floodplains and the associated tributary stream systems that facilitated transport, as well as supplying a source of water and food. Native American communities, which often included major ossuaries, agricultural lands, and access to inland fauna and flora, developed on the higher banks along the estuarine shoreline of the lower Coastal Plain.[26] In addition, some of the larger coastal islands, including Kitty Hawk, Colington, Roanoke, Hatteras, Shackleford, and Bogue islands, contain seasonal subsistence camps for collecting shellfish. Many of these coastal Woodland archaeological sites are today being eroded by storms and drowned by ongoing sea-level rise.

After European Settlement

From 1584 to 1587 Sir Walter Raleigh's expeditions sailed into the salty estuarine waters of Currituck, Roanoke, and Albemarle Sounds looking for the "New World." There were at least five inlets through the Outer Banks barrier islands north of Roanoke Island, as indicated on the 1590 map of John White and Theodor de Bry.[27] The openings through the barrier islands were inlets for the settlers and outlets for the Roanoke-Albemarle drainage discharge, which was not connected to the Pamlico Sound drainage system. The ships probably came through the "Roanoke Inlet," which at that time was located due east of Roanoke Island and followed a deep channel northwest, passing adjacent to the high bluffs and overlying dune field along the north shore of Roanoke Island. The Roanoke Island shoreline at that time extended about one-half mile farther north than today's shoreline, which is still severely eroding.[28]

The colonists set out to explore their newfound land and search for the components of new wealth: sassafras, clay, copper, and gold. In March 1586, Ralph Lane led his team of twenty-nine men westward in two double wherries (fifteen-person rowboats) to find a "fabled land of mountains and gold called Chaunis Temoatan, far up the River Morotico" (Roanoke River) and beyond the territory of the Moratucks to the territory of the Mangoaks, where Chaunis Temoatan was located. The spring thaw on the serpentine "River of Morotico hath so violent a current from the west and southwest that it made me almost of opinion that with ores it would scarce be navigable," wrote Thomas Harriot.[29] This expedition, as with others to come, failed in the face of the natural dynamics, as the wild and untamed Roanoke River was in its annual spring flood stage.

The North Carolina coastal system in the sixteenth century was a wilderness dominated by low and wet pocosin swamplands and remote estuaries and rivers. The ephemeral inlets through the highly mobile barrier islands opened, migrated, and closed in response to individual storm events. Sea level was about three feet lower than today and rising, and the newly named Pamlico and Albemarle Sounds were saltwater estuaries. These two drowned river drainage systems were not yet connected. Today's Croatan Sound did not yet exist; rather, it was a drowning Croatan Creek that occupied "the narrows" flowing off the vast shallows of Roanoke Marshes connecting Roanoke Island to the mainland (fig. 1.4). The detailed geologic history of the evolution of Croatan Sound is supported by the historic maps and local oral traditions of early Wanchese residents, who walked over the Roanoke Marshes to the mainland with only a few planks across the small tidal channels.[30]

The navigable inlets north of Roanoke Island began to shoal and became ephemeral and unreliable for shipping by the latter half of the 1700s. By 1808 only Roanoke Inlet remained open, but it was shallow and ephemeral (fig. 1.4C). Roanoke Inlet finally closed permanently by 1817 in the vicinity of Whalebone Junction, with two important results. First, without any inlets, the Albemarle and Currituck Sounds and their tributary estuaries became freshwater, along with major shifts in both the flora and fauna. This dramatic change in the ecosystem led directly to the emergence of new bass fishing and wildfowl hunting industries within Currituck Sound and to the extensive occurrence of surviving fresh-water bald cypress trees that are now drowned in the shallow waters around the perimeter of the Albemarle Sound coastal system. Second, without a direct outlet to the ocean, the freshwater discharge from the Roanoke-Albemarle drainage system was forced to flow through the Croatan Narrows, flooding across the interstream divide and into the Pamlico Sound drainage system with its outlets to the ocean.

As the natural dynamics of sea-level rise and storms brought evolutionary changes to the coastal system, these impacted human settlement in the region. During the first three centuries of European settlement the inlets and estuarine waterways were the highways. In 1705/6 Bath, located on the Pamlico River with access to the Atlantic Ocean via Ocracoke Inlet, was incorporated as North Carolina's oldest town. The North Carolina assembly established Edenton in 1722 as North Carolina's first capital, due to availability of shipping through the northern inlets and its proximity to Jamestown and Chesapeake Bay. However, by the mid-1700s the northern inlets became unreliable for shipping. Four inlets began to shoal and close, jeopardizing Edenton's access to the ocean. In response the North Carolina assembly in 1753 established Portsmouth as the official port of entry on the south side of the larger and more stable Ocracoke Inlet. In the 1760s Governor William Tryon moved the North Carolina capital to New Bern on the Neuse River, which had direct access to shipping through Ocracoke Inlet.

The Dismal Swamp Canal, connecting the Chesapeake Bay and Albe-

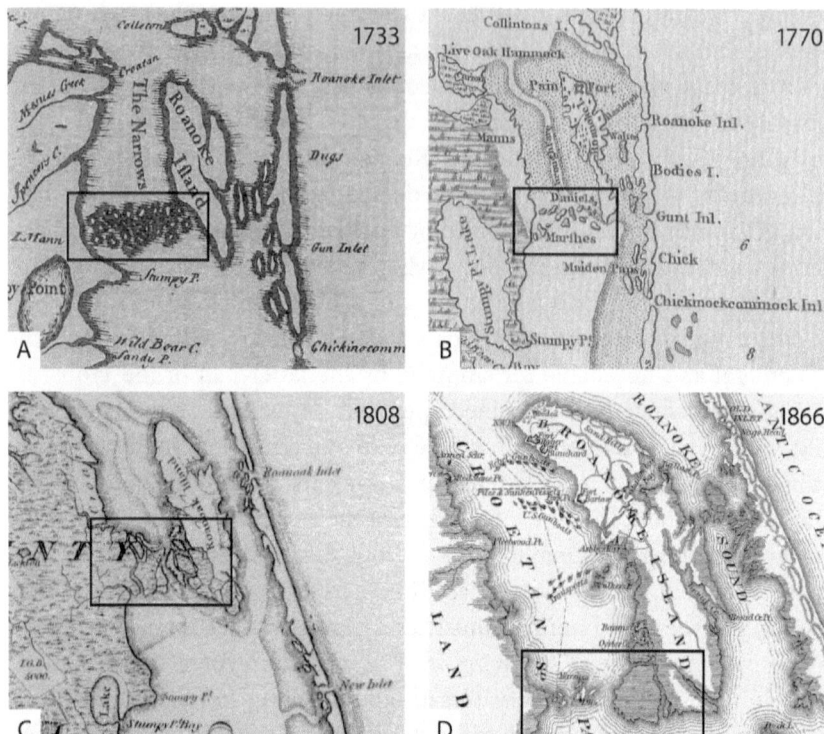

FIGURE 1.4. Four historic maps of the Roanoke Island coastal area show the dramatic changes in the coastal landscape that occurred in little more than a century due to the combined processes of frequent storms and ongoing sea-level rise. "The Narrows," shown in A and diagrammed in B and C, is the narrow channel of Croatan Creek that flows north into Albemarle Sound. The black box shows the Roanoke Marshes interstream divide that separated the Albemarle and Pamlico drainage basins. With closure of all ephemeral inlets through the barrier islands north of Roanoke Island by about 1817, the Roanoke-Albemarle drainage was forced to flow through The Narrows into Pamlico Sound and discharge to the ocean through existing inlets south of Roanoke Island. This flow severely eroded Croatan Creek through time to form the wide and deep Croatan Sound, and flooded across and through the Roanoke Marshes connecting the Albemarle and Pamlico Sound estuarine systems. Croatan Sound was now open for navigation between the estuaries and ready for the maritime battles of the Civil War (D). The maps in the first three panels are Moseley 1733 (A), Collet 1770 (B), and Price and Strother 1808 (C). D is an 1866 modified copy of the original 1862 map in the Union and Confederate Navies official records (*War of the Rebellion*, 1882, ser. 1, vol. 6, p. 554a).

marle Sound for the first time, was constructed and opened for small-scale shipping in 1805. This canal gave new life to the towns of Edenton and Elizabeth City and the agricultural and forestry industries of the Albemarle region. From the middle to late 1700s land-based roadways were developed between communities and migration began expanding into the Piedmont Province. Even the North Carolina capital was moved again, this time to the present location in Raleigh in 1792. In the mid-1800s railroads added another link to the infrastructural expansion within North Carolina. Finally the state's heavy dependence upon its coastal waterway system began to disappear.

With closure of all the northern inlets, the Roanoke-Albemarle discharge had no direct outlet to the Atlantic Ocean. This forced the discharge to flow through the Croatan Narrows and to flood across the Roanoke Marsh interstream divide, increasing shoreline erosion laterally and vertically to form the modern Croatan Sound (fig. 1.4D). Thus, the Roanoke-Albemarle and Pamlico drainage systems were connected and with time opened major navigation channels between the two drainage basins.[31] In 1836 the first screwpile lighthouse was built at the entrance to the expanding Roanoke Marsh channels. By the time of the Civil War a large portion of Roanoke Marshes had been eroded away and Croatan Sound was a major navigable waterway (fig. 1.4D). This opening allowed the Union general Ambrose Burnside to move forty-eight transport ships, nineteen warships, and 13,000 troops into Croatan Sound during the Civil War in a successful effort to capture Roanoke Island. Today, the two-hundred-year-old Croatan Sound is not only one of North Carolina's major waterways but also a dramatic example of rapid coastal system change in response to ongoing storm activity and rise in sea level.

NATURAL DYNAMICS VERSUS HUMAN OCCUPATION

The expulsion of North Carolina's dominant Tuscarora Nation at the end of the Tuscarora War in 1711–13 opened North Carolina's vast pocosin environments for full-scale modification and development (see table 1.1).[32]

The post–Tuscarora War history is one of clearing, ditching, dredging, draining, diking, and damming of the interior wetlands of North Carolina's lower Coastal Plain. Scientists estimated that before European settlement North Carolina contained about eleven million acres of wetlands, including estuarine and freshwater marshes, riverine-floodplain swamp forests, and upland pocosin swamp forests.[33] Of this original acreage, about 2.5 mil-

TABLE 1.1. Drainage history of North Carolina's Coastal Plain pocosins: Three centuries of swampland development

1711–13	Tuscarora Indian War opened North Carolina's "Land of Water" for settlement of the Coastal Plain and westward.
1728	William Byrd surveyed the North Carolina–Virginia boundary through the Great Dismal Swamp and proposed its drainage for agricultural development.
1763	George Washington and associates bought 46,464 acres of the Great Dismal Swamp; the Great Dismal Swamp Land Company dug the Washington Ditch in an effort to produce rice from 1776 to 1789.
1784	Construction began on the Dismal Swamp Canal from Chesapeake Bay to Albemarle Sound, creating a dike that held water to the west and drained land to the east for agriculture; the canal was completed in 1805.
1786–88	Josiah Collins brought enslaved West Africans to dig the Somerset Canal between the Scuppernong River and Lake Phelps to establish Somerset Place Plantation, drain the pocosin wetlands, harvest timber, and develop agricultural cropland.
1787	The North Carolina governor appointed a drainage board for Hyde County to drain wetlands for agriculture, including Lake Mattamuskeet.
1795	George Washington sold his share of the Great Dismal Swamp Land Company due to agricultural failures.
1825	North Carolina established the State Literary Fund: all state-owned swamplands were turned over to the fund, including Lake Mattamuskeet, with money from development and sale to be used for public education.
1826	The State Literary Fund recommended that Lake Mattamuskeet be drained and developed.
1837–42	The State Literary Fund contracted a seven-mile ditch from Lake Mattamuskeet to Wysocking Bay to lower the water table 3.5 feet and reduce the lake from 140 to 80 square miles.
1850	U.S. Congress passed the Swamp Lands Act, authorizing transfer of 20 million acres of swamp to Florida and 28.5 million acres to states along the Mississippi River for drainage and reclamation, reflecting the national mood to eliminate wetlands as exploration and development migrated south and west.
1867–1900	Post–Civil War interest in swamplands in North Carolina shifted from agriculture to logging.
1909	The North Carolina General Assembly passed a law to establish water drainage districts.
1911–28	Fifty-three water drainage districts were established in North Carolina, covering 700,000 acres, with 500,000 acres of swamp ditched and drained.

TABLE 1.1. Continued

1913–26	A plan was formed to dig 130 miles of drainage ditches and build a pumping plant to drain Lake Mattamuskeet for agriculture and construct New Holland Village on the lake bed; all three attempts to drain the lake (1916, 1920, and 1926) failed.
1934	New Holland Farms, Inc., sold 49,925 acres of Lake Mattamuskeet to the U.S. Fish and Wildlife Service for a wildlife refuge.
Post-1945	Because most major timber had been harvested on private swamplands, logging companies sold holdings to paper companies for pine production and the next period of extensive ditching and draining.
1973	George Washington's former property in the Great Dismal Swamp became a U.S. National Wildlife Refuge.
1973–80	The energy crisis led to evaluation of swamp-forest peat deposits as an alternative fuel resource; initial efforts in the Albemarle-Pamlico Peninsula failed.
2000–2007	Plans were made for regional landfills in numerous eastern North Carolina pocosin swamplands from urban areas outside of North Carolina.
2007	The North Carolina General Assembly passed a law to limit regional landfills in coastal swamplands.

lion acres consisted of upland pocosin swamp forests, an Algonquin concept meaning "swamp on a hill." By the mid-1980s North Carolina wetland acreage had dropped by 49 percent, to only about 5.7 million acres. However, the good news is that today the North Carolina Coastal Plain contains ten U.S. National Wildlife Refuges, four U.S. National Park facilities, one U.S. National Forest, seven North Carolina State Parks, and vast acreages of North Carolina game lands, most of which are in former ditched and drained pocosins. Even though the swamplands are highly modified landscapes, they are now preserved.

During the early portion of North Carolina's human history the coastal system was dominated by small sustainable villages. With time, regional economies began to develop around the wealth of the natural resources. The lower Coastal Plain depended on the rapid expansion of forestry and agriculture industries and was supported by a major shipping industry through the Civil War and into the early part of the twentieth century. During this same period the barrier island economies were largely driven by small-scale fisheries, boat building, salvage, lifesaving, and military-related industries.

By the late nineteenth and early twentieth century, major modifications of the barrier island and inlet system began with the rapid development of

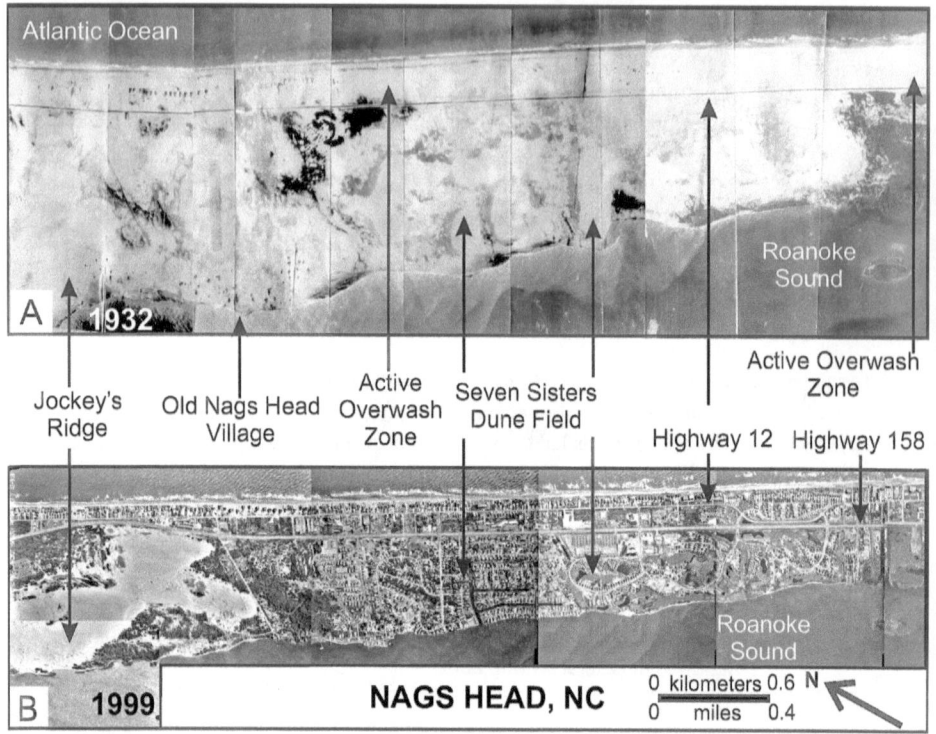

FIGURE 1.5. Two aerial photographs of the Nags Head village on the northern Outer Banks show the expansion of Old Nags Head from the shores of Roanoke Sound to the oceanfront with growth and development of the modern tourism industry. Notice the substantial decrease in distance from the shoreline to North Carolina Highway 12 from 1932 to 1999. The nineteenth-century oceanfront houses have been moved westward several times in response to shoreline recession, and most land areas and associated dune fields have been urbanized since 1932, with the exception of Jockey's Ridge.

a new tourism economy. Coastal tourism began in New Hanover County in the late 1800s, as indicated by the dramatic growth in population. Similar coastal growth started only after World War II in Carteret County. In addition, North Carolina's development of deepwater ports early in the 1900s in both of these counties shifted all shipping away from northeastern North Carolina.

Because of the relative isolation of the northeastern coastal system and shifts in transportation from waterways to railroads, paved roads, and ports, the region's economy languished (fig. 1.5A). The new coastal economy based on tourism of the Outer Banks did not begin until the latter half of the 1900s when adequate infrastructure had been developed. Construction of new highways, bridges, power, and water and sewage treatment facilities associated with the Outer Banks communities led to the post-1980 growth and booming beach economy (fig. 1.5B). In contrast, during the same time period many of the Inner Banks counties generally experienced a decline in both population and basic economy.

During the last glacial maximum (18,000 years ago) the North Carolina coastline was 15 to 60 miles to the east and 410 feet below its current location (fig. 1.2). Since then the coastline has migrated upward and westward to the present barrier island location (fig. 1.2), due to storms and rising sea level. Segments of the Outer Banks and other ocean shorelines continue to have explosive growth, along with receding shorelines (fig. 1.6A) at rates that require ever-increasing construction of sand-bag walls (fig. 1.6B) and pumping of beach replenishment sand in attempts to hold a quasi-permanent development line on the islands.[34] Since the Tuscarora War, 1711–13, the efforts to engineer and stabilize North Carolina's Land of Water have escalated the region's conflict between the natural dynamics of change and the complex commercial and economic landscape that has developed.

Since the mid-1930s, engineering efforts have escalated in an effort to stabilize shorelines and stop the migration of the Outer Banks.[35] But the bulldozers, sand-bag walls, and constructed barrier-dune ridges have minimized overwash and prevented possible inlets that would have built both the elevation and width of many barrier islands. Thus, the present coastal highway and associated economic developments that are largely near mean sea level on a mobile sand pile are at ever-increasing risk (fig. 1.6). As sea level continues to rise, there is an increasing likelihood that large segments of the barrier islands will be devastated by massive storm overwash and development of new inlets, before collapsing into a series of shallow shoals.[36] In spite of extensive engineering efforts, the ocean shorelines of the barrier islands continue their westward recession (fig. 1.6A).

There will always be a shoreline and a coastal system wherever an ocean intersects a landmass, and these have always moved in response to changing climatic and geologic conditions. The potential economic impact of storms and changing coastal systems depends on the topography, land-use patterns, and development density. However, both the historical and recent economic development practices in North Carolina's coastal system have largely ignored the dynamics of natural change. Centuries of engineering the low swamplands and the more recent introduction of an upland style of business economy (highways, megahouses, hotels, and condominiums) on mobile piles of barrier sands have created the potential for a catastrophic failure in response to a large-scale hurricane such as Hurricane Sandy in

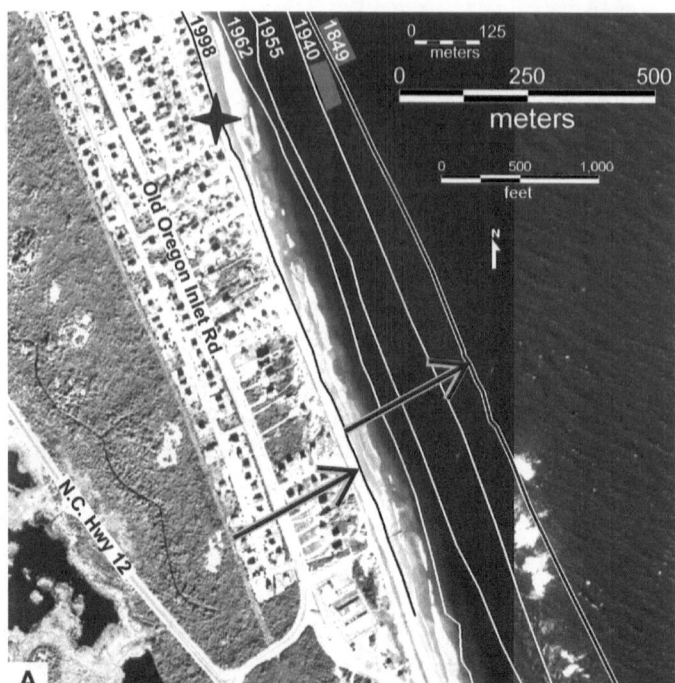

FIGURE 1.6. (A) A 1998 aerial photograph of a portion of South Nags Head on Bodie Island displays the location of the 1849 surveyed shoreline (double white line) relative to the shoreline location in 1998 (black line). The locations of other shorelines (single white lines) were obtained from georeferenced aerial photographs and are shown in recessional sequence from 1940, 1955, and 1962. The ocean shoreline has receded up to one thousand feet during 149 years, an average annual erosion rate up to seven feet per year. (B) A 2008 image shows a housing development built in the late 1980s to early 1990s. Sand-bagged houses were flanked by the ocean, septic tanks and access road destroyed, and the houses finally abandoned and demolished. The black star is the same location in both panels.

2012. Escalating urbanization within this dynamic system almost guarantees massive economic losses with every major storm event.

VISION FOR THE FUTURE OF A DYNAMIC AND CHANGING COASTAL SYSTEM

North Carolina's coastal economy is largely dependent upon a mixed commerce of agriculture, forestry, and tourism that is perched on a dynamic system of low wetlands and mobile barrier islands. Large portions of these ecosystems are being overwhelmed by storms and rising sea level at the same time as the coastal population has boomed in the twenty-first century (fig. 1.5). Thus, North Carolina finds itself in the throes of a "perfect conflict": an escalating battle between dramatic use and alteration of the landscape and the natural dynamics of coastal change.

To avoid catastrophic losses of life, economy, infrastructure, and property, North Carolina, like other coastal regions of the world, will need to develop responsible land-use plans for its coastal system of barrier islands, estuaries, wetlands, and adjacent uplands. Such a proposal, "North Carolina Land of Water" (NC LOW), was set forth in 2011.[37] NC LOW is a geographic region consisting of interdependent ecosystems dominated by large-scale changes resulting from ongoing processes of sea-level rise, high-energy storms, and severe human modification (fig. 1.7). These energetic processes of change have molded the human history, continue to impact the present culture, and will have an increasing effect on the nature of North Carolina's future coastal culture and economy. NC LOW is a new paradigm based on an integrated coastal system that is flexible and adaptable to change. With a science-based economic paradigm and a population of educated managers, politicians, and citizenry, North Carolina can adapt to these changes and maintain a viable and sustainable economy within a dynamic and changing coastal system. This initiative is built on an integrated natural, cultural, and economic resource base that will build connectivity throughout the coastal system, utilizing a multimodal transport system by water, air, and land.

The history of North Carolina's coastal region and its associated human culture is a product of the continual interplay of geologic, ecologic, and human processes acting upon North Carolina's dynamic coastal system. The NC LOW concept for economic development is a diversified, enhanced, and sustainable coastal economy that adapts to the natural processes necessary to preserve the coastal resources upon which that economy depends.[38]

North Carolina's unique coastal system has challenged the engineering prowess of many great minds through the centuries: Thomas Harriot and

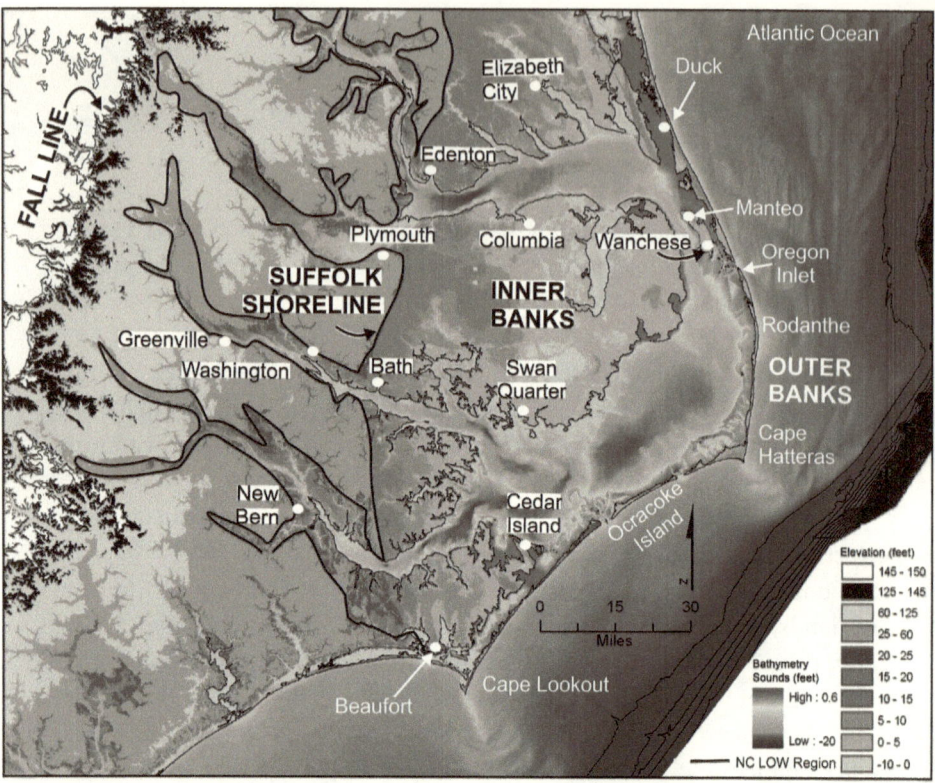

FIGURE 1.7. This gray-scale topographic map of northeastern North Carolina shows the location of the North Carolina Land of Water (NC LOW) coastal system. The "Land of Water" extends from the Outer Banks on the east, westward to the paleo-Suffolk Shoreline and up the major drainage floodplains to the fall line, and from the Virginia state line south to Beaufort Inlet. The North Carolina Coastal Plain rises slowly westward from the Lower Coastal Plain to the Upper Coastal Plain (moderate to light grays) and then rises abruptly across the fall line (black boundary zone) and onto North Carolina's Piedmont Province.

John White, who mapped the northeastern North Carolina region for Sir Walter Raleigh in 1585; George Washington, who initially tried to drain the Great Dismal Swamp in the latter half of the eighteenth century; Archibald DeBow Murphey, who attempted to reopen inlets through the Outer Banks in the antebellum period; and the redoubtable U.S. Army Corps of Engineers, which has fought the dynamics of nature from the nineteenth to the twenty-first century. With a fuller understanding of the state's coastal region from a geologic and ecologic point of view, North Carolina's future challenge will be to devise a coastal management and development system that can advance in harmony with the realities of this magnificent facet of its geologic heritage and resource dynamics.

NOTES

1. P. J. Godfrey and M. M. Godfrey, *Barrier Island Ecology of Cape Lookout National Seashore and Vicinity, North Carolina*, National Park Service Monograph Series, no. 9 (Washington, D.C., 1976); R. Dolan and H. Lins, *The Outer Banks of North Carolina*, U.S. Geological Survey Professional Paper 1117-B (1986); S. R. Riggs, W. J. Cleary, and S. W. Snyder, "Influence of Inherited Geologic Framework upon Barrier Beach Morphology and Shore Face Dynamics," *Marine Geology* 126 (1995): 213–34; O. H. Pilkey, W. J. Neal, S. R. Riggs, C. A. Webb, D. M. Bush, D. F. Pilkey, J. Bullock, and B. A. Cowan, *The North Carolina Shore and Its Barrier Island: Restless Ribbons of Sand* (Durham, N.C.: Duke University Press, 1998); S. R. Riggs and D. V. Ames, *Drowning the North Carolina Coast: Sea-Level Rise and Estuarine Dynamics*, N.C. Sea Grant College Program, publ. no. UNC-SG-03-04 (Raleigh, N.C., 2003); S. R. Riggs, D. V. Ames, S. J. Culver, and D. J. Mallinson, *The Battle for North Carolina's Coast: Evolutionary History, Present Crisis, and Vision for the Future* (Chapel Hill: University of North Carolina Press, 2011).

2. D. S. Phelps, "Archaeology of the North Carolina Coast and Coastal Plain: Problems and Hypothesis," in *The Prehistory of North Carolina: An Archaeological Symposium*, ed. M. A. Mathis and J. J. Crow (Raleigh: North Carolina Division of Archives and History, 1983), 1–51; I. R. Daniel and C. R. Moore, "Current Research into the Paleo-Indian and Archaic Periods of the North Carolina Coastal Plain," in *The Archaeology of North Carolina: Three Archaeology Symposia*, ed. C. R. Ewen, T. R. White, and R. P. S. Davis Jr., North Carolina Archaeological Council publ. no. 20 (Raleigh, N.C., 2011), 3-1–3-24; C. R. Moore and I. R. Daniel, "Geoarchaeological Investigations of Stratified Sand Ridges along the Tar River, North Carolina," in Ewen et al., *Archaeology of North Carolina*, 1-1–1-42; D. G. Anderson and K. E. Sassaman, *Recent Developments in Southeastern Archaeology: From Colonization to Complexity* (Washington, D.C.: Society for American Archaeology, 2012).

3. G. S. Dunbar, *Historical Geography of the North Carolina Outer Banks*, Coastal Studies Institute Series, no. 3 (Baton Rouge: Louisiana State University Press, 1958); D. Stick, *The Outer Banks of North Carolina* (Chapel Hill: University of North Carolina Press, 1958); D. Stick, *Roanoke Island: The Beginnings of English America* (Chapel Hill: University of North Carolina Press, 1983); Riggs et al., *Battle for North Carolina's Coast*.

4. Riggs et al., *Battle for North Carolina's Coast*.

5. Ibid.

6. *Geologic Map of North Carolina* (Raleigh: North Carolina Geological Survey, 1985), 1 sheet, scale = 1:500,000; R. E. Sheridan and J. A. Grow, eds., *The Atlantic Continental Margin: U.S.*, vol. I-2 of *The Geology of North America* (Boulder, Colo.: Geological Society of America, 1988); W. A. Thomas, R. D. Hatcher, and G. W. Viele, *The Appalachian-Ouachita Orogen in the United States*, vol. F-2 of *The Geology of North America* (Boulder, Colo.: Geological Society of America, 1990); F. R. Press, J. Sever, and T. H. Jordan, *Understanding Earth*, 4th ed. (New York: Freeman, 2004); W. A. Thomas, "Tectonic Inheritance at a Continental Margin," *GSA Today* 16, no. 2 (2006): 4–11.

7. *Geologic Map of North Carolina*; Sheridan and Grow, *Atlantic Continental Margin*;

Thomas et al., *Appalachian-Ouachita Orogen*; J. W. Horton and V. A. Zullo, eds., *The Geology of the Carolinas: Carolina Geological Society Fiftieth Anniversary Volume* (Knoxville: University of Tennessee Press, 1991); Press et al., *Understanding Earth*; Thomas, "Tectonic Inheritance."

8. Riggs et al., "Influence of Inherited Geologic Framework"; P. R. Parham, S. R. Riggs, S. J. Culver, D. J. Mallinson, and J. F. Wehmiller, "Quaternary Depositional Patterns and Sea-Level Fluctuations," *Northeastern North Carolina: Quaternary Research* 67, no. 1 (2007): 83–99; S. R. Riggs, *Shoreline Erosion in North Carolina Estuaries*, publ. no. UNC-SG-01-011 (Raleigh: North Carolina Sea Grant College Program, 2001).

9. Riggs et al., *Battle for North Carolina's Coast*.

10. J. Imbrie and K. P. Imbrie, *Ice Ages* (Cambridge, Mass.: Harvard University Press, 1979); M. Williams, D. Dunkerley, P. De Deckker, and J. Chappell, *Quaternary Environments*, 2nd ed. (New York: Oxford University Press, 1998); R. S. Bradley, *Paleoclimatology: Reconstructing Climates of the Quaternary*, 2nd ed. (San Diego: Academic Press, 1999); W. F. Ruddiman, *Earth's Climate: Past and Future*, 2nd ed. (New York: Freeman, 2008).

11. W. F. Ruddiman and H. E. Wright, eds., *North American and Adjacent Oceans during the Last Deglaciation*, vol. K-3 of *The Geology of North America* (Boulder, Colo.: Geological Society of America, 1987); H. H. Lamb, *Weather, Climate, and Human Affairs* (New York: Routledge, 1988); E. C. Pielou, *After the Ice Age* (Chicago: University of Chicago Press, 1991); B. G. Anderson and H. W. Borns, *The Ice Age World* (Oslo, Norway: Scandinavian University Press, 1994).

12. B. P. Horton, W. R. Peltier, S. J. Culver, R. Drummon, S. E. Englehart, A. C. Kemp, D. Mallinson, E. R. Thieler, S. R. Riggs, D. V. Ames, and K. H. Thomson "Holocene Sea-Level Changes along the North Carolina Coastline and Their Implications for Glacial Isostatic Adjustment Models," *Quaternary Science Reviews* 28 (2009): 1725–36; Riggs et al., *Battle for North Carolina's Coast*; E. R. Thieler, D. S. Foster, E. A. Himmelstoss, and E. J. Mallinson, "Geologic Framework of the North Carolina, U.S.A., Inner Continental Shelf and Its Influence on Coastal Evolution," *Marine Geology* 348 (2014): 113–30.

13. D. Mallinson, S. R. Riggs, E. R. Thieler, S. J. Culver, D. S. Foster, D. R. Corbett, K. Farrell, and J. F. Wehmiller, "Late Neogene and Quaternary Evolution of the Northern Albemarle Embayment (Mid-Atlantic Continental Margin, U.S.A.)," *Marine Geology* 217 (2005): 97–117; D. J. Mallinson, S. J. Culver, S. R. Riggs, E. R. Thieler, D. Foster, J. Wehmiller, K. Farrell, and J. Pierson, "Regional Seismic Stratigraphy and Controls on the Quaternary Evolution of the Cape Hatteras Region of the Atlantic Passive Margin, U.S.A.," *Marine Geology* 268 (2010): 16–33; Thieler et al., "Geologic Framework "; Riggs, *Shoreline Erosion in North Carolina Estuaries*.

14. O. H. Pilkey and R. Young, *The Rising Sea* (Washington, D.C.: Island Press, 2009); Riggs et al., *Battle for North Carolina's Coast*.

15. Horton et al., "Holocene Sea-Level Changes."

16. S. R. Riggs and D. V. Ames, *Effect of Storms on Barrier Island Dynamics, Core Banks, Cape Lookout National Seashore, North Carolina, 1960–2001*, U.S. Geological Survey Scientific Investigations Report 2006-5309 (U.S. Department of the Interior, 2007); Riggs et al., *Battle for North Carolina's Coast*.

17. R. Dolan, H. Lins, and B. Hayden, "Mid-Atlantic Coastal Storms," *Journal of Coastal*

Research 4, no. 3 (1988): 417–33; P. J. Robinson, *North Carolina Weather and Climate* (Chapel Hill: University of North Carolina Press, 2005).

18. Stick, *Outer Banks*; Stick, *Roanoke Island*; Jay Barnes, *North Carolina's Hurricane History* (Chapel Hill: University of North Carolina Press, 2001).

19. Riggs and Ames, *Drowning the North Carolina Coast*; Riggs and Ames, *Effect of Storms on Barrier Island Dynamics.*

20. Lamb, *Weather, Climate, and Human Affairs*; Pielou, *After the Ice Age*; S. J. Williams, K. Dodd, and K. K. Gohn, *Coasts in Crisis*, U.S. Geological Survey Circular 1075.

21. Imbrie and Imbrie, *Ice Ages.*

22. Stick, *Outer Banks*; Stick, *Roanoke Island*; Riggs and Ames, *Drowning the North Carolina Coast.*

23. Imbrie and Imbrie, *Ice Ages*; Pielou, *After the Ice Age*; Ruddiman, *Earth's Climate.*

24. Daniel and Moore, "Current Research"; Anderson and Sassaman, *Recent Developments in Southeastern Archaeology.*

25. Phelps, "Archaeology of the North Carolina Coast"; Moore and Daniel, "Geoarchaeological Investigations."

26. Phelps, "Archaeology of the North Carolina Coast."

27. W. P. Cumming, *North Carolina in Maps* (Raleigh: North Carolina Department of Archives and History, 1966); W. P. Cumming, *Mapping the North Carolina Coast: Sixteenth-Century Cartography and the Roanoke Voyages* (Raleigh: North Carolina Department of Cultural Resources, Division of Archives and History, 1988).

28. Riggs and Ames, *Drowning the North Carolina Coast*; D. J. Mallinson, C. W. Smith, S. J. Culver, S. R. Riggs, and D. V. Ames, "Geological Characteristics and Spatial Distribution of Paleo-Inlet Channels beneath the Outer Banks Barrier Islands, North Carolina, U.S.A.," *Estuarine, Coastal, and Shelf Science* 88 (2010): 175–89; Thieler et al., "Geologic Framework."

29. Quoted in Stick, *Roanoke Island*, 145.

30. Riggs and Ames, *Drowning the North Carolina Coast*; Riggs, *Shoreline Erosion in North Carolina Estuaries*; S. R. Riggs, G. L. Rudolph, and D. V. Ames, *Erosional Scour and Geological Evolution of Croatan Sound, Northeastern North Carolina*, North Carolina Department of Transportation, rep. no. FHWA/NC/2000-002 (Raleigh, N.C., 2000); Riggs et al., *Battle for North Carolina's Coast.*

31. Riggs et al., *Erosional Scour and Geological Evolution of Croatan Sound*; Mallinson et al., "Late Neogene and Quaternary Evolution."

32. Phelps, "Archaeology of the North Carolina Coast"; Anderson and Sassaman, *Recent Developments in Southeastern Archaeology.*

33. K. A. Wilson, *North Carolina Wetlands: Their Distribution and Management*, North Carolina Wildlife Commission Project W-6-R (Raleigh, N.C., 1962); C. J. Richardson, *Pocosin Wetlands* (Stroudsburg, Pa.: Hutchinson Ross, 1981); Environmental Defense Fund, "Carolina Wetlands," unpublished report (Raleigh, N.C.); T. E. Dahl, *Wetlands: Losses in the United States, 1780s–1980s*, U.S. Fish and Wildlife Report to Congress (Washington, D.C., 1990).

34. Godfrey and Godfrey, *Barrier Island Ecology*; C. H. Everts, J. P. Battley, and P. N. Gibson, *Shoreline Movements: Cape Henry Virginia to Cape Hatteras, North Carolina, 1849–1980*, U.S. Army Corps of Engineers Technical Report CERC-83-1 (1983); S. D. Heron, T. F.

Moslow, W. M. Berelson, G. A. Steele, and K. R. Susman, "Holocene Sedimentation of a Wave-Dominated Barrier-Island Shoreline: Cape Lookout, North Carolina," *Marine Geology* 60 (1984): 413–34; Dolan et al., "Mid-Atlantic Coastal Storms"; B. T. Gutierrez, S. J. Williams, and E. R. Thieler, "Potential for Shoreline Changes due to Sea-Level Rise along the U.S. Mid-Atlantic Region," U.S. Geological Survey Open-File Report 2007-1278 (2007), http://pubs.usgs.gov/of/2007/1278; Mallinson et al., "Regional Seismic Stratigraphy"; S. J. Culver, C. A. Grand Pre, D. J. Mallinson, S. R. Riggs, D. R. Corbett, J. Foley, M. Hale, L. Metger, J. Ricardo, J. Rosenberger, D. G. Smith, C. W. Smith, S. W. Snyer, D. Twamley, K. Farrell, and B. P. Horton, "Late Holocene Barrier Island Collapse: Outer Banks, North Carolina, U.S.A.," *Sedimentary Record* 5 (2007): 4–8; S. R. Riggs, D. V. Ames, S. J. Culver, D. J. Mallinson, D. R. Corbett, and J. P. Walsh, "Eye of a Human Hurricane: Pea Island, Oregon Inlet, and Bodie Island, Northern Outer Banks, North Carolina," in *Identifying America's Most Vulnerable Oceanfront Communities: A Geological Perspective*, ed. J. T. Kelley, O. H. Pilkey, and J. A. G. Cooper, Geological Society of America, Special Paper 460 (Boulder, Colo., 2009), 43–72; Riggs et al., *Battle for North Carolina's Coast*.

35. Riggs et al., "Eye of a Human Hurricane"; Riggs et al., *Battle for North Carolina's Coast*; S. R. Riggs and D. V. Ames, "Consequences of Human Modifications of Oregon Inlet to the Down-Drift Pea Island, North Carolina Outer Banks," *Southeastern Geology* 48, no. 3 (2011): 103–28.

36. Mallinson et al., "Late Neogene and Quaternary Evolution"; Culver et al., "Late Holocene Barrier Island Collapse"; Gutierrez et al., "Potential for Shoreline Changes due to Sea-Level Rise"; Riggs et al., "Eye of a Human Hurricane"; Riggs et al., *Battle for North Carolina's Coast*; Riggs, *Shoreline Erosion in North Carolina Estuaries*.

37. Riggs et al., *Battle for North Carolina's Coast*.

38. Ibid.

VOYAGES TO CAROLINA

EUROPEANS IN THE INDIANS' OLD WORLD

Michael Leroy Oberg and David Moore

For many years, historians telling the story of early North Carolina have focused on the efforts of English explorers backed by Sir Walter Ralegh[1] to establish a foothold on the Outer Banks. The state's history, all too often, thus seems to begin when these ill-fated colonists arrive. But there are alternatives to this Anglocentric narrative. The first Europeans who arrived in what became "Virginia," then "Carolina," and finally North Carolina—Spaniards in the west and the English along the coast—sojourned in a world where Native American rules prevailed. The early history of North Carolina is as much an Indian as it is a European story.

Students of the encounter between natives and newcomers in North Carolina are often quite familiar with John White's paintings of the Algonquian towns of Secotan and Pomeiooc, but they know almost nothing about Otari, Yssa, Dudca, and Guatari or Quinahaqui, Guaquiri, and Joara, all towns in the Carolina Piedmont described by Spanish explorers almost two decades before Ralegh's first efforts to plant an outpost along the coast.[2]

No Spanish adventurer in the region wrote with the ethnographic curiosity of Thomas Harriot, the scientist and explorer who penned those indelible accounts of the encounter at Roanoke, but if we look at the surviving Spanish accounts, alongside the archaeological record, much indeed might be learned. These Spaniards, warlike, governed in nearly every aspect of their life by fervent religious beliefs that justified violence toward the region's native peoples, and ever aggressive, began their explorations in the American Southeast in the early 1520s. Juan Ponce de León attempted an initial settlement on the southwest Florida coast in 1521. Five years later, Lucas Vázquez de Ayllón failed in his attempt to establish a colony of around six hundred people, somewhere along the Gulf Coast of modern Georgia. In 1528, the expedition led by Pánfilo de Nárvaez and four hundred soldiers came to ruin on the Gulf Coast. One decade later, Hernando de Soto and his survivors spent several years stomping through the Southeast, followed by the lesser known expedition of Tristán de Luna y Arellano in 1559–60.[3] Of these, only the relatively large force led by de Soto passed through the Piedmont region of North Carolina, though scholars continue to debate the exact route he followed.[4]

Surely these expeditions affected the native communities through which they passed. The de Soto narratives show that the Spaniards demanded from Indians food and labor and resorted quickly to mind-numbing levels of violence. The Spanish may have carried with them into the interior epidemic diseases like smallpox that took an enormous toll in Indian lives, though the nature and timing of these epidemics remain a matter of debate.[5] There is much that we cannot know. Only the arrival in the Piedmont of Juan Pardo, a Spanish captain at the head of more than one hundred men, allows us to see something of the Indians' world in the Carolina interior.

Pardo's expedition grew out of the early jockeying between the Spanish and their imperial rivals for control of the southeastern coast. Pedro Menéndez de Avilés, the governor of La Florida (defined, at the time, as all of North America north of Mexico), founded the town of St. Augustine on the Florida coast in 1565. He then moved decisively against the French, beginning with the seizure of Fort Carolina on the northern coast of Florida. He next moved north up the coast to today's Parris Island, South Carolina, where in the spring of 1566 he established Santa Elena, intended to be his capital city.[6] Pardo arrived in Santa Elena from Spain in July with an army of 250 men to reinforce the outpost following a mutiny of Menéndez's original forces. Menéndez lacked the food to feed all these men but possessed a clear plan for settlement of La Florida. Pardo and his men, if dispatched into the interior, could help solve both problems.[7]

Menéndez instructed Pardo to take "as many as one hundred and twenty soldiers, harquebusiers, and crossbowmen" along "the road which seems to you most convenient and direct to go to Zacatecas and the mines of San Martin" in northern Mexico, "trying to make all friendship with the caciques," or native leaders, "who may be on and along the way." Menéndez expected Pardo to stay for several days at a time "in order that the caciques of the surrounding country may go to see you."[8]

It was, to Menéndez, a campaign to "pacify and calm the caciques or Indians of all the land and to attract them to the service of God and of His Majesty and likewise to take possession of the land in his royal name." Conquest and Christianity marched hand in hand. The men accompanying Pardo kept records on the region they hoped to integrate into a Spanish North American empire (fig. 2.1). They noted the names of the caciques, some of whom traveled one hundred miles to meet with Pardo. They recorded the gifts the Spaniards bestowed upon those native leaders and Pardo's demands that

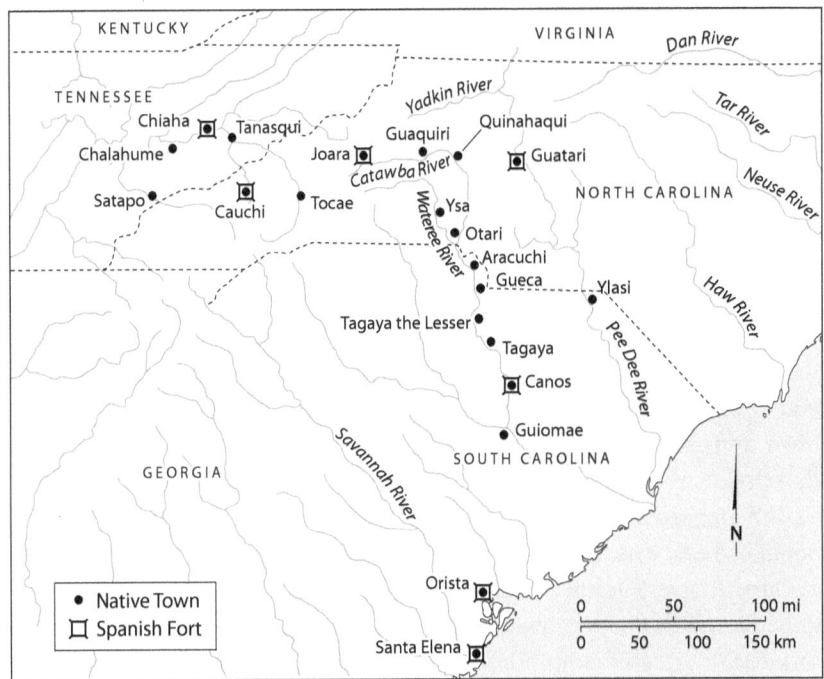

FIGURE 2.1. Indian towns visited by Juan Pardo's second expedition in 1567–68.

these leaders compel their people to provide the Spaniards with food and build for them housing.⁹

Who are these native peoples encountered by de Soto and Pardo in the North Carolina Piedmont? It is clear from the archaeological evidence that a large population of prehistoric Native Americans lived throughout the middle and upper Catawba Valley in scattered settlements in the fifteenth and sixteenth centuries.¹⁰ These were people known to archaeologists as Mississippians, groups organized into chiefdoms supported by an agricultural subsistence base of maize, beans, and squash. Several of the larger towns in this region also featured small earthen platform mounds on top of which a chief's house would be placed.

To the Spanish, these people inhabited villages identified by the names of their respective chiefs—names that emerge in history as the first indigenous peoples described by Europeans in the region that became North Carolina. Who are they relative to the eighteenth-century Piedmont peoples described by John Lawson? This is a difficult question to answer definitively, but the names of the native leaders with whom Pardo met along his route offer the most interesting and compelling clues. These names serve as markers of lin-

Europeans in the Indians' Old World 43

guistic and ethnic identity, as well as indicators helping to establish some understanding of the social structure of the Carolina Piedmont peoples.[11]

As to their ethnic identity, ceramic evidence suggests that these people were related to Muskogean-speaking Indians to the south in Georgia and South Carolina. Linguistic analysis of the chiefs' names indicates that most of the village leaders Pardo met in North Carolina spoke Siouan/Catawban languages, others spoke Iroquoian (probably ancestral Cherokees from the western North Carolina mountains), and a few, perhaps, Eastern Muskogean and Yuchian.[12] Their names are associated with titles implying various degrees of authority. Juan de la Bandera, Pardo's notary, records more than 120 *oratas* (translated as "lesser lords" and probably meaning a village headman) and only three *mico* (translated as "great lords"): Joara Mico, Guatari Mico, and Olamico (from Chiaha). The Spanish sources allow us to conclude that these three individuals held more regional authority than the *oratas*.[13]

The archaeological data along with the linguistic clues suggest a highly populated and complex indigenous cultural landscape in the mid-sixteenth century. Archaeological evidence also indicates that widespread depopulation followed in the seventeenth century, rendering more difficult our efforts to identify these communities. However, it seems likely that the descendants of most of the sixteenth-century Catawba Valley peoples were among those identified in 1700 by the English surveyor John Lawson as the Esaw, Wateree, Sugaree, and others, located along the modern-day North Carolina/South Carolina border in the vicinity of Charlotte, North Carolina. By the 1720s, the English identified these people as Catawbas. A more definitive analysis of the ethnic identity of the sixteenth-century western North Carolina Piedmont peoples must await further archaeological investigations.[14]

Nonetheless, Pardo's expeditions provide the first glimpse of these North Carolina Piedmont peoples. Pardo and his men advanced into the interior beginning in the fall of 1566, traveling north from Santa Elena and ultimately following the Wateree River. He found several of the towns described by de Soto twenty-six years before. He continued northward, entering the North Carolina Piedmont by way of the Catawba River Valley. In late December, arriving at Joara, an ancestral Catawban town in the foothills of the Appalachians, Pardo saw snow in the mountains to the west and decided to wait to cross the mountains in the spring. He and his men remained in Joara for two weeks while he constructed Fort San Juan and renamed Joara Ciudad de Cuenca, after his hometown in Spain. The construction of Fort San Juan marked the establishment of the first European settlement in the interior of what is now the United States, nearly twenty years before the English landed at Roanoke Island and almost forty years before they settled Jamestown.[15]

Pardo left a garrison of thirty men at the fort under the command of Sergeant Hernando Moyano de Morales. With the remainder of his army, Pardo began the return trip to Santa Elena, establishing three additional forts near native villages on the journey. He hoped to return later that year.[16]

During Pardo's absence Sergeant Moyano received a threat from a mountain chief that he would kill and eat the Spaniards.[17] In response, Moyano left ten men stationed at Fort San Juan, taking the remaining twenty of his men along with warriors from Joara to attack the Chisca Indians in eastern Tennessee. It is difficult to understand Moyano's motivation for such an action; Charles Hudson suggests that Moyano may have felt seriously threatened or may have used this as an opportunity to prospect for gold and silver.[18] He may also have acted at the urging of Joara Mico in order to settle a previous grievance between the tribes. After engaging the Chiscas, Moyano briefly explored the area of eastern Tennessee and ultimately built a small fort in the native town of Chiaha, possibly located near present-day Dandridge, Tennessee. He then sent word that he would remain at Chiaha to await Pardo's spring return.[19]

Meeting with Menéndez in Santa Elena, Pardo described a bountiful interior. The land at Joara, he wrote, "is very good," and nearby Quinhanaqui has "very fine bottomlands and a high volume river passes through it." Menéndez was encouraged by these reports. He ordered Pardo to return to the interior, find the most direct route to Spain's silver mines in northern Mexico, establish sound relations with the native peoples he encountered, and "take possession of the land in the name of the King of Spain." Pardo visited nearly twenty villages on the return march to Joara.[20]

In the meantime, Moyano had gotten himself into trouble. Pardo learned on September 24, 1567, that Chisca warriors surrounded Chiaha. Over the next six weeks, Pardo and his army traveled into the mountains of western North Carolina and eastern Tennessee. They relieved the stranded Moyano and his men, and together they continued the mission to Mexico. However, after passing though several other towns and following negotiations for assistance from the chief of the town of Satapo, Pardo began to suspect that a number of native leaders were gathering warriors to ambush the Spanish army. As a result, he and his men decided to end their mission to the west.[21]

Pardo still fully intended to meet Menéndez's instructions and to solidify a permanent Spanish presence in this region of La Florida. Thus, he began to build a chain of forts to add to Fort San Juan at Joara. As he returned eastward, his men built Fort San Pedro in Chiaha and Fort San Pablo, perhaps along the French Broad River between the modern-day towns of Asheville and Marshall, North Carolina. Pardo left twenty-six men at Fort San Pedro and eleven men at Fort San Pablo and returned to Joara with his remaining soldiers. Pardo spent nearly three weeks at Joara, resting, conducting diplomacy with native leaders who came to visit, and gathering provisions before heading east again. He renamed the town of Guatari (possibly located in the vicinity of modern-day Salisbury, North Carolina) "Cuidad de Salamanca," and his men built Fort Santiago, which he garrisoned with around thirty men. Next, moving south toward Santa Elena, he returned to Cofitachequi, which he renamed "Cuidad de Toledo," and built Fort Santo Tomás. The sixth and final fort, Fuerte de Nuestra Señora, he built just north of Santa Elena at the native town of Orista, a site Pardo renamed "Villa de Buena Esperança." And fully aware that there was still insufficient food at Santa Elena to supply his remaining troops, he dispatched most of them back to Fort Santo Tomás and to several other smaller native towns. Pardo finally arrived at Santa Elena with just a few remaining men on March 2, 1568.[22]

Pardo surely thought he had accomplished much of his mission to control La Florida for Menéndez. The Spanish forts, however, did not last long. The men stationed in the six forts had little to offer their hosts in terms of additional trade goods. They received no support from Santa Elena once Pardo departed from them. It is likely that the Indians expected the Spaniards to continue to supply trade goods in return for the food they provided for the men garrisoned in the forts, but no more trade goods were to come. Certainly, the natives did not understand or accept the pretense of a Spanish "conquest" of their towns and their countryside. At some point, the relatively peaceful relations between hosts and guests ended. In May 1568, three months after Pardo arrived back in Santa Elena, word came that the Indians had attacked and destroyed the interior forts. Only one of Pardo's men survived.[23]

Unfortunately, the Spanish documents provide few clues of what the Spanish settlements and forts looked like, but we can assume that the forts resembled Fort San Felipe that Pardo's men built at Santa Elena before they marched inland in 1566. It consisted of a rectangular, palisaded fortification surrounded by a steep-sided ditch or moat. The population of Santa Elena was distributed in houses outside the fort itself. Archaeologists have located only one of Pardo's six forts, San Juan, at the Berry site in Burke County, North Carolina. Excavations conducted there since 2001 shed important light on this early encounter between natives and newcomers.[24]

At Berry, archaeologists have uncovered evidence of five structures arranged around a plaza. These square buildings measure approximately seven to nine meters on a side, and though slightly larger than domestic native structures, they were built on a similar plan. Each of the buildings was burned, and no attempt was made to rebuild them. Evidence from the burned timber frames shows that many of the timbers were cut with metal axes. More than two hundred mid-sixteenth-century Spanish artifacts have been found around these five buildings, including a variety of ceramic vessels, wrought iron, iron chain mail links, and one piece of plate armor, as well as nails, lead balls, sprues, clothing hooks, copper aglets, and pieces of an iron steelyard scale. Notably, while there are a few glass beads and one iron knife, the vast majority of the Spanish artifacts are goods that the Spanish reserved for themselves and did not trade to the Indians.[25]

These buildings constituted Ciudad de Cuenca, Pardo's first settlement in the interior. Archaeological evidence now indicates that Fort San Juan was built immediately beside the five buildings. A portion of a large moat has been revealed, and future excavations should identify the entire fort structure.[26]

Something, however, clearly went very, very wrong between the Spaniards and their hosts. Evidence from the Berry site shows that the Indians swept all five buildings clean before setting the structures ablaze. Early evidence suggests that the Joarans raised an earthen platform mound over the destroyed fort, perhaps as an indication of Mico Joara's newly acquired stature as one of the leaders against the unwelcome intruders.[27]

As Pardo advanced westward beginning in 1566, he expressed optimism that the native peoples of the interior might be integrated into Spain's Christian, New World empire. He described native leaders who traveled great distances to trade and to greet the Spanish party. The Indians, Pardo might have concluded, welcomed the Spanish. The caciques accepted Spanish gifts, and they supplied food and shelter for the Spanish. At the town of Aracuchi in the fall of 1567, for instance, "the cacique of the place, who was called Aracuchi Orata" showed to Pardo a "new wooden house" containing within it "an elevated room with a certain quantity of maize." This all was for the Spanish crown, Pardo's interpreter conveyed to him. The cacique said that he gathered the corn and built the house for the Spanish and pledged his obedience for the future. He would neither consume nor take away "any amount of the maize except with the permission of His Majesty or of one who has his power."[28]

A Spanish dream, this: compliant native peoples, awaiting the arrival of the Spanish and bestowing all they owned upon them with selfless generosity. Perhaps native peoples understood Spanish firepower and their penchant for violence and chose the path of least resistance. But there are other explanations, and it is not necessary to view these interactions as passive acquiescence to Spanish imperialism. On the contrary, they are best understood as diplomatic measures by natives who wished to assess the potential relationship with the Spanish. The native peoples Pardo encountered viewed the Spanish army as a movable feast or, in the words of Robin Beck and his colleagues, as "an array of resources, one with the potential to be mobilized by indigenous peoples toward a range of political, economic, and military ends."[29] From this perspective, it is also possible to view hostile native responses to the Spanish incursion not primarily as an automatic resistance to the Spanish threat but as calculations among competing leaders to position themselves politically with relation to competing leaders in other regional towns.[30]

The Spanish built their forts, placed their garrisons, and dreamed their imperial dream only because native peoples in the interior allowed them to settle there. They invited the Spanish to enter their villages. They complied with the initial requests for food and shelter, and they continued to assess the potential utility of these new "resources" as Pardo and his men moved westward. In this sense, the very act of building houses for the Spanish army constituted a gesture of autonomy among and between competing chiefs who gathered at each town to meet with Pardo.[31] Yet another example of native agency is exhibited in Moyano's forays against the Chisca towns in southwest Virginia and east Tennessee. Because warriors from Joara accompanied Moyano and his men, it seems likely that the Indians drew Moyano into these military forays at the behest of Mico Joara to gain an advantage against rival regional leaders. Spanish troops became proxies in a struggle between indigenous players.[32]

Native intention and calculation are most clearly demonstrated in the destruction of Pardo's six inland forts, probably by planned and coordinated attacks. While we do not know the proximate cause of the attacks, there are clues in Bandera's reports that relations between the soldiers and native women may have caused disputes.[33] It is also very likely that the native hosts regarded the constant support for the forts without accompanying reciprocation from the Spanish as no longer sustainable. This realization, combined with interpersonal misunderstandings, may have sparked the destruction. Indian leaders decided that they had had enough. They acted according to their own needs, their assessments of the needs of their followers, and their expectations for the future.

■ Two decades after Pardo's failure, English mariners would sack Spanish possessions along the coast of La Florida and the Caribbean. The native allies of the Spanish offered no assistance to their colonial overlords. Spanish imperialism in North America could not succeed without the assistance or, at a minimum, the acquiescence of native peoples. The English might have learned from this at Roanoke. Thomas Harriot was indeed a careful observer of the Algonquian peoples the English settled among in 1585. But despite his great curiosity and, by the standards of his time, his open-mindedness, he told us only part of the story. There is much that he did not describe. When he explained how the Carolina Algonquians blew tobacco smoke upon their fish weirs, he could not or would not plumb the depths of the reasoning behind this ritual.[34] When he tells us that Algonquians "either pownes, or paynt their forhead, cheeks, chynne, bodye, armes, and legs" with a variety of images in a number of colors, he did not explain why. And he only hints at how the Indians perceived the "invisible bullets" fired at them by the English and the diseases that whipsawed through their villages, leaving many dead— in some villages twenty, in some forty, and in one six score.[35]

Harriot's work does make clear, however, that at Roanoke Island the English intruded into a world that was very different from their own, one that bristled with a way of thinking and knowing foreign to Elizabethan Englishmen. They intruded into an Algonquian world when Wingina's people guided them to their village on the northern tip of Roanoke Island and allowed them to establish their settlement a short distance away. Roanoke is best understood as an Algonquian story, not an English one. While English settlers in 1607 would later struggle to establish a town along a river that both bore the name of an English king, and while Calvinist extremists fleeing their homes first for Leiden and then for America would settle places in New England named after the towns they left at home, Ralegh's sojourners visited Croatoan, Hatorask, Dasemunkepeuc, Secotan, and Roanoac. It was the Algonquians of the Outer Banks who drove the narrative, provided the setting, and, in a sense, determined its outcome. It was they who sealed the fate of Ralegh's Roanoke ventures, which makes it all the more important that we understand something of the Carolina Algonquians' "Old World."[36]

When we recast the story of Roanoke in this manner, it becomes clear that the English came to Roanoke Island not so much as colonizers and explorers but as invited guests. After the English arrived in the summer of 1584, with little sense of what to do next, Indian scouts sent from Roanoke hung about the Outer Banks for three days and then approached the English reconnaissance voyage led by Philip Amadas and Arthur Barlowe, initiating the processes of exchange and ritual that transformed the newcomers from strangers into kin. Ultimately, Granganimeo, the "brother" of the Roanoke weroance Wingina, and clearly a weroance in his own right, invited the En-

Europeans in the Indians' Old World 49

glish to visit the small village on Roanoke Island, a site some distance up the Pamlico Sound, which we have no reason to believe the English would otherwise have found.[37]

At Roanoke Island, this ritual process continued, with confident Algonquians greeting, welcoming, and sizing up a small number of nervous newcomers, who clung to their weapons while dinner was served. The Algonquians on Roanoke clearly saw the English as potential allies in their wars with their native neighbors—Indian communities on the Outer Banks had conflicts and relationships with their neighbors that did not disappear merely because the English arrived. Granganimeo and his supporters, Barlowe wrote, "offered us very good exchange for our hatchets and axes, and for knives, and would have given any thing for swords."[38] Granganimeo took a tin dish the English offered him and wore it about his neck, suggesting that it would protect him from his enemies' arrows. (Wingina, his superior in some capacity, was unable to meet the English at this time for he was, tellingly, recovering from wounds suffered in battle.) When the English fired their guns, Granganimeo and his followers "would tremble thereat for very feare, and for the strangeness of the same." The Algonquians marveled at English weaponry that demonstrated tremendous power. It was loud, dramatic, and capable of immense damage on those occasions when it found its target. They tried, unsuccessfully, to persuade Amadas and Barlowe to deploy these weapons against their enemies.[39]

If the Indians perceived the English to have value as potential friends for a people at war, the source of this belief lay in the power Granganimeo's people perceived in the objects and items the English possessed, technologies that Harriot said left the Algonquians wondering, in a famous phrase, if the English were "gods or men."[40] The Roanokes were clearly intrigued by the newcomers. A small group of men in strange ships arrive off their shores. They bring with them a technology suggesting that they possessed great power—a concept that Harriot later learned the natives called *montoac*—to do things that ordinary humans could not do. That power interested Granganimeo and Wingina particularly within the context of their rivalries with their native neighbors.[41] The famous Theodor de Bry map (1590) has misled many historians, anthropologists, and archaeologists who have written about these early colonizing ventures with a view of the native peoples as belonging to different "tribes": de Bry depicts such groupings on his map. The reality was more complex. Villages came together on occasion in alliance, but they also fought, apparently with some frequency. In these struggles the English and their technology might be useful. But Granganimeo and Wingina needed first to know more, so they sent two men, Manteo and Wanchese, to accompany the Englishmen to their homeland to learn what they could about them and to report back what they found.[42]

By the time these two envoys returned to Roanoke Island in the summer of 1585, along with the men Ralegh had sent to establish an outpost on American shores, they each had arrived at very different interpretations about the meaning of the English. Manteo, impressed by the power of the English, remained steadfast in his connection to the newcomers and saw in them a powerful ally. Wanchese, on the other hand, had concluded after his sojourn in England that these men posed a mortal threat to his people's way of life. He promptly abandoned the English and returned to Wingina once the newcomers arrived on the Outer Banks in the summer of 1585.[43]

Other Algonquians, at Roanoke and elsewhere, wavered between these two poles, as they attempted to understand the newcomers and to assimilate them into their accustomed ways of dealing with and relating to outsiders. After the English arrived, the newcomers explored the Carolina sounds. They attacked Wingina's enemies at Aquascogoc over the theft of a silver cup and, perhaps, another hostile village somewhere along the northern bank of the Albemarle Sound.[44] If the Aquascogoc attack seemed unnecessarily savage and violent, the burning of the town may well have demonstrated to Wingina that he could find the English useful in his conflicts with his neighbors, an extremely dangerous weapon if he could control them. He likely met with Manteo, whose account of the English contrasted starkly with that of Wanchese. Wingina announced that he would allow the English to establish a post on the northern end of Roanoke Island, close to the village there. Wingina thus kept the Englishmen near his people and effectively isolated from native rivals who may have wished to establish relations with the newcomers on their own. Wingina would attempt to control access to Ralegh's colonists and the powerful trade goods that they carried. Indeed, copper has been frequently remarked upon, but it appears to have been the other items—the mathematical instruments, the compasses, and the "perspective glasse whereby was shewed manie strange sights," along with guns, books, writing and reading, clocks, "and manie other things that we had"— that "were so strange unto them" that they attracted the Algonquians to the English colonists.[45]

The familiar image of stalwart European explorers climbing from their boats, splashing through the surf, and planting the flag to claim the new world does not entirely fit the reality of what happened at Roanoke. Once again, English explorers came to Roanoke Island not as discoverers but as invited guests. They settled on Roanoke Island because Wingina allowed them to do so. They did not have the power to dictate to native peoples the

Europeans in the Indians' Old World

terms under which they took possession of American soil. They took what they were given.

Harriot tells us that the initial relations in 1585 were peaceful. Wingina and other Roanokes traded with the newcomers, acquiring the magical and otherworldly items—items infused with *montoac*—that allowed their English allies to do things that ordinary human beings could not. Yet if the English technology deeply impressed the Roanokes and left them wondering whether the newcomers were, in Harriot's words, gods or men, the power of English disease, which quickly made its presence felt, perplexed and frightened them.[46]

Some of Wingina's followers believed that the English controlled the disease, that it was something that might be deployed as a weapon—invisible bullets fired by the English. This belief was not fueled by what an earlier generation of historians might have dismissed as superstition but, rather, by a calculated consideration of the power that the English displayed and the Algonquians' understanding of why bad things happened. They asked the English to send the diseases among their enemies so that they might die as well.

The Roanoke Indians fell ill from these diseases. It spared nobody, Harriot wrote. Operating on a cultural logic that held that there were no accidents, that bad things happened for a reason often tied to the failure or ineffectiveness of one's rituals, or to the malevolence of spiritually powerful figures, the Indians living closest to the English began to experiment, so Harriot tells us. Their own priests, shamans, and conjurers could not halt the spread of the disease, so some Roanokes began to adopt English rituals. Our rituals lack power, they may have reasoned, so perhaps their rituals are superior. Wingina and his followers tried to understand the sources of English power and to incorporate that power into their accustomed ways of living. They attempted to understand the reasons for the misfortunes that had befallen them. They joined the English in prayer. They learned to sing their psalms. They rubbed the English Bible, the evident material center of English Christian ritual, on their bodies. Many of them, Harriot wrote, were "glad to touch it, to embrace it, to kiss it, to hold it to their breasts and heads, and stroke over all their body with it," showing, in Harriot's view, "their hungry desire of that knowledge which was spoken of." They assessed carefully how best to protect the interests of their community when confronted by visitors who appeared to have the power to do things that Algonquians could not.[47]

Doing so, of course, required a significant willingness to experiment. For Wingina this effort must have been profoundly disillusioning. The English prayed, read from books, and gathered together to worship their God. They did not fall ill. They did not die. English power and English rituals, however, provided few answers for the increasingly beleaguered Roanokes. Indeed, English *montoac*, it seemed, could manifest in violence, in death, and in suffering. The arrival of the English coincided with prolonged drought on the Outer Banks, and the English did nothing in response to Algonquian pleas to allow it to rain once again. Wingina, like Wanchese before him, arrived at the conclusion that his people's problems stemmed from contact with the English. In so doing, he operated on a very old logic.[48]

Ralph Lane, the governor of the 1585 colony, tells us what happened next. Wingina changed his name and his identity and became Pemisapan, and he withdrew from Roanoke Island. He led his people away from the newcomers to his village at Dasemunkepeuc, away from the newcomers whom he had welcomed but who had brought such misery to his people. Lane, however, read much more into this act and concluded that Pemisapan had organized a conspiracy to wipe out the English settlement, but he appears to have learned this only from Pemisapan's native rivals. These rivals, with Skiko, the captive son of the Choanoac weroance Menatonon, at the center, sowed suspicion of the Roanoke leader. The English could count on the Choanoacs, Skiko said, but they should fear Pemisapan's plot to wipe out their settlement. So Lane attacked, a murder that too many historians still feel was justified. Lane's men crossed the sound at nightfall. They entered the village and met with the Indians. Lane gave the watchword, "Christ Our Victory," and the English opened fire. His men wounded Pemisapan, and after the weroance fled, they ran him down in the woods, killed him, and took his head as a trophy. Less than two weeks later, Lane's harried colonists, with few resources and even fewer friends, clambered aboard Francis Drake's fleet and fled from a Roanoke Island that appeared extremely unforgiving.[49]

The killing of Pemisapan, like so much of the early history of North Carolina, is a little-known part of the story, but it was this act—the killing of a weroance—that in many ways determined the fate of Ralegh's Roanoke ventures. Nothing was the same as a result of this act. A small holding party left by Sir Richard Grenville in the summer of 1586 was quickly wiped out by Wanchese and his followers. They sought vengeance and destroyed the English. When John White returned to Roanoke Island in 1587, an episode that clearly demonstrates White's unfitness for command and his weakness as a leader, his colonists had been on the island for only a short amount of time before one of his principal men, George Howe, was found stuck like a pincushion with dozens of Algonquian arrows, his head pulverized by the warriors' weapons. White's sources again identified Wanchese as the leader of the hostile forces. White's attempts to secure justice resulted in an uncomfortable encounter on Croatoan Island, where the colonists confronted the legacy of the previous colony's violence: maimed Indians injured by Lane's men the year before. No native attended the council White called to "receive" the Indians and to forgive and forget their past misdeeds. When he retaliated for the killing of Howe, White's misdirected wrath inadvertently fell upon the last Indians in the region willing to speak with the English, Manteo's Croatoan kin. White, a coward and a weakling despite his significance as an artist, blamed the victims.[50]

Facing hostile Indians, short supplies, and, perhaps, English colonists staggered by their leader's gross cowardice and incompetence, White returned home to England in 1587. When he finally returned to Roanoke in the summer of 1590, on his granddaughter Virginia Dare's third birthday, the colonists were gone. White and his men saw in the sand fresh footprints of Algonquians who had heard the Englishmen arrive. When these natives fled from the island, they deprived White of his last, best opportunity to find out what had happened. Surely they knew.[51]

Instead of finding the people he had left behind, White found only the famous signs carved into posts by his countrymen and the ransacked remains of his material wealth, which the colonists had not buried deep enough to conceal from the Indians. But Ralegh's colonists were lost only to those Europeans who failed to find them. Indian people knew what had happened to them, but only small traces of what they knew reached the Englishmen who wrote the documents on which historians rely. Whether the colonists moved to the Chesapeake, to the north shore of the Albemarle Sound, or to the Chowan River Valley or migrated throughout the southern interior distributing Dare Stones hither and thither, there has emerged something of a consensus that wherever they found shelter, they fell victim to an attack by the Powhatan leader now most commonly called Wahunsonacock but better known simply as Powhatan. Some of the colonists, the scant evidence suggests, survived this attack. If they were lucky, they found shelter in native communities, into which they necessarily would have been assimilated to survive. The descendants of these few survivors would have been socialized in native village communities in the eastern woodlands. They became Algonquians, and only in the sense of their ancestry could they be considered any longer English.[52]

■ We make choices about the stories we want to tell. We can tell the story of valiant Spanish *adelantados* or of Sir Walter Ralegh and the Roanoke ventures. We can discuss Spanish dreams of empire or a misguided attempt to extend in some small way English influence into the Atlantic world, a first act in an attempt to establish an Anglo-American empire. We can speak of the Spanish discovery of the interior or the opening frame in a story of the expansion of the English world abroad into a number of alien peripheries, marchlands, frontiers—whatever phrase you want to use.[53] Out of the processes of conflict and accommodation that occurred there, as the historian Bernard Bailyn and many others have pointed out, new creole structures emerged, shaped by the interaction between the newcomers and a number of other populations.[54] But at Roanoke the colonists controlled no territory. The several dozen Spanish soldiers in the Piedmont clung tenuously to outposts in the heart of indigenous territory. The glories Menéndez sought in the interior, or the empire promoter Richard Hakluyt the Younger trumpeted and Ralegh claimed with the queen's blessings, were indeed puny things. They were illusions, easily dispelled when the newcomers wore out their welcome.

Much of the early writing of the history of North Carolina, and of all of colonial America for that matter, expresses a teleological belief that assumes the inevitability of European triumph and advance, an almost Turnerian view of American history, of a frontier expanding relentlessly westward, eliminating all in its path. But Joara and Roanoke, however fleetingly, offer an opportunity to consider other outcomes, one where the Indians did not disappear and did not retire in the face of settlement. In these early encounters, the Indians won. In the interior and on the Carolina coast, the region's native peoples played a larger role in driving the story than previous students of North Carolina's past have acknowledged. At Joara and at Roanoke, Europeans intruded into an indigenous world, one where their settlements could endure only as long as native peoples allowed them to. The Spanish brought trade goods and military technology that made them appear as potentially valuable allies to native peoples living in a world of warfare. When that supply of trade goods ceased, and when Spanish aggressions increased, native peoples in the interior acted to rid themselves of a European presence that brought more problems than benefits. Pardo's men would have recognized their relative powerlessness as they attempted to flee from their small fortifications late in the 1560s, if not earlier. Indian rules prevailed. At Roanoke, Granganimeo and Wingina allowed the English access to their territory. They sent emissaries to accompany the newcomers home to England. They experimented with the rituals of the colonists' religion to secure the benefits that they believed the English received. They sought peace and an alliance, on indigenous terms. Wingina became Pemisapan after the colonists' diseases slashed their way through his community, killing many of those Indians who had worked most closely to accommodate the English. European technology, meanwhile, left him and his people debating whether the colonists were "gods or men." When English demands for food surpassed what he could safely provide during a period of sustained drought, Pemisapan withdrew to the mainland and decided to feed the colonists no longer. That decision was not an easy one to reach—we can look closely at the documents and sense something, faintly through the membrane of time, of the conversations and rich debates that took place in Algonquian villages around the Carolina sounds—and we can see if we choose the cultural imperatives that drew some native peoples to fear the English but, at the end, others to hate them and wish them gone. Ralph Lane, reliant upon information from the Roanokes' rivals who wanted to supplant them as the main trading partner of the English, concluded that Pemisapan had orchestrated a massive Indian uprising. To preempt this threat Lane ordered the assault that led to the weroance's death. This murder doomed Lane's colony and subsequent English efforts to settle and hold the island.

The early Europeans who visited what became North Carolina traversed wide ranges of territory. They could settle and remain, however, only where they had the cooperation and assistance of native peoples. Following these initial early European encounters with North Carolina's native peoples, a number of themes emerge that historians and archaeologists may fruitfully explore in the future. Indeed, some are already doing so.[55] Whereas the founding of Jamestown in 1607 began a new era of sustained contact between natives and Europeans, it is clear that the establishment of Charles Town in 1670 accelerated these forces especially on North Carolina native peoples. From this moment on, native North Carolinians were forced to negotiate the destructive dynamics of intense slave raiding by South Carolinians and their native allies, as well as the new ecological and economic impacts of the deerskin trade. These and other factors would drastically alter the cultural and political landscapes of North Carolina's native peoples and force native leaders and communities to confront a new and complex world into the eighteenth century and beyond.

NOTES

1. Sir Walter spelled his name most commonly "Ralegh." That spelling is used in this chapter.

2. For White's artwork, see Kim Sloan, *A New World: England's First View of America* (Chapel Hill: University of North Carolina Press, 2007). The documents relevant to an understanding of Ralegh's Roanoke ventures were compiled and published in David B. Quinn, ed., *The Roanoke Voyages, 1584–1590*, 2 vols. (London: Hakluyt Society, 1955). For Spanish ventures in the interior of present-day North Carolina, see Charles M. Hudson, *The Juan Pardo*

Expeditions: Exploration of the Carolinas and Tennessee, 1566-1568 (Tuscaloosa: University of Alabama Press, 2005).

3. For these ventures, see the chapters in Jerald T. Milanich and Susan Milbrath, eds., *First Encounters: Spanish Explorations in the Caribbean and the United States, 1492-1570* (Gainesville: University of Florida Press, 1989).

4. On de Soto see Charles Hudson, Marvin T. Smith, and Chester DePratter, "The Hernando de Soto Expedition: From Apalachee to Chiaha," *Southeastern Archaeology* 3 (Summer 1984): 65-77; Chester DePratter, Charles Hudson, and Marvin T. Smith, "The De Soto Expedition: From Chiaha to Mabila," in *Alabama and the Borderlands, from Prehistory to Statehood*, ed. Reid Badger and Lawrence Clayton (Tuscaloosa: University of Alabama Press, 1985), 108-27; Charles Hudson, *Knights of Spain, Warriors of the Sun* (Athens: University of Georgia Press, 1997); and Charles Hudson, Marvin Smith, David Hally, and Chester DePratter, "Coosa: A Chiefdom in the Sixteenth-Century Southeastern United States," *American Antiquity* 50, no. 4 (1985): 733-37.

5. Paul Kelton, *Epidemics and Enslavement: Biological Catastrophe in the Native Southeast, 1492-1715* (Lincoln: University of Nebraska Press, 2007), 1-101.

6. Eugene Lyon, "Pedro Menéndez's Plan for Settling La Florida," in Milanich and Milbrath, *First Encounters*, 151-59.

7. Eugene Lyon, *The Enterprise of Florida: Pedro Menendez de Aviles and the Spanish Conquest of 1565-1568* (Gainesville: University of Florida Press, 1976), 41-43.

8. Juan de la Bandera, quoted in Hudson, *Juan Pardo Expeditions*, 256.

9. Ibid., 255. It should also be noted that Pardo's only chaplain, Sebastian Montero, was left with four soldiers at Guateri to proselytize the Indians. Ibid., 26.

10. Robin A. Beck Jr. and David G. Moore, "The Burke Phase: A Mississippian Frontier in the North Carolina Foothills," *Southeastern Archaeology* 21 (Winter 2002): 192-205; David G. Moore, *Catawba Valley Mississippian: Ceramics, Chronology, and Catawba Indians* (Tuscaloosa: University of Alabama Press, 2002), 185-95.

11. Karen M. Booker, Charles M. Hudson, and Robert L. Rankin, "Placename Identification and Multilingualism in the Sixteenth-Century Southeast," *Ethnohistory* 39, no. 4 (1992): 399-451; Hudson, *Juan Pardo Expeditions*, 67-112; Robin A. Beck, *Chiefdoms, Collapse, and Coalescence in the Early American South* (Cambridge: Cambridge University Press, 2013), 59-95.

12. Hudson, *Juan Pardo Expeditions*, 83.

13. Ibid., 61-67; Beck, *Chiefdoms*, 79.

14. Beck, *Chiefdoms*, 161-78; Mary Elizabeth Fitts, "Mapping Catawba Coalescence," *North Carolina Archaeology* 55 (2006): 1-59.

15. Robin A. Beck Jr., David G. Moore, and Christopher B. Rodning, "Identifying Fort San Juan: A Sixteenth-Century Occupation at the Berry Site, North Carolina," *Southeastern Archaeology* 25, no. 1 (2006): 65-77.

16. Hudson, *Juan Pardo Expeditions*, 25-26.

17. Charles Hudson in *Juan Pardo Expeditions* (28-29) suggests this is a Chisca chief. The Chiscas are an enigmatic, perhaps nomadic group located on the western Virginia and North Carolina border in the mid-sixteenth century. See Steven C. Hahn, "The Mother of Necessity: Carolina, the Creek Indians, and a New Order in the American Southeast, 1670-1763," in *The*

Transformation of the Southeastern Indians, 1540–1760, ed. Robbie Ethridge and Charles Hudson (Jackson: University of Mississippi Press, 2002), 93.

18. Hudson, *Juan Pardo Expeditions*, 26–27.

19. Ibid., 29.

20. Ibid., 29–45.

21. Bandera, quoted in ibid., 272.

22. Ibid., 35–46.

23. Ibid., 175.

24. Beck et al., "Identifying Fort San Juan."

25. Ibid.; Christopher B. Rodning, Robin A. Beck Jr., and David G. Moore, "Conflict, Violence, and Warfare in La Florida," in *Native and Spanish New Worlds: Sixteenth-Century Entradas in the American Southwest and Southeast*, ed. Clay Mathers, Jeffrey M. Mitchuem, and Charles M. Haeckeer (Tucson: University of Arizona Press, 2013), 242–43.

26. Robin A. Beck Jr., Christopher B. Rodning, and David G. Moore, "Finding Fort San Juan: New Discoveries at the Berry Site, North Carolina," paper presented at the Seventieth Annual Meeting of the Southeastern Archaeological Conference, November 7–10, 2013, Tampa, Fla.

27. Continuing archaeological investigations at Berry suggest that Fort San Juan and an earthen mound structure are constructed immediately adjacent to each other if not intruding one upon the other. However, the timing and precedence of these constructions are not yet clearly understood.

28. Bandera, quoted in Hudson, ed., *Juan Pardo Expeditions*, 262.

29. Robin A. Beck Jr., Christopher B. Rodning, and David G. Moore, "Resisting Resistance: Juan Pardo and the Shrinking of Spanish *La Florida*, 1566–1568," in *Enduring Conquests: Rethinking the Archaeology of Resistance to Spanish Colonialism in the Americas*, ed. Matthew Liebman and Melissa S. Murphy (Santa Fe, N.M.: School for Advanced Research Press, 2011), 28.

30. Ibid., 33.

31. Ibid., 30–31.

32. Hudson, *Juan Pardo Expeditions*, 27–29.

33. A similar dynamic is described by Juliana Barr in her coverage of Spanish missions in eastern Texas a century later. See Barr, "A Diplomacy of Gender: Rituals of First Contact in the 'Land of the Tejas,'" *William and Mary Quarterly*, 3rd ser., 61 (July 2004): 393–434.

34. Harriot, in Quinn, *Roanoke Voyages*, 345.

35. Ibid., 372.

36. See Neal Salisbury, "The Indians' Old World: Native Americans and the Coming of Europeans," *William and Mary Quarterly*, 3rd ser., 53 (July 1996): 435–58.

37. This point is developed in Michael Leroy Oberg, *The Head in Edward Nugent's Hand: Roanoke's Forgotten Indians* (Philadelphia: University of Pennsylvania Press, 2007).

38. Quoted in Quinn, *Roanoke Voyages*, 100–101.

39. Ibid.

40. Harriot used variants on this phrase twice in his report. Ibid., 376–79.

41. Ibid., 91.

42. Michael Leroy Oberg, "Between 'Savage Man' and 'Most Faithfull Englishman': Manteo and the Early Anglo-Indian Exchange, 1584–1590," *Itinerario* 24 (2000): 146–69.

43. Ibid.

44. Quinn, *Roanoke Voyages*, 191.

45. Ibid., 375–76.

46. On the specific outbreak of disease at Roanoke, see Peter B. Mires, "Contact and Contagion: The Roanoke Colony and Influenza," *Historical Archaeology* 28 (1994): 32–34.

47. Quinn, *Roanoke Voyages*, 377–78.

48. Ibid., 378; Michael Leroy Oberg, "Gods and Men: The Meeting of Indian and White Worlds on the Carolina Outer Banks, 1584–86," *North Carolina Historical Review* 76 (October 1999): 382–83.

49. Quinn, *Roanoke Voyages*, 265–94; Oberg, *Head in Edward Nugent's Hand*, 81–100.

50. Quinn, *Roanoke Voyages*, 525–31.

51. Ibid., 611–16.

52. In addition to the sources mentioned above, see Lee Miller, *Roanoke: Unlocking the Mystery of the Lost Colony* (New York: Arcade, 2000); James Horn, *A Kingdom Strange: The Brief and Tragic History of the Lost Colony of Roanoke* (New York: Basic Books, 2010); Thomas Parramore, "The 'Lost Colony' Found: A Documentary Perspective," *North Carolina Historical Review* 78 (January 2001): 67–83; and David La Vere, "The Chowan River 'Dare Stone': A Re-evaluation," *North Carolina Historical Review* 86 (July 2009): 251–81.

53. Michael Leroy Oberg, *Dominion and Civility: English Imperialism and Native America, 1585–1685* (Ithaca, N.Y.: Cornell University Press, 1999), chap. 1.

54. See the essays in Bernard Bailyn and Philip D. Morgan, eds., *Strangers within the Realm: The Cultural Margins of the First British Empire* (Chapel Hill: University of North Carolina Press, 1993).

55. Beck, *Chiefdoms*; Ethridge and Hudson, *Transformation of the Southeastern Indians*; Robbie Etheridge and Sheri M. Shuck-Hall, eds., *Mapping the Mississippian Shatter Zone: The Colonial Indian Slave Trade and Regional Instability in the American South* (Lincoln: University of Nebraska Press, 2009).

INTERCOLONIAL CONFLICT AND COOPERATION DURING THE TUSCARORA WAR

Stephen Feeley

Colonial studies have increasingly focused on the distinctiveness of experiences in different regions, and yet scholarship on North Carolina remains overshadowed by colonial neighbors near and far. Often ignored in its own right, North Carolina does not fit easily into other regional narratives either. Geographically proximate and politically linked to South Carolina, North Carolina was not really part of the Deep South. Nor was it part of the Chesapeake. Its backcountry was settled by many of the same population flows of Scots-Irish, German, and nonconformist English settlers as Pennsylvania's, but describing North Carolina alongside the Middle Colonies yields diminishing returns. Its coastal connections, smugglers, and pirates mean that North Carolina can even be plugged—albeit, tenuously—into a Caribbean portrait. And so after short obligatory mention of the failed Roanoke settlement, colonial North Carolina often recedes into the histories of better-known neighbors or is excluded altogether.

One solution is to embrace these multiple connections, exploring how the region served as a crossroads where multiple narratives overlapped. Viewing North Carolina as a hybrid does not relegate it to some placid backwater lacking its own history. Instead the mixture created a turbulent pool where currents competed and merged to create a story worth telling. To borrow another metaphor, North Carolina was less a vale of humility between two mountains of conceit than an arena into which loftier neighbors descended to struggle over and impose their views.

Emblematic of these patterns is the Tuscarora War.[1] In broad histories it is often ignored or dwarfed by more familiar conflicts such as Bacon's Rebellion in Virginia, King Philip's (or Metacom's) War in New England, or the Yamasee War in South Carolina. But far from being local or limited in scope, even a basic outline of events reveals that the war was a maelstrom capable of drawing the attention and efforts of multiple colonies.

Fighting began in September 1711. Tuscaroras from the town of Catechna had captured Christoph von Graffenried, founder of New Bern, and John Lawson, an influential surveyor. When talks with the captives broke down, Tuscarora, Coree, Neuse, Bear River, and other Indians who had gathered at Catechna (hereafter referred to as the Catechna Alliance) executed Lawson and launched a devastating surprise attack against settlements along the Pamlico, Neuse, and Trent Rivers and Core Sound. Disorganized and lacking supplies and troops, North Carolina turned to other colonies for assistance. South Carolina sent two armies, largely composed of Indians, sacking Tuscarora communities and destroying vital forts at Catechna in April 1712 and at Neoheroka in March 1713 (see fig. 3.1). Meanwhile, Virginia took the lead in engaging diplomatically with several predominantly neutral Tuscarora "Upper Towns," paving the way for eventual treaties with many Tuscaroras after the fall of Neoheroka. Other members of the Catechna Alliance continued sporadic fighting as late as 1715. During and after the war as many as two thousand Tuscaroras fled to the Susquehanna Valley in Pennsylvania and near Oneida Lake in New York, where they were adopted as the "Sixth Nation" of the Iroquois Confederacy, prompting worries by officials as far away as New York that "the war betwixt the people of North Carolina and the Tuscarora Indians is like to embroil us all."[2]

And yet the Catechna Alliance did not seek or expect such a broad conflict. Thomas Pollock, North Carolina's acting governor at the war's end, explained the "chief cause" of the war:

> For the Indians, being informed by some of the traders, that the people that lived here were only a few vagabond persons, that had run away out of other governments, and had settled hear of their own head, without any authority, so that, if they cut them off, there would be none to help them, this, with the seeing our own differences rise to such a height that we (consisting of only counties) were in armes each against the other, encouraged them to fall upon the county of Bath not expecting they would have any assistance from this county, or any other English plantations [i.e., colonies].[3]

These expectations raise the issue of how Indians perceived relations between and within the colonies. Indians in eastern Carolina had every reason to expect that colonies and factions would disagree, leaving one another isolated and vulnerable. And in truth, intercolonial conflicts did surface throughout the Tuscarora War, in important ways not readily apparent in a cursory overview of events.

The divisions were more than just a matter of competition over trade or

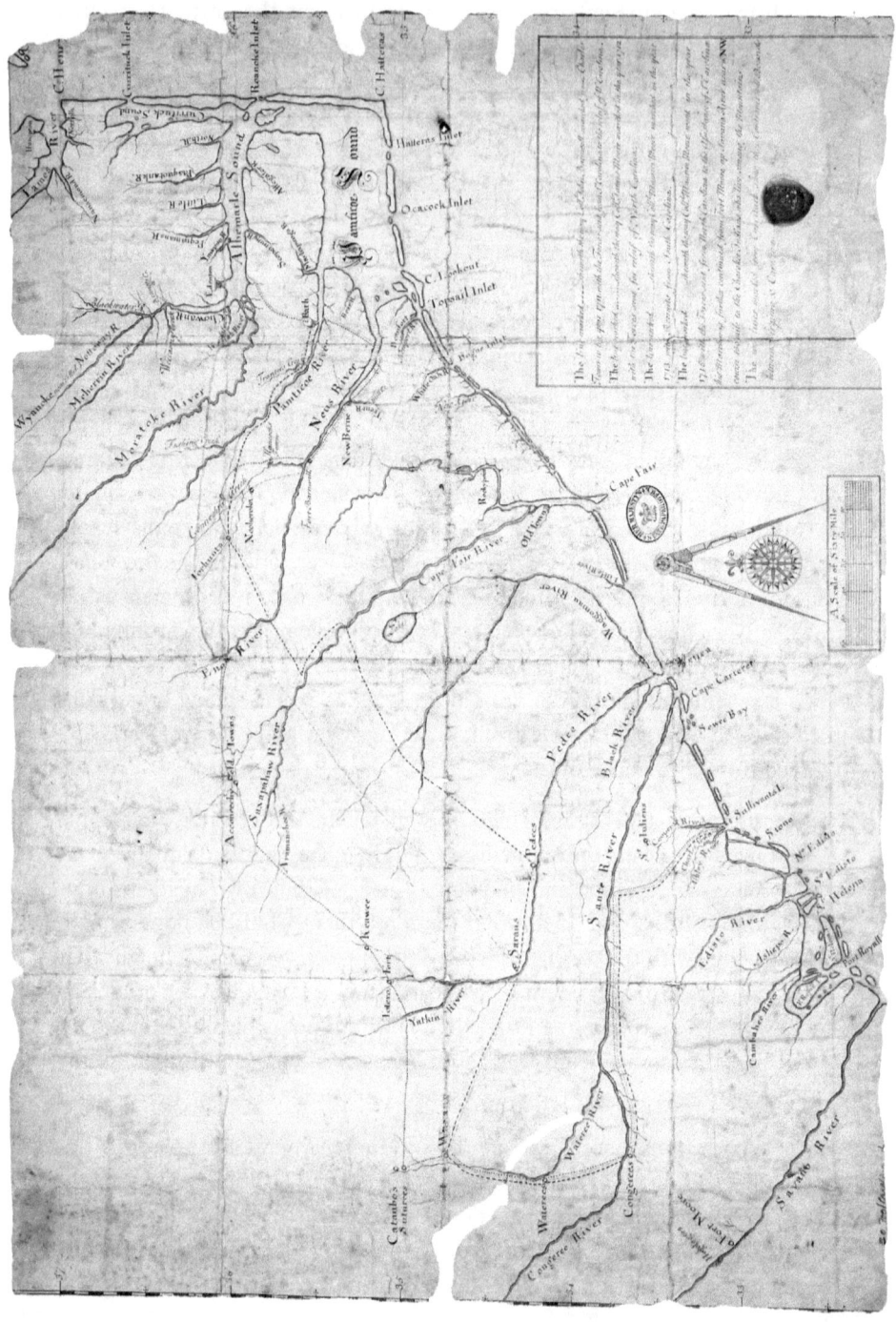

borders, although these played a prominent role, and instead call attention to the different approaches colonies took toward ordering their frontiers.[4] Scholarship by Richard White, James Merrell, Eric Hinderaker, and others has shown that frontiers did not just happen.[5] They were constructed and fought over. No two were exactly alike. During the 1710s, the period of the Tuscarora War, Virginia, North Carolina, South Carolina, and Iroquoia each had their own sense of hierarchy, legal justice, and fair punishment; their own sense of how trade should be fairly conducted; separate notions of who controlled the land and how people related to it; and different understandings of work and labor. In going to war, the Catechna Alliance hoped to gain a greater say on these issues. When outsiders entered the Tuscarora War, they each carried with them and tried to impose their own separate models.

The result was a conflict within the conflict over which model would prevail. Recognizing these splits adds to our understanding of the Catechna Alliance's goals. Ultimately, the infighting and divisions did not spare the Tuscaroras but did play an important role in determining the war's course and outcome. It was these multiple layers of contention—the struggles not only between the Catechna Alliance and its enemies but also among its enemies, native and white, from North Carolina, Virginia, South Carolina, and beyond—that made the Tuscarora War a milestone in determining North Carolina's cultural landscape.

■ From its beginning, North Carolina's frontier policies bore the mark of other colonies. If outsiders later wanted to imprint their visions on North Carolina, in part it was because that colony's policies long seemed malleable and in flux. English settlement in North Carolina began in the mid-seventeenth century as traders and settlers from Virginia established trading posts and then plantations and small communities in North Carolina's Albemarle region.[6] Therefore, North Carolina's early land and Indian policies can best be understood as part extension of and part reaction to Virginia's approaches.

At its core, Virginia's policies relied on the close supervision of what it referred to as its "tributary" Indians. For example, in the 1677 Treaty of Middle Plantation after Bacon's Rebellion, leaders of at least nine Virginia native

(*opposite*) FIGURE 3.1. This map from the British Archives, nominally dated 1715, charts the successive campaigns led by South Carolina's veteran Indian warriors against North Carolina's Tuscarora settlements and fortifications between 1711 and 1715. Internal evidence suggests that the map may date from as late as 1725.

groups submitted to Virginia's governor and promised an annual symbolic tribute of twenty beaver skins. In return, they were guaranteed fields and settlements within reservations and the right to go "oystering, fishing, and gathering Tuccahoe,... wild oats, rushes,... or any thing else for their natural Support not usefull to the English." Trade was to be "continued, limited, restrained, or laid open" according to the governor's wishes. Finally, tributaries agreed to report "any march of strange Indians," to "strengthen and joyne" the colonial militia, and to act as slave catchers, policing the fringe of the region's increasingly African chattel-based plantation system.[7]

For Virginia tributary Indians it was a precarious position. They found limited autonomy in many aspects of life and worried that Virginians would unilaterally abandon promises, finding excuses to seize them or their lands.[8] Accusations of murder by several Nanzatico men in 1704 quickly turned into a pretext for the enslavement and expulsion of that entire nation.[9] Living on this knife's edge, tributaries nonetheless found some protection by serving as important symbols of the Virginia governor's authority and reach, embodying the sort of paternal control the government dreamt of wielding in a region where churches, courts, prisons, and other emblems of control were few and far between.[10] Virginia's experience with Bacon's Rebellion, during which a breakdown in Indian affairs precipitated internal rebellion, toppling the government and prompting the flight of hundreds of servants and slaves, demonstrated the broad importance of well-regulated Indian relations.

To an extent North Carolina adopted these lessons. In 1676 proprietors of Carolina asked the governor and council of "that parte of our province called Albemarle"—soon to be North Carolina—to "send us by the next opportunity a true account of what tribute or payment are rendered by any of our people or officers from any of the Indians."[11] Over time North Carolina made treaties with various Indian groups, including Chowans, Mattamuskeets, the Bay River Indians, and others. Documents are fragmentary but suggest that North Carolina negotiated a treaty with the Tuscaroras in 1672 and again in 1704.[12] As with Virginia, such agreements offered protections from encroachment and promises of peace and outlined patterns of trade. Occasionally they offered more specific clauses, such as an agreement in which the Bay River Indians agreed to care for shipwrecked sailors who washed upon their shores.[13]

But in actual practice, many of North Carolina's agreements went partially or wholly ignored, leaving Indians unprotected and provoking one named Wehuna in 1703 to ask "whether the English did intend to make war or no."[14] Virginia's governor wrote to North Carolina, warning that the Indians were learning that "there is no dependence on our Treaties."[15] For

Indians trying to make sense of North Carolina's actions, by the 1710s it seemed that North Carolina seemed to zig one way and zag the other. Part of the inconsistent frontier policy owed to the colonial government's own internal weaknesses. Squabbles over religion, land, and control of the assembly culminated in Cary's Rebellion, which ended only months before the Tuscarora War.

But this apparent laxity in Indian relations was not entirely accidental and reflected a sort of policy in its own right. To grow, North Carolina hoped to lure settlers directly from Virginia or to compete for the same pool of migrants from Europe.[16] To make their colony more attractive the assembly passed laws making settlers immune to past debts, offering guarantees of religious freedom, and easing enforcement of vestry acts, beckoning a minor flood of debtors, runaway servants, pirates, Quakers, and other dissenters.[17] Even when North Carolina did sign agreements with Indians, abiding by those provisions was not a priority for officials, if it was possible at all. In a sense, having no policy—or one that was hardly enforced—was the policy.[18] The challenge to Virginia's frontier policies was not lost on officials, who complained that North Carolina was drawing away its populace, creating a lawless zone, and undermining Indian relations.[19]

Indians in the region personally witnessed tensions between these two frontier systems in numerous ways, perhaps most clearly through those colonies' long-running border dispute. Reversing the maxim that good fences make good neighbors, for Virginia and North Carolina bad boundaries made dreadful neighbors. The feud dated back to the colony's beginning. North Carolina had two charters, one from 1663 and another in 1665, each containing different language regarding the Virginia border. The discrepancy essentially created a nearly forty-mile-wide ribbon of land claimed by both colonies.[20] Land speculation, always an important source of revenue for colonial elites, became uncertain. Administration became a nightmare as settlers routinely switched loyalties depending on which colony's tax collectors came calling.[21]

As the area's principal and original inhabitants, Indians were drawn into the conflict, observing tensions between Virginia and North Carolina firsthand. In its description of the border, the 1665 charter referenced a "Weyanoke Creek." But nobody could agree on what river or stream actually was Weyanoke Creek. Presumably it was named for the Weyanoke Indians, but they had repeatedly relocated before dispersing among other native groups.[22] Beginning in 1707 Virginia and North Carolina sent out commissioners, among them John Lawson, to interview Indians about the missing creek. Commissioners bribed, begged, and threatened Indians to support

Conflict and Cooperation during the Tuscarora War 65

their version of geography, all the while giving Indians ample opportunity to witness the true depth of the colonies' squabbles.²³

Especially involved in the dispute were the Meherrins, a group near the Virginia–North Carolina border zone with whom the Tuscaroras frequently intermingled. To strengthen territorial claims, Virginia reached out, claiming sovereignty over Meherrins as tributaries and offering moral if not actual military support.²⁴ Predictably, North Carolina was furious. In 1703 North Carolina complained that Meherrin Indians "do daily commit great injuries to the inhabitants of... [North Carolina] by destroying their stocks and burning their timber and houses and refusing to ... render obedience ... under pretense that they are tributary to Virginia."²⁵ When sixty North Carolina settlers retaliated by imprisoning Meherrins and tearing down their homes, Virginia's Council responded in outrage: "We might with as much justice treat those [settlers] who ... pretend to belong to Carolina ... with the same severity as you have used those poor Indians since we have at least as much Reason to believe them within the bounds of Virginia as you have to imagine the Meherrin Indians to be within yours."²⁶ Meherrins received messages of support from Virginia, which urged them to stand strong against the North Carolinians.²⁷

Disputes also spilled over into the Indian trade—natives' main point of connection with the two colonies. In 1708 when Virginia tried to punish Tuscaroras accused of a frontier murder by levying an embargo, Tuscaroras turned to North Carolina traders for powder, arms, and supplies. Virginia was left sputtering against the "inhabitants of Carolina who have by the supplies they have hitherto given the Tuscaroro Indians have frustrated the effect of the late proclamation."²⁸ Likewise, in 1691 when a Virginia trader named Daniel Pugh kidnapped and sold several Tuscaroras onto ships bound for Caribbean sugar plantations, Tuscaroras took advantage of colonial divisions by appealing for help to North Carolinians.²⁹ Virginia traders, on the other hand, were sometimes accused of encouraging the Tuscarora Indians to "cutt off the [North Carolina] inhabitants of Pamtico and News."³⁰

Proving the direct effects of such encouragement—if the invitations happened at all—is difficult. But it is certain that, when Tuscaroras and other Indians at Catechna contemplated war, they had strong reason to believe that Virginia would stay out or might even offer tacit support. Among the Indians in attendance at Catechna on the eve of the Tuscarora War was a Meherrin Indian named Nick Major. Months earlier Nick Major had been "strictly" interrogated by John Lawson on behalf of North Carolina and a cluster of other commissioners about the disputed border.³¹ At Catechna the two met again, this time as captor and captive, just before that ill-fated surveyor's execution sparked the war.[32]

In predicting conflict between the two colonies, Indians at Catechna were largely correct. During the war Virginia supported North Carolina, but in the most dilatory manner possible. Virginia's governor, Alexander Spotswood, spent most of his energies shoring up Virginia's own defenses and overseeing that the war did not spread among tributary Indians living there. Spotswood raised six hundred militia plus thirty cavalry but never sent them to North Carolina.[33] Instead the two colonies fell to arguing over how to fund the troops.[34] Perhaps, Spotswood suggested, North Carolina could mortgage the disputed boundary land as payment?[35] Spotswood did try to intimidate representatives from the seven neutral Tuscarora communities of the Upper Towns to remain out of the fighting or perhaps even take up arms against Catechna.

Even then, Spotswood's main goal was for these Tuscarora Upper Towns to declare their allegiance to Virginia, thereby bolstering that colony's regional authority in an evolving scheme Spotswood referred to as his "new project for securing our frontiers."[36] The plan was essentially an expanded version of Virginia's previous tributary model. According to this vision, tributary Indians would relocate alongside strategically placed forts; trade would be monitored and monopolized; movement would be curtailed; resident schoolmasters would lead courses in cultural and religious reeducation; hostages would be schooled at the College of William and Mary. Taken together, boasted Spotswood, these policies "will create in them a liking to our Laws and Governm't ... secure a necessary dependence on this colony ... banish their present savage customs" and, in "a generation or two," "bind them ... to be good subjects and useful neighbours."[37]

Spotswood had mixed success with Virginia's existing tributaries—Saponis clustered as ordered alongside the giant new edifice of Fort Christanna. But others, like the Nottoways and Meherrins, refused. These troubles aside, it was the Upper Town Tuscaroras that were to be central to this plan. Not only were Tuscaroras more populous than any existing Virginia tributary group, but they had also previously undercut Virginia's policies by engaging in illegal trade, diplomacy, and sporadic skirmishes with Virginia's tribes. Now they would be brought to heel. Before unveiling his scheme to several Upper Town representatives, Spotswood put on a show of leading his militia through maneuvers, afterward bragging optimistically that "I could not hope for a more favourable Conjecture to meet this demand than now when they are under great apprehension of our Resentments for the late Barbaritys committed in Carolina, and the impressions made on them by the appearance of so great a force as I then show'd them."[38]

But whether intentionally or because of internal divisions, the Upper Towns proved to be masters at stalling—never accepting or putting off Virginia's ambitions. Towns signed agreements but then trotted out long strings of excuses for failing to abide by most of the provisions.[39] Spotswood became increasingly frustrated that his project might fail. For its part North Carolina's government decried the lack of more tangible support from Virginia. Starving English settlers along North Carolina's Neuse River directly petitioned Virginia's government, appealing to Spotswood's "paternal Tenderness" for a "Considerable forse of men, armes and ammunition."[40] In reply, Spotswood sent only "a copy of the said Treaty" so that they "may see what care this Government hath already taken for their Relief"—hardly the response they hoped for.[41] Indians who predicted divisions between Virginia and North Carolina would have been correct. The very fact that the Tuscarora Upper Towns reached out in the beginning months of the war to Virginia, not to North Carolina, suggests recognition of this rift.

Nonetheless, even limited involvement by Virginia mattered. In previous disputes, Tuscaroras could always count on trade from one colony or the other. But during the war the vital flow of trade goods and ammunition from Virginia virtually dried up.[42] Moreover, even though the Upper Towns never fell into line with Spotswood's plans, by negotiating the governor had made it less likely that they would take up arms.[43] One can imagine a very different course of the war if the Catechna Alliance had been able to enlist the Upper Towns—likely representing half the Tuscarora population—and Virginia tributaries such as the Meherrins and Nottoways with whom Tuscaroras frequently associated. As late as spring 1712, members of the Catechna Alliance bragged about expecting military "relief" from the Upper Towns—assistance that never materialized, in part stymied by Virginia's diplomatic maneuvers.[44]

Moreover, Virginia's diplomacy helped set the stage for talks with Tom Blount, leader of a Tuscarora town called Ucouhnerunt on the Pamlico River. Blount stood out even among other Upper Town leaders in his willingness to treat with Virginia and North Carolina. It was Blount who tricked and captured Hancock, "King" of Catechna, and as a mark of goodwill handed him over to North Carolina authorities for execution. In the war's latter days when North Carolina officials recognized that they lacked the resources to capitalize on South Carolina's military successes, it was Blount with whom they negotiated a peace.[45] In doing so, North Carolina's acting governor Thomas Pollock hitched onto and adopted not only Virginia's diplomatic efforts but also a frontier framework that relied on tributary Indians. The cornerstone of this system would be Tuscarora Indians—at least those willing to make peace, accept punishment, and hail Blount as their king. They in turn would kill, expel, or force into negotiations holdouts among the Tuscaroras and other Indians from the Catechna Alliance who continued their fight from the coastal swamps. Ultimately some Tuscaroras would oppose the agreements and flee, adding to the exodus to Iroquoia.

From 1712 into 1714 the two governors coordinated closely, exchanging frequent letters as they dealt with Blount. But even as North Carolina adopted Virginia's tributary approach, the partnership broke down. Both colonies agreed that the Tuscaroras must become tributaries—but *whose* tributaries? Could authority be divided? Old debates over the border continued, now magnified by the realization that sovereignty over the borderland's Indian communities might tip the scales on the question of who controlled the land. The partnership between the governors descended into what can only be described as name-calling, each accusing the other of being "highly prejudicial," "very disrespectful," "ill deserving," "unjust," and "destructive to her Majesty's subjects."[46]

The squabble created negotiating space for the Tuscarora leader, Tom Blount. Harsh language concealed efforts by both North Carolina and Virginia to ease demands for punishment of Tuscaroras and instead broaden promises of clemency in return for loyalty. Blount wavered but ultimately signed an agreement with North Carolina.[47] The agreement transformed Blount's Tuscaroras into North Carolina tributaries, confined to a reservation and politically dependent.[48] But North Carolina, weakened by divisions and war, could not afford the missionaries, enforced schooling, forts, soldiers, and tightly regulated trade fairs envisioned by Spotswood. Lacking the populous Tuscaroras, who were so vital to his own schemes, Spotswood's "new project" was vitally weakened and soon faced political opposition at home. Exacerbating problems, Blount's Tuscaroras, now ensconced as tributaries just across the border in North Carolina, resumed troublesome military, economic, and political ties with Indian groups supposedly loyal to Virginia.[49]

■ Word of the Tuscarora War reached South Carolina in late October 1711. Most of the actual fighting occurred between Tuscaroras and forces nominally led by South Carolina. Over the next two years it was South Carolina that sent two armies—mostly composed of Yamasees, Cherokees, Catawbas, and other Piedmont Siouan groups—that sacked the Tuscarora homeland. Tragically for the Tuscaroras, an alliance including not only Virginia and

North Carolina but also South Carolina and its native allies would have been difficult to anticipate. Nonetheless, just as Virginia used the war as an opportunity to try to strengthen its frontier organizational model, South Carolina leapt into the fray hoping to implement its own system of policies.

Although politically linked to North Carolina, these southern neighbors carried a different set of norms and assumptions.[50] More than that of any other British colony, South Carolina's frontier approach was driven by a distant trade in skins and especially slaves. Allan Gallay provides the astounding statistic that, prior to 1717, more Indian slaves were exported from the docks of Charleston than black African slaves were imported.[51] At first glance, reliance on the slave trade hardly seems like the basis of a sturdy frontier system. Indeed, the slave trade, as described by Robbie Ethridge and other historians of the "shatter zone," wreaked havoc and destabilized native communities across the interior South.[52] Entire societies gave way and reshaped themselves before the onslaught.

Nonetheless, for South Carolina the slave trade system perversely provided its own sense of logic, acting as a sort of ordering principle. It was a tool for punishing Indian enemies, for enforcing the loyalty of native neighbors, and for rewarding allies with guns and ammunition. Cycles of debt and dependency orbited around traders based out of Charleston and nearby Goose Creek. Simultaneously, the slave trade served as a way to undercut South Carolina's European competitors in French Louisiana and Spanish La Florida by devastating the Indian groups upon whom those colonies depended. In contrast to North Carolina's somewhat laissez-faire approach to Indian relations, South Carolina's might be described as a sort of public-private partnership, with semiofficial agents leading armies of white traders and native allies, both drawn by the prospect of acquiring slaves for market. Occasionally officials struggled to rein in the worst abuses, but the trade was a tool too valuable and versatile to abandon entirely. Thus, in 1702 Governor James Moore led a few dozen English colonists and about thirteen hundred Creeks and Yamasees to besiege St. Augustine and pillage nearby Guale mission towns. Two years later Moore led a similar assault against mission towns among the Apalachee. Such attacks continued until by around 1713 Florida's *republica de indios* was reduced to shambles.[53]

Differences between North Carolina and Virginia were but a spat compared to rifts between Virginia and South Carolina. For over a decade before the Tuscarora War, Virginia and South Carolina had been engaged in a ferocious battle for Indian trading partners, especially Creeks and Cherokees in present-day Georgia, Alabama, and Tennessee. Particularly galling for South Carolina was the fact that Virginia pack trains—some with two hundred or more horses—in cutting south of the Appalachians, were passing through the Carolinas and poaching "their" Indian clients. In response South Carolina threw up legal roadblocks: a bill aimed to hobble Virginians by banning horses from entering the colony from the north; punitive duties; and a requirement on the eve of the war forcing Virginia traders to make a long, expensive detour to receive clearance in Charleston.[54] Virginia traders such as Robert Hix risked finding their storehouse among the Shuterees empty, its cache of nearly fifteen hundred deerskins confiscated by South Carolina agents.[55]

South Carolina was willing to apply the methods and logic of the slave trade not just against the French and Spanish but also against fellow English competitors, particularly Virginian traders. In 1707 and 1708 South Carolina rushed guns, flints, powder, shot to several piedmont Siouan Indian groups to defeat the Savannah Indians (as Shawnees were locally known) who were important trade partners of Virginians. The attacks helped solidify South Carolina's ties with the Siouans, bankrupted several Virginia traders, and captured numerous Savannah slaves. The remnants fled north to the Susquehanna Valley on the edge of Iroquoia and Pennsylvania.[56] Indians across eastern North America had often taken advantage of divisions between colonial powers, but here was a counterlesson on the dangers of being unintentionally caught in the middle of such a conflict—a lesson whose import would become even clearer during the Tuscarora War.

Tuscaroras witnessing such disputes might hope that South Carolina would avoid any war requiring alliance with Virginia. But instead South Carolina seized the Tuscarora War as an opportunity. Virginia's pack trains depended on Tuscaroras and other North Carolina Indian communities as important way stations en route farther southwest. Destroying these communities, South Carolina realized, could cripple Virginia's trade. South Carolina's assembly explicitly linked the two issues, describing the "great mischief and danger to this province by the intrusions and approaches of the Virginia Traders trading with the Indians living within the limits of and in amity with this Government" in the same address that they announced entry into the Tuscarora War.[57]

In 1712 Colonel Jack Barnwell led the first force from South Carolina. An experienced trader, surveyor, and soldier, he later spent the next decade earning a reputation for raids into Florida. His army consisted of thirty-three white traders and a wide assortment of Carolina Indian groups—just shy of five hundred Yamasees, Hog Logees, Apalachees, Corsaboys, Waterees, Sugarees, Catawbas, Shuterees, Waxsaws, Congarees, Sattees, Reddees, Winyaws, Cape Fear Indians, Hoopengs, and Wareperes.[58] As the raids set out, Francis

Le Jau, an Anglican minister in South Carolina, recorded that "we think to destroy the whole Nation, that is kill the men and make the women and children slaves, this is the way of our Warrs upon the like provocations."[59]

Virginia's diplomatic efforts had carefully differentiated between communities of the Catechna Alliance actually involved in the fighting and those Upper Towns with whom Virginia had the greatest trade. But the first South Carolina expedition led by Barnwell came as a hammer, indiscriminately smashing those communities. Two hours were spent torching the "great town Innennits." Another fort called Narhontes, along with its cadre of defiant women who fought to the death, fell before the assault.[60] Both of these towns had signed neutrality agreements with Virginia.[61] None would ever again serve as trading stations for Virginia traders.

Barnwell's force marched through the Tuscarora heartland, destroying homes, burning crops, but mostly taking slaves—several hundred if his count is correct. A bloody confrontation at a well-constructed Tuscarora fort at Catechna led to a short-lived armistice, which collapsed when either Barnwell or his Indian allies, under the guise of further talks with the Corees, seized nearly two hundred for enslavement.[62]

In the official journal of his exploits, Barnwell carried on a running condemnation of Virginia. Had Virginians incited the war? Had they supplied Tuscaroras? Demonstrating intercolonial tensions, Barnwell tortured Tuscarora prisoners to find out. Ultimately, he accused Virginia traders of buying "horses skins and plunder" for four hundred buckskins' worth of ammunition.[63] Barnwell's critique was not aimed merely at Virginians possibly abetting the Tuscaroras but at the system that Spotswood was trying to implement. Learning of Virginia's diplomatic efforts, Barnwell scoffed that Virginians believed "they had obtained a glorious victory, when ... they begged a most ignominious treaty of those cowardly miscreants, which they were so gracious to grant upon Condition to have goods at a cheaper rate and their children brought up at the College."[64]

In response, Virginia's council condemned Barnwell's journal as a "scurrilous paper" full of "false and unjust reflections on this Government" and derided Barnwell's raids and "clapt up" treaty as clumsy affairs unlikely to bring real peace.[65] Likewise, Spotswood intimated that South Carolina's Indian allies, motivated by the slave trade, could not be trusted. When at one point Virginia did consider sending militia, North Carolina officials panicked: "If the [Virginia] forces join [with South Carolina's] their may chance some differences fall out to the hindrance and detriment of the action"[66]—a polite way of saying that, for these clashing colonies, the Tuscarora War was not big enough for the two of them.

North Carolina had its own history of antagonism with South Carolina, one that became even more evident during the fighting. Barnwell wrote that he "had such a tale to tell of barefaced villainy's daily committed here [in North Carolina]" that he could only report home about it privately, face-to-face.[67] A missed rendezvous by North Carolina left Barnwell's force hungry, angry, and resentful. Sixty-seven North Carolinians joined Barnwell's army, but he considered even them a "country cowardly crew," many of whom fled in combat and thus were "deservedly shott ... in their arses."[68] Barnwell did himself no favors when upon arriving in North Carolina he apparently joined in party politics, stirring the embers of the recent Cary Rebellion—leading some to speculate that he wished to stage a coup and make himself governor.[69] Later in the Tuscarora War, North Carolina sent another request to South Carolina for aid—with one caveat: that Barnwell *not* lead the second expedition.[70]

Like the first, the second South Carolina expedition—the one that ultimately destroyed Neoheroka in the last large-scale battle of the war—was composed almost entirely of Indian warriors.[71] At its head was Colonel James Moore, son of the former governor who had built his prestige on slaving raids into Florida. As the force gathered, South Carolina's assembly salivated at the thought of "the great advantage ... [there] may be made of slaves there being many hundreds of them women and children may we believe 3 or 4 thousand."[72] Despite the apparent enthusiasm, close observers would have noticed a fault line stemming from South Carolina's reliance on Indian warriors.

An underlying feature of South Carolina's frontier strategy was that, even as the slave trade preyed upon some Indian groups, it ideally drew others closer as allies and partners. Barnwell had used the first expedition to recruit several groups to South Carolina's interest for the first time, like the Saras and Saxapahaws, whom Barnwell recommended to the governor as "brave men and good."[73] Likewise, Moore's expedition included on its lengthy roster of native allies the notable addition of a large Cherokee contingent, a group whom South Carolina had long hoped to peel away from Virginia traders.

Nonetheless, tactics generating short-term unity could breed long-term distrust. On the eve of the Tuscarora War, South Carolina's entire Indian slave trade complex teetered on the brink of collapse. Indians gained temporarily from access to South Carolina's trade and guns but over time faced drowning in a sea of debt and doubts that they too might ultimately be enslaved. By 1711, Yamasees collectively owed about 100,000 deerskins, larger than South Carolina's yearly export total.[74] In August 1711, Yamasee fears prompted commissioners to send assurances, but traders continued to prosecute debts.[75] Scant months before the war, Yamasees, Waxhaws, Essaws, and Catawbas—the same groups who formed a bulk of Barnwell's expedition—conferred in Savannah Town to discuss rumors that their lands would be seized.[76]

South Carolina Indians carried such fears into the Tuscarora War, behaving in ways that complicate the label "allies." After illegally harboring an escaped Indian slave, one Waxhaw Indian fled the law and his creditors by joining the expedition; he died in North Carolina.[77] Commissioners learned about another Indian, a slave who had already paid half of his manumission and had gone "to Warr to gett the remayning Part of his Freedom."[78] Rather than exhibiting any sort of blind loyalty, such Indians proved to be independent actors, often capturing enough slaves to ease their debt and then immediately disappearing toward home—hardly a model of a cohesiveness.[79] And yet, rather than making common cause, the desperate circumstances of such Indians added to the violence of their assaults on the Catechna Alliance.

Ultimately, Yamasees, Catawbas, and other Piedmont Siouans did rise against South Carolina—not during the Tuscarora War but almost immediately afterward in the Yamasee War beginning in 1715. Does this suggest that the Catechna Alliance, in planning their own war, predicted the Yamasee War, or expected that it would take place simultaneous with their own uprising? Certainly not. Historian William Ramsey has convincingly argued that the precise timing of the Yamasee War owed to the particular circumstances of a breakdown in diplomacy that occurred in 1715 in the Yamasee Town of Pocotaligo.[80] But records do show that at the beginning of the Tuscarora War the Catechna Alliance did try to convince Saxapahaws "to join with them against the English."[81] Likewise, they may have imagined that other discontented Indians would decline to take up arms alongside South Carolina.[82] Unfortunately, the proposed alliance never occurred and the Saxapahaws joined Barnwell—adding to the Tuscaroras' list of enemies.

Nonetheless, during the Tuscarora War South Carolina's tactics put divisions on display. South Carolina's previous raids intentionally wreaked havoc on French and Spanish settler communities around Mobile and Fort Augustine. But in the Tuscarora War South Carolina's native partners would be operating in and around the colonial settlements of supposed allies. Yamasees, Siouans, and Cherokees found themselves quartered among settlers bearing little love for Indians and possessing few supplies to offer. Hungry warriors ate through scarce provisions and dispersed "without orders" to rove and forage, eating "all the Catle wherever they have come."[83] Potential "friendly fire" incidents were a constant risk. According to North Carolina's governor, settlers "[were in] such a ferment that they were more ready to Fall upon the South Carolina Indians, than march out against the enemy."[84] After the fall of Neoheroka, North Carolina turned back a third native army out of concerns that tensions with erstwhile allies might "cause an insurrection against the government."[85]

The long-term significance of this refusal by Governor Pollock should not be overlooked. Militarily, South Carolina's invasions had been undeniably effective against the Catechna Alliance. At the fall of Neoheroka, Moore tersely reported: "Enemies destroyed as follows—prisoners 392, scolps 192 out of the sd fort—and at least 200 killed and burnt in the fort—and 166 kill'd and taken out of the fort on the scout."[86] Survivors fled—some to Iroquoia; some to the hills, hovering on the edge of starvation; and others to the swamps, where they launched deadly retaliatory raids. South Carolina's shatter zone had come north. Unchecked, low-level fighting could continue indefinitely, offering South Carolina fertile ground for future slaving expeditions, providing opportunities for that colony to consolidate military and economic bonds with Indian allies, and leaving the trade routes south from Virginia an economic wasteland. It was in this context, and faced with this terrifying prospect, that North Carolina's leadership balked, paving the way for the survival of Tuscaroras and other Indians as tributaries in eighteenth-century North Carolina.

■ Divisions beset North Carolina itself. Just as it is best not to think of the Tuscaroras as a single polity but instead a loose coalition of towns, Tuscaroras almost certainly viewed North Carolina as an assortment of separate groups and communities: enclaves of Quakers, Anglicans, and nonsectarians; Englishmen, Germans, Swiss, and French Huguenots; aspiring planters and runaway servants and debtors. What towns there were usually lacked roads to connect them. Northerly Albemarle and southerly Pamlico and Neuse settlements could communicate only via water, but suitable boats were always in short supply. North Carolina's politics had long been beset by "perpetual broils."[87] One contemporary groused it had long "been the common practice there to resist and imprison their governors."[88] The Neuse and Pamlico settlements—closest to the bulk of fighting in the Tuscarora War—especially were of "such a factious temper, that they were ready to follow anyone that will head them."[89] Such splits contributed to the so-called Cary Rebellion, mere months before the Tuscarora War, during which accusations flew of partisans holding "traitorous correspondence with the Tuscarora Indians," going from town to town urging them to join the conflict on one side or the other.[90]

Thus, members of the Catechna Alliance would not have seen themselves as going to war against all white settlers, against a united British Empire, against multiple colonies, or even against the entity "North Carolina." This war was meant to be intensely local. A sense of this can be gleaned from Tuscarora captives who told Barnwell that they had learned from "Virginia traders" that "the people massacred were outlandish men and not English" and that they "doubted not to make peace with the English soon and they were then about it."[91] Captured by Yamasees and interrogated by South Carolinians, these Tuscarora detainees seemed befuddled that the war had gotten so tragically out of hand.

What, then, did Tuscaroras and others Indians within the Catechna Alliance actually anticipate and hope to achieve in planning the war? The allusion to peacemaking is a clue. What is known as *the* Tuscarora War needs to be viewed in the context of previous conflicts, now more or less forgotten, each of which could have escalated into *a* "Tuscarora War" but did not, instead ending in peaceful affirmations. In 1672, Tuscaroras "killed some English dwelling on the So. shore in Carolina," leading militia to assemble for several short campaigns. Hostilities simmered until thirty Tuscarora "kings" met colonial leaders to arrange a peace.[92] In 1689, Tuscaroras threatened to "sett the whole Country in a flame" after runaway Virginia slaves killed a Tuscarora. In this case Tuscaroras ultimately accepted a hefty load of trade goods as "satisfaction."[93] In 1704 mere rumors that Tuscaroras and Bear River Indians considered war because they were "of late dissatisfied with the inhabitants" of the Neuse and Pamlico river settlements spurred North Carolina's governor to call "all the Indian Kings and Rulers to meet ... [whereupon] they agreed upon a firm peace."[94]

It is in this context of a limited conflict with an aim toward peacemaking that the Tuscarora War needs to be understood. On the war's eve, when the surveyor John Lawson and Christoph von Graffenried, the founder of New Bern, were captured traveling near Catechna, the first impulse was to hold an all-night council negotiating with the captives. Initially, Indians there mistook Graffenried for the governor of North Carolina, adding to hopes for meaningful diplomacy. Only the next morning, when Lawson got into a shouting match with Core Tom (leader of a community whose land the surveyor had stolen) and seemed to renege on the previous night's agreements, did the Indians execute Lawson. The Indians who gathered at Catechna kept Graffenried alive, however, and later refined their agreement into a six-point treaty, hashing out settlement patterns, hunting rights, and trade protocols along with mutual promises to "henceforth be good friends."[95] Having secured Graffenried's promises "to live on good terms with them," the Catechna Alliance launched attacks to ensure those agreements would be followed and to force negotiations with other communities.[96]

This first attack was successful, almost shockingly so. More puzzling are the several months afterward. The Catechna Alliance fell into a sort of holding pattern of skirmishes and plundering raids—almost marking time, it seems, waiting for peace overtures that never came. The problem was, there was hardly any viable entity left with whom to make that peace. North Carolina's government collapsed into ineffectiveness and infighting as the wounds of the recent Cary Rebellion reopened. New Bern, only recently founded on unsteady footing and already on the verge of a Jamestownesque starving time, split into two rival refugee camps, each warily on guard against "wild Indians" and "wild Christians."[97] The treaty with Graffenried went disregarded as the mark of a coward or a traitor.[98] Pacifist Quakers refused to pay war taxes or take up arms.[99] Inhabitants of Albemarle either could not or would not help.

By autumn or winter of 1711 the Catechna Alliance had *won* the war they had set out to fight. As late as March 1712 Tuscaroras had called out to canoes bearing Barnwell's wounded men, speaking "kindly to them, and told them they hoped before long to be good friends."[100] But lacking a way to end it, the war continued. This next stage—a war against Virginia, South Carolina, numerous Indian groups, and eventually a more cohesive North Carolina—this was a war that they had not expected. This was the war that the Catechna Alliance lost.

Hindsight does not allow us to blame the Tuscaroras for lack of perfect foresight. The Catechna Alliance had predicted divisions, and divisions there were. But instead of shielding the Tuscaroras, divisions meant that the war ushered in a moment when the region became a battleground between various understandings of what the frontier should be. The outcomes of these struggles lasted well into the eighteenth century. Nonetheless, even though Tuscaroras and other members of the Catechna Alliance were not victors, they never allowed themselves to be plugged neatly into patterns imposed by outsiders. Virginia's dreams of gaining Tuscaroras as tributaries never came to fruition. Tuscaroras who remained with Blount in North Carolina proved themselves to be troublesome tributaries, a source of tension with settlers and neighboring colonies. Still other Tuscaroras would not abide and fled the region altogether, creating a new sort of crisis when they joined the Iroquois Confederacy.

■ Even a brief examination of the Tuscarora War reveals how attention to Indians can serve to integrate North Carolina into broader colonial narratives. Indians had their own social geography that predated European colonizers. More often than not, Indians refused to abide by the newcomers' maps. Or they recognized and took advantage of boundaries between colonies for the splits they were—seams in an imperfect facade of imperial authority. For historians of North Carolina, this means a dose of Indian studies, properly applied, can serve as an antidote to parochialism, forcing attention to the colony's place in broader networks of trade, culture, and politics.[101]

Even if scholars confine their geographic bounds to North Carolina, greater attention to Indian affairs can reshape and flesh out previously ignored histories. Studies of slavery, race, gender, politics, and class in North Carolina have all benefited from such inclusion, highlighting the need for more such scholarship.[102] Finally, at the most basic level North Carolina stands out today for having the largest American Indian population of any state east of the Mississippi—a fact that needs to be recognized and taken into account. These North Carolinians deserve to have their history told.[103]

NOTES

1. For useful accounts of the Tuscarora War, see Herbert Richard Paschal, "The Tuscarora Indians in North Carolina," M.A. thesis, University of North Carolina, 1953; Thomas C. Parramore, "With Tuscarora Jack on the Back Path to Bath," *North Carolina Historical Review* 64 (April 1987): 115–38; Thomas C. Parramore, "The Tuscarora Ascendancy," *North Carolina Historical Review* 59 (October 1982): 307–26; and Christine A. Styrna, "The Winds of War and Change: The Impact of the Tuscarora War on Proprietary North Carolina, 1690–1729," Ph.D. diss., College of William and Mary, 1990. The most recent detailed treatment is David La Vere, *The Tuscarora War: Indians, Settlers, and the Fight for the Carolina Colonies* (Chapel Hill: University of North Carolina Press, 2013). For a fuller account of the issues described in this essay, see Stephen Feeley, "Tuscarora Trails: Indian Migrations, War, and Constructions of Colonial Frontiers," Ph.D. diss., College of William and Mary, 2007, esp. chaps. 2–6.

2. John R. Brodhead and Edmund Bailey O'Callaghan, eds., *Documents Relative to the Colonial History of the State of New York*, 15 vols. (Albany, N.Y.: Weed, Parsons and Co., 1853–73), 5:343. The concerns of New York governor Robert Hunter especially reflected worries of French and Iroquois involvement. Unfortunately, time and space constraints prevent a full discussion on Iroquois influence and participation in the Tuscarora War. Despite linguistic and cultural similarities Tuscaroras and members of the Five Nations had a long period of warfare until 1711. The recent peace may have freed Tuscaroras to consider war against colonists. Despite frequent colonists' fears of direct Iroquois intervention, their actual role in the Tuscarora War was ambiguous, reflecting internal divisions within the Five Nations and among the Tuscaroras. Iroquois warriors offered and in at least one case gave military aid to the Catechna Alliance; Iroquois spokesmen attempted to spur New York officials to help broker a peace; most significant, the Iroquois Confederacy used the conflict as an opportunity to assimilate Tuscaroras fleeing the conflict, broadening their influence, even while briefly threatening the stability of the "covenant chain" alliance with the British colo-

nies. Some Tuscaroras, notably Tom Blount, resented these outsiders' interference during and after the war. See Feeley, "Tuscarora Trails," esp. chaps. 7 and 9. For Tuscarora-Iroquois relations also see Douglas W. Boyce, "'As the Wind Scatters the Smoke': The Tuscaroras in the Eighteenth Century," in *Beyond the Covenant Chain: The Iroquois and their Neighbors in Indian North America, 1600-1800*, ed. Daniel Richter and James H. Merrell (Syracuse: Syracuse University Press, 1987), 151–63.

3. Quoted in William L. Saunders and Walter Clark, eds., *Colonial Records of North Carolina*, 30 vols. (New York: AMS Press, 1968–78), 2:40 (hereafter *CRNC*).

4. By "frontier" I refer to both geographic border regions and the social space created by dealings with peoples considered outsiders and on the metaphorical edge of political and legal control. Because of its focus on intercolonial conflicts, this essay approaches frontier models primarily from a colonial perspective. In other works I have emphasized the ways that Tuscaroras worked to shape their own frontiers with colonies and other Indian groups. See Stephen Feeley, "'Before Long to Be Good Friends': Diplomatic Perspectives of the Tuscarora War," in *Creating and Contesting Carolina: Proprietary Era Histories*, ed. Michelle LeMaster and Bradford J. Wood (Columbia: University of South Carolina, 2013), 140–63.

5. Richard White, *The Middle Ground: Indians, Empires, and Republics in the Great Lakes Region, 1650-1815* (Cambridge; N.Y.: Cambridge University Press, 1991); James H. Merrell, *The Indians' New World: Catawbas and Their Neighbors from European Contact through the Era of Removal* (New York: Norton, 1989); Eric Hinderaker, *Elusive Empires: Constructing Colonialism in the Ohio Valley, 1763-1800* (Cambridge: Cambridge University Press, 1997).

6. The early decades of North Carolina remain underserved by scholarship. See Noeleen McIlvenna, *A Very Mutinous People: The Struggle for North Carolina, 1660-1713* (Chapel Hill: University of North Carolina Press, 2009). Also useful are essays in LeMaster and Wood, *Creating and Contesting Carolina*.

7. For tributaries, see W. Stitt Robinson, "The Tributary Indians in Colonial Virginia," *Virginia Magazine of History and Biography* 67 (January 1959): 49–64 (hereafter *VMHB*); and Merrell, *Indians' New World*. The text of the 1677 Treaty of Middle Plantation appears in "Treaty between Virginia and the Indians, 1677," *VMHB* 14 (January 1907): 289–96; and W. Stitt Robinson, ed., *Virginia Treaties, 1607-1722*, vol. 4, *Early American Indian Documents: Treaties and Laws, 1607-1789* (Frederick, Md.: University Publications of America, 1983), 82–88. For the 1646 treaty, see Robinson, *Virginia Treaties*, 67–71.

8. Helen C. Rountree, *Pocahontas's People: The Powhatan Indians of Virginia through Four Centuries* (Norman: University of Oklahoma Press, 1996), 89–187; Edward DuBois Ragan, "Where the Water Ebbs and Flows: Place and Self among the Rappahannock People," Ph.D. diss., Syracuse University, 2006.

9. Henry R. McIlwaine, ed., *Executive Journals of the Council of Colonial Virginia*, 6 vols. (Richmond, Va.: Virginia State Library, 1925), 2:383–86, 390, 396–98, 456; 3:5–6, 98 (hereafter *EJCCV*). Also see Ragan, "Where the Water Ebbs and Flows," 383–86.

10. For brief examples of efforts, successful and failed, to exert such control, see William P. Palmer, ed., *Calendar of Virginia State Papers and Other Manuscripts, 1652-1781*, 11 vols. (Richmond: Virginia State Library, 1875–93), 1:131–33. For emblems of control, see Rhys Isaac, *The Transformation of Virginia, 1740-1790* (Chapel Hill: University of North Carolina Press for the Institute of Early American History and Culture, 1982).

11. *CRNC*, 1:230.

12. Parramore, "Tuscarora Ascendancy," 313; Paschal, "Tuscarora Indians in North Carolina," 28; "Relating to the Indians," in *North Carolina Historical and Genealogical Register*, ed. J. R. B. Hathaway, 3 vols. (Edenton, N.C., 1900–1903; repr., Baltimore: Genealogical Publ. Co., 1970), 2:193–94 (hereafter *NCHGR*); John Lawson, *A New Voyage to Carolina* (London: 1709; repr., Chapel Hill: University of North Carolina Press, 1967), 211–12.

13. "Articles of Agreement with the Bay River Indians, September 23, 1699," *NCHGR* 1:598–99. Originals are in "Indians: Treaties, Petitions, Agreements, and Court Cases (1698–1736)," Colonial Court Records, box 192, North Carolina State Archives, Raleigh.

14. *NCHGR*, 2:194.

15. Governor Spotswood to the Ministry of Queen Anne, February 1710/11, quoted in Douglas W. Boyce, "Notes on Tuscarora Political Organization, 1650–1713," M.A. thesis, Department of Anthropology, University of North Carolina at Chapel Hill, 1971, 7.

16. North Carolina also hoped to compete for potential settlers against Pennsylvania, which likewise advertised broad religious tolerance.

17. Styrna, "Winds of War and Change," 47. Although these freedoms were first proposed as part of John Locke's idealistic vision of New World settlement contained in his Fundamental Constitutions, their effect in spurring settlement was a clear motivation. Two contemporary estimates in 1708 and 1709 put the percentage of Quakers at between one-seventh and one-tenth of the total population (*CRNC*, 1:600–603, 686–87, 708–15; 4:xv). Many of the Quakers in the colony were also converts rather than immigrants. For pirates being "kindly entertained in Carolina," see *CRNC*, 1:475.

18. Feeley, "'Before Long to Be Good Friends,'" 142–43.

19. Henry Read McIlwaine, ed., *Journals of the House of Burgesses of Virginia*, 12 vols. (Richmond, Va.: Colonial Press, E. Waddey Co., 1910), vol. 2:1659–1693, 75; *EJCCV*, 3:367.

20. For a basic account of the dividing-line dispute, see William K. Boyd, ed., *William Byrd's Histories of the Dividing Line betwixt Virginia and North Carolina* (Raleigh: North Carolina Historical Commission, 1929), xvi–xxiv.

21. Ibid., xvii; *CRNC*, 1:357–58.

22. For accounts of the Weyanokes' movements, see William G. Stanard, "The Indians of Southern Virginia, 1650–1711: Depositions in the Virginia and North Carolina Boundary Case," *VMHB* 7 and 8 (April and July 1900): 337–58 and 1–11; and Benjamin Harrison, "Deposition of Benjamin Harrison in Regard to Indian Affairs, 1707," *VMHB* 5, no. 1 (1897): 47–50. See also Lewis R. Binford, *Cultural Diversity among Aboriginal Cultures of Coastal Virginia and North Carolina* (New York: Garland, 1991), 162–76; J. Leitch Wright, *The Only Land They Knew: American Indians in the Old South* (New York: Free Press, 1981), 91–92; and Daniel L. Simpkins, "Aboriginal Intersite Settlement System Change in the Northeastern North Carolina Piedmont during the Contact Period," Ph.D. diss., University of North Carolina at Chapel Hill, 1992, 257–83.

23. *CRNC*, 1:746–49; Stanard, "Indians of Southern Virginia"; Harrison, "Deposition." For examples of cajoling, bribery, and trying to get Indians drunk, see *CRNC*, 1:740, 743.

24. Such tributary relationships, asserted Virginia, provided "argument that the lands in dispute do belong" to Virginia. Alexander Spotswood, *The Official Letters of Alexander Spotswood*, ed. R. A. Brock, 2 vols. (Richmond: Virginia Historical Society, 1857), 1:25.

25. *CRNC*, 1:570.

26. Ibid., 1:671.

27. Ibid., 1:668. For a fuller treatment of the Meherrins' involvement in this dispute, see Shannon Lee Dawdy, "The Meherrins' Secret History of the Dividing Line," *North Carolina Historical Review* 72 (October 1995): 386–415.

28. *EJCCV*, 3:207.

29. Ibid., 1:147, 157–58.

30. Ibid., 2:390.

31. Stanard, "Indians of Southern Virginia," *VMHB* 8 (July 1900): 6–10.

32. *CRNC*, 2:644.

33. William Byrd, *The Secret Diary of William Byrd of Westover, 1709-1712*, ed. Louis B. Wright and Marion Tinling (Richmond, Va.: Dietz Press, 1941), 423.

34. A brief summary of these disputes from Spotswood's point of view can be found at Spotswood, *Letters*, 1:170.

35. *CRNC*, 2:7.

36. Spotswood, *Letters*, 2:51.

37. Ibid., 2:57. See also ibid., 1:121–23; and Feeley, "'Before Long to Be Good Friends,'" 149.

38. *CRNC*, 1:816–17.

39. See, e.g., *EJCCV*, 3:300–303.

40. *CRNC*, 1:819–20.

41. *EJCCV*, 3:300–301; Byrd, *Secret Diary*, 488.

42. *CRNC*, 1:879.

43. Towns that had negotiated with Virginia reported that they were hesitant to take up arms against Barnwell's expedition. See Byrd, *Secret Diary*, 499.

44. John Barnwell, "Journal of John Barnwell," *VMHB* 5, no. 4 (1898): 391–402, and *VMHB* 6, no. 1 (1898): 42–55. For reference to relief by the Upper Towns, see Barnwell, "Journal," *VMHB* 6, no. 1 (1898): 47.

45. A preliminary treaty was negotiated in November 1712, but talks fell apart with the arrival of the second expedition from South Carolina. Negotiations resumed in earnest in the spring and summer of 1713 after the fall of Neoheroka. "Preliminary Articles ... 25 November, 1712," in Thomas Pollock Papers, North Carolina State Archives, transcribed in appendix B of Paschal, "Tuscarora Indians in North Carolina." Another copy of the treaty appears in the John Devereux Papers, Land Records, 1712-72, North Carolina State Archives.

46. *EJCCV*, 3:347; *CRNC*, 1:896; 2:57, 73–75; Palmer, *Calendar of Virginia State Papers*, 1:172; Feeley, "'Before Long to Be Good Friends,'" 152.

47. Virginia later made itself party to North Carolina's treaty. *EJCCV*, 3:396–98. Spotswood negotiated a separate treaty with other Tuscarora communities hesitant to submit to Blount, but its provisions went ignored almost immediately. For these failed efforts, see Alexander Spotswood [?], "Examination of Indians, 1713 [?]," *VMHB* 19 (July 1911): 272–75; *EJCCV*, 3:363; and "Spotswood's Treaty with Tuscaroras," in Robinson, *Virginia Treaties*, 211–16. See also "Treaty between Virginia and Tuscarora Nation, February 27, 1713," in Fulham Palace Papers Relating to the American Colonies, microfilm, reel 4, vol. 11, Southern Historical Collection, University of North Carolina, Chapel Hill.

48. See, e.g., *CRNC*, 23:87–88.

49. Feeley, "Tuscarora Trails," esp. chap. 9.

50. North Carolina and South Carolina shared the same charter and proprietors. Although each had separate councils and assemblies, at various times either North Carolina and South Carolina shared a governor or North Carolina operated under a deputy governor.

51. Alan Gallay, *The Indian Slave Trade: The Rise of the English Empire in the American South, 1670–1717* (New Haven, Conn.: Yale University Press, 2002), 288–314.

52. Robbie Ethridge and Charles Hudson, eds., *The Transformation of the Southeastern Indians, 1540–1760* (Jackson: University Press of Mississippi, 2002); Robbie Ethridge and Sheri Marie Shuck-Hall, eds., *Mapping the Mississippian Shatter Zone: The Colonial Indian Slave Trade and Regional Instability in the American South* (Lincoln: University of Nebraska Press, 2009).

53. William L. Ramsey, *The Yamasee War: A Study of Culture, Economy, and Conflict in the Colonial South* (Lincoln: University of Nebraska Press, 2008), 37; John Worth, "Razing Florida: The Indian Slave Trade and the Devastation of Spanish Florida," in Ethridge and Shuck-Hall, *Mapping the Mississippian Shatter Zone*, 295–311.

54. Verner Winslow Crane, *The Southern Frontier, 1670–1732* (repr., New York: Norton, 1981), 154–56; Gallay, *Indian Slave Trade*, 212; Thomas Cooper, ed., *Statutes at Large of South Carolina*, 10 vols. (Columbia: A. S. Johnston, 1836–41), 2:164, 357. For forcing traders to detour, see W. L. McDowell, ed., *Journals of the Commissioners of the Indian Trade, September 20, 1710–August 29, 1718* (Columbia: South Carolina Department of Archives and History, 1955), 14, 16. For considerations of such matters in 1711, prior to the outbreak of the Tuscarora War, see South Carolina Commons House Journals, February 13, 1711 (1706–11): 526–27, and Green Transcripts, February 2, 1711 (1706–11): 515–17, South Carolina Department of Archives and History (all such references are to the microfilm edition found in "Microfilm Collection of the Early State Records," prepared by the U.S. Library of Congress).

55. Merrell, *Indians' New World*, 52–53; *EJCCV*, 3:177–78, 201, 217, 235.

56. Gallay, *Indian Slave Trade*, 210–12; Chapman James Milling, *Red Carolinians*, 2nd ed. (Columbia: University of South Carolina Press, 1969), 85–89; Merrell, *Indians' New World*, 56–57.

57. *CRNC*, 1:823; South Carolina Commons House Journals, Green Transcripts, November 3, 1711 (1706–11): 589–90. Seizures of Virginia traders' wares continued apace during the Tuscarora War (South Carolina Commons House Journals, May 16, 1712[?], [1712–16]: 30–33). Spotswood, *Letters*, 1:171–72, describes the competitive edge South Carolina traders gained because of the Tuscarora War.

58. For arrangement of the army, see Barnwell, "Journal," *VMHB* 5, no. 4 (1898): 393–94.

59. Frank J. Klingberg, ed., *The Carolina Chronicle of Dr. Francis Le Jau* (Berkeley: University of California Press, 1956), 122–23.

60. For detailed summaries of Barnwell's expedition, see Parramore, "With Tuscarora Jack," 115–38; Gallay, *Indian Slave Trade*, 267–73; and Paschal, "Tuscarora Indians in North Carolina," 72–89. For archaeological attempts to trace his route, see John E. Byrd and Charles L. Heath, "The Rediscovery of the Tuscarora Homeland: A Final Report of the Archaeological Survey of the Contentnea Creek Drainage, 1995–1997" (Greenville, N.C.: East Carolina University, David S. Phelps Archaeology Laboratory, 1997).

61. Parramore, "With Tuscarora Jack," 122–28, notes the impact of these attacks on diplomacy in Virginia. Also see *EJCCV*, 3:293–95. Innennits appears in this record as "Chouna-

nitz." Narhontes was a fort associated with Torhunta appearing as "Taughoutnith" in this record.

62. For Barnwell's treaty, see Barnwell, "Journal," *VMHB* 6, no. 1 (1898): 53–54. For speculation on who may have seized the Coree Indians, see Gallay, *Indian Slave Trade*, 274–75.

63. Barnwell, "Journal," *VMHB* 5, no. 4 (1898): 398, and *VMHB* 6, no. 1 (1898): 52, 53.

64. Barnwell, "Journal," *VMHB* 5, no. 4 (1898): 400.

65. *EJCCV*, 3:318; Spotswood, *Letters*, 1:150, 169–70.

66. *CRNC*, 2:19

67. Barnwell, "Journal," *VMHB* 6, no. 1 (1898): 55.

68. Ibid., 45.

69. *CRNC*, 2:19–20, 46.

70. Ibid., 1:843, 899.

71. Joseph Barnwell, "The Second Tuscarora Expedition," *South Carolina Historical and Genealogical Magazine* 10 (January 1909): 33–48.

72. South Carolina Commons House Journals, August 6, 1712 (1712–16): 90–96. Also see *CRNC*, 1:900.

73. Barnwell, "Journal," *VMHB* 5, no. 4 (1898): 394. South Carolina's governor later met with some of these Saxapahaws, "who came to desire the protection of this Government and to have liberty to settle themselves amongst our Northern Indians. They have brought me a present of sixty odd skins ... [and] some Scalps they have brought from the Enemies" (South Carolina Commons House Journals, April 9, 1712 [1712–16]: 19). South Carolina's General Assembly also extended relations to other Indians during the conflict by sending messages "to our Northern Indians the Esaws and Wacksaws to assure them of our protection and that we will take the best methods we can to keep them from the insults of their Enemies and encourage to plant good quantities of corn to supply our forces in case we shall have occasion to send any that way" (South Carolina Commons House Journals, April 4, 1712 [1712–16]: 8).

74. William L. Ramsey, "'Something Cloudy in Their Looks': The Origins of the Yamasee War Reconsidered," *Journal of American History* 90 (June 2003): 55; Gallay, *Indian Slave Trade*, 249.

75. McDowell, *Journals*, 14.

76. Ibid., 14, 28, 31.

77. Ibid., 33.

78. Such participation was technically illegal, but in this case an exception was made because it was a fait accompli. McDowell, *Journals*, 23, 33.

79. Barnwell, "Journal," *VMHB* 5, no. 4 (1898): 399; South Carolina Commons House Journals, April 9, 1712 (1712–16): 19.

80. Ramsey, "'Something Cloudy.'"

81. Barnwell, "Journal," *VMHB* 5, no. 4 (1898): 394.

82. For a description of tensions amid South Carolina's Indian allies during this period and their manifestations during the Tuscarora War, see Steven J. Oatis, *A Colonial Complex: South Carolina's Frontiers in the Era of the Yamasee War, 1680–1730* (Lincoln: University of Nebraska Press, 2004), 83–111.

83. *CRNC*, 2:4, 6–7.

84. Ibid., 2:6–7.

85. Ibid., 2:52–53.

86. Ibid., 2:27.

87. Ibid., 1:686.

88. Ibid., 1:798.

89. Ibid., 1:804.

90. Ibid., 1:776–75, 802. For divisions in North Carolina, see McIlvenna, *A Very Mutinous People*.

91. Barnwell, "Journal," *VMHB* 5, no. 4 (1898): 398.

92. From George Fox, *Selections from the Epistles of George Fox* (Cambridge: Trustees of Badiah Brown's Benevolent Fund, and the Managers of the Mosher Fund of the New England Yearly Meeting of Friends, 1879), 154; and Paschal, "Tuscarora Indians in North Carolina," 28.

93. William Byrd, "Letters of William Byrd, First," *VMHB* 26 (January 1918): 28.

94. *NCHGR*, 2:194; Lawson, *New Voyage*, 211–12. Similar rumors in Virginia also spoke of possible Nottoway-Tuscarora collusion. *EJCCV*, 3:453.

95. Christoph Von Graffenried, *Account of the Founding of New Bern*, Vincent H. Todd, ed. and trans. (Raleigh: North Carolina Historical Commission, 1920), 281. For a fuller treatment of diplomacy and peacemaking efforts, see Feeley, "'Before Long to Be Good Friends.'"

96. Graffenried, *Account*, 269.

97. Ibid., 236.

98. Ibid., 237–40.

99. *CRNC*, 2:40.

100. Barnwell, "Journal," *VMHB* 6, no. 1 (1898): 47.

101. Excellent examples of works in this regard include Merrell, *Indians' New World*; Crane, *Southern Frontier*; Ethridge and Hudson, *Transformation of the Southeastern Indians*; and Peter Wood, Gregory A. Waselkov, and M. Thomas Hatley, eds., *Powhatan's Mantle: Indians in the Colonial Southeast* (Lincoln: University of Nebraska Press, 1989).

102. A brief list of examples includes Kirsten Fischer, *Suspect Relations: Sex, Race, and Resistance in Colonial North Carolina* (Ithaca, N.Y.: Cornell University Press, 2002); McIlvenna, *A Very Mutinous People*; Gerald M. Sider, *Living Indian Histories: Lumbee and Tuscarora People in North Carolina* (Chapel Hill: University of North Carolina Press, 2003); Gallay, *Indian Slave Trade*; and various essays in LeMaster and Wood, *Creating and Contesting Carolina*.

103. Figures from Tina Norris, Paula Vines, and Elizabeth M. Hoeffel, "The American Indian and Alaska Native Population: 2010," *2010 Census Briefs*, January 2012, 7, http://www.census.gov/prod/cen2010/briefs/c2010br-10.pdf (accessed May 2015). For a brief introductory survey of North Carolina's Indian peoples, see Theda Perdue and Christopher Arris Oakley, *Native Carolinians: The Indians of North Carolina*, rev. ed. (Raleigh: North Carolina Department of Cultural Resources Office of Archives and History, 2010).

THE CONUNDRUM OF UNFREE LABOR

Bradford J. Wood and Larry E. Tise

BOUND LABOR IN "POOR CAROLINA"

After his arrival in North Carolina in 1765, newly appointed lieutenant governor William Tryon wrote a detailed letter about his new American home, including some reflections on the institution of slavery in the colony.[1] He noted that the colony had more free settlers than slaves but asserted that the "Negroes are very numerious[,] I suppose five to one White Person in the Maritime Counties." While Tryon recognized that settlers in the backcountry owned far fewer slaves, he believed this was merely because their "Poverty prevents their purchasing of Slaves." In the wealthier coastal areas he found that planters typically owned 50 to 250 slaves, and the institution was so pervasive that "when a man marries his Daughters he never talks of the fortune in Money but 20 30 or 40 Slaves is her Portion." Tryon probably overstated the concentration of slaves in the Tidewater region, where free people typically outnumbered slaves, but it is more revealing that he perceived North Carolina to be a place where economic life revolved around bound labor.

Tryon also recognized that his description suggested an important question, writing, "I suppose you will expect to be informed what return is Made for the expence of Supporting such a Number of Slaves in the Province." He identified a number of uses for slave labor and described the colony's distinctive naval stores industry but still gave an inadequate answer. While North Carolina's slave populations remained small compared with those in the Caribbean or on the largest plantation holdings in nearby colonies, they exceeded the economic demand for bound labor in a colony that produced only small quantities of marketable goods, such as rice, tobacco, and indigo.

North Carolina included a few colonists who imagined themselves as planters, and some bound laborers from its earliest years, but starting in the first half of the eighteenth century the colony's Tidewater elite followed the lead of other Atlantic World colonizers who embraced the plantation system. Neither contemporaries nor modern historians have been much impressed by the scale or profitability of North Carolina plantations, yet by the late eighteenth century North Carolina had become a planter-dominated place with all of the trappings of a slave society.[2] By 1770 at least 40,000 and perhaps well over 50,000 slaves were held in the colony.[3] While this number might seem paltry compared with those in neighboring Virginia and South Carolina, it is significant within the context of colonial British America at this time—comparable, for example, to the combined slave population of all of the New England and Middle Colonies and more than the entire enslaved populations of a dozen other small British colonies on the mainland and in the Caribbean.[4]

Still, in relatively remote North Carolina the arrival of the plantation system remained tenuous and incomplete and has to be understood in relationship to developments in other plantation colonies (and later to other plantation states). Considering North Carolina in this way helps recast the spread of the plantation system as a deliberate choice made by planters who participated in ongoing conversations about culture, wealth, and status. Historians writing about other colonies have often treated the spread of the Atlantic plantation system as a seemingly inevitable outcome of economic forces. In fact, in many colonies decision making depended on a wider range of factors, involved more contingency, and proved to be more complicated at almost every level. Especially on the margins of colonial America—such as in North Carolina—the development of a plantation system proved to be more of an open proposition than a foregone conclusion.

Scholars have usually treated the expansion of the plantation system into North Carolina as an extension of activities in nearby Virginia and South Carolina. While they are undoubtedly in part correct, some of the most important factors in this process owed more to the expansion of the British Atlantic World and the pervasive influence of the plantation system and its promises of economic opportunity by the late seventeenth century. The history of colonial North Carolina, and of the British Atlantic World more generally, is filled with ambitious dreamers and entrepreneurs who tried to create plantations in challenging places with unpromising natural environments, often against more prudent advice and in the face of formidable authorities.[5] In North Carolina, the arrival of the plantation system was less an economic calculation than an unquestioned set of assumptions about the path to success in the British Atlantic World. Instead of understanding slavery and other forms of bound labor as an economic choice, these are probably better understood as resulting from a cultural drive—as much about mastery as about balancing accounts, even though it was clearly about both. North Carolina property owners rarely asked and probably never doubted whether they would purchase forced labor. They sometimes seemed more and perhaps unduly obsessed with the question of how they could obtain forced labor in a relatively poor colony with limited prospects.

North Carolina, moreover, as a geophysical entity lacked the terrain, other than in the extreme northeast and southeast corners, to build and sustain a plantation economy on the scale of the West Indies or of other southern states. But that did not keep a number of ambitious North Carolinians from adapting the same plantation ideal that spread across British West Indian islands and the southern coastal regions of North America. Although even the most aggressive North Carolina planters experienced difficulty in acquiring slave labor to work staple crop plantations and until the nineteenth century lacked a reliable transportation infrastructure for moving crops to market, they nevertheless held the ideal of producing cash crops and acquiring wealth closely in their gaze. Seeing the opulence of their compatriots across the Carolina and Virginia borders, they just worked that much harder to harvest tobacco, rice, cotton, and timber products, hoping to gain their own fortunes through the feeding of ravenous world markets.

In addition to being a more complicated geophysical environment than those other plantation lands in the Indies and along the southeastern coast, North Carolina had other characteristics that made the creation of a prosperous plantation society a formidable challenge. Because more than half of North Carolina's coastal region was water, not land, it was not possible, except along the Cape Fear River, to build lines of rich plantations, each with its own concentration of big house, slave quarters, and tillable lands. North Carolina's plantations were widely scattered, semi-independent from one another, and beyond the possibility of creating a system of security that could assure the whereabouts of every slave, every free black, and hosts of other folk with varying degrees of whiteness, brownness, or darkness who plied the shallow, watery realms of the coast.[6] And the farther one went from the coast—to the end of the coastal plain and beyond—land was divided into smaller and smaller parcels whose owners never embraced the plantation ideals of the folk who settled along the coast.

■ In the middle of the seventeenth century, when the first English colonists moved past the Great Dismal Swamp onto promising farming lands around the Albemarle Sound that would become North Carolina, the British plantation system was still being invented on the distant Caribbean island of Barbados. In another generation, plantations and African slaves would start to seem commonplace in Virginia and a half dozen other British colonies. Prior to the emergence of a distinctive plantation culture, those colonists who styled themselves as "planters" usually operated on a relatively small scale and relied mostly on family labor or on indentured European labor. Early settlers in the Albemarle region would have been very familiar with indentured servitude. In all likelihood many or even most of them initially crossed the ocean as servants themselves.[7] Consequently, would-be planters who wanted more hands to work their land would have defaulted to indentured servitude as the most established and widespread means of obtaining larger labor forces.

If indentured servitude seemed to be a predictable and easy choice for early Albemarle planters, it had at least one overwhelming shortcoming: indentured servitude depended heavily on the engine of transatlantic migration. The vast majority of white laborers who lived and worked in mainland British America arrived as bound migrants. But North Carolina in these early years attracted very few laborers from transatlantic migration.[8] This dynamic ensured that North Carolina could never rely on indentured servants for anything approaching the scale of bound labor in mid-seventeenth-century Virginia and Maryland.

Nevertheless, white servants did not disappear from the Albemarle until well into the eighteenth century. During the 1760s, as much as one out of every three households in Bertie County included someone classified as a servant, though few households had more than one servant—and none had more than four. Surviving sources make it difficult to determine how many of these servants were migrants with indentures, apprentices, bound-out orphans, or criminals. But however they were legally bound originally, there were white bound laborers in North Carolina at least to the period of the American Revolution.[9]

Early North Carolina landowners could not draw large numbers of bound laborers, even by paying their passage across the Atlantic, partly because they were in a disadvantageous competitive position with Virginians. Since any bound servants would have to arrive overland from Virginia once they landed in America, the costs of passage were greater for Carolinians. Given the expense of obtaining bound laborers, Carolina settlers of necessity followed the same strategies as farmers in New England and the Middle Colonies: they relied primarily on work done by their own families.[10] While widespread land ownership with a shortage of labor may have presented a challenge, before the end of the seventeenth century some Albemarle colonists began consolidating resources, marketing surplus crops, and seeking new business opportunities. Assertive and sometimes ruthless men such as Seth Sothell, Thomas Pollock, Samuel Swann, and Edward Moseley pursued the same ambitions as elites throughout the British American world.[11]

Within a few years of the settlers' arrival in the Albemarle, anyone who lived in Virginia would also know about the enslavement of Africans, and the wealthiest men in Virginia were starting to show a preference for enslaved labor instead of servants.[12] In fact, slavery had a place in the earliest visions of the Carolina Proprietorship in the 1670s and 1680s and seemed relevant in initial plans for both the northern (Albemarle) and southern Carolina settlements (Cape Fear and Charles Town). In 1664, Peter Carteret, a distant cousin of one of the proprietors, traveled from England to the Albemarle to take over two poorly managed plantations: Colleton Island and Powell's Point. Carteret's correspondence makes it clear that he was expected to model these plantations after the system in place in Barbados, to market crop staples in the West Indies, and, in the process, to obtain African slaves or indentured servants through this trade.[13] After a couple of years Carteret left, the landowners gave up, and the two plantations failed. But these experiments provided a clear if fleeting glimpse of early visions for an extensive plantation system in North Carolina. Carteret's Albemarle peers would have been aware both of the shift toward more slaves in Virginia and of efforts to make North Carolina and other colonies more like Barbados. During these early decades of slow growth, many considered the possibility that North Carolina as well might develop into a plantation colony.

Making plantations proved more difficult than imagining them, however, and finding labor presented the biggest challenge. Before African slaves could be purchased in large numbers, settlers in many colonies relied on indigenous peoples to provide workers.[14] In the southern British colonies, some settlers and peripatetic traders tapped into native slave-trading markets to make impressive profits by delivering enslaved Indians to labor on plantations.[15] North Carolina colonists never purchased as many native slaves as their neighbors in South Carolina and Virginia, and the reasons remain obscure. Native traders controlled the indigenous slave trade in the southeast, so North Carolinians probably could not buy larger numbers of slaves from unwilling neighbors.

Most of the scattered references to indigenous slaves in the Albemarle date to the years after 1690, when more documents survived, and none of the native groups in the region appears to have been extensive slave traders in the region during those years. This may reflect native cultural choices, limits to the appeal of trade with the Albemarle, demographic forces, geographic obstacles, or some combination of all of those things. Despite these possible checks on the indigenous slave trade in the Albemarle, for at least a generation Native American laborers would have been a common sight on plantations.[16] If late seventeenth-century record keepers strongly associated the label "Negro" with slavery, available sources might well hide many of those bound laborers that colonists might otherwise have called "Indian."[17]

But this also resulted from the fact that North Carolinians never adopted the virtual scorched-earth policies of South Carolina's Indian warriors and slave traders of either killing or enslaving every Indian who lived anywhere within its colonial boundaries. Nor did North Carolinians implement a policy like that of Virginia of subjugating Indian populations and giving them reservation lands where they could live in relative harmony and peace. Although North Carolina invited South Carolina's slavers to enter its lands in 1712 and 1713 for purposes of subduing and removing an enraged nation of Tuscarora Indians (and many coastal land-hungry speculators eagerly joined the fray), it was never the policy of North Carolinians to eradicate the resident Indian population. North Carolina—with many square miles of what was considered unusable land—instead drove its large permanent Indian populations into regions of swamps, dismals, and marchlands. And there they remained from the colonial era until the twenty-first century.[18]

Colonists in the Albemarle far more frequently identified their slaves as Africans, and the forces at work in the British Atlantic world made it far more likely that North Carolina plantations would be worked by African hands. Headright counts, court records, and contemporary comments all indicate that at the start of the eighteenth century North Carolina had several times as many African slaves as indigenous slaves or indentured servants. In these records indentured servants seem to have outnumbered indigenous slaves.[19] The enslaved African population probably exceeded a thousand by this time. Meanwhile, in nearby South Carolina and Virginia, as well as some other British colonies, African slaves were far more numerous and had become a rapidly growing demographic.[20] The first surviving legal code regulating bound labor in North Carolina emerged in a 1715 revision of laws and applied not only to Africans but also to any "Negro, Mulatto or Indyan Slave" and included provisions for white servants.[21]

During these early decades, North Carolina property owners cobbled together workforces from different sources and made use of indentured servants, indigenous slaves, and enslaved Africans based primarily on their availability rather than any clear preference for one or the other. Nor had they yet devised a systematic plantation economy strategy. For example, in 1680 the inventoried estate of Valentine Bird included "Mary ye Indian," a "Women Servant named Ann farmer" with four years to serve, and nine other slaves referred to as "negroes."[22] Thomas Pollock's unusually large labor force of more than seventy provides a more detailed example, including five identified as natives in headrights and thirty-seven African headrights. Life among these diverse bound peoples must have presented intriguing and complicated opportunities for cultural exchange.

Pollock's letters also demonstrate his persistent and usually frustrated desire to purchase more slaves. Over a third of Pollock's surviving letters express an interest in buying slaves, and they make it clear that obtaining labor was his highest business priority. Instead of acquiring large numbers of slaves from Africa, he bought them a few at a time from Boston and other colonial ports. Instead of obtaining significant numbers of indigenous slaves in North Carolina, he imported Native American workers from elsewhere.[23] Pollock wrote these letters as Native American labor declined even more in North Carolina due partly to the aftermath of the Tuscarora War and South Carolina's Yamasee War, though some Indians would linger among the enslaved population for years.[24]

By the time of Pollock's death in the early 1720s, he and other North Carolina colonists had also designed a plantation system to fully exploit their bound laborers. Because North Carolina planters could not grow large quantities of a single profitable staple crop—such as tobacco in the Chesapeake or rice in the South Carolina Low Country—they had to improvise a more flexible and opportunistic plantation economy.[25] For almost another century and a half, North Carolina planters remained ever alert to employ their slaves in producing high-demand and profitable products, while their counterparts in other plantation colonies searched to find sufficient labor to produce their profitable staples. Sometimes planters worked in traditional agricultural settings, growing tobacco in the northeast when it might prove profitable, rice along the Cape Fear where it might have enough water and warm weather, or wheat and maize any place in the colony when and where they could be readily marketed.[26] Many planters participated in an integrated and elaborate system of forest industries that proved especially profitable in the Lower Cape Fear. The work, often lonely and autonomous, did not require large gangs of slaves and often did not pay well enough to purchase them.[27] Other slaves carved out a way of life in the watery world of the Tidewater as boatmen, sailors, or fishermen.[28] Far to the west in the Piedmont a small handful of Africans even experienced religious and cultural conversions and became members of Moravian congregations.[29] But in all but the most exceptional settings and circumstances, bondage became the normative status for peoples of African descent across North Carolina, in all regions and economic situations.

Even while they sought more work for their slaves, North Carolina planters also tried desperately to buy more Africans. The large majority of North Carolina's slaves arrived overland in a poorly documented internal slave trade across the boundaries with adjacent colonies.[30] One of the best records of slave purchases in colonial North Carolina can be found in the letters of Scottish merchant and planter James Murray.[31] Murray arrived on the Cape Fear River in 1735 from London. By the third decade of the eighteenth century the assumed connection between slavery and colonial prosperity in the British colonial world was strong enough that Murray made a rapid decision to purchase slave labor. For about five years he steadily wrote letters to slave traders in Antigua, but with few results.[32] Next, Murray turned his attention to South Carolina slave markets and wrote to buy slaves from one merchant firm over a dozen times in two years. After a hiatus of a few years, Murray returned to North Carolina in the 1750s and tried unsuccessfully to organize a direct trade in slaves between North Carolina and Bance Island on the coast of West Africa.[33] But then in the 1760s Murray relocated to Massachusetts and sold his few dozen slaves in the Cape Fear region for less than he believed they were worth. References in Murray's letters also make it clear that for many years Murray's plantation must have been as much a West African place as a Scottish one and that most of its inhabitants arrived after being sold somewhere else, probably not long after leaving Africa.

By the late colonial period, slavery had undergone an impressive expansion across North Carolina. The largest plantations in the colony were small compared with West Indian sugar plantations, but slave ownership was nevertheless widespread. By the time of the American Revolution somewhere around 1,000 North Carolina households owned ten or more slaves.[34] In the handful of counties with the largest concentrations of wealth and power, most households owned slaves. Plantations, especially in the important Lower Cape Fear region, operated on a scale comparable to those in the South Carolina Low Country, perhaps with a similar level of enforced brutality. North Carolina's slave laws and plantation management practices showed little variation from those in the two slave societies to the north and south even though the colony lacked a powerful economic rationale for the plantation system. North Carolina's economy was actually much more like that of other colonial societies lacking a staple crop. In most of those, both slavery and the plantation system withered with the eventual rise of antislavery opinions and abolitionist movements.[35] In contrast to those lands where slavery diminished as the most logical form of securing labor, North Carolinians embraced slavery and plantations as their preferred system of labor—even if they did so somewhat less enthusiastically than their neighboring Virginians or South Carolinians. Although the American Revolution dislodged many forms of bound labor across much of the new United States, the most complete form of bound labor, slavery, continued to spread and thrive in North Carolina.

THE IMPERATIVE OF SLAVERY IN THE STATE OF NORTH CAROLINA

There was another matter—an oddly complicating factor—that probably served as a reverse stimulus in the slow march of North Carolina toward a slave-based plantation economy. Among the initial white settlers who began spilling southward from the Chesapeake region into the realm that became North Carolina in the late seventeenth century were a very noisy and headstrong group of people who identified themselves as Quakers. Almost as soon as King Charles II issued the Carolina Charter to eight of his most worthy creditors in 1663, this newly emerging band of energetic Protestants, calling themselves Friends, began pouring into corners of the British Empire where they could practice their particular form of Christianity in peace and quiet. Sensing that the new land of Carolina might be a place where they could listen for the spiritual Inner Light that animated them into action—thus to quake—some of these people moved into the unstructured and as yet unformed colony just south of the Virginia border. Other Carolinians—eager for religious succor—were converted by the visiting and dynamic Quaker evangels William Edmondson and George Fox. From wherever they came these Quaker settlers were just as avaricious to acquire wealth as any other soul who went to the new land. They thus shared the appetite of other early Carolina residents to establish plantations stocked with bound labor that could produce crops for an Atlantic market.[36]

Yet by the 1760s North Carolina's Quakers shared a growing conviction with other Friends throughout America and beyond that slaveholding was a personal sin that they could no longer practice. The North Carolina Yearly Meeting concluded in 1768 that "the having of Negroes is become a Burthen to such as are in Possession of them." Quaker opinions on slavery in North Carolina refused to relent on that point, so by the spring of 1776 a cluster of large slaveholding Friends in northeastern North Carolina decided to manumit their slaves. But their hearts hardened on the subject of slavery at a very unpropitious moment. The thirteen colonies south of Canada making up British America were already at war with mother England and were on the verge of declaring their independence. For Quakers to release clusters of slaves at this precise moment was viewed as madness by other slaveholders across coastal North Carolina. In 1777 the newly formed revolutionary state assembly quickly condemned Carolina's Quaker emancipationists. It granted citizens the authority to "take up" any of the freed slaves and deliver them to county courthouses to be jailed until they could be sold at the courthouse door and thus be reenslaved.[37]

It was, of course, in these same years that both North Carolina and American revolutionaries both sought independence and propounded a new brand of ideas about liberty, freedom, and equality. The extent to which these notions—declared as the inalienable rights of man—would extend to slaves, Indians, women, freed blacks, and persons of mixed races would be worked out in the first decades after independence while individual states and the United States as a federal union defined their legal traditions.

If North Carolina's fervently antislavery Quakers thought they would inherit a larger freedom to manumit their slaves in the newly independent nation, they were wrong. When another wave of emancipation fever infected Carolina Quakers in the 1790s, their timing turned out to be equally unfortunate. As they resumed manumitting even larger numbers of slaves in 1792 and 1793, their philanthropic gestures began at the same moment that the slaves of the French island of San Domingue (later to become Haiti) rose up against their masters. Well-armed and rebellious slaves burned hundreds of plantation houses and chased most of their masters off the island in the direction of ports in the United States.

Once again, fearing that the revolutionary upheaval that enveloped Haiti could inspire a general uprising of slaves in North Carolina, the General Assembly—still made up of slaveholding planters—closed virtually every remaining loophole Quakers pursued in attempting to liberate their slaves. Sheriffs were encouraged to search for these "lurking" slaves who had been illegally manumitted by Quaker enthusiasts and to seek out those who sought refuge in the vast Dismal Swamp on the North Carolina–Virginia border.[38]

The concept of seeking out escaped slaves and returning them to their masters is endemic to slave societies of every era, ancient or modern. But the notion of "taking up" individuals who had been freed by their masters—for whatever reason and by whatever method—seems to have been invented in North Carolina specifically to recapture persons emancipated by Quakers. Building upon ancient laws and customs, North Carolina's majority slaveholding lawmakers blunted every effort of Quakers to free their slaves from 1777 until the 1820s. By that time most Friends had either transferred the ownership of their slaves to the North Carolina Yearly Meeting to be colonized in Africa or decided to migrate from the state to places like Ohio and Indiana where they had a better chance of freeing their slaves.

During this same first half century of American independence, the state's

General Assembly, instead of eliminating slaveholding, abolished every form of manumission (the legal process for emancipating slaves) by any person and by any method whatsoever—no matter the person's religious persuasion. Following the second great wave of Quaker manumissions in the 1790s, the assembly stipulated in 1796 that "meritorious service" as adjudged by a county court could be the only grounds for manumission. Five years later owners wanting to free such a slave had to post a hundred-pound bond as security for the good behavior of a freed slave.

By 1830 would-be emancipators had to post a $1,000 bond for each slave manumitted and had to guarantee that the freed person departed North Carolina for good within ninety days. Any freed slave who did not leave North Carolina could be "taken up" by a county sheriff and sold back into slavery. Moreover, any person thus freed who wished to go back to North Carolina to visit family or friends was subject to seizure and sale as well. Because many nonslave states passed laws at the same time prohibiting the entry of freed slaves, both North Carolina and the American nation, instead of moving toward the abolition of slavery, marched steadily toward the abolition of manumission. By the 1830s, not only was it virtually impossible for a slaveholder to free slaves but it was also nearly as difficult to find a place in the United States where that person could legally reside.[39]

But the growing imperative of slavery in North Carolina and other Southern states did not end with roadblocks to manumission (see fig. 4.1). Partially out of a fear of slave insurrections and the possible complicity of previously freed blacks in such uprisings, by the early 1830s North Carolina seemed to be drifting inexorably toward a day when there would be only two orders of inhabitants within its boundaries: free whites and enslaved blacks. Whereas in colonial North Carolina one could find white bound labor in the form of legally indentured servants, in the state of North Carolina and much of the South it became both law and practice for whites to be free and all persons who were not white—blacks, Indians, and people of mixed races—either to be slaves or to be treated much as if they were slaves.[40]

This expanding order of things contradicted what seemed to be an abundance of individual free mulattos and blacks who were able to achieve economic independence and prominence in North Carolina in the years leading up to the Civil War. John Carruthers Stanly (1774–1846), an emancipated free black in New Bern, is often cited by historians as a North Carolina success story. Beginning as a barber, Stanly became a prosperous planter, real estate dealer, and even a prominent slaveholder in his own right, at one time owning 163 slaves. Thomas Day (c. 1801–61), another free black, lived and worked in Caswell County, where he became North Carolina's most promi-

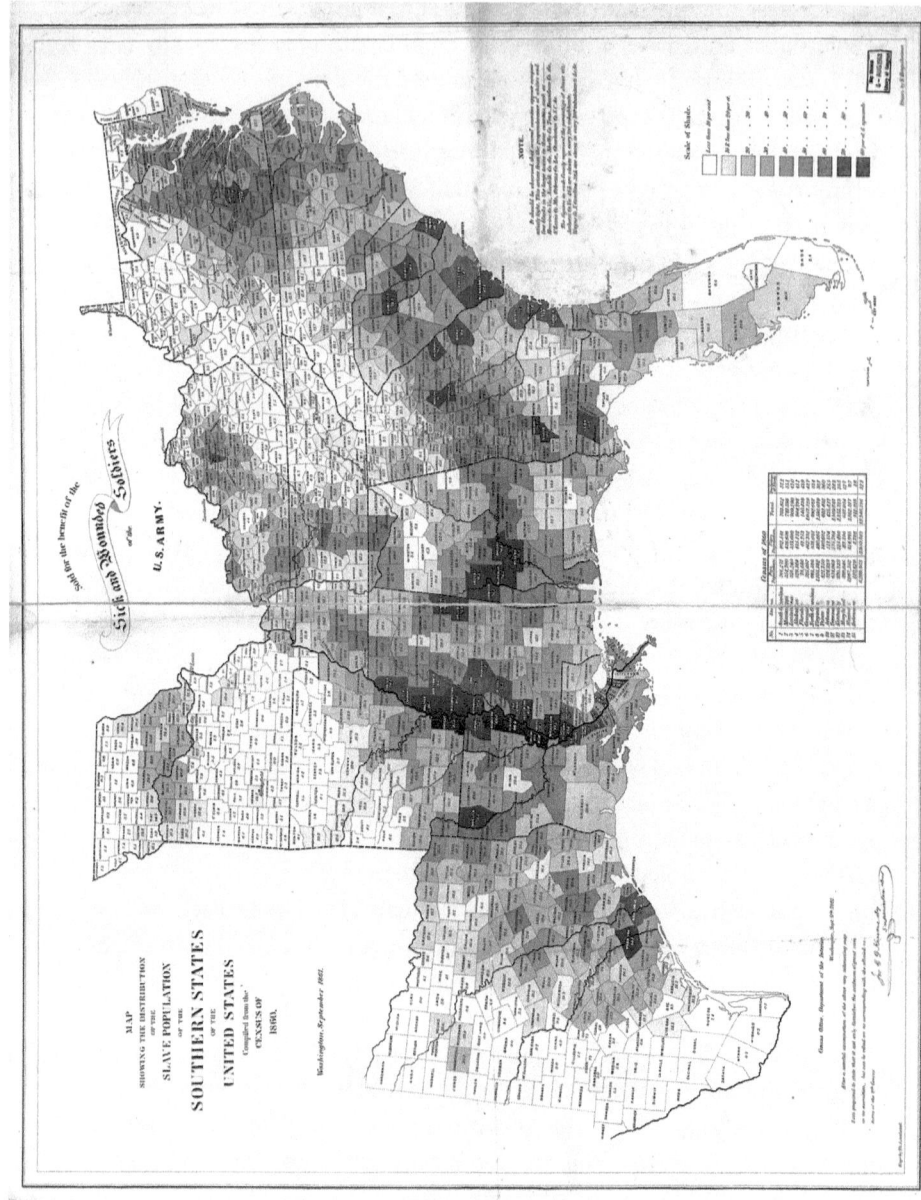

nent cabinet and furniture maker prior to the Civil War. Employing both white and black apprentices and employees, Day turned out hundreds of pieces of furniture of his own unique design and fabricated fine interior woodwork both for plantation homes and in ornate public buildings on the campus of the University of North Carolina. Even a North Carolina slave in Chatham County, George Moses Horton (1797–1884), achieved national fame as a well-published poet on life, liberty, and beauty from the 1820s until the Civil War, when he was finally emancipated.[41]

Even while these gems of humanity came forth in North Carolina—largely due to their individual genius and indomitable drive—the trajectory of North Carolina law and custom from the 1830s until the Civil War was to tighten control of all humans in the state who were not white with a system that was tantamount to enslavement. While it would be challenging to find a politician or state leader who openly espoused a formal legal policy of enslaving free blacks, Indians, and mixed race people living inside the state, it is not difficult at all to discern the drift of lawmaking toward an unspoken imperative of slavery.[42]

North Carolina's evolving system of laws began putting manacles on the legal standing and rights of those who had long been free. For example, in the first decade following the American Revolution when slaves were manumitted they were given all of the rights of free persons: they were "in every respect declared to be a freeman ... as if they had been born free." But beginning in 1791 they were instead set free "as others of their colour who were born free." The law was amended again by 1816 to stipulate that they were set free "as other free persons of color." In other words, as of 1784—the year after the Revolution ended—a newly freed slave was given all of the rights of other Americans. But beginning in 1816, a freed slave was placed in the category of "other free persons of color" whose rights in America were slowly being chipped away.[43]

The erosion of the rights of free blacks followed rapidly after 1816. The ability of persons of "negro, Indian, Mulatto or of mixed descent" to provide testimony in court was limited in 1821. Beginning in 1831 free blacks were forbidden "from gaming with slaves" and from preaching or exhorting

(*opposite*) FIGURE 4.1. This 1860 official U.S. Census map documented the percentage of slave inhabitants in every county of the South where slaveholding still existed. Although the percentages in North Carolina ranged from a high of 68 percent in Warren County to a low of 2.1 percent in Watauga (with 39.5 percent in Wake), it was clear that slavery was a deeply entrenched institution across the state on the eve of the Civil War. Courtesy of the Library of Congress.

in public; in 1832, from "hawking or peddling" without a license; in 1837, from serving in the state militia "except for musicians" and from meeting with other free blacks for the purposes of drinking or dancing; in 1841, from possessing "any Shot gun, Musket, Rifle, Pistol, Sword, Dagger or Bowie knife"; and in 1845, from selling "ardent spirits to any person whatsoever." Other laws sought to prevent white citizens from circulating publications that might foment insurrection among slaves or free blacks (1837) and from selling "spirituous liquors" to free blacks.[44]

In addition to these limitations on the lives and social habits of free blacks, another set of restrictive laws were even more frightening. A long string of laws specified other grounds on which free blacks could be "taken up" and sold into slavery. While many American states—North and South—limited the immigration of freed slaves into their boundaries prior to the Civil War, North Carolina was especially aggressive in discouraging black arrivals. In 1826 North Carolina declared that "any free negro or mulatto" migrating into the state could be taken up and sold into servitude for a period of ten years. Five years later the state applied this same provision to any slave manumitted in North Carolina, which by then was becoming increasingly impossible. Freed slaves had to leave North Carolina within ninety days after they were freed or they could be taken and sold at the courthouse door back into slavery. And after they left the state, if they should return to North Carolina for any purpose whatever, they could be sold back into slavery. If this were not enough, the same proviso was extended to any free blacks living in the state. Even though a black individual might have been free from birth and their parents, too, if they left North Carolina for more than ninety days and then returned, they also could be taken up by the county sheriff and sold into slavery.[45]

When the Quakers freed slaves in years past, North Carolina lawmakers could justify a policy of taking up these particular ex-slaves on the grounds that they had been manumitted in an illegal manner. But arresting and enslaving individuals who had previously enjoyed a life of freedom in America was a massive expansion of a newly designed system of social control. The same 1826 law that controlled the migration of free blacks also took aim at those remaining in North Carolina but who did not seem to move quickly enough to suit the proclivities of the state's white majority. Special laws were designed for those free blacks who did not appear to be pursuing an income-producing occupation. County courts were suddenly required to hire out for three years any free black who spent "his or her time in idleness or dissipation." If, at the end of that time, this same free black returned to a life of idleness, he or she could be hired out again and then again at the judgment of the court. This law had a further provision that not only put a free black perceived to be living in idleness at risk but also gave authority to the county court to bind the children of free blacks without "some honest industrious occupation" to even longer periods of legal servitude. Determined to be absent the support of "industrious" parents, these children were deemed virtual orphans and could be legally bound into an apprenticeship until they reached adulthood.[46] Whether or not this law was intended to dismantle free black families, it indeed disrupted those of Indians who occupied lands coveted by ambitious white farmers.[47]

The scrutiny and potential endangerment of the lives of free blacks went further in the face of potential slave insurrections. Following the Nat Turner slave rebellion of August 1831 just across the North Carolina border in Virginia, in which fifty-five whites were killed, rumors of other rebellions crisscrossed North Carolina. Fearing that North Carolina's swamps and forests might be filled with runaway slaves and free blacks organizing to massacre whites, the General Assembly passed a new set of laws placing suspicion on the back of every free black in the state. Slave patrols were authorized to "take up" any "negroes" suspected of being runaway slaves. North Carolina's unique laws of "taking up" suspected slaves meant that these persons could be sold into slavery if no master showed up to claim ownership of the apprehended blacks. Black sailors arriving as crew members or passengers on ships stopping in North Carolina ports were subject to being taken up and sold if they did not depart on the same ship. Just as slaves came under suspicion if they were away from their owner's plantation or place of business, free blacks—without identity documents or a white person's authentication—could find themselves under suspicion of being a runaway or party to a real or fabricated crime. Such a purported crime was spelled out in a new 1837 law providing that a free black convicted of "intent to commit a rape upon the body of a white female shall suffer death without benefit of clergy" (i.e., commutation).[48]

By the early 1830s when a plantation ideal for good or ill was firmly seated in the minds of North Carolinians, there was also emblazoned in their minds a fear of having an unfettered population of African slaves roaming across the state. While Indian wars were a distant memory in North Carolina by the 1830s, plenty had heard tales of the battles with Indians on America's frontiers. While they were feeling the tremors of slave rebellions in Virginia and rumors of other slave conspiracies in South Carolina, they also witnessed on their western borders the removal of angry Cherokees from their mountain homelands to distant territories across the Mississippi River. Yet many of those proud Cherokees resisted removal and hid in remote valley haunts.

Nor could Carolinians fail to notice the thousands of Indians who were scattered around North Carolina border regions on lands and in swamps not commandeered by the state's intrepid brigades of planters and farmers.

While the residual populations of Indians surviving colonial wars mainly avoided contact with potential white oppressors, there were Chowans on the Chowan River and Meherrins along the Roanoke River. Remnants of the once mighty Tuscarora nation still lived in Bertie County. Other clusters of Indians were spread along the Virginia border with nearly forgotten names—Enos, Sauras, Occaneechis. Along the South Carolina border there were other thousands of Indians, also avoiding notice as much as possible—the Waccamaws, a large cluster of unnamed Indians in Robeson County, and more remnants of the departed Tuscarora and Catawba nations. Without reservation lands or an inherited tribal structure, these fragments of former nations survived only through increasingly vague and mysterious oral traditions and in their facial characteristics and light, but not white, skin tones.

Finally, there were the free blacks—many of African descent, but mulattos too from the miscegenation of white men and black slave women, as well as free black and slave men taken into physical union by white women. Into this mix of nonwhites there appeared other progeny of different types of unions: white men and women bore children with Indians, giving birth to mestizos—more frequently recognized in Spanish nations than in the United States. Indians and Africans also came together to birth yet other nonwhite progeny. By the 1830s there was virtually every skin color under the sun in North Carolina and elsewhere in the United States—mixtures of the many faces of Africa, the hues and smooth skins of Indians, and the ruddy, swarthy, or pocked complexions of Europeans. While historians might argue for generations on whether America was a melting pot of cultures, it was by the 1830s already a genetically altered stew of peoples with a well-mixed majority of whites and a well-stirred minority of peoples who were not white.

Whether America's white male leaders stumbled into it or it was a consequence of coming to grips with the evolving political economy and racial diversity of the United States, a handy solution to their concerns emerged in the 1820s that was quickly embraced in North Carolina and across the nation. The solution was actually very simple: rather than having a complicated set of laws written specifically for whites, blacks, Indians, free blacks, mulattos, mestizos, and other nonwhite mixtures of beings that had emerged in the American population, why not just call all of these people "persons of color"? That was the first corollary of the solution. The second was just as straightforward: because "persons of color" for a whole variety of reasons were deemed not worthy of participating in the political life of the United States, why not establish a body of laws that would keep these people under surveillance and control? And the third corollary in this new equation was equally uncomplicated: because there is no place for these folk as potential citizens in the United States, why not relocate them to some other places (Indians), colonize them in Africa (freed slaves and free blacks), or create a caste system for them that is tantamount to slavery (all those persons of color who refuse to leave)?

Thus, from the 1820s forward, North Carolina (but not alone) began the process of creating (or perhaps merely solidifying) a social system that included only three kinds of persons: free men (white men), free persons of color (blacks and people of mixed race who were not slaves), and slaves. At the same time, legally and socially North Carolina drifted toward a system that had essentially only two kinds of beings: free men and slaves. In this carefully designed social framework (again not elaborated only in North Carolina), women had limited legal rights and were thus made legal appendages to men. The rights of "free persons of color" came to be similarly restricted between the 1830s and the Civil War until their status (except for being sold as property) was little different from that of slaves.[49]

The process of doing this was insidious—even if it was not entirely conscious. For example, one of North Carolina's earliest laws respecting those who would eventually become "persons of color"—the 1746 law on servants and slaves—defined the status of "all Negroes, Mulattoes, bond and free, to the Third Generation, and Indian Servants or Slaves." When the law was revised immediately following the Declaration of Independence in 1777, the net was spread wider to include "Negroes, Indians, Mulattoes, and all Persons of mixed Blood, descended from Negro and Indian Ancestors, to the fourth Generation inclusive (though one Ancestor in each Generation may have been a white Person) whether Bond or free."[50]

Racial designations were obviously getting way too complicated. When the North Carolina General Assembly began simplifying categories in the 1820s and 1830s toward a new construction of the state's society, these same laws were said to pertain to "free negroes, mulattos or free persons of color" (1831). By 1837 a separate reference to "mulatto" was dropped. And when various observers pointed out that there were some free negroes or mulattos who looked alarmingly white, the legislators came back in 1854—a century and a half before the development of DNA testing—with a clearer (though obviously subjective) definition: "All free persons descended from negro ancestors, to the fourth generation inclusive, though one ancestor of each generation may have been a white person, shall be deemed free negroes and persons of mixed blood." Thus, legally, they were thenceforth thereafter free persons of color and not white.[51]

If there were any question about what was meant in these laws, North Carolina held a state constitutional convention in 1835 to explain how this new structure was intended to work. Called initially to create a more equitable distribution of the electorate and of elected state representatives across the entire geography of the state, the General Assembly issuing the call for a convention was very specific about who was invited and what needed to be amended in the state's original constitution of December 1776. The only North Carolinians who could vote for delegates to the convention were "free white men, of the age of twenty one years, who shall have been resident in the State one year previous to ... the election." When the convention met in 1835, it was thus an assembly consisting of "Representatives of the Freemen of the State of North Carolina." And by direction of the General Assembly and the voters, among the first items of business to be considered by the convention was "to abrogate or restrict the right of free negroes or mulattoes to vote for members of the [North Carolina] Senate or House of Commons." Although it took a good deal of debate, the convention proceeded to do just that. While in retrospect this might seem a harsh and radical step on the part of the state's leaders, North Carolina was actually the last Southern state to exclude free blacks from voting and nearly the last state, North or South, in the nation to do so.[52]

By putting such a provision in the new state constitution, North Carolina both abolished the right of free persons of color to vote and their rights and ability to participate on an equal footing with all other "free white men" of the state. By excluding free persons of color from citizenship in North Carolina, another whole cascade of consequences came into play. Just as North Carolina had expanded a colonial authority for sheriffs and citizens to "take up" runaway slaves and slaves freed by Quakers, the state began extending this same practice in the direction of free persons of color. Even before the constitutional convention of 1835, as noted earlier, North Carolina's counties were granted authority in 1826 to take up any free Negro or mulatto who spent "his or her time in idleness and dissipation" either to be bound out or to be sold into slavery. The same law permitted counties to bind out the children of free blacks without "some honest industrious occupation."[53]

The screws of authority over the lives of free persons of color tightened regularly from that time forward. In 1832 any person of color who could not pay a duly levied fine or a contracted debt could be "hired out" to the highest bidder. The successful bidder was then granted the same authority over that person as if he or she were an apprentice or a bound servant. In 1837 any citizen was authorized to "take up" a person of color for living in idleness. If that person could not pay the costs of court for his prosecution, he could also be hired out to the highest bidder. If a free black should be convicted of a crime, he or she was required to be sold at the courthouse door for a period of five years. The sentence was automatically doubled if the person should abscond during the term of service. By 1854 county courts were not merely authorized to bind out the children of idle free persons; "it shall be the duty" of the courts, a new law provided, to bind out the children of free Negroes who "do not habitually employ their time in some honest industrious occupation."[54]

The historic squelching and limitation of the rights of free blacks in North Carolina is not a new finding. Indeed, one of the pioneering studies of this subject was conducted by the noted historian John Hope Franklin during the last years of the Great Depression and beginning of the Second World War. Working under research conditions at the North Carolina State Archives where he was segregated from white researchers and placed in a separate room out of view, Franklin compiled the records for his first of many books on slavery and race in America. Published in 1943 under the title *The Free Negro in North Carolina, 1790–1860*, Franklin set out to tell the story of how North Carolina was more tolerant of free blacks than other Southern states—at least in the period from the American Revolution through the 1820s.[55]

But, Franklin, too, found that things then changed dramatically. In the 1820s and 1830s North Carolina embraced many of the restrictive laws on free blacks that were appearing elsewhere in both the North and the South. The impulse to send free blacks and freed slaves out of North Carolina to anywhere else—to a "free" state or to Africa—grew enormously from the 1830s forward—just as Northern states closed their doors to free blacks and as most free blacks in the North decided that they would have nothing to do with African colonization. As he observed this huge, historic shift in North Carolina, Franklin—ever a genial soul who wanted to find good in the heart of every man—sadly titled his last chapter "An Unwanted People." Whereas he found North Carolina once to be a place where "free Negroes" (and he lumped all free persons of color together in his book—Indians too) could live and even thrive, following the 1835 constitutional convention of "the Freemen of North-Carolina," the state became a no-man's land for free persons of color. Franklin thus concluded his book questioning the twentieth-century characterization of North Carolina as historically a state of liberal tendencies.[56]

A gentle, peace-loving historian from beginning to end, Franklin stopped short of drawing out the implications of North Carolina's drift toward a two-level society between the American Revolution and the Civil War. Deep within North Carolina's earliest roots there seemed to be a preference for cultivating crops and producing goods for export with bound labor. If there had not been wealthy planter societies both to the north and to the south of North Carolina and also around the Atlantic World, maybe North Carolina would have gone in another direction when the supply of white indentures dried up. Maybe North Carolina would have headed elsewhere if its entire Indian population had been virtually eradicated as it was in places like New England, Pennsylvania, and South Carolina. Maybe it would have chosen a different course if its small population of Quakers had not attempted to free their slaves at moments when the state's white planters were frightened to the core that they were about to suffer a bloody rebellion of slaves, probably being led by a legion of free blacks and Indians, who would cut the throat of every white man, rape every white woman, and kidnap every white child.

But those were courses not taken in the strangely situated land that became North Carolina. Bound labor became the norm; slavery became an imperative. The first was to secure work. The second was as much to control what was perceived as dangerous alien populations as to generate work. Both were pursued in a manner that would have determining implications not only for the way North Carolinians chose sides in the face of the Civil War and but also for figuring out what to do with freed persons of color after the Civil War, how it would build a segregated society in the 1890s, how it would design a system of factories to bring an industrial base to the state, and how it would resist the integration of schools and of civil society in the 1960s. It is as if North Carolinians watched to see what others were doing around them and then chose a pattern that either avoided the pitfalls of their neighbors or outdid those other folk in their contrariness not to suffer change.

NOTES

1. William Tryon to Sewallis Shirley, in *Correspondence of William Tryon and Other Selected Papers*, ed. William S. Powell, 2 vols. (Raleigh, N.C.: Division of Archives and History, 1980–81), 1:136–43. The letter has also been published in William S. Powell, ed., "'Tryon's Book' on North Carolina," *North Carolina Historical Review* 34 (July 1957): 406–15.

2. On slavery in colonial North Carolina, see Marvin L. Michael Kay and Lorin Lee Cary, *Slavery in North Carolina, 1748–1775* (Chapel Hill: University of North Carolina Press, 1995); Jeffrey J. Crow, *The Black Experience in Revolutionary North Carolina* (Raleigh, N.C.: Division of Archives and History, 1977); Jeffrey J. Crow, Paul D. Escott, and Flora J. Hatley, *A History of African Americans in North Carolina*, rev. ed. (Raleigh, N.C.: Division of Ar-

chives and History, 2002); Alan D. Watson, "Impulse toward Independence: Resistance and Rebellion among North Carolina Slaves, 1750-1775," *Journal of Negro History* 63 (October, 1978): 317-28; Bradford J. Wood, *This Remote Part of the World: Regional Formation in Lower Cape Fear, North Carolina, 1725-1775* (Columbia: University of South Carolina Press, 2004), 34-38, 98-102, 135-39, 163-68, 174-216, 233-40; and Jon F. Sensbach, *A Separate Canaan: The Making of An Afro-Moravian World in North Carolina, 1763-1840* (Chapel Hill: University of North Carolina Press, 1998).

3. An estimate of 40,000 follows Kay and Cary, *Slavery in North Carolina*, but Peter H. Wood puts the number at 52,000 in "The Changing Population of the Colonial South: An Overview by Race and Region, 1685-1790," in *Powhatan's Mantle: Indians in the Colonial Southeast*, ed. Peter H. Wood, Gregory A. Waselkov, and M. Thomas Hatley (Lincoln: University of Nebraska Press, 1989), 38.

4. The dozen colonies were Rhode Island, New Hampshire, Nova Scotia, Bermuda, the Bahamas, Antigua, St. Kitts, Montserrat, Nevis, the Virgin Islands, Delaware, and Georgia.

5. Similar experiments occurred in a variety of places and times in the history of British colonization but with mixed results. In this sense, North Carolina planters shared much in common with Barbadians before sugar, Virginians before tobacco, settlers on Providence Island before the Spanish, South Carolinians before rice, dairy farmers in the Narragansett River Valley of Rhode Island, and the malcontents in early Georgia.

6. This is well documented in David S. Cecelski, *The Waterman's Song: Slavery and Freedom in Maritime North Carolina* (Chapel Hill: University of North Carolina Press, 2001). The activities of people of darker hues—slave, free, Indian, mulatto—are obvious from the dozens of laws passed by the General Assembly of North Carolina, many of them designed for local waterways. See William L. Byrd III, comp., *Against the Peace and Dignity of the State: North Carolina's Laws Regarding Slaves, Free Persons of Color, and Indians* (Westminster, Md.: Heritage Books, 2007), e.g., 222-29 (1831-32), 303-4 (1835), 340-42 (1847), 401-2 (1854).

7. On indentured servants in the Chesapeake, see Lorena S. Walsh, *Motives of Honor, Pleasure, and Profit: Plantation Management in the Colonial Chesapeake, 1607-1763* (Chapel Hill: University of North Carolina Press, 2010), 373-86; and James Horn, *Adapting to A New World* (Chapel Hill: University of North Carolina Press, 1994), 251-92. The best discussion of indentured servitude in North Carolina is Alan D. Watson, "A Consideration of European Indentured Servitude in Colonial North Carolina," *North Carolina Historical Review* 91 (October 2014): 381-406.

8. See Christopher Tomlins, *Freedom Bound: Law, Labor and Civic Identity in Colonizing English America, 1580-1865* (Cambridge: Cambridge University Press, 2010), 29-66. For the classic overview of indentured servitude, see David Galenson, *White Servitude in Colonial America: An Economic Analysis* (Cambridge: Cambridge University Press, 1984).

9. Watson, "Consideration of European Indentured Servitude," 388-90; Watson's discussion summarizes the best available evidence for any North Carolina county. Alan D. Watson, "Household Size and Composition in Pre-revolutionary North Carolina," *Mississippi Quarterly* 31 (Winter 1978): 558-59. We have not made use of the population estimates for indentured servitude suggested by Marvin L. Michael Kay and Lorin Lee Cary because, as Watson explains, their methodology is flawed. See Kay and Cary, "A Demographic Analysis of Colo-

nial North Carolina with Special Emphasis upon the Slave and Black Populations," in *Black Americans in North Carolina and the South*, ed. Jeffrey J. Crow and Flora J. Hatley (Chapel Hill: University of North Carolina Press, 1984), 104–7, 112–15.

10. Evidence of this family migration pattern can be found in the numerous headrights given to landowners for the importation of people bearing the same surnames. See Carolina B. Whitley, *North Carolina Headrights: A List of Names, 1663-1744* (Raleigh: North Carolina Office of Archives and History, 2008).

11. For a case study along these lines, see Bradford J. Wood, "Thomas Pollock and the Making of an Albemarle Plantation World," in *Creating and Contesting Carolina: Proprietary Era Histories*, ed. Michelle LeMaster and Bradford J. Wood (Columbia: University of South Carolina Press, 2013), 211–33.

12. John C. Coombs, "The Phases of Conversion: A New Chronology for the Rise of Slavery in Early Virginia," *William and Mary Quarterly* 68 (July 2011): 332–60; John C. Coombs, "Beyond the 'Origins Debate': Rethinking the Rise of Virginia Slavery," in *Early Modern Virginia: Reconsidering the Old Dominion*, ed. Douglas Bradburn and John C. Coombs (Charlottesville: University of Virginia Press, 2011), 239–78.

13. See the numerous relevant letters in William S. Powell, ed., *Ye Countie of Albemarle in Carolina* (Raleigh, N.C.: Department of Archives and History, 1958), 6–8, 11–12, 30–32, 56–62.

14. The dominance of enslaved African labor in the United States after the early eighteenth century makes the use of indigenous labor seem anomalous, but it was more commonplace and more important earlier and in the Spanish, Portuguese, and French empires in America (see, e.g., chapter 3 of this volume).

15. Alan Gallay, *Indian Slave Trade: The Rise of the English Empire in the American South, 1670-1717* (New Haven, Conn.: Yale University Press, 2003); Alan Gallay, ed., *Indian Slavery in Colonial America* (Lincoln: University of Nebraska Press, 2010), 1–32, 67–108, 207–49; Christina Snyder, *Slavery in Indian Country: The Changing Face of Captivity in Early America* (Cambridge, Mass.: Harvard University Press, 2012), 1–151.

16. Little has been written about these indigenous slaves in North Carolina, but see David La Vere, *The Tuscarora War: Indians, Settlers, and the Fight for the Carolina Colonies* (Chapel Hill: University of North Carolina Press, 2013), 51–53, 115, 198–99; and Wood, "Thomas Pollock," 217–18.

17. It is impossible to know how common this slippage may have been, but the terms appear to have been fluid at this time. The fact that neither Carolina colony could rely on a systematic trade in slaves from Africa until several decades into the eighteenth century makes it plausible that scholars have mistaken many Native American slaves for Africans in both colonies.

18. One can trace this story in Stephen D. Feeley, "Tuscarora Trails: Indian Migrations, Wars, and Constructions of Colonial Frontiers," Ph.D. diss., College of William and Mary, 2007, 180–209, 270–316; La Vere, *Tuscarora War*, 178–210; and Theda Perdue and Christopher Arris Oakley, *Native Carolinians: The Indians of North Carolina* (Raleigh, N.C.: Office of Archives and History, 2010), 27–39.

19. Whitley, *North Carolina Headrights*, provides all of the headright information. Relevant higher court records can be found in Mattie Erma Edwards Parker, William S. Price Jr.,

and Robert J. Cain, eds., *Colonial Records of North Carolina*, 2nd ser., 11 vols. (Raleigh, N.C.: Division of Archives and History, 1963–81), vols. 2–6. See also Wood, "Thomas Pollock," 218.

20. Crow et al., *African Americans in North Carolina*, 3.

21. "An Act Concerning Servants and Slaves," in *The Colonial and State Records of North Carolina*, ed. William L. Saunders, Walter Clark, and Stephen B. Weeks, 26 vols. (Raleigh: State of North Carolina, 1886–1914), 23:62–66.

22. Bryan J. Grimes, *North Carolina Wills and Inventories, Copied from the Original Records and Recorded Wills and Inventories in the Office of the Secretary of State* (Raleigh, N.C.: Edwards and Broughton Printing, 1912), 472–74. For other estates with similarly mixed workforces, see ibid., 13–15, 273–76, 357–60, 560–61.

23. Wood, "Thomas Pollock," 216–18.

24. La Vere, *Tuscarora War*, 198–99.

25. For a regional case study of this process, see Wood, *This Remote Part of the World*, 174–216.

26. Ibid., 181–87, 195–99; Kay and Cary, *Slavery in North Carolina*, 40–43; James M. Clifton, "Golden Grains of White: Rice Planting on the Lower Cape Fear," *North Carolina Historical Review* 50 (October 1973): 365–93.

27. Wood, *This Remote Part of the World*, 174–95, 199–212; Robert Outland III, *Tapping the Pines: The Naval Stores Industry in the American South* (Baton Rouge: Louisiana State University Press, 2004).

28. Cecelski, *Waterman's Song*.

29. Sensbach, *A Separate Canaan*.

30. Gregory E. O'Malley, "Beyond the Middle Passage: Slave Migration from the Caribbean to North America, 1619–1807," *William and Mary Quarterly* 66 (January 2009): 125–72; Kay and Cary, *Slavery in North Carolina*, especially 19–22, 307–8; Walter E. Minchinton, "The Seaborne Slave Trade of North Carolina," *North Carolina Historical Review* 71 (January 1994): 1–61; Wood, *This Remote Part of the World*, 38–40.

31. These letters will be included in Bradford J. Wood, ed., *James Murray in North Carolina* (in preparation by the North Carolina Office of Archives and History). All citations here are to that manuscript, but pending its publication the relevant original letters are all available in the James Murray Letters and James Murray Robbins Papers in the Massachusetts Historical Society, Boston, Mass. Murray's letters regarding the slave trade have also been analyzed in Gregory E. O'Malley, *Final Passages: The Intercolonial Slave Trade of British America, 1619–1807* (Chapel Hill: University of North Carolina Press, 2014), 194–200.

32. James Murray to David Tullideph, February 21, 1736, and April 15, 1736; Murray to Henry McCulloh, May 28, 1736; Murray to Walter Tullideph, June 23, 1736; Murray to William Ellison, July 10, 1736; all in Wood, *James Murray in North Carolina*.

33. James Murray to Richard Oswald, June 16, 1752, July 19, 1756, and November 26, 1757, all in Wood, *James Murray in North Carolina*.

34. This estimate is based on a comprehensive survey of all surviving county tax lists and lists of taxables for the colonial period and extrapolates using the population estimates included in Kay and Cary, *Slavery in North Carolina*, 221–27.

35. The most logical reference point may be the vast and growing literature on the end of slavery in the American North. For example, a model driven by purely economic factors

would make it difficult to explain why slavery persisted on the Chowan, Neuse, and Cape Fear Rivers but was eliminated on the Hudson, Delaware, or Narragansett.

36. The most reliable source for tracing the phenomena of Quakers in early North Carolina is still the pioneering work of Stephen B. Weeks, *Southern Quakers and Slavery: A Study in Institutional History* (Baltimore: Johns Hopkins Press, 1896).

37. This tangled and difficult story can be pieced together through the rich body of documents contained in Michael J. Crawford, *The Having of Negroes Is Become a Burden: The Quaker Struggle to Free Slaves in Revolutionary North Carolina* (Gainesville: University Press of Florida, 2010), 76–88, 112–19.

38. For the new round of manumissions and the extensive responses on the county level where Quakers lived, see William L. Byrd III, *North Carolina Slaves and Free Persons of Color—Perquimans County* (Westminster, Md.: Heritage Books, 2005), 165–69, 172–75, 183–84. See also William L. Byrd III, *North Carolina Slaves and Free Persons of Color—Pasquotank County* (Westminster, Md.: Heritage Books, 2006), 390–92.

39. For the string of antimanumission laws, see Byrd, *Against the Peace and Dignity of the State*, 132–33, 144–45, 214–16. There have been many studies of legal impediments introduced by nonslave states to prevent the immigration of freed slaves. Among the most interesting, with many parallels to North Carolina's pattern of lawmaking, is Beverly C. Tomek, *Colonization and Its Discontents: Emancipation, Emigration, and Antislavery in Antebellum Pennsylvania* (New York: New York University Press, 2011), esp. 18–42, 63–92.

40. Throughout much of the twentieth century North Carolina historians and many outside observers have argued that North Carolina was different from other southern states when it came to the subject of slavery; that slave practices in the state were not nearly as severe as in other states; that there was more freedom of opportunity for free blacks; and that there was more antislavery sentiment in the state. (Note by Larry Tise: I too, was long in this school of thought. See Larry E. Tise, "Confronting the Issue of Slavery," in *The North Carolina Experience: An Interpretive and Documentary History*, ed. Lindley S. Butler and Alan D. Watson (Chapel Hill: University of North Carolina Press, 1984), 193–216; the present chapter represents a revision of my earlier work.)

41. John C. Stanly's story was noted prominently by John Hope Franklin in his pioneering book, *The Free Negro in North Carolina, 1790–1860* (Chapel Hill: University of North Carolina Press, 1943), 31–32, 126–28, 149–50, 161–62. Loren Schweninger filled in many details on the remarkable career of Stanly in "John Carruthers Stanly and the Anomaly of Black Slaveholding," *North Carolina Historical Review* 67 (April 1990): 159–92. Thomas Day's life and many unique designs have been well celebrated in Patricia Phillips Marshall and Jo Ramsay Leimenstoll, *Thomas Day: Master Craftsman and Free Man of Color* (Chapel Hill: University of North Carolina Press, 2010). On George Moses Horton, see Joan R. Sherman, ed., *The Black Bard of North Carolina and His Poetry: George Moses Horton* (Chapel Hill: University of North Carolina Press, 1997); and the older groundbreaking work by Richard Walser, *The Black Poet* (New York: Philosophical Library, 1966).

42. That North Carolina's lawmakers were aware they were creating a new status for blacks and mixed-race Carolinians is clear in the transcripts of the 1835 North Carolina Constitutional Convention. See *Proceedings and Debates of the Convention of North-Carolina, Called to Amend the Constitution of the State, Which Assembled at Raleigh, June 4, 1835* (Raleigh, N.C.: Joseph Gales and Son, 1836), esp. 61–69 (June 13, 1835).

43. Byrd, *Against the Peace and Dignity of the State*, 91 (1784), 117 (1791), 141 (1800), 163 (1816).

44. Ibid., 180 (defendants), 216 (gaming with slaves), 224–25 (exhorting in public), 226–27 (hawking), 270 (musicians), 302 (drinking or dancing), 313 (musket, dagger), 317 (ardent spirits), 274 (circulate literature), 420 (sell liquors).

45. Ibid., 199–202, 214–16.

46. Ibid., 199–202.

47. For a documentation of how these laws were used to displace the Mattamuskeet Indians from their lands around Lake Mattamuskeet, see Patrick H. Garrow, *The Mattamuskeet Documents: A Study in Social History* (Raleigh, N.C.: Division of Archives and History, 1975).

48. Byrd, *Against the Peace and Dignity of the State*, 218–19, 222–24, 305.

49. The interpretation offered here of North Carolina's process of limiting the rights and freedoms of free blacks is an extrapolation and expansion of the theories developed over the years most notably by Ira Berlin, especially in his classic work *Slaves without Masters: The Free Negro in the Antebellum South* (New York: New Press, 1992).

50. Byrd, *Against the Peace and Dignity of the State*, 35, 66–67, 72–73.

51. Ibid., 199–202, 268–69, 401–2.

52. Ibid., 245–51. Prior to North Carolina's bar on voting by free blacks the following states had restricted voting to "white" citizens alone: Alabama (1819), Connecticut (1818), Delaware (1792), Illinois (1818), Indiana (1816), Kentucky (1799), Louisiana (1812), Maryland (1810), Mississippi (1817), Missouri (1820), New Jersey (1807), New York (1820), Ohio (1802), South Carolina (1790), Tennessee (1834), Virginia (1830). Pennsylvania followed North Carolina's example (1838), as did other newly established states: Arkansas (1836), California (1849), Florida (1838), Iowa (1846), Texas (1845), and Wisconsin (1848). As of the onset of the Civil War only the following states did not legally restrict free black residents from voting: Georgia (although no blacks, by custom and social practice, were permitted to vote), Maine, Massachusetts, New Hampshire, Rhode Island, and Vermont. See Alexander Keyssar, *The Right to Vote: The Contested History of Democracy in the United States* (New York: Basic Books, 2000), 349–53.

53. Byrd, *Against the Peace and Dignity of the State*, 199–202. See also *Proceedings and Debates of the Convention of North-Carolina*, 61–69.

54. Byrd, *Against the Peace and Dignity of the State*, 225–26, 303–7, 365–66.

55. Franklin, *Free Negro in North Carolina*. For John Hope Franklin's experiences in doing his research at the North Carolina State Archives, see Franklin, "A Sense of Time and Place," in *Public History in North Carolina, 1903-1978*, ed. Jeffrey J. Crow (Raleigh, N.C.: Division of Archives and History, 1979), 75–80.

56. Franklin, *Free Negro in North Carolina*, see esp., chap. 6, "An Unwanted People," 192–221.

LAND TENURE AS REGULATOR GRIEVANCE AND REVOLUTIONARY TOOL

Carole Watterson Troxler

ENTERING A HISTORIAN'S NO-MAN'S-LAND

Early on the last Monday of September 1770, dusty paths and byways in the town of Hillsborough already were crowded with more people than usually attended the district court. Their shouting prompted vendors to cry louder as they opened stalls and uncovered carts and wagons. Soon smells would ripen with the heat of the day—fruit and its libations, horses and walkers, even the few rotting leaves that feet disturbed in their out-of-the-way accumulations. Court had opened on Saturday, and a petition addressing the subject of juries had been delivered to the presiding judge. He had laid it aside, promising to respond later. Today was the first session in which cases might be tried, and that was the reason for the crowds. More than 170 men had signed the petition, and its contents were widely known. Garrulous and rambling, it repeated the complaint that jurymen selected for the district court were prejudiced to a man. County justices of the peace selected them, the long-accepted practice. The petitioners maintained that, at the time, jurors routinely protected the interests of the justices, whether the justices' connections were with the plaintiff or the defendant. Of direct concern were "Regulator" spokesmen who, both in and out of court, had accused county officers of misconduct and faced indictments as a result.

The courthouse grounds were packed before the court opened at eleven o'clock, and men crammed shoulder to shoulder inside. Immediately, a delegation of Regulator spokesmen asked to address the court and demanded the trial of their indicted leaders by new juries, not the jurors the county justices had appointed. That was their only demand. The frightened judge kept his seat at their request and allowed them to control the proceedings for the rest of the day, an action he disavowed after making his escape that night.[1]

The day brought forth some of the best-known violence of North Carolina's Regulator movement of the 1760s through 1771. Some of the crowd dragged men from the courthouse and whipped them through the streets, having come into court prepared with clubs, cowhide whips, and switches cut from trees. They attacked others outside the courthouse, but none of the victims were random targets. The judge recorded ten names of the "many" men he said the mob whipped. The names he recorded were justices of the peace, former sheriffs, merchants, registrars, and militia officers. Each of them fit two or more of these categories.[2]

For more than four decades now, historians have embraced North Carolina Regulators and their issues as a fertile field for investigating aspects of the late colonial Southern backcountry.[3] Studies have revealed rapid settlement by farmers and herders in the 1750s, mainly in clusters identified by kinship, ethnicity, and religion. Their various Protestant identities had taken political shape in seventeenth-century wars in the British Isles and Europe. British-based groups revered the legislation concerning personal freedoms, limits on the monarchy, and freedom of religion that had followed the Revolution of 1688–89, seeing in it some vindication of their forebears' struggles. They still resented the official role of the Church of England, which that legislation had reinforced. The considerable Calvinism and pietism within the Scottish, English, and Scots-Irish bodies gave them some common ground with German, Swiss, and French congregations scattered among them.[4]

The settlements were rural entities, not towns like Hillsborough. Even the Moravian towns in northern Rowan County were designed to provide outlets for craft goods and trading for farmers in the surrounding Moravian congregations. Studies have identified the cosmopolitan commercial patterns that came into the backcountry with merchants and lawyers, who largely were based in eastern North Carolina and Tidewater Virginia. Moreover, the easterners fostered the establishment of social and political structures that favored planters, merchants, and their networks, not the bulk of the farmer/settlers. Attendant stresses gave rise to class tensions. There were widespread accusations that officials took illegal fees, along with bitter dissatisfaction with the malfunctioning machinery of land granting and complaints against the taxes and fees that supported Anglican clergy. Throughout the 1750s and 1760s, it became increasingly clear that the governing bodies with authority to address the backcountry ills (the elected lower house of the colonial legislature and the respective county courts in the interior) would not do so. Indeed, the closed circle of power linking the eastern-dominated lower house with generally corrupt courthouse rings in the interior was the basic political reality of late colonial North Carolina. The September 1770 court riot in Hillsborough was one result.

The Regulator-related studies have heightened clarity and appreciation for present-day encounters with the late-colonial southern backcountry, in

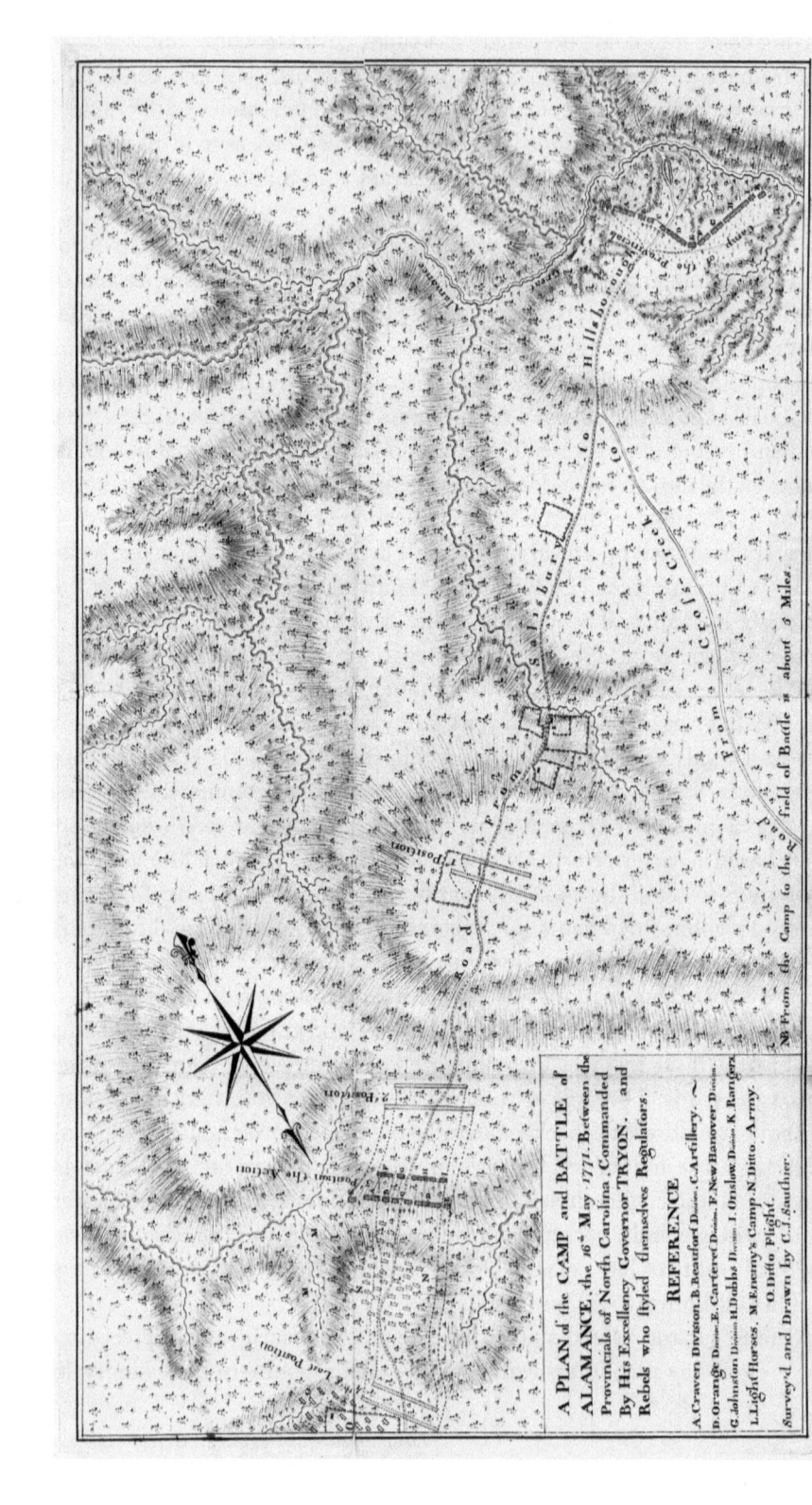

particular the North Carolina Piedmont. Today, that world is more accessible than ever for the general public, academics, and younger students. What is missing is sufficient exploration of any relationship between the Regulator movement and the American Revolution. For more than a century, scholars have avoided the terrain between the suppression of the Regulators at the 1771 Battle of Alamance and the emergence and success of the independence movement a few years later (see fig. 5.1).

There are historical reasons for this restraint. In short, the false image of British troops defeating Regulators fighting for freedom four years prior to the Battle of Lexington served sectional purposes after 1850. Moreover, the image achieved a popular life of its own. By the early twentieth century, it was solidly entrenched in resistance to research findings of the infant historical profession in North Carolina.

In the 1850s, perception of the Regulators and Alamance fell prey to growing sectional tension. Already, as the historian R. D. W. Connor would observe in the 1920s, antebellum writers "wrote history from patriotic motives," and professional writers, other than journalists, "were looked at askance."[5] The "patriotic motives" that dominated the 1850s were, first, to call the attention of North Carolina people to their honorable history and, second, to claim primacy in events of the Revolutionary War, challenging New England's priority. Two books of this nature appeared in 1851, intended for different audiences. Calvin H. Wiley produced *The North Carolina Reader* for school and home use. He would direct the new system of publicly funded "common schools" beginning in 1852 as the state's first superintendent of public instruction. Having grown up among descendants of the Regulators in Guilford and Alamance Counties, Wiley had published in 1847 a popular work of fiction that linked the Regulator movement and the Revolution. Even so, he chose his words carefully in the home and school volume. He revered "the first fight in the great cause which ten years later united all the colonies," but he made no sectional observation. One of several letters to the editor recommending the book in the widely read *North Carolina Standard*

(*opposite*) FIGURE 5.1. Plan of the camp and Battle of Alamance, May 16, 1771, by Claude Joseph Sauthier. One of the most accomplished landscape architects and battlefield cartographers of the Revolutionary War era, the Swiss-born Sauthier sketched Governor William Tryon's military maneuvers across North Carolina throughout the War of the Regulation in 1771. He also followed Tryon to the colony of New York, where in the service of British forces he prepared clandestine maps of George Washington's encampments and battlefield plans. Original, Governor Tryon's Order Book, North Carolina State Archives.

praised Wiley specifically for "not dismiss[ing] Regulators who died at Alamance as traitors and rebels." The writer likewise made no sectional claim.[6]

The other work was less accessible to the little-educated public, but coming from a seasoned lawyer, politician, and federal public servant, John Hill Wheeler's two-volume *Historical Sketches of North Carolina, from 1584 to 1851* carried immediate credence, despite its hasty judgments and pro-Democratic bias.[7] Wheeler used more original manuscripts from the colonial period (housed on both sides of the Atlantic) than earlier writers had examined. Even so, historian H. G. Jones has noted that Wheeler's *Historical Sketches* "has been characterized as having perpetuated more error than any nineteenth-century history of the state."[8] Wheeler quoted British records for vivid details of illegal extractions and high-handed court tactics, thereby presenting the virtues of the Regulators' cause. Like Wiley, his implicit comparison with Northern revolutionary events was prudent. Wheeler wrote, "Had this battle [Alamance] terminated differently (and five years afterwards this would have been the case), the banks of Alamance [Creek] would be venerated as another Bunker Hill." In addition, he perpetuated the assumption that Governor Tryon's force that defeated the Regulators consisted of British troops.[9] Wheeler had spent several years as superintendent of the Charlotte branch of the U.S. Mint, and he used his *Historical Sketches* to encourage enthusiasm for the "Mecklenburg Declaration of Independence." Wheeler concluded that his volumes proved the primacy of North Carolina as the first English colony, the first colony to have the blood of its people shed by "royal troops," and the first "to throw off the yoke of English oppression."[10]

Two years later, three other prominent North Carolinians brought forth a volume that sharpened the observations of Wiley and Wheeler into an instrument to challenge New England's credit for leading the independence movement. Two were former governors, and the third was Francis L. Hawks, an Episcopal minister in New York City with whom the project originated. A New Bern native, Hawks identified strongly with the South and recruited his friends William A. Graham and David L. Swain to join him in a series of lectures before the New-York Historical Society, of which Hawks was a member. The subject was the importance of the Old North State in the revolutionary cause. They pointedly linked the Mecklenburg Declaration with the Battle of Alamance as North Carolina initiatives predating Northern ones. In 1853, they published the lectures in both states as *Revolutionary History of North Carolina*.[11] Extracts and paraphrases from the *Revolutionary History* found their way into newspapers in 1858–59 as challenges to the primacy of encounters at Bunker Hill and Lexington. All of them paired Alamance with the Mecklenburg claims. Efforts of the Greene Monument

Association, which sought to mark the Guilford Battleground, consistently enhanced their arguments with descriptions of the 1771 battle at Alamance as the "first battle" of the Revolution.[12]

After the Civil War, a new flurry of insistence that Alamance had been the first battle of the Revolution appeared in newspapers following the 1875 centennial celebration of the Lexington battle. Publications in South Carolina, Virginia, Maryland, Kansas, and Tennessee carried such items as "Celebrating in the Wrong Places" and "Alamance: A Detailed Account of the First Battle of the Revolution." In addition, North Carolina papers widely reprinted the Raleigh *Sentinel*'s "Historical Facts Worth Remembering about North Carolina," which featured Alamance and the Mecklenburg Declaration. A few brief articles treating the Regulators and Alamance circulated as useful fillers for midwestern and western papers, and by the 1890s they had spread to Oregon.[13]

Meanwhile in 1880, recognition of "first battle" status had become formalized. Almost concurrently it was challenged, and lines became drawn that would harden in the following decades. Civic-minded promoters in Alamance County erected a marker on the privately owned battleground, proclaiming the Battle of Alamance to have been the first battle of the Revolution. The 1880 commemoration featured Durham manufacturer and philanthropist Julian Shakespeare Carr, along with promoters of the Guilford Battleground and other dignitaries. In the same year, John W. Moore published the most extensive treatment of the state's history to that time. Moore sympathized with the Regulators' grievances, but he found no fault with Tryon's suppression of them. He explained his position by blaming Herman Husband, the pro-Regulator spokesman and writer, for fomenting a lawless insurgency. He called Husband "a base and designing man," a troublemaker by nature, and looked for no further issues. Moore saw no evidence of Regulators' opposition to crown rule. He did not characterize Tryon's forces as British, and he narrated their movements as militia units.[14] The 1880 events—the marker and Moore's publication—were not essentially antagonistic, but three lawyers writing in the 1890s failed to see any legal principles in the Regulator agitation and pointed out the Regulators' adherence to British authority. "The quarrel of the Regulators was with obnoxious officials, not at all with the government," one wrote; "they always professed themselves loyal subjects of King George." Further, he denounced as "sentimental slush" any notion that "the same spirit inspired the Regulators that inspired the Sons of Liberty or the Lexington Minute Men." Tryon's star remained high as a hard-pressed defender of order.[15]

None of this meshed with "first battle" identity and the fresh spurt of newspaper articles lauding it. Moreover, newspaper writers in the 1890s renewed the sectional theme. Their "patriotic motives" (to use Connor's 1920s term for pre–Civil War writing) now were to honor the Confederacy and the resistance it had embodied. Newspapers seized the "first battle" position to pay homage to Confederate leaders, the Confederate dead, and the targets of Governor William Woods Holden's suppression of the Alamance-Caswell Insurrection in 1870.[16] Moreover, Rev. Thomas D. Gregory, a prolific and vivid writer known for his opposition to the formation of a third party in North Carolina, advocated the "first battle" position as well. Themes of his letters to the editors of Democratic papers were "White Men, Think" and "The People's Party Snare."[17] Gregory's brief but sensationalist article "The Battle of Alamance" was widely printed in newspapers, as were descriptions of the battleground marker, along with its inscription, "First Battle of the Revolution."[18]

Also in the 1890s, a transformation occurred in researching colonial North Carolina history with the state's publication of *Colonial Records of North Carolina*. The ten-volume series resulted from several decades of copying official records and correspondence, largely in British repositories. Transcribed and printed, the documents made possible a closer investigation of the Regulator movement, and a Trinity College professor, John Spencer Bassett, produced one in 1895. Bassett cited and quoted documents. His was not a rhetorical presentation. He concluded that the revolt had been brought on by eastern domination and local corruption, with no connection with the Revolution.[19] Even before Bassett's publication, the editor of the *Colonial Records* remarked that, for him, "the most surprising thing ... about the war of the Regulation ... is not that it began and had its being, but that it was so ruthlessly stamped out by North Carolina troops, especially that this was done by the people of the Eastern portion of the Province."[20]

Bassett's dull distinction between a "popular upheaval" (his category for the Regulator movement) and a "revolution" left a sea of disconnection between the newly forming historical profession in the state and the public perception of history, with its enjoyment of markers and newspaper drama. To people living in the Regulator area, it may have appeared that something of value to them was being threatened or denied. If so, a physician who lived briefly among them addressed the need. William Edwards Fitch was a North Carolina native who as recently as 1900 had lived in Savannah. Visiting patients in Alamance and adjacent counties soon thereafter, he encountered respect for the Regulators among descendants of people who had been adults in 1771. He may have encountered consternation or even confusion as well. His informants vividly described the 1880 marker dedication and freely shared their opinions and other observations.

Drawing largely on this material, Fitch published an earnest and attractive book in 1905 and reprinted it in 1912, after he had moved to New York City. A reviewer for the *New York Times* had encountered the "first battle" claim already and did not question it. Other newspapers gave the book warm reviews, noting only the claims for the Battle of Alamance and the Mecklenburg Declaration.[21] A review article by the historian Theodore Clark Smith, however, demonstrated the gap between the professors and the public. Clark included the book in a survey for the *Atlantic Monthly* of more than twenty-five recent books treating the colonial period. While he sympathized with the Regulators, Smith concluded that "the value of the book lies wholly in the original documents reprinted from the North Carolina Colonial Records." Even they had been selected "to justify preconceived ideas." Smith continued, "Unfortunately for the writer's thesis, the documents he cites show that the uprising was purely against local misgovernment, and that the governor—a fiend incarnate—was supported by the legislature and the eastern counties *which later led the revolt against British authority*. Scarcely any attempt is made to account for this fact." In short, he dismissed Fitch's work as a "product of ill-founded local enthusiasm."[22]

The divergence between popular writers and professional historians that Fitch seized has deterred students of history from looking for links between the Regulator movement and the Revolution. Suggestions that links might have existed have been derided out of hand in scholarly circles—except for occasional curiosity for "whether" Regulators "became" loyalists or revolutionaries. The Regulators were finished in 1771, and research after Alamance had to focus on the revolutionaries. One can understand why graduate students in particular and other young scholars in general would not risk appearing to be a neo-Fiske.

The remainder of this essay focuses on one frustration—land—that motivated meetings, petitions, political action, and violence of men who called themselves "Regulators." Grievances they raised remained unaddressed following their defeat. A few years later, revolutionary leaders acknowledged a need to satisfy some of the festering backcountry issues in order to secure support for the Revolutionary War in the interior of North Carolina. The study spotlights Orange County and draws a few related observations from other counties to explore revolutionaries' use of land insecurity as a tool for enlisting support and intimidating the reluctant. Dynamics regarding security of land tenure reflect continuities of local power in the Piedmont for three decades before and during the Revolutionary War. The essay is intended to spur research in other Regulator counties and to open scholarly conversations in the long-standing no-man's-land between understanding the Regulator movement and comprehending the American Revolution.

LAND AND LOCAL POWER AS REGULATOR GRIEVANCES

A variety of injustices were claimed by mid-eighteenth-century residents of North Carolina's "backcountry," as the area inland from the coastal power base was called. It was commonplace for sheriffs and other local officers to charge illegal fees for their services. The inability of non-Anglican clergy to perform legally sanctioned marriages in royal colonies such as North Carolina was an inconvenient reminder of the networks of landed families and wealthy merchants in the British Isles who influenced and protected church, military, and colonial appointments for their sons and clients. Scarcity of money heightened the state of unrest. Merchants and lawyers were quick to sue, and they set up shop near hastily built courthouses in the large new interior counties (Granville and Johnston in the 1740s, Anson, Orange, and Rowan in the 1750s, and Mecklenburg in 1762). Moreover, it was hard to establish legal ownership of land in much of the colony's interior.

Most people farmed and herded and did not want to be evicted from the land they used. A family could settle, build a house, and grow crops without buying land, but they had no assurance of securing title to the land they had settled. Land was cheap, but getting a legal title to it was frustrating and complicated. Typically, a few men controlled local land offices and law enforcement in the new counties of the Piedmont frontier, and they could demand illegal payments for their services. These county networks kept their power through political and business partnerships with groups in the elected lower house of the North Carolina legislature, although backcountry counties had few representatives there. Piedmont farmers distrusted the eastern interests that controlled the legislature and were allied with the backcountry courthouse rings. It was in the new Piedmont counties that the Regulator movement developed.

Even before the name "Regulator" came into use in North Carolina, there were sporadic disturbances against networks of land speculators and county officials. For most of the region in the mid-eighteenth century, it was hard or impossible to know if someone had title to a particular site, regardless of whether anyone appeared to be using it. Uncertainty was embedded in the colony's original proprietary status and its change to a royal colony in 1729. In 1663, King Charles II had created a colony comprising present-day North

Carolina and South Carolina, plus lands to their west, and granted it to eight lords proprietors. The colony was their reward for assisting with the restoration of the English monarchy and the Church of England in 1661.

Under an interregnum during the 1650s, a lightly supervised but official church had embodied a loose, populist form of Protestantism with no bishops. The proprietors' ownership of Carolina symbolized their continued cooperation with England's restored king and church. By 1729, sixty-six years later, the original lords proprietors were long dead, and political changes had made proprietary control of Carolina obsolete. The Revolution of 1688–89 had seen Parliament offer the crown to a different branch of the royal family. At the same time, Parliament secured the liberties of individuals, provided limited toleration for non-Anglican Protestants, and continued to reserve top positions in the military, church, and administration for sons of the landed elite. Furthermore, insufficient proprietary attention to Carolina contributed to difficulties there. The proprietors separated the colony into North Carolina and South Carolina in 1712, and in 1729 the crown bought the rights of seven of the lords proprietors from their descendants.

Quickly, the first royal governors of North Carolina granted tracts of land to influential speculators. Grants of thousands of acres each included great swaths of the backcountry. Recipients—or their heirs and creditors—sporadically sent agents into the interior to sell parcels, but their surveys and legal documents were flimsy. Moreover, some absentee landlords preferred to rent out their investments rather than to sell them piecemeal. They continued to do so until revolutionaries confiscated the large tracts in the 1770s. For newcomers seeking land in the 1750s and 1760s, squatting was a common practice. Some settlers stayed long enough to get a crop or two and then moved on. Others stayed with their "improvements" (such as orchards, cleared fields, and buildings) in hopes of purchasing the land.

Henry Eustace McCulloh became a target of wide resentment. A self-acknowledged exploiter of men and women, McCulloh was agent and attorney for his father, a London merchant whose holdings of more than a million acres blanketed the central and western Piedmont. The elder McCulloh had helped Gabriel Johnston secure the governorship of North Carolina in 1734 and had been rewarded with land grants. By 1750, McCulloh agents were said to be "hawking [land] about in small quantities thro' all the back parts of the Province and quite thro' America even to Boston." During the next two decades, McCulloh's easiest money came from selling land to the very families whose settlement and work had increased the land's price. Contiguous McCulloh tracts of 100,000 acres each dominated the present-day counties of Stanly, Cabarrus, Mecklenburg, Iredell, Rowan, Montgomery, Davidson, and Davie. Two other McCulloh tracts centered on today's Wake County and land in western Alamance and eastern Guilford Counties.[23] The latter consisted of 12,500 acres, including the site near Alamance Creek where Regulators would assemble and be defeated in 1771.

Rather than buy from the hated agents of absentee speculators, it was easier, cheaper, and more secure to obtain ungranted (or "crown") land. For most of the area where the Regulator movement developed, however, available land was not crown land. It was Granville land, owned by descendants of the one Carolina proprietor who had not sold their land rights to the crown in 1729. In 1744, King George II settled with John Carteret, Earl Granville, granting him one-eighth of the original Carolina land. In effect, the "Granville Tract" or Granville District was the northern half of North Carolina, extending sixty to seventy miles south of the Virginia border. Governor Gabriel Johnston and Earl Granville appointed surveyors to establish the Crown-Granville boundary. They started at Bath and were well into the Piedmont by April 1746. The survey halted at Cold Water Creek in present-day Cabarrus County. Except for an extension in 1753, the line was not continued farther until 1772, after the Regulator movement. The location of the line east of Cold Water Creek was known well enough in 1753, 1762, and 1768 for the colonial legislature to cite it as boundaries when it created Rowan, Mecklenburg, and Tryon Counties, but there could be uncertainty on the ground.[24]

A surveyor recalled in 1753 that "in the year 1746 I was up in the Country that is now Anson, Orange and Rowan Counties, there was not then above one hundred fighting men [but] there is now at least three thousand for the most part Irish Protestants and Germans and dayley increasing."[25] Indeed, Germans and Scots-Irish were conspicuous among the newcomers, though many of them were second or even third generations in families that had settled on the Pennsylvania frontier, known in the early eighteenth century as "the best poor man's country" for its good cheap land and the colony's religious toleration. Land prices rose sharply with the birth rate, however, and the next generation moved into nearby Virginia or North Carolina in search of affordable farmland. Further, during the French and Indian War in the 1750s, clashes in western regions of Pennsylvania and Virginia added to the push toward the new "best poor man's country" in the Carolina interior. Already, long-established trade corridors known as Indian trading paths provided access. Portions of these bridle paths widened into wagon roads as heavier migration poured into what future Regulator leader Herman Husband would call the second Pennsylvania.

Land-hungry newcomers encountered small circles of public officials in the new counties; the legislature had made interior counties large to diminish their aggregate representation in the lower house, and a few men enjoyed power over large areas. The land-granting personnel, whether agents of absentees or of the Granville land office, were enmeshed with local officials. All of them were in a position to exploit the new arrivals and anyone else without a clear title to land.

In the Granville District, the land prices were low, as they were in crown land. Eight pounds and four shillings Virginia currency, or about six pounds sterling, would buy 640 acres of "good" land in 1760, a cost of about five shillings per acre. The quitrent of two shillings per one hundred acres was the same rate as for crown lands and was not enforced in any case. The biggest problem was the dishonest and abusive manner in which Granville lands commonly were administered. Earl Granville never had or claimed any governing authority in the area. The Granville tract was simply a source of income that he had inherited. He turned its management over to men in business for themselves, who then turned the duties over to other men in business for *them*selves.

The influence that Granville agents Francis Corbin and Thomas Childs, successively, held in Orange County is reflected in the names by which the new county seat was known. The first Orange County courthouse was built near the east bank of the Haw River, but after the legislature created Rowan out of western Orange County in 1754, the Orange justices of the peace relocated their meetings to a more central site on the Eno River.[26] Before the name "Hillsborough" was adopted, the Eno seat was known briefly as Corbinton and then as Childsboro. Land seekers complained vigorously about both agents.[27]

A deputy Granville agent in Rowan County, James Carter, was known for pocketing entry fees from men who had made improvements on land; Carter failed to register improvements or any other claims. He was free to demand payoffs and otherwise reward favorites with grants, as he was surveyor as well as agent and register of deeds. Also as a trustee of the new town of Salisbury, he could distribute its lots.[28]

McCulloh managed sales in his largest western tracts through men who were prominent among the incoming Scots-Irish settlers. His choice of Moses and Benjamin Alexander and their relatives as agents and allies in greater Anson County (soon to yield Mecklenburg and Tryon Counties in its western portions) recognized the emerging pattern of county-level power in the 1750s: multiple office-holding land speculators with ties to Virginia and eastern North Carolina. Prominent members of the Polk family added to McCulloh's Tryon/Mecklenburg network in the 1760s. John and Thomas

Frohock were their counterparts in greater Rowan County. They enjoyed a family tie with the McCullohs and held land responsibilities for Granville and the crown as well as McCulloh. With several judicial offices and command of the county militia, John Frohock's local power meshed with the eastern-dominated assembly in which he served.

For such backcountry kingpins and their allied merchants, justices of the peace, and militia captains, membership in the elective lower house of the colonial assembly was essential. The administration that regulated county officials was not the distant Board of Trade in London. Oversight resided in the county court, the district court, and the colonial assembly itself. Of these, the lower house of the assembly and the justices of the peace in the county courts held the greatest power. The upper house was the governor's council, appointed by the Board of Trade, generally on the advice of the governor and council. The lower house, called the Commons House of Assembly, paralleled the elected House of Commons in London. In the third quarter of the eighteenth century, the lower house was the dominant branch of the government, exercising some powers by charter and some by tradition. It initiated most bills and, like the British House of Commons, had exclusive power to initiate and amend money bills.

The North Carolina lower house more than any other unit controlled and distributed power in the counties. Justices of the peace were appointed by the governor, normally from names handed him by members of the lower house. Justices usually held office for two years and could succeed themselves. The legislature determined how many justices a county would have, thereby creating new appointments. Typically, the representatives from a county had first approval of its new justices or commission renewals for its current ones. Like the justices, other county officers—coroners, registers of deeds, clerks, and sheriffs—held commissions from the governor but were suggested by justices and county representatives in the lower house. Colonial sheriffs were very powerful, and justices could determine who would be sheriff. The governor routinely appointed the sheriff from three nominees provided by the justices. Sheriffs and justices were assisted by constables, whom the justices appointed. Justices named the jurors for county courts and district superior courts. The district courts usually met twice a year at Edenton, New Bern, Wilmington, and Halifax. The Piedmont got a district court in 1762, when the legislature established the Salisbury District, and in 1767 a sixth was added at Hillsborough.

Social deference and class consciousness were normal expectations, and the crude appearance and behavior of some local officials shocked visitors in the backcountry. At the Granville County court in 1753, an English merchant was surprised to see that "The J——s on the Bench appeared like Gladiators Stript Ready for fighting." Further west, he noted, "[I] got to Orange Court house, where was Sundry people assembled and their Appearance did not prejudice me much in their favour but I soon understood they were j- - - -ces of this Court wch disapated our fears a little."[29] A study of class distinctions has observed that, even by the early 1770s, the "ruling class was new and not firmly entrenched in [the] recently settled and fast growing" Piedmont.[30]

In those counties where the Regulator movement was strongest, the justices of the peace owned 40 percent of both land and enslaved laborers. Officers in the county militia and overseers of roads, many of whom were justices, were among the wealthier residents as well. The governor appointed the top militia commanders; they in turn appointed officers of the various companies. Justices appointed overseers of roads to supervise the work crews who cut roadways through the heavy forests and kept their vegetation in check. Men living in the district of the road were required to serve on the road crews, but there were automatic exemptions for justices, members of the assembly, and overseers. A slaveholder could provide an enslaved substitute to work the roads. Militia musters required about two weeks a year, and roadwork typically took an additional two weeks.[31]

In Britain and in the colonies, lawmakers kept land taxes low or nonexistent by offering officials legitimate opportunities for making money from their offices instead of paying them salaries. Every administrative unit had a "fee table," which listed, for example, the amount of money an official would receive for registering one deed or the payment a sheriff or constable would collect for riding to someone's residence and serving a writ. The person for whom the public service was rendered paid the fees. The Board of Trade set the fee table for each colony and included it among the general instructions to a governor at the time he took office. Fees were consistently low throughout the colonies. There might be exceptions for areas of low population, in which it would be expected that few fees could be collected. In the North Carolina Piedmont, the officially sanctioned fees were low. The trouble came when officials ignored the fee table and collected what they could get away with. Such abuse not only exacerbated class tensions but also called forth objections on constitutional grounds, most notably recorded in Granville County in 1765.[32]

Violence was near the surface of the new and changing communities, and ritual violence was part of traditional peasant cultures.[33] Some Regulators and their allies used force in 1768 after efforts to secure their goals peacefully failed. Local officials promptly retaliated, and some Regulators attacked officers of the law, disrupted court proceedings, and refused to pay taxes and fees throughout 1769–70. As well, several Regulators and their sympathizers were elected to the lower house in November 1769—a futile move, given the sectional imbalance and the alarm that Governor William Tryon and the majority in the legislature displayed. Determined to end the backcountry unrest speedily and authorized by the legislature to do so, Tryon led eastern units of the North Carolina militia into the backcountry in 1771. They were joined by smaller Piedmont units, commanded largely by the local power brokers.

On May 16, 1771, when about 2,000 Regulators and sympathizers who had assembled near Alamance Creek in western Orange County refused Tryon's orders to surrender and disband, his militia force roundly defeated them. Many received pardons in the ensuing weeks after taking an oath of allegiance. A few of the Regulators' enemies died or moved away, as did Tryon, who became governor of New York. His replacement, Josiah Martin, made satisfying Regulator grievances a priority. Beginning in 1772, Martin actively courted their former leaders. By 1775, however, the new governor's priority was his contest with eastern leaders of the legislature for the direction of North Carolina.[34]

LAND AND LOCAL POWER AS REVOLUTIONARY TOOLS

Issues that gave rise to the Regulator movement were not settled by the defeat at Alamance; therein is the basic connection between the Regulator movement and the Revolution. The various grievances that drove the Regulators still were alive after revolutionaries began putting together a state government following the Declaration of Independence. Land remained foremost.

When the Revolution began, the political sympathies of the Piedmont were uncertain. Most of the men who led the Revolution in North Carolina had sided with Tryon in putting down the Regulators. They had been part of the eastern-dominated legislature and the courthouse rings against whom the Regulators had raged. If the Piedmont—Regulator country—were to support the cause of independence, some accommodation had to be made toward settling the issues that had fueled the Regulator movement. Not all people living in the interior were Regulators or sympathized with them, as evidence of social tension during the 1760s suggests. After the Battle of Alamance, however, outrage over the disproportionate bloodshed enhanced popular sympathy for the Regulators, as did the militia's retributions on targeted communities. Entire families, congregations, and communities left their homes, deepening the sense of disruption.³⁵ John Adams noted that "the back part of North Carolina" resisted the Revolution because of "hatred" former Regulators held for "their fellow-citizens." Herman Husband himself supported the Revolution in Pennsylvania, where he relocated following Alamance, but he shunned the North Carolina revolutionaries. Roger Ekirch's 1981 study of politics and society in North Carolina before the Revolution concluded that "in few other colonies did revolutionaries go to war with so little popular support."³⁶

In the summer of 1775, revolutionary leaders addressed Regulator political concerns in a conciliatory manner. Sensitive to their legacy of eastern domination of North Carolina affairs, revolutionary leaders brought their third "provincial congress" (the body they had developed out of the old lower house in two previous sessions) directly into the backcountry and convened at Hillsborough. The body declared amnesty and protection for those who had "engaged in the late Insurrection" and sent a delegation among them, including a popular preacher who had worked with Regulators, "to remove any ill impressions" they harbored against "associating in the common Cause of America."³⁷ At the touchy juncture of politics and land ownership, the Third Provincial Congress specified that occupiers of land in the Granville District who had no title but who had made improvements on the land could vote for members of the next provincial congress. As voters they were, for the time being, on equal terms with "Freeholders in the other counties." The congress's strong message elicited a corresponding response: so many men came out to vote in Orange County in October 1776 that only about one-fourth of them were able to do so.³⁸

After the adoption of a revolutionary state constitution in 1776, county courts reemerged with little change in their personnel or in their relationship with members of the legislature and the eastern North Carolina establishment. For the most part, individuals and networks who had dominated backcountry counties before the Revolution continued to do so as local militia leaders, justices of the peace, and sheriffs. Likewise, they maintained their pre-1776 control over credit, large landholdings, and unfree workers. Across the southern backcountry, scattered resistance against revolutionary tendencies had flared in 1775 and 1776, but revolutionaries had restrained it or made local compromises, even tolerating neutrality in some cases until the network of local revolutionary militia units emerged, generally in 1777. Throughout 1777 and 1778, county-level exercise of state power regarding taxes, oaths of allegiance, and militia service tightened dragnets around neutrals, foot draggers, and resisters alike, denouncing them all as "the disaffected." The result was a jumble of scattered confrontations and counteractions that spiraled into widespread civil war as the focus of the war shifted south by 1779.[39]

Politically, land was the crucial issue, for which revolutionary leaders held the cards. Theirs was the political framework that ensured or threatened the landholder's legal title. As the political and military crisis intensified, legislators and county officials began addressing land issues directly. The legislature set up a land entry process whereby, beginning in 1778, a man could "enter," or register a claim to purchase, a tract of land from the state.[40] This procedure was the long-standing crown practice, followed also in the Granville tract. Much of the Regulator area was in the Granville tract, and its land office had been closed since 1763, when the earl's death left his estate in disarray. The crown ceased granting land in 1773 with the intention of rationalizing the process throughout the colonies. In North Carolina, previous purchases from speculators were largely in various states of recorded legality, so the stakes for entering land were high. The procedure required an oath of allegiance to the state. Just as using the new currency that revolutionaries had created, registering a land claim with the state government was an investment of support, but it had far greater consequences for the investor if the colonies won their bid for independence. On the other hand, should the revolutionaries be defeated and their acts declared illegal and null, what had people who obtained title to their farms from the revolutionaries to lose, if they had not had a legal claim before the Revolution? There was a rush to enter land claims. For farmers who already had clear title to their land, however, the logic of revolution was less compelling.[41]

Some men who expressed fear over revolutionaries seizing their land were overheard and were reported to justices of the peace. Two episodes in Rowan County in 1778 illustrate attitudes and consequences. Elijah Lyons spoke too freely before going to bed in a tavern, declaring "our Assembly had no Right to open ye Land Office & that if any man would Molest him or take away his land he would shoot him." James Dickey of Orange County responded that Lyons did not have the power to disobey the legislature. Then Lyons boasted that he could raise a company of men in twenty-four hours, declaring "there would be other Laws in ye Land before long." Sobered and contrite the following morning, Lyons went upstairs to Dickey's room and made an ineffectual apology. Dickey had Lyons brought before the Rowan County court, with the result that Lyons raised a company for the revolutionary militia.[42]

The blacksmith James Forbush had a similar experience. He had been summoned to the Rowan County court in August 1777 "upon suspicion of being unfriendly to this state," along with seven others; all of them took the oath of allegiance that was part of a treason act passed four months earlier. It replaced a bland 1776 oath and allowed no mental hedging in supporting "the Independent government" of North Carolina "against George the Third and his successors." Further, the oath taker vowed to "disclose" to state authorities "any ... Attempts, committed or intended against the State, which shall come to my Knowledge."[43] A customer's complaint about a land entry drew Forbush into a conversation that, like Lyons' speech in the tavern, was overheard and led to the blacksmith's arrest. A man named Spears or Sears complained that Captain John Johnston of the Rowan Regiment of Militia had made an entry for the land where Spears lived. Johnston had boasted that he would not take £500 for his claim. Forbush tried to console Spears by telling him of "ye great faits of Lord howe" against Washington. A third man challenged Forbush's account and reminded him of his oath against such talk. "Forbush answard & said that Nothing Never Conserned him so much as takeing that oath," according to the man's deposition.[44] Taken to court and put into the militia, Forbush soon led a movement for companies to elect their officers. The captain of Forbush's company happened to be John Johnston, against whom Spears had complained. One hundred and three men participated in an unauthorized election and requested the commander of the Rowan Regiment, Colonel Francis Locke, to approve it. Forbush was their spokesman.[45] During 1778, the year of these events, Johnston was filing entries for eighteen tracts in Rowan County, totaling more than seven thousand acres.[46]

The county-administered machinery of entering land as the first step to a grant was one facet of the new state power over land tenure. Threat of confiscation was another. Several laws authorizing confiscation of land and other property were passed during 1776–83. Only one of them, passed in 1779, named individuals whose property was to be seized. The list included the McCullohs and Edmund Fanning, the former Orange County multiple office holder whom Husband had characterized as "our chief enemy and Cause of our oppression." The other confiscation legislation affected more landholders, for it left interpretation of causes for action to the county and district superior courts. Across the state during the war, county courts cited men to "show cause why their estates be not forfeited," and some of these cases reached the district superior courts.[47]

Militia captains and county courts used the summonses to get "disaffected" men to take the state oath and join the militia or Continental service. Some men satisfied their summons privately to a justice, leaving little or no record, so it is not clear how many of the summonses yielded confiscations and how many yielded soldiers.[48] At least in Lincoln County, the three-

Land Tenure as Regulator Grievance 127

man committee on confiscation listed names for the court to summon, in addition to the ones justices and militia captains named in court. The men might not be on their lands, having been chased away or killed in the vendettas that marked the war by 1780–81.[49] Typically, the summonses occurred after local fighting slowed or ceased, mostly in 1782 following hiatuses in the county courts during the height of local conflicts. Overall, the summons process appears not to have dislodged as many landholders as had the land entries of 1778–79 and the subsequent violence. Entries and summonses could work hand in hand, even if separated by years. Court citations for victims of land entries appear to have been common, and they call for careful study of county and district court records.

There is some information about German and Swiss Baptists (or Dunkers) in this regard. The largest of their six settlements was in the forks and tributaries of the Uwharrie River in Randolph (Guilford until 1779) and Rowan Counties. When Rowan revolutionaries drew militia districts, they included Dunker residents in a district for which all constables, justices of the peace, tax assessors, tax collectors, and militia officers were nonresident revolutionaries. Rowan Dunkers circulated a neutrality and nonviolence statement among themselves in 1778 and were chastised in the county court. Those who persisted in their principles of nonviolence and refused to take oaths—most of the Dunkers in the Uwharrie area—found themselves without civil rights in 1778. Entries were made on the lands of at least fifteen Dunkers, including two widows, in the Rowan County section of the Uwharrie in August 1778. The tracts included holdings of multiple households. In November 1782 and February 1783, Colonel Griffith Rutherford of the Rowan Regiment of Militia secured court summonses of 163 men, many of them Dunkers, to "show Cause ... why their Estates should not be Confiscated." None of them appeared and so "defaulted." There was a Dunker move en masse to present-day Davidson County at this time, and litigation continued until 1800.[50]

Meanwhile, Dunkers on McCulloh land in Randolph County likewise refused to take the oath. When the confiscated McCulloh lands in Randolph County were sold after the war, the nonjurors (that is, those who had refused to take the oath) were unable to offer bids for the lands they had improved, and their parcels went to speculators. By late 1787, a nucleus of this group was settling in present-day Ashe County.[51] Dunker groups elsewhere in the Piedmont were more willing than the Uwharrie brethren to take the "affirmation" that the state allowed nonjuring religious groups to take instead of an oath. This suggests that nonviolence, not avoidance of any oath or affirmation, was the root of their nonjuring. Elsewhere, some Dunkers took the affirmation, and some fought. Even so, land occupied by Dunkers in Tryon/Lincoln and Mecklenburg Counties were notable prey of county officers there, as were Quaker farms in Surry County. Even the Wachovia tract was threatened, in spite of the wartime modus vivendi between Moravian leaders and officials of Surry, Rowan, and Guilford Counties.[52]

If the Uwharrie Dunkers had taken oaths (and not disqualified themselves in any other way), they would have been able to challenge their predators. To defend a preexisting claim, one filed a caveat against the entry, stating the basis of the prior claim. One might cite a purchase-lease agreement, an acquisition from the Granville office, or a right by prior possession and improvements. The volume of caveats filed against land entries shows that many of the entries were contested. Various court records indicate also that entries and caveats were accompanied by charges of trespass, forcible entry, and assault. Such disputes suggest that Piedmont residents were fighting over land well before they stood in military formation against each other or against outsiders.[53] The new state land act provided for settlement of such disputes. Sheriffs selected land juries to hear both claimants under the authority of the justices of the county court. In contested land cases, sheriffs and justices mattered.

The 1776 state constitution continued the practice of justices selecting the sheriff. As well, justices of the peace continued to be appointed by the governor on the advice of the county's members of the lower house of the General Assembly (now called the House of Commons). The state constitution forbade multiple office holding in general but made exceptions for justices and militia officers, who long had held more than one office. Thereby, local authority continued to facilitate courthouse rings connected with the legislature, as they had before and during the Regulator years. Ultimately, the makeup of the county officers and justices remained in the hands of the county's representatives in the lower house of the General Assembly, as it had been during the Regulator era.

The new state constitution made the General Assembly more powerful than the governor. Significantly, the legislature elected the governor for a one-year term. The legislature itself, however, was subject to annual elections for members of both the House and the Senate. Only free men who owned at least fifty acres could vote for state senators, but all free men who held land or paid "public taxes" could vote for members of the House. The General Assembly, elected every year, stood between the county officers and the state executive and controlled both.

In the Regulator area, county alliances mirrored the lineup of local officials before the Revolution. In Guilford County, for example, the revolutionary and postwar courthouse ring included at least two men who had been Regulators, but the others had stood against Regulators as justices and militia officers.[54] In Orange County, the first justices of the peace under state authority included at least five men who had been justices before 1767. (Colonial Orange County court minutes after 1766 have not survived.) The eighteen other first state-authorized justices for Orange County included several with surnames from the pre-1766 roster of magistrates.[55] Orange County in 1777 included only present-day Orange, Alamance, and Durham Counties; during the Regulator scare, the legislature had created Chatham, Wake, and Guilford Counties from Orange, and Caswell County followed in 1777.

ORANGE COUNTY: PAYING TAXES TO OWN LAND

The constitution approved by the Fifth Provincial Congress in December 1776 enabled free male householders to vote for members of the House of Commons. This action addressed a franchise issue that lingered from the Regulator years throughout the Granville District: a widespread lack of clear title to land. My research has found no direct evidence that allowing the householder, as distinct from the landowner, to vote for members of the lower house carried any understanding that the householder would in time come to own his land as payment for standing with the revolutionaries. Even so, in Orange County at least, that was the outcome.

Making tax lists was part of the dynamic. For most taxpayers, taxes were levied on men, enslaved persons, land, cattle, and horses. It is the "land" category that is politically significant. State law set the terms of the tax. Local justices who were the court-appointed tax assessors for their districts decided whether a householder should be listed as a landowner for tax purposes. Most of the names on the Orange County tax lists during the Revolutionary War appear neither in the prewar land records (not surprising in view of their incomplete nature) nor in the land entry records, which were carefully kept and survive. Obviously, it was in the state's interest to have as many people pay tax on "their" land as possible, motivation for the tax assessor to encourage men who had no legal claim to the land to go ahead and list it anyway. For much of the land there were conflicting claims, either formally lodged as entry and caveat or informally contested by rival claimants who might never reach the courthouse with their claims. Who decided which claimant listed the land? Tax districts were small enough for the justice/tax assessor to know all the taxpayers he listed. The keeper of the district tax list was also a guardian of the Revolution. Moreover, he was part of a control network linking county officials with the legislators who selected them and with the voters who selected the legislators. There was little wartime change in the Orange County justices, other county officials, and representatives in the General Assembly. Where change occurred, it could be accounted for in large part by military or other official demands. The householder, as defined by the tax list, was also a voter. If a man's name was on the tax list, he could vote. He might also expect state sanction of his landholding.[56]

In Orange County's Hawfields area in particular, the continuity of land issues between the Regulator and revolutionary years compels examination. How typical such continuity was throughout the Regulator area is a question for further research. In Orange County, if a man with no title to land was listed for land tax and his name remained on the list, every year the tax assessor listed land under his name increased his likelihood of owning it.

Samuel Strudwick's weakening grasp on much of the Hawfields lends insight on this process. The circumstances of Strudwick's ownership of Piedmont land goes back to the early eighteenth century and the governorship of George Burrington (1724–25, 1731–34). Burrington fed speculators "blank patents" in the 1720s and amassed at least 18,400 acres himself, including much of the Hawfields. Burrington obtained some or all of this land from Edward Moseley, a London orphan who became arguably the most influential North Carolina politician of the first half of the eighteenth century and one of the first to take large grants on the trading paths across the backcountry. Burrington died in 1759, killed at age seventy-seven by a robber while walking in a London park. Much of his estate quickly passed through his son's hands to pay the son's gambling debts. Strudwick's father, a London merchant, bought Burrington's land in the Hawfields and in New Hanover County in 1761. Apparently, Samuel Strudwick bought other Hawfields land as well that dated back to the blank patents. He took possession of the land in 1764 and moved permanently to North Carolina in 1767, building residences in Orange and New Hanover Counties. Promptly, Strudwick became a member of Governor William Tryon's council, a justice, and a militia officer.[57]

How the absent Burrington administered his valuable lands is unknown. Strudwick, by contrast, was not an absentee. In the spring of 1768, when the Regulator movement was gaining momentum, the occupants of Strudwick's land organized. In April, Francis Nash and Thomas Hart urged their business partner Edmund Fanning to advise Tryon to send a military force from eastern North Carolina into the heart of Regulator country, advice Tryon was to refuse for three years. Nash and Hart, thinking of other landlords as well as Strudwick, implored:

Land Tenure as Regulator Grievance 131

We really think it a matter worthy the Governor's notice, as we are apprehensive a force must be brought from some other part of the Province. ... In short sir, the matter is of so new & of so extraordinary a nature to us that we are at the greatest loss what is to be done, but certain we are, that unless some measures can be fallen upon, of suppressing ... those who have offended, no man will be safe among us in the possession either of his life or property. ... And as an instance of the Evil & destructive consequence ... we are creditably informed that Mr Strudwicks Tenants almost to a man have entered into an association among themselves to keep forcible possession of his lands and for that purpose, had a meeting yesterday in the Hawfields.[58]

During the 1771 military campaign against the Regulators, Strudwick was a lieutenant general in Tryon's militia.[59] Following a post-Alamance quiescence, people living on Strudwick's Hawfields land resumed their efforts to cast off his landlordship during the Revolution. They did so by listing and paying taxes on the land they occupied and by obstructing several parties of surveyors Strudwick sent into the area to document their trespasses. For Strudwick to be able to use the revolutionary courts to enforce his ownership, he had to make some acknowledgment of the Revolution and not give any indication of resisting it. He was among those who did not rush to take the state oath when the 1777 law made it mandatory on all free males over the age of sixteen. Accordingly, the county court ordered him and several others to take the oath. Apparently, he took it quietly before a neighboring justice of the peace, which was the usual way, for he was named to the District Superior Court grand jury pool a few months later, his first public function under the new government.

By all appearances, Strudwick came to terms with his allegiance and its risks in a cautious and subdued manner. In the summer of 1777, he spent a month in quiet seclusion in Salem, rooming in the tavern, worshiping with the Moravians, reading an English translation of an account of their Greenland missions, and no doubt, thinking. After the first few days, his Salem hosts assumed he was there to avoid taking the state oath, and they avoided the subject of politics.[60]

By 1780, Strudwick was on the offensive, with the legal and political assistance of revolutionary leader Thomas Burke, suing people for illegally occupying his lands and obstructing the surveyors. More than once the superior court ordered new surveys of the 24,000 acres for which Strudwick provided legal documentation. In these court-ordered surveys, each side named a surveyor. Still the surveys were stopped. Strudwick described to Burke one incident: "The Chain was cutt by a Fellow of no property," while the persons in whose interest he acted had stepped away from the surveyors. "Too much intimidated to join the links and make a second attempt, [the surveyors demand] a Guard for the Security of their persons."[61] Strudwick struck back in the next court, October 1780, obtaining an order for Sheriff Alexander Mebane Jr. to protect the survey party with a posse. Mebane seems to have had a friendly relationship with Strudwick, having bought 214 acres on Back Creek from him in 1772 and paying a fair price. Whatever Sheriff Mebane did with a posse, the survey did not go on, and in the November county court Strudwick tried to protect himself financially. His method played into the hands of his "tenants."

Strudwick petitioned the county court to be taxed on 100 acres of land instead of 24,000. He declared that the land was being taxed twice: he listed it on the tax inventory, but the "Sundrie Persons" occupying the land also listed it. His reasoning was that he could not sell, rent, lease, cultivate, or use the land in any way and therefore should not be charged taxes on it. The people who had the use of it could pay the taxes. The court recorded no response to Strudwick but apparently referred the matter to the General Assembly, for Strudwick petitioned that body early in 1781, repeating his request. The assembly complied in February, allowing Strudwick to avoid the tax. Did Strudwick understand the strategy of his challengers? It is likely. The legislature's resolution noted, "This resolve shall not be considered in any sense to affect the title of these lands." By this time, the war was being fought in Orange County, with elements of the forces of Charles Lord Cornwallis and Nathanael Greene skirmishing widely in the area. Everything was up in the air until October and Yorktown. Strudwick did not wear down easily. In October 1782, the Hillsborough District Superior Court ordered another survey and repeated the county court's order that the sheriff use "the power of the county" to protect the survey party. Meanwhile, the campaign to own the land outright by paying tax on it had continued through the war. It had never been separate from the survey obstructions. Two of the three men whom Strudwick mentioned as directing the obstruction in 1780 were tax assessors at the time.[62]

Strudwick left an image of himself during his beleaguered days when he confided his land troubles to his lawyer, Thomas Burke, in September 1780. Burke was helping Strudwick buttress his legal documentation for all his New Hanover and Orange County lands, but Strudwick's mind was on the place where he lived on Haw Creek. Someone, he said, had filed a land entry for it. And "one Bowles ... has got a new patend [patent, or grant] for a small plantation lying in sight of my house." James Bowles had entered eighty acres on the waters of Haw Creek in November 1778 and received it as a grant in September 1779. On the land for which Bowles now had a deed, Strudwick had planted corn and an orchard. Bowles, Strudwick related, "came and told me he intended in a few days to fetch away the peaches to distill. On my saying I would not consent to it, he answered he could get a Posse to assist him, which I suppose he will: and it is very probable the other man who has got a Patend for my house will raise another (or the same) Posse, and drive us into the woods." Strudwick asked Burke's legal advice. In a postscript, Strudwick apologized for not going to Burke in person but, he explained, "at the one time the dread of losing my house, and at another that of loosing my peaches, keeps me almost a Prisoner at home." Despite his fears, Samuel Strudwick handsomely survived the loss of much of his land and passed his estate to his heirs when he died in the Hawfields in 1797.[63]

Strudwick's presence and his acquiescence to the state government facilitated his use of its courts to try to save his land. His case was exceptional. Generally, owners of large grants comparable to his were absentees, and the state legislature confiscated their holdings in 1779. The 1779 statute named persons whose property it confiscated, and it authorized commissioners of confiscated estates in each superior court district to inventory the property with an eye to future sales. When commissioners of confiscated estates sold land and movable property at auction, it was a separate process from entering land for a state grant, and it was not much used in the Piedmont until after the Revolutionary War. The disposition of one of Edmund Fanning's tracts in the Hawfields illustrates the easy process by which residents who paid taxes during the war could enter land that was not already claimed by other revolutionaries, even when it had not yet been confiscated. Further, the episode illustrates the continuity of title difficulties stemming from early eighteenth-century grants. It displays farmers' fears of powerful litigators as well.

Fanning already owned land elsewhere in Orange County when he bought a 10,000-acre tract in the Hawfields, north and west of Strudwick's, in 1770. Fanning bought it at a court-ordered sale presided over by Sheriff John Butler. The superior court ordering the sale was not the Hillsborough court but the superior court for Halifax District, where Fanning was not a touchstone for controversy. A debt suit by George Lathbury against the estate of Governor Sir Richard Everard's grandson had resulted in the court's order to the Orange County sheriff to sell the Everard family's holdings. Everard had granted the tract to himself while governor in the 1720s. Fanning bought an undivided share of the 10,000-acre tract in 1770, paying slightly more than £930 in proclamation currency.[64] Together, Fanning's and Strudwick's Hawfields holdings included perhaps half of present-day Alamance County and stretched into present-day Orange County.

Fifteen men petitioned the legislature in 1789 claiming ownership of portions of Fanning's Hawfields tract. They said they had purchased the land from Granville. Their fear was that it would be sold as Fanning's confiscated property. Granville documentation exists for only one of the claimants, and all fifteen had made entries for state grants of the land in 1778 without obstruction, prior to the 1779 law confiscating Fanning's property. Their request was successful.[65]

A year after the Hawfields men secured their claims, Michael Holt petitioned the legislature regarding nearly 2,400 acres of the McCulloh lands west of the Haw River. Holt's dealings with the legislature were more complex than the petitions of the Hawfields farmers who had entered land on Fanning's tract prior to its confiscation. Like Strudwick, Holt had cut a large figure before and during the Regulator upheaval. Also like Strudwick, Holt had been slow to cast his lot with the revolutionaries. Even so, the adaptation of both men to the new political formalities ensured continuation of their elite status.

Holt (1723–99) was a son of the elder Michael Holt (d. 1767) and Elizabeth Scheible, Rhineland natives who had married and reared a family in Virginia before buying Granville land along the Great Trading Path, west of where it crossed the Haw River at Pine Ford and near the first Orange County courthouse. They moved there with some of their sons in the 1750s.[66]

After the Revolutionary War, the younger Michael Holt bought the McCulloh land not from the commissioners of confiscated lands but from James Williams, who had purchased it from one of the commissioners, William Moore, in 1784. Two years earlier, Williams and two other men had formed a partnership to buy most of the McCulloh lands to be sold in Hillsborough District; they agreed to pay certificates and money to Moore and to post bond for the remainder, some £3,000. Who among the three partners paid is not known, but Moore conveyed twelve tracts west of the Haw River to Williams in May 1784. Williams absconded to Georgia, leaving an erstwhile partner, John Estis, as sole security for the £3,000. Meanwhile, Holt had purchased the tracts from Williams. In 1789, Estis got the legislature to authorize him to sell the lands to pay the state. In this way, Holt's purchase was rendered insecure.[67]

Holt and two other men who had bought land from Williams petitioned the legislature in 1790 to rescind its resolution insofar as it applied to those lands.[68] Most of the 2,379 acres Holt had purchased was along Alamance and Stinking Quarter Creeks, with some on nearby Gun and Varnal's Creeks.

Variations in size and price of the twelve tracts indicate that they were not wilderness land but active farms with improvements. Apparently, they were homes of Holt's neighbors, who had not filed land entries for them during the revolutionary crisis. In purchasing the farms from Williams, Holt was protecting the holdings and improvements where his neighbors had lived for more than a generation. The speculator Williams and his partners had been middlemen, but in effect, Holt prevented the farms from being sold as confiscated McCulloh lands. It was a solid investment for Holt, with clear ownership in his hands by 1790.[69]

Like the Scots-Irish east of the Haw River, the largely German residents on its west side had displayed discontent during the Regulator years, and the site of the Battle of Alamance lay in their midst. The area had not produced striking support for the Revolution, however. Cornwallis had been comfortable enough in the area for his forces to spend a week there after leaving Hillsborough in the winter of 1781, the time of greatest military intensity in what Cornwallis called "the Regulator country." Moravians in Wachovia were friends of Germans in the area, but in 1782 a Moravian writer remarked on their reputations as "tories." Moreover, a descendant of Holt, living in the Alamance-Stinking Quarter area in the mid-nineteenth century, recorded an oral tradition that prosperous German farmers there had been targets of extortion by Orange County militia commander Colonel William O'Neal.[70] These factors raise the likelihood that the farms Holt bought in this particular McCulloh tract were homes of people who had been reluctant to follow the county's officials during the war years.

The Hawfields petitioners had filed entries for state grants during the war. Residents of the farms that Holt bought had not. Perhaps the latter felt secure because of action they or their parents had taken more than a decade earlier. In 1763–66, about 130 people who were buying land west of the Haw River from Henry McCulloh had made purchase-lease agreements for tracts of about 350 acres each with McCulloh. This included but was not limited to the Alamance-Stinking Quarter region. The tracts were on McCulloh land that the Crown-Granville survey had found to be in the Granville tract. Typically, purchasers paid two-thirds, with the remaining one-third functioning as a mortgage. Recording the agreements prevented the tracts from being sold by the Granville land office. (In 1755, McCulloh and Granville had agreed that McCulloh's purchasers were to be exempt from the ongoing survey of the Crown-Granville boundary.) Holt had worked for McCulloh during that time, and Holt's parents had facilitated the paperwork for these mortgages at their store and blacksmith operation.[71] Whether the buyers had paid off their mortgages to McCulloh by the time of the Revolution is not known, for that segment of land records did not survive the war, but Germans in the area paid the land tax during the conflict.[72] The large-scale community effort in 1763–66 suggests that German farmers living on the watercourses of Alamance and Stinking Quarter Creeks may have thought their land tenure was secure already when revolutionaries opened land offices. Among the continuities apparent in these decades of land transactions is the liaison Holt's family provided between German-speaking farmers and the respective colonial and revolutionary officialdoms.

Michael Holt the younger had been whipped during the September 1770 riot in Hillsborough with which this essay began. He had been a land agent for McCulloh since 1762, and that may explain the attack. A justice of the peace and militia captain as well, Holt was conspicuous in the county power structure during the Regulator upheaval. In 1775 he wrote McCulloh, who was in England, "You may be sure I am your real friend you may be sure I will do all I can for you." He added, "It is hard times and likely to be harder for the whole country is in an uproar concerning Boston all for battle like they were in the Regulation as for myself I will have no hand in it."[73] After the war, Holt remained in McCulloh's employ. The latter's son, trying to get possession for the confiscated McCulloh land that remained unsold, wrote the elder McCulloh from Holt's home on Alamance Creek, "I am concerned for security of the paperwork. At present it is in possession of Mr Holt, whom I count on entirely to look after your interest."[74]

The Battle of Alamance took place on Holt's property, and wounded Regulators were treated in his home by Tryon's orders. Holt came to champion the Regulators soon after their defeat. Prior to the outbreak of the Revolution, he talked about the Regulators at length to an English visitor, convincing him that the Regulators had not been responsible for the ills they suffered and that they "were, and still are among the worthiest, steadiest, and most respectable friends to British government and real constitutional freedom."[75]

Holt opposed the Revolution at its inception, leading a militia company from Orange County to join the loyalist force that was defeated at Moore's Creek Bridge. He was well placed to be pardoned by other Orange County officials, with whom he had served for more than a decade, and he provided beef for Greene's forces in 1781.[76] Holt adapted to the Revolution and expanded his landholding as a result. After the legislature cleared Holt's title to the McCulloh land in 1790, his neighbors rented or purchased their farms from him or his heirs. Their payments continued well into the nineteenth century, contributing to the capital accumulation by which Holt's grandson, Edwin Michael Holt, pioneered textile manufacturing in the Piedmont in the 1830s. Like many other targets of Regulator ire, Michael Holt well understood the continuities of local power and found a way to benefit from the tumultuous transition from colonial to republican government.

NOTES

1. Richard Henderson to William Tryon, Granville County, September 29, 1770, in William L. Saunders, ed., *Colonial Records of North Carolina*, 10 vols. (Raleigh: P. M. Hale et al., 1886–90), 8:242–44 (hereafter *CRNC*); deposition of Ralph McNair, October 9, 1770, *CRNC*, 8:245.

2. Judge Richard Henderson named Thomas Hart, Alexander Martin, Michael Holt, John Litterell, Col. [James] Gray, Major [Thomas] Lloyd, Francis Nash, John Cooke, Tyree Harris, and Edmund Fanning. Ibid., 8:242.

3. Marvin L. Michael Kay, "The Payment of Provincial and Local Taxes in North Carolina, 1748–1771," *William and Mary Quarterly* 26 (April 1969): 218–40; James Penn Whittenburg, "Backwoods Revolutionaries: Social Context and Constitutional Theories of the North Carolina Regulators, 1765–1771," Ph.D. diss., University of Georgia, 1974; Marvin L. Michael Kay, "The North Carolina Regulation, 1766–1776: A Class Conflict," in *The American Revolution: Explorations in the History of American Radicalism*, ed. Alfred F. Young (DeKalb: Northern Illinois University Press, 1976), 71–123; Marvin L. Michael Kay and Lorin Lee Cary, "Class, Mobility, and Conflict in North Carolina on the Eve of the Revolution," in *The Southern Experience in the American Revolution*, ed. Jeffrey J. Crow and Larry E. Tise (Chapel Hill: University of North Carolina Press, 1978), 109–51; A. Roger Ekirch, *"Poor Carolina": Politics and Society in Colonial North Carolina, 1729–1776* (Chapel Hill: University of North Carolina Press, 1981); Mark H. Jones, "Herman Husband: Millenarian, Carolina Regulator, and Whiskey Rebel," Ph.D. diss., Northern Illinois University, 1982.

4. Writing in 1994, Alan D. Watson analyzed the historiography of the Regulator movement since 1814 in three sequential phases, broadly reflecting trends in the profession nationwide: a revolutionary or proto-revolutionary interpretation, an east-west sectional approach, and analyses employing sociological, economic, and psychological concepts in the 1970s through the early 1990s. Watson, "The Origin of the Regulation in North Carolina," *Mississippi Quarterly* 47 (Fall 1994): 567–600. See also Carole Watterson Troxler, *Farming Dissenters: The Regulator Movement in Piedmont North Carolina* (Raleigh: North Carolina Department of Cultural Resources, 2011), 167–70, 188. In 2002, Marjoleine Kars drew on work of the previous twenty-five years to analyze the Regulator experience from three prisms: economics, religion, and politics. Kars, *Breaking Loose Together: The Regulator Rebellion in Pre-revolutionary North Carolina* (Chapel Hill: University of North Carolina Press, 2002). Troxler presents a Regulator narrative reaching into the 1780s and focusing on land and the broad culture of religious dissent in *Farming Dissenters*.

5. R. D. W. Connor, *North Carolina: Rebuilding an Ancient Commonwealth 1584–1925*, 4 vols. (Chicago: American Historical Society, 1929), 1:612.

6. *North Carolina Standard* (Raleigh), November 8, 1851; Calvin Henderson Wiley, *The North Carolina Reader* (Philadelphia: Lippincott, Grambo and Co., 1851). The novel was Wiley, *Alamance, or the Great and Final Experiment* (New York: Harper and Brothers, 1847).

See also Michael O'Brien, *Conjectures of Order: Intellectual Life and the American South, 1810-1860*, 2 vols. (Chapel Hill: University of North Carolina Press, 2004) 1:346-50.

7. William S. Powell, ed., *Dictionary of North Carolina Biography*, 6 vols. (Chapel Hill: University of North Carolina Press, 1979-96), s.v. "John Hill Wheeler" (hereafter *DNCB*); John Hill Wheeler, *Historical Sketches of North Carolina, from 1584 to 1851*, 2 vols. (Philadelphia: Lippincott, Grambo, and Co., 1851).

8. *DNCB*, s.v. "John Hill Wheeler."

9. Wheeler, *Historical Sketches*, 2:19.

10. Ibid., 2:469.

11. Francis L. Hawks, David L. Swain, and William A. Graham, *Revolutionary History of North Carolina to Which Is Prefixed a Preliminary Sketch of the Battle of the Alamance* (Raleigh: W. D. Cooke; New York: G. P. Putnam, 1853). Swain and Graham treated Moore's Creek Bridge and the 1780-81 campaign, respectively, and Hawks presented the Mecklenburg Declaration and argued that the Regulators instigated the Revolution. For Hawks, see O'Brien, *Conjectures of Order*, 1:43-44, 2:648-50.

12. A common theme was, "Why is the battle of Lexington on the lips of every boy in the Union, and perhaps not one in a thousand ever heard of the battle of Alamance?" *Weekly Standard* (Raleigh, N.C.), November 28, 1860 (quotation), March 24, 1858, June 15, 1859; *Semi-weekly Standard* (Raleigh, N.C.), July 17, 1858, October 23, 1858; *Wilmington Journal*, July 2, 1858; *Western Democrat* (Charlotte, N.C.), October 4, 1859.

13. *Tarborough Southerner*, May 14, 1875; *Wilmington Journal*, May 14, 1875, citing *the Baltimore Gazette*; *Newberry (S.C.) Herald*, June 2, 1875; *Weekly Kansas Chief* (Troy), May 20, 1875; *Fairfield Herald* (Winnsboro, S.C.), May 12, 1875; *Morning Oregonian* (Portland), July 30, 1893.

14. John Wheeler Moore, *History of North Carolina from the Earliest Discoveries to the Present Time* (Raleigh: Alfred Williams and Co., 1880), 109 (quotation), 125-28.

15. Francis Nash, *Hillsboro: Colonial and Revolutionary* (Raleigh, N.C.: Edwards and Broughton, 1903), 12 (quotation); Alfred Moore Waddell, *A Colonial Officer and His Times, 1754-1773* (Raleigh, N.C.: Edwards and Broughton, 1890); W. H. Bailey Sr., "The Regulators of North Carolina," *American Historical Register* 3 (1895-96): 313-34, 464-71, 554-67; Watson, "Origin of the Regulation."

16. *Durham Daily Globe*, May 22, 1894; *Asheville Daily Citizen*, May 24, 1894; *Gold Leaf* (Henderson, N.C.), May 31, 1894, August 4, 1898; *Weekly Union (S.C.) Times*, January 5, 1894.

17. *Fayetteville Observer*, August 11, September 15, 1892; *News and Observer* (Raleigh, N.C.), August 4, 1892, November 20, 1894.

18. The copy in the *Opelousas (La.) Courier*, August 18, 1906, indicates a reprint from the *New York American*. *El Paso Herald*, May 21, 1912; *Wahpeton (N.D.) Times*, November 20, 1913; *Chickasha Daily Express* (Indian Territory [Okla.]), May 29, 1914; *Bridgeport (Conn.) Times and Evening Farmer*, April 4, 1919; *St. Mary Banner* (Franklin, La.) June 28, 1919; *Daily Missoulian* (Mont.), February 14, 1909.

19. John S. Bassett, "The Regulators of North Carolina (1765-1771)," in *Annual Report of the American Historical Association for the Year 1894* (Washington, D.C.: Government Printing Office, 1895), 141-212.

20. *CRNC*, 8:iii.

21. William Edwards Fitch, *Some Neglected History of North Carolina, Being an Account of the Revolution of the Regulators and of the Battle of Alamance, the First Battle of the American Revolution* (New York and Washington: Neale, 1905); *New York Times*, March 25, 1905; *Baltimore Sun*, May 9, 1914.

22. Theodore Clark Smith, "The Scientific Historian and Our Colonial Period," *Atlantic Monthly* 98 (January 1, 1906): 702–11 (quotation 705, emphasis added).

23. *CRNC*, 4:1086 (quotation); *CRNC*, 8:230; Charles G. Sellers Jr., "Private Profits and British Colonial Policy: The Speculations of Henry McCulloh," *William and Mary Quarterly* 8 (October 1951): 548; Daniel Frederick Blower, "The Orange County and Mecklenburg County Instructions: The Development of Political Individualism in Backcountry North Carolina, 1740–1776," Ph.D. diss., University of Michigan, 1984, 228–40; Kars, *Breaking Loose Together*, 39; *DNCB*, s.v. "Henry Eustace McCulloh"; William S. Powell, James K. Huhta, and Thomas J. Farnham, eds., *The Regulators in North Carolina: A Documentary History, 1759–1776* (Raleigh, N.C.: Department of Archives and History, 1971), 31–32. A transcription of selections from Henry Eustace McCulloh's correspondence is Stewart Dunaway, *Henry McCulloh and Son Henry Eustace McCulloh* (n.p., Lulu.com, 2011).

24. *CRNC*, 4:807; Thornton W. Mitchell, "The Granville District and Its Land Records," *North Carolina Historical Review* 70 (April 1993): 103–29; W. N. Watt, *The Granville District* (Taylorsville, N.C.: n.p., 1992); William P. Cumming, "Wimble's Maps and the Colonial Cartography of the North Carolina Coast," *North Carolina Historical Review* 46 (April 1969): 157–70.

25. *CRNC*, 5:24.

26. Carole Watterson Troxler and William Murray Vincent, *Shuttle and Plow: A History of Alamance County, North Carolina* (Graham, N.C.: Alamance County Historical Society, 1999), 51–55; Minutes of the Court of Pleas and Quarter Sessions (hereafter CPQS), Orange County, 1752–54, North Carolina State Archives, Raleigh.

27. "Hillsborough" honored the first secretary of state for the colonies, the earl of Hillsborough. For abuses in the Granville District administrations of Corbin and Childs, see George Stevenson's entries in *DNCB*, s.vv. "Francis Corbin" and "Thomas Childs."

28. Roger Ekirch, "'A New Government of Liberty': Herman Husband's Vision of Backcountry North Carolina, 1755," *William and Mary Quarterly*, 34 (October 1977): 632–46.

29. John Saunders, "Journal of a Journey to Pee Dee," North Carolina State Archives.

30. Kay and Cary, "Class, Mobility, and Conflict," 145.

31. Kay, "North Carolina Regulation," 71–123; Marvin L. Michael Kay and William S. Price Jr., "'To Ride the Wood Mare': Road Building and Militia Service in Colonial North Carolina, 1740–1775," *North Carolina Historical Review* 57 (October 1980): 361–409; Kay and Cary, "Class, Mobility, and Conflict."

32. The schoolmaster George Sims, writer of the "Nutbush Address," urged his readers and listeners: "Let us appear what we really are, To wit, free subjects by birth, endeavouring to recover our native rights according to law, and to reduce the malpractices of the Officers of our Court down to the standard of law." William K. Boyd, ed., *Some Eighteenth Century Tracts concerning North Carolina* (Raleigh, N.C.: Edwards and Broughton, 1927).

33. For traditions of ritual violence that were used during the Regulator uprising and the

Revolution, see Wayne E. Lee, *Crowds and Soldiers in Revolutionary North Carolina: The Culture of Violence in Riot and War* (Gainesville: University Press of Florida, 2001); and E. P. Thompson, *Customs in Common* (New York: New Press, 1993), 1–15, 517–19.

34. For former Regulator leaders during 1772–75, see Troxler, *Farming Dissenters*, 124–32.

35. For the role of nonviolence in the Baptist dispersion, see Troxler, *Farming Dissenters*, 149–52.

36. Ekirch, *"Poor Carolina,"* 211 (quotations).

37. *CRNC*, 10:169.

38. *CRNC*, 10:211, 932–33.

39. Jeffrey J. Crow, "Liberty Men and Loyalists: Disorder and Disaffection in the North Carolina Backcountry," in *An Uncivil War: The Southern Backcountry during the American Revolution*, ed. Ronald Hoffman, Thad W. Tate, and Peter J. Albert (Charlottesville: University Press of Virginia, for U.S. Capitol Historical Society, 1985), 125–29; Carole Watterson Troxler, "Refuge, Resistance, and Reward: The Southern Loyalists' Claim on East Florida," *Journal of Southern History* 55 (November 1989): 566–75.

40. *North Carolina Gazette*, January 2, 1778; Walter Clark, ed., *The State Records of North Carolina*, vols. 11–25 (Raleigh, N.C.: P. M. Hale et al., 1886–1907), 24:43–48 (hereafter *SRNC*).

41. Abstracts of the earliest state land entries and grants, arranged by counties and published by Albert B. Pruitt, Pat Shaw Bailey, and others, are entry points to the manuscript records in Secretary of State Record Group, North Carolina State Archives.

42. Deposition of James Dickey, March 12, 1778, Rowan County Civil and Criminal Cases, North Carolina State Archives; pension application of Mark Dedmon, transcribed by Will Graves, http://revwarapps.org/w3960.pdf (accessed March 2015).

43. *SRNC*, 23:985, 24:11.

44. Deposition of John Haggen, July 27, 1778, Rowan County Civil and Criminal Cases.

45. Locke sent the list to Johnston, remarking, "They have Seen that you Refused to hold any alection I am apt to believe that you may point out where they have mistaken them Selves." Locke requested that, at the next muster, "you … [or] your Lieutenant Can … Show the Onresebellness of their power to hold any Such Election. You are to Set Down the Eage; Sise, Complackson and Ocpeseon of the draft; you are to prepotion the Cloathen amonst your Company and let Every man know what part to Rease & upon this their failer or refusel in that Case I have to Send a warnt against Souch failler that will reas it of their goods You will Send their List Down as soon as you Can." At the time, Rowan and Guilford Continentals were permitted to elect two captains in each county. *SRNC*, 13:444, 24:154.

46. Rowan County Land Entries, North Carolina State Archives, 49, 174, 882, 926, 1052, 1055, 1331, 1336, 1425, 1427, 1429, 1430, 1520, 1522, 1526, 1532, 1533, 1536, 1953. Another captain by this name entered lands in Randolph County. The law limited the size of entries to 640 acres but placed no limit on the number an individual could claim. *SRNC*, 24:44.

47. Boyd, *Some Eighteenth Century Tracts*, 307 (first quotation); *SRNC*, 24:263 (second quotation); Treasurer's and Comptroller's Papers, boxes 2–5, North Carolina State Archives; National Archives United Kingdom, Audit Office 12/91, extract from Office of Secretary of State of North Carolina, copy in British Records, North Carolina State Archives (hereafter NAUK).

48. Examples appear in CPQS, Rowan County, 1773-86, May 7, 1782, November 7-8, 1782; Salisbury District Superior Court, 1782-86, Minute Docket, September term, 1782, North Carolina State Archives.

49. Lincoln County Miscellaneous Papers, 1764-1923, September 19, 1782, December 21, 1782, n.d. [January 1783], North Carolina State Archives; Crow, "Liberty Men and Loyalists," 131, 139, 170; Betty Linney Waugh, *The Upper Yadkin in the American Revolution: Benjamin Cleveland, Symbol of Continuity* (Wilkesboro, N.C.: Wilkes Community College, 1971).

50. CPQS, Rowan County, 1773-86, November 1782, February 1783 (quotation); *SRNC*, 19:926-27; Carole W. Troxler, *The Loyalist Experience in North Carolina* (Raleigh, N.C.: Division of Archives and History, 1976), 18; John S. Davenport, unpublished manuscript shared with author, 1977, 30-34.

51. Davenport manuscript, 42; Roger E. Sappington, "Two Eighteenth-Century Dunker Congregations," *North Carolina Historical Review* 47 (July 1970): 179-80, 200-203.

52. Adelaide L. Fries, ed., *Records of the Moravians in North Carolina*, 11 vols. (Raleigh, N.C.: Edwards and Broughton, 1922-69), 2:897, 1027-29, 1032, 1044-48; Davenport manuscript, 42.

53. Robert L. Ganyard, *The Emergence of North Carolina's Revolutionary State Government* (Raleigh, N.C.: Division of Archives and History, 1978), 87; Hillsborough District Superior Court: Dockets, Minute Dockets of the Superior Court, 1768-83, North Carolina State Archives; CPQS, Orange County, Trial Docket, 1780-83; Hillsborough District Superior Court: Civil Action Papers, box 51, Civil Actions Concerning Land (1778-1806), North Carolina State Archives; CPQS, Randolph County, 1770-85.

54. *CRNC*, 7:702, 8:273-74; Powell et al., *Regulators*, 368-73, 540; Fred Hughes, *Guilford County, N.C.: A Map Supplement* (Jamestown, N.C.: Custom House, 1988), 6-8; Albert Bruce Pruitt, *Abstracts of Land Entrys [sic]: Guilford Co., NC, 1779-1796, and Rockingham Co., NC, 1790-1795* ([Cary, N.C.]: A. B. Pruitt, c. 1987).

55. CPQS, Orange County, 1765, 1777-78; Pat Shaw Bailey, *Land Grant Records of North Carolina*, Vol. 1, *Orange County, 1752-1885* (Graham, N.C.: n.p., 1990); John L. Cheney Jr., ed., *North Carolina Government, 1585-1974: A Narrative and Statistical History* (Raleigh, N.C.: Department of the Secretary of State, 1981), 201-7; *DNCB*, s.vv. "Thomas Burke," "John Butler," and "Nathaniel Rochester"; Powell et al., *Regulators*, 368-73, 540.

56. Only one tax appraiser specified which acreage he listed had been granted and which had been entered only or entered and surveyed. Orange County District Tax Lists, March 1770-83, microfilm copies in North Carolina State Archives; Pat Shaw Bailey, *Land Grant Records*, Orange County; CPQS, Orange County, 1777-84; Cheney, *North Carolina Government*, 201-11.

57. *DNCB*, s.vv. "George Burrington" and "Samuel Strudwick"; William S. Powell, ed., *The Correspondence of William Tryon and Other Selected Papers*, 2 vols. (Raleigh, N.C.: Division of Archives and History, 1980-81), 2:5.

58. *CRNC*, 7:710-12.

59. Powell, *Correspondence of William Tryon*, 1:19.

60. Fries, *Records of the Moravians*, 3:1135, 1159, 1365-66.

61. *SRNC*, 15:409; *Register of Orange County, North Carolina, Deeds, 1752-1768 and 1793*, transcribed by Eve B. Weeks (Danielsville, Ga.: Heritage Papers, 1984).

62. *SRNC*, 17:661; CPQS, Orange County, 1779–81; Hillsborough District Superior Court, Minute Dockets, October 1782.

63. *SRNC*, 15:410 (quotation); Bailey, *Land Grant Records*, Orange County, 5; *DNCB*, s.v. "Samuel Strudwick."

64. After Fanning went to New York with Tryon in 1771, he turned the land over to agents to lease or sell. Orange County Deed Book, 3:441, 462, 492, North Carolina State Archives.

65. Petitions, 1789, Legislative Papers, box 31, General Assembly Session Records, North Carolina State Archives; land grant to George Hodge, September 1779, Land Grant Records of North Carolina, Office of the Secretary of State, North Carolina State Archives; Bailey, *Land Grant Records*, Orange County; *SRNC*, 24:263; Orange County Deed Book 3:462.

66. Troxler and Vincent, *Shuttle and Plow*, 47–49.

67. Williams and Estis were newly appointed Hillsborough town commissioners when they made the purchase; the third partner was Nicholas Long Jr., son of a Halifax County planter and revolutionary quartermaster. *SRNC*, 24:622–24; Audit Office 12/91, NAUK; Orange County Deed Book 3:100–101, 108–13, 116, 118; *DNCB*, s.v. "Nicholas Long."

68. *SRNC*, 21:984–85, 998, 1034, 1042.

69. Holt was taxed for only 650 acres in 1780. Orange County Tax, Chatham District, 1780, North Carolina State Archives.

70. O'Neal's reputation is treated in Carole Watterson Troxler, *Pyle's Defeat: Deception at the Racepath* (Graham, N.C.: Alamance County Historical Association, 2003), 38–43, 80; Eli Washington Caruthers, *A Sketch of the Life and Character of the Rev. David Caldwell* (Greensborough, N.C.: Swaim and Sherwood, 1842), 213–15; Audit Office 12/91, NAUK; and Salem Memorabilia, July 1782, Moravian Archives Southern Province, Winston-Salem, N.C.

71. Orange County Deed Books 1 and 3; *SRNC*, 21:984–85, 998, 1034, 1042; CPQS, Orange County, 1752–53.

72. Orange County Register of Deeds, 1752–68, and Orange County Tax, St. Asaph's District, 1780, microfilms in North Carolina State Archives.

73. Michael Holt to Henry Eustace McCulloh, March 15, 1775 (quotation), and Henry Eustace McCulloh to Edmund Fanning, September 18, 1762, Fanning and McCulloh Papers, Southern Historical Collection, Wilson Library, University of North Carolina at Chapel Hill; *Virginia Gazette*, January 14, 1773, January 21, 1773, January 28, 1773; memorials of Henry Eustace McCulloh, Audit Office 13/bundle 117, copy in English Records, North Carolina State Archives; Michael Holt to Henry Eustace McCulloh, November 28, 1784 [Land Tract 11, 1784 reports], Fanning and McCulloh Papers.

74. George McCulloh to Henry Eustace McCulloh, April 10, 1795, Fanning and McCulloh Papers.

75. John Ferdinand Dalziel Smyth, *A Tour in the United States of America*, 2 vols. (London, 1784; repr., New York: Arno Press, 1968), 1:228.

76. Powell et al., *Regulators*, 246; *CRNC*, 10:441–43, 601, 827–28; *SRNC*, 11:350.

EVANGELICAL GEOGRAPHIES OF NORTH CAROLINA

Charles F. Irons

George Fox, when he glided up the Pamlico Sound into the Perquimans River in late 1672, saw the same sights and sounds as did other immigrants and visitors to North Carolina. He may have noticed a subtle difference in smell when the brackish water gave way to freshwater, and he certainly gazed upon the many-knobbed cypresses crowding the water's edge as he approached the shore. But Fox, like other Protestant evangelists and religiously motivated immigrants to North Carolina, had a second sight; he not only noted the "woods, & swamps, & many cruell boggs & watery places" through which he passed but also saw networks of like-minded believers as well as communities of potential converts. Though he had not been to Carolina before, he had intelligence of this "spiritual geography" from members of the Society of Friends in Virginia, local informants such as Nathaniel Batts, and Quaker correspondents around the world. Thus, passing by now-vanished Batts Island, he noted in his journal that "there is some friendly people" up the Perquimans and reported on a meeting by the riverside at Quaker Joseph Scott's house. Alert also to the possibility of extending this network to new peoples and places, he "went among ye Indians" and preached his Gospel.[1] Fox was one of hundreds of Protestant missionaries to travel to North Carolina in the seventeenth through the nineteenth centuries who helped shape the spiritual geography of the Old North State.

In many ways, religion, specifically Evangelical Protestantism, was like dye in the blood, revealing nonstate pathways for the circulation of ideas into and out of North Carolina. The movement of people is difficult enough to track by itself, but the changing ways in which Tar Heels imagined themselves in relation to those in other states and in the rest of the world is even more elusive. Evangelicalism, however, draws out these hidden cartographies, showing how North Carolinians understood their relationships to other places and institutions. In this light, the account of Fox's visit is significant not for his role as a potential immigrant but for the ligaments he revealed connecting dissenters in the northeastern part of the state to transnational networks. Scholars of North Carolina and of the South in general have endeavored in recent years to deprovincialize Carolina and Southern history by emphasizing global connections.[2] Scholars of religious history, for their part, have shown that Evangelical North Carolinians participated in global networks long before the economic upheavals of the twentieth century.[3] This essay not only synthesizes some of their work, using Evangelicalism to emphasize the Atlantic sensibilities of generations of Tar Heels, but also sketches black and white Evangelicals' sometimes convergent, sometimes divergent participation in networks within the state and nation. It narrates also Evangelicals' metaphorical movement from the margins to the center of the state's political and cultural life, and their partially successful attempt to consolidate Evangelical cultural authority in strong institutions.

Protestant missionaries and religiously motivated immigrants over time changed the ways in which they understood the spiritual geography of North Carolina and its connection to the wider world. In the colonial period, dissenting missionaries took advantage of a weak Anglican establishment to extend hemisphere-wide networks into the colony. Many residents in these early Evangelical outposts held values more in synch with their coreligionists across the Atlantic than with Carolina elites. After independence, however, Evangelical Protestant pioneers expanded beyond their initial beachheads and focused on building networks within the state and ultimately connecting them to new, national denominations. Baptists and Methodists predominated, in roughly equal measure, but a variety of smaller sects, such as Lutherans, German Reformed, members of the Christian Connection, also contributed to make a de facto Protestant establishment. As cultural gatekeepers and natives of the state instead of interlopers, white Evangelicals began to affirm rather than challenge hierarchies of race, class, and gender. Significantly, they also began sending rather than receiving missionaries, a process in which black Evangelicals ironically played a prominent role given their increasing marginalization at home. In the late antebellum period, the institutions Evangelical Protestants had built to protect and extend their geographic reach began to fracture along creedal, sectional, and racial lines. White Carolinians found that their imagined communities had shrunk considerably and walked away from relationships with their Northern coreligionists, while black Tar Heels instead took advantage of new possibilities during and after the Civil War to form independent churches and to forge new relationships with national, black-controlled denominations.

DIVERSITY AND MOTION, 1663–1776

Anglicans in North Carolina never created a strong establishment, thereby opening the colony to Protestant interlopers from around the world. Charles II gave permission in the 1663 charter to the lords proprietors to grant "such indulgencies and dispensations" as they thought appropriate to settlers who could not in good conscience conform to the "Liturgy, forms, and Ceremonies of the Church of England." The proprietors themselves went even further in the Fundamental Constitutions of 1669. Resigned that "those who remove from other parts to Plant there will unavoidably be of different opinions concerning matters of Religion," they decreed that "any Seven or more persons agreeing in any Religion shall constitute a church or profession," creating a welcoming environment for sectarians of every kind who wanted to make inroads into Anglican and Indian territory.[4] Loyal churchmen in the assembly did pass the 1701 Vestry Act to support the Anglican Church, but this rearguard action was not enough to close Carolina's borders to missionaries and immigrants of every persuasion. Quakers like Fox were the first to set up outposts of dissenters, gathering hundreds of Friends in the northeastern corner of the colony and becoming a powerful political faction by the first decade of the eighteenth century.[5] While Quakers and other smaller sects remained a feature of the religious landscape, their rapid growth tapered, and members of various "Evangelical" Protestant sects took over their position by the late eighteenth century.[6]

Evangelicals were especially successful in the backcountry of the Carolina Piedmont, fertile country largely beyond the reach of either legislators or Anglican priests. In the model of George Whitefield, the archetypal evangelist of the eighteenth century, they set out to win converts in North Carolina and to integrate them into larger circles of shared commitment within the Atlantic world. At this point, the colony itself was not important as a discrete theater of Evangelical activity; to the extent that religious leaders kept records of their movements, they elided colonial boundaries as often as they noted them.

Leaders of the Unitas Fratrum, or Moravian Church, based in Herrnhut, Saxony, demonstrated the global scope of Evangelicals' geographic imagination when they purchased land for a new settlement in North Carolina. Bishop August Spangenberg served as agent for the brethren and journeyed from Edenton deep into the Carolina interior in late 1752 in search of a suitable 100,000-acre parcel. The farther from Edenton he traveled in search of a piece of land large and desirable enough for his purposes, the more Spangenberg noted the attenuation of the threads connecting his proposed settlement to trade routes and to the Moravians' North American headquarters in Bethlehem, Pennsylvania. To procure salt and other necessities, he calculated, "they must go from here [a massive plot centered around modern-day Winston-Salem and christened Wachovia], to Charlestown, South Carolina, about 300 miles ... or else they must go to Bolings Point, Virginia, on a branch of the James River, about 300 miles from here." Spangenberg concluded his spatial musings with a declaration of faith in God's capacity to overcome the distance. An anonymous Moravian artist working at approximately the same time gave stunning visual form to the interconnectedness of Moravian settlements, sketching in *The Settlement Scene* (1758), a landscape of sixty-three Moravian towns and villages from around the world brought together under one sky—including four buildings from Wachovia. Moravians imagined themselves more tightly connected to one another than to their neighbors of other faiths.[7]

By the American Revolution, roughly a thousand immigrants as well as dozens of converts had vindicated Spangenberg's confidence in God's provision and made Wachovia home. These residents lived in one of two different types of communities: congregation towns called *Ortsgemeinen*, or *Landgemeinen* (farm towns). Moravians from settlements in Pennsylvania, Maine, and Maryland each came to the colony for the purpose of establishing a *Landgemeinen*, again demonstrating the porosity of colonial boundaries. Members of the society built meetinghouses surrounded by a cemetery and a garden at the center of each of these communities (Friedburg, Friedland, and Hope, respectively) and welcomed potential converts to the community as partial members. These pioneers may have been on the margins of political power in colonial North Carolina, but they built enduring, globally connected communities and established a tradition of dissenting religious practice on the frontier.[8]

Shubal Stearns, a charismatic evangelist who had been operating in Virginia, arrived not far from Wachovia in 1755 and quickly cultivated a dense network of Baptist churches in the Piedmont, outstripping his Moravian neighbors in numbers and influence. Settlers typically sought to locate on or near the water, but the South's creeks and rivers held special meaning for Baptists like Stearns, who often named their churches after the outdoor sites where they baptized new members (among North Carolina's first congregations were Bear Creek, Deep River, Falls of Tar, etc.). Stearns established Sandy Creek Baptist Church along a stream in what is now the town of Liberty. While he did bring with him from Virginia a small band of family and friends (including his brother-in-law and able lieutenant, Daniel Marshall), Stearns intended to expand his little church's network by converting his unchurched neighbors rather than by attracting like-minded immigrants. Marching to the tune of Stearns's high, nasal voice, the Separate Baptists launched immediately upon their arrival what was arguably the most remarkable church-planting campaign in Carolina history. Within seventeen years, Stearns and his co-laborers not only gathered over six hundred members into their first congregation but also planted forty-two new churches in the region (including congregations in Virginia and South Carolina), forever changing the religious geography of their adopted home.[9]

Baptists were radically congregational in theory but profoundly connectional in practice, knitting together believers across space by sharing ministers, forming associations to resolve challenging questions, and forever dividing congregations as membership enabled them to plant "daughter" churches nearby. Believers in the early- to mid-eighteenth century sought primarily to form relationships with other Baptists and only later sought to elaborate colony- or state-specific institutions. A few strands connected some North Carolina Baptists to those in other colonies even before Stearns arrived; believers from South Carolina, for example, had planted a "daughter" church named Abbot's Creek on a tributary of the Yadkin River in 1753. Stearns's own connections extended far north but were mainly centered over the line in Virginia. In 1758, representatives from Sandy Creek and other Separate Baptist congregations in North Carolina institutionalized their relationships with one another by forming the Sandy Creek Baptist Association. The association was one of the first in North America, antedated only by the Philadelphia Association (1707) and the Charleston Association (1751). Soon, delegates were receiving churches from Virginia and messengers from as far afield as Pennsylvania and South Carolina. By 1770, in fact, the number of participating churches from South Carolina and Virginia had grown so large that delegates to the annual meeting divided the Sandy Creek Association into thirds along colonial lines, anticipating somewhat the organization of conventions along state lines in the antebellum period.[10]

Presbyterians did not experience the rapid success their Separate Baptist rivals did, in part because the first Presbyterian immigrants did not receive meaningful support from their coreligionists in other colonies. Most of the earliest Presbyterians to arrive in North Carolina were Scots or Scots-Irish, who left their homes in large numbers following crop shortages beginning in 1718. These new arrivals sought land, first in western Pennsylvania and subsequently south and west along the Shenandoah Valley and into Virginia and the Carolinas. Presbyterian settlers along the Eno and Haw Rivers in the 1730s tried to prevail upon fellow believers in the Synod of Philadelphia (1707) to provide them with a minister, but members neither of this group nor of the competing New Light Synod of New York (1741) were able to send anyone on a permanent basis. Several missionaries visited North Carolina's numerous Presbyterian societies for short periods in the 1740s and early 1750s, but they did not offer long-term leadership. Permanent ministers such as Hugh McAden and David Caldwell finally began to arrive in the late 1750s, though few communities were lucky enough to attract a qualified preacher. As late as 1768, members of seven proto-congregations (Sugar Creek, Fifth Creek, Bethel, the Jersey Settlement, Centre, Poplar Tent, and Rocky River) offered an annual salary of 160 pounds but were still unable to attract an ordained minister from the North. Despite these disappointments, by 1770 there were seven ministers, enough to form the Presbytery of Orange.[11]

The men and women who worshipped with the Moravians, Separate Baptists, or Presbyterians—or in Lutheran, Quaker, Pietist, or independent congregations—transformed the backcountry of North Carolina from a frontier to a thriving agricultural economy with a diverse mix of mostly Protestant religious traditions. Whereas Bishop Spangenberg had worried about finding trading partners, Wachovia itself soon developed into a hub of exchange for Moravians and non-Moravians alike. George Soelle, a Moravian minister, marveled at the cacophony of religious voices echoing across the region in 1771. North Carolinians "appear to me like Aesop's crow which inflated itself with other birds' feathers," he wrote, "They have Moravian, Quaker, Separatist, Dunkard principles, know everything and know nothing, look down on others, belong to no one, and spurn others."[12] Residents of the Piedmont thus did not have a common creed, but they did share animosity (or at least distrust) for the nominally established Anglican Church and for the eastern elites who championed it. When farmers began to feel frustration at the royal government for not attending to the interests of their growing region in the late 1760s, it was no surprise that they rallied behind a nonconformist minister to protest.

Herman Husband provides a nice bookend to the colonial period, for he dramatized the extent to which Evangelicals from different transatlantic movements created a distinctive subculture in the western portion of the state. The island communities that missionaries and immigrants had planted overlapped by the 1760s to form in the interior a more individualistic, marginally more egalitarian alternative to the Anglican, politically connected Coastal Plain. Quakers in the North Carolina Yearly Meeting were among the most radical; they began discussing their obligation to enslaved Carolinians in 1758 and even dared by the 1770s to question the justice of slaveholding itself.[13] In another sign of a more democratic ethos, Martha

Stearns Marshall, sister of Shubal Stearns and wife of Daniel Marshall, was one of several women who took to the pulpit in defiance of a ban on female preaching.[14] Most Evangelicals, however, confined their egalitarianism to white men. A former Quaker leader (and onetime Presbyterian), Husband rallied his fellow farmers to protest high taxes payable only in specie, compulsory public service, remote courts, and a number of other policies he felt made backcountry residents second-class citizens. Historians debate the extent to which Husband assailed eastern privileges because of his religious commitments and rightfully cite the fact that some Evangelicals remained on the side of Governor William Tryon. Some historians, however, find Husband's own explanation for his decision to challenge what he perceived as unjust laws compelling. "When the Opposition to the Stamp Act began," he wrote in 1770, "I was early convinced that the Authors who Wrote in favor of Liberty was Generally Inspired by the Same Spirit that we Relegeous Professors Called Christ."[15] In other words, Husband drew a direct connection between the embrace of Evangelical Christianity and opposition to arbitrary hierarchy. Other North Carolinians must have drawn a similar association, based on the rapid expansion of Evangelicalism across the state in the years during and following the American Revolution.

EVANGELICALISM AND POWER, 1776–1835

Evangelicals continued their recruitment of new members and elaboration of new institutions in the years during and immediately following the American Revolution, and the "religious map" shifted as Evangelicals blanketed the state and built statewide organizations that became powerful instruments for influencing their fellow Carolinians. On a national level, churchgoers in the 1780s formed new, American jurisdictions, cutting transatlantic bonds and locating their areas of responsibility within the bounds of the new nation-state.[16] State lines, which Evangelicals had regarded as arbitrary boundaries a century earlier, became more important containers of church activity. At the same time, unlike dissenters before the Revolution who had been able to position themselves as outsiders challenging Anglican authority, North Carolina Evangelicals themselves became the insiders after independence and formed a de facto Protestant establishment. In 1776 framers of the new state constitution abandoned any language about the Anglican Church or tax support for any particular denomination, but they did stipulate "that no person who shall deny the being of God, or the truth of the Protestant religion, or the divine authority of either the Old or New Testament ... shall be capable of holding any office, or place of trust or profit, in the civil department, within this State."[17] As religious and political insiders, Evangelicals defended hierarchies of race, class, and gender, as well as of creed, more vocally than they had done in the past—though women, Roman Catholics, Jews, and people of color pushed back with some limited success. At the same time, when white and black Evangelicals renewed Atlantic connections by sending out missionaries from North Carolina, they ironically facilitated the creation of new ways of thinking about race.

Methodists embodied the rapidity of Evangelical ascendancy in the wartime and postwar period when they developed strong networks across the state, and not just in the dissenter-friendly west. Circuit riders, the itinerant ministers who carried their message to every nook and cranny of the new country, saw the landscape as a puzzle—a riddle about how to fit as many appointments as possible on a "circuit" that they rode (or, occasionally, walked). They came to North Carolina in the months before the Revolution as reformers within the Anglican Church and expanded dramatically after independence when they became a separate denomination. Whereas Presbyterians had not been able to secure outside assistance in the 1740s, Methodists benefited from the beginning of their ministry in the Tar Heel state from strong out-of-state leadership and a steady supply of new ministers. The spiritual heirs of John Wesley were almost obsessive record keepers, and they documented their statistical progress in detailed annual minutes. The first time North Carolina appeared in the records was in May 1776, when the clerk reported 683 "members in society." The record keeper did not identify the locations of any worship services, but he did indicate that Edward Dromgoole, Francis Poythress, and Isham Tatum served as the itinerants.[18]

Methodists in North Carolina had already organized ten circuits and were making dramatic gains both within areas formerly controlled by the Anglican Church and in the more diverse Piedmont and points west by 1784, the year in which American Methodists made a formal break with their English brethren. Itinerants served circuits centered around Yadkin, Caswell, Salisbury, Halifax, Wilmington, New River, Tar River, Roanoke, New Hope, and Guilford, and some ministers from Virginia (in the hinterland of Norfolk) served both Virginia and North Carolina congregations. Including the elders supervising the itinerants, the nascent Methodist Episcopal Church had managed to put more than a dozen full-time missionaries on the ground in less than ten years. By 1796, the missionaries and their homegrown successors worked nineteen North Carolina circuits and had enrolled 7,425 white and 1,288 "colored" persons as members.[19] For the Wesleyans, as for members of other denominations, the list of full members severely underrepresented the number of persons actually attending worship. Church officials maintained rigorous membership requirements throughout the antebellum period, with the result that full members represented only a fraction of the total "adherents" to a given tradition; in the Methodist case, the ratio was at least 2.5 additional adherents for every full member.[20] Methodists continued to rationalize the distribution of their staff and reallocated ministerial positions annually. National leaders, meeting in General Conference every four years, divided the circuits into annual conferences that roughly corresponded to state lines. Despite its separate circuits and impressive growth, the North Carolina Conference did not achieve full separation from the Virginia Conference until 1837, at which time it claimed 19,208 total members.[21]

Methodists and other Evangelicals made the limits of their egalitarianism clear during this period, perhaps not coincidentally as they gained adherents and set up congregations in the more slaveholding eastern portion of the state. Dromgoole corresponded with many fellow Methodist ministers who wrote on the topic of slavery; his friend Devereaux Jarratt (who ultimately cast his lot with the Episcopalians, after much soul-searching) explained in 1788 white Evangelicals' decision to avoid poking the hornet's nest of antislavery. Jarratt made it clear to Dromgoole that, like an increasing number of clerics, he prized white unity above the rights of enslaved blacks. "I hope you wont understand that I am writing to you to prove the innocency or lawfulness of Slavery," he protested. "No. I know not your opinion on it, nor do I wish to know. Be it your Opinion what It will, I do not even wish to alter it. If our sentiments should not be alike in it, I agree to disagree, & never say a word about it. I stand neuter, I neither persuade nor dissuade any one to this or that in the case. And tho I have received many a keen letter, I have never answered one."[22] Jarratt and Dromgoole were corresponding in the wake of the General Conference's decision to rescind a rule passed in 1784 barring slaveholding local preachers from membership, a startling retreat from antislavery on the national level.[23] Significantly, black North Carolinians joined Methodist (as well as Baptist and, to a lesser extent, Presbyterian) churches despite white Evangelicals' rejection of religiously motivated antislavery. By 1837, for instance, 3,896 of the 19,208 men and women who had chosen to pursue full membership within the Methodist North Carolina Conference identified as "colored."[24] Evangelicals were expanding their networks across the color line.

Presbyterian Henry Pattillo, based in Hillsborough from 1765 through 1773 and near Henderson from 1780 through his death in 1801, penned one of the more prominent defenses of slavery in postrevolutionary North Carolina, an excellent example of Evangelicals' investment in racial privilege. In 1787 Pattillo published his *Plain Planter's Assistant*, a spiritual almanac of sorts, in which he addressed the obligations that devolved on citizens of the new country. He assumed hierarchy as natural in his little book, exhorting the heads of household who made up his primary audience to pay special attention to the various constituencies for whom he held them responsible, encouraging them to ask: "1. Is it well with thyself? 2. Is it well with thy wife? 3. Is it well with your children? 4. Is it well with your servants?" Pattillo naively asserted that, after the Revolution, patriot planters had become so humane in their practices that enslaved people had nothing to resent about their bondage. "But the slaves of my *Plain Planter*, are among the happiest of human beings," he rhapsodized. "Well clothed, and well fed; a warm cabbin, and comfortable bedding; with their hearty thriving children, growing up under their eye. Their daily labour they scarcely feel, being void of all the distressing cares of life."[25]

While Pattillo was thus engaged in wishful thinking about the benevolence of slaveholding, more Presbyterians were moving into the state. North Carolina Presbyterians had become numerous enough to form the Concord Presbytery in 1795 and in 1813 organized the Synod of North Carolina to oversee presbyteries in the eastern (Fayetteville), central (Orange), and western (Concord) portions of the state. In 1815 these three presbyteries claimed 3,859 communicants. Because Presbyterians were even more restrictive than Baptists or Methodists in their definition of membership, this figure represented a reach of at least 16,000 Carolinians.[26] David Ker, a recent immigrant from Ireland and a Presbyterian minister, both illustrated the continuing relevance of Atlantic connections and became the inaugural professor at the newly chartered University of North Carolina in 1794. When the first student arrived from Wilmington (the university drew patrons from across the state), Ker was still the only faculty member and greeted him alone. Over the next several years, more Presbyterian ministers would join the faculty, including Elisha Mitchell, Robert Chapman, and James Phillips, as well as the institution's first president, Joseph Caldwell. The preponderance of clergymen provoked some North Carolinians to worry that Presbyterians were exercising undue sectarian influence over the state's future leaders. In 1822, Caldwell defended the institution against the charge that he had given "an ascendant influence to presbyterianism in our college." "It is probable," he claimed, "that not one young man is likely to have his sentiments changed on the subject of denomination in religion while he is here."[27] Nonetheless, Caldwell presided over a cadre of largely Presbyterian intellectuals who taught a generation of future leaders of the state.

Baptists may not have occupied professorships in Chapel Hill, but they were also busy in the interval between independence and 1835 crafting institutions with a statewide reach (see figs. 6.1 and 6.2). While Baptist divisions into Anti-missionary and Free Will factions make it more difficult to estimate the scale of Baptist growth, one of the denomination's twentieth-century chroniclers estimated that the heirs of Shubal Stearns had already founded more than 250 churches by 1830, grouped into nineteen regional associations.[28] As was the case nationally, Baptists first organized beyond the association level to advance the cause of missions by pooling their resources, with education being a close second as a priority. Carolinians started their first extracongregational effort to promote missions in 1805, the Philanthropic Baptist Missionary Society. When national leaders of the denomination formed the Triennial Convention in 1814 (formally known as the General Missionary Convention of the Baptist Denomination of the United States for Foreign Missions, the Baptist analog to the national institutions formed by members of other denominations in the 1780s), Carolinians formed the North Carolina Baptist Society for Foreign Missions.

North Carolina Baptists concluded the 1830s in triumph, establishing three institutions with a high profile even outside Baptist circles. Following the example of their coreligionists in Virginia and South Carolina, Baptists formed in 1830 an organization powerful enough to unify Baptists across the state. The Baptist State Convention of North Carolina met for the first time on March 26, 1830, in Greenville. Many of the prime movers in this initiative hailed from the eastern part of the state, demonstrating how completely Baptists had erased the association of the east with Anglicanism and the west with dissenters. Thomas Meredith, one of the seven ministers present at the founding, and Charles Skinner, one of the seven laypersons, both hailed from the flatlands of Perquimans County. Meredith had drafted the constitution, which declared "the primary objects of this Convention shall be the education of young men called of God to the ministry, and approved of by the churches to which they respectively belong; the employment of missionaries within the bounds of the State and cooperation with the Baptist General Convention ... in the promotion of Missions in general." At the time of the convention's genesis, one of the founders claimed that there were 15,000 members and fourteen associations in the state, excluding Anti-missionary congregations.[29] Among the very earliest fruits of the convention's work were two institutions that would serve both Baptists and others well, the *Biblical Recorder* and Wake Forest College. Each depended for its success upon the liberality of Baptists from across the state and the ability of men and women from Down East to the mountains to imagine common cause with one another as North Carolinians.

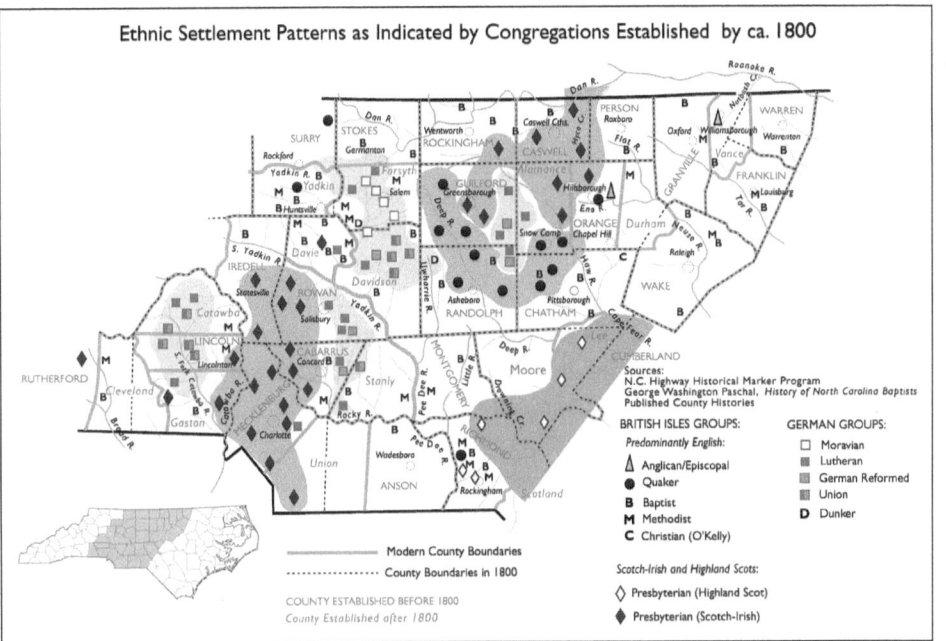

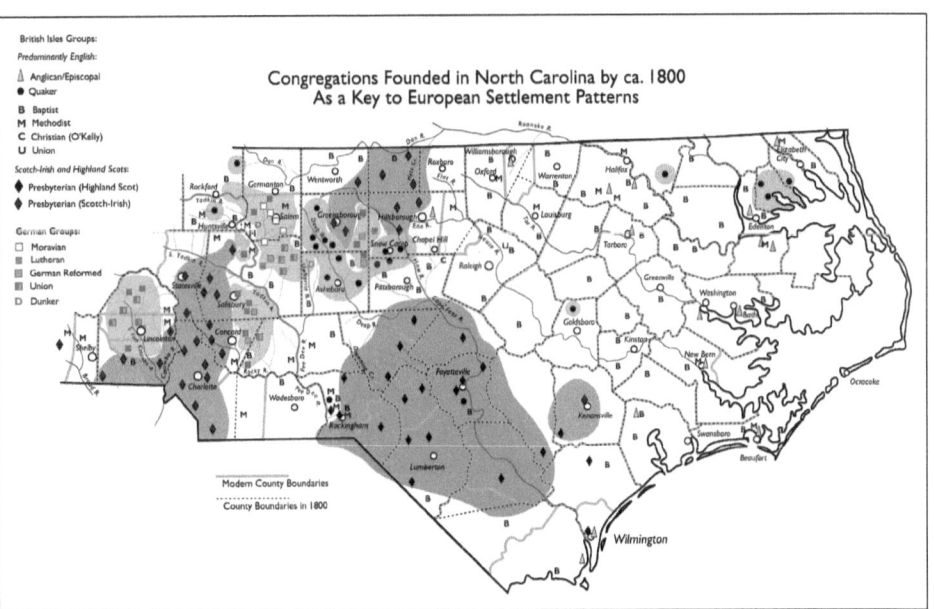

FIGURES 6.1 AND 6.2. These two maps by architectural historian Michael Southern trace ethnic settlement patterns and the establishment of various churches in eastern North Carolina and the Piedmont, c. 1800. Reproduced with the permission of Michael Southern.

African Americans found ways to participate in the multiplication of Evangelical institutions and even helped establish new transatlantic connections to West Africa. From the beginning of the modern missions' movement in 1814, U.S. Evangelicals had turned their attention overseas in the hopes of bringing "heathen" nations to Christ. Under the auspices of the American Colonization Society (1816/17), black Southerners had a key part to play in this enterprise.[30] The society established Liberia on the west coast of Africa as a destination for free black emigrants as well as enslaved individuals manumitted for the sole purpose of emigration. More black North Carolinians traveled to Liberia than did residents of any other state save Virginia before the Civil War. John Day, brother of the famous free black furniture maker Thomas Day, was only the most famous emigrant with North Carolina connections. The letters Day sent back to religious leaders in the United States constituted one of many tangible links these pioneers forged between North Carolina and Liberia.[31]

Baptists, Methodists, and to a lesser extent Presbyterians enjoyed so much success in building stronger organizations and participating in prominent ventures like the University of North Carolina that Tar Heels from other faith traditions felt pressure to convert. A Jewish couple, Henry and Rebecca Lazarus, wrote from Raleigh to Rebecca's sister, Ellen Mordecai in Richmond, about Rebecca's contemplated conversion to Christianity in the summer of 1835. "This my dear Ellen is likely to prove an eventful day to me," Rebecca confessed. "I have as you know, long been in an uneasy & anxious state of mind, caused by the change in my religious sentiments, & the impossibility under existing circumstances of acting up to them. These considerations have operated so powerfully on my mind, that I have at length resolved by a bold effort to disclose my sentiments to our dear father & pray for his indulgence & pardon."[32] Ministers from non-Evangelical traditions who did not emphasize Evangelical tenets such as the importance of being born again or the primacy of scripture likewise had a hard time carving a place for themselves. North Carolina's Episcopalians clung tenaciously to high church practices and found that they had an incredibly difficult time attracting new members as a result. In 1830 they listed a paltry thirty-one parishes in their annual report; representatives from only fourteen showed up at the meeting. The weak diocesan administration was unable to collect membership rolls from every church; the partial list, 576 communicants with thirteen parishes reporting, was not inspiring.[33]

From an institutional perspective, the 1830s represented the pinnacle of achievement for church builders from the Methodist, Baptist, and Presbyterian traditions. Evangelicals would maintain for decades a majority of the religious practitioners of the state, but rarely if ever again would the Evangelical "market share" be engrossed so completely by so few organizations. Leaders of the North Carolina Conference, Baptist State Convention, and Synod of North Carolina were each able to prevent major schism in their respective denominations for a season, with the result that the Evangelical witness within the state had more organizational coherence than it would even a decade later. Evangelicals had conquered the state and were consolidating their influence within it, at the same time that they strengthened connections with national denominations and became a source rather than a destination of international missionaries.

FRAGMENTATION AND PERSISTENCE, 1835–1875

When delegates to North Carolina's 1835 constitutional convention removed language from the state's charter prohibiting non-Protestants from serving as elected officials, they were demonstrating their high regard for fellow delegate and Roman Catholic William Gaston rather than trying to displace Evangelical Protestantism as the chief religious tradition of the state.[34] Nevertheless, the act was symbolic. Evangelicals grew in number from 1835 through the Civil War (and resumed their expansion afterward), but they also dealt with a number of persistent schisms that pitted practicing Evangelicals within the state against one another. The powerful organizations that were both engines and emblems of Evangelical success earlier in the century could not hold back divisions based on creed, region, or race. Often as a part of the same processes, the national denominations with which Carolinians were affiliated also fragmented. Tar Heel Evangelicals remained connected to Americans outside of their state, but to ever narrower segments of the population.

The Methodist, Presbyterian, and Baptist divines who built statewide and national organizations achieved success in part because they drafted codes of discipline, wrote hymnals, adopted creeds, and otherwise created standardized expressions of their faith around which the faithful could rally. The trouble with such rallying points, of course, was that marginalized persons or groups within the various denominations could define themselves against the very standards or new practices that the institution builders erected to preserve unity. When Evangelicals formed splinter groups before the 1830s, they typically followed precisely this pattern. In the 1760s and 1770s, for example, Baptists in North Carolina and Virginia argued so much over adherence to the Philadelphia Confession of Faith (1742), predestination, and other topics that they divided into Regular and Separate factions.[35] In 1792,

Methodist Elder James O'Kelly rebelled at the heavy hand of superintending bishops in the Methodist Episcopal Church as well as the church's compromise on slavery and broke off to form the "Republican Methodists."[36] This trend accelerated as church leaders formed stronger institutions. In the Methodist tradition, for instance, Carolinians in the Roanoke Conference spoke out against the power of their bishops and of the itinerants beginning in 1824. Their work culminated in the formation (alongside dissidents from other states) in the Methodist Protestant Church in 1828.[37]

Baptists dealt with a series of similar disruptions as some members reacted against the new practices of the nineteenth century. Some churchgoers did not approve of any "new measures" such as missionary societies to induce conversion, for they appeared presumptuous in the face of their Calvinist convictions.[38] Members of four associations, most prominently the storied Kehukee Association, rejected coordinated missionary efforts entirely. Alexander Campbell and his father Thomas also found the Missionary, Bible, Sunday School, and Tract Societies objectionable. Alexander Campbell believed them to be "engines" of "priestly ambition" and struck out against them publicly in 1823 when he began to publish the *Christian Baptist* (later the *Millennial Harbinger*). Thomas Campbell was the first of the Campbellites to visit North Carolina, in 1833. He headed straight for the lion's den, Thomas Meredith's Edenton Baptist Church, where he took the pulpit and taught, among other things, "that all Articles of Faith, Church Covenants, Church Constitutions, Rules of Decorum, System of Discipline, etc., are unnecessary, unscriptural and hurtful."[39] As Campbellites urged other churches to disavow the new practices of the nineteenth century, more Baptist (and some Presbyterian and Methodist) members left to join new "Union" churches, most of whom became known as "Disciples of Christ." With no insignificant irony, the Disciples formed their own statewide convention in 1857.[40]

Ecclesiology, however, was only one of several axes of division. In the late 1830s and 1840s, white Evangelicals in North Carolina joined with their coreligionists from other slave states in withdrawing from national denominations to form sectional ones more congenial to slaveholder interests. North Carolina Presbyterians, Baptists, and Methodists did not take the lead in any of these schisms, nor did they hesitate before joining the new proslavery jurisdictions. In advance of a full separation between the Old and New Schools of the Presbyterian Church, for instance, delegates to the Presbytery of Concord's fall meeting in 1836 made it clear that they would prefer to divide than quarrel with Northern abolitionists. "Rather than surrender the truth, or perpetuate the present distracting agitation," they resolved, "we will feel bound to submit to a division of the Church, upon any plan which may be found most conducive to peace and good order." North Carolina Presbyterians overwhelmingly sided with the proslavery Old School in the 1837 separation.[41]

White Methodists and Baptists made a break with their respective national organizations less than a decade later. In an August 23, 1845, editorial in the pages of the *Biblical Recorder*, the acting board of the Baptist State Convention of North Carolina made a case for separation from their Northern brethren. In contrast to the anti-institutional Campbellites, the Baptists in 1845 explicitly affirmed the denominational machinery they had created in partnership with their Northern coreligionists but insisted that they could not collaborate with those who held that slaveholding was sinful. As they expressed it, "We fully concur in the argument exhibited on different occasions in publications at the South showing the decisions above referred to, to be unconstitutional and unscriptural — at variance with the spirit of christianity, and a violation of our rights as men — inasmuch as we are virtually punished for not concurring with our would-be reformers on the question of slavery."[42]

Methodists, too, foundered on the shoals of the all-important political and religious question of slavery, dividing in the 1840s into Northern and Southern branches. When Bishop James O. Andrew inherited enslaved men and women, Northern Methodists at the General Conference of 1844 demanded that he "desist" from the exercise of his episcopal duties until he divested himself of his property in persons. Southern Methodists could not bear either the insult to Bishop Andrew or the implication that slaveholding was so villainous that it disqualified one for the bishopric. North Carolina's delegates signed on to a resolution authored by South Carolinian William Capers in which they explained that "for various reasons enumerated, the objects and purposes of the Christian ministry and church organization cannot be accomplished by them under the jurisdiction of this General Conference as now constituted." Accordingly, white Southerners formed the Methodist Episcopal Church, South at an organizational meeting in Lexington, Kentucky, in 1846.[43] Smaller sects generally followed the pattern set by the larger denominations. The North Carolina and Virginia Christian Conference, the institutional home of the descendants of O'Kelly, resolved in 1854 "that we pity those members of the Christian church in the free States, who have departed from our cherished principles ... we will no more cooperate with them until they return to the platform first adopted by the Christian Church in the United States."[44] When the major denominations fractured along slaveholding lines, white Evangelicals in North Carolina experienced a second attenuation of out-of-state bonds. After the Revolution, they had exchanged transatlantic for national ties (before reestablishing some transatlantic ties through mission work); in the sectional crisis, they exchanged national for regional connections.

African American Tar Heels did not have a choice of whether or not to remain in fellowship with Northern whites during the sectional schisms, but many of them quickly took advantage of expanded religious choices during the Civil War and Reconstruction. Missionaries from the Northern branch of the Methodist Episcopal Church and the African Methodist Episcopal (AME) and AME Zion (AMEZ) Churches were among those who accompanied the Union army south. Southern Methodist minister L. S. Burkhead took careful notes of how one AME missionary, Chaplain W. H. Hunter of the U.S. Colored Troops, took over his pulpit at Wilmington's Front Street Methodist Church in February 1865. "One week ago you were all slaves; now you are all free," Hunter preached to uproarious applause. "Thank God the armies of the Lord and of Gideon has triumphed and the Rebels have been driven back in confusion and scattered like chaff before the wind."[45] Impressed by Hunter's message of empowerment, more than six hundred men and women first tried to seize the property of Front Street Methodist from the white membership and subsequently withdrew to form St. Stephen's AME Church. Elsewhere in North Carolina, AMEZ ministers were the ones assisting black Methodists in forming new churches. James Walker Hood, who traveled to North Carolina as a missionary from Bridgeport, Connecticut, not only helped organize several AMEZ congregations but also became one of the most important Reconstruction-era leaders among the state's freedmen. Hood chaired, for instance, the first Freedmen's State Convention in late September 1865.[46] When black Methodists left their churches to form AME or AMEZ congregations, they were exchanging bonds with white Methodists in North Carolina for stronger bonds of affinity with black Methodists across the nation. Ultimately, as James Campbell has chronicled, black Methodists also established new international ties on their own terms through mission work in Africa.[47]

Black Baptists in North Carolina did not necessarily affiliate immediately with an organization national in scope like the AME or AMEZ Churches, but they nonetheless formed yet another layer of religious networks in the state when they withdrew from white-controlled churches in massive numbers.[48] The pace at which black Baptists withdrew varied. In some churches, such as Bethel Baptist Church in Perquimans County, black members received permission to leave relatively quickly. At an August 1866 congregational meeting, "an order was passed granting letters of dismission to our colored brethren and sisters to organize a church to themselves."⁴⁹ In other congregations, North Carolinians of color waited before making a break.

For instance, in 1867 the Chowan Association retained 1,726 of the 3,175 black members listed in 1861 (54 percent), the Cape Fear Association increased the number of black members from 656 in 1860 to 708 in 1867 (a gain of 8 percent), and the Raleigh Association still held onto 818 of its 883 antebellum black members in 1867 (93 percent).⁵⁰ By the late 1870s, however, almost all black members had left white-controlled churches. Perhaps more importantly, even though black Baptists may have struggled nationally to coordinate their activities, they were successful on the state level. In 1867, representatives from independent black Baptist churches organized the Educational and Missionary Convention of North Carolina in Goldsboro.⁵¹

Evangelicals in North Carolina in the 1870s belonged to more denominations with more complex ties stretching out of the state—some based on creed, others on a combination of creed and race or region. Despite this fragmentation, on a cultural level Evangelicals continued to dominate the religious life of the state. Moreover, the denominational mix in terms of denominational families, rather than individual denominations with a shared governance structure, remained fairly stable. Taken together, Baptist, Methodist, and Presbyterian churches still accounted for 87 percent of the 718,310 seats in houses of worship recorded in the U.S. Census of 1890.⁵² Unlike the 1830s, however, when the North Carolina Conference, the State Convention, and the Synod of North Carolina could speak for the vast majority of the state's churchgoing population, Evangelicals by the 1870s relied on officers of more than a dozen denominations to represent them, reflecting the country's own painful divisions. The denominational map would become even more complicated, and the matrix of interstate and international connections more complex, in the late nineteenth century and beyond. New religious groups, some Evangelical Protestant and others not, penetrated the state and created new ties binding Carolinians to outsiders. Pentecostals embodied this trend, carrying their charismatic Gospel into the state in the first years of the twentieth century.⁵³

NOTES

1. Entry for September 26, 1672 ("ye 26th of ye 9th moth"), in *Journal of George Fox*, ed. Norman Penney, 2 vols. (1911; repr., New York: Octagon Books, 1973), 2:235-36.

2. See, e.g., James L. Peacock, Harry L. Watson, and Carrie R. Matthews, eds., *The American South in a Global World* (Chapel Hill: University of North Carolina Press, 2005); and Cornelis A. van Minnen and Manfred Berg, eds., *The U.S. South and Europe: Transatlantic Relations in the Nineteenth and Twentieth Centuries* (Lexington: University Press of Kentucky, 2013). In recent years scholars have taken this enthusiasm for transatlantic con-

nections back to the Civil War era, with such titles as David T. Gleeson and Simon Lewis, eds., *The Civil War as Global Conflict: Transnational Meanings of the American Civil War* (Columbia: University of South Carolina Press, 2014); and Don Doyle, *The Cause of All Nations: An International History of the American Civil War* (New York: Basic Books, 2014).

3. In addition to the titles cited further below, good examples include Jon F. Sensbach, *A Separate Canaan: The Making of an Afro-Moravian World in North Carolina, 1763-1840* (Chapel Hill: University of North Carolina Press, 1998); and Claude Clegg III, *The Price of Liberty: African Americans and the Making of Liberia* (Chapel Hill: University of North Carolina Press, 2004).

4. "[1663] Charter to the Lords Proprietors of Carolina," in John Cheney, ed., *North Carolina Government: A Narrative and Statistical History* (Raleigh: North Carolina Department of the Secretary of State, 1981), 107-8, 138.

5. For an account of Cary's Rebellion, the conflict that both epitomized and helped curtail Quaker political influence, see Noeleen McIlvenna, *The Struggle for North Carolina, 1660-1713* (Chapel Hill: University of North Carolina Press, 2009), 126-47.

6. "Evangelical" remains a somewhat capacious term. The operable definition here, with noted exceptions, follows Mark Noll, D. W. Bebbington, and George Rawlyk, *Evangelicalism: Comparative Studies of Popular Protestantism in North America, the British Isles, and Beyond, 1700-1900* (New York: Oxford University Press, 1994), 6. Noll et al. identify four defining characteristics of Evangelicalism: "biblicism (a reliance on the Bible as ultimate religious authority), conversionism (a stress on the New Birth), activism (an energetic, individualistic approach to religious duties and social involvement), and crucicentrism (a focus on Christ's redeeming work as the heart of essential Christianity)."

7. Quotation from "August Spangenberg: The Moravian Diary," quoted in Andreas Lixl, ed., *Memories of Carolinian Immigrants: Autobiographies, Diaries, and Letters from Colonial Times to the Present* (Lanham, Md.: University Press of America, 2009), 37-38. For works on the North Carolina Moravians especially sensitive to geography, see Leland Ferguson, *God's Fields: Landscape, Religion, and Race in Moravian Wachovia* (Gainesville: University Press of Florida, 2009); and S. Scott Rohrer, *Hope's Promise: Religion and Acculturation in the Southern Backcountry* (Tuscaloosa: University of Alabama Press, 2005). For *The Settlement Scene*, see Ferguson, *God's Fields*, 73.

8. S. Scott Rohrer, *Wandering Souls: Protestant Migrations in America, 1630-1865* (Chapel Hill: University of North Carolina Press, 2010), 110-14.

9. Maloy A. Huggins, *A History of North Carolina Baptists, 1727-1932* (Raleigh: General Board of the Baptist State Convention of North Carolina, 1967), 50-52 and app. A; John Sparks, *The Roots of Appalachian Christianity: The Life and Legacy of Elder Shubal Stearns* (Lexington: University Press of Kentucky, 2001), esp. 59-65. Much of this progress happened in the first few years of Stearns's arrival; he had already baptized nine hundred souls by 1757.

10. Huggins, *History of North Carolina Baptists*, 65-70.

11. Ernest Trice Thompson, *Presbyterians in the South*, Vol. 1, *1607-1861* (Richmond, Va.: John Knox Press, 1963), 61-65; Walter H. Conser Jr. and Robert J. Cain, *Presbyterians in North Carolina: Race, Politics, and Religious Identity in Historical Perspective* (Knoxville: University of Tennessee Press, 2012), 31-40; Herbert Snipes Turner, *Church in the Old Fields: Hawfields Presbyterian Church and Community in North Carolina* (Chapel Hill: University of North Carolina Press, 1962), 46-51.

12. George Soelle diary, October 19, 1771, quoted in Marjoleine Kars, *Breaking Loose Together: The Regulator Rebellion in Pre-revolutionary North Carolina* (Chapel Hill: University of North Carolina Press, 2002), 93.

13. Stephen B. Weeks, *Southern Quakers and Slavery: A Study in Institutional History* (1896; repr. New York: Bergman, 1968), 206–7.

14. Sparks, *Roots of Appalachian Christianity*, 30–31. In 2007, the Cooperative Baptist Fellowship of North Carolina inaugurated the Martha Stearns Marshall Month of Preaching to highlight female preaching within the Baptist tradition.

15. Herman Husbands, *An Impartial Relation of the First and Causes of the Recent Differences in Public Affairs* (1770), quoted in Kars, *Breaking Loose Together*, 124. Marjoleine Kars argues for a more prominent role for religious actors than do some other scholars. On Presbyterian opposition, see Conser and Cain, *Presbyterians in North Carolina*, 41–45.

16. For instance, Methodists met in 1784 to form the Methodist Episcopal Church; Presbyterians in 1787 to form the Presbyterian Church in the United States of America; and Episcopalians in 1789 to form the Protestant Episcopal Church in the United States of America.

17. "Constitution of North Carolina of 1776," in Cheney, *North Carolina Government*, 814.

18. *Minutes of the Annual Conferences of the Methodist Episcopal Church, for the Years 1773–1828* (New York: T. Mason and G. Lane, 1840), 7. Name misspelled "Dromgole" in minutes.

19. Ibid., 22, 69.

20. Ratio derived from H. K. Carroll, *The Religious Forces of the United States* (New York: Christian Literature Co., 1893), xxxv. Carroll's figures are notably lower than those used by Robert A. Baird in *Religion in America* (New York: Harper and Brothers, 1844), 264–65.

21. *Minutes of the Annual Conferences of the Methodist Episcopal Church, for the Years 1829–1839*, 4 vols. (New York: T. Mason and G. Lane, 1840), 2:525–26.

22. Devereaux Jarratt to Edward Dromgoole, March 22, 1788, Edward Dromgoole Papers (no. 230), Southern Historical Collection, University of North Carolina at Chapel Hill.

23. For a general survey of the Methodists' retreat from moderate antislavery, see Donald G. Mathews, *Slavery and Methodism: A Chapter in American Morality, 1780–1845* (Princeton, N.J.: Princeton University Press, 1965); for Upper South Evangelicals' shifts on slavery more generally, see Charles F. Irons, *The Origins of Proslavery Christianity: White and Black Evangelicals in Colonial and Antebellum Virginia* (Chapel Hill: University of North Carolina Press, 2008).

24. *Minutes of the Annual Conferences, 1829–1839*, 2:525–26.

25. Henry Pattillo, *The Plain Planter's Assistant; Containing an Address to Husbands and Wives, Children and Servants; With Some Helps for Instruction by Catechisms; and Examples of Devotion for Families: With a Brief Paraphrase on the Lord's Prayer* (Wilmington, N.C.: James Adams, 1787), 7, 22–23. On Pattillo, see also Turner, *Church in the Old Fields*, 52–78; on this moment in Presbyterian thought, Jewel L. Spangler, "Proslavery Presbyterians: Virginia's Conservative Dissenters in the Age of Revolution," *Journal of Presbyterian History*, 98, no. 2 (Summer 2000): 111–24.

26. Conser and Cain, *Presbyterians in North Carolina*, 48; *Minutes of the General Assembly of the Presbyterian Church in the United States of America, from Its Organization A.D. 1789 to A.D. 1820 Inclusive* (Philadelphia: Presbyterian Board of Publication, 1847), 603; Carroll, *Religious Forces*, xxxv.

27. Joseph Caldwell to ?, April 20, 1822, Joseph Caldwell Papers (no. 127), Southern Historical Collection.

28. Huggins, *North Carolina Baptists*, 264.

29. This account of the convention's formation follows Huggins, *North Carolina Baptists*, 227–33; membership estimate, 223.

30. Charles F. Irons, "Zion in Black and White: Missionary Work in the Old South," in *The Old South's Modern Worlds: Slavery, Region, and Nation in the Age of Progress*, ed. L. Diane Barnes, Brian Schoen, and Frank Towers (New York: Oxford University Press, 2011), 209–27.

31. Eric Burin has assembled the most complete reckoning of migrants sponsored by the American Colonization Society. Of the 10,138 individuals in his data set (covering 1820–60), 1,312 hailed from North Carolina, compared with 3,444 from Virginia. Burin, *Slavery and the Peculiar Solution: A History of the American Colonization Society*, (Gainesville: University Press of Florida, 2005), tables 4 and 5.

32. Henry and Rebecca M. Lazarus to Ellen Mordecai, July 29, 1835, Mordecai Family Papers (no. 847), Southern Historical Collection. See also Emily Bingham, "Though Knowest Not What a Day May Bring Forth: Intellect, Power, Conversion, and Apostasy in the Life of Rachel Mordecai Lazarus (1788–1838)," in *Religion in the American South: Protestants and Others in History and Culture*, ed. Beth Barton Schweiger and Donald G. Mathews (Chapel Hill: University of North Carolina Press, 2004), 67–98.

33. *Journal of the Proceedings of the 14th Annual Convention of the Protestant Episcopal Church in the State of North Carolina* (Fayetteville, N.C.: Edward J. Hale, 1830), 9–14.

34. Ronnie W. Faulkner, "Constitution of 1835," North Carolina History Project, http://northcarolinahistory.org/encyclopedia/constitution-of-1835/ (accessed April 21, 2014). For the text of the amended provision, see "Amendments of 1835," in Cheney, *North Carolina Government*, 822.

35. Sparks, *Roots of Appalachian Christianity*, 39–40; Irons, *Origins of Proslavery Christianity*, 39, 69.

36. O'Kelly promptly began a ministry in North Carolina; for a contemporary treatment of the schism that stresses the institutional dynamics, see Russell E. Richey, "Francis Asbury, James O'Kelly, and Methodism's Growing Pains," *Virginia United Methodist Heritage: Bulletin of the Virginia Conference Historical Society* 27, no. 2 (2001): 24–40.

37. Edward J. Drinkhouse, *History of Methodist Reform: Synoptical of General Methodism, 1703 to 1898*, 2 vols. (Norwood, Mass.: Norwood Press for the Board of Publication of the Methodist Protestant Church, 1899), 2:84–87, 201–2.

38. For the timeline, see Huggins, *North Carolina Baptists*, 222–23., For the best single-volume treatment of the growth of reform initiatives such as benevolence and mission societies in the South, see John W. Kuykendall, *Southern Enterprize: The Work of National Evangelical Societies in the Antebellum South* (Westport, Conn.: Greenwood Press, 1982).

39. Huggins, *North Carolina Baptists*, 219–21; Charles Crossfield Ware, *North Carolina Disciples of Christ: A History of Their Rise and Progress, and of Their Contribution to Their General Brotherhood* (St. Louis: Christian Board of Publication, 1927), 58–64. Quotation from Alexander Campbell in 1823, quoted in Garnett Ryland, *The Baptists of Virginia, 1699-1926* (Richmond: Virginia Baptist Board of Missions and Education, 1955), 246.

40. Ware, *North Carolina Disciples of Christ*, 124–27.

41. Thompson, *Presbyterians in the South*, 391.

42. "Statement and Appeal to the Baptists of North Carolina," *Biblical Recorder*, August 23, 1845.

43. *Journal of the General Conference of the Methodist Episcopal Church Held in the City of New York, 1844* (New York: G. Lane and C. B. Tippett, for the Methodist Episcopal Church, 1844), 135.

44. *Minutes of the Annual Session of the North Carolina and Virginia Christian Conference* (1854), Belk Archives, Elon University.

45. L. S. Burkhead, "History of the Difficulties of the Pastorate of the Front Street Methodist Church, Wilmington, N.C., for the Year 1865," *Trinity College Historical Society Historical Papers* 8 (1908–9): 35–118; quotations, 42.

46. For the best account of Hood's ministry in North Carolina, see Sandy Dwayne Martin, *For God and Race: The Religious and Political Leadership of AMEZ Bishop James Walker Hood* (Columbia: University of South Carolina Press, 1999). For religion and Reconstruction more generally, Roberta Sue Alexander, "North Carolina Churches Face Emancipation and the Freedmen: An Analysis of the Role of Religion during Presidential Reconstruction, 1865–1867," *University of Dayton Review* 9, no. 3 (1972): 47–65.

47. James T. Campbell, *Songs of Zion: The African Methodist Episcopal Church in the United States and South Africa* (Chapel Hill: University of North Carolina Press, 1998).

48. On the challenge of building a national denomination, see James Melvin Washington, *Frustrated Fellowship: The Black Quest for Social Power* (1986; repr. Macon, Ga.: Mercer University Press, 2004).

49. Minutes of August 1866, Bethel Baptist Church (Perquimans County), CRMF 151, North Carolina Baptist Historical Society, Wake Forest University, Winston-Salem, N.C.

50. *Minutes of the Sixty-First Annual Session of the Chowan Baptist Association ... 1867* (Raleigh, N.C.: Hufham and Hughes, 1867); *Minutes of the Annual Session of the Cape Fear Association ... 1867* (Raleigh, N.C.: Mills and Hughes, 1867); *Minutes of the Sixty-Second Annual Session of the Raleigh Baptist Association ... 1867* (Raleigh, N.C.: Biblical Recorder Publishing Co., 1867).

51. J. A. Whitted, *A History of the Negro Baptists of North Carolina* (Raleigh, N.C.: Edwards and Broughton Printing Co., 1908), 34, http://docsouth.unc.edu/church/whitted/whitted.html.

52. Historical Census Browser, University of Virginia, Geospatial and Statistical Data Center, http://mapserver.lib.virginia.edu/collections/stats/histcensus/index.html (accessed April 23, 2014).

53. Randall Stephens, *The Fire Spreads: Holiness and Pentecostalism in the American South* (Cambridge, Mass.: Harvard University Press, 2008).

MONEY IN THE BANK
AFRICAN AMERICAN WOMEN, FINANCE, AND FREEDOM IN NEW BERN, NORTH CAROLINA, 1868–1874

Karin Zipf

"Should [I] die with money in the bank it is to go to Gatsey Cole." These were the instructions of Gatsey Williams when she opened a bank account at the New Bern branch of the Freedman's Savings and Trust Company on June 5, 1874. She did not intend to pass her savings to her husband, Sharper J. Williams. Her husband, a farmer in New Bern, likely knew of her account, as he had one too. Instead, she directed it to her namesake, probably a cousin or niece. Williams specified that Gatsey Cole lived in Goldsboro with her mother, Katie Cole, and likely she included these instructions as a gift to her namesake or to pay back some debt to the Cole family.[1]

There is no surviving record to show that bank authorities honored Gatsey Williams's request. They may not have followed her wishes as, except in limited cases, North Carolina law in 1874 dictated that husbands generally controlled their wife's property. Also, it is likely that the Williams's savings, along with those of many thousands of other Americans, vanished into the ether of the economic recession in 1873. The National Freedman's Savings and Trust Company, a victim of mismanagement and default, closed its doors in July 1874. However, Gatsey Williams's request, her husband's tacit approval, and the bank cashier's willingness to record her wishes indicate that freedmen and freedwomen embraced meanings of property that recognized a degree of married women's independence and autonomy, concepts that challenged prevailing North Carolina law.

Federal records are a treasure trove for the North Carolina historian. Records of corporate banks chartered by Congress offer historians important evidence about not only the state's economic history but also its social and cultural history. Even the seemingly barest of economic data offer insight into historical meanings of property, patterns of ownership, gender relations, work, inheritance, and family. The Freedman's Savings and Trust Company deposit registers thus offer special access into the past, especially

TABLE 7.1. Recorded gender of depositors to Freedman's Savings and Trust Company, New Bern branch

DEPOSITORS	MALE (%)	FEMALE (%)	TOTAL
All depositors	1,301 (70.5)	545 (29.5)	1,846
From New Bern	620 (70.2)	263 (29.8)	883
From James City	81 (69)	36 (31)	117
From the countryside and surrounding counties	286 (71.5)	114 (28.5)	400

Source: *Freedman's Bank Database; Zipf, "Promises of Opportunity," 100.*

when considered alongside the rich and substantive records of the Bureau of Refugees, Freedmen, and Abandoned Lands, Southern Claims Commission, and U.S. Pension records.

The bank application records include many specifics on each depositor. For example, on their applications, Gatsey (age forty) and Sharper (age fifty-four) Williams provided their residence as Lane's Branch in New Bern and previous residences in Bertie and Wayne Counties. Sharper Williams listed his occupation. The couple had no children. Gatsey listed no parents, and Sharper claimed his parents as deceased. The cashier who took and processed the application noted Gatsey's complexion as "black" and her husband's as "dark." On his application, Sharper signed his full name, and Gatsey signed hers with an "X."

Recent historiography on the economic and cultural transitions of African Americans from slavery to freedom allow researchers the deep context necessary for understanding the challenges of emancipation buried in these records. The data, then, offer historians clues into gendered meanings of property and work and encourage further inquiry for new areas of research in North Carolina's past.[2] Approximately two-thirds of the New Bern bank application records have survived. This essay examines the data from the existing records. Women account for nearly one-third (545) of the 1,846 extant depositor records from the New Bern branch of the Freedman's Savings and Trust Company (table 7.1). In 1870, these 545 women represented only a fraction of the 3,829 freedmen and freedwomen living in New Bern, and an even smaller proportion of the 12,116 freedmen and freedwomen who lived in Craven County.

Yet a population sample of about 4 percent is still a considerable pool worthy of inquiry. This essay reports on two chief findings from an analysis of the bank data. First, the data indicate that, after slavery, African American women claimed significant economic autonomy and influence in public spaces and at work. Second, the data strongly confirm findings in recent scholarship that in emancipation freedmen and freedwomen adapted free labor and free market principles to their extralegal values of property derived in slavery. This congruence of free labor ideology and extralegal custom helps explain why African American male delegates to the North Carolina 1868 constitutional convention spearheaded proposals and legislation supporting women's rights to property, suffrage, and divorce.[3]

FREE LABOR IDEOLOGY, UNIONISM, AND THE FREEDMAN'S SAVINGS AND TRUST COMPANY IN NEW BERN

The directors of the Freedman's Savings and Trust Company opened North Carolina's first branch bank in New Bern in January 1866. New Bern's proclivity toward Unionism throughout the war had set a strong foundation of support for a bank for freedpeople. The city had been a stronghold of Whiggism before secession. The Civil War had fueled Unionist spirits. Confederate sympathizers fled in 1862 when Union General Ambrose E. Burnside captured New Bern and transformed it into the center of Federal occupation in eastern North Carolina. Refugees fleeing their masters gathered on confiscated and abandoned lands. Out of 10,000 contrabands throughout the state, 7,500 camped around New Bern. From among these refugees and other sympathetic whites, Burnside mustered two colored and two white Union regiments.[4]

Many future depositors had settled among nearly 3,000 refugees at the Trent River settlement. Reverend Horace James, superintendent of Negro affairs in North Carolina, established the camp from abandoned lands south of New Bern to accommodate the refugees that were pouring behind Union lines. Throughout the war many Trent River settlement inhabitants remained self-sufficient. A few months after the close of the war James marveled at the progress the freedmen and freedwomen had made in establishing a permanent and self-supporting settlement. "Many of the people," he reported, "are laying up property, own mules, horses and carts, or are keeping little shops, or running some mechanical trade ... in fact, the village is now self-supporting." The income of the people, he said, exceeded the expenses in the form of rations by several hundred dollars. The community also consisted of other buildings, including a Freedmen's Bureau office, a school, a blacksmith shop, a hospital, and several churches. By the war's end the settlement, later renamed James City for its founder, had become an established part of New Bern's community, and the freedmen and freedwomen there joined the black

FIGURE 7.1. With the Union occupation of eastern North Carolina early in the Civil War, thousands of slaves fled to New Bern. Shown here are the headquarters of Vincent Collyer, superintendent of the poor, in *Frank Leslie's Illustrated Newspaper*, June 14, 1862. Photograph courtesy of the North Carolina Collection, University of North Carolina at Chapel Hill.

majority in the area. By 1870 African Americans comprised 59 percent of the county populace and 66 percent of the city residents.[5]

Although Union occupation had infused people and energy into New Bern, the city's financial atmosphere was a disaster. The war had devastated North Carolina banks. Confederate bonds were worthless, state bonds were depreciated, and credit sources were limited. New Bern's banking facilities, the Merchants Bank, the Bank of Commerce, and a branch of the Bank of North Carolina, had sputtered through the Civil War. Although these institutions had managed to survive the conflict, congressional action in Washington sealed their doom by declaring a 10 percent levy on all notes issued by state banks. This act, plus the enormous losses in Confederate and state bonds and notes, caused every state bank to cease operations. Charles Slover and Alonzo T. Jenkins, respective presidents of the Merchants Bank and Bank of Commerce, kept their banks afloat at least until 1867 but eventually succumbed to the desperate times. The state's branch bank closed in 1865. The entire state system was bankrupted by 1868 and liquidated by 1874. In 1866, the North Carolina legislature chartered one savings bank, the New Bern Savings Institution, which never opened primarily because it lacked sufficient capital. During the early postwar years the dearth of capital impeded the development of agriculture, commerce, and shipping. Even less cash existed for retention in a nascent interstate savings bank for the former slaves.[6]

Four new banks opened in New Bern shortly after the New Bern branch of the Freedman's Savings and Trust Company began to accept deposits. These four banks did not compete with the freedpeople's bank, which was strictly a savings institution. Records suggest that the several banks operated relatively harmoniously alongside the Freedman's Savings and Trust Company. The first bank, operating under the requirements of the National Bank Act of 1863, was the First National Bank of New Bern (1866). Capitalized from mostly Northern sources at $100,000, twice that required of Congress, this bank declared a 7 percent yield on each account. Three private banks, considered less financially stable because they required no charter or other form of approval by state authorities, opened in 1867. All three banks, the S. T. Jones and Company, Disosway and Guion, and R. H. Rountree and Company, operated on relatively congenial terms with the Freedman's Savings and Trust Company. The cashier for each company conducted at least one transaction with the bank during its tenure in New Bern, probably for goodwill measures.[7]

New Bern's five brand-new banks helped stoke the free labor economy in New Bern. The banking authorities who ran them shared a common mission with other former Unionists, Republicans, and military officials in the community: to instill among New Bern's former slaves and slaveholders Northern beliefs in a free labor ideology and to educate them on the principles of a free market economy. In 1867, Congress divided the Southern states into five military districts and outlined a strict process for each state's readmission to the Union. Among these requirements, Congress required each state to rewrite its constitution in conformity with the Reconstruction Amendments.[8] Agents of the Freedmen's Bureau, a branch of the military known as the Bureau of Refugees, Freedmen, and Abandoned Lands, served a critical role in the free labor economy. They enforced labor contracts and mediated disputes between whites and former slaves to protect freedpeople's claims to freedom. Bureau agents saw themselves as defenders of the 1866 Civil Rights Act, a U.S. law that invalidated the Black Codes, a series of state laws that the bureau's assistant commissioner Eliphalet Whittlesey, head of North Carolina operations, argued would allow Southern whites to "re-establish slavery just as it was before ... [or] they would enact laws which would make the blacks virtually slaves." Repulsed by slavery, bureau agents encouraged free labor relations. According to historian Thomas Holt, bureau agents pursued free labor relations "not merely to make ex-slaves work, but to make them into a working class, that is, a class that would submit to the market because it adhered to the *values* of a bourgeois society, regularity, punctuality, sobriety, frugality, and economic rationality." These labor values also shaped the way military authorities and agents mediated such family issues as marriage, divorce, child custody, and women's roles at work and in the home. Northern ideas about free labor also operated alongside Northern attitudes about the nuclear family and women's place in the domestic arena.[9]

The Freedman's Savings and Trust Company thus operated in this nascent postwar banking environment as a savings institution designed to instill free labor ideology among the newly freed men and women in New Bern and its vicinity. The directors of the bank had designed the facility to be a simple mutual savings bank established for the benefit of the former slaves. Politicians and bank officials embraced the idea that the freedpeople, mired for generations in slavery, must first learn good saving habits before entering more entrepreneurial activities such as borrowing, investment, and extending credit on their own. Congress chartered the bank on March 3, 1865. The act declared that the company would receive deposits "by or on behalf of persons heretofore held in slavery in the United States, or their descendants, and investing the same in the stocks, bonds, Treasury notes, or other securities of the United States." The bank was a nonprofit concern that had no stockholders; depositors owned all of the bank's assets in proportion to the deposits of each. The Freedman's Savings and Trust would receive the freedpeople's deposits, invest everything except a sizable available fund in government securities, and return all the profits to the freedpeople in the form of interest, a rate that over the years fluctuated from 0 to 6 percent. In the 1870s bank officials restructured the company to invest in real estate, which, in 1873, spelled the company's doom. But these early paternalistic intentions tried to give the freedpeople some sense of limited ownership, much like a parent would for a child.[10] The newly freed slaves evidenced plenty of thrift and economic rationality, mainly in their pursuit of land and home ownership. In his annual report for the year 1867, Lieutenant Colonel Stephen Moore, a Freedmen's Bureau agent, remarked that the freedmen "have all an intense desire to own land, and often stand in their own light, by working two or three acres of land for themselves in preference to hiring themselves out for $12 per month and board." Bank cashier Charles A. Nelson painstakingly recorded what depositors did with their money when they removed it from their accounts. He reported that depositors spent $9,240 for land in seventy-seven purchases, averaging 15 acres each. Sixty-six freedpeople used their money to buy houses (total $10,667.44), farm improvements (total $15,668.91), and on general business ($87,068.28). He listed $1,275 for education and $14,539.09 for personal and family comfort. Another $6,600 was spent on liquor, tobacco, and "fast living," chiefly by ex-soldiers receiving bounties. Agriculture and commerce were big business in New Bern. Bank records suggest that depositors used their funds to invest in real estate and engage in the emerging commercial economy.[11]

Bank officials worked closely with the Freedmen's Bureau military disbursing station to make it simple for veterans and their widows to deposit funds in the Freedman's Savings and Trust. Nelson had his office in the same building as Freedmen's Bureau agent Major Andrew Coats, who operated the military disbursing station. Nelson's proximity to Coats allowed people to receive, cash, and deposit their bounty and pension checks all in the same building. By August 1867, soldiers and their dependents began receiving their long-awaited disbursements. Of seventeen discharged soldiers from Company A of the Fourteenth U.S. Colored Heavy Artillery who received their bounty money on January 12, 1868, five deposited money at the bank. Because every bounty check for these soldiers equaled $200.00, it is likely that each man's first deposit was substantial. By 1874, discharged military personnel and their families were still receiving checks and depositing them in the bank. Not all of the depositors informed the bank cashier the source of their money. Approximately one hundred depositors listed sons and husbands who served, some of whom died while enlisted. Jane Newby, whose son died while serving the Union, deposited part of his $206.04 bounty check at the bank. Others mentioned that their prolonged military service had just ended. A few prompted Nelson to write "portion of bounty" as comments on their deposit cards.[12]

Women married to deceased soldiers collected their husband's pension only as long as they did not remarry. With that income, women could remain independent. Of the 545 women in this study, 148 (27 percent) were widows, though not all benefited from pensions. To claim this money, a woman filed a "Widow or Dependent Mother" claim form with military disbursement officer Coats. Once the claim was processed, the widow or mother could receive eight to twelve dollars per month, and according to the pension notice, this payment would "continue during life, unless she shall again marry, in which case it is no longer payable after the date of such marriage."[13]

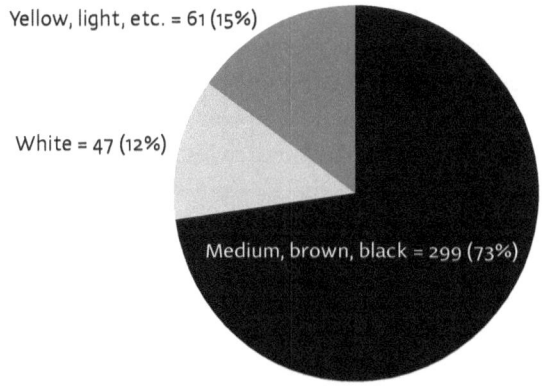

FIGURE 7.2. Recorded complexions of female depositors to Freedman's Savings and Trust Company, New Bern branch, 1869–1874. From Zipf, "Promises of Opportunity," 108, fig. 3.1.

Bounty money provided the means for women across racial lines to open accounts. For identification purposes, bank cashiers listed depositors' complexions, as illustrated in figure 7.2. Of 407 female depositors for whom the cashier listed a complexion, 360 (88 percent) were black, brown, yellow, or light skinned, and 47 (12 percent) identified as white. Many of the white women were the wives and daughters of local Republicans and merchants. Others were the widows and daughters of soldiers who had died while enlisted in one of the area's two Union regiments for white men. Some Northern states accepted married women's claims to property in both law and custom; thus, New Bernians were more tolerant than most Southerners to the idea of married women's separate property ownership.[14]

Parmelia Bateman, a white woman, opened an account and deposited her deceased husband's bounty money in December 1869. He had served in the First Federal Regiment of North Carolina Troops and died at a Union military hospital while stationed at Morehead City. Triphemia Haskett's aunt, Mary F. Pittman, opened an account as Triphemia's guardian and deposited the money that the young girl's father had earned for his service in Company F of the Second North Carolina Regiment. Annie Coats, wife of Freedmen's Bureau agent Andrew Coats, opened and closed six accounts at the bank, while Emma Nelson, wife of bank cashier Nelson, opened two accounts in her own name. Nelson's mother, Jane C. Nelson, also opened an account. The family of I. Edwin West, a white Republican who served as the clerk of superior court in 1868, opened three accounts, one for each of his two daughters and another by his wife Annie. Wives of other prominent white Republicans opened accounts, including Emeline Kehoe, who was married to Robert C. Kehoe, New Bern's coroner in 1868, and Harriet Lehman, wife of Robert C. Lehman, a local attorney.[15]

The U.S. Pension Office required proof of marriage, which some couples that had married in slavery could not provide. Celia Simmons, who opened a bank account, received $500.00 on behalf of her husband Nicholas Simmons. Celia claimed that during the war she and Nicholas ran away to New Bern and lived in a shanty together. Not long after arriving there, Nicholas enlisted and was killed. Simmons's pension checks were stopped in May 1873 because the pension office said that it could not determine whether Celia and Nicholas had actually "lived together as husband and wife." It was a facile reason to end her pension checks, as slaves were forbidden to marry and, often, could or would not provide white witnesses to lend the kind of credibility that white Union officers wanted for the file.[16]

Unless they were sure a potential husband could provide at least as much security, soldiers' widows and mothers refused to remarry. Margaret Dudley, an African American, fought to protect her right to her dead husband's pension checks. Since 1850, Margaret and her husband Elias had lived together as husband and wife. Together they raised four children, and in 1864 Elias enlisted and was killed. Margaret collected his bounty and monthly pension, and on September 15, 1871, she opened an account at the Freedman's Savings and Trust. As time passed, Margaret opened and closed three more accounts until the bank closed in 1874. With her money she purchased a small lot and a house in New Bern for herself and her children. To supplement her income, she took in sewing and wash and kept boarders.[17]

Life continued relatively uninterrupted for Margaret and her family until 1873, when the pension office discontinued her checks without an apparent reason. Margaret voiced her complaints to the pension office. "I think my Pension was stoped," she reasoned, "by the alledged charge I had remarried. This was not or is not true. I have never remarried, was never but once and that was to Elias Dudley my deceased husband." Special Agent G. N. Ragsdale, a federal officer for the pension office, reported that she had married one of her boarders, John Ireland, a railroad worker, and had had a child by him. Margaret, however, argued that Ragsdale had fabricated the charge. "I never had any intention of marrying him never thought of any such thing." Thanks to an affidavit from her pastor, Samuel Foy (another depositor), who stated he had no knowledge of a marital union between Margaret and Ireland, Margaret's pension of $12.00 a month was reinstated. Margaret Dudley probably did not think that her relatively generous pension checks were worth losing to John Ireland's meager wages as a railroad worker. After all, she had to provide for four children. For Margaret Dudley and a few other black women, remaining a widow was an attractive alternative to remarrying.[18]

The Freedman's Savings Trust officials, military officers, and Freedmen's Bureau agents worked closely with one another to encourage their vision of free labor ideology and free market principles in the former slaves. Labor contracts reflected Northern values in free labor ideology. U.S. Army pensions in bank accounts affirmed free market principles. In New Bern, these officials had purposefully intended women's participation in the free labor economy yet had not expected that women, by the many hundreds, would assume such prominent roles in the free market economy by banking their cash at the Freedman's Savings and Trust Company.

MEANINGS OF PROPERTY IN FREEDOM

Freedmen and freedwomen embraced the bank, a free market concept, because it harmonized with their views of property before the war. In slavery, the freedpeople had developed sophisticated understandings of property, both legal and extralegal. Before the war, generations of slaves acutely understood both the vagaries of an economic system that defined them as chattel and learned how to adapt in a society that legally refused to recognize their claims to property.

Among slaves, property ownership was common. The median claim in the Southern Claims Commission by former slaves was $300.00. Masters permitted property ownership among slaves because the practice allowed plantations to operate more smoothly and efficiently. Moses Grandy, who escaped slavery in North Carolina, explained that masters generally allowed slaves to clear land for themselves because the slaves' land clearings produced a buffer for the master's crops against damage by raccoons and squirrels. Historian Dylan C. Penningroth argues that, although considered "customary," slaves' property ownership occurred at the discretion and convenience of the master and did not reflect a master's benevolence toward slaves. Brutal treatment easily coexisted with customary practices of property ownership in slave communities.[19]

Slaves and, later, freedpeople recognized property ownership as dynamic and integral to social ties and community obligations. Slaves and freedpeople keenly understood trade, marketing, and wild swings in currency. Many slaves distrusted Confederate currency and demanded payment in commodities such as salt and silver or converted their capital into material goods. In both slavery and freedom, African American women dominated markets, where they sold butter, eggs, and finished goods. In an extralegal environment, claim to property rested upon relations with other slaves. Slaves produced property together, and they claimed partnerships and cooperation with family members and extended kin. As an extralegal practice, slaves and freedmen also reinforced their claims to ownership by public occasions and public display of their property. Even the law sometimes endorsed masters' right to permit slaves to own property. The North Carolina Supreme Court upheld the practice of masters permitting slaves to mark ownership of hogs that roamed on others' land. These public displays created witnesses to property claims that encouraged public recognition of their ownership. They also employed sophisticated inheritance practices. Slaves and freedpeople left property to one another based on obligations that sometimes extended across past generations. Gatsey Williams's bequest may have represented her payment of a debt to Gatsey Cole that reached back a generation or more between their mothers or grandmothers.[20]

Both in slavery and in freedom women made use of these practices to acquire property. Whites' Victorian standards of property ownership vested in the English common law practice of coverture and disallowed married women's claim or control of property. However, coverture never had the same influence over African American women. Men still had a tendency to claim all household property as their own, but extralegal custom gave women some power to defend their claims. Before and after the war, African American women participated in markets and used public occasions such as weddings to reinforce their claims to property brought into marriage. During Reconstruction, they enforced their rights to ownership in divorce or broken engagements by taking husbands to court and presenting witnesses to defend their claims to property. Bank records clearly reflect women's complex understandings of property ownership. Officials required depositors to list names of close family members for inheritance purposes. However, women documented not only their children's names but also extended kin and even deceased kin to demonstrate their social meaning of property, inheritance, and obligations that crossed generations.[21]

A typical application by a woman included a veritable diary of her social connections and genealogy of her descent. Consider these two applications:

> 2432 Record for Eliza Stanton. Date of Application Nov. 4, 1871. Born and raised in Perquimans County. Residence—15 miles from Elizabeth City, N.C. Age 30. Black complexion. Self-employed at farming, etc. Husband, Levi Stanton, soldier, unknown whereabouts. I married Hannibal Whitty last August. One child, John Parker (dead). Father, John Boise (dead). Mother Esther Stanton, lives with me. Brother, Thomas, lives in Washington, D.C. Sisters Mela and Dinah "sold before war." Signature made with an (x).

1479 Record for Becky Godding, mother of Richard Godding. Date of Application Feb. 4, 1870. Born and raised in Sampson County, N.C. Residence—now on the Dudley place, 5 miles up the Trent River. Age 60. Brown complexion. Her occupation—cooking, etc. "not much of anything." Her first husband was Bily Otridge, who died 27–28 years ago. Her present husband is Robin Hobbs. Children by her first husband included Sally, who was sold; Tilly, who died; Mary Ann, who died; Richard, who died; John, who died. Children by her second husband include Isaac, 23; Silvy, married to Lawrence Asky; Eliza Hobbs; Boyt, who died. Her father was Richard Riall, who died 10 years ago in Sampson County. Her mother, Mary Riall, about 80, was living last fall at Goshen, Sampson County. Her bother [sic] Isaac died and her brother Simon was sold. Her sisters include Arbor, who married Peter King, and lives at Rufus Monk's Place, Goshen; Daphne, married to Madison Moore; Milly, married to Stephen Lane, first, and to an Evans, secondly; Jane, married to Faison L. Bryant. Her signature by an (x).[22]

The records of Eliza Stanton and Becky Godding are similar in many respects. Both women lived in rural areas well outside of New Bern. At the time of application, both had second husbands. Godding's first husband had died decades earlier in slavery, and the whereabouts of Stanton's first husband, a soldier, were unknown. Stanton and her husband likely were sharecroppers, indicated by the phrase "self-employed at farming." Godding, at age sixty, probably worked part time as a domestic. The phrase "not much of anything," made in reference to her employment, might be her words or those of the bank cashier who recorded her application. The applications provide remarkable detail about the women's identity. In addition to their marital and occupational status, the records note current and previous places of residence, age (but not birth dates), and skin color. Becky Godding notes that she is the mother of Richard Godding, likely another bank depositor who may have opened an account in or before October 1869, the date when the extant New Bern records begin. At some point Godding closed this account, reopening it September 26, 1871.[23]

Extralegal customs emanate from the record as well. The records suggest Stanton's and Godding's attitudes about kinship and property. These two entries demonstrate freedwomen's meticulous documentation of their family ties that transcend Northern values in inheritance and linear descent. Freedwomen rooted their social identity and economic obligations not only in their spouses and children but also in those dead or sold decades previously. These claims provide far more information than that necessary by law. North Carolina law vested married women's property in their husbands. North Carolina intestate and inheritance laws for men and single women privileged living children first and, if none, parents and siblings. By these rules, the law did not require bank authorities to record such detail.

Becky Godding and Eliza Stanton recorded another custom: they recognized property claims of family who were sold away. Eliza Stanton had no living children to inherit from her, so bank officials found it pertinent to note that she had three known living heirs, her husband, her mother, and her brother living in Washington, D.C. Yet she also claimed two sisters "sold before the war," likely hoping that if they turned up in the event of her death, they might make claim to her estate. Becky Godding's record is even more complex. Strictly speaking, her second husband, Robin Hobbs, and his children were entitled to her property. Her first husband and all but one of her children were long deceased. She named others lost to the auction block. The whereabouts of her daughter Sally by that first marriage were unknown because she was "sold away." North Carolina law prohibited Sally from any claim, anyway, for two reasons. First, Godding's original marriage was extralegal and Sally had no legal record of claim. Second, North Carolina law vested the property in Robin Hobbs, her husband by her second marriage.

Sally would have no claim by law, yet Godding recorded her name anyway. Men also noted relatives "sold away." Of the approximately 1,500 depositors in this study, 175 listed relatives "sold away." Some freedpeople had endured this horror many times. Simon Croom reported that five of his brothers and two of his sisters had been sold. James Allen told Nelson that his sisters "was took away from folks when I was five years old, don't know about them." Harriet Smith's sisters Ciddy and Chloe were sold away before the war. Julia Ann Foy commented that her father, Simon, had been "sold before I was grown," and Wright Whitfield's father, Jacob, was "carried away to Alabama when I was small." In yet a further blow, Whitfield's wife, Minna, was "carried away before the war." Eliza Scott encountered equally great hardships. Both her first husband, Moses, and her second husband, Abram, were sold away. In addition, she lost four brothers to the auction block. Godding, like other women and men, probably hoped that the act of recording the names of her missing kin (including Sally and her brother, Simon) not only identified their claims to her property but, more important, created written documentation that might increase her chances of finding them again.[24]

Godding, Stanton, and other freedpeople named their deceased kin as well. Obviously the dead could not inherit, but deceased kin represented ties to genealogical networks that reinforced identity among freedpeople. These genealogical networks reminded the living of social and economic obligations that transcended generations. Sometimes women documented their kinships meticulously, but sometimes they also withheld information. Depositor Fannie Artis, age twenty-four and also a sharecropper, did so when she opened her application on April 25, 1871. She had two known living heirs, a six-month-old son and a sister. She had lost her husband in 1864, and her father had escaped to Ohio when she was a child. When she named her son, John Edward, the cashier made note that she "don't [sic] want to tell who father is." Artis may have refused this information out of embarrassment or shame based upon the circumstances of John Edward's birth. Most likely she refused to name the father because she rejected any extended obligations to him or his kin.[25]

Freedwomen thus carried their extralegal beliefs and customs about property into emancipation. Bank records show that women (as well as men) accepted the concept of married women's property ownership independent of their husbands. The records also indicate that women reinforced their prewar extralegal beliefs about property, inheritance, and social obligations by meticulously recording their deceased relatives and family members lost in slavery.

MEANINGS OF WORK IN FREEDOM

The Freedman's Savings and Trust Company records not only provide insights into freedwomen's values about property but also clearly indicate their attitudes about their occupations, assertiveness with employers, and the compromises they made in terms of balancing family responsibilities and work. At the New Bern branch, records indicate that women, both skilled and unskilled, acquired cash through their labor and saved their wages. Among the bank depositors, 17 percent worked as washerwomen and nearly 19 percent listed their occupation as cook. Another 15 percent said they were "farming for self," indicating that they helped their husbands who farmed their own land or worked as sharecroppers or tenant farmers. Others worked as seamstresses, domestics, nurses, hotel and dining room waiters, and laborers, indicating that the women who conducted business at the bank obtained the same kinds of jobs as black women throughout the South (see table 7.2).[26]

In the case of the New Bern branch, women depositors represented distinct occupations from three geographic areas in the Craven County vicinity: New Bern (urban), James City (the former refugee camp), and the countryside (rural). Among the 545 female depositors, black and white, 263 lived in New Bern. The bank, though, managed to attract 114 women from the countryside and 36 women from James City. Compared with the number

TABLE 7.2. Recorded occupations of nonwhite female depositors to Freedman's Savings and Trust Company, New Bern branch

OCCUPATION	NUMBER	OCCUPATION	NUMBER
Cook	57	Wash/sew	2
Washerwoman	53	Wash/spin/cook	1
Farmer	47	Farmer/cook	1
Seamstress	29	Farmer/keeps house	1
Domestic	27	Wash/iron	1
Keeps house	20	Dishwasher	1
Nurse	11	Doctoress	1
Field hand	8	Clerk	1
Laborer	7	Merchant	1
Teacher	7	Guardian	1
Waiter	6	Midwife	1
Vendor	5	Merchant	1
Spinner	4	Sausage maker	1
Wash/cook	4	Stallkeeper	1
Baker	2	Student	1

Source: *Freedman's Bank Database*; Zipf, "Promises of Opportunity," app., table 3.2.

of male depositors from each region, the gender ratio is consistently three women for every ten depositors (see table 7.1).[27]

NEW BERN DEPOSITORS

In the city, women bank applicants worked jobs proportionately equivalent to those jobs women worked in the general population. Of 1,416 black women over age eighteen listed in the 1870 census, 690 (48.7 percent) stayed at home. Another 41.3 percent listed working-class occupations such as cook, laundress, housekeeper, domestic servant, and fieldworker. Female depositors in New Bern selected jobs from these same categories. As indicated in table 7.3, female depositors usually worked as washerwomen, cooks, domestic servants, waiters, and seamstresses. Although washerwomen comprised the largest number of women who worked in any one field (40), the number of cooks was nearly the same (39), and the number of seamstresses and domestics (numbering 24 and 19, respectively) followed not far behind.[28]

Regardless of occupation, marital status sometimes determined a woman's ability to save money. Most women depositors at the New Bern branch were married or widowed (fig. 7.3). Not all women listed their marital status. Of those who did, 32 percent identified themselves as married, 27

TABLE 7.3. Recorded occupations of nonwhite female New Bern residents who were depositors to Freedman's Savings and Trust Company, New Bern branch, 1869–1874

OCCUPATION	NUMBER	OCCUPATION	NUMBER
Washerwoman	40	Field hand	2
Cook	39	Clerk	1
Seamstress	24	Dishwasher	1
Domestic	19	Merchant	1
Housework	13	Midwife	1
Nurse	8	Sausage maker	1
Waiter	6	Stallkeeper	1
Teacher	6	Student	1
Vendor	3	Wash/cook	1
Laborer	3	Wash/iron	1
Baker	2	Wash/sew	1
Farmer	2		

Source: *Freedman's Bank Database*; Zipf, "Promises of Opportunity," app., table 3.2.

percent identified themselves as widowed, and 14 percent identified themselves as single. By the same token, among men who listed their status, the number of single men was much higher, 30 percent. These data indicate that married and widowed women, thanks to their husbands' income or military pay, usually were more likely to open accounts than single women who probably had less disposable income. Young, single men, typically better paid than their female counterparts, opened accounts more often than single women. Freedmen's Bureau agent Stephen Moore noted one example of the inequalities in male and female field laborers' compensation. Male workers usually received ten to fifteen dollars per month while female workers generated four to eight dollars per month.[29]

In freedom, women purposefully specialized in specific domestic fields. By their choice of domestic work, freedwomen asserted their autonomy as employees (not servants or slaves) who worked for employers (not masters or mistresses) in a workplace (not a plantation household or "big house"). Freedwomen asserted this specialization of labor to counter many decades of forced intimacy in domestic work defined by slaveholding families. Thavolia Glymph has shown that relations between mistresses and slaves represented a brutal and barbaric power struggle where mistresses sought to enforce their own "ideology of domesticity" that defined white women as gentle, kind, and civilizing over their "lazy" and "disobedient" slaves, no matter how hard they worked. Within this paradigm, white mistresses culti-

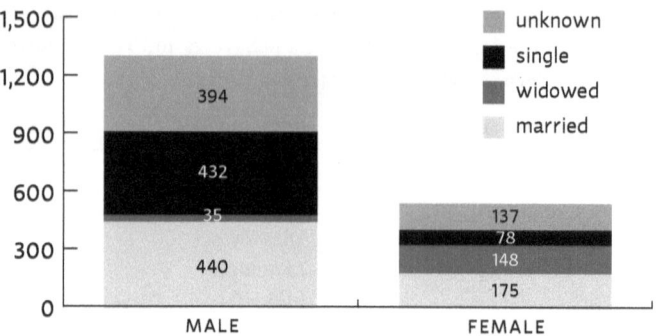

FIGURE 7.3. Recorded gender and marital status of depositors to Freedman's Savings and Trust Company, New Bern branch. From Zipf, "Promises of Opportunity," 120, fig. 3.2.

vated the image of themselves as submissive and gentle Southern belles on pedestals, while in reality they brutalized their slaves and committed barbaric violence against them. They justified their brutality, Glymph argues, in the name of civilization. In freedom, women preferred labor arrangements based on their chosen skills and their family arrangements. To the frustration of whites, they moved from job to job, engaged in work stoppages, and refused to offer the undying attention and loyalty desired by their employers. They rejected the most arduous or demeaning labor, brought their children along, and asserted themselves with their employers—and, as the bank records confirm, they refused to do work for which they had not been hired.[30]

Women's occupations were dynamic, as women chose or faced circumstances that required them to move to different lines of work. Schoolteacher and missionary Rachel Thomas also worked as a domestic between teaching appointments. One of six female teachers who opened accounts, Thomas lived in New Bern and opened the Normal School in James City, where she taught. She succeeded in obtaining a teaching commission from the American Freedmen's Union Commission of New York that included a salary of $20.00 per month. On November 19, 1869, she opened an account and continued to teach at the Normal School. Originally from Plymouth, North Carolina, she settled in New Bern with her husband, Robert, and taught her only child (Robert's stepchild), twelve-year-old Fanny, to read. Unfortunately, Thomas's funding was cut, and she had to find other work. In 1870 she landed a job as a domestic servant for the bank cashier Charles Nelson. Refusing to work in the household of a white Southern woman, she chose a job working for the Republican from Maine who, like herself, was dedicated to the freedpeople's improvement. In 1872 she accepted a position with the American Missionary Association in Rocky Mount. There, she continued to teach and also to raise funds for the building of a church.[31]

Laundering ranked highest among all women, rural and urban, who banked. A total of sixty women laundered for pay. Fifty-three women listed "washerwoman" as an occupation, and another seven listed washing along with another skill, such as cooking or spinning. Washing was among the lowest paid occupations, at only two or three dollars a week, about the same rate paid to a female field laborer. Historian Jacqueline Jones describes the work as "exceedingly heavy and hot, and especially unpleasant in the South's already steamy climate." But crucially, it offered the most autonomy by allowing women to take on multiple "clients" rather than to work for a single employer. Women could negotiate their pay against the cost of equipment, such as tubs, soap, starch, and irons. Also, it enabled women to perform their work at home, where they could look out for their children and tend to their domestic chores. Finally, the work was plentiful. Across the South, even the most ordinary white wage earner's family engaged a washerwoman. Middle-class families hired a washerwoman and a cook, and upper-class and elite families hired housekeepers and child nurses.[32]

Another benefit of washing clothes was that it allowed women to work in a communal environment with other women as they performed the same work. Children sometimes joined in to help by drawing the water and setting up the pot in the yard. Women boiled the clothes in the pot, scrubbed them on a washboard, and then rinsed, starched, strung out, hung up, and ironed the clothes. In this communal environment, women could share stories about the work, connect friends and family to employers, teach each other how to bargain, and encourage one another how to save money. For example, on March 5, 1870, Phyllis Neal, a twenty-nine-year-old washerwoman for the Manly family, opened an account at the bank. She had married her husband Marcus only a year earlier. Two days later, Phyllis's sister, Emeline Banks, who washed and ironed for the Roberts and Emanuel families, opened an account. Phyllis, after opening her own account, probably told her sister about the bank and encouraged her to visit it. Emeline, only one year older than her sister, had been married for thirteen years to her husband George. They had three children: Emma Catherine, age six; Innis Newton, age three, and John Junius, age four months. Emeline probably needed Phyllis as an extra set of eyes on her children while they worked.[33]

Figure 7.4 identifies the marital status and occupations of women depositors identified as nonwhite. The first cluster in the bar graph identifies jobs such as domestic, cook, nurse, and laborer that required women to work

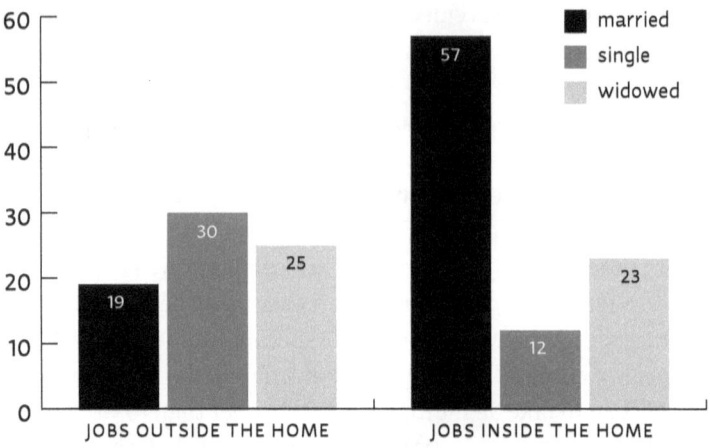

FIGURE 7.4. Recorded marital status and occupations of nonwhite female depositors to Freedman's Savings and Trust, New Bern branch. From Zipf, "Promises of Opportunity," 122, fig. 3.3; app. 3.4.

outside the home. The second cluster identifies jobs that allowed women to work at home, including washerwoman, seamstress, farmer, housekeeper, baker, and teacher. During Reconstruction, some of the categories were fluid. For example, women who listed themselves as a farmer often identified as "self-employed," and teachers could bring their children with them to school. The data illustrate that married women often chose work that they could perform at home.[34]

Women's networks, such as those formed around the washtubs, also politicized women to engage as community leaders. After the war, women's cooperatives formed throughout the South. Sometimes these cooperatives served as trade unions to teach women skills, encourage them to bargain with employers, and to help set wage minimums. In some cities, these cooperatives engaged in picketing, protests, and strikes. On July 31, 1877, women domestics in Galveston, Texas, picketed Chinese steam laundries. In July 1881, washerwomen in Atlanta formed a "Washing Society" that struck for almost two weeks during the International Cotton Exposition in demand of a standard rate of pay. Six women were arrested, but not before white women had joined the strike. In New Bern, there is no evidence of picketing or strikes, but African American seamstresses had organized by forming "The Cooperative Sewing Society," which opened an account in December 1870. This club was organized by Rev. Noble Johns (also a depositor) and other male and female congregation members from the Hancock Street Methodist Episcopal Zion Church. It likely originated as a charitable organization to teach women skills and to sew for the poor. While its membership remains unknown, bank records indicate that twenty-four African American seamstresses opened bank accounts at the New Bern branch.[35]

Bank records provide a new and untapped source for evidence of African American women's contributions to community organizations. Societies and associations established accounts at the bank and occasionally listed women in executive positions. All of the trustees and executive officers listed in the bank deposit records for the churches were male, but women joined men in the top ranks at schools, charitable associations, and temperance unions. Several women depositors held prominent positions in local organizations. Among a list of about two dozen black temperance union officers listed in the *New Bern Daily Times* on October 5, 1873, six were female and two, Charlotte Maxwell and Mary J. Williams, held bank accounts. In November 1870, Charlotte Connor, president of the Faith and Charity Society, instructed the association's treasurer, Abram Connor, to deposit the society's funds at the bank. Treasurer Susan Brown and her successor Mary Jourdan maintained accounts at the bank for the "Infant Singing School," at the request of the school's male president, Allen G. Oden. Teacher Emma Norris on her own opened an account for the "School Exhibition Fund" on April 16, 1872.[36]

Unlike their white counterparts, black women who served as teachers and leaders of benevolent and charitable associations did not always come from the ranks of the affluent. Indeed, the freedpeople had not created the sharp distinctions between the middle class and the working class that predominated among whites. Several of the depositors who led organizations came from the working class. Charlotte Maxwell, a temperance union officer, worked as a domestic servant. Mary Jane Williams, Maxwell's associate, labored as a cook, as did Mary Jourdan, who established the Infant Singing School. Nellie Fowle, who helped support her husband and her eight-month-old daughter, divided her time between teaching school and working as a seamstress. Most women, like the ones who established the Cooperative Sewing Society, often worked through their churches. This information, gleaned from the bank records, illustrates that black female leaders crossed class as well as gender lines within the black community.[37]

JAMES CITY AND RURAL DEPOSITORS

Most women who opened accounts at the New Bern branch lived in the city. However, nearly one-third of female depositors traveled into town from James City and the surrounding countryside to visit the bank. These women, mostly widows, worked as farmers, and few worked in jobs out-

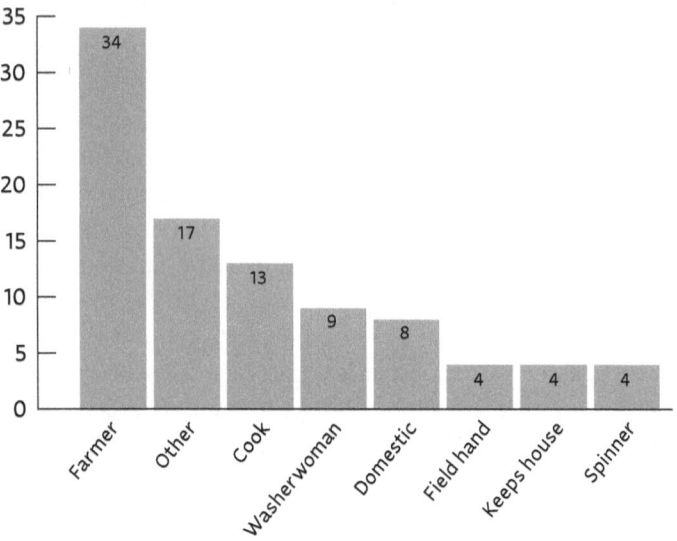

FIGURE 7.5. Recorded occupations of nonwhite female depositors from the countryside to Freedman's Savings and Trust, New Bern branch. From Zipf, "Promises of Opportunity," 135, fig. 3.4; app. 3.7.

side the home, except as part-time work. In James City, a population nearly devoid of whites except the occasional bureau agent or missionary teacher, women enjoyed an autonomy that allowed them to own land, rent, or farm on shares. One seventy-year-old woman, Margaret Salter, distinguished her title as "doctoress, or mid-wife." Over 50 percent of the female depositors in the countryside who listed their marital status were widowed. Of these sixty-one women, thirty-four named a husband or son who had died while enlisted in the Union army. Figure 7.5 shows that most of these women farmed. Of the ninety-three female depositors from the countryside who listed occupations, thirty-four worked as "self-employed farmers," including twenty-two widows. These women likely sharecropped or paid for small plots of land from their husband's bounty or pensions.[38]

Jane Edwards represents one example of the widowed farmer. This forty-nine-year-old woman, of dark brown complexion and whom the bank cashier described as tall and thin in stature, farmed on her own land on Island Creek in Jones County. While enslaved, Jane had suffered the pain of separation when her mother was "sold into the back country," and in 1864 her husband, Stephen, died. When her son, Fred, died after being discharged from the Union army, Jane collected his bounty money and set up a household for her three remaining children: Shade, age seventeen; Mary, age fifteen; and Eliza, age eleven. All three children were able-bodied and probably helped Jane farm her plot of land.[39]

The bank data confirm the most recent scholarship on freedwomen's farm labor during Reconstruction. Historians once argued that women "withdrew" from the marketplace after slavery to work in the domestic arena away from the control of whites. Recently, historians have found this claim to be an overstatement. Women did not "withdraw" from the marketplace. Instead, they asserted themselves as laborers, engaged in the contract labor system, and refused to perform "double duty" in domestic production for employers as they had as slaves. Rural life offered widows and single women a degree of autonomy, especially for those who used their deceased husband's or son's pension to buy land. Some widowed and single women chose the freedom of James City or more rural environs. It is an exaggeration to say that they retreated from the marketplace and into the private sphere.[40]

Married women farmers rarely opened bank accounts. Freedmen's Bureau agents enforced gender roles that privileged husbands' claims to their wife's property and labor. Marriage contracts had institutionalized men's privileges and obligations as household heads. When a woman married, her identity subsumed into that of her husband's. Scholars have shown that where conflict occurred between husbands and wives, bureau agents often upheld the men's prerogative. Military authorities required married freedwomen to abandon the independent provision of crops and the signing of labor contracts independent of their husbands. Bank records also confirm this trend. Only 7 percent (30) of rural depositors were married women, a statistic that strongly indicates that husbands in the countryside held power over their wife's claims to property and income.[41]

In sum, the bank records indicate that women in New Bern and the surrounding countryside asserted new meanings of work and labor in freedom. They participated in the economy as workers in a wide variety of occupations, purposefully specialized in certain domestic skill sets to exert their autonomy amongst employers, understood themselves as instrumental in the community, and took leadership positions, including roles of economic influence, in community organizations. Bank records also indicate that widowed and single women in New Bern, James City, and the countryside enjoyed a certain autonomy as farmers, enough to open a bank account. The data also show a near absence of rural married women from the records. Law, custom, and decisions made by military officials continued to privilege husbands over wives, at least in the rural countryside.

AFRICAN AMERICAN MEN ADVOCATE FOR WOMEN'S RIGHTS

The congruence of women's participation in the workplace and extralegal customs about property likely explains why several prominent African American men spearheaded reforms in marriage and property laws and championed women's rights as citizens. In January 1868, the North Carolina Constitutional Convention assembled to rewrite the North Carolina Constitution and bring it into alignment with the Reconstruction Acts. With former Confederates disfranchised, the state elected 120 delegates, at least thirteen of whom were African American. The purpose of the convention was to redraft the state's social compact to reflect more accurately the responsibilities and rights of North Carolina's male citizenry, both black and white, rich and poor. Much of the discussion involved the 1866 Civil Rights Act, enfranchisement, reorganization of government to include free schools, and coordination of public charities. As the delegates first convened, specific attention to women's rights was nowhere on the list.[42]

Yet as the convention progressed, African American delegates pursued numerous reforms, often at odds with their white Republican counterparts, that benefited women. African American delegates introduced divorce petitions, proposed reforms in married women's property and dower rights, and submitted legislation in favor of woman's suffrage. Faced with widespread backlogs in the county court system, twenty-seven aggrieved citizens, both men and women, filed divorce petitions hoping for relief from the constitutional convention. White Republicans dismissed the petitions, calling them trivial and out of the convention's purview. Yet James Henry Harris and James Walker Hood, two prominent African American leaders from eastern North Carolina, kept these petitions alive. Harris headed a "Special Committee on Divorce" and found himself besieged with requests. Under his direction, the committee approved fifteen divorces, many of them advanced by women.[43]

African American men advanced other reforms, including a married women's property law. The initial bill practically reversed coverture by granting married women the same rights to property as single women. White Republicans kicked up a storm against the proposal yet conceded a compromise to dilute a husband's claim to his wife's property by declaring him a trustee, rather than sole owner, of her estate. Another reform proposed by Hood, first as a constitutional provision and later as legislation, secured women's rights to the "privy examination." By this law, the state required county officials to conduct a private examination whenever husbands conveyed the homestead and abandoned lands. Hood's persistent efforts in successive legislatures by 1869 expanded this law to require a married woman's consent whenever her husband conveyed property owned by the husband "at any time during coverture."[44]

Some African American men actively campaigned for woman's suffrage. Abraham Galloway, an African American delegate and former slave from New Hanover County, worked tirelessly to secure rights for African American men and for all women. As a convention delegate, he supported Harris and Hood on the divorce and property legislation. He continued his work for women's rights as a North Carolina state senator. In 1869 and again in 1870, he proposed constitutional amendments to grant woman's suffrage. He pressed for property reform, and he supported proposals against domestic abuse. Galloway's vision of gender equity was rare for his day, yet he and his colleagues sedulously pressed a wide variety of reforms in divorce, property reform, suffrage, and women's autonomy over their bodies. Though they left little written evidence about their views of gender equality, their combined legislative record suggests that the gendered realities of Reconstruction as demonstrated in the bank records helped to shape their political agenda.[45]

CONCLUSION

In freedom, African American women took command of their emancipation. The data in the Freedman's Savings and Trust Company records strongly support this assertion. Women drew from the realities of their past experiences to define their lives during Reconstruction. They shaped their own meanings of property, work, and family relations. Their actions seem modest. In hindsight, a washerwoman negotiating with her "clients" or the influence wielded by a cooperative society of seamstresses pales in comparison to the speeches, sermons, and legislation of men. But for this demographic, that is, women who had once suffered the worst indignities of forced servitude, these examples of everyday assertion shaped the meaning of freedom: for them it meant dignity, fair compensation, and autonomy in self, family, and community. The bank data reflect that process, a creative synchronization of free labor ideology and extralegal customs where women claimed their rights to their property and labor. Prominent African American men supported women's claims in their determined advocacy for women's rights. Republican whites may have recognized African American men as the "voice" of the freedpeople, but with money in the bank, women spoke loudly too.

NOTES

1. Bill Reaves, *The North Carolina Freedman's Savings and Trust Company Records* (Raleigh: North Carolina Genealogical Society, 1992), 321. In 1994, I compiled and digitized Reaves's data featured in this chapter, hereafter referred to as Freedman's Bank Database. Reaves abstracted the bank records from surviving registers of three branches, including deposit records from Raleigh, New Bern, and Wilmington, of which the originals are housed in the Records of the Comptroller of the Currency, RG 101, National Archives and Records Administration, Washington, D.C. The surviving deposit records from New Bern begin with account no. 1327, opened in October 1869, and end with account no. 4157, for which the date of application was not recorded but was probably entered sometime in June 1874, just before the branch closed. The records preceding account no. 1327 have been lost. Reaves reports that the records are on microfilm roll M816.4. Currently, all North Carolina deposit records are housed on microfilm roll M816.18, Records of the Comptroller of the Currency. See also Carl R. Osthaus, *Freedmen, Philanthropy, and Fraud* (Urbana: University of Illinois Press, 1976), 147-49, 173.

2. Dylan C. Penningroth, *The Claims of Kinfolk: African American Property and Community in the Nineteenth Century South* (Chapel Hill: University of North Carolina Press, 2003); Thavolia Glymph, *Out of the House of Bondage: The Transformation of the Plantation Household* (New York: Cambridge University Press, 2008); and Catherine Bishir, *Crafting Lives: African American Artisans in New Bern, North Carolina, 1770-1900* (Chapel Hill: University of North Carolina Press, 2013).

3. The extant records of the New Bern Freedman's Savings and Trust Company includes a total of 2,820 existing depositor applications, about 745 of which are identifiable by name and marital condition as female. Approximately 200 of these 745 are duplicates or continued accounts. This data set presented in this article does not include duplicates, continuations, or incomplete records. This chapter originates in the author's earlier work, Karin Lorene Zipf, "Promises of Opportunity: The Freedman's Savings and Trust Company in New Bern, North Carolina," M.A. thesis, University of Georgia, 1994.

4. Alan D. Watson, *A History of New Bern and Craven County* (New Bern, N.C.: Tryon Palace Commission, 1987), 437; Joe A. Mobley, *James City: A Black Community in North Carolina* (Raleigh: North Carolina Department of Cultural Resources, 1981); Louis H. Manarin, ed., *Guide to Military Organization and Installations: North Carolina, 1861-1865* (Raleigh: North Carolina Confederate Centennial Commission, 1961), 1-3; Barton A. Myers, *Rebels against the Confederacy: North Carolina's Unionists* (New York: Cambridge University Press, 2014); Judkin Browning, *Shifting Loyalties: The Union Occupation of Eastern North Carolina* (Chapel Hill: University of North Carolina Press, 2014); Wayne Durrill, *War of Another Kind: A Southern Community in the Great Rebellion* (New York: Oxford University Press, 1994); Lesley J. Gordon, "'In Time of War': Unionists Hanged at Kinston, North Carolina, February 1864," in *Guerrillas, Unionists and Violence in the Confederacy*, ed. Daniel Sutherland (Fayetteville: University of Arkansas Press, 1999), 44-58.

5. Mobley, *James City*, 29, 43.

6. T. Harry Gatton, *Banking in North Carolina: A Narrative History* (Raleigh: North Carolina Bankers Association, 1987), 51; Watson, *History of New Bern and Craven County*, 541-42; Rev. L. Branson, ed., *North Carolina Business Directory* (Raleigh, N.C.: J. A. Jones, 1869), 46-47.

7. In its 1866 quarterly report, the First National Bank of New Bern referred to its depositors as "stockholders" and its interest rate as a "dividend." "Quarterly Report of the Condition of the National Bank of New Berne," October 6, 1866, Guion Papers, North Carolina State Archives, Raleigh, N.C.; Gatton, *Banking in North Carolina*, 52–53; Watson, *History of New Bern and Craven County*, 541; Freedman's Bank Database; Reaves, *North Carolina Freedman's Savings and Trust Company Records*, 86, 12, 209.

8. Karin L. Zipf, *Labor of Innocents: Forced Apprenticeship in North Carolina, 1715–1919* (Baton Rouge: Louisiana State University Press, 2005), 96. Horace W. Raper examines the Reconstruction Acts in *William W. Holden: North Carolina's Political Enigma* (Chapel Hill: University of North Carolina Press, 1985), 59–126.

9. Zipf, *Labor of Innocents*, 63; Leslie A. Schwalm, *A Hard Fight for We: Women's Transition from Slavery to Freedom in South Carolina* (Urbana: University of Illinois Press, 1997), 235–36, 351; Roberta Sue Alexander notes Whittlesey's discontent with the Black Codes in *North Carolina Faces the Freedmen: Race Relations during Presidential Reconstruction, 1865–1867* (Durham, N.C.: Duke University Press, 1985); Thomas Holt, "'An Empire over the Mind': Emancipation, Race, and Ideology in the British West Indies and the American South," in *Region, Race, and Reconstruction: Essays in Honor of C. Vann Woodward*, ed. J. Morgan Kousser and James M. McPherson (New York: Oxford University Press, 1982), 287–88.

10. Legislators refused to bestow it lending authority because its directors felt that the freedmen must first learn good savings habits. Carl Osthaus claims that Congress limited the bank as a savings institution. Congressional authorities, he argues, believed that "the ex-slaves, now free to do as they pleased, might sink deep into poverty and degradation through their own improvidence unless something was done to educate them in the habits of work, thrift, and self-sufficiency." Osthaus, *Freedmen, Philanthropy, and Fraud*, 5, 147–49, 173.

11. Annual Report of the Sub-assistant Commissioner Lieutenant Colonel Stephen Moore, September 25, 1867, Reports of Operations (Annual), Records of Bureau of Refugees, Freedman and Abandoned Lands, 1865–72, RG 105, M843.22, National Archives, Washington, D.C. (hereafter Freedman's Bureau Records); Catherine W. Bishir examines the African American New Bern artisanal community in *Crafting Lives: African American Artisans in New Bern, North Carolina, 1770–1900* (Chapel Hill: University of North Carolina Press, 2013), 223–26. See also Loren Schweninger, *Black Property Owners in the South, 1790–1915* (Urbana: University of Illinois Press, 1990), 172, 236; Barbara Jeanne Fields, *Slavery and Freedom on the Middle Ground* (New Haven, Conn.: Yale University Press, 1985), 178–79; and Osthaus, *Freedmen, Philanthropy, and Fraud*, 130.

12. Zipf, "Promises of Opportunity," 46–50; Osthaus, *Freedmen, Philanthropy, and Fraud*, 35; Major Andrew Coats to Brevet Lieutenant Colonel Jacob F. Chur, January 16, 1868, February 4, 1868, Registered Letters Received, Freedmen's Bureau Records, RG 105, M843.10; Reaves, *North Carolina Freedman's Savings and Trust Company Records*, 72.

13. Zipf, "Promises of Opportunity," 127; "Widow or Dependent Mother" pension notice for Celia Simmons, September 4, 1869, pension file of Nicholas Simmons, Records of the Veterans Administration, RG 15, National Archives, Washington, D.C.

14. Zipf, "Promises of Opportunity," 105–8; Woody Holton, "Equality as Unintended Consequence: The Contracts Clause and the Married Women's Property Acts," *Journal of Southern History* 81 (May 2015): 313.

15. Zipf, "Promises of Opportunity," 109; Watson, *History of New Bern and Craven County*, 438; Reaves, *North Carolina Freedman's Savings and Trust Company Records*, 14, 48, 59, 83, 141, 175, 205, 207, 225, 253.

16. Report of Special Examiner J. Speed Smith, November 24, 1890, and Pension Commissioner M. A. Baker to the Pension Office, Department of the Interior, May 27, 1873, pension file of Nicholas Simmons.

17. Affidavit of Margaret Dudley, May 27, 1874, pension file of Elias Dudley, Records of the Veterans Administration; Reaves, *North Carolina Freedman's Savings and Trust Company Records*, 131, 206, 269, 299.

18. Affidavit of Samuel Foy, July 14, 1873, affidavit of Margaret Dudley, and Special Agent G. N. Ragsdale to Commissioner of Pensions J. H. Baker, circa 1874, all in pension file of Elias Dudley; Reaves, *North Carolina Freedman's Savings and Trust Company Records*, 14.

19. Dylan C. Penningroth, *The Claims of Kinfolk: African American Property and Community in the Nineteenth-Century South* (Chapel Hill: University of North Carolina Press, 2003), 6, 12, 46, 57–67.

20. Ibid., 80–97, 119.

21. Ibid., 106–7, 123.

22. Reaves, *North Carolina Freedman's Savings and Trust Company Records*, 29, 145.

23. Ibid., 134.

24. Zipf, "Promises of Opportunity," 104–6; Reaves, *North Carolina Freedman's Savings and Trust Company*, 83, 37, 74, 100, 107.

25. Reaves, *North Carolina Freedman's Savings and Trust Company Records*, 99–100.

26. Zipf, "Promises of Opportunity," 111; Tera W. Hunter, *"To 'Joy My Freedom": Southern Black Women's Lives and Labors after the Civil War* (Cambridge, Mass.: Harvard University Press, 1998); Leslie Schwalm, *Hard Fight for We*; Noralee Frankel, *Freedom's Women: Black Women and Families in Civil War Era Mississippi* (Bloomington: Indiana University Press, 1999); Jacqueline Jones, *Labor of Love, Labor of Sorrow: Black Women, Work, and the Family, from Slavery to the Present* (New York: Basic Books, 1985).

27. Zipf, "Promises of Opportunity," 111–14.

28. Mark S. Mitchell, "A History of the Black Population of New Bern, North Carolina, 1862–1872," M.A. thesis, East Carolina University, 1980, 65–66; Freedman's Bank Database; Zipf, "Promises of Opportunity," 114.

29. The data in figure 7.3 reflect a total 538 deposit applications by women. Seven additional deposit applications do not appear in the data because they represent accounts appointed by women for a guardian or as a trustee. Freedman's Bank Database; Zipf, "Promises of Opportunity," 116–18, chart 120, appendix, table 3.3.

30. Schwalm, *Hard Fight for We*, 108, 205–13; Glymph, *Out of the House of Bondage*, 8–10, 64–65.

31. Annual Report of the Sub-assistant Commissioner Lieutenant Colonel Stephen Moore; Craven County Census, 1870, in Eula Pearl Beauchamp, *1870 Census, Craven County, North Carolina* (New Bern, N.C.: E. P. Beauchamp, 1990; Freedman's Bank Database; Rachel Thomas to George Whipple, October 27, 1872, doc. 103105, American Missionary Association Archives, box 127 (North Carolina, 1873 January–1875 December), Amistad Research Center, Tulane University, New Orleans, La.; Reaves, *North Carolina Freedman's Savings and Trust Company Records*, 8, 57.

32. Freedman's Bank Database; Zipf, "Promises of Opportunity," 123–24; Jones, *Labor of Love, Labor of Sorrow*, 90–125; Hunter, *"To 'Joy My Freedom,"* 52–62.

33. Hunter, *"To 'Joy My Freedom,"* 62; Jones, *Labor of Love, Labor of Sorrow*, 90, 125; Reaves, *North Carolina Freedman's Savings and Trust Company Records*, 36–37; Freedman's Bank Database.

34. Freedman's Bank Database; Zipf, "Promises of Opportunity," 122, app. 3.4.

35. Martha Jones, *All Bound Up Together: The Woman Question in African American Public Culture, 1830–1900* (Chapel Hill: University of North Carolina Press, 2007), 4–7, 122–23; Hunter, *"To 'Joy My Freedom,"* 71–92; Reaves, *North Carolina Freedman's Savings and Trust Company Records*, 50, 73; Freedman's Bank Database; Zipf, "Promises of Opportunity," 143.

36. Zipf, "Promises of Opportunity," 142–45; Reaves, *North Carolina Freedman's Savings and Trust Company Records*, 23, 70, 182, 184, 258.

37. Zipf, "Promises of Opportunity," 142–45; Reaves, *North Carolina Freedman's Savings and Trust Company Records*, 7.

38. Freedman's Bank Database; Zipf, "Promises of Opportunity," 130–33, chart 138, app. 3.7; Reaves, *North Carolina Freedman's Savings and Trust Company Records*, 244.

39. Freedman's Bank Database; Zipf, "Promises of Opportunity," 133–34; Reaves, *North Carolina Freedman's Savings and Trust Company Records*, 58.

40. Jacqueline Jones has made the argument about women "withdrawing" from labor to work in the domestic arena in *Labor of Love, Labor of Sorrow*, 58–59, 104–5. Scholars since have challenged this idea. See also Schwalm, *Hard Fight for We*, 7–8, 177, 205–8, 236. Glymph rejects the theory that women "withdrew" from labor into a "private" sphere and instead demonstrates that women bargained, negotiated, and reorganized household labor during Reconstruction. Glymph, *Out of the House of Bondage*, 139, 149–51.

41. Penningroth discusses gendered conflict in families over property claims during Reconstruction in *Claims of Kinfolk*, 179–85. Laura F. Edwards discusses bureau agents' enforcement of husbands' prerogatives over wives in *Gendered Strife and Confusion: The Political Culture of Reconstruction* (Urbana: University of Illinois Press, 1997), 198–217. See also Zipf, *Labor of Innocents*, 68.

42. Karin Zipf, "No Longer under Cover(ture): Marriage, Divorce, and Gender in the 1868 Constitutional Convention," in *North Carolinians in the Era of the Civil War and Reconstruction*, ed. Paul D. Escott (Chapel Hill: University of North Carolina Press, 2008), 194.

43. Ibid., 198, 208.

44. Ibid., 210–12.

45. Ibid., 208.

EDUCATIONAL CAPITAL AND HUMAN FLOURISHING
NORTH CAROLINA'S PUBLIC SCHOOLS AND UNIVERSITIES, 1865–2015

Glenda Elizabeth Gilmore

Charlotte Mayor Anthony Foxx had three minutes and thirty-six seconds to welcome the Democratic National Convention to his city in 2012. Foxx called Charlotte a place of "energy and commerce," a place where "business and government work together and make things happen." Then he talked about *why* Charlotte is so successful. He did not attribute that success to NationsBank and First Union becoming the largest banks in the nation, Bank of America and Wells Fargo, respectively. Nor did he dwell on all those law firms, Charlotte Douglas International Airport, Nucor Steel, Family Dollar, or Duke Energy.

Instead he talked about West Charlotte High School. He attributed Charlotte's commercial success in the twenty-first century to its response to school desegregation in the early 1970s. Indeed, many think that Charlotte became the city it is today because civic-minded black and white Charlotteans came together "across kitchen tables" and "gave a generation a gift: a chance to go to school together," to quote Foxx. He took that chance as a teenager, realizing that "education could expand my mind and transform my life."[1]

Foxx eloquently made the argument that North Carolina's formidable educational capital, reflected in its public schools, community colleges, and universities, generates most of the state's "energy and commerce." In fact, his premise has been an article of faith in the state since 1900: the state's success depends on making the public school system the best possible educational institution in the nation.

Nevertheless, fifteen years into the twenty-first century, North Carolinians find themselves embroiled in heated discussions of public school and university reform and cuts in funding. Few North Carolinians would consider abolishing public education altogether. Beyond that relative consensus, disputes abound over what the nature of the relationship between the state and its publicly funded schools should be.

In 2015, the state of North Carolina was having a difficult time doing three things at once: cutting its budget, maintaining its commitment to education, and encouraging policies that result in integrated schools that serve all of the state's citizens. Many fair-minded people think that it is impossible to accomplish all three. Some think that the public school system does not really need a commitment from all of the state's citizens to sustain it. And there are some who have no more strength for the fight after the twenty-five-year-long evisceration of the gift that they gave North Carolina's children: a chance to go to school together. The current crisis feels new, made more desperate by the recent recession, the worst that many have ever experienced. However, crises abound in the history of North Carolina's public schools and universities, crises that the state's citizens met in the past.

A long view of the state's educational history reinforces Foxx's argument that prosperity depends on the state's commitment to educating its children in truly public schools, even in hard times. Moreover, educational funding must be robust in the state budget if North Carolina's commerce is to succeed. Today's budgetary problems pale compared to the fiscal crisis of early Reconstruction, when the state stepped up to its responsibility to educate freedpeople, or to the Great Depression year of 1938, when the state added a twelfth grade to all of its high schools. Nor are the challenges posed by educating all North Carolinians—white, black, Asian, or Latino—together any different from what they were during segregation or during desegregation in the 1960s and 1970s.

North Carolina's school system, from preschool to doctoral programs, provides the state an asset: educational capital, metaphorically and actually. The problem is that the profit it produces is long in coming, and it is difficult to annualize. That profit is measured by the production of engaged citizens, a trained workforce, and self-supporting families. No business models account for amortizing Greensboro's Grimsley High School's goodwill, nor are there any financial forecasts to predict how cutting teachers' salaries will affect the value of the product: an educated North Carolinian. The state's educational capital can be exhausted quickly if its citizens mismanage the schools, neglect any part of the population, or turn away from what North Carolinians in 1900 called "universal education."

For the past 150 years, there was never a time in North Carolina without strife over the state's public schools, most of it centered on money and the exigencies of racial politics. Moreover, these adversities bred opportunities. Since the Civil War, black North Carolinians' efforts to better educate their children resulted in better schools for both whites and blacks, which in turn fueled the engines of commerce. Considerable white opposition always existed. Occasionally, as in Anthony Foxx's teenage years, widespread white and black cooperation and shared visions transformed policy and practice in the state.

Problems such as poverty, segregation, desegregation, and resegregation produced achievements that arose as a by-product of the productive friction generated in solving them. The long process of extending good public education in equal measure to everyone bequeathed to North Carolina an enviable public school and university system. This argument holds up despite a shameful history of segregation and, especially after 1900, unequal provision for black pupils.

It may seem counterintuitive to argue that the strength of public education in North Carolina has resulted in large part from the African American fight for inclusion. The traditional story is that white people controlled resources and ultimately "gave" black people access to them after the 1954 *Brown v. Board of Education* decision. In other words, the story has centered on what white people did for black people. Turning that narrative on its head reveals the ironic story of what black people did for white people by challenging exclusionary and racist policies and politics at every turn to build a better public school system.

FIVE PERIODS OF EDUCATIONAL HISTORY

The history of education in North Carolina falls roughly into five time periods characterized by different political contexts. First, from 1865 until 1900, black leadership forced the state to reopen schools after the Civil War and then to make them relatively equal, albeit segregated. Black North Carolinians campaigned for longer school years and for coeducation, which led to better education for poor white women excluded from existing male schools. African Americans demanded two-year teacher training institutions where there had been none, better school buildings, and more rigorous academic programs. One could even argue that during these first thirty-five years, public education for poor black people at some levels outdistanced that available to poor whites, particularly women.

The second phase dates from the late 1890s when a white supremacy movement fought back and cast black North Carolinians out of politics yet improved the white schools. The push to keep the state's schools separate and make them more unequal lasted until roughly 1935. Because one of the tools the white supremacists used to prevent African Americans from voting was a literacy test, the new regime pledged in 1900 to educate illiterate white North Carolinians and to appropriate more funds for public schools. Thus, one could argue that African American success in the latter half of the nineteenth century forced white supremacists to increase educational spending for white schools. Moreover, the new white leadership blatantly distributed funds unequally, and black schools deteriorated in the first thirty-five years of the twentieth century. Despite this terrible reversal of fortune, two positive things happened for African Americans in the period. First, Northern philanthropies entered the state to underwrite teacher training, build better school buildings, and fund black high schools. Second, African Americans migrated out of the state to Northern urban areas and became a force in national politics.

In the third period, from about 1935 to roughly 1960, African Americans began to file suits against "separate but equal" education, based on the principle that black public education was unequal. The threat of lawsuits and national political action forced the state to allocate more money to the black schools that they had eviscerated since the turn of the twentieth century. White leaders sought to convince the courts that the state's segregated separate school systems were in fact equal, and they hoped that by putting money into black schools they could delay the implementation of desegregation. After *Brown v. Board of Education* in 1954, white North Carolinians in power in Raleigh and in city and county school systems focused on limiting segregation on the ground in individual schools and argued that *Brown* did not require equal schools.

In the fourth period, from the 1960s to the 1990s, court and community action plans for meaningful desegregation brought a series of innovations to North Carolina schools. Magnet schools, International Baccalaureate schools, and improved facilities resulted. As Sarah Thuesen points out in *Greater than Equal: The African American Struggle for Schools and Citizenship in North Carolina, 1919–1965*, *Brown* was "incomplete."[2] In the process of desegregation, African American educators lost influence in most places, and emphasis on keeping white students in the public school system drove many policy decisions.

In the fifth period, after 1990 to the present, without the productive friction of black challenges to white power structures, educational policy slipped from public view, schools resegregated, and alternatives to public schooling grew. Black underrepresentation in the state legislature and in educational administration meant that African Americans had perhaps less than proportional input into education than earlier. As schools resegregated, all of the state's poor became underserved, elite support for public schools eroded, and various constituencies promoted parental choice over universal education.

RECONSTRUCTING PUBLIC EDUCATION, 1865–1900

In 1839, with $1.5 million in federal aid, the North Carolina General Assembly established a public school system. When the Civil War began, 3,000 schools served about 68 percent of white school-age children. The school year lasted a mere four months, and the ungraded schools offered roughly six years of education. North Carolina's decision to secede and fight in the Civil War destroyed the school system, and from 1861 to 1865 there were no reliable state paychecks for the 2,700 teachers, all of whom were men, and most of whom had already left the classroom to join Confederate forces.[3]

During early Reconstruction white leaders obstructed the reopening of the common schools. Governor Jonathan Worth warned early in January 1866: "If we educate white children at public expense, we will be required to educate the negroes in like manner.... I think the com.[mon] school system had better be discouraged and thus avoid the question as to educating the negroes."[4]

The state's African Americans agitated to open the public schools. In September 1865 more than one hundred African Americans gathered at the Freedmen's Convention in Raleigh where convention president James Walker Hood announced: "We have waited long enough for our rights. The best way is, to give the colored men rights at once and then they will practice them and the sooner know how to use them.... These are the rights we want that we will contend for—and that by the help of God, *we will have*!" One of those rights, the convention argued, was "education for our children."[5] After the first election in which African Americans could vote, the General Assembly of 1868–69 included twenty-one black legislators, and black men continued to serve until the turn of the century.

For three years, Governor Worth and white members of the General Assembly fought against funding a public school system. The superintendent of schools, elected under federal occupation, was a Northern minister named S. S. Ashley, who favored integrated schools. Late in 1868 he reported, "Almost nothing was being done for public schools."[6] To Governor Worth, having a white integrationist Northerner as superintendent of schools was bad enough, but worse was the fact that Hood, the Freedman's Convention president, served as assistant superintendent of schools from 1868 to 1871. Finally, in 1869, under Governor William W. Holden, the General Assembly passed a "separate school law" that outlawed racially mixed public schools and appropriated a small sum to fund common schools on a segregated basis. The four-month school year that they established lasted another thirty years.

As state assistant superintendent for education, Hood founded public schools and searched for teachers. By 1871, 49,000 black students attended public schools. Thousands attended other schools as well. The Freedmen's Bureau, American Missionary Association (AMA), black religious denominations, and groups of African American parents all sponsored schools that educated black North Carolinians and gave them an advantage over poor whites during early Reconstruction. Freedmen's Bureau school inspector John Alvord noted, "There is only here and there in the state a schoolhouse for the whites, of very inferior description, and with long distances between."[7] Some white parents sent their children to the Freedmen's Bureau schools. Nonetheless, one AMA educator noted that most white families "would go without any schooling at all rather than bear up against the ridicule that meets them for going to a freedmen's school."[8] A U.S. Sanitary Commission representative in Wilmington, North Carolina, who came south to establish schools for white children, marveled, "The prejudices of this land are marvelous. The jealousy as marvelous. Their pride as great as their necessity."[9]

The 1869 law provided, in theory, equal allocation of tax dollars on a per pupil basis for both black and white children and equal pay for black and white teachers. In practice, African Americans regularly sued local school officials who tried to circumvent the law by allocating money to schools proportionally on the basis of each race's tax payments to the county. In 1886, the North Carolina Supreme Court ruled these tax prorating schemes unconstitutional, and relative racial equality prevailed in allocations and teacher salaries until 1900.

Eager for more than four months of school, black families extended the year in two ways: by "getting up a school" during the months between planting and harvesting and by moving close to AMA and denominational schools that conducted longer school years. "Getting up a school" meant parents raised money to hire a teacher to extend the school year by several months. Fayetteville native (and later acclaimed author) Charles Waddell Chesnutt looked for work at such a subscription school outside of Charlotte when he was only fifteen.

Teenage Anna Julia Cooper was another such teacher. During Reconstruction, she left after spring term at St. Augustine's College in Raleigh to teach in a parent-funded summer school in Chatham County, where she encountered a really smart thirteen-year-old named Simon Green Atkins. She brought him back to enroll at St. Augustine's, from which he graduated in

1880 at the age of seventeen, and he went on to found Winston-Salem State University. St. Augustine's structure represented the second way that black North Carolinians extended the four-month school year and progressed beyond the public grammar schools. In 1867, the Episcopal church founded St. Augustine's Seminary to educate freedpeople, and a score of other denominations organized similar schools. They began with grammar school education; however, unlike public schools, they offered additional years of high school and sometimes an additional two years of teaching or ministerial training.[10] White teachers staffed these schools in the 1870s, but by the 1880s most had some black teachers.

In 1880, James Walker Hood and his colleagues in the African Methodist Episcopal Zion church founded their own high school and college, Livingstone, staffed with black teachers. In addition, seven AMA schools operated across North Carolina, more than in any other state. These schools lengthened the school year, extended the number of years of schooling beyond grammar school, and catered to freedpeople of all ages. Eula Wellmon Dunlap's experience at Lincoln Academy, an AMA school in Kings Mountain, illustrates black families' devotion to education. Her father moved the family to Kings Mountain so that they could attend the school, which Eula entered as a three-year-old. "For a while Father, Mother, sister, and I all went to school.... I spent most of my time marking on paper and playing with blocks. Several married couples went to school." Eula graduated from high school at Lincoln Academy.[11] When Anna Julia Cooper's protégé Simon Green Atkins graduated from St. Augustine's, he headed back home to Chatham County to teach in a public school. Four years later he became a Livingstone professor.[12]

At a time when no coeducation existed above grammar school for whites, the dire need for black teachers meant that private black colleges admitted women on an equal basis with men. The contrast between black coeducational colleges and southern white female academies in the 1870s and 1880s could not have been starker. White women's colleges did not offer the classical educations that black women gained access to at places like St. Augustine's or Livingstone. One white educator noted in 1888, "No one would dare propose, with any hope of success that [white] women be admitted to the University and leading denominational colleges of the state."[13]

In 1877, when the General Assembly appropriated money to found a normal school for African Americans in Fayetteville, it became the second state-supported institution of higher learning. The University of North Carolina, established in Chapel Hill in 1789, had been the first. It apparently did not occur to most legislators that women would attend Fayetteville. When the

General Assembly found out that black women made up the majority of Fayetteville's first class, they protested the use of state funds to educate them. The principal held firm and told them, "The presence of females has a refining influence on the manners of the males,... [women were the] brightest students and the most promising teachers."[14] The term lasted nine months.

The success of Fayetteville Normal resulted in appropriations during the 1880s for other normal schools for African Americans at Plymouth, Goldsboro, Salisbury, and Franklinton. The state also funded the Croatan Normal School to provide Lumbee teachers, while maintaining segregation. The normal schools ran grammar schools in which the teachers-in-training practice-taught. Consolidating black normal schools geographically, the state established one at Elizabeth City in 1891 and, with the help of the Slater Fund, in Winston-Salem in 1895. Simon Atkins, Anna Julia Cooper's pupil, moved from Livingstone College to found Slater Industrial and State Normal School there.[15] All black normal schools were coeducational, and all were free if students pledged to teach in North Carolina.

Until the state opened Woman's College in Greensboro in 1892, public white teacher training for women mostly took place in summer institutes that lasted four weeks and for which the state appropriated $4,000 each year.[16] Certainly scores of private schools existed in the state that included high school and some college, many of them only for females, but the average farm girl's family would have found it difficult to afford private schooling and may not have seen any sense in it. No public school for white children extended above grammar school until 1899, when Greensboro Senior High School opened. Before the Civil War, none of the state's teachers were women. By 1891, only 40 percent were female. The teaching force in both black and white schools feminized incrementally, and the state's teachers were 86 percent female by 1920. The state began supporting coeducation for whites at Cullowhee Normal School in 1905.[17]

ILLITERACY AND UNIVERSAL EDUCATION, 1900–1935

With only four-month-long schools that students could attend for six years, in 1890 North Carolina had the highest white illiteracy rate in the nation. In 1900, 19 percent of adult white men in the state were illiterate, as were 53 percent of black men. That year and again ten years later, the state's public school system ranked last in the nation, according to ten measures of educational flourishing.[18] The shame of leading the nation in illiterates permeated the state, and it fit quite conveniently with the new politics of aggressive white supremacy. After thirty-five years of black improvement and success, the white sons of Confederate veterans determined in 1898 to drive black North Carolinians out of politics.

Charles Brantley Aycock was one of a triumvirate, including Josephus Daniels and Furnifold M. Simmons, who masterminded the turn-of-the-century white supremacy campaign. The irony was that disfranchising black North Carolinians through a bogusly administered literacy test forced the state to increase funding to white schools so that the one out of five illiterate white men and their illiterate sons could pass it. Improving public schools for white people was a cornerstone of the white supremacy elections of 1898, 1900, and 1902. Even so, the General Assembly so doubted their ability quickly to reform schooling that they extended a grandfather clause to poor white men. If your grandfather could vote before 1867, you could too, without passing the literacy test, at least until 1915, when the U.S. Supreme Court found the law unconstitutional.[19]

It would be an error to claim that at least some of the white supremacists, especially Charles Aycock, were disingenuous about pledging the state's resources to white education, and James Leloudis has successfully chronicled this middle-class push for public school improvement.[20] In fact, Aycock always recalled the burden that he had felt as a sixteen-year-old when he stepped off a stagecoach on Franklin Street in Chapel Hill, to come to the University of North Carolina with the weight of his family's hopes on his shoulders. His mother, Serena, was illiterate and signed her name with an X. Aycock's commitment extended to African American education. When, during his term as governor, the General Assembly proposed an amendment to the state constitution to implement another spurious prorated taxation scheme to starve black schools, Aycock attacked it, saying, "The amendment proposed is unjust, unwise, and unconstitutional. It would wrong both races, would bring our State into the condemnation of a just opinion elsewhere, and mark us as a people who have turned backward.... Let us not seek to be the first State in the Union to make the weak man helpless."[21]

If other white supremacist politicians made false promises to fund education to get poor white men to vote their race rather than their class interests, Aycock had not been among them. When he took the governor's seat in January 1901, he reaffirmed his commitment:

> I pledged the State, its strength, its heart, its wealth, to universal education. I promised the illiterate poor man, bound to a life of toil and struggle and poverty, that life should be brighter for his boy and girl than it had been for him and the partner of his sorrows and joys. I pledged the wealth of the State to the education of his children. Men of wealth, representa-

tives of great corporations, applauded eagerly my declaration.... I have found no man who is unwilling to make the State stronger and better by liberal aid to the cause of education. Gentlemen of the Legislature, you will not have aught to fear when you make ample provision for the education of the whole people.[22]

Aycock fought a losing battle in the long run. When he died speaking at the podium in Alabama on April 2, 1912, his last word was "education." Aycock embodied the ambiguities of public education in the white supremacist regime.

Predictably, after African American disfranchisement, the legislature began to appropriate more money for white schools and proportionately less for black schools. With no statewide voting rights, African Americans had lost the power they had held in the nineteenth century in the Department of Public Instruction and General Assembly. Meanwhile, education for whites improved rapidly. Passage of compulsory attendance laws in 1907 made a difference, as did increases in appropriations to lengthen the school year to 96 days for blacks and 107 for whites.

But the state had to dig strenuously to get out of the hole that it had dug for itself. In the decade between 1900 and 1910, North Carolina went from forty-eighth in the nation for white adult illiteracy to forty-sixth. Eighteen percent of all North Carolinians and 12 percent of white North Carolinians could not read and write. The low scores of white Southerners on Intelligence Quotient tests in World War I sparked greater laments.[23]

As state appropriations for black schools failed to keep pace with white schools from 1900 to 1930, northern philanthropists sprang into action. With dwindling public school funds to both black schools and teacher training, they made serious financial commitments to the state from about 1908 until the Great Depression. The Anna T. Jeanes Fund proposed to each county that it would fund one-half of a traveling home economics teacher's salary if the county would pay the other half. Twenty-two counties employed Jeanes teachers, and the fund's contribution went from $2,144 in 1909 to $12,728 by 1921. The Rockefeller Foundation's General Education Board paid the salary of the white supervisor for the state's "Negro Rural Schools" and funded private black high schools across the state.[24]

Black parents despaired of the government ever building decent school buildings, so they built facilities themselves and *gave* them to the county. For example, in the academic year 1915–16, statewide thirty-two black schools were built and thirty improved at a total cost of $29,000. African Americans themselves contributed over $21,000 of the total: $15,293 in cash and the rest in labor. They deeded their own land and existing buildings to the county. When the Mecklenburg County school board chairman told complaining black parents that the "board was willing to help those who help themselves" and would pay for half of the cost of public schools if the black community paid for the other half, black parents built six schools. In 1917, the Julius Rosenwald Fund fostered these self-help efforts by appropriating $5,000 to stimulate public school building for African Americans. The fund promised to pay a third, the black community had to raise a third, and then the state had to pay a third of the cost of the building out of taxes. They built twenty-one schools that first year (figs. 8.1 and 8.2).[25]

In other words, African Americans donated school facilities to the state and counties, over and above the taxes that they paid. In fact, they paid a tax share disproportionately higher than their educational allocations, as the white superintendent of African American normal schools proved in 1909.[26] Nonetheless, black North Carolinians privately paid for 30 percent to 50 percent of the cost of their school buildings. And then they deeded them over to the county for no compensation other than the chance for their children to attend "public" schools.

The first black public high school in the state was Charlotte's Second Ward High, established in 1923, and in the same decade the black normal schools became teachers' colleges. Simon Green Atkins, the young Chatham County boy whom Anna Julia Cooper had brought to St. Augustine's in 1876, turned the Slater Industrial and State Normal School into Winston-Salem Teachers College in 1925.

MAKING SEPARATE MORE EQUAL FOR ALL, 1935–1960

By 1938, black and white high schools served most of the state's children, but they went only through the eleventh grade. Many students wanted to apply to college in northern or western states, where twelve years was the norm, but found that they had to take an extra year of high school outside of the state to be accepted. The story of how the state came to fund the final year of high school demonstrates how African American educational campaigning forced white power brokers to improve education for everyone.

Throughout the 1930s, a series of court cases portended that the unequal funding system might soon be found unconstitutional. African Americans did not frontally attack the "separate" part of "separate but equal"; rather, they attacked the "equal" fantasy. While attacking educational disparities, other African Americans filed suits to restore voting rights to African Americans.

 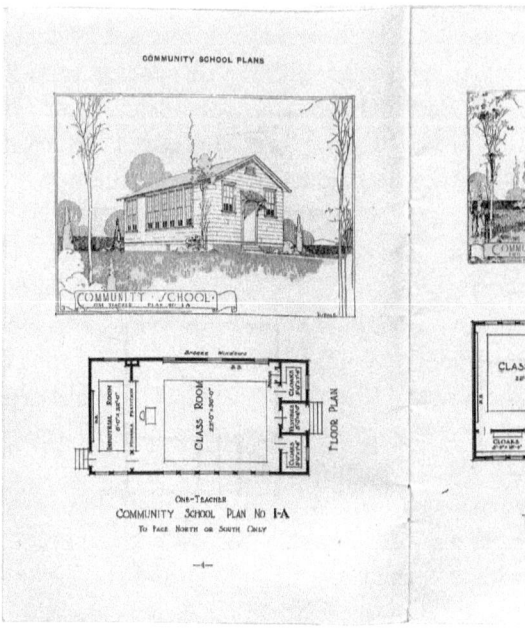 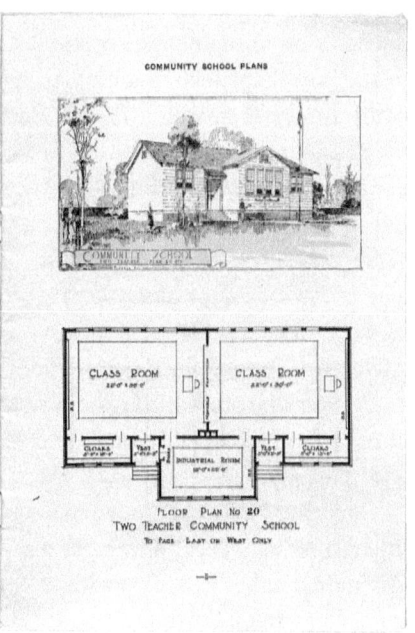

FIGURES 8.1 AND 8.2. Shown here are typical designs for Rosenwald schools: an idealized campus for a community school (cover) and plans for one- and two-teacher schools. From *Community School Plans*, bulletin no. 3, 1924, Julius Rosenwald Fund. Drawings courtesy of the North Carolina State Archives.

Jasper Alston Atkins, Simon Atkins's son, was one of them. Jasper, known as Jack, was born on August 8, 1898, attended Slater Normal and Technical School in Winston-Salem, and graduated from Fisk University as valedictorian in 1919. He then enrolled in Yale Law School, where he served as editor of the *Yale Law Journal* and was elected to the Order of the Coif. He graduated with honors in 1922. While his dad Simon was busy turning Slater into Winston-Salem Teachers College, Jack was in Texas litigating the case *Grovey v. Townsend*, involving the right of African Americans to vote in municipal primaries. Jack Atkins argued the case before the U.S. Supreme Court in 1935 and won. He then returned to Winston-Salem to serve as an administrator at Winston-Salem Teachers College.[27]

Meanwhile, a Missouri case, *Missouri ex rel. Gaines v. Canada*, reached the Supreme Court in 1938, and the court ruled that separate school systems must actually *be* equal. The court found that if a state funded a school for whites, it must fund one for blacks as well. The decision applied most directly to the absence of opportunity. For example, North Carolina funded a law school for whites, but not one for blacks. Most white politicians soon realized that keeping the schools separate would depend on making them equal.

The crisis for the North Carolina General Assembly came when Durham native Pauli Murray was rejected from the University of North Carolina School of Public Welfare and Social Work at Chapel Hill because she was black. Murray, who was named an Episcopal saint in 2013, challenged the decision in her characteristic fashion. She went to the press, threatened to sue, and kept insisting on visiting Chapel Hill and demanding to meet with university president Frank Porter Graham. She put also pressure on the president of the North Carolina College for Negroes, James E. Shepard, to back up her application. There was no graduate social work at the North Carolina College.

Shepard avoided Murray, but he used her application to the University of North Carolina and the Missouri verdict to secure increased funding for his segregated college. He sent North Carolina's governor, Clyde Hoey, a copy of a telegram from a black newspaper that demanded that Shepard comment on the Missouri case. Both Shepard and Hoey knew just how unequal North Carolina's schools really were, and Murray's application presented Shepard with the perfect opportunity to press for more money.[28]

Governor Hoey responded to Shepard and Murray by calling for "courses" in law, medicine, and pharmacy at North Carolina College, with additional graduate courses in agriculture at North Carolina Agricultural and Technical College in Greensboro. Significantly, Hoey asked the General Assembly to equalize salaries between black and white teachers in the public schools, which they began to do very gradually, at a pace that would not close the gap until 1945.[29]

In 1938, North Carolina remained one of only six states that did not provide a twelfth year of high school, so to sugarcoat the pill that Hoey asked white taxpayers to swallow—allocating money for black colleges and teachers' salaries in the Great Depression—he proposed an additional year of high school for all. Thus, Pauli Murray's attempt to enter the University of North Carolina helped produce a twelfth year of high school to bring North Carolina into step with the rest of the nation.

MAKING GOOD ON *BROWN*, 1960–1990

World War II delayed the momentum of the separate-but-equal cases, but when *Brown v. Board of Education* and *Brown II* finally made segregation illegal in 1955, people like Jack Atkins and Pauli Murray expected North Carolina to obey the law and integrate its schools. Nonetheless, those who went to North Carolina's public schools during the period understood that a variety of political maneuvers defied the court's ruling. Schemes like freedom of choice and the Pearsall Plan, which disingenuously shifted the responsibility for desegregation from the state to each of the one hundred counties, prevented any meaningful integration until the late 1960s.

By then Winston-Salem, for example, had made little progress in creating a unitary school system. In 1955 it had consolidated city and county schools to blunt the effect of integrating a city school system in a town that was almost 50 percent black. In 1969 there were seven inner city schools with no white pupils. All of those black schools, unbelievably, were Rosenwald schools that had been constructed from 1914 to 1923. In stark contrast, the suburbs hosted fifteen schools, all built in the late 1940s, 1950s, and 1960s. In 1969, two were completely white and two completely black; Sherwood Forest had 823 students, one of whom was black; and one school met integrated criteria. None of these conditions equaled the legal definition of a desegregated or unitary school system.

In 1968 Jack Atkins had finally had enough—thirteen years after *Brown*, forty-six years after he had graduated with honors from Yale Law School, fifty-four years after he had graduated from Slater, and ninety-eight years after Anna Julia Cooper had brought his dad, Simon Atkins, from Chatham County to St. Augustine's to get the high school education that the state would not provide. Atkins filed suit against the Winston-Salem/Forsyth County School District and the city on behalf of his publicly schooled grandchildren, arguing that the school system must improve historically black school facilities. When the court ruled that Jack Atkins had no standing as a grandfather, his daughter and her husband became the plaintiffs in *Allen v. State Board of Education of North Carolina*.[30]

Collaborating with white civil rights lawyer Norman B. Smith of Greensboro, Atkins's daughter sued to prevent the system and the city from issuing bonds and from spending any more money on schools unless they first improved the historically black—indeed, still almost all black—schools and came up with a plan to achieve "an equal and unitary" school system. That meant approximating the county's racial percentages in each school's pupil assignments and equalizing school facilities. Jack Atkins may have handed over plaintiff status to his daughter, but he continued to write briefs and work with Norman Smith.

The defendants used two primary defenses at each level. In response to Atkins's complaint that the municipality bore responsibility to "eliminate unwholesome surroundings where schools are located in Negro neighborhoods," the city responded that it did not, although it created those conditions by imposing restrictive covenants, zoning to the disadvantage of black neighborhoods, and failing to enforce codes.

Second, William F. Womble Sr., attorney for the school system, took the position that after *Brown* the system no longer had any responsibility to make majority black schools equal to majority white ones. He argued: "The only proper relief in a case where a dual school system is alleged and proved is to have the dual system disestablished and to have each school operated in a non-discriminatory manner." In other words, once black and white separate school systems merged on paper, regardless of whether they achieved real integration or not, Womble argued, no legal reason compelled the city to make formerly black dilapidated schools, now filled with predominantly black pupils, equal to formerly white well-maintained schools, still filled with white pupils. To Womble, *Brown* eliminated both separate and equal. After decades of arguing for "separate but equal," Womble's new argument justified a system that was "unsegregated and unequal."[31]

Civil rights lawsuits, even unsuccessful ones, changed the South by focusing on persistent inequality and by convincing politicians that it would be in their best interests to eliminate it. For example, Atkins and Smith lost their first trial, and the U.S. Fourth Circuit Court of Appeals affirmed the loss. Atkins wrote the writ of certiorari to petition for a U.S. Supreme Court hearing, which was refused.[32] By the time that the Supreme Court declined to hear Jack Atkins's appeal in 1971, the Winston-Salem system had begun using busing as a desegregation tool and had closed all the ancient Rosenwald schools except one. Then the city poured the pent-up $24 million that had been tied up during Atkins's lawsuit into building new integrated schools to which white and black pupils rode the bus. The only historically black school that survived was the beautiful Rosenwald-designed building named Simon G. Atkins High School (figs. 8.3 and 8.4).

Lawsuits like Jack Atkins's and the successful *Swann v. Charlotte-Mecklenburg Board of Education* case in Charlotte brought to light the enormous disparities between formerly black and white schools and, after about 1970, resulted in a productive push for bonds and building schools in the state's urban areas. Judge James B. McMillan, the federal district court judge who ordered in *Swann* that buses could be used as a desegregation tool, said that he had no idea of what abysmal conditions existed in black schools until the litigants and the judge visited Piedmont Middle School, only two miles from the courtroom.[33] After *Swann*, black and white parents dedicated themselves to making Piedmont one of the best schools in Charlotte.

Improving Piedmont Middle School, in a black neighborhood but close to three exclusive white neighborhoods, illustrates how white community leaders and parents found a way to buy into school desegregation in the early 1970s. Scholar Charles Willie describes this dynamic at the local level as "goal displacement," explaining, "The primary responsibility for developing school desegregation plans *that protect the rights of blacks* was transformed into a primary responsibility to develop school desegregation plans *that are the least offensive to whites.*"[34] For a while, when Anthony Foxx went to high school, Charlotte managed to use goal displacement to produce a high level of community involvement in the schools. This involvement led to educational innovation that would never have happened without integration. It pioneered magnet schools, which legal scholar Judy Scales Trent reminds us came about as an incentive for integration even as they accomplished goal displacement by keeping white parents committed to the school system. Without integration imperatives, white parents would have resisted taking their children out of neighborhood schools, even to send them across town for an International Baccalaureate program or to a facility with excellent technology labs.[35]

In Charlotte, the bold move of sending white students from the city's elite suburbs across town to historically black West Charlotte High School resulted in administrators and parents lavishing attention on Foxx's high school. African American principal Bill McMillan remembered, "I think every superintendent, every school board [across the state], wanted West Charlotte to be highly successful.... One, it was the only remaining histori-

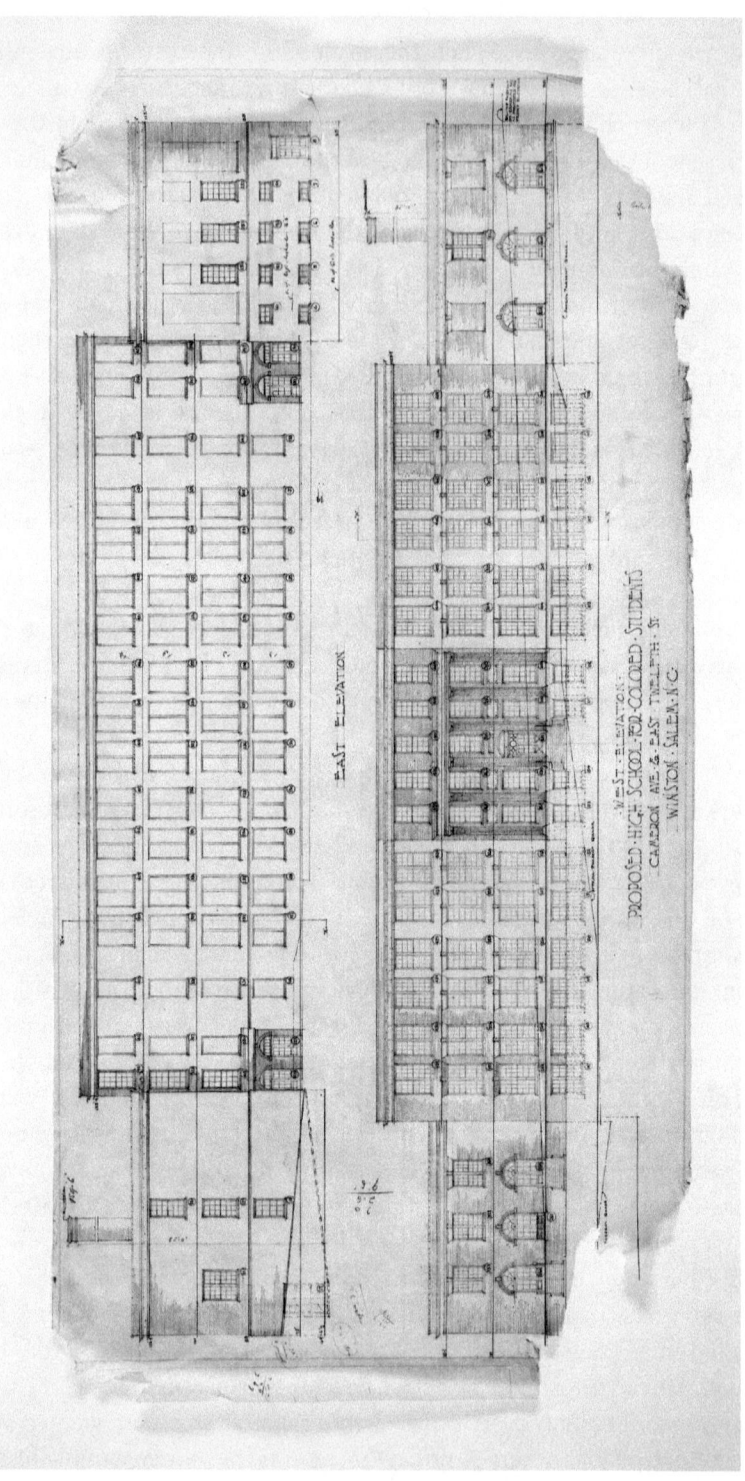

FIGURES 8.3 AND 8.4. North Carolina built more Rosenwald schools than did any other southern state. Generally, they were one-, two-, or three-classroom frame structures. Simon G. Atkins High School (1931) in Winston-Salem was atypical. Shown here are the east and west elevations (*above*) and the basement plan (*opposite*) from 1929 ar-

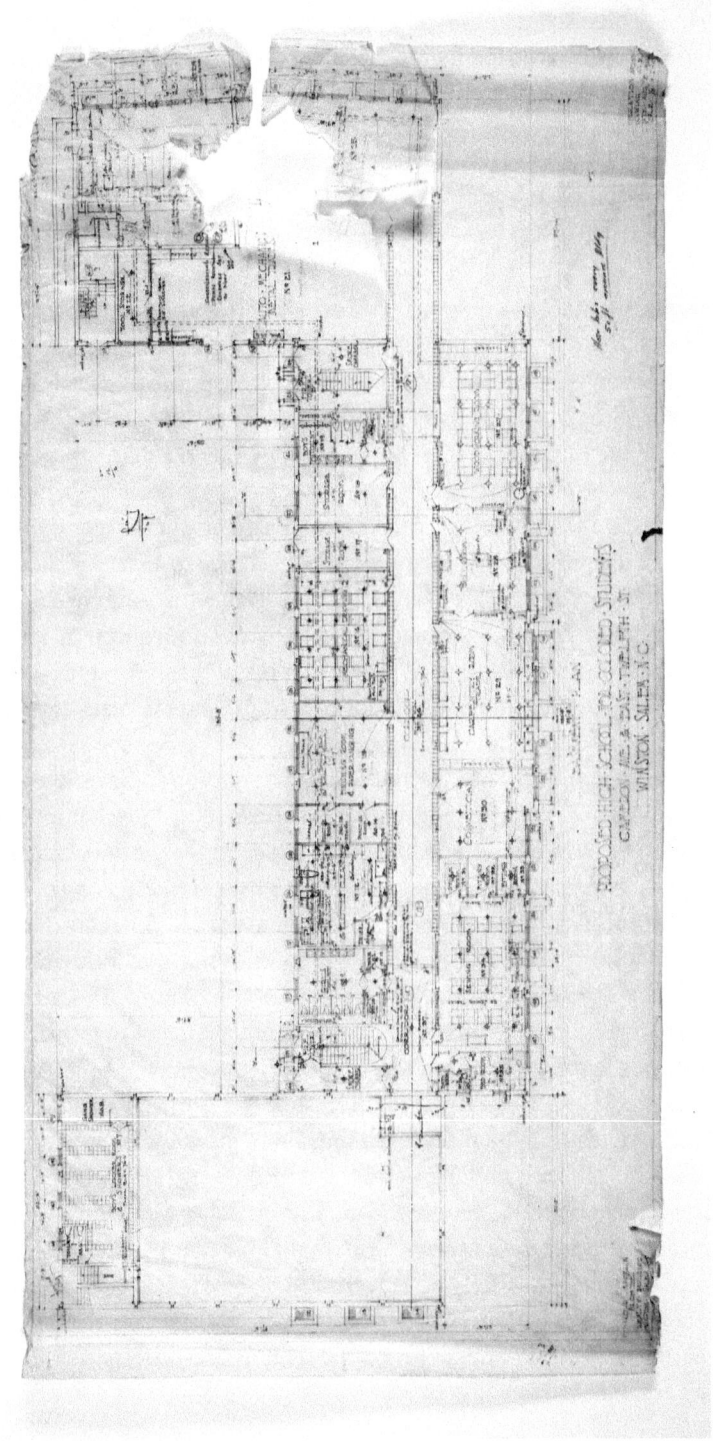

chitectural drawings by Harold Macklin. Four decades later the school became the subject of a civil rights lawsuit. Drawings from the William Roy Wallace Collection, North Carolina State University Libraries, Special Collections. Reproduced with permission.

cally black high school. [We] had to make sure that parents, students, teachers, administrators [were involved]. West Charlotte was the center; so goes West Charlotte, so goes the desegregation."³⁶ Principal McMillan understood goal displacement and put it to work for his school, while keeping in mind African Americans' needs.

DISMANTLING THE "COMMON" SCHOOL, 1990 TO THE PRESENT

The unitary school systems that African American challenges built existed from the early 1970s until the 1990s, when they succumbed to a combination of reactionary politicians, antibusing advocates, the enrollment of children in private schools made viable for the first time in the South by the post-1980 economic boom, the growth of home schooling, and a demographic contingent of out-of-state newcomers who expected neighborhood schools. After 1990, the state lost the historical consciousness of what integration had bequeathed, the gift that "gave a generation a chance to go to school together." In that decade, the courts began issuing decisions that had the effect of upholding resegregation. For example, U.S. District Judge Robert Potter, who had fought the desegregation of public schools in the 1960s and 1970s, ruled in 1999 that the Charlotte-Mecklenburg School System must stop using race as a basis for pupil assignment.

Between 1991 and 2016, as the state's population increased 33 percent, the numbers of children in conventional private schools, either independent or religious, nearly doubled, from 53,372 to 97,721—almost 8 percent of total students. Home schooling grew exponentially as well after 1991. That year, only 4,127 pupils, or 0.4 percent, were home schooled. In 2016 74,563, or almost 6 percent, of the state's school-age children were home schooled. By 2016, 1,008,419 students studied in traditional public schools, and 64,540, or 6 percent, attended charter schools, up from 3 percent in 2012. Almost 87 percent of the state's children still attended conventional public schools in 2012, but four years later, in 2016, only 81 percent of students did.³⁷

These trends suggest that North Carolina's public schools are fracturing and that education is no longer universal in the way that Charles Aycock or *Swann* attorney Julius Chambers fought to make it. Many politicians today assume that integration is not a worthy goal, or that neighborhood schools are a panacea, or that charter schools and vouchers will produce academic excellence, or that the most vocal elements of their constituency will be home schoolers. They budget for public schools and universities along these fault lines.

On a recent trip to the United States, Aung San Suu Kyi, the heroic Burmese dissident leader, lamented the "lost generations" of Burmese students over the fifty years of military rule. In the 1950s, as a newly independent country, Burma had a promising public school system based on that of their former British colonizers, along with the best university in Southeast Asia. First, the military government cut salaries for public school teachers, causing them to "lose respect" in the community. Teachers could not live on public school salaries and had to teach in private schools. Aung San Suu Kyi argued, assuming that Americans would agree, that a democratic nation needs its public school teachers to be respected members of the state structure and that privatizing education demonstrates that the state does not respect its teachers. Before long, she said, Burmese children came to see their teachers as hirelings. In the end, the lack of support for public schooling destroyed Burma's school system. No longer are there young people in Burma who are ready to go to college and university. "We have," she said, "lost generations of students, and our people have been badly educated." By starving its public school system, her nation depleted its store of educational capital.

Over the past century, North Carolina dug itself out of its position as the worst state educationally and the most likely place to find white illiterates by channeling its resources into what North Carolinians called the "common schools." They were common schools not because they were ordinary but because they belonged to all North Carolinians in common. If North Carolina's citizens no longer have schools in common, it may not take very long to reverse a century and a half of progress and spend the state's educational capital in the pursuit of short-term profit.

Current attacks by North Carolina public officials on educational funding and educators' control of public schools and universities will, to recall Charles Aycock's words, "bring our State into the condemnation of a just opinion elsewhere, and mark us as a people who have turned backward." Indeed, in July 2013 the *New York Times* headlined an editorial condemning the state's cuts to education as "The Decline of North Carolina." The first of 1,328 comments written by "J. Maron, Raleigh, NC" read: "I'm a native Tar Heel. These days I feel as if I'm watching the death of someone I've loved intensely all my life. Such sadness."[38] The state's history proves that its schools flourish when its citizens are all in them together: working on shortcomings, learning from differences, pooling resources, and, quite simply, going to school together.

NOTES

This chapter is adapted from the speech "Educational Capital and Human Flourishing: North Carolina Schools, 1865–1970" delivered at the North Carolina Department of Cultural Resources conference "Defining the Contours of the Old North State," October 2012, Chapel Hill, N.C. I thank Stephon Richardson for his excellent research assistance.

1. "Charlotte Mayor Anthony Foxx at the 2012 Democratic National Convention," posted September 12, 2012, http://www.youtube.com/watch?v=J41L7uqNffc (accessed February 15, 2017.).

2. Sarah Caroline Thuesen, *Greater than Equal: African American Struggles for School and Citizenship in North Carolina, 1919-1965* (Chapel Hill: University of North Carolina Press, 2013), 203.

3. Guion G. Johnson, *Ante-bellum North Carolina, 1790-1860* (Chapel Hill: University of North Carolina Press, 1937), 277–82. For the best overview of postbellum black education, see James D. Anderson, *The Education of Blacks in the South, 1865-1935* (Chapel Hill: University of North Carolina Press, 1988).

4. Jonathan Worth to William A. Graham, January 12, 1866, in *The Correspondence of Jonathan Worth*, vol. 1, ed. Joseph Gregoire de Roulhac Hamilton (Raleigh: North Carolina Historical Commission, 1909), 467.

5. *Convention of Freedmen of North Carolina* (Raleigh: The Convention, 1865), 4–5, 14.

6. Edgar W. Knight, *Public Education in the South* (Boston: Ginn and Co., 1922), 367–70; Frenise Logan, "The Legal Status of Public School Education for Negroes in North Carolina, 1877-1894," *North Carolina Historical Review* 32 (July 1955): 346–57.

7. State Superintendent's Monthly School Reports, October 1866, M844 roll 13, RG 105, Bureau of Refugees, Freedmen, and Abandoned Lands, National Archives and Records Administration, Washington, D.C.; J. W. Alvord, *Third Semi-annual Report on Schools for Freedmen, January 1, 1866* (Washington, D.C.: Government Printing Office, 1868), 3–11.

8. Fisk P. Brewer to George Whipple, February 6, 1867, American Missionary Association Papers, Amistad Research Center, Tulane University (New Orleans, La.).

9. D. C. Cashman, *Headstrong: The Biography of Amy Morris Bradley* ([Wilmington, N.C.?]: Broadfoot Publishing, 1990), 159–76; Robert A. Margo, *Race and Schooling in the South, 1880-1950: An Economic History* (Chicago: University of Chicago Press, 1990), 26.

10. *A Record of Fifty Years, 1867-1917: St. Augustine's School* (Raleigh, N.C.: Edwards and Broughton, n.d.). On Anna Julia Cooper, see Cooper, *A Voice from the South*, repr. ed. (New York: Oxford University Press, 1990); Karen A. Johnson, *Uplifting the Women and the Race: The Educational Philosophies and Social Activism of Anna Julia Cooper and Nannie Helen Burroughs* (New York: Garland, 2000); and N. C. Newbold, *Five North Carolina Negro Educators* (Chapel Hill: University of North Carolina Press, 1939).

11. Quoted in Glenda Elizabeth Gilmore, *Gender and Jim Crow: Women and the Politics of White Supremacy, 1896-1920* (Chapel Hill: University of North Carolina Press, 1996), 36.

12. Ibid., 35.

13. Ibid., 37.

14. Ibid., 38.

15. *Second Annual Catalogue of the North Carolina State Colored Normal Schools for 1905-'06* (Raleigh: E. M. Uzzell & Co., for the North Carolina State Board of Education, 1906), 7–17.

16. *Report of the State Superintendent of Public Instruction, 1890* (Raleigh, N.C., 1890). For the best discussion of school building and of women's education, see James L. Leloudis, *Schooling the New South: Pedagogy, Self, and Society in North Carolina, 1880–1920* (Chapel Hill: University of North Carolina Press, 1996). See also Elizabeth Bowles, *A Good Beginning: The First Four Decades of the University of North Carolina at Greensboro* (Chapel Hill: University of North Carolina Press, 1967); and Pamela Dean, "Covert Curriculum: Class, Gender, and Student Culture at a New South Women's College," Ph.D. diss., University of North Carolina at Chapel Hill, 1994.

17. Leloudis, *Schooling the New South*, xiii; Western Carolina University website, www.wcu.edu/celebrate125/history.html (accessed February 15, 2017). For an overview of the feminization of the teaching force, see Joel Pearlmann and Robert Margo, *Women's Work? American Schoolteachers, 1650–1920* (Chicago: University of Chicago Press, 2001).

18. Helen Edmonds, *The Negro and Fusion Politics in North Carolina, 1894–1901* (Chapel Hill: University of North Carolina Press, 1951), 229.

19. Henry Leon Prather, *Resurgent Politics and Educational Progressivism in the New South: North Carolina, 1890–1913* (Rutherford, N.J.: Fairleigh Dickinson University Press, 1979). For a bibliography on the white supremacy campaign in North Carolina, see Gilmore, *Gender and Jim Crow*.

20. Leloudis, *Schooling the New South*.

21. Charles Brantley Aycock, "Speech to the General Assembly, 1903," R. D. W. Connor and Clarence Poe, *The Life and Speeches of Charles Brantley Aycock* (Garden City, N.Y.: Doubleday and Page, 1912), 135.

22. Knight, *Public Education in the South*, 427–28.

23. *Report of the Superintendent of Public Instruction, 1910* (Raleigh, N.C., 1910).

24. Valinda W. Littlefield, "'A Yearly Contract with Everybody and His Brother': Durham County, North Carolina, Black Female Public School Teachers, 1885–1927," *Journal of Negro History* 79 (Winter 1994): 37–53; Littlefield, "'I Am Only One, But I Am One': Southern African American Women Schoolteachers, 1884–1954," Ph.D. diss., University of Illinois, 2003; Lance G. E. Jones, *The Jeanes Teacher in the United States, 1908–1933* (Chapel Hill: University of North Carolina Press, 1937); Anderson, *Education of Blacks in the South*.

25. Thomas W. Hanchett, "The Rosenwald Schools and Black Education in North Carolina," *North Carolina Historical Review* 65 (October 1988): 387–427; Joseph K. Hart, "'The Negro Builds for Himself': The Rosenwald Schools: An Episode in the Epic of Education," *Survey* 52 (September 1, 1924): 563–67, 596.

26. George-Anne Willard, "Charles Lee Coon (1868–1927): North Carolina Crusader for Educational Reform," Ph.D. diss., University of North Carolina at Chapel Hill, 1974.

27. "Biographical Sketch," Jasper Alston Atkins Papers, Manuscripts and Archives, Sterling Library, Yale University, New Haven, Conn.

28. "Dedicate Nine New Buildings," December 6, 1937, f566, b8, Frank Porter Graham Papers, Southern Historical Collection, Wilson Library, University of North Carolina at Chapel Hill; James Shepard to Clyde Hoey, December 15, 1938, quoted in Augustus Merrimon Burns, "Graduate Education for Blacks in North Carolina, 1930–1951," *Journal of Southern History* 46 (May 1980): 204; Augustus Merrimon Burns, "North Carolina and the Negro Dilemma," Ph.D. diss., University of North Carolina at Chapel Hill, 1968, 124–25; Jerry Gershenhorn, "Stalling Integration: The Ruse, Rise, and Demise of North Carolina

College's Doctoral Program in Education, 1951–1962," *North Carolina Historical Review* 82 (April 2005): 155. See also Gershenhorn, *"Hocutt v. Wilson* and Race Relations in Durham," *North Carolina Historical Review* 77 (July 2001): 275–308. On Murray's desegregation attempt, see Glenda Elizabeth Gilmore, *Defying Dixie: The Radical Roots of Civil Rights* (New York: Norton, 2008), 247–90.

29. "Hoey Asks for N.C. Graduate Schools," clipping from *Journal and Guide* (Norfolk, Va.), January 14, 1939, in f382, b15, Pauli Murray Papers, Arthur and Elizabeth Schlesinger Library, Radcliffe Institute for Advanced Study, Harvard University, Cambridge, Mass.; Burns, "Graduate Education for Blacks," 204–5; Burns, "North Carolina and the Negro Dilemma," 77–80.

30. *Allen v. State Board of Education of North Carolina*, folders 1–9, box 1, Atkins Papers; *Atkins v. State Board of Education of North Carolina*, 418 F. 2d 874, http://openjurist.org/418/f2d/874.

31. Supplemental brief of the city of Winston-Salem in support of the motion to dismiss and for summary judgment (served November 23, 1971), box 4, Atkins Papers.

32. *Atkins v. State Board of Education*.

33. James B. McMillan, interview by the author, October 11, 1989, Southern Oral History Program, C-0067, Southern Historical Collection.

34. Charles Vert Willie, *School Desegregation Plans that Work* (Westport, Conn.: Praeger, 1984), 164.

35. Judy Scales Trent, "A Judge Shapes and Manages Institutional Reform: School Desegregation in Buffalo," *NYU Review of Law and Social Change* 119 (1989): 17.

36. Bill McMillan, interview by Pamela Grundy, October 26, 2000, K0824, Southern Oral History Program.

37. Figures compiled from the statistics published by the N.C. Department of Administration. Public school enrollment figures 1991 at http://www.ncdnpe.org/hhh500.aspx (accessed September 15, 2012). Public school and charter school enrollment at http://www.dpi.state.nc.us/docs/fbs/resources/data/factsfigures/2015-16figures.pdf (accessed February 15, 2017). Private schools in 1991 at https://ncdoa.s3.amazonaws.com/s3fs-public/documents/files/hhh540.pdf; in 2016 at https://ncdoa.s3.amazonaws.com/s3fs-public/documents/files/2015-2016%20Conventional%20Schools%20-%20Stats%20Report_0.pdf (accessed on February 15, 2017). Home schooling statistics for 1991 at http://ncdoa.s3.amazonaws.com/s3fs-public/Documents/hhh216.pdf; for 2016, at https://ncdoa.s3.amazonaws.com/s3fs-public/documents/files/15-16%20Home%20School%20Report_0.pdf (accessed February 15, 2017).

38. "The Decline of North Carolina," *New York Times*, July 9, 2013, http://www.nytimes.com/2013/07/10/opinion/the-decline-of-north-carolina.html?module=Search&mabReward=relbias%3Ar&r=0.

LINTHEAD STOMP

CAROLINA COTTON MILL HANDS AND THE MODERN ORIGINS OF HILLBILLY MUSIC

Patrick Huber

"Mountaineer musicians of western North Carolina who know little of cities except by legend and who play by native instinct will come to Charlotte today to perpetuate their art for an invisible audience of hundreds of thousands of people," proclaimed a front-page article in the *Charlotte Observer* on August 9, 1927. "They will make records for the Victor Talking Machine company for distribution in a dozen nations, it was declared yesterday by Ralph S. Peer, scout for the company. Folk-lore songs and banjo selections by artists of the soil who have never read a note but through whose music runs the passion of river torrents and mountain feuds and the melody of valley meadows are to be recorded."[1] A Victor recording crew from Camden, New Jersey, had arrived in Charlotte that August as part of a three-city expedition to the Southeast, and the firm's stopover there marked the first such field-recording session ever held in this important southern commercial and industrial hub. Charlotte sits at the center of the southern Piedmont, a crescent-shaped region of rolling hills between the Appalachian Mountains and the Atlantic Coastal Plain that extends southward from Richmond, Virginia, through the central Carolinas and northern Georgia to Birmingham, Alabama. By 1927, this region, the most urban and heavily industrialized area of the American South, reigned as the world's leading textile-manufacturing center. With almost six hundred mills within a hundred-mile radius, Charlotte had attracted tens of thousands of white migrants from the surrounding Piedmont and mountain counties in the late nineteenth and early twentieth centuries. As a result of the dense clustering of working-class communities, Charlotte and nearby textile towns flourished as hotbeds of musical activity. Over the course of six days in August 1927, in a makeshift studio set up in the auditorium of the Charlotte Observer Building, Peer and his two engineers recorded a total of twelve acts, including such North Carolina and Virginia textile string bands as the Carolina Tar Heels, Kelly Harrell and the Virginia String Band, and Red Patterson's Piedmont Log Rollers. Although the forty-six selections captured at this session represented a remarkable variety of southern music, most of the recordings were classified as what was then called "hillbilly music" or, less pejoratively, "old-time music," the forerunner of American country music.[2]

Since the early 1920s, Victor and other major phonograph companies had marketed such records in their advertisements and catalogs as expressions of the authentic folk music of the rural South, particularly the mountain South. "These old tunes rarely get into the cities," explained Victor's 1924 *Olde Time Fiddlin' Tunes* catalog, "but mountain folk have sung and danced to them for generations." To market these records effectively to rural and working-class white consumers, nearly all of the major companies released hillbilly records prior to the mid-1930s in specially designated numerical series, and their associated marketing labels, including OKeh's "Old Time Tunes," Vocalion's "Old Southern Melodies," and Paramount's "Olde Time Tunes—Southern Series," underscored the supposedly regional folk character and ancient vintage of this music. Such marketing labels, as well as the quaint pastoral images of the barn dances, log cabins, and stands of mountain pines that often graced the covers of hillbilly record catalogs and promotional brochures, all harked back to a preindustrial rural South that was deeply embedded in the popular imagination.[3]

But the evocative and appealing imagery of this promotional literature obscured the modern, urban-industrial origins of the hillbilly music recorded in Charlotte and other southeastern cities. Historians and folklorists have long considered this musical genre to be essentially a commercialized form of traditional rural folk music that originated in southern farming communities and mountain hollows, often isolated from or little influenced by the main currents of modern American life and mass culture. But within central North Carolina and throughout the rest of the southern Piedmont, hillbilly music actually emerged in a rapidly modernizing society of cities and towns, railroads, two-lane highways, hydroelectric plants, and factories. Bill C. Malone and other historians have identified the mass migration of rural and working-class white Southerners to midwestern and West Coast cities during World War II as one of the central themes of country music's historical development. But scholars have paid far less attention to the equally significant forces of industrial development, urban growth, and southern migration in the half-century before World War II that just as profoundly shaped this commercial music.[4] Even to this day, scholars often view hillbilly music as the product of the traditional rural South and overlook the importance of modern influences, especially urban and industrial ones, on this music, particularly the recordings made by southeastern mill-hand musicians. However, the hillbilly music that sprang forth from the Piedmont's cities and towns is, in fact, as thoroughly modern in its origins and evolution as its quintessentially modern counterpart, jazz.

Arguably, working-class white Southerners exerted their greatest influence on American culture by broadcasting and recording hillbilly music between 1922 and 1942.[5] Indeed, these contributions marked the first time that Southern white working people played a significant role in shaping American popular music and mass culture, and no group of Southerners did more to create this commercial music than Piedmont textile mill hands. To be sure, many hillbilly musicians earned their livings as farmers and sharecroppers, coal miners, railroaders, building-trades craftsmen, or even as doctors, lawyers, and merchants. But, as Malone has noted, Piedmont textile workers comprised the single largest occupational group to sing and play in front of radio and recording studio microphones before World War II. Between 1922 and 1942, singers and musicians from Piedmont textile villages played on, conservatively, more than 1,500, or 6 percent, of the approximately 23,000 hillbilly records released in the United States. Although the occupational backgrounds of many hillbilly artists remain unknown, nearly 110 performers who worked, at one time or another, in southeastern cotton mills made commercial hillbilly recordings. More than half of them were North Carolinians, including such now-celebrated artists as Charlie Poole, Gwin Foster, David McCarn, J. E. Mainer, Wade Mainer, and Dorsey Dixon (see table 9.1).[6]

Within central North Carolina and the rest of the southern Piedmont, much of the hillbilly music heard on prewar phonograph records and radio broadcasts emerged from the new urban-industrial culture created chiefly by the textile industry. Beginning in the 1880s and accelerating during the 1900s and 1910s, businessmen and town boosters across the region embraced industrial capitalism as the engine that would bring progress and economic development to a New South still recovering from the devastation of the Civil War. As a result, cotton mills sprouted up all across the Piedmont, first along the region's swift-running rivers and then, increasingly after 1900, with the harnessing of the hydroelectric power of these same rivers, in the region's fast-growing cities and towns. "The Piedmont region," proclaimed the Southern Railway's 1909 *Textile Directory*, "is one of the great cotton manufacturing districts of the world and has such prominence in this industry that the territory of the Southern railway [sic] between Danville, Va., and Atlanta, Ga., a distance of 400 miles, has been referred to as one long cotton mill village." Other industries contributed to the re-

TABLE 9.1. North Carolina mill hands who made hillbilly music recordings, by hometown, 1925–1942

ALBEMARLE
Sam Poplin

BOONVILLE
Earl Nance

BURLINGTON / GREENSBORO
John F. Butler
Buchanan H. "Buck" Butler
Jack Caudle
Jay Hugh Hall
Roy Hall
Okel E. Moore (later Evans)

CANTON
Tommy Magness

CHARLOTTE / CONCORD
Lester "Pete" Bivins
"Daddy" John Love
Joseph Emmett "J. E." Mainer
Wade Mainer
Claude "Zeke" Morris

DURHAM
Sam Pridgen
Norwood Tew

GASTONIA / BELMONT / SHELBY
Luke Baucom
Harvey Ellington
David O. Fletcher
Gwin Foster
Charles Freshour
Roy "Whitey" Grant
Shannon Grayson
Arval Hogan
Howard Long
David McCarn
Palmer Rhyne
Reid Summey

George Wade
Wilmer Watts
Percy "Frank" Wilson

HICKORY / NEWTON
Julius "Nish" McClured
Horace Propst
Homer "Pappy" Sherrill

LEAKSVILLE / SPRAY / DRAPER
Lonnie Austin
Esmond Harris
Dallas Hubbard
Hamon Newman
Charlie Poole
Posey Rorer
Odell Smith
Walter "Kid" Smith
Norman Woodlieff

LEXINGTON
Dewey Cooper
Tom Cooper

ROCKINGHAM
Beatrice (née Moody) Dixon
Dorsey M. Dixon
Howard Dixon
James Mirtz "Mutt" Evans
Frank Gerald
Jimmie Tarlton

RUTHERFORDTON / SPINDALE
Dee Christopher Cole
Thomas O. "Tom" Hendrix
Guy B. Howard Sr.
John W. Starnes

STATESVILLE
Charlie Parker

Source: Based on Doug DeNatale and Glenn Hinson, "The Southern Textile Song Tradition Reconsidered," Appendix B, in Songs about Work: Essays in Occupational Culture for Richard A. Reuss, edited by Archie Green, Special Publications of the Folklore Institute, no. 3 (Bloomington: Folklore Institute, Indiana University, 1993), 104–7, augmented with the author's own research into census records and various other public documents, historical newspapers, and secondary sources.

gion's burgeoning economy, including cigarette and tobacco manufacturers in Richmond and Durham and furniture factories in High Point and Hickory. But none of them dominated the region that sociologist Rupert Vance called the "Piedmont Crescent of Industry" more than textile production. By 1929, the southern Piedmont contained almost fourteen hundred textile mills, three-fourths of them clustered in the Carolinas, that employed more than a quarter million workers, most of whom were either rural migrants from economically collapsing upcountry and mountain farms or only a generation removed from that rural life. With this surge of industrial growth, the southern Piedmont officially surpassed long-dominant New England to become the world's greatest center of textile manufacturing, producing approximately two-thirds of the cotton cloth manufactured in the United States.[7]

With the construction of cotton mills and the gathering of displaced white farm families to tend their whirring spindles and beating looms, a new world of cities and towns, roaring factories, and crowded mill villages rapidly emerged.[8] And within these mills and their villages, entire families, including children as young as six and seven years old (prior to the enactment of Progressive Era child labor laws), became industrial workers. Before the passage of the New Deal's National Industrial Recovery Act in 1933, southern mill hands worked ten- to eleven-hour shifts, five days a week, plus a half-day on Saturdays, tending clattering weaving looms and spinning frames in stiflingly hot, lint-choked conditions for some of the lowest industrial wages in the nation; townspeople and farmers alike disparagingly called these workers "lintheads" or "factory trash." Most mill hands, approximately 70 percent in 1929, resided in mill-village housing, which textile firms constructed and then rented to their employees. After 1900, as electricity began to replace water as the power source in these factories, mill villages were often built on the outskirts of cities and towns, and depending on the size of the workforce, these communities might contain anywhere from a few dozen houses laid out along a central dirt road in the rural countryside to several hundred closely spaced cottages neatly arranged in rows along paved streets in suburban areas.[9]

Although textile workers came under the close surveillance of the mill superintendents and their staffs of ministers, social workers, and recreation directors, they nonetheless enjoyed a greater array of cultural advantages in these villages than in the rural countryside. During World War I, textile wages soared to all-time highs, sometimes tripling between 1915 and 1920, and mill hands were soon purchasing a variety of consumer products, often on installment plans. With their wages, they could also afford to participate avidly in the nation's blossoming mass culture. By the mid-1920s, affordable Model T automobiles and the powerful media of radios, phonographs, mass-circulation magazines and newspapers, and Hollywood motion pictures had initiated southern mill hands into modern America's mass culture and also reoriented daily life in Carolina mill villages. "Since 1920 life in the mill village has shared in the general twentieth-century change," Marjorie Potwin observed in *Cotton Mill People of the Piedmont: A Study in Social Change* (1927). "We have the auto and the movies and the radio, the lipstick and the boyish bob. We have an almost overwhelming complexity of old customs and old standards with new ways and new ideas.... Granny wears a sunbonnet and came to the mill in a farm wagon, the young'uns wear georgette and silk hose and own a Ford car, Grandpaw chaws terbacker and fiddles, Grandson smokes cigarettes and takes home jazz records for the Victrola."[10]

The momentous social and economic changes that remade central North Carolina and the rest of the southern Piedmont in the half century following Reconstruction, particularly the integration of mill hands into the nation's mass culture and consumer economy, played a significant role in shaping the development of hillbilly music. The music that mill workers performed on radio and records during the 1920s and 1930s emerged from this swiftly modernizing world and the often wrenching working-class experiences of social dislocation, mass migration, class formation, urban life, industrial work, race relations, and labor strife. When hard-pressed farm families left the countryside to find work in the Piedmont's bustling cities and textile towns, they brought with them their fiddles, banjos, guitars, and assorted musical traditions, and although many of them were already accomplished singers and musicians when they arrived, their exposure to a wide range of musical influences, along with their access to factory-made instruments, radios, phonographs, sheet music, songbooks, and musical instructional booklets, led to a flourishing musical culture within Carolina mill villages. Mill-hand singers and musicians certainly continued to learn new songs and tunes in face-to-face exchanges with friends, neighbors, and coworkers in Piedmont textile villages, but they also augmented their evolving repertoires with material learned directly from phonograph records and radio broadcasts. By the mid-1920s, the singer and five-string banjo player Charlie Poole, of Spray, North Carolina, could count among his musical influences not only other local practitioners of these arts but also the "classic" banjo virtuoso Fred Van Eps and the vaudeville singing star Al Jolson, whose music he had heard only on phonograph records (see fig. 9.1). Exposure to a greater variety of new musical selections and musical styles spawned rapid innovations in which musicians blended local fiddling and string-band traditions

FIGURE 9.1. Hillbilly music had its origins in the dusty textile mills of North Carolina's Piedmont. Shown here are Charlie Poole (*left*) and the North Carolina Ramblers (Posey Rorer [*center*], and Roy Harvey [*right*]), 1927. Photograph courtesy of Kinney Rorer.

with the contemporary sounds of the nation's commercial music to create a wildly popular hillbilly music that has been described as "the most playful and democratic of mill workers' contributions to the popular culture of the nation and the world."[11]

Several factors account for Piedmont mill hands' dominance in the hillbilly music industry prior to World War II. Because of the region's proximity and rail accessibility, its cluster of closely spaced cities, and the rich pool of musical performers these cities attracted, New York–based record companies focused their searches for new talent and their field-recording sessions in the major cities of the Piedmont South, where hundreds of thousands of textile workers lived.[12] But other factors intrinsic to the southern textile industry also help explain these musicians' overrepresentation on hillbilly records. One such factor was the remarkable concentration of string bands, brass bands, vocal quartets, and other musical ensembles that thrived in Piedmont mill villages. In the rural countryside, fiddlers and banjo pickers had long furnished the music for square dances, corn shuckings, barn raisings, and other social affairs. But the gathering of hundreds, sometimes even thousands, of workers in a single mill village offered mill hands greater opportunities both to form musical groups and to perform for appreciative audiences. In fact, although hillbilly music is usually characterized as a rural or rural-derived musical expression, the formation of string bands with actual names and regular members was chiefly an urban phenomenon, particularly in the Piedmont South. "Everybody tried to make the old-time music at the cotton mills," recalled guitarist and singer Roy "Whitey" Grant, who worked at Gastonia, North Carolina's Firestone Cotton Mills before joining the long-lived radio string band the Briarhoppers in 1941 on station WBT-Charlotte. "A lot of the boys that we knew, or heard of, after we came in formed bands. They would get together in the cotton mills and the first thing you know they would form bands. On Saturday or Sunday, when the mill wasn't running, they had a little band stand up there and would draw a big crowd." Although mill hands usually worked exceedingly long hours prior to 1933, their leisure time and close proximity to other musicians afforded them the chance to practice their music more regularly and thus to become proficient, accomplished entertainers.[13]

Piedmont textile musicians and bands also enjoyed numerous opportunities to play their music publicly for neighbors and coworkers. Within their own mill communities and in surrounding cities and towns, these performers supplied the entertainment for picnics, parades, fairs, dances, political rallies, religious revivals, union meetings, and even civic club luncheons. Even in smaller textile towns, organizations such as fraternal lodges, American Legion posts, Boy Scout troops, churches, and Bible study classes often engaged textile bands to play for fund-raisers in exchange for a percentage of the gate receipts. Playing at these events allowed mill-hand singers and musicians to hone their musical skills and sometimes to earn extra cash. Moreover, such performances enhanced their musical reputations within their communities, often opening the door to recording contracts, radio programs, and additional concert bookings. For many, a career as a professional entertainer was far more attractive and financially rewarding than industrial work, and the monotonous routine, long hours, and low wages of textile work inspired hundreds of ambitious singers, fiddlers, guitarists, and banjo pickers to try to escape their dead-end mill jobs through music making.[14]

During the mid- to late 1920s, the expansion of radio stations across the southern Piedmont spurred the demand for entertainers who could perform on live broadcasts. Atlanta, Charlotte, and Richmond, all of which boasted multiple stations, soon became important regional broadcasting centers that attracted hundreds of aspiring singers and musicians, many of them North Carolinians, who sought a chance to play over the airwaves. By the mid-1930s, Piedmont radio stations were regularly broadcasting a variety of hillbilly music programs, including WBT-Charlotte's *Crazy Barn*

Dance, a Saturday-night jamboree sponsored by the regional division of the Crazy Water Crystals Company, the Texas-based manufacturer of a popular laxative. But even those performers fortunate enough to land a sponsored fifteen-minute daily radio show or a spot on a Saturday-night barn dance usually did not receive a salary. Instead, they capitalized on their radio exposure to book and advertise their personal appearances at ten- and twenty-five-cent-admission shows in theaters and schoolhouses across the southern Piedmont, where the region's textile mills and other manufacturing plants had gathered thousands of working-class families into concentrated pockets of music fans. The wages those industries paid allowed musicians and string bands to play before paying audiences within a one-hundred-mile radius virtually every night of the week.[15]

By the mid-1920s, as a result of intensive road-building campaigns, thousands of miles of two-lane, hard-surfaced roads crisscrossed the southern Piedmont, making it possible for musicians and string bands to travel to far-flung recording sessions, radio dates, and live performances. Stretching through the heart of Virginia, the Carolinas, and Georgia, U.S. Route 29 "tied the principal towns and secondary roads together" in the region, historian Allen Tullos has noted, and "paved the way for some of the first hillbilly bands to earn their livings performing at a Spartanburg high school auditorium one night, at a Gastonia mill recreation center the next evening, and on a Charlotte radio station the following morning." By 1935, dozens of radio string bands with names like J. E. Mainer's Crazy Mountaineers, the Briarhoppers, the Honolulu Strollers, Dr. Bennett's Smoky Mountain Boomers, and Raymond Lindsey's Combinators were barnstorming throughout the southern Piedmont, staging one-night shows for audiences of appreciative textile mill hands, tobacco workers, and farmers. Although it usually paid double or triple a weaver's weekly wages, the life of a touring musician on the "kerosene circuit" was difficult. "Back in those days you just rode and rode and played and played," explained fiddler Homer "Pappy" Sherrill, who fronted a Hickory, North Carolina, radio string band during the mid-1930s. "It didn't matter how small the buildings were, you played 'em anyway, and just put on the full show. And you got up there and picked your heart out—with no p.a. system, sweat running off your elbows, you couldn't hardly feel the strings on the fiddle. Man, that was rough days then.... We'd put on two shows sometimes, and it'd be midnight before we even got away from there."[16]

Some mill hands developed a high degree of musical aptitude as a result of extensive "industrial welfare" programs sponsored by Piedmont mills. Such programs, common among larger, more progressive textile firms before

World War I, were designed to help rural migrants assimilate to mill-village life, offer recreational outlets for employees and their families, and, most important, promote employee loyalty to the company during times of labor shortage. Between the 1890s and the mid-1920s, such firms often engaged full-time musical directors to provide workers and their children with violin, guitar, mandolin, and singing lessons. "No Mill Company Lays More Stress upon the Musical Feature than the Carolina Cotton & Woolen Mills," proclaimed a 1920 Charlotte *Mill News* article. The Carolina Company, which operated a chain of ten mills in the adjoining towns of Leaksville, Spray, and Draper (all of which were consolidated and incorporated, in 1967, as Eden), North Carolina, employed a musical director and several assistants to teach music classes and oversee mill-sponsored organizations such as "Hawaiian guitar clubs, mandolin clubs, guitar clubs for girls, glee clubs, [and] three male quartets." "There are 1,000 people taking voice, in class or group singing," the *Mill News* reported. "The children are taught in community 'sings' of from 500 to 800. Group singing is one of the features upon which stress is particularly laid. The people are urged to come and sing. And they are taught simple old time songs, classical selections, religious songs, and jazz tunes of the day.... In the violin classes the same methods are used as are taught in the New York city public schools." Mill sponsorship of such bands and formal musical instruction not only introduced textile workers and their children to a wide range of classical and popular music but also fostered high levels of musical literacy and musicianship. As a result, thousands of employees and their family members learned to play musical instruments and to read musical notation. Moreover, as part of their welfare programs, textile firms often sponsored community brass bands, orchestras, string ensembles, gospel quartets, and occasionally even minstrel troupes, all of which were composed of employees. Although most such groups performed chiefly at company picnics, community concerts, school closings, and other local events, at least a couple of them managed to make phonograph records: the Tubize Royal Hawaiian Orchestra, sponsored by Tubize Artificial Silk Company of Hopewell, Virginia, recorded six issued sides for OKeh in 1929 (two of which appeared in the label's "Old Time Tunes" series), and the Proximity String Quartet, which may have been sponsored by the Proximity Manufacturing Company of Greensboro, North Carolina, waxed two sides for Columbia at a 1928 field session in Johnson City, Tennessee.[17]

Even the very nature of industrial labor and the organization of the textile industry encouraged the development of a vibrant musical culture in Piedmont mill communities. Tending weaving looms and spinning frames, for example, required dexterity and nimble fingers, and although some unfortunate musicians had their musical careers abruptly ended by amputated fingertips, crushed hands, and other occupational accidents, the physical demands of such work exercised and developed the same fine motor skills used in playing the guitar, fiddle, and banjo. Furthermore, the perpetual movement of dissatisfied workers from one mill to the next prior to the mid-1920s reinvigorated the musical culture of mill villages through the continuous introduction of new singers and musicians who brought with them different repertoires and styles. With their concentrations of hundreds and sometimes thousands of workers, North Carolina mill villages, like those across the rest of the Piedmont South, formed important sites for the exchange of a varied assortment of songs and tunes, musical styles, and instrumental techniques among aspiring musicians. And the relatively cosmopolitan character of southeastern mill villages—which drew together workers with various musical skills and repertoires from all across the Piedmont and Southern Appalachia as well as, to a lesser degree, from other parts of the nation—contributed to the rich musical diversity heard on hillbilly records and radio broadcasts.[18]

Work itself often inspired and formed the subject matter for songs. In October 1929, for example, a Belmont, North Carolina, string band billed as Wilmer Watts and the Lonely Eagles recorded such a song for Paramount titled "Cotton Mill Blues," an adaptation of George D. Stutts's poem "A Factory Rhyme," originally published in his chapbook *Picked Up Here and There* (1900). On their recording, Watts and the band confronted the social stigma attached to textile workers, complaining that "uptown people" call them "trash" and the "ignorant factory set."[19] Carolina mill hands also wrote their own songs based upon their daily frustrations and hardships working in the mills. Dorsey Dixon, of East Rockingham, North Carolina, composed several occupational songs, most notably "Weave Room Blues," in which he recounted his difficulties in operating his looms as well as his struggles to raise a family on his weaver's wages. "Working in a weave room, fighting for my life, / Trying to make a living for my kiddies and my wife," he sang on his 1936 Bluebird recording of the song. "Some are needing clothing and some are needing shoes, / But I'm getting nothing but the 'weave room blues.'" Eventually, Dixon recorded two additional textile songs of his own composition on prewar hillbilly records. Altogether, North Carolina mill hands made commercial recordings of ten such occupational songs between 1929 and 1938. Several of these songs, including David McCarn's "Cotton Mill Colic" and Dixon's "Weave Room Blues," entered oral tradition and circulated within southern textile communities during the Great Depression and then, after World War II, became enshrined as classic protest songs within the urban folk music revival and the American labor movement.[20]

Not only was the hillbilly music created by Piedmont textile workers the product of a modern, urban-industrial world, but, as the above occupational songs suggest, much of this music also offered social commentary on this new emerging world. Hillbilly records present compelling narratives and images of the modernizing South from the perspectives of those who felt the effects of industrial development most strongly but who also left few written documents detailing their experiences. As a commercial product, however, these records cannot be considered the pure, unmediated expression of white working-class Southerners, for, as cultural historian George Lipsitz reminds us, among other examples of production control, recording companies "censored lyrics" and "insisted that performers imitate previous commercial successes rather than giving free rein to their own creativity." Nonetheless, these records do offer glimpses of how Piedmont mill-hands-turned-musicians engaged with and negotiated modernity in their daily lives. In doing so, these records both broaden and deepen historians' understanding of the creation of the modern South by contributing long-absent working-class voices to the larger public dialogue about modernity that so engaged elite cultural observers such as Henry Ford, F. Scott Fitzgerald, H. L. Mencken, and the Vanderbilt Agrarians during the Jazz Age and the Great Depression.[21]

Much of the hillbilly music created by North Carolina mill hands, for example, illuminates their conflicted, often ambivalent responses to the emerging modern South and to the changing configurations of white working-class life and culture. Perhaps one of the best examples of this is David McCarn's "Cotton Mill Colic," which he recorded at a 1930 RCA-Victor field session in Memphis, Tennessee. Born in Gaston County, North Carolina, in 1905, the son of mill-hand parents, McCarn began working in the mills after dropping out of school at the age of twelve. But he soon came to despise textile work and spent much of his late teens and early twenties rambling around the United States.[22] McCarn wrote "Cotton Mill Colic" in 1928 during a severe economic depression in the southern textile industry, and in the song he drew upon his own specific struggles and grievances as a Gastonia mill hand. He titled it "Cotton Mill Colic," he later explained, because "colic," in the Carolina vernacular, meant to "complain" or "gripe," and, as he admitted, "I was colicking about the hard times and the cotton mills, you know. So that seemed a pretty fit word for the song."[23] Although couched in humor, "Cotton Mill Colic" expressed a deep sense of working-class resentment and alienation seldom heard on commercial recordings of the 1920s and 1930s:

When you buy clothes on easy terms,
The collectors treat you like measly worms.
One dollar down, and then, Lord knows,
If you don't make a payment, they'll take your clothes.
When you go to bed, you cain't sleep,
You owe so much at the end of the week.
No use to colic, they're all that way,
Pecking at your door till they get your pay.
I'm a-gonna starve, ever'body will,
'Cause you cain't make a living at a cotton mill.

When you go to work, you work like the devil,
At the end of the week, you're not on the level.
Payday comes, you pay your rent,
When you get through, you've not got a cent,
To buy fatback meat, pinto beans,
Now and then you get turnip greens.
No use to colic, we're all that way,
Cain't get the money to move away.
I'm a-gonna starve, ever'body will,
'Cause you cain't make a living at a cotton mill.

Twelve dollars a week is all we get,
How in the heck can we live on that?
I got a wife and fourteen kids,
We all have to sleep on two bedsteads.
Patches on my britches, holes in my hat,
Ain't had a shave since my wife got fat [became pregnant?].
No use to colic, ever' day at noon,
The kids get to crying in a different tune.
I'm a-gonna starve, ever'body will,
'Cause you cain't make a living at a cotton mill.

They run a few days and then they stand [i.e., shut down],
Just to keep down the working man.
We cain't make it, we never will,
As long as we stay at a lousy mill.
The poor're gettin' poorer, the rich're gettin' rich,
If I don't starve, I'm a son of a gun.
No use to colic, no use to rave,
We'll never rest till we're in our grave.

> I'm a-gonna starve, nobody will,
> 'Cause you cain't make a living at a cotton mill.²⁴

Unlike most other contemporary textile songs, "Cotton Mill Colic" is not specifically about the daily miseries of factory labor. Instead, it concerns itself with working-class consumption—or, rather, the lack of it—and the vicious downward cycle of debt and poverty that ensnared tens of thousands of textile mill families. Mill hands occupied an impossible economic position, McCarn suggested, because the longer they worked in the mills, the deeper into debt they sank. Beyond these class resentments, he also used the song to explore an important gender dilemma that plagued male textile workers. In "Cotton Mill Colic," McCarn complained about mill managers' refusal to pay him a living wage with which he can purchase not only those little luxuries he desires, such as a shave at the barbershop, but also those barest of life's necessities, such as food and clothes for his wife and children. Mill hands' paltry wages, McCarn asserted, emasculated working men by preventing them from fulfilling their traditional masculine roles as family breadwinners.²⁵

If a considerable amount of the hillbilly music recorded by North Carolina mill hands offered contemporary responses to the emerging modern South, the records also revealed, not surprisingly, that these singers and musicians responded in a variety of ways to this new world in the making. But the differences have often been downplayed or ignored in the scholarly literature, especially that of the 1920s and 1930s, which consistently characterized southern textile workers as a largely homogeneous group.²⁶ In fact, such workers actually constituted a comparatively diverse population, one that was often sharply divided by occupational skill and experience, gender, ethnicity, political views, religious beliefs, personal ethics, and career aspirations. Similarities clearly existed among them, but differences played a critical role in shaping both their lives and the ways in which they understood their world. Certain cultural trends and behaviors associated with the rise of the automobile, to take one example, distressed devout fundamentalist Christians such as Dorsey Dixon, who performed on radio and records between 1934 and 1938 with his younger brother Howard in a guitar-and-steel-guitar duo called the Dixon Brothers. For more than thirty-five years Dixon struggled to earn a living in the cotton mills of the Carolina Piedmont, but by calling he was a guitarist, singer, and songwriter who believed that his special mission in life was to spread the gospel through music. Throughout his life, he wrote or arranged more than one hundred sacred and secular songs as part of this mission, and several of his most popular compositions of the 1930s criticized what he saw as a profoundly disturbing trend of modern southern life: the erosion of bedrock Christian morals.[27]

Nowhere did Dixon explore this theme more compellingly than in his most famous song, "I Didn't Hear Anybody Pray," better known as "Wreck on the Highway," the title of Roy Acuff's 1942 hit version. Dixon wrote the song, probably in late 1937, based upon a deadly automobile accident that occurred on U.S. Highway 1 near his hometown of East Rockingham. After his shift at the Entwistle Mill ended, he went to view the wrecked sedan in which two local residents had been instantly killed. "I was looking in on the floorboard," Dixon later recalled, "and I seen bottles—broken bottles—and blood all mixed up there. 'Course, they probably was Coca-Cola bottles. But it was glass, you know, all broken to pieces and mixed up with blood there on the floorboard of that old wrecked car. And the thought came across my mind that many times cars had wrecked and killed people and that whiskey was mixed up with the broken glass and blood. And that's how I was inspired to write ['I Didn't Hear Anybody Pray']." A few months later, on January 25, 1938, Dixon and his brother Howard recorded his new song at an RCA-Victor field session in Charlotte. "Whiskey and glass all together / Was mixing with blood where they lay," Dixon sang on one of the verses. "Death played her hand in destruction, / But I didn't hear nobody pray."[28]

Dixon's composition is more than just another hillbilly song about a fatal drunk driving accident. As one music scholar has noted, "What is even more horrifying [to Dixon] than the violence itself is the reaction of those who run out from their homes to witness the tragedy—namely, their failure to lift even a single voice in prayer for the souls of the dead and the dying." If McCarn's "Cotton Mill Colic" complains about the inability of mill hands to participate fully in America's consumer culture, Dixon's "I Didn't Hear Anybody Pray" is about the dangers that befall those who indulge too much in "worldly" amusements and, as a result, lose their way spiritually. In this song, then, Dixon transformed a grisly scene on a small southern highway into a sweeping indictment of what he feared was an increasingly secular and godless society.[29]

Other mill-hand musicians, in contrast, celebrated the liberating pleasures and freedoms of modern life. One striking example is the Three Tobacco Tags' mildly risqué 1938 recording, "How Can I Keep My Mind on Driving." This string trio, like the Dixon Brothers, also emerged from the Carolina Piedmont's textile mill culture; its original members—guitarist Reid Summey and mandolin players George Wade and Luke Baucom—all had worked in Gastonia cotton mills prior to becoming full-time radio and recording artists. Between 1934 and 1937, the band regularly performed on the same Saturday-night hillbilly radio program as the Dixon Brothers, WBT's *Crazy Barn Dance*. But unlike the Dixons, who adhered to an older, more traditional gospel-inflected sound, the Three Tobacco Tags gravitated toward the popular music of the day. Indeed, their "How Can I Keep My Mind on Driving" appears to be a version of a 1936 song of that same title by the Tin Pan Alley songwriter and music publisher Fred Fisher, who composed such pop standards as "Peg o' My Heart," "Dardanella," and "Come Josephine in My Flying Machine."[30] The Three Tobacco Tags recorded "How Can I Keep My Mind on Driving" on the same day, January 25, 1938, at the same Charlotte field session at which, only an hour or so before, the Dixon Brothers had waxed "I Didn't Hear Anybody Pray." But the Three Tobacco Tags' song offers a starkly different reaction to the automobile than does the Dixon Brothers' song. The opening stanza of "How Can I Keep My Mind on Driving," in which a flustered automobile driver addresses the police officer who has just pulled him over, goes:

> Say, how can I keep my mind on driving
> When my gal is driving me mad?
> How can I keep my mind on steering
> When my gal is steering me bad?
> How can I keep shifting my gears
> When my gal keeps pecking my ears?
> How can I keep throwing my clutch
> When my gal keeps clutching so much?
> I keep yelling, I keep telling
> T'ain't no time to neck.
> She don't listen, just keeps kissing,
> That's why I'm a wreck.
> Oh, take away my driver's license,
> I won't be mad; in fact, I will be glad.
> How can I keep my mind on driving
> When my gal is driving me mad?[31]

Clearly, the Three Tobacco Tags take a much more liberal, lighthearted attitude toward the automobile, independent women, changing sexual behaviors, and run-ins with the law than the fundamentalist Dixon Brothers were likely to take. Despite their obvious differences, though, "I Didn't Hear Anybody Pray" and "How Can I Keep My Mind on Driving" both reveal a genuine recognition that automobiles had ushered in significant changes in daily southern life. These changes may be pleasurable, as in the Three Tobacco Tags' song, or they may be deeply troubling, as in the Dixon Brothers' song.³² But this pair of recorded hillbilly songs offers a glimpse of the diverse attitudes held by Piedmont mill hands and, equally important, exposes some of the multiple, often ambivalent ways that these workers grappled with the birth of the modern South.

David McCarn, Dorsey Dixon, the Three Tobacco Tags, and most of their fellow mill-hand musicians spent much of their lives in small southern cities and textile towns. Their experiences, however, combined with their contact with the powerful mass media of commercial radio and phonograph records, enabled them to engage, through their music and, in some cases, their songwriting, in serious cultural conversations about some of the most significant social changes then transforming Carolina working-class life. Indeed, mill-hand musicians were undoubtedly children of the modern age, for they were among the first generation of Southerners to be deeply influenced by automobiles, movies, radios, phonograph records, and mass-circulation newspapers and magazines. All of these modern innovations offered textile workers glimpses of a world far beyond the tenant farms, mountain hollows, and rural hamlets that had circumscribed their parents' and grandparents' lives. Piedmont mill hands not only avidly participated, as much as their wages allowed, in the nation's expansive mass culture, but they also inscribed their working-class culture upon this same mass culture. As inhabitants of an emergent modern cotton-mill world, these musicians combined the collective memories of the rural countryside with the upheavals of urban-industrial life to create a distinctive American music that spoke to the changing realities of working-class life in the early twentieth-century South.

Examining the significant role that textile workers played in the creation and development of hillbilly music helps move us beyond the traditional narrative of North Carolina history in important ways. Understanding how textile workers, as singers, musicians, and songwriters but also as fans and consumers, contributed to the growth of the hillbilly music industry before World War II creates a richer, more complicated historical narrative through the addition of new, long-excluded voices to that narrative. Hillbilly music also reveals how their experiences of mass migration, industrial labor, urban life, class formation, and race relations, combined with the region's increasing integration into the nation's mass culture, shaped their working-class lives and communities. Since the 1970s, a growing collection of richly textured histories of Piedmont textile workers has done much to illuminate the experiences and struggles of this marginalized group of working-class white Southerners during the late nineteenth and early twentieth centuries.³³ Most of these regional and community studies focus on mill hands' experiences on the factory floor, on the picket line, and in the voting booth. But few studies consider, in any substantive way, what workers did on their front porches, in YMCA community centers, dance halls, and roadhouses, and at minstrel shows, Fourth of July picnics, and church revivals.[34] Focusing on textile workers as both active producers and consumers of American popular music reveals the myriad ways that ordinary working people shaped the mass culture of North Carolina, the American South, and, indeed, the entire United States and beyond. Such an approach also helps dismantle pernicious stereotypes of working-class white Southerners as socially unsophisticated, culturally backward, and hopelessly ignorant.

Whether Carolina mill hands were listening to or even performing it, hillbilly music helped workers cope with the sometimes bewildering challenges of modern life. Mill hands created new identities for themselves in part around their production and consumption of this commercial music, and some uprooted rural migrants may have turned to hillbilly music to help them acclimate to their new working-class lives and assuage those anxieties spawned by social dislocation, industrial employment, and shifting social attitudes and morals. This music also nurtured a strong sense of community and regional identity among Piedmont mill hands, anchoring them in what must have, at times, seemed a turbulent and uncertain new world. The hillbilly music they heard on radio barn dances and phonograph records, some of it performed by local musicians who were their friends and neighbors, "put millhands across the region in touch with each other" and "bolstered a sense of unique, regionwide identity," wrote Jacquelyn Dowd Hall and her coauthors in *Like a Family: The Making of a Southern Cotton Mill World* (1987). Comparatively few transcriptions of 1930s hillbilly radio programs survive, but 78-rpm hillbilly records, a more permanent cultural artifact, offer historians a means of understanding how Carolina mill hands experienced, negotiated, and responded to the far-reaching economic and social revolutions that had transformed the southern Piedmont from a region of small farms and market towns into the world's greatest textile-manufacturing district in less than two generations.[35]

Although hillbilly music rose to national popularity during World War II to become what *Time* magazine in 1943 called the "dominant popular music of the U.S. today," after the war singers and musicians from southern textile backgrounds played a progressively smaller role in this music, at least at the national level. Several factors account for their diminished participation, chief among them the corporate consolidation of the country music industry in Nashville during the late 1940s and early 1950s and, relatedly, the end of the prewar field-recording expeditions that had allowed so many Carolina textile musicians and string bands to make records without leaving the

South.[36] A number of postwar changes in the southern textile industry also contributed to the declining presence of mill-hand musicians in commercial country music, particularly the dismantling of Piedmont textile villages and the subsequent disintegration of their distinctive mill culture.[37] A few postwar music stars did emerge from the mills, most notably the five-string banjo virtuoso Earl Scruggs, of Cleveland County, North Carolina, one of the leading architects of the new postwar genre of bluegrass music. For all intents and purposes, though, the heyday of Piedmont mill-hand musicians within the national music scene had passed. Today, as a result of plant closings, automation, and relocations of companies overseas, southern textile mills employ fewer workers than at any time since the end of World War II, and the once-vibrant occupational culture that gave rise to hillbilly music in the Piedmont nearly a century ago has largely vanished. "Padlocked gates and knee-high grass surround many of the textile mills that were the lifeblood of this region for much of this last century," remarked the *Charlotte Observer* in 2001. "The scars—like the silent brick smokestacks—will remain for some time. Few parts of America are suffering as much from the economic slowdown as the textile belt that runs through the western Carolinas and into northern Georgia. Textile job losses are among the worst since the Great Depression."[38] Although scores of cotton mills sit abandoned, and crippled textile towns face uncertain economic futures, echoes of the distinctive hillbilly music that Piedmont mill hands forged during the 1920s and 1930s, now widely reissued on compact discs and available on Internet downloads, continue to reverberate throughout the United States and, indeed, the world.

NOTES

For their encouragement, suggestions, and assistance in the preparation of this essay, I am indebted to Kathleen Drowne, Jacquelyn Dowd Hall, Leon Fink, James Leloudis, Glenn Hinson, David Whisnant, Robert Cantwell, the late Archie Green, Tom Hanchett, Pamela Grundy, Kinney Rorrer, Norm Cohen, Tony Russell, the late Ed Kahn, David M. Anderson, Steve Weiss, Harry L. Watson, and Marshall Wyatt. I owe special thanks to Larry E. Tise, William S. Price Jr., and Jeffrey J. Crow for inviting me to participate in their series of conferences and to contribute to this important anthology. This essay is adapted from my 2008 book, *Linthead Stomp: The Creation of Country Music in the Piedmont South.*

1. "Records Made in Charlotte to Perpetuate Mountain Ballads," *Charlotte Observer,* August 9, 1927. See also the follow-up article, "Musicians Trek from Mountains to City to Record Old Ballads of Hill Country," *Charlotte Observer,* August 10, 1927.

2. Tom Hanchett, "Recording in Charlotte, 1927–1945," in *The Charlotte Country Music Story,* ed. George Holt (Charlotte: North Carolina Arts Council, 1985), 12–16; Thomas W. Hanchett, *Sorting Out the New South City: Race, Class, and Urban Development in Char-*

lotte, 1875-1975 (Chapel Hill: University of North Carolina Press, 1998), 2, 90-96; Brian Rust, comp., *The Victor Master Book Vol. 2: 1925-1936* (Stanhope, N.J.: Walter C. Allen, 1970), 146-48.

3. *Olde Time Fiddlin' Tunes* (New York: Victor Talking Machine Co., 1924), n.p.; Archie Green, "Commercial Music Graphics: Four," *John Edwards Memorial Foundation Newsletter* 4 (March 1968): 8-13; Tony Russell, *Country Music Records: A Discography, 1921-1942* (New York: Oxford University Press, 2004), 25.

4. See, e.g., Bill C. Malone's brief discussion of the mass media and industrial influences on prewar hillbilly music in *Don't Get above Your Raisin': Country Music and the Southern Working Class* (Urbana: University of Illinois Press, 2002), 31-36. Hillbilly music itself was a modern invention, a commercial music genre created in the mid-1920s in large part by U.S. record companies that relied upon bureaucratic organizational structures and state-of-the-art technologies to produce, advertise, and distribute their recordings of this mass-mediated music. See, e.g., Patrick Huber, "Black Hillbillies: African American Musicians on Old-Time Records, 1924-1932," in *Hidden in the Mix: The African American Presence in Country Music*, ed. Diane Pecknold (Durham, N.C.: Duke University Press, 2013), 47-48, 52-53.

5. On the birth and formative period of the hillbilly music industry, see, e.g., Archie Green, "Hillbilly Music: Source and Symbol," *Journal of American Folklore* 78 (July-September 1965): 204-28; Bill C. Malone, *Country Music U.S.A.*, rev. ed. (Austin: University of Texas Press, 1985 [1968]), 31-75; and Charles K. Wolfe, "The Birth of an Industry," in *The Illustrated History of Country Music*, ed. Patrick Carr (New York: Random House / Time Books, 1995 [1980]), 33-75.

6. Malone, *Don't Get above Your Raisin'*, 34-35; Patrick Huber, comp., "Southern Textile Workers on Hillbilly Records, 1923-1942," unpublished list, compiled in 2006 and revised in 2013 (a copy of which remains in the author's possession). For a nearly complete list of these artists, see Patrick Huber, *Linthead Stomp: The Creation of Country Music in the Piedmont South* (Chapel Hill: University of North Carolina Press, 2008), 283-95. The total number of approximately 23,000 domestic hillbilly releases is based on four samplings I conducted of the discographical information found in Russell, *Country Music Records*; records released in foreign markets, such as Canada, England, Ireland, Australia, and India, are excluded from this total.

7. Harriet L. Herring, *Welfare Work in Mill Villages: The Story of Extra-mill Activities in North Carolina* (Chapel Hill: University of North Carolina Press, 1929), 17, 25, 43; *Textile Directory* (1909), quoted in *Atlanta Constitution*, June 15, 1909; Rupert B. Vance, *Human Geography of the South: A Study in Regional Resources and Human Adequacy* (Chapel Hill: University of North Carolina Press, 1932), 275, 301-15; Ben F. Lemert, *The Cotton Textile Industry of the Southern Appalachian Piedmont* (Chapel Hill: University of North Carolina Press, 1933), 3, 137-38. On the Piedmont South and its industrialization during the late nineteenth and early twentieth centuries, see also Holland Thompson, *From the Cotton Field to the Cotton Mill: A Study of the Industrial Transition in North Carolina* (New York: Macmillan, 1906); Broadus Mitchell and George Sinclair Mitchell, *The Industrial Revolution in the South* (Baltimore: Johns Hopkins University Press, 1930); Rupert B. Vance, *All These People: The Nation's Human Resources in the South* (Chapel Hill: University of North Carolina Press, 1945), 279-317; David L. Carlton, *Mill and Town in South Carolina, 1880-1920* (Baton Rouge: Louisiana State University Press, 1982); Jacquelyn Dowd Hall, James Lelou-

dis, Robert Korstad, Mary Murphy, Lu Ann Jones, and Christopher B. Daly, *Like a Family: The Making of a Southern Cotton Mill World* (Chapel Hill: University of North Carolina Press, 2000 [1987]); and Allen Tullos, *Habits of Industry: White Culture and the Transformation of the Carolina Piedmont* (Chapel Hill: University of North Carolina Press, 1989).

8. On the urbanization of central North Carolina and the southern Piedmont generally, see Hall et al., *Like a Family*, 25; Gerald L. Ingalls, "Urbanization," in *The North Carolina Atlas: Portrait of a New Century*, ed. Douglas M. Orr Jr. and Alfred W. Stuart (Chapel Hill: University of North Carolina Press, 2000), 105; Vance, *Human Geography of the South*, 32–33; and Lemert, *Cotton Textile Industry*, 36–37.

9. Janet Irons, *Testing the New Deal: The General Strike of 1934 in the American South* (Urbana: University of Illinois Press, 2000), 15. On southern mill villages, see Hall et al., *Like a Family*, 114–20, 126–27; and I. A. Newby, *Plain Folk in the New South: Social Change and Cultural Persistence, 1880–1915* (Baton Rouge: Louisiana State University Press, 1989), 244–53.

10. John Salmond, "Aspects of Modernization in the Loray Mill Strike of 1929," in *Varieties of Southern History: New Essays on a Region and Its People*, ed. Bruce Clayton and John Salmond (Westport, Conn.: Greenwood Press, 1996), 169–76; Hall et al., *Like a Family*, 183, 185, 196, 252–55; Bertha Carl Hipp, "A Gaston County Cotton Mill and Its Community," M.A. thesis, University of North Carolina, 1930, 45–47; Frances Hampton, "New Leisure: How Is It Spent? A Study of What One Hundred Twenty-Two Textile Workers of Leaksville, Spray, and Draper Are Doing with the New Leisure Created by the N.R.A., as Applied to Certain Types of Activities," M.A. thesis, University of North Carolina, 1935, 61–63, 75–77; Marjorie Potwin, *Cotton Mill People of the Piedmont: A Study in Social Change* (New York: Columbia University Press, 1927), quotation on 34 and 64.

11. Carol J. Oja, "The USA, 1918–45," in *Modern Times: From World War I to the Present*, ed. Robert P. Morgan (Englewood Cliffs, N.J.: Prentice Hall, 1993), 208; Charlie Poole Jr., interview by Eugene W. Earle and Archie Green, Mountain Home, Tenn., August 13, 1962, FT-20002/4383, Southern Folklife Collection, Wilson Library, University of North Carolina at Chapel Hill; Kinney Rorrer, *Rambling Blues: The Life and Songs of Charlie Poole* (Danville, Va.: McCain Printing Co., 1992 [1982]), 37–38, 65; George Lipsitz, *Rainbow at Midnight: Labor and Culture in the 1940s* (Urbana: University of Illinois Press, 1994), 310; Hall et al., *Like a Family*, 377 (quotation).

12. Of the approximately one hundred field-recording sessions at which record companies made hillbilly recordings between 1923 and 1932, a total of forty-three took place in the Piedmont cities of Richmond, Charlotte, Winston-Salem, Atlanta, and Birmingham. Indeed, firms sponsored more than five times as many field sessions in the Piedmont as they did in Southern Appalachia—long considered the wellspring of commercial hillbilly music. See Patrick Huber, comp., "Southern Field-Recording Sessions of Hillbilly Music, 1923–1932," unpublished list, compiled in 2006 and based upon tabulations from Russell, *Country Music Records* (a copy of which remains in the author's possession). For accounts of some of the North Carolina sessions, see, e.g., Bob Carlin, *String Bands in the North Carolina Piedmont* (Jefferson, N.C.: McFarland, 2004), 151–53; and Hanchett, "Recording in Charlotte," 12–16.

13. Hall et al., *Like a Family*, 174; Roy "Whitey" Granted quoted in Vincent J. Roscigno and William F. Danaher, *The Voice of Southern Labor: Radio, Music, and Textile Strikes, 1929–1934*, Social Movements, Protest, and Contention, vol. 19 (Minneapolis: University

of Minnesota Press, 2004), 48; Doug DeNatale and Glenn Hinson, "The Southern Textile Song Tradition Reconsidered," in *Songs About Work: Essays in Occupational Culture for Richard A. Reuss*, ed. Archie Green, Special Publications of the Folklore Institute, no. 3 (Bloomington: Folklore Institute, Indiana University, 1993), 96.

14. Della Coulter, "The Piedmont Tradition," in Holt, *Charlotte Country Music Story*, 7–8, 9–11.

15. John W. Rumble, "Charlotte Country: A Sixty Year Tradition," in Holt, *Charlotte Country Music Story*, 4–5; Pamela Grundy, "'We Always Tried to Be Good People': Respectability, Crazy Water Crystals, and Hillbilly Music on the Air, 1933–1935," *Journal of American History* 81 (March 1995): 1591–1620; "Recording and Radio: WRVA and the 1929 Richmond OKeh Sessions," *Virginia Cavalcade* 51 (Summer 2002): 136–42; Wayne W. Daniel, *Pickin' on Peachtree: A History of Country Music in Atlanta, Georgia* (Urbana: University of Illinois Press, 1990), 109–26, 127–51; Carlin, *String Bands in the North Carolina Piedmont*, 172–96.

16. Tullos, *Habits of Industry*, 2; Homer "Pappy" Sherrill quoted in Coulter, "Piedmont Tradition," 10.

17. Rorrer, *Rambling Blues*, 18–20; *Mill News* (Charlotte, N.C.), October 14, 1920; Herring, *Welfare Work in Mill Villages*, 112–13, 141–44; Gregg D. Kimball and Ron T. Curry, "On the Beach of Waikiki: Hopewell's Tubize Royal Hawaiian Orchestra," *Virginia Cavalcade* 51 (Summer 2002): 112–23; Ted Olson and Tony Russell, liner notes to *The Johnson City Sessions, 1928–1929: "Can You Sing or Play Old-Time Music?,"* four-CD boxed set (Bear Family Records BCD 16083), 36–37; Russell, *Country Music Records*, 714.

18. Jennings J. Rhyne, *Some Southern Cotton Mill Workers and Their Villages* (Chapel Hill: University of North Carolina Press, 1930), 18, 105–21; Hall et al., *Like a Family*, 107–9. A 1926 investigation by the Women's Bureau of the Department of Labor indicated that the annual labor turnover rate in southern textile mills ran as high as 190 percent. See Paul Blanshard, *Labor in Southern Cotton Mills* (New York: New Republic, 1927), 60. A 1926–27 Gaston County, North Carolina, study, for example, found that, although almost three-fourths of the five hundred textile families surveyed were natives of North Carolina, among them were also a few Texans, Louisianans, Oklahomans, Pennsylvanians, Arizonans, Ohioans, Indianans, and even one Italian immigrant. See Rhyne, *Some Southern Cotton Mill Workers*, 46, 47–48, 54–55, 68–69, 70.

19. Archie Green, *Wobblies, Pile Butts, and Other Heroes: Laborlore Explorations* (Urbana: University of Illinois Press, 1993), 297–99, 312–15. Wilmer Watts and the Lonely Eagles' "Cotton Mill Blues" can be heard on *Gastonia Gallop: Cotton Mill Songs and Hillbilly Blues: Old-Time Music from Gaston County, North Carolina, 1927–1931* (Old Hat Records, Old Hat CD-1007).

20. Huber, *Linthead Stomp*, 24, 166, 218, 220. Dixon's "Weave Room Blues" can be found on Bear Family Records' four-CD boxed set, *The Dixon Brothers: "A Blessing to People"* (Bear Family Records BCD 16817DK). The complete list of Carolina mill-hand musicians' prewar recordings of textile songs, in chronological order, is "Cotton Mill Blues" (Wilmer Watts and the Lonely Eagles, 1929), "Cotton Mill Colic" (David McCarn, 1930), "Poor Man, Rich Man" (David McCarn, 1930), "Serve 'Em Fine" (David McCarn and Howard Long, as Dave and Howard, 1931), "The Weaver's Blues" (Jimmie Tarlton, 1932), "Weave Room Blues" (Dixon Brothers, 1936), "Cotton Mill Blues" (Daddy John Love, 1936), "Spinning Room Blues" (Dixon Brothers, 1936), "Weaver's Life" (Dixon Brothers, 1937), and "Cotton Mill Blues"

(Lester "Pete" Bivins, as Lester [The Highwayman], 1938). See DeNatale and Hinson, "The Southern Textile Song Tradition Reconsidered," Appendix A, 102-4.

21. Lipsitz, *Rainbow at Midnight*, 311-12; James C. Cobb, "From Rocky Top to Detroit City: Country Music and the Economic Transformation of the South," in *You Wrote My Life: Lyrical Themes in Country Music*, ed. Melton A. McLaurin and Richard A. Peterson, Cultural Perspectives on the American South, vol. 6 (Philadelphia: Gordon and Breach, 1992), 64.

22. On McCarn, see William Henry Koon, "Dave McCarn," *John Edwards Memorial Foundation Quarterly* 11 (Winter 1975): 167-76; and Huber, *Linthead Stomp*, 162-215.

23. David McCarn, interview by Archie Green and Ed Kahn, Stanley, N.C., August 19, 1961, FT-20002/4100, Southern Folklife Collection. The word "colic," as used by McCarn to mean "complain," does not appear in Norman E. Eliason, *Tarheel Talk: An Historical Study of the English Language in North Carolina to 1860* (Chapel Hill: University of North Carolina Press, 1956), nor is it included in J. A. Simpson and E. S. C. Weiner, eds., *The Oxford English Dictionary*, 2nd ed. 20 vols. (Oxford: Clarendon Press, 1989).

24. Huber, *Linthead Stomp*, 162-63, 190-91, 200-203. McCarn's "Cotton Mill Colic" can be heard on *Gastonia Gallop*.

25. Huber, *Linthead Stomp*, 202-3.

26. Southern mill hands have been consistently characterized as a homogeneous group, especially in the sociological and economic studies of the region's textile industry published during the 1920s and 1930s. Writing in 1928, for example, the economist Lois MacDonald described textile workers as a "uniform" population—"native born, Southern, and rural"—and spoke of "the mind of the workers," as if their attitudes and thoughts formed a monolithic consensus. See MacDonald, *Southern Mill Hills: A Study of Social and Economic Forces in Certain Textile Mill Villages* (New York: Alex L. Hillman, 1928), 69, 104, 135, 146.

27. On Dixon, see Huber, *Linthead Stomp*, 216-73.

28. Dorsey M. Dixon, interview by Archie Green and Ed Kahn, East Rockingham, N.C., August 20, 1961, FT-20002/4075-4076, Southern Folklife Collection. On Dixon's now-classic song, see Tony Hilfer, "'Wreck on the Highway': Rhetoric and Religion in a Country Song," *John Edwards Memorial Foundation Quarterly* 21 (Fall/Winter 1985): 116-19; and Huber, *Linthead Stomp*, 237-40. The Dixon Brothers' original 1938 recording of this song can be found on *The Dixon Brothers*.

29. Billy Altman, liner notes, *Something Got a Hold of Me: A Treasury of Sacred Music* (RCA 2100-2-R) (quotation); Huber, *Linthead Stomp*, 239.

30. On the Three Tobacco Tags, see Ivan M. Tribe, liner notes, *Songs of the Tobacco Tags, Vol. 1* (Old Homestead OHCS 156); and Patrick Huber and Marshall Wyatt, booklet notes to *Gastonia Gallop*. Unfortunately, I have been unable to compare the Three Tobacco Tags' 1938 recording to the 1936 sheet music of Fisher's song, published by his own firm, the Fred Fisher Music Company of New York.

31. The song can be heard on Old Homestead's *Songs of the Tobacco Tags, Vol. 1*.

32. For a larger discussion of Southerners' conflicted responses to the automobile, see Blaine A. Brownell, "A Symbol of Modernity: Attitudes toward the Automobile in Southern Cities in the 1920s," *American Quarterly* 24 (March 1972): 20-44.

33. For some of the best of these studies, see, e.g., Hall et al., *Like a Family*; Newby, *Plain Folk in the New South*; Tullos, *Habits of Industry*; Douglas Flamming, *Creating the Modern South: Millhands and Managers in Dalton, Georgia, 1884-1984* (Chapel Hill: Univer-

sity of North Carolina Press, 1992); Gary M. Fink, *The Fulton Bag and Cotton Mills Strike of 1914-1915: Espionage, Labor Conflict, and New South Industrial Relations* (Ithaca, N.Y.: ILR Press, 1993); Bryant Simon, *A Fabric of Defeat: The Politics of South Carolina Millhands, 1910-1948* (Chapel Hill: University of North Carolina Press, 1998); Irons, *Testing the New Deal*; G. C. Waldrep III, *Southern Workers and the Search for Community: Spartanburg County, South Carolina* (Urbana: University of Illinois Press, 2000); and Clifford M. Kuhn, *Contesting the New South Order: The 1914-1915 Strike at Atlanta's Fulton Mills* (Chapel Hill: University of North Carolina Press, 2001). For an overview of this historical literature, see Robert H. Zieger, "Textile Workers and Historians," in *Organized Labor in the Twentieth-Century South*, ed. Robert H. Zieger (Knoxville: University of Tennessee Press, 1991), 35-59.

34. Exceptions here include Hall et al., *Like a Family*, esp. 135-37, 237, 249-55, 257-62; and Roscigno and Danaher, *Voice of Southern Labor*, esp. 26-27, 29-30, 46-70.

35. Hall et al., *Like a Family*, quotation on 261-62; Grundy, "'We Always Tried to Be Good People,'" 1592.

36. "Bull Market in Corn," *Time* 42 (October 4, 1943): 33. On the expansion of the hillbilly music industry during World War II and the postwar rise of Nashville as its center, see, e.g., Malone, *Country Music, U.S.A.*, 177-200; and Martin Hawkins, *A Shot in the Dark: Making Records in Nashville, 1945-1955* (Nashville, Tenn.: Vanderbilt University Press and Country Music Foundation Press, 2006), esp. 221-44.

37. Harriet L. Herring, *Passing of the Mill Village: Revolution in a Southern Institution* (Chapel Hill: University of North Carolina Press, 1949), 6, 9-12.

38. *Charlotte Observer*, September 17, 2001. On the decline of the southern textile industry and the economic crisis it now faces, see Timothy J. Minchin, *Fighting against the Odds: A History of Southern Labor since World War II* (Gainesville: University Press of Florida, 2005), 144-46, 158-64; John Gaventa and Barbara Ellen Smith, "The Deindustrialization of the Textile South: A Case Study," in *Hanging by a Thread: Social Change in Southern Textiles*, ed. Jeffrey Leiter, Michael D. Schulman, and Rhonda Zingraff (Ithaca, N.Y.: ILR Press, 1991), esp. 181-88; and Rhonda Zingraff, "Facing Extinction?," in Leiter et al., *Hanging by a Thread*, 199-216.

TAR HEEL POLITICS IN THE TWENTIETH CENTURY

THE RISE AND FALL OF THE
PROGRESSIVE PLUTOCRACY

Karl E. Campbell

North Carolina politics has long perplexed academics and journalists alike. In the twentieth century North Carolina earned a reputation as the most progressive state in the South. Its commitment to public education, good government, and social moderation stood out in a region better known for rock-ribbed conservatism. Yet the positive image of the Old North State existed side by side with contradictory social and economic realities. During the first half of the twentieth century North Carolina became the most industrialized southern state, but it also had the nation's largest rural farm population. It boasted of nationally respected institutions of higher education such as the University of North Carolina, Duke, and Wake Forest, yet it also had one of the worst high school dropout rates in the country. In the 1950s North Carolina was praised for its moderate response to the *Brown v. Board of Education* decision, yet two decades later reporters described it as the least changed of the former Confederate states. In 1975 Thad Beyle, a political scientist at the University of North Carolina at Chapel Hill, observed that these contrasting tendencies "suggest the difficulties in generalizing about the state since it is neither simply 'Liberal' or 'Conservative.'" North Carolina, he concluded, could only be called "a Progressive Paradox."[1]

North Carolina's distinctive politics required a unique approach, and in 1949 one of America's preeminent political scientists provided one. In his seminal book *Southern Politics in State and Nation*, V. O. Key Jr. titled his chapter on North Carolina the "progressive plutocracy." Key observed that the state enjoyed "a reputation for progressive outlook and action in many phases of life, especially industrial development, education, and race relations."[2] But he also described the state's dominant leadership as a plutocracy of businessmen, bankers, and lawyers who maintained strict control over the state's government. The progressive plutocracy did not welcome democratic participation, especially from labor unions or civil rights groups. When confident in their power, the business elite extended government services to benefit the state's citizens, but their paternalism ended when their control was threatened. Thus, Key's theory helped resolve the central dilemma of North Carolina's political history. The state's progressivism was not a contradiction to its plutocratic government but was enabled by it.[3]

Retracing the rise and fall of the progressive plutocracy is the key to understanding North Carolina political history in the twentieth century. There is, however, much more clarity about the beginning of the story than about its end. The economic oligarchy that came to power with the Wilmington Uprising of 1898 and the election of Governor Charles B. Aycock in 1900 consolidated its hold on state government through the following decades. It survived a dramatic transition from one political machine to another in the late 1920s and managed to repel most challenges to its authority until after World War II. But a combination of social and economic transformations in the postwar years eventually weakened and brought down the progressive plutocracy, although the timing and cause of its demise are still very much in debate. Indeed, confusion about what happened to the progressive plutocracy in the latter half of the twentieth century is so great that some scholars have abandoned Key's model altogether and turned again to the paradigm of paradox to describe Tar Heel politics.[4]

The problem, however, is not with the concept of a progressive plutocracy but with our confusion about the political structure that sustained it. Political scientists have developed an analytical tool that can help us better understand the political changes of the twentieth century—the theory of political realignment. Ironically, the scholar recognized as the father of realignment theory is none other than Key.[5] The theory suggests that individual elections should be seen not as discrete events in which the outcome is primarily determined by the exigencies of the moment—such as campaign strategies, dynamic personalities, debate performances, and other specific events—but as part of a larger political system. These political systems represent distinct eras of related elections in which the issues, the factions, the ideologies, and the behavior of both leaders and voters are relatively consistent. Such a political system may last for twenty or thirty years, or even longer, until a major transformation occurs—a realignment—in which a new political system is established.[6]

A great deal of political science literature is dedicated to explaining, and debating, various aspects of realignment theory, but there is general consensus about how realignments occur. At the beginning of a realignment period the established political system contains two parties or factions that are divided along a set of issues and philosophies rooted in past battles. During the second stage of a realignment, new issues arise that cut across the former line of cleavage that defined the old parties, and the existing political system has difficulty adjusting to the new realities. In the last stage, the old system disintegrates and a new political system is born. Sometimes a realignment is expressed in a dramatic critical election, such as Franklin Delano Roosevelt's decisive victory in 1932. But more frequently a realignment is much slower and develops in stages. For instance, many political scientists believe that the realignment of the formerly solid Democratic South to the Republican majority of the early twenty-first century took several decades stretching from the turbulent 1960s to the Reagan revolution of the 1980s or even longer.[7]

Realignment theory is not limited to partisan political change but is a valid concept for analyzing the transformation of all political systems, including ones in which the competition is between factions within a single party. Such was the case in North Carolina for most of the twentieth century. Reconstructing the story of the progressive plutocracy as the creation, maintenance, and dissolution of a unique political party system resolves many of the ambiguities of North Carolina political history, especially during the gradual realignment in the decades after World War II.

THE BIRTH OF A POLITICAL SYSTEM

The most significant political event of the first half of the twentieth century in North Carolina actually occurred several years before the new century began. The political coalition that would become the progressive plutocracy was born in the tragic election of 1898. Through a combination of racist propaganda and vigilante violence, the Democratic Party defeated a biracial, class-based, and genuinely reformist insurgency of Populists and Republicans. Two days after the election, a pro-Democratic mob of angry whites staged a coup d'état in Wilmington, North Carolina, killing approximately sixty African Americans and overthrowing the last significant Populist-Republican local government in the state. Two years later, in 1900, the Democrats solidified their power by electing their chief political strategist, Furnifold M. Simmons, to the U.S. Senate and their most eloquent spokesman, Charles B. Aycock, to the governorship. The Democrats also amended the North Carolina Constitution to disfranchise most blacks and many poor whites with a literacy test and poll tax. The victorious Democrats had destroyed the Populist Party, reduced the Republican Party to minority status, and ended any real threat of biracial reform to the status quo for years to come.[8]

The dramatic events of 1898 and 1900 have all the markings of a true political realignment. North Carolina's former political system in the 1880s had been divided between two parties. The Democrats represented the former planters of Down East and the industrialists in the Piedmont. The Republicans included African Americans, former Unionists in the western mountains and foothills, and some New South elites (the Democrats and Republicans of that time bear almost no resemblance to the political parties that share their names today). In the early 1890s the economic crisis of the farmers challenged the existing party system when the new Populist Party fused with the Republicans and gained brief control of state government. The violent events of 1898 and subsequent consolidation of Democratic power in 1900 created a new political system defined by white supremacy, one-party rule, and a new brand of Democrats who dominated North Carolina politics for the next six decades. The principal characteristics of this new political system included an established elite leadership (the progressive plutocracy), consistent political factions, a generally predictable electorate, regular political mechanisms, and an emerging ideological framework.[9]

The Democratic Party that emerged from what Furnifold Simmons called "the revolution" of 1898–1900 introduced a new generation of political leadership to North Carolina.[10] Simmons remained in the U.S. Senate for thirty years, serving as both the state's senior senator and political boss. Charles Aycock became known as the education governor by initiating an aggressive (but unequal) program of school construction for both white and black students during his term (1901–5), while also implementing Jim Crow segregation and overseeing the disfranchisement of African American voters. The editor of the Raleigh *News and Observer*, Josephus Daniels, who played a major role in whipping up the racist whirlwinds of 1898 and 1900, became the most important newspaperman in the state and a powerbroker in his own right. Indeed, every occupant of the North Carolina Executive Mansion between 1900 and 1925 was associated in some way with the white supremacy campaigns at the turn of the century. These men led the first generation of the progressive plutocracy.[11]

In addition to an established elite leadership, fairly consistent political factions within the progressive plutocracy were included in the new political system. The Republicans, defeated in 1898, remained a significant minority party that controlled some mountain and urban localities and attracted about one-third of the votes in statewide elections. They continued to be just enough of a threat to reinforce some unity among the ruling Democrats. The real competition for power was limited to infighting between various factions and personalities within the dominant Democratic Party. While no clear boundaries divided these Democratic factions, there tended to be tensions between the rural-based landholders in the east and the rising industrialists of the Piedmont, as well as between those who favored greater progressive reforms and those who opposed them. Cultural issues, however, did not divide political leaders into definitive camps. Before World War II emotional crusades for and against prohibition, teaching Darwin in the public schools, and woman's suffrage attracted followers from all classes, political persuasions, and geographical sections of the state. White supremacy was taken for granted.[12]

The electorate shrank considerably in the new political system, which further enhanced the power of the progressive plutocracy. Approximately 80,000 black and white men were disfranchised in North Carolina by the literacy tests and poll taxes passed in 1900. Of the 120,000 African American men who were eligible to vote in 1896, fewer than 6,000 remained on the rolls by 1902. Voter turnout dropped dramatically as well. While over 85 percent of men had voted in 1896, fewer than 50 percent of those who remained eligible bothered to cast a ballot in 1904. Those who did vote tended to follow established political allegiances and geographical patterns. In the early years of the twentieth century power flowed upward as elite politicians gained even more control over state government.[13]

The stability of the political system was enhanced by the presence of Furnifold Simmons's political machine. Simmons was a clever strategist who understood the political mechanisms of his day. He built his organization by controlling patronage, dispersing campaign funds, and determining who was next in line to run for important offices such as governor, congressman, and senator. In a time when illiteracy was high and travel difficult, Simmons exerted power through networks of local leaders, the courthouse gangs who could rally supporters, host barbeques, dispense cash, offer favors, threaten retribution, and get their followers to the polls. Simmons's reach extended into the farthest harbors and hollows of North Carolina.[14]

The Simmons machine faced several challenges to its authority, but the nature and scope of these insurgencies demonstrate the durability of the political system. Only once during its thirty-year reign did the Simmons machine not win a gubernatorial election. In 1908 W. W. Kitchin, a popular six-term congressman from a prominent eastern political family, challenged Locke Craig, Simmons's designated candidate for governor. Kitchin represented the rural and more progressive wing of the Democratic Party that was frustrated by the machine's putting the desires of the business class over the needs of the common man. After an exhausting four-day battle at the Democratic convention, Kitchin won the nomination on the sixty-first ballot. His victory came only after Josephus Daniels orchestrated a backroom deal in which Kitchin promised to support Craig as next in line for the Executive Mansion. Four years later, however, Governor Kitchin broke the truce by trying to unseat Simmons himself from the U.S. Senate. After a mean-spirited primary campaign, Simmons defeated his most significant rival and returned to the Senate, from where he managed North Carolina politics for another eighteen years.[15]

Historians have struggled to decide whether insurgents such as Kitchin (and later outliers including Ralph McDonald, "Our Bob" Reynolds, Kerr Scott, and Frank Porter Graham) should be considered members of the progressive plutocracy. Key's original definition implied that they were not. Following his example, most scholars have equated membership in the progressive plutocracy with belonging to the conservative Democratic machine. Such a narrow definition is too restrictive. Often these challengers had been former members of the Democratic machine. Sometimes they would rejoin the dominant coalition after their insurrection. Scholarly work subsequent to Key's original understanding of the progressive plutocracy suggests that the term should include all the members of the ruling hegemony, no matter if they were in the dominant Democratic faction, a reformist insurgent, or even a Republican (at least after the Republican Party in North Carolina rejected its historic commitment to civil rights in the early 1920s and fully embraced white supremacy).[16] Predictable divisions within a political system are more a sign of strength than of weakness, especially if the combatants play by the same rules and agree on the same fundamental values.

The presence of a dominant ideology, or a set of defining issues, is another characteristic of an authentic political system. The progressive plutocracy ran the state on the basis of racism, religion, and reform. White supremacy was the absolute foundation of the new progressive plutocracy. Conservative Evangelical Protestantism provided its moral energy, especially in the crusade for prohibition. Progressivism was its central philosophy, or at least a southern variant of the reform movement popular in many sections of the country during the early years of the twentieth century. Progressivism defies easy definition. According to historian George Tindall, the basic tenets of the original progressive movement included democratic reform, efficient government, corporate regulation, social justice, and the extension of government services. Tindall suggested that several of these progressive principles did not last long in the South. The push for greater democracy, corporate regulation, and social justice did not find favor with North Carolina's political elite.[17]

In the early years of the twentieth century, the progressive plutocracy's commitment to genuine reform was tenuous, and the ideological framework of the political system was not yet fully developed. The Democratic Party promoted the expansion of public schools in part as a means to educate illiterate whites so that they could pass the literacy test and gain access to the polls before the grandfather clause, which exempted white men whose grandfathers had had the right to vote, expired in 1908. "Our motive was political as well as humanitarian," Furnifold Simmons explained.[18] Many Democrats distrusted the more liberal aspects of the Progressive movement. Simmons represented the more conservative end of the spectrum, while Aycock and Kitchin pushed for a more robust program of government reform. After two decades of debate the factions within North Carolina's Democratic Party found agreement on only two components of Progressivism: government efficiency and the extension of state power to provide increased public services to its citizens.

George Tindall labeled this uniquely southern strand of the reform movement "business progressivism." The southern Democrats' commitment to New South industrialism blended nicely with the progressive ideas that good government should promote the infrastructure needed by business and expand both education and health programs to create a more dependable workforce. The key, of course, was that the progressive plutocracy had to maintain political control of the industrialization process and prevent any disruption to its system of racialized capitalism.[19]

THE PROGRESSIVE PLUTOCRACY AT HIGH TIDE

Historians point to the 1920s as the decade in which North Carolina emerged as the most progressive state in the South, but the turning point came during World War I. It was during the Great War that the progressive plutocracy fully committed to the ideology of business progressivism. Thomas Bickett entered the Executive Mansion just a few months before the United States entered the war. He had campaigned on a platform of progressive reform significantly more aggressive than any member of the Simmons machine had previously proposed. Among his recommendations was a restructuring of the tax system, an end to the crop lien, electoral reforms, increasing teacher salaries, a longer school year, limits on child labor, reorganization of state agencies, more spending on roads and hospitals, and the creation of a state public welfare system. To get the North Carolina General Assembly to enact so many progressive measures would have been challenging at any time, but the coming of a world war appeared to undercut the governor's plans.[20]

Bickett enthusiastically embraced the war effort and used the opportunity to advance his progressive agenda. The governor crisscrossed the state delivering a series of emotion-packed patriotic speeches in which he tied support for the war overseas to support for his reform agenda at home. He reminded the mothers in the audience that they "may never again look with tear-dimmed eyes at the boys you held once so close and whose tiny feet you led and whose lips you taught to say 'Now I lay me.'"[21] He evoked the country's duty to the boys who were fighting or who had died overseas: "When the American soldier sacrificed every individual right, abandoned every personal pleasure and buried every personal profit for the common good, he breathed new life into the principle that no individual in the United States has any right the assertion of which would prove fatal to the welfare and happiness of all the people.... From every soldier's sepulcher there comes to this Nation the solemn warning, 'If you break faith with us who died, we shall not sleep.'"[22]

Governor Bickett's strategy worked brilliantly and forged a new ideological consensus on the principles of business progressivism. Even Senator Simmons jumped on the reform bandwagon. During the war years the state legislators passed thirty-five of the forty-three measures Bickett proposed. Just months after the armistice the Raleigh *News and Observer* concluded that the Bickett administration had established "a new high record for gubernatorial influence."[23] Bickett himself commended the General Assembly for "its sympathy with the new tides running in the hearts of men" and praised it for being the first in the Union to endorse a League of Nations and the first to ratify the federal prohibition amendment. Other notable progressive actions in North Carolina included the creation of a graduated income tax, the state's first public welfare system, increased expenditures for teachers' salaries and state agencies, and an extension of the school term to six months.[24]

But business progressivism had its limits. Bickett opposed the woman's suffrage amendment and the North Carolina legislature declined to approve it, missing the opportunity to be the final state needed for ratification.[25] The governor claimed to support organized labor in public pronouncements, but he still criticized major national strikes, valued law and order over protecting worker's rights, and put his administration firmly on the side of "capital" over "labor."[26] Bickett was also a white supremacist. He reminded the General Assembly that "in North Carolina we have definitely decided that the happiness of both races requires that white government shall be supreme and unchallenged in our borders." But the governor added a note of paternalism: "Power is inseparably linked with responsibility; and when we deny to the negro [sic] any participation in the making of laws, we saddle upon ourselves a peculiar obligation to protect the negro [sic] in his life and property, and to help and encourage him in the pursuit of happiness."[27]

When Cameron Morrison replaced Thomas Bickett as governor of North Carolina in 1921, most observers expected a sharp turn away from business progressivism. Morrison had a reputation as one of the most conservative members of the Simmons machine. The reform faction of the Democratic Party was so worried about Morrison's election that it rallied behind a brash young challenger named O. Max Gardner in the Democratic primary. According to author Rob Christensen, Gardner probably won the most votes on the first ballot, but the Simmons machine stole the election with thousands of fraudulent absentee ballots from the mountain counties. Once he became governor, however, Morrison surprised his critics by completely embracing the principles of business progressivism. His reform agenda included radical increases in public spending for the state universities, local school buildings, and improvements to the state ports, but he is best known as "the good roads governor" because of his administration's dramatic program of highway construction. All told he coaxed an extraordinary $65 million out of the legislature for the building and improvement of roads, an amount only $10 million less than the federal government's budget for the same purpose during the same time.[28]

Morrison's governorship demonstrated that the political system of the progressive plutocracy had reached a new level of maturity. The electorate had been reduced in size and influence, and voting behavior was predictable. The cleavages within the Democratic Party were well defined. Both the conservative and reform factions operated within the basic ideological framework of business progressivism. The Simmons machine ran the state but not without competition from within the Democratic Party and from the minority Republicans, which compelled organizational discipline and kept the Democrats attuned to changing times.

But in the late 1920s challenges both inside and out of North Carolina would threaten the stability of this political system. Perhaps most worrisome to the progressive plutocracy was the constant agitation by African Americans who never relented in their attacks on Jim Crow segregation. The discontent of mill workers and rural farmers provided additional concerns, as did the passage of the Nineteenth Amendment that brought women to the polls and new issues into the political arena. National political dynamics also threatened to destabilize Tar Heel politics as black voters began to shift their allegiances from the Republican to the Democratic Party, part of a broader transformation that would come to fruition after the election of Franklin Delano Roosevelt in the 1930s. But even before the Roosevelt revolution the changing national political climate contributed to the end of the Simmons machine and gave birth of a new political dynasty in North Carolina. It did not, however, lead to a new political system.[29]

The election of 1928 represented high drama on both the national and state political stage. The presidential election pitted Republican Herbert Hoover against Democrat Al Smith. The differences between them were stark. Hoover, a Quaker and a conservative, ran on a ticket of continuing the pro-business, laissez-faire policies of the Republican Party. Smith, a Catholic and a liberal, opposed prohibition and supported immigration. In North Carolina the seventy-six-year-old Simmons could not tolerate Smith's Catholicism and "wet" position against prohibition. He threw the full weight of his Democratic political machine against Smith and managed to help the Republican Hoover carry North Carolina on his way to the White House. It was the only election between 1872 and 1968 that the Tar Heel State voted for a Republican candidate for president. O. Max Gardner, whose first bid for governor had been stolen in 1920, earned the endorsement of the Simmons machine in 1928, but he was unwilling to join the old political boss's crusade against Al Smith. The resulting schism within the Tar Heel Democratic Party marked the beginning of the end for Simmons's dynasty. Hoover's coattails carried two North Carolina Republicans into the U.S. Congress, but Gardner cruised to victory not only with the support of his own political organization but also with the newfound admiration of loyal Democrats across the state. Two years later, in 1930, Simmons lost his Senate seat to Josiah Bailey, a former political ally. Gardner replaced Simmons as the most powerful politician in the state.[30]

No politician better exemplifies the progressive plutocracy than Governor O. Max Gardner. He had become a millionaire textile mill owner before entering politics and was well connected within the businessmen class of North Carolina. In some ways the election of Gardner marked the arrival of a new generation of leaders in the progressive plutocracy. He was the first gubernatorial candidate that did not run against Reconstruction or evoke fears of "Negro domination" associated with the Wilmington Race Riot. Gardner responded to the Great Depression with an aggressive plan that centralized government power, protected business interests, and offered assistance to the struggling citizens of the state, all without sacrificing any of the ruling elite's power. He also reformed the political process by adopting the "Australian" or closed ballot that would make the heavy-handed ballot stuffing practiced by the Simmons machine more difficult. In other ways, however, Gardner represented a continuation of the progressive plutocracy. While he decried the outspoken racism of his political opponents, he did nothing to advance civil rights during his political career. When faced with violent labor strikes in Marion and Gastonia, the governor called out the National Guard to protect both the private property and the power of the mill owners.[31] In spite of Gardner's earlier criticisms of the Simmons machine he established his own political organization through his use of patronage and control of the newly centralized state bureaucracy. The "Shelby Dynasty," named for his hometown in Cleveland County, dominated North Carolina politics for over twenty years. Gardner was a paradox, just as North Carolina politics seemed a paradox by the middle of the twentieth century. Indeed, some scholars believe that Key had Gardner and the Shelby Dynasty in mind when he originally coined the phrase "progressive plutocracy."[32]

Like Simmons before him, Gardner ran his political organization from the nation's capital. At the end of his four years as governor Gardner moved to Washington, D.C., where he represented the interests of North Carolina businessmen, worked in support of the New Deal, and managed political developments back home. The transition from one political machine to another did not represent the weakness of the progressive plutocracy political system but, rather, demonstrated its strength. A new generation of business-oriented plutocrats picked up right where the last generation had left off. The same basic factional divisions, political mechanisms, leadership, and ideology remained in place. Gardner had just as much success controlling the Executive Mansion as had his predecessor. In spite of several significant challenges in specific elections, especially from the insurgent reformer Ralph McDonald, who gave the Shelby Dynasty a real run for its money in 1936, Gardner handpicked every one of the state's governors from when he left office in 1933 until the year after his death in 1947.[33]

O. Max Gardner's control over North Carolina was never absolute, but it remained dominant even as his national political influence increased. A man of deep faith, personal grace, and a quick sense of humor, Gardner became a central figure in the Washington social and political scene. He developed a close friendship with President Franklin Roosevelt and served in both the Roosevelt and Truman administrations. In 1947 President Truman appointed Gardner ambassador to the Court of St. James. Tragically, Gardner died from a sudden heart attack the night before he was to set sail for England.[34]

THE DISINTEGRATION OF THE POLITICAL SYSTEM

Historians have struggled to explain Tar Heel politics after World War II. Some scholars point to a dynamic individual politician or a specific critical election as the pivotal turning point, such as the victory of Governor Kerr Scott in 1948 or the defeat of Senator Frank Porter Graham in 1950. Others focus on partisan politics and the rise of the Republican Party in the 1970s, giving Senator Jesse Helms star billing. There is little agreement on chronology, terminology, or which themes should shape the narrative. Realignment theory suggests that the story line should follow the fall of the progressive plutocracy and the creation of a new political system. The timing of that realignment depends on when the defining characteristics of the progressive plutocracy's party system ceased to be relevant, including its leadership, factions, political mechanisms, electoral behavior, and dominant ideology.

Some of these characteristics are easier to trace than are others. Clearly the Shelby Dynasty outlived the man who created it.[35] After Gardner's death in 1947 his political organization continued to dominate Tar Heel politics for another decade. Likewise, the progressive plutocracy maintained its leadership of state government for even longer, although its power faded long before the Republican Party began winning statewide elections in 1972. Of course, the Shelby Dynasty and the progressive plutocracy were never the same, no matter how closely they were linked in the public mind during the 1930s and 1940s. The first was a specific political machine born in 1928; the second was the elite leadership of the larger political system that came to power in 1900.

Such political distinctions probably meant little to the one man who disliked and defeated them both, although finding the right vocabulary to describe Kerr Scott is difficult as well. Scott was born on the family farm near the Haw River in Alamance County. His family had been active in North Carolina politics since before Governor Aycock came to office in 1901 and was generally associated with the reform faction of the progressive plutocracy. Kerr Scott entered politics when Governor Gardner appointed him state commissioner of agriculture in the middle of the Great Depression. He built a reputation as a tobacco-chewing, "possum 'n' taters"–eating good ol' boy. His willingness to fight for the common man earned him a significant following in the rural areas of the state. He began to assemble his own political organization that he nicknamed the "Branchhead Boys" because it was made up of those who lived in the rural areas at the branch heads of creeks and rivers, not the city dwellers who lived downstream. In 1948 he surprised the political establishment by running for governor against the handpicked candidate of Gardner's Shelby Dynasty. He surprised even more people when he won.[36]

The election of 1948 was significant in national politics as well. Conventional wisdom held that President Harry Truman stood little chance of winning reelection, but his surprising victory over Thomas Dewey reaffirmed the power of the recently formed Roosevelt Democratic coalition in presidential politics. Truman won in spite of the defections of the left and right wings of his party. Liberals, disenchanted with Truman's moderation, followed Henry Wallace into the Progressive Party. Southern conservatives, incensed by the pro–civil rights plank in the Democratic Party platform, nominated Strom Thurmond to lead their Dixiecrat crusade. Although both insurrections were unsuccessful, the willingness of diehard segregationists to bolt the Democratic Party over civil rights foreshadowed the eventual rise of the Republican Party in the South. Most Tar Heel Democrats stuck with Truman and the Democratic Party, but the conservative Thurmond gained the most votes in the black belt counties Down East, the same counties in which the moderate Kerr Scott performed the best, demonstrating growing contradictions in North Carolina's political system.[37]

Kerr Scott's victory, and his subsequent actions as governor, represented a significant challenge to the ruling elite. Scott exaggerated only a little when he described his political success as "the bottom layer overturning the top."[38] Governor Scott was significantly more liberal than his predecessors in the reform wing of the progressive plutocracy. Indeed, it is unclear if he should be considered a member of that elite leadership or a rebel who broke from its ranks. His "Go Forward" program included paving 15,000 miles of farm-to-market roads, new school construction, new public health programs, expanded port facilities, increased rural electrical service, and more than 75,000 rural phone installations. Of course, these programs cost money, and the governor spent the state's surplus built up during World War II in just two years. When conservatives complained about his call for modest tax increases, Scott shot back, "The people are demanding that something be done to lift them out of the mud."[39] These actions pushed the outer limits of the state's progressive tradition by their scope more than by their substance. The Go Forward program was larger but not radically different from the reforms advocated by former governors Kitchin, Bickett, Morrison, and Gardner.

In other areas, however, Governor Scott broke new ground. He upset traditional gender boundaries by appointing Susie Sharp North Carolina's first woman superior court judge. He outraged the business community by calling for repeal of the anti-union right-to-work law. And most ominous, he threatened traditional race relations by assigning the first African American to the State Board of Education and publicly supporting equal pay for all black and white state employees, although equalization of funding for public education was a generally supported strategy by white leaders to preserve the separate but equal principle in face of multiple court challenges. These recommendations had little chance of succeeding during Scott's administration, but they signaled a break from the ideological framework of the progressive plutocracy and the political system it dominated.[40]

The most famous of Governor Scott's challenges to the political status quo came in his response to the death of Senator J. Melville Broughton. In a surprising move Scott named the state's most prominent liberal, Dr. Frank Porter Graham, as Broughton's replacement. Dr. Frank, as he was affectionately called by his admirers, was the president of the University of North Carolina and had been an outspoken ally of textile workers' right to unionize. His defense of the university as a place of free expression, even for African American intellectuals such as the black poet Langston Hughes, had angered many of the state's leading conservatives, who looked on him with suspicion. Governor Scott's appointment of Graham to the Senate set off an explosion in Tar Heel politics.[41]

Graham took his Senate seat in 1949 and immediately faced a campaign for reelection in 1950. His opponent in the Democratic primary, Willis Smith, an attorney and former president of the American Bar Association, represented the mainline conservative interests of the Shelby Dynasty. To convince working-class whites to vote against Graham, who better represented their economic interests, the Smith campaign suggested that Graham was a closet communist and secretly favored racial integration. In fact, Graham was a moderate on racial issues but not an integrationist, at least not publicly. In spite of the smear campaign Graham earned 48.9 percent of the vote, just short of the 50 percent necessary to win the primary, and Smith seemed reluctant to call for a runoff. Then things turned nasty. A conservative newsman named Jesse Helms ran radio advertisements urging Smith supporters to rally at the candidate's house. That night a large, enthusiastic crowd convinced Smith to challenge Graham in a second primary. A group calling itself "Know the Truth Committee" circulated placards that in part read: "White People Wake Up Before It Is Too Late."[42] Smith supporters fabricated stories, lied about Graham's record, and even passed around a doctored picture showing Mrs. Graham dancing with a black man. The attacks worked, and the voters of North Carolina elected Smith by a substantial majority.[43]

The vicious Senate campaign of 1950 is clearly an important political event in North Carolina politics, but its significance has been overstated.

Some scholars contend that Graham's defeat widened the growing rift between the factions within the Democratic Party to the point that there was no longer a clearly recognizable progressive plutocracy in North Carolina. Furthermore, Jesse Helms and other Smith supporters became the core of a new, more aggressively conservative faction that would eventually become the Republican Party, while Graham's supporters, including Terry Sanford and Jim Hunt, became the nucleus of the future Democratic Party.[44]

The elections of 1948 and 1950, however, were more foreshadowing than realignment. Helms and the Republicans did not win their first major election until 1972, twenty-two years after Graham's defeat. The Shelby Dynasty did not fade after Kerr Scott but reclaimed the Executive Mansion with the election of William Umstead in 1952. The issues debated during the 1952 elections, as well as in 1954 when Scott won a seat in the U.S. Senate, returned to regular disagreements between the business interests and reformers. There was no repeat of the virulent race-baiting of the Graham–Smith primary in either election. Both factions of the Democratic Party—the Shelby Dynasty and the Branchhead Boys, which now dominated the reform wing of the party—accepted the ideology of business progressivism but disagreed on how far to extend it. Thus, North Carolina did not experience a dramatic break with its past during Kerr Scott's governorship. The progressive plutocracy not only survived but thrived throughout the decade of the 1950s. The major characteristics of the party system remained in place.

But the introduction of new crosscutting issues in 1948 and 1950 did represent the first stage of a realignment process, especially the growing rift between the hard-line and moderate segregationists over how best to defend Jim Crow. There had always been tensions between the radical and paternalistic racists within the progressive plutocracy.[45] Furnifold Simmons did not share Charles Aycock's commitment to expanding educational opportunities to both races, and O. Max Gardner's Shelby Dynasty did not approve of the extreme racist rhetoric employed by the former Simmons machine. But there had never been any significant disagreement on the foundational belief in white supremacy. After World War II, however, the certainty of a segregationist future had been shaken by Presidents Roosevelt and Truman's executive orders, the federal Civil Rights Commission, a series of Supreme Court decisions, and most important, the growing momentum of the civil rights movement.

Perhaps most troubling to white supremacists in North Carolina was the hint of compromise in the moderate language of Kerr Scott and Frank Porter Graham, conciliatory tones that seemed too much in harmony with the direction of the national Democratic Party. The progressive plutocracy, and the political system that sustained it, had been built on the uncompromising tenet that African Americans had no place in Tar Heel politics. Any change in that consensus among Democratic leaders threatened to bring down the whole political system. Ironically, however, the downfall of the progressive plutocracy eventually came as much from the racist right as from the moderate middle. In the new context of postwar America the unapologetic and aggressive white supremacy of Jesse Helms and his allies in the Smith campaign threatened to undercut the favorable business climate upon which the progressive plutocracy depended.[46]

The debate between radical and moderate segregationists in North Carolina intensified after 1954 when the Supreme Court ruled in *Brown v. Board of Education* that racially segregated schools were inherently unequal. Even then public disagreement was muted. Elsewhere in the South opportunistic leaders found political gold by mining old veins of Confederate pride and digging up long-held fears of miscegenation. Appeals for calm competed with battle cries of resistance. But in North Carolina, Governor William B. Umstead only stated that he was "terribly disappointed" in the ruling, and he established an Advisory Committee on Education to recommend ways in which the state could preserve its segregated schools.[47] His response was typical of the progressive plutocracy. He tried to reassure worried white North Carolinians that the state's natural business leadership would protect their privileged racial status. Umstead, however, was a sick man, having suffered a heart attack soon after his inauguration two years earlier. Within a few months he would be dead, and it would fall to his lesser known lieutenant governor, Luther H. Hodges, to lead the Old North State's defense of segregation.

Hodges was a political novice who had been asked to run for lieutenant governor by leaders of the Shelby Dynasty who feared the consequences of Umstead's poor health. Hodges, who had risen from poverty to become one of the most successful textile manufacturers in the nation, had recently announced his retirement from Marshall Field and Company at the age of fifty-two. He had a confident manner and was completely comfortable speaking in public. He came across well on radio but even better on television, which for the first time had carried presidential and state political advertisements in the election of 1952. He knew all the major businessmen in the state and was well connected politically. He believed in business progressivism and racial segregation. Hodges was the quintessential progressive plutocrat.[48]

Not since O. Max Gardner had North Carolina experienced a businessman governor so intent on restructuring government and promoting growth. After learning that the state ranked forty-fourth among the forty-eight states

FIGURE 10.1. The progressive plutocracy in its twilight. *Left to right*: Archie K. Davis (president of the Research Triangle Foundation), Mrs. Meade Willis, Frank Borden Hanes, Mrs. Robert M. Hanes, and Governor Luther H. Hodges attending the groundbreaking for the Hanes Research Laboratory in Research Triangle Park, 1960. Photograph courtesy of the North Carolina State Archives.

in per capita income, Hodges launched the most aggressive industrial recruitment campaign in the South. To attract investment he cut taxes, started industrial training centers (the forerunner of the state's community college system), led business-hunting trips across the United States and Europe, and established innovative private-public investment projects, the most famous being the Research Triangle Park. He also passed the first minimum wage in the state's history. But true to the tradition of the progressive plutocracy, he disliked unions and sent the National Guard to restore law and order when textile workers went on strike at the Harriet-Henderson mills.[49]

Hodges delighted the businessmen in the Shelby Dynasty, but he frustrated its politicians. He was a uniquely independent governor whose sudden rise to power did not saddle him with the political debts most politicians owe from years of deal making. Hodges often boasted that he ran for office "with no political tie-ups or commitments," and he regularly made appointments based on applicants' merit instead of their politics, a practice that infuriated the old boy networks and courthouse gangs.[50] Hodges's neglect of the patronage machine, and his own lack of interest in building a personal political dynasty, killed off what was left of the Shelby Dynasty. The resulting power vacuum was yet another sign of a developing realignment.[51]

The segregation question was also of little interest to Luther Hodges. His passion was economic development, and he considered the furor over the *Brown* ruling to be a dangerous distraction from the real issue of creating jobs. But the governor was just as adamant as his predecessors that white supremacy must be protected. Hodges continued Umstead's Advisory Committee on Education—better known as the Pearsall Committee for its chairman, Thomas Pearsall—and supported its recommendation for a pupil assignment law that gave local school boards the power to determine where students would attend school. The law cleverly decentralized the state's education system, which meant that African Americans would have to bring suit in every one of over one hundred autonomous local school districts. Hodges hoped black North Carolinians would agree to voluntary segregation, and he responded angrily when they emphatically refused. He reconstituted the Pearsall Committee, removing its three black members, and then strongly endorsed its new proposal to allow local school districts to close their public schools by a majority vote. It also provided vouchers for white parents to send their children to private schools if necessary. These proposals, nicknamed the Pearsall Plan, passed the legislature with Hodges's enthusiastic support. In September 1956 he went on statewide television to urge the state's voters to pass the constitutional amendments required to implement it. The referendum passed by an overwhelming vote of 471,657 to 107,757, but it attracted the largest margin of support in the eastern black belt counties where historically the populist reformers, and more recently Kerr Scott, had performed best. A few months later, in November, Luther Hodges won reelection by the largest margin in the state's modern electoral history.[52]

The Pearsall Plan ranks as one of the progressive plutocracy's greatest victories. Hodges and the state's business elite managed to postpone any substantial challenge to the state's racial segregation for over a decade while appearing to be more sensible than the militant segregationists popping up all across Dixie. When twelve black students integrated three urban school districts in Greensboro, Winston-Salem, and Charlotte with relatively minor violence in 1957, the national press praised North Carolina for its moderation. For a brief time it appeared that the business oligarchy that had ruled the state since 1900 would retain its unchallenged hold on power.[53]

But a closer examination of the Pearsall Committee and its impact on Tar Heel politics suggests the opposite conclusion. Instead of fortifying the power of the progressive plutocracy the Pearsall Plan undercut its foundation—the uncompromising agreement on white supremacy. Infighting between militant white supremacists and the pragmatic segregationist majority within the Pearsall Committee had almost derailed the plan before it was presented. Implicit in the committee's strategy was the understanding that some token integration would have to be allowed to prevent intervention by the federal government. Hodges and the majority of the committee members accepted tokenism as a tactical retreat necessary to maintain the larger system of racial capitalism, a middle way between impractical massive resistance and unacceptable racial integration. On Hodges's political right the militant white supremacists saw it as surrender. Jesse Helms, Thomas Ellis (legal counsel to the Pearsall Committee), and I. Beverly Lake Sr. (a former state assistant attorney general) attacked the governor and the Pearsall Plan as a capitulation to the NAACP and the abandonment of the southern way of life. On Hodges's political left racially moderate, but not quite liberal, politicians such as Kerr Scott (now serving in the U.S. Senate) and his protégée Terry Sanford (Scott's campaign manager and a state senator) rallied behind Hodges and supported the Pearsall Plan. They defended it as a safety valve to forestall both federal intervention and a white backlash that might close the public schools. The split among these factions was irreconcilable, and it would widen with each new civil rights battle. The elite consensus on white supremacy was over, and so was the progressive plutocracy. Luther Hodges was the last governor that can be considered a member of that historic cohort of Tar Heel leaders.[54]

In 1960, four years after the Pearsall Plan and ten years after the bitter Graham–Smith Senate campaign, Terry Sanford walked into the board of elections office to file his name as a candidate for governor. Sanford was making a secret, symbolic declaration of political war against the conservatives who had smeared Graham in 1950. Under his lapel, just out of sight, Sanford had pinned a Frank Porter Graham for Senate button to his suit. Sanford's gesture illustrates both the emotional legacy of Graham's defeat and the last stage of the realignment process.[55]

Opposing Sanford in the Democratic primary of 1960 was I. Beverly Lake Sr. Lake had worked in the Hodges administration and had helped shape the state's legal reaction to the *Brown* ruling, but he had become increasingly disillusioned with the moderate tone of North Carolina's antiintegration strategy. Lake was an uncompromising and unapologetic segregationist, and he intended to turn the state hard to the right. He had the support of Jesse Helms, Tom Ellis, and other conservatives within the Democratic Party, many of whom had supported Smith in 1950. In the center of the political spectrum, positioned between Sanford and Lake, were two more traditional candidates in the mold of the old progressive plutocracy: John

Larkins, an experienced legislator and former state Democratic chairman, and Malcolm Seawell, North Carolina's attorney general. Larkins and Seawell were pragmatic segregationists. Even though they attracted the support of the major business interests in the state, and in spite of Governor Hodges's endorsement of Seawell, neither candidate gained any traction. A decade earlier, one of these moderately conservative gentlemen would have won the endorsement of the Shelby Dynasty and moved into the Executive Mansion. But in the new politics of 1960 the middle would not hold.[56]

Both Sanford and Lake knew that the outcome of the Democratic primary depended on the issue of race. Three days before Sanford announced his candidacy, four students from North Carolina A&T State University started their sit-in at the Woolworth's lunch counter in Greensboro. When Lake launched his campaign a month later on March 1, 1960, protests against segregation in downtown Raleigh could be seen from his office window. Lake tried to define the contest as a choice between Sanford's supposedly pro-integration views and his own staunch opposition to civil rights. Sanford countered by suggesting that Lake would move the state in a radical direction that would endanger its public schools, growing economy, and moderate reputation. Lake warned about the horrors of racial integration. Sanford pledged to improve public education. Lake had enough support to force a second primary, but Sanford's well-organized campaign, and his assurance that he was not an integrationist, brought him a solid victory.[57]

Since 1900 the winner of the Democratic primary was assured of beating the Republican challenger in the fall elections. Not in 1960. Sanford boldly chose to endorse presidential candidate John F. Kennedy at the Democratic convention against the wishes of the majority of North Carolina's delegation, who backed Lyndon B. Johnson. Sanford's move further splintered the state's already fractious Democratic Party. When Kennedy won the nomination, many North Carolinians expressed negative feelings about his Catholicism, liberalism, and support for civil rights. The Republican candidate for governor, Robert Gavin, took advantage of the opportunity and attacked Sanford as a member of the "radical-socialist wing of the Kennedys."[58] The issues now being served up by the candidates in the general election were much expanded from the typical fare in Tar Heel politics. Both Kennedy and Sanford carried the state, but by the narrowest of margins. No longer could the Republicans be ignored in Tar Heel politics.[59]

The election of 1960 marked the end of a twelve-year realignment period. The first phase of the realignment began with the campaigns of 1948 and 1950 and the reintroduction of the crosscutting issue of race. The traditional geographical voting tendencies of the eastern rural counties to vote for populist reformers were gradually transformed by increased racial concerns. The traditional factions within the progressive plutocracy—the majority conservative or machine wing versus the reform insurgents—had been shaken up by the success of Kerr Scott and then, after a brief respite, further unsettled by the impact of the *Brown* decision and the civil rights movement. What once had been a fight over the expansion of business progressivism became a battle between radical and moderate segregationists over the extent of white supremacy. Luther Hodges's political independence killed off a weakened Shelby Dynasty, and the Pearsall Plan served as a catalyst for the dissolution of the elite political leadership V. O. Key Jr. had called the progressive plutocracy.

By 1960 a new generation of leaders and voters, many who had served in World War II, witnessed the emergence of a new political party system. The old guard was gone. Frank Porter Graham was in New York City working for the United Nations, and Luther Hodges left for Washington, D.C., to become President Kennedy's secretary of commerce. Senators Willis Smith and Kerr Scott had died in office. The Republican Party, long reduced to minority status in North Carolina, now had a real shot at winning elections. Changing economic conditions, the civil rights movement, and escalating tensions overseas brought new issues into the public debate. Even the mechanisms of the political process had changed. Television, first used in the 1952 campaigns, began to replace radio and newspapers as the primary source of political information. Media consultants and political polling first appeared in Terry Sanford's campaign in 1960. All of these new technologies served to weaken the influence of the traditional good ol' boy networks and courthouse gangs. The process of political realignment that had begun a decade earlier had come to fruition.[60]

CONCLUSION

When Governor Terry Sanford moved into his office in the State Capitol in 1961, he once again made a symbolic gesture to identify with the progressive tradition in Tar Heel politics. He hung four portraits in his office—Charles Aycock, O. Max Gardner, Kerr Scott, and Frank Porter Graham. While the Sanford administration can be seen as a modern extension of business progressivism, the governor cannot be considered a member of the old plutocracy of business elites that ran North Carolina for the first six decades of the twentieth century.[61] The progressive plutocracy, and the political system that supported it, passed from the scene as Sanford took center stage. But the state's progressive reputation outlived the plutocratic leadership that created it. The ideology of business progressivism—the idea that state government should be run efficiently, support business interests, and extend services for the benefit of its citizens—not only survived into the Sanford administration but became the rhetorical cornerstone of every subsequent governor through the end of the twentieth century. Whether one believes that this progressivism should be seen as a legitimate description or a mythical exaggeration of the state's reputation, it certainly remained a central issue in the new political system.[62]

Scholars have described the post-1960 political system in various ways, but most agree with political scientist Alexander Lamis that the South experienced a long period of transition in which Republicans gradually overwhelmed the Democratic Party.[63] In North Carolina, however, the usually helpful categories of Republican and Democrat are not sufficient to explain the dynamics of the new political system. Sociologist Paul Luebke suggested that, beginning with the Sanford administration, North Carolina's politicians and business leaders have chosen policies consistent with one of two competing ideological movements: modernizers or traditionalists. Modernizers favored moderate reform of the state's social and economic relations in order to advance the growth of new business opportunities in technology, finance, and manufacturing. According to Luebke the modernizers tend to come from the urban areas of the state, especially the industrial Piedmont. Traditionalists resisted any alteration in southern racial, economic, or social relations. They were based in the state's small towns and in rural and agrarian sections, and they enjoyed the support of the established industries, such as textiles, furniture, and agriculture. While modernizers supported an activist government to promote infrastructure and especially education, the traditionalists favored limited government, fewer taxes, and old-fashioned family values. Modernizers may be more willing than traditionalists to accept African Americans and women into their ranks, but they are not enthusiastic supporters of social movements that challenge the status quo.[64]

While there are significant differences between modernizers and traditionalists in the political system since 1960, Luebke argued that they are actually two sides of the same coin because they represent two different brands of conservatism. Neither modernizers nor traditionalists support the liberal or populist agenda of expanding equality or redistributing wealth and power at the expense of the paternalistic but self-sustaining elite. Luebke also warned against thinking of modernizers and traditionalists as synonymous with Democrats and Republicans because elements of both groups can be found in both political parties. For instance, Republicans included both modernizers such as Governors James E. Holshouser and traditionalists like Senator Jesse Helms, while the Democrats included both traditionalists like Senator Sam Ervin and modernizers such as Governor James B. Hunt Jr. By the end of the century, however, the political system had sorted itself out, with modernizers dominating the Democratic Party while traditionalists and conservative-leaning modernizers battled for control of the Republican Party.[65]

Throughout the twentieth century, and even into the early twenty-first century, North Carolinians have been far more willing to send ideologically driven politicians to Washington, D.C., than to Raleigh. Fire-breathing conservatives and pitchfork populists occasionally won election to the U.S. House or Senate, but Tar Heel voters have historically elected pragmatic centrists to run their state government.[66] By the 1990s that trend began to diminish in the state legislature. Ideological divisions increased at the same time that Republicans began challenging Democrats for control of the General Assembly. By the turn of the twenty-first century the Republican caucus had become increasingly the home of traditionalists while the Democrats generally remained modernizers. But North Carolina's governors continued to reflect the tradition of business progressivism, and they consistently embraced the modernizer ideology despite their party label.

That trend ended with the election of Governor Pat McCrory in 2012. Before running for governor, McCrory had earned a reputation as the pragmatic, moderate, Republican mayor of Charlotte. Yet during his gubernatorial campaign McCrory presented himself as an energetic conservative, and in the first years of his administration he embraced traditionalist ideology. Political commentators frequently pointed out that McCrory's election was of historical importance because it was the first time in over one hundred years that the state had been run by a Republican governor and a Republican legislature. But such observations were misleading. The two parties had so completely switched positions over the past century that describing the political turning point of 2012 as a return to Republican rule caused more confusion than enlightenment. Much more significant was the fact that, for the first time in over one hundred years, both the governor and the legislature openly repudiated business progressivism in favor of a conservative, antigovernment traditionalism. Whether the McCrory administration represented a major realignment of Tar Heel politics or a revealing anomaly in the state's political system will be a topic of debate for future scholars. No one, however, should confuse Governor McCrory and his Republican allies with the progressive plutocracy. That chapter in North Carolina's political history ended long before the twenty-first century began.

NOTES

1. Thad L. Beyle, "The Paradox of North Carolina," in *Politics and Policy in North Carolina*, ed. Thad L. Beyle and Merle Black (New York: MSS Information Corp., 1975), 12. On North Carolina's paradoxical reputation, see Jack Bass and Walter DeVries, *The Transformation of Southern Politics: Social Change and Political Consequences since 1945* (New York: Basic Books, 1976), 218–47; Rob Christensen, *The Paradox of Tar Heel Politics* (Chapel Hill: University of North Carolina Press, 2008); William H. Chafe, *Civilities and Civil Rights: Greensboro, North Carolina, and the Black Struggle for Freedom* (New York: Oxford University Press, 1980); and H. G. Jones, "North Carolina, 1946–1976: Where Historians Fear to Tread," in *Writing North Carolina History*, ed. Jeffrey J. Crow and Larry E. Tise (Chapel Hill: University of North Carolina Press, 1979), 211–18.

2. V. O. Key Jr., *Southern Politics in State and Nation* (New York: Alfred A. Knopf, 1949), 205–6.

3. Ibid.

4. For a sampling of general interpretations of recent North Carolina political history, see Thomas Eamon, *The Making of a Southern Democracy: North Carolina Politics from Kerr Scott to Pat McCrory* (Chapel Hill: University of North Carolina Press, 2014); Christensen, *Paradox of Tar Heel Politics*; Thomas F. Eamon, "The Seeds of Modern North Carolina Politics," in *The New Politics of North Carolina*, ed. Christopher A. Cooper and H. Gibbs Knotts (Chapel Hill: University of North Carolina Press, 2006), 15–37; Paul Luebke, *Tar Heel Politics, 2000* (Chapel Hill: University of North Carolina Press, 1998); William Link, *North Carolina: Change and Tradition in a Southern State* (Wheeling, Ill.: Harlan Davidson, 2009); and Jack D. Fleer, *North Carolina Government and Politics* (Lincoln: University of Nebraska Press, 1994).

5. Scholars often point to Key's first article on critical elections as his breakthrough work: V. O. Key Jr., "A Theory of Critical Elections," *Journal of Politics* 17 (February 1955): 3–18. However, an article he published some years later is more relevant to this essay: Key, "Secular Realignment and the Party System," *Journal of Politics* 21 (May 1959): 198–200.

6. The literature on realignment theory is vast and often contradictory, but a general consensus has emerged over the past decade around the basic theory. See Theodore Rosenof, *Realignment: The Theory That Changed the Way We Think about American Politics* (New York: Rowman and Littlefield, 2003). For realignment theory applied to recent southern politics, see Charles Presby, "The Reshaping of the Political Party System in North Carolina," in Cooper and Knotts, *New Politics of North Carolina*, 61–85; and Alexander P. Lamis, *Southern Politics in the 1990s* (Baton Rouge: Louisiana State University Press, 1999), 392–406.

7. Lamis, *Southern Politics*, 147–57.

8. See LeRae Sikes Umfleet, *A Day of Blood: The 1898 Wilmington Race Riot* (Raleigh: North Carolina Office of Archives and History, 2009); David S. Cecelski and Timothy B. Tyson, eds., *Democracy Betrayed: The Wilmington Race Riot of 1898 and Its Legacy* (Chapel Hill: University of North Carolina Press, 1998); and Jeffrey J. Crow, Paul D. Escott, and Flora J. Hatley, *A History of African Americans in North Carolina* (Raleigh, N.C.: Office of Archives and History, 1992), 113–18.

9. Paul D. Escott, *Many Excellent People: Power and Privilege in North Carolina, 1950–1900* (Chapel Hill: University of North Carolina Press, 1985).

10. Christensen, *Paradox of Tar Heel Politics*, 21.

11. Ibid., 31; Oliver Hamilton Orr Jr., *Charles Brantley Aycock* (Chapel Hill: University of North Carolina Press, 1961); Lee A. Craig, *Josephus Daniels: His Life and Times* (Chapel Hill: University of North Carolina Press, 2013).

12. Key, *Southern Politics*, 223–28; Christensen, *Paradox of Tar Heel Politics*, 41. William Link sees a general division between modernizers and traditionalists starting in the 1920s, but it was not until the 1950s that cultural divisions began to reinforce political factions. See Link, *North Carolina*, 314; and Luebke, *Tar Heel Politics*, 19.

13. Deborah Beckel, *Radical Reform: Interracial Politics in Post-Emancipation North Carolina* (Charlottesville: University of Virginia Press, 2011); Luebke, *Tar Heel Politics*, 8.

14. Kenneth Joel Zogry, "Furnifold M. Simmons," in *The North Carolina Century: Tar Heels Who Made a Difference, 1900-2000*, ed. Howard E. Covington and Marion A. Ellis (Charlotte, N.C.: Levine Museum of the New South, 2002), 418.

15. Christensen, *Paradox of Tar Heel Politics*, 46–47; Craig, *Josephus Daniels*, 207–11.

16. Glenda Elizabeth Gilmore, "False Friends and Avowed Enemies: Southern African Americans and Party Allegiances in the 1920s," in *Jumpin' Jim Crow: Southern Politics from Civil War to Civil Rights*, ed. Jane Dailey, Glenda Elizabeth Gilmore, and Bryant Simon (Princeton, N.J.: Princeton University Press, 2000), 219–32.

17. George B. Tindall, "Business Progressivism: Southern Politics in the Twenties," *South Atlantic Quarterly* 62 (Winter 1963): 92–106; Beckel, *Radical Reform*, 183.

18. Quoted in Christensen, *Paradox of Tar Heel Politics*, 42. See also J. Morgan Kousser, *The Shaping of Southern Politics: Suffrage Restriction and the Establishment of the One-Party South, 1880-1910* (New Haven, Conn.: Yale University Press, 1974).

19. Tindall, "Business Progressivism"; Christensen, *Paradox of Tar Heel Politics*, 48–61. The South's defense of its uniquely racialized capitalism is discussed in Jason Morgan Ward, *Defending White Democracy: The Making of a Segregationist Movement and the Remaking of a Racial Politics, 1936-1965* (Chapel Hill: University of North Carolina Press, 2011).

20. Thomas Bickett, "Inaugural Address," January 11, 1917, in *Public Letters and Papers of Thomas Walter Bickett, Governor of North Carolina, 1917-1921*, ed. R. B. House (Raleigh, N.C.: Edwards and Broughton, 1923), 1–15.

21. Thomas Bickett, "A Debt of Honor," November 11, 1919, in House, *Public Letters and Papers*, 208.

22. Ibid., 207.

23. "Governor Bickett's Administration Represents New High Record of Legislative Achievement," *News and Observer* (Raleigh, N.C.), April 20, 1919, quoted in House, *Public Letters and Papers*, 283.

24. Tindall, "Business Progressivism," 98; Thomas Bickett, "An Inspiring Record," in House, *Public Letters and Papers*, 287–92 (quote on 279).

25. Bickett long opposed woman's suffrage, but with passage of the Nineteenth Amendment all but certain he suggested that "it would be the part of wisdom and of grace for North Carolina to accept the inevitable and ratify the amendment." Thomas Bickett, "Women's Suffrage," in House, *Public Letters and Papers*, 62.

26. House, *Public Letters and Papers*, 292–97.

27. "Legislation for Negroes, Seventh Message of Governor T. W. Bickett to the Special Session of the General Assembly of 1920," August 23, 1920, in House, *Public Letters and Papers*, 72–73.

28. Lydia Charles Hoffman, "Cameron Morrison," in Covington and Ellis, *North Carolina Century*, 495–98; Christensen, *Paradox of Tar Heel Politics*, 48–55; Craig, *Josephus Daniels*, 385–86. But Morrison remained true to his social conservatism: he condemned woman's suffrage, fearing it would lead to black women's voting; did nothing to stop the growth of the KKK; attacked the evils of liquor; and sided with the fundamentalists in their crusade against the teaching of evolution. His actions demonstrate once again that cultural issues did not define the political system of the progressive plutocracy.

29. Gilmore, "False Friends and Avowed Enemies," 219–32; Ward, *Defending White Democracy*.

30. Christensen, *Paradox of Tar Heel Politics*, 56–61.

31. Joseph L. Morrison, *Governor O. Max Gardner: A Power in North Carolina and New Deal Washington* (Chapel Hill: University of North Carolina Press, 1971), 52–83; Allen Jay Maxwell, foreword to *Public Papers and Letters of Oliver Max Gardner*, comp. Edwin Gill, ed. David Leroy Corbitt (Raleigh, N.C.: Council of State, 1937), vii–lii; Christensen, *Paradox of Tar Heel Politics*, 64–68.

32. Christensen, *Paradox of Tar Heel Politics*, 108.

33. Ibid., 76–78, 84–101, 106–8.

34. Morrison, *Governor O. Max Gardner*, 131–69, 241–70.

35. After Gardner's death the leadership of the Shelby Dynasty fell not to one man but to a group of well-connected businessmen and politicians who had been part of the organization for many years. Among them were banker and civic leader Robert Hanes from Winston-Salem and the head of the state's Democratic Party, B. Everett Jordan. Interestingly, Jordan was married to Kerr Scott's cousin and had been a key member of the Branchhead Boys, Scott's political organization, until he had a falling out with Scott over the appointment of Frank Porter Graham to the U.S. Senate in 1950.

36. Julian Pleasants, *The Political Career of W. Kerr Scott: The Squire from Haw River* (Lexington: University Press of Kentucky, 2014); William D. Snider, "The Scotts of Haw River," in Covington and Ellis, *North Carolina Century*, 519.

37. Eamon, *Making of a Southern Democracy*, 22.

38. Snider, "The Scotts of Haw River," 519.

39. Christensen, *Paradox of Tar Heel Politics*, 116

40. Ibid., 115–20. On school equalization, see Sarah Caroline Thuesen, *Greater than Equal: African American Struggles for Schools and Citizenship in North Carolina, 1919–1965* (Chapel Hill: University of North Carolina Press, 2013).

41. Graham had also worked for both the United Nations and the Oak Ridge Institute of Nuclear Studies—the first suspected by conservatives to be a den of communists and the second a repository of some of the nation's most sensitive atomic secrets—which made him a target of national conservatives who feared he was too "pinkish" to be trusted. See Julian M. Pleasants and Augustus M Burns III, *Frank Porter Graham and the 1950 Senate Race in North Carolina* (Chapel Hill: University of North Carolina Press, 1990).

42. Milton Ready, *The Tar Heel State: A History of North Carolina* (Columbia: University of South Carolina Press, 2005), 354.

43. Pleasants and Burns, *Frank Porter Graham*.

44. "There was a fervor and a passion about Kerr Scott and the change he would make in

our lives," future governor Jim Hunt later recalled, "that is very unusual in politics." Christensen, *Paradox of Tar Heel Politics*, 153. The case for the Kerr Scott era being the pivotal turning point in recent Tar Heel politics is implied in many sources but most clearly stated in Julian M. Pleasants, "A New Day for N.C.: Kerr Scott and the Gubernatorial Campaign of 1948," paper presented at the conference "'To Gain Attention to Their Various Claims,' Historical Political Campaigns in North Carolina," University of North Carolina at Chapel Hill, September 14, 2012.

45. On the "long history" of the evolving tensions between radical and pragmatic segregationists in the South, see Ward, *Defending White Democracy*.

46. Several scholars have examined the growing conflict between the more moderate pragmatic segregationists who discouraged excessive racial conflict in order to promote business modernization and the uncompromising militant white supremacists who opposed any strategic accommodation as surrender. See Bruce Schulman, *From Cotton Belt to Sunbelt: Federal Policy, Economic Development, and the Transformation of the South, 1938-1980* (Oxford: Oxford University Press, 1991); Joseph Crespino, *In Search of Another Country: Mississippi and the Conservative Counterrevolution* (Princeton, N.J.: Princeton University Press, 2007); and William A. Link, *Righteous Warrior: Jesse Helms and the Rise of Modern Conservatism* (New York: St. Martin's Press, 2008).

47. Umstead's remarks are discussed in Chafe, *Civilities and Civil Rights*, 65.

48. See A. G. Ivey, *Luther H. Hodges, Practical Idealist* (Minneapolis, Minn.: Denison, 1968); and Luther H. Hodges, *Businessman in the Statehouse* (Chapel Hill: University of North Carolina Press, 1962).

49. Hodges, *Businessman in the Statehouse*.

50. "Prepared Remarks," TV Charlotte, May 29, 1952, Luther H. Hodges Papers, folder 1876, Southern Historical Collection, Wilson Library, University of North Carolina at Chapel Hill.

51. Christensen, *Paradox of Tar Heel Politics*, 158.

52. On the Pearsall Plan, see Anders Walker, *The Ghost of Jim Crow: How Southern Moderates Used Brown v. Board of Education to Stall Civil Rights* (New York: Oxford University Press, 2009), 56-66.

53. Chafe, *Civilities and Civil Rights*, 67-80.

54. Walker, *Ghost of Jim Crow*, 56-66. Governor Luther H. Hodges, Thomas J. Pearsall, Paul A. Johnson, Robert I. Giles, and E. L. Rankin Jr., "Transcription [of] Session on History of the Integration Situation in North Carolina," September 3, 1960, Governor's Office, State Capitol, Raleigh, Southern Oral History Program, Southern Historical Collection.

55. Howard E. Covington Jr. and Marion A. Ellis, *Terry Sanford: Politics, Progress and Outrageous Ambitions* (Durham, N.C.: Duke University Press, 1999), 208.

56. The best source on the campaign of 1960 is John Drescher, *Triumph of Good Will: How Terry Sanford Beat a Champion of Segregation and Reshaped the South* (Jackson: University Press of Mississippi, 2000).

57. See Eamon, *Making of a Southern Democracy*, 58-68; Christensen, *Paradox of Tar Heel Politics*, 181-84; and Drescher, *Triumph of Good Will*.

58. Christensen, *Paradox of Tar Heel Politics*, 185.

59. See Eamon, *Making of a Southern Democracy*, 68-77.

60. Covington and Ellis, *Terry Sanford*; Robert R. Korstad and James L. Leloudis, *To Right These Wrongs: The North Carolina Fund and the Battle to End Poverty and Inequality in 1960s America* (Chapel Hill: University of North Carolina Press, 2010), 39–42.

61. Christensen, *Paradox of Tar Heel Politics*, 186.

62. A previous generation of scholars strongly endorsed the notion that North Carolina was the most progressive southern state. See, e.g., William S. Powell, *North Carolina through Four Centuries* (Chapel Hill: University of North Carolina Press, 1989). Recent scholarship has been more critical. See Chafe, *Civilities and Civil Rights*; and Luebke, *Tar Heel Politics*.

63. Lamis, *Southern Politics*.

64. Luebke, *Tar Heel Politics*, 19–24.

65. Ibid., 207–36.

66. Christensen, *Paradox of Tar Heel Politics*, 315–16.

DEFYING *BROWN*, DEFYING PEARSALL
AFRICAN AMERICANS AND THE STRUGGLE FOR PUBLIC SCHOOL INTEGRATION IN NORTH CAROLINA, 1954–1971

Jerry Gershenhorn

On May 17, 1954, the U.S. Supreme Court ruled unanimously in *Brown v. Board of Education* "that in the field of public education the doctrine of 'separate but equal' has no place. Separate educational facilities are inherently unequal."[1] Although this ruling marked the successful culmination of a two-decade-long struggle to overturn *Plessy v. Ferguson* (1896), it was not the end but the beginning of another long struggle by African Americans and their allies to ensure implementation of the court's decision. In North Carolina, in response to the *Brown* decision, white government officials and their supporters redoubled their efforts to stop or delay racial integration of the schools. The North Carolina General Assembly enacted the pupil assignment law and the Pearsall Plan, which placed legal and logistical roadblocks to racial integration. African Americans renewed their efforts to integrate public schools through lawsuits, direct action, and grassroots political mobilization. Black lawyers, journalists, activists, students, and parents, with black community support, fought courageously to surmount the obstacles placed in their path by white segregationists and end America's educational apartheid. Thus white segregationists defied *Brown*, while civil rights activists sought to defy Pearsall.

While many white North Carolinians have long claimed a progressive political outlook, white officials' actions in response to *Brown* were more devious than progressive. While North Carolina's top officials did not refuse to desegregate all schools or employ the virulent rhetoric heard in the Deep South, the state's policies were designed to perpetuate a dual system of public education. And, despite North Carolina's progressive reputation, the state was among the slowest to integrate its schools.

In response, black activists engaged in a monumental struggle, which ultimately broke through the barriers constructed by segregationist officials. The revival of the civil rights movement by the sit-ins, which began in Greensboro in 1960, played a crucial role in integrating public schools. Movement activists took to the streets to fight for the desegregation of all public facilities, including the schools. Black freedom fighters and their allies succeeded in winning passage of the Civil Rights Act of 1964, which among other things provided black attorneys with a new ally in the U.S. Justice Department. During the late 1960s and early 1970s, successful NAACP lawsuits led to U.S. Supreme Court decisions that sped up school integration. But when white officials finally began to implement integration in the public schools, they did so in ways that employed white control to fire many black teachers and principals and close many black schools, which led to another round of black protest.

Since the 1980s, several important works on the black struggle for equal and integrated education in North Carolina have given us a better understanding of these efforts. In *Reading, Writing, and Race: The Desegregation of the Charlotte Schools* (1995), Davison Douglas recounts the protracted legal struggle to integrate Charlotte city and Mecklenburg County schools in the twenty years after the *Brown* decision. Douglas argues that black protest yielded limited gains in desegregation of public schools during the late 1950s and early 1960s. But during the late 1960s and early 1970s, African Americans "gained in the courtroom what they could not possibly have gained in the streets; one of the most thoroughly integrated urban school systems in the United States."[2]

In his important work on the late 1960s battle over the direction of education in Hyde County, in eastern North Carolina, *Along Freedom Road: Hyde County, North Carolina, and the Fate of Black Schools in the South* (1994), David Cecelski analyzes a local black protest movement that rejected white domination of the integration process, which ignored the needs of black students, educators, and institutions. African Americans in Hyde County organized a successful protest movement to save two black schools that were threatened with closing by the white-controlled school board.[3]

Years earlier, William Chafe had debunked the myth of North Carolina's progressivism in *Civilities and Civil Rights: Greensboro, North Carolina, and the Black Struggle for Freedom* (1980). In this important study of a local protest movement, Chafe examines thirty years of struggle against racial injustice in a state that despite its progressive reputation would be more accurately described as reactionary.[4]

Nonetheless, despite these important works, two more recent surveys of North Carolina history, Milton Ready's *The Tar Heel State: A History of North Carolina* (2005) and William Link's *North Carolina: Change and Tradition in a Southern State* (2009), which are often used in college classes on

North Carolina history, have minimized the important role played by black students and their parents, black attorneys, and the black community in the struggle for educational integration.[5] A more comprehensive understanding of the modern civil rights movement requires more attention to the post-1954 African American struggle for equity and integration in public education in the face of segregationists' tactics to delay public school integration. This struggle, moreover, was a vital component of the long black freedom struggle in North Carolina.

In North Carolina in 1954, white politicians, almost all Democrats, controlled the state and local governments. All 170 members of the General Assembly were white, with no black members since 1900, when white supremacists had pushed through amendments to the North Carolina Constitution—poll tax, literacy test, grandfather clause—that disfranchised African Americans. During the 1950s and early 1960s, city councils and local school boards were either all white or in a few instances had one black member. Although voter registration campaigns had increased black voting in North Carolina from the 1930s to the 1950s, the literacy test and white Democratic Party control of the registration process restricted black voting, particularly in the eastern part of the state, where most of the state's African Americans lived.

In this context, the *Brown* ruling that racially segregated schools were unconstitutional filled many black Carolinians with great hope that a new day had come. Robert Williams of Monroe, North Carolina, recalled, "At last I felt that I was part of America and that I belonged.... That was what I had wanted, even as a child." Williams believed "that this was the beginning of a new era in American democracy."[6]

But a new era in American democracy would not come quickly or easily because white state officials took action to block implementation of the *Brown* decision. Governor William Umstead pronounced his disagreement with the decision, calling it "a clear and serious invasion of the rights of the sovereign states."[7] And every member of North Carolina's all-white General Assembly voted in favor of a resolution that claimed that public school integration would lead to the destruction of public education in the state.[8]

In December 1954, a committee appointed by Governor Umstead asserted that "the mixing of the races forthwith in the public schools throughout the state cannot be accomplished and should not be attempted."[9] Luther H. Hodges, who had succeeded Umstead as governor after the latter man's death in November, praised the committee's conclusion.[10] The committee recommended that the North Carolina General Assembly pass a law that would "give local school boards control of enrollment and assignment of children in the state's public schools."[11] Passed in April 1955, the pupil assignment act made it much more difficult for civil rights lawyers to challenge public school segregation because instead of suing the state, they would have to sue each of North Carolina's 173 school districts, thus slowing down the process.[12] The act proved very effective at bogging down lawsuits for desegregation as the federal courts required that "plaintiffs must exhaust their administrative remedies provided by the act and that rights must be asserted as individuals, not as a class before applying to a Federal court for relief."[13] Ten states passed pupil placement laws in the middle to late 1950s.[14]

Then, in May 1955, the U.S. Supreme Court aided the segregationists' cause by issuing its implementation decision, calling for desegregation "with all deliberate speed" and failing to set a timetable for integration.[15] Furthermore, federal courts interpreted the *Brown* decision and determined that it did not require "integration in the schools, but only prohibited enforced segregation."[16]

Black leaders and organizations mobilized in opposition to the stalling tactics of the state's government. In January 1955, Kelly Alexander, president of the North Carolina NAACP, attacked the pupil assignment bill and announced plans to contravene the anti-integration tactics employed by state and local governments.[17] Three months later, the North Carolina Teachers Association, the state's black teachers' association, announced its opposition to the state legislature's plans to delay school integration.[18] In July 1955, black civil rights and labor leaders, ministers, businessmen, teachers, and parents in Durham petitioned the city's school board to assign students to schools without regard to race.[19]

In February 1955, black Durham banker and attorney John H. Wheeler testified against the pupil assignment plan before the General Assembly's Joint Committee on Education. He argued that the plan was designed to "avoid the execution of the Supreme Court's decision and to slow down or retard the process of integration."[20] Cheered on by two hundred black supporters, he rejected the notion that white North Carolinians would never send their children to integrated schools, noting that the U.S. Army had operated integrated schools at its installations, including at Fort Bragg in Fayetteville, North Carolina, since 1951. Wheeler insisted that school integration had worked in other cities and would work in North Carolina if the state's leaders took forthright action to enforce federal law.[21] And evidence supports Wheeler's statement on both counts. Hundreds of school districts in Washington, D.C., Delaware, Maryland, Missouri, and other border states had "quickly and peacefully integrated their classrooms."[22] Furthermore, public opinion polls in North Carolina showed that, while a minority

FIGURE 11.1. This political cartoon by Hugh Haynie of the *Greensboro Daily News*, c. 1956, shows how the Pearsall Plan, instigated by Governor Luther H. Hodges, generated both intense support and opposition after the U.S. Supreme Court in *Brown v. Board of Education* (1954) ordered the desegregation of public schools. © Greensboro News and Record. All rights reserved.

of white voters were vociferously opposed to school integration, most whites were neither actively in favor of nor actively opposed to integration.[23]

Meanwhile, some white officials counseled compliance with the *Brown* decision. Greensboro school superintendent Benjamin L. Smith publicly announced his support for compliance with the Supreme Court decision. In a 1954 speech, he said that integration was "not a preferential matter. It is not up to us to decide whether—simply how and when to adjust to a decision already made." He urged his audience to support school boards, superintendents, and principals as they adjusted to the *Brown* decision.[24] Similarly, in June 1955, North Carolina Appeals Court judge John J. Parker wrote Governor Hodges: "It is the duty of all law-abiding men to accept and obey the law as laid down by the Supreme Court."[25] U.S. representative Thurmond Chatham of Winston-Salem pledged "to work with all groups in seeing that the law of our land is carried out without bitterness or rancor."[26] Congressman George A. Shuford of Asheville said, "Regardless of what may be anyone's personal feelings or beliefs, the policy of non-segregation now is the law of the land,... and it is up to all of us to obey the law."[27]

Nonetheless, Governor Hodges and the General Assembly took further action to stop school integration. In April 1955, the General Assembly appointed an all-white committee, headed by Thomas Pearsall, a former North Carolina speaker of the house, to act in defiance of *Brown*. This committee, known as the Pearsall Committee, proposed a constitutional amendment that would authorize the state to pay for a student to go to a private school if the student's parents refused to send their child to an integrated school. It would also permit the state to close a school if it determined that integration would lead to "intolerable" conditions.[28] Hodges campaigned for General Assembly passage of this Pearsall Plan. Calling the Supreme Court decision "an unlawful seizure of power ... in derogation of the Constitution of the United States," he vowed that the North Carolina government would "use every legal means ... to insure that the effects" of the court's decision were "not forced on our state."[29]

Black activists and organizations attacked the Pearsall Plan. In May 1956 the North Carolina Teachers Association, along with black religious and community organizations with over 700,000 members, called for integration, rejecting the Pearsall Plan and criticizing the Pearsall Committee for excluding blacks from serving as members.[30] At the special session of the General Assembly on the Pearsall Plan, John Wheeler argued that the Pearsall Plan, not school integration, would "undermine and destroy the public school system." He called the proposed bills "anti-democratic" and "evidence of bad faith and defiance of the supreme law of the land." Wheeler noted that

North Carolina, which ranked in the bottom 10 percent in education among American states, could ill afford to run two school systems.[31] Similarly, Louis Austin, black editor of Durham's *Carolina Times*, denounced the Pearsall Plan as "a plan concocted by its author and backed by the Governor of this state for one expressed purpose, and that is defiance of the U.S. Supreme Court's ruling on segregation."[32]

Although Wheeler argued that the state's resistance to integration would keep out business investment and hurt economic growth, this did not occur. North Carolina politicians like Hodges and his successor as governor, Terry Sanford, were relatively successful in creating the illusion that North Carolina was a moderate southern state and therefore avoided a negative reaction from business interests that would have retarded economic growth. Richmond, Virginia, banker Preston Holmes noted that North Carolina "had new plant investment in 1958 totaling $253 million, while Arkansas, with its massive resistance and unsettled conditions, had only $25.4 million in 1958," a substantial decline from the previous two years.[33]

Despite a large black vote against the Pearsall Plan, the constitutional amendments were passed by a four-to-one margin.[34] A large-scale radio and television campaign orchestrated by the governor and his supporters in favor of the Pearsall amendments helped ensure passage.[35] In addition, the continued disfranchisement of most African Americans in eastern North Carolina was a significant factor in suppressing the anti–Pearsall Plan vote. In fact, the largest margin in favor of the amendments was in North Carolina's eastern counties.[36] The only major city to reject the education amendments was Winston-Salem, where the black vote was crucial. For example, in three large black precincts in that city, the amendments were defeated by a thirty-to-one margin.[37] In implementing the pupil assignment act and the Pearsall Plan, North Carolina acted like other southern states that sought to block implementation of the *Brown* decision.

In 1957, Governor Hodges sought to further weaken pro-integration forces in the state by backing proposed legislation to suppress the NAACP in North Carolina. The black community, led by Kelly Alexander, who testified against the bill, condemned attempts to suppress the organization. Despite Hodges's support and House approval, the state senate rejected a bill to require the NAACP to divulge its membership and financial records to the legislature because of fears it would lead to a federal response imposing integration.[38] Consequently, North Carolina did not enact restrictions on the operation of the NAACP, as did ten southern states. It also did not end the requirement of public education, as did four southern states, nor did it cut off state funding to desegregated schools, as four states did.[39] Interestingly,

Hodges's attacks on the NAACP had an unintended impact as they spurred more blacks to join.[40]

Meanwhile, local black attorneys with community backing pressured school boards to enforce school integration. According to Christina Greene, "Between 1956 and 1960 NAACP youth in Durham canvassed neighborhoods while black women drew on a long tradition of community work to persuade wary residents to join school desegregation lawsuits."[41] The Durham Committee on Negro Affairs and the local NAACP signed up hundreds of African Americans to apply to transfer their children to all-white schools.[42] In July 1955, the black community petitioned the Durham City School Board to assign students to schools without regard to race.[43] Black attorneys challenged the constitutionality of the Pearsall amendment, filing desegregation lawsuits in Montgomery, McDowell, and Caswell counties in 1956.[44] The same year, the Winston-Salem NAACP threatened to file a desegregation law suit, which led the city's school board to agree to start desegregating schools in fall 1956. When the school board broke the agreement, the lawsuit was filed.[45] Similarly, in Mecklenburg County, the local NAACP branch and the Charlotte and Mecklenburg County Parents Committee on Education pushed for desegregation of schools. In June 1957, forty-one students filed for transfers to white schools.[46]

In these desegregation lawsuits, black plaintiffs showed great courage in the face of harassment by white segregationists. In Greensboro, black parents who joined desegregation cases were physically threatened, received threatening phone calls, and were threatened with losing their jobs.[47] In 1955, in Montgomery County, a white man assaulted a black activist who had tried to enroll five black students at a white school.[48] After blacks in the county who worked in local mills sued, one company's executives attended the hearing in order to intimidate the plaintiffs.[49] In 1956, the Raleigh school superintendent threatened to fire a teacher unless she withdrew her application for a transfer of her daughter to an all-white junior high school; the teacher withdrew her application.[50] Similarly, when Joseph Holt Sr. and Elwyna Holt applied for a transfer of their son Joseph Jr. to Raleigh's all-white Broughton High School, the family received a bomb threat and Joseph Sr. "lost his job." The Holts were not deterred and sued the school board in 1958, but the judge ruled against them because they did not appear in court. Their lawyers "feared that the board members might try to intimidate them." In 1959, when the Durham school board rejected transfer applications from black students "regardless of whether they had appeared before the school board, Thurgood Marshall quipped that their only chance would have been to be 'neither here nor there.'"[51]

Despite these setbacks, during the late 1950s black legal pressure convinced several school boards to admit a handful of black students to previously all-white public schools. In 1957, the Greensboro, Charlotte, and Winston-Salem school boards admitted twelve black students to previously all-white schools.[52] Two years later, backed by petitions by hundreds of black Durhamites and 225 transfer requests by black students and their parents, lawsuits filed by NAACP and local attorneys compelled the Durham city board of education to admit six black students to white schools in 1959.[53]

White officials agreed to desegregate these schools to forestall federal court orders to integrate schools on a larger scale. Thomas Pearsall recalled, "After the [1956] election we knew we had to move on integration or the court would come in."[54] Attorney William T. Joyner, vice-chairman of the Pearsall Committee, explained to the (all-white) North Carolina Bar Association that token desegregation was "a small price to pay" for keeping most schools segregated. He "said he had nightmares about ending up in a federal court trying to defend a school board that had rejected transfers by Negro students in a state that had never had a single Negro student admitted to any one of the approximately 2,000 white schools in North Carolina."[55] As historian Davison Douglas has shown, in North Carolina "token integration, unaccompanied by defiant rhetoric, enabled the state to escape judicial intervention in a manner that other, more defiant southern states did not."[56] This token desegregation helped North Carolina argue that its pupil assignment law and Pearsall Plan were constitutional because the state had permitted some black students to attend white schools. The *Charlotte News* asserted, "The Charlotte City School Board has acted to preserve the schools. It has acted to prevent massive court decree integration."[57] In desegregating schools in three cities, North Carolina joined the border states and three other southern states, Arkansas, Texas, and Tennessee.[58]

The young black integration pioneers in the late 1950s bravely faced tremendous resistance from segregationists and put their bodies on the line in the struggle for freedom. In Greensboro in September 1957, the five black children, ten to sixteen years of age, who desegregated Gillespie Park School courageously walked past a group of Ku Klux Klansmen, who screamed nasty epithets at them. Inside the school, the students "had to run a gauntlet of insults and epithets each time they walked the halls on their way to classrooms."[59] Within a week of the start of school that September, a dynamite explosion occurred at the home of two of the students who had desegregated the Greensboro school.[60]

Right after the Greensboro school board's announcement in July 1957 that Josephine Boyd would desegregate Greensboro High School, her family began receiving threatening phone calls, some from KKK leaders. Segregationists threw objects down the Boyd's chimney, their tires were slashed, their pet dogs were killed, and a tree was cut down to block their driveway. And the police did nothing. Boyd's father's snack bar, which he operated near a black public school, was burned to the ground. Josephine recalled seeing her father cry for the first time.[61] On the walk to school on the first day of classes, Josephine and her mother were surrounded by "angry, hostile" whites. As she heard the angry screams, Josephine "felt the hatred. It seemed to seep up from the sidewalks to smother me.... It was terrifying."[62] Inside the school, white students pelted her with eggs and told her to leave the school. Teachers did nothing to protect her. One time, when white students pushed her into the lockers, she fought back, but the teachers punished her, not those who had attacked her.[63]

In Charlotte, Dorothy Counts bravely faced a torrent of harassment as she broke the color line at Harding High School in 1957.[64] On the first day of class, two of Charlotte's White Citizens' Council leaders "encouraged students to prevent Counts from enrolling."[65] White students threw rocks and sticks, yelled epithets, and spat at Counts.[66] The *New York Times* reported that, in the face of these attacks, Counts demonstrated "a quiet dignity that made theories of Negro inferiority seem grotesque." During the second week of classes, Counts was "pelted with debris" and "her father's car window was shattered." With the principal ignoring the attacks on Counts, her parents withdrew her and enrolled her "in an integrated school in Philadelphia."[67]

Andree McKissick, just eleven years old when she enrolled at Carr Junior High School in Durham, recalled that "it was pretty frightening." She said she felt like the target of "a continual assault," including "verbal abuse ... the entire time I was there."[68] One time, "twelve white boys surrounded" her "and spat at her on her way to English class." Her teacher refused to intervene. McKissick recalled, "I had to fight with my brain, always sitting in the front row, always asking questions." She emphasized, "Some of us were psychologically damaged in the process [of integration], but some of us have grown quite strong and resilient."[69]

Although parents had to consent to their children requesting transfers to previously all-white schools, in several cases it was the students who initiated the transfer requests. Joycelyn McKissick, who helped desegregate Durham High School, recalled that the "[black] youth in Durham were highly motivated" to fight for their rights.[70] At least one Durham student, "strong-willed" Lucy Mae Jones, volunteered to desegregate a school despite her mother's opposition.[71]

The black community provided essential support and protection for the students who desegregated schools. To shield its young trailblazers from violence at the hands of white mobs, the Durham Committee on Negro Affairs arranged transportation for several of the students for the entire year to make sure that they would be safe from attack.[72] And "Joycelyn McKissick fondly recalled the two black women cafeteria workers who helped her survive those initial days of desegregation."[73] Black churches provided spiritual and material support. In 1959, every day after school, the Durham students would meet at "Union Baptist Church or St. Joseph's AME Church to pray and to sing together with members of the community, sharing their stories of harassment and finding in one another's company the courage to forge ahead."[74] In Greensboro, the Methodist Youth Fellowship provided Josephine Boyd with spiritual and emotional support, and her church bought clothes for her.[75]

Family support was also crucial to the students' physical and emotional well-being. Charmaine McKissick-Melton recalled that her mother, Evelyn McKissick, who fought for school integration in Durham, "watched over all of these brave kids. 'Don't mess with my children,' is what she always used to say, 'because I'm going to be there to tell you about it.'"[76] Black attorney Floyd McKissick recalled, "To clean those kids up everyday and pray with them at night and send them back to school every day was one hell of a fight."[77]

In addition to desegregating North Carolina schools, black students, including forty from Durham, participated in the April 1959 Youth March on Washington for Integrated Schools. About 26,000 high school and college students marched that day. Josephine Boyd, who had helped desegregate Greensboro's schools in 1957, attended a White House conference as part of the march. She reported that "President Eisenhower sent word that he would never be satisfied until the last vestige of racial discrimination has disappeared in this country."[78] Unfortunately, Eisenhower rarely backed those words with substantive action.

Black North Carolina attorneys played a key role in integrating public schools. Conrad Pearson, who had filed the first lawsuit to integrate a white university in the south back in 1933, served as lead counsel in several desegregation lawsuits in the state.[79] He worked with hundreds of black parents and their children, who beginning in 1955 sought to compel the Durham City School Board to desegregate the city schools. For years, Pearson and his co-counsels pursued integrated schools while the white-dominated school board stonewalled and delayed. Pearson helped pressure the Durham school board to admit the first group of black students to white schools in 1959. When the school board rejected the black parents' applications for large-scale transfers of black students to the white schools, Pearson, joined by NAACP attorney Jack Greenberg, among others, filed a lawsuit, which was delayed for over seven years by nine district court trials and numerous appeals.[80] The obstacles faced by the lawyers in the Durham case were typical. In fact, "by the spring of 1959, fewer black students were attending white schools in North Carolina than in September 1957."[81]

In the gubernatorial campaign of 1960, neither of the leading candidates supported compliance with the *Brown* decision. Although historians have praised Terry Sanford, the ultimate victor in the race, for his moderate position on integration, he backed Hodges's policies of stalling integration, including the Pearsall Plan and the pupil assignment law. It was only in contrast to his opponent, I. Beverly Lake, that Sanford appeared moderate. Lake, a former state assistant attorney general, virulently opposed integration, calling for a return to totally segregated schools through a program he called "voluntary segregation." He said he would create a "'climate of opinion' in the state which would prevent desegregation." Further, he said he would outlaw the NAACP. Trying to endear himself to white voters, Sanford called himself a segregationist and said that the *Brown* decision was "distasteful to him."[82]

As governor, despite his liberal reputation, Sanford did little to speed up the integration of schools in North Carolina. In 1962 the U.S. Commission on Civil Rights revealed that only 11 of 173 North Carolina school districts had any black students in desegregated classes, and in those districts, less than 0.1 percent of the black students were in desegregated schools.[83] In the fall of 1964, at the end of Sanford's term, the state's superintendent of public instruction reported that less than 1 percent of all black students were attending previously all-white schools and less than 0.2 percent of all white students were attending previously all-black schools.[84] Despite North Carolina's claims of progressivism, it operated one of the least integrated school systems in the South, ranking "behind Florida, Tennessee, Texas and Virginia by 1965."[85]

Meanwhile, black college students in North Carolina revived the civil rights movement, demanded the end of racial segregation, and fought the continued intransigence of white officials. The movement to integrate public schools was a central component of the wider struggle to integrate all public facilities. In fact some of the first North Carolina students to integrate schools were leaders in sit-ins to integrate other public facilities. And many African American activists simultaneously fought for integrated schools, restaurants, parks, and other public facilities. George Simkins Jr., a Greensboro dentist and local NAACP leader, led a protest to integrate a public golf course in 1955, sued to integrate Greensboro's Moses Cone Hospital in 1962, and filed a lawsuit to integrate the city's public schools in 1970.[86] Joycelyn McKissick, who had helped desegregate Durham High School in 1959, joined three other students in a 1962 sit-in to integrate the Howard Johnson's restaurant in Durham. The arrest and convictions of the four students triggered a massive protest with over 1,000 demonstrators outside the Durham restaurant in August 1962. Marva Bullock, a plaintiff in the school desegregation lawsuit in Durham, protested segregation at a downtown store, where she was assaulted by a segregationist.[87]

Although the sit-ins that began in Greensboro in 1960 narrowly focused on integrating downtown lunch counters, during the next few years movement activists expanded their goals to include the integration of all racially segregated public facilities, including public schools. For example, in 1961 black students in Charlotte launched a nine-day boycott of an all-black junior high school in response to the continued segregation of schools.[88] In 1963, in Winston-Salem, NAACP and Congress of Racial Equality protesters demanded integration of public schools and the assignment of black faculty to historically white schools.[89] That summer, the eastern North Carolina field director of the Southern Christian Leadership Conference, Golden Frinks, led hundreds of African Americans, who marched and boycotted schools and white businesses in Williamston, demanding integration of public schools, hospitals, and all public accommodations, as well as equal employment opportunities in Martin County. Black protesters refused to back down despite police use of fire hoses and cattle prods, job termination by white employers, and Ku Klux Klan rallies.[90]

These protests in North Carolina, along with others throughout the South, as well as the March on Washington in 1963, pressured Congress to pass the Civil Rights Act in 1964, which banned racially segregated public facilities and reinforced the federal role in integrating public schools. The inclusion of Title VI in that legislation marked a turning point in the integration of public schools, as it empowered the U.S. Attorney General to file lawsuits to integrate schools and authorized the federal government to withdraw funds from districts that violated integration orders. In April 1965, Congress passed the Elementary and Secondary Education Act, sending more than $1 billion in aid to schools, which reinforced Title VI because school systems now risked losing substantial federal funding if they refused to integrate. In response to the Civil Rights Act, the North Carolina attorney general announced in February 1965 that each of the state's school districts was required to issue a desegregation plan.[91] According to Gary Orfield, "Enforcement of the new law by the Johnson administration and the Warren

Court turned a region in which school segregation was almost total into the nation's most integrated within five years of the issuance of the first desegregation guidelines."[92]

Although local white officials in the state continued to stonewall, unrelenting pressure exerted by black protests, lawsuits, court decisions, and increasingly strict desegregation guidelines issued by the U.S. Office of Education of the Department of Health, Education, and Welfare (HEW), led to change. In March 1966, new HEW guidelines required results, not just a plan. For example, if 5 percent of black students "had transferred to a desegregated school" during the previous year, then 15 percent "would be expected to do so the following year," or federal funds would be lost.[93] Continued black protest against the slow pace of school desegregation compelled the HEW to take action. In 1966, U.S. Commissioner of Education Harold H. Howe II said, "A revolution is brewing under our feet.... It is largely up to the schools to determine whether the energies of that revolution can be converted into a new and vigorous source of American progress, or whether their explosion will rip this nation into two societies."[94]

Meanwhile, the North Carolina government continued to block federal enforcement of integration. In 1965 it adopted the so-called freedom of choice plan, which provided freedom of choice for whites only, as they could choose their schools, but if blacks sought entrance to white schools, administrative roadblocks were placed in their way. By 1968, 85 percent of black students were still attending black schools.[95]

A major breakthrough occurred in 1968, when the U.S. Supreme Court ruled in a Virginia case, *Green v. County School Board*, that school districts had to prove that schools were racially mixed and that schools were not identifiable as white schools or black schools.[96] North Carolina's freedom of choice plan could not meet those requirements because almost all schools in the state continued to be racially identifiable. Consequently, in 1968, in *Boomer v. Beaufort County Board of Education*, civil rights lawyers, including North Carolina's Conrad Pearson, Julius Chambers, and James Ferguson, successfully argued that the state's freedom of choice plan violated the *Green* decision. The court's decision mandated that Beaufort County schools operate based on attendance zones and required that black and white students living in those attendance zones be assigned to the requisite schools.[97]

Some North Carolina school districts continued to violate the federal mandates. Although Greensboro was among the first three North Carolina cities to desegregate its schools in 1957, its school board resisted substantial integration during the late 1960s. As late as 1971 Greensboro was one of five school districts in North Carolina that were still "not in compliance with federal civil rights guidelines." In 1970 George Simkins and ten other black parents sued the school board, demanding immediate integration. The following year, a federal court required that Greensboro integrate its schools in the fall of 1971.[98]

Charlotte attorney Julius Chambers played a leading role in finally ending North Carolina's operation of a dual system of public schools. In 1966, representing three black families, Chambers won a case that overturned the Pearsall Plan, as he "successfully challenged the legality of granting expense vouchers for private schools."[99] Four years later he was suing over thirty North Carolina school districts to integrate their schools.[100] In 1971, Chambers won a landmark case when he argued before the U.S. Supreme Court that busing was a constitutional method to integrate public schools in *Swann v. Charlotte-Mecklenburg Schools*.[101]

By the middle to late 1970s, the combined efforts of black students, their families and their communities, black attorneys, and the larger civil rights movement had succeeded in integrating North Carolina schools. But this success was tempered by the fact that school boards, still dominated by whites, had implemented integration to the detriment of black schools, black principals, and black teachers. Many black schools were closed by white-dominated school boards, with many black principals and teachers being let go, as black students integrated historically white schools.[102]

Undaunted, black activists and attorneys mobilized to protect black educators and black schools. Black attorneys filed lawsuits on behalf of black teachers who were fired by white officials as schools integrated. In Hendersonville, in 1966 a lawsuit yielded an appeals court decision that reinstated seventeen black teachers.[103] In 1969 E. B. Palmer, secretary of the North Carolina Teachers Association, urged black educators to fight back against the termination of teachers and principals by white-dominated school boards. Palmer reported that the percentage of teachers in Charlotte who were black dropped from 44 percent in 1966 to 22 percent in 1969. Further, Charlotte schools hired only 17 black teachers of a total of 722 new teachers for the 1968–69 school year. Black teachers were regularly fired instead of being assigned to predominantly white schools.[104] In March 1971, *Carolina Times* editor Louis Austin called on the North Carolina Teachers Association to pursue legal action to protect black principals from being replaced by whites, who were "not as qualified or prepared."[105] In Hyde County, from 1968 to 1969, the black community mounted a five-month-long protest movement to reopen two historically black high schools and save the jobs of many black educators.[106]

We now know that the *Brown* decision was merely a start, not the end of the movement for integration. Ultimately, decades of struggle by black students, parents, lawyers, and the larger black community were necessary to break the back of public school segregation in North Carolina. And although racial integration has not necessarily been a panacea for the public schools, it has yielded important gains in black education, as high school graduation rates rose and more black students attended and graduated from college.[107]

NOTES

1. Harvard Sitkoff, *The Struggle for Black Equality, 1954–1992* (New York: Hill and Wang, 1993), 22.

2. Davison M. Douglas, *Reading, Writing, and Race: The Desegregation of the Charlotte Schools* (Chapel Hill: University of North Carolina Press, 1995), 253–54.

3. David S. Cecelski, *Along Freedom Road: Hyde County, North Carolina, and the Fate of Black Schools in the South* (Chapel Hill: University of North Carolina Press, 1994).

4. William H. Chafe, *Civilities and Civil Rights: Greensboro, North Carolina, and the Black Struggle for Freedom* (New York: Oxford University Press, 1980).

5. Milton Ready, *The Tar Heel State: A History of North Carolina* (Columbia: University of South Carolina Press, 2005); William Link, *North Carolina: Change and Tradition in a Southern State* (Wheeling, Ill.: Harlan Davidson, 2009).

6. Quoted in Timothy B. Tyson, *Radio Free Dixie: Robert F. Williams and the Roots of Black Power* (Chapel Hill: University of North Carolina Press, 1999), 73.

7. Quoted in Max K. Gilstrap, "Governor 'Disappointed': Umstead Calls Desegregation Rule Unfortunate," *Christian Science Monitor*, July 13, 1954, 5.

8. I. Beverly Lake Sr., interview by Charles Dunn, September 8, 1987, interview C-0043, Southern Oral History Program Collection (no. 4007), http://docsouth.unc.edu/sohp/C-0043/C-0043.html.

9. Quoted in Jeffrey J. Crow, Paul D. Escott, and Flora J. Hatley, *A History of African Americans in North Carolina* (Raleigh: North Carolina Department of Cultural Resources, 2008), 167.

10. "Address by Governor Luther Hodges before Joint Session of the General Assembly of North Carolina, Meeting in Special Session," in *Journal of the House of Representatives of the General Assembly of the State of North Carolina, Extra Session 1956 and Regular Session 1957* (Raleigh: M. S. Littlefield, 1957), 10, https://archive.org/details/journalofhouseof19561957. For Hodges, see also Anders Walker, "'Legal Means': Luther Hodges Limits Brown in North Carolina," in *The Ghost of Jim Crow: How Southern Moderates Used Brown v. Board of Education to Stall Civil Rights* (New York: Oxford University Press, 2009), 49–84.

11. Crow et al., *History of African Americans in North Carolina*, 167.

12. Ibid., 168; Richard E. Day, "North Carolina," in *Civil Rights U.S.A.: Public Schools Southern States, 1962: Staff Reports Submitted to the United States Commission on Civil Rights and Authorized for Publication* (Washington, D.C.: Government Printing Office, 1962), 65.

13. Day, "North Carolina," 66.

14. James T. Patterson, *Brown v. Board of Education: A Civil Rights Milestone and Its Troubled Legacy* (New York: Oxford University Press, 2001), 100.

15. Crow et al., *History of African Americans in North Carolina*, 169.

16. Day, "North Carolina," 67.

17. "Public School Desegregation Battle Plans Drawn in N.C.," *Baltimore Afro-American*, January 22, 1955, 8.

18. Victor L. Gray, "Integration Theme of N. C. Teachers," *Baltimore Afro-American*, April 9, 1955, 2.

19. "To the Board of Education of the Public School District of Durham," July 11, 1955, box 13, William J. Kennedy Papers, Southern Historical Collection, Wilson Library, University of North Carolina at Chapel Hill.

20. Crow et al., *History of African Americans in North Carolina*, 168–69.

21. Jay Jenkins, "School Bill Opposed by Negroes," *News and Observer* (Raleigh, N.C.), February 23, 1955, 1, 2; Howard E. Covington Jr. and Marion A. Ellis, *Terry Sanford: Politics, Progress, and Outrageous Ambitions* (Durham, N.C.: Duke University Press, 1999), 159. Black supporters included representatives of the North Carolina Teachers Association, the General Baptist State Convention, the Free and Accepted Prince Hall Masons, and three black city councilmen. Jenkins, "School Bill Opposed by Negroes," 2.

22. Sitkoff, *Struggle for Black Equality*, 23. See also Peter William Moran, "Border State Ebb and Flow: School Desegregation in Missouri, 1954–1999," in *With All Deliberate Speed: Implementing Brown v. Board of Education*, ed. Brian J. Dougherty and Charles C. Bolton (Fayetteville: University of Arkansas Press, 2008), 175–98; and Janell Drone, "Desegregation and Effective School Leadership: Tracking Success, 1954–1980," *Journal of African American History* 90 (Autumn 2005): 410–12.

23. William H. Chafe, *The Unfinished Journey: America since World War II*, 5th ed. (New York: Oxford University Press, 2003), 154. According to a poll of white residents of Guilford County, "18 per cent of the population was ready to resist desegregation at all costs; another 18 per cent wished to push ahead much faster with integration. The vast majority, however, were in the middle." Chafe, *Civilities and Civil Rights*, 59.

24. "Speech by Benjamin L. Smith to the Kiwanis Club," c. 1954, Civil Rights Greensboro Collection, University of North Carolina at Greensboro Digital Collections, http://library.uncg.edu/dp/crg/item.aspx?i=987#complete.

25. John J. Parker to Luther Hodges, June 1, 1955, box 19, Luther Hodges Papers, North Carolina State Archives, Raleigh, N.C.

26. Quoted in Charles Dunn, "An Exercise of Choice: North Carolina's Approach to the Segregation-Integration Crisis in Public Education," M.A. Thesis, University of North Carolina, 1959, 8–9, box 3, Thomas J. Pearsall Papers, Southern Historical Collection.

27. Quoted in ibid., 9.

28. Crow et al., *History of African Americans in North Carolina*, 169–70.

29. "Address by Governor Luther Hodges," 8–9.

30. Peebles-Wilkins, "Reactions of Segments of the Black Community," 116.

31. Quoted in A. M. Rivera Jr., "Negro Group Terms School Bills 'Economic Suicide,'" box 3, Reed Sarratt Papers, Southern Historical Collection; 1956 Extra Session, North Carolina General Assembly, AV Collection, CD, TR 1-10, 1-11, box 1, North Carolina State Archives; "Citizens' Report to the North Carolina Legislature," *Norfolk Journal and Guide*, August 11, 1956, 9.

32. "Vote against the Pearsall Plan," *Carolina Times*, September 8, 1956, 2.

33. Quoted in Douglas, *Reading, Writing, and Race*, 39.

34. "Voters Approved Pearsall School Plan," *News and Observer* (Raleigh, N.C.), September 9, 1956, 1; "Hodges Pleased by Margin of Victory for School Plan," *News and Observer* (Raleigh, N.C.), September 10, 1956, 1.

35. Numerous letters attest to this point in folder titled "Segregation," box 130, Luther Hodges Papers.

36. "Hodges Pleased by Margin of Victory," 2. For disfranchisement of blacks in eastern North Carolina through unfair application of the literacy test and "systematic discrimination by eastern county registrars," see Julian M. Pleasants and Augustus M. Burns III, *Frank Porter Graham and the 1950 Senate Race in North Carolina* (Chapel Hill: University of North Carolina Press, 1990), 84.

37. "Local Vote on Pearsall Plan Suggests Situation Calm Here," *Winston-Salem Journal*, September 10, 1956, box 3, Sarratt Papers.

38. Douglas, *Reading, Writing, and Race*, 40; "Anti-NAACP Bills Will Not Stop Struggle for Equality Says Kelly M. Alexander," *Carolina Times*, June 1, 1957, 1; "The North Carolina Legislature's Attack on the NAACP," *Carolina Times*, June 1, 1957, 2; "'Hodges-ocracy' Yields to Democracy in N.C. Senate," *Carolina Times*, June 15, 1957, 1.

39. Douglas, *Reading, Writing, and Race*, 33.

40. "Governor Hodges for President of NAACP," *Carolina Times*, February 11, 1956, 2.

41. Christina Greene, "'The New Negro Ain't Scared No More!': Black Women's Activism in North Carolina and the Meaning of Brown," in *From the Grassroots to the Supreme Court: Brown v. Board of Education and American Democracy*, ed. Peter F. Lau (Durham, N.C.: Duke University Press, 2004), 246.

42. "Durham Ministers Ban All Segregated Places," *Carolina Times*, May 11, 1957, 1; Christina Greene, *Our Separate Ways: Women and the Black Freedom Movement in Durham, North Carolina* (Chapel Hill: University of North Carolina Press, 2005), 72.

43. "To the Board of Education of the Public School District of Durham."

44. "Scheme Faces Court Test," *Carolina Times*, September 22, 1956, 2; "Oral History Interview with J. Kenneth Lee by Kathleen Hoke," June 6, 1990, Civil Rights Greensboro Collection, http://library.uncg.edu/dp/crg/oralhistitem.aspx?i=541; "Caswell County Scene of Suit," *Carolina Times*, December 15, 1956, 1.

45. "Court Action Is Not Best Way to Settle School Problem," *Winston-Salem Journal*, September 29, 1956, box 3, Sarratt Papers.

46. "Desegregation Is Pressed in Charlotte," *Carolina Times*, June 15, 1957, 1.

47. "Oral History Interview with Otis L. Hairston, Sr. by Eugene Pfaff," June 1, 1979, Civil Rights Greensboro Collection, http://library.uncg.edu/dp/crg/oralHistItem.aspx?i=518.

48. Sarah Caroline Thuesen, *Greater than Equal: African American Struggles for Schools and Citizenship in North Carolina, 1919-1965* (Chapel Hill: University of North Carolina Press, 2013), 213.

49. "Oral History Interview with J. Kenneth Lee."

50. "Teacher Scared out of Integration Try," *Carolina Times*, November 10, 1956, 1.

51. Thuesen, *Greater than Equal*, 221-22.

52. Crow et al., *History of African Americans in North Carolina*, 171.

53. Jack Greenberg, *Crusaders in the Courts: How a Dedicated Band of Lawyers Fought for the Civil Rights Revolution* (New York: Basic Books, 1994), 260; "Delegation Presents

Request to School Board Asking Elimination of Segregation for Use as Solution to Problem of Crowded Schools Here," *Carolina Times*, April 18, 1959, 1.

54. Quoted in "Rocky Mount Lawyer Parried Blow of '54 Ruling," *News and Observer* (Raleigh, N.C.), November 7, 1976, box 3, Pearsall Papers.

55. Betty Jamerson Reed, *School Segregation in Western North Carolina: A History, 1860s–1970s* (Jefferson, N.C.: McFarland, 2011), 37; Day, "North Carolina," 72. In Virginia, a federal appeals court overruled Virginia's pupil assignment act in 1957 because "it was backed up by inflexible segregation laws and practices." Day, "North Carolina," 72.

56. Davison M. Douglas, "The Rhetoric of Moderation: Desegregating the South during the Decade after Brown" (1994), Faculty Publications paper 116, William and Mary Law School Scholarship Repository, scholarship.law.wm.edu/facpubs/116/, 133.

57. Day, "North Carolina," 73.

58. Douglas, "Rhetoric of Moderation," 131.

59. "School Officials Hail Restraint," *Carolina Times*, September 7, 1957, 1; Jim Schlosser, "A Brave Act That Changed Citys [sic] Schools," *News and Record* (Greensboro, N.C.), September 4, 2007, http://triadhomes.news-record.com/content/2007/09/04/article/a_brave_act_that_changed_citys_schools (accessed June 7, 2012). The *Carolina Times* reported, "The abusive phrases ranged ... from 'Hey Nigger ... Go home ... Get on Black Sambo.'" "School Officials Hail Restraint."

60. "School Violence Explodes: Dynamite Set Off at Home of Pupils in Mixed School," *Carolina Times*, October 5, 1957, 1.

61. Josephine Ophelia Boyd Bradley, "Wearing My Name: School Desegregation, Greensboro, North Carolina, 1954–1958," Ph.D. diss., Emory University, 1995, 376–86.

62. Ibid., 366.

63. Ibid., 372, 378.

64. Day, "North Carolina," 74.

65. Douglas, *Reading, Writing, and Race*, 72.

66. Ibid.; "Negro Student Heckled at Charlotte; Arkansas Governor Voices Arrest Fear," *News and Observer* (Raleigh, N.C.), September 5, 1957, 1.

67. Douglas, *Reading, Writing, and Race*, 72.

68. Quoted in Matthew E. Milliken, "No Normal First Day of School," *Herald-Sun* (Durham, N.C.), online, ca. 2010, http://www.heraldsun.com/view/full_story/9228952/article-51-years-later—recalling-the-courage-of-desegregation? (accessed June 3, 2012).

69. Quoted in "Durham to Mark 30th Anniversary of School Integration," *Dispatch* (Lexington, N.C.), August 30, 1989, 12.

70. Joycelyn McKissick, interview by Chris D. Howard, March 15, 1983, tape 27a, box 4, Chris D. Howard Papers, Duke University Archives, Durham, N.C.

71. "Durham to Mark 30th Anniversary of School Integration."

72. "To Our Community Leaders," October 30, 1959, box 49, William A. Clement Papers, Southern Historical Collection; "Five Negroes Enter Schools," *Carolina Times*, September 5, 1959, 1.

73. Greene, "'The New Negro Ain't Scared No More!,'" 253.

74. Osha Gray Davidson, *The Best of Enemies: Race and Redemption in the New South* (Chapel Hill: University of North Carolina Press, 2007), 93–94.

75. Bradley, "Wearing My Name," 384, 391.

76. Charmaine McKissick-Melton, "Looking Back 50 Years—Durham school desegregation," *Herald-Sun* (Durham, N.C.), June 1, 2010, http://paulimurrayproject.org/looking-back-50-years-durham-school-desegregation/ (accessed June 3, 2012).

77. Floyd McKissick, interview by Chris D. Howard, November 30, 1982, tape 17, box 3, Howard Papers.

78. Quoted in "Greensboro Girl Goes to White House: 26,000 Demonstrate in D.C.," *Carolina Times*, April 25, 1959, 1, 8; "Marchers Run Afoul of Jim Crow," *Carolina Times*, April 25, 1959, 1.

79. On the 1933 case, see Jerry Gershenhorn, "*Hocutt v. Wilson* and Race Relations in Durham, North Carolina, during the 1930s," *North Carolina Historical Review* 78 (July 2001): 275–308.

80. Douglas, "Rhetoric of Moderation," 138.

81. Douglas, "Rhetoric of Moderation," 132.

82. Walt Damtoft, "N. Carolina Governor Race Fought Out on Desegregation," *Washington Post*, June 24, 1960, A17.

83. Day, "North Carolina," 63.

84. "Integration Gains in North Carolina," *Christian Science Monitor*, December 4, 1964, 3.

85. Peebles-Wilkins, "Reactions of Segments of the Black Community," 117. North Carolina was barely "ahead of Alabama, Arkansas, Louisiana and South Carolina" in integrated schools. Ibid., 119.

86. Jane Cary Chapman Peck, "School Desegregation in Greensboro, North Carolina, 1954–1971: A Case Study in Purposive Social Change," Ph.D. diss., Boston University, 1974, 224, 230, 355–57.

87. "Four in Sit-In Sent to County Roads for 30 Days," *Carolina Times*, August 11, 1962, 1; "In Race Struggle: Durham Discovers 'New Unity': Nearly 1,500 Take Part in Bias Protest," *Carolina Times*, August 18, 1962, 1, 2; Greene, "'The New Negro Ain't Scared No More!,'" 246, 256.

88. Michael B. Richardson, "'Not Gradually . . . But Now': Reginald Hawkins, Black Leadership, and Desegregation in Charlotte, North Carolina," *North Carolina Historical Review* 82 (July 2005): 360–62.

89. Aingred G. Dunston, "The Black Struggle for Equality in Winston-Salem, North Carolina: 1947–1977," Ph.D. diss., Duke University, 1981, 153–54.

90. David C. Carter, "The Williamston Freedom Movement: Civil Rights at the Grass Roots in Eastern, North Carolina, 1957–1964," *North Carolina Historical Review* 76 (January 1999): 12, 22–23, 26–31.

91. Douglas, *Reading, Writing, and Race*, 113–14.

92. Gary Orfield, "The 1964 Civil Rights Act and American Education," in *Legacies of the 1964 Civil Rights Act*, ed. Bernard Grofman (Charlottesville: University of Virginia Press, 2000), 89–90.

93. Douglas, *Reading, Writing, and Race*, 124–25.

94. Quoted in J. Harvie Wilkinson III, *From Brown to Bakke: The Supreme Court and School Integration: 1954–1978* (New York: Oxford University Press, 1979), 105.

95. Crow et al., *History of African Americans in North Carolina*, 171–72.

96. Douglas, *Reading, Writing, and Race*, 128.

97. Crow et al., *History of African Americans in North Carolina*, 172; *Boomer v. Beaufort County Board of Education*, 294 F. Supp. 179 (1968), http://www.leagle.com/decision/1968473294FSupp179_1431/BOOMER%20v.%20BEAUFORT%20COUNTY%20BOARD%20OF%20EDUCATION.

98. Chafe, *Civilities and Civil Rights*, 220–22.

99. Peebles-Wilkins, "Reactions of Segments of the Black Community," 114, 116.

100. Peck, "School Desegregation in Greensboro," 358.

101. Raymond Wolters, *Race and Education, 1954–2007* (Columbia: University of Missouri Press, 2008), 139–43.

102. Cecelski, *Along Freedom Road*, 7–13.

103. "Enfield Teacher Is Awarded Damages in Dismissal Case," *Carolina Times*, June 11, 1966, 1.

104. "NCTA Secretary Scores Black Teacher in Halifax County," *Carolina Times*, June 14, 1969, 1.

105. "Protection for Black Teachers," *Carolina Times*, March 13, 1971, 2A.

106. Cecelski, *Along Freedom Road*, 8, 160–62.

107. Patterson, *Brown v. Board of Education*, 188.

IT'S EASIER TO PICK A YANKEE DOLLAR THAN A POUND OF COTTON

TOURISM AND NORTH CAROLINA HISTORY

Richard D. Starnes

In the fall of 1964, Governor Terry Sanford convened a group of business leaders to discuss the future of tourism in North Carolina. In a three-day journey across the state with stops in Greenville, Winston-Salem, and Asheville, attendees heard about tourism's economic impact and potential strategies to increase the flow of visitors. Speakers included bus company executives, newspaper travel editors, government officials, hoteliers, and attraction owners such as Grandfather Mountain's Hugh Morton. The conference centered on expanding the state's tourism trade and the promise of tourism for North Carolina's economy. Greensboro businessman and former director of the North Carolina Department of Conservation and Development Hargrove "Skipper" Bowles opened the discussion by noting that tourism was a billion dollar a year industry in the state, attracting more than 27 million visitors and representing a vital component of the state's economy. The environment, roads, hotels and motels, restaurants, and an advertising campaign honed since the 1930s all provided a strong foundation, but Bowles understood that the state was in fierce competition for tourists. To remain competitive, Bowles advised his audience to greet visitors enthusiastically and with a smile. "Welcome to North Carolina, the greatest vacation land in the Union," he suggested. "What'll you have? I'll give you maps and directions on any kind of fishing, boating, mountains, seashore, [and] golf. Indians, cigarette factories, cowboys, historic sights [*sic*] galore, battleship—we have it all." To attract tourists and keep them coming back, the industry needed to mobilize and professionalize and to view what had been largely locally based businesses as part of a statewide enterprise. A service station attendant, according to Bowles, "can do a lot of good hard selling while he is cleaning the windshield." Bowles predicted that tourism would continue to grow more important for the state's economy, and with good reason. "It's easier to pick a Yankee dollar," Bowles reflected, "than a pound of cotton."[1]

Skipper Bowles understood the importance of tourism to North Carolina. Although he may have overstated the ease by which money could be made by catering to visitors, he was correct about its economic influence, past and future. He also realized that the state's distinctive history, vibrant culture, and diverse environment provided the foundations of tourism development. In 2013, the North Carolina Department of Commence reported that tourism "directly supported 197,690 jobs" and generated more than $3.0 billion in federal, state, and local tax revenue. That same year, "domestic travelers spent $20.2 billion across the state."[2] As a result of its economic power, economists, politicians, and business leaders have long been interested in Tar Heel tourism, and more recently, historians have become interested as well. Because it exists at the nexus of so many social forces, the study of tourism as a cultural, economic, and historical catalyst has opened fresh avenues of inquiry and has encouraged historians to interpret old stories in new ways.[3]

Tourism has existed in North Carolina since at least the early nineteenth century, but it remains a topic well outside the traditional state historical narrative. Despite its absence in most state histories, tourism provides an important opportunity to reconsider North Carolina's past. Tourism is the story of people, of seasonal migrations, workers, visitors, and the politics of identity. It rests within the state's broader economic and cultural history, offering historians opportunities to explore how businesses, public policies, and communities interacted in pursuit of visitors. It also reshapes our understanding of social dynamics, the environment, and culture by considering how the state was packaged and sold to visitors. Skipper Bowles recognized that even a gas station attendant could help bring visitors back to the Old North State, but historians now recognize that tourism offers a window to better understand the experience of the state and its people.

Since the beginning two essential themes—the evolution of a tourist landscape and the creation of attractions based on the state's history and culture—have defined and shaped North Carolina's experience. Neither operated in a vacuum but, rather, combined to create vibrant local and regional tourism industries. The state's natural climate provided the earliest foundation for the North Carolina tourist landscape. With lofty mountains, a majestic coast, and a Piedmont filled with forests and interwoven with rivers, North Carolina could offer visitors a rich diversity of topographies and climates. Tourism promoters did not simply present the landscape for visitor enjoyment. The state's environments were preserved, enhanced, altered, and in some cases destroyed to optimize visitor experiences. In this way, tourism emerged as a powerful force in the state's environmental history. But for tourists and those who sought to profit from them, the landscape extended beyond the natural environment. Visitors demanded easy access and amenities like accommodations, restaurants, and entertainment venues to enhance their leisure experiences. Boosters realized this and built and promoted Tar Heel destinations through vivid imagery and evocative language in a variety of promotional campaigns. Over time, the natural and the built environments and the images used to sell them combined to create a tourist landscape where leisure became a profitable commodity.[4]

By the early nineteenth century, tourists had discovered the state's distinctive and attractive environment. Low Country planters fleeing the fever season began annual pilgrimages to the North Carolina mountains. These were more than leisure travelers. Sometimes as early as mid-May these elites started north before the malarial swamps posed serious risks, and they took their entire households with them. When they arrived at Flat Rock, Asheville, or other mountain communities, they took up residence in stately homes matching their station, where slaves provided the labor and masters and mistresses continued active social calendars. In these summer months the presence of planters such as Mitchell King, Wade Hampton, and C. G. Memminger transformed mountain communities. Flat Rock was known as the "Charleston of the Mountains," and wealth, status, and culture set these seasonal residents apart from the local community. This antebellum precursor to second-home communities not only provided a foundation for subsequent mountain tourism but also demonstrated how tourism emerged as a social and economic catalyst in antebellum North Carolina.[5]

The mountain environment and climate began to attract others who hoped to enjoy the region and emulate the planter's leisure lifestyle but could not afford to maintain two households. To serve these visitors, resorts emerged in Hendersonville, Highlands, and other mountain towns. Like at other antebellum healing springs, places like the Hot Springs Hotel in Madison County and the Sulphur Spring Hotel near Asheville offered guests desirable accommodations, impressive food and entertainment, and the opportunity to take the waters, admire the scenery, and enjoy the company of their peers for a few weeks or for a season. In the summer the Sulphur Spring Hotel entertained guests with gourmet meals, hunting and fishing, carriage rides in the countryside, and music from an orchestra of free black musicians from Charleston and Columbia, South Carolina. Charles Lanman, a noted antebellum travel writer, proclaimed Sulphur Springs "one of the most popular watering-places in the South, not only on account of medicinal quality of the water, but on account of the surrounding scenery" as well as "the style in which people are entertained." Crafting a tourist landscape that blended nature and amenities would remain central to North Carolina's tourism experience.[6]

By the late nineteenth century, the expansion of the railroad, the state's growing reputation as a health destination, and a burgeoning demand for leisure travel broadened and deepened North Carolina tourism. Like tobacco, textiles, and furniture, tourism emerged as a transformative New South industry. Members of the industrial middle class began to vacation in record numbers and wanted to experience nature as part of their sojourns but also demanded entertainment and creature comforts. The tourist landscape evolved to serve this market.[7] To compete in this increasingly national tourism marketplace, North Carolina resorts sought to establish themselves in potential tourists' imaginations. Writing under the pen name Christian Reid, novelist and travel writer Frances Tiernan used her 1875 novel *"The Land of the Sky," or Adventures in Mountain By-ways* to highlight North Carolina's majestic mountains and valleys near Asheville. "If you want fresh air and glorious scenery—the greatest this side of the Yosemite," she wrote, "you must go to Western North Carolina to find them." She also highlighted Asheville's high-quality accommodations and emerging society culture, noting that the city "is a decidedly civilized place." Her novel and its images provided local boosters with a promotional slogan that remained in use for well over a century.[8] An 1890 illustrated guidebook to western North Carolina published by Asheville photographer Thomas Lindsey seized on Tiernan's imagery, seeking "to combine every item of information that would be of interest to the tourist and Health-seeker, or visitor to this beautiful 'Land of the Sky.'" "To us," Lindsey told his readers, "the 'Land of the Sky' is a limited and well-defined expression. The fervor of enthusiasm in the worship of nature has given to it substantial and well-defined metes and bounds." Offering more than natural beauty, tourists would find a place with all the latest infrastructure, including electric lights, a gas system, and a booming business district "not surpassed by a Southern city," with modern resort hotels that were "gay at night, and music and dancing is 'the order of the day' for all who enjoy it."[9] In 1912 the Chamber of Commerce of Wilmington, North Carolina, told potential visitors that "as a summer resort and as a place of residence, Wilmington may claim to be unequalled in the South." Beautiful and popular, nearby Wrightsville Beach was "one of the finest on the Atlantic coast and a thousand bathers are often seen at one time," and reports of tourist facilities matched descriptions of the coastal environment. Boosters touted access to and accommodations at Wrightsville Beach, boasting of "a high speed electric road" with "about forty cars in service" that connected Wilmington to the nearby beaches. While there, tourists could wade in the waves or enjoy Lumina, "one of the finest pavilions of its kind on the Atlantic coast," where they could dance, dine, and relax beside the sea. As North Carolina tourism expanded, pamphlets, postcards, and promotional campaigns evolved with changing visitor demands, but an agreeable climate, natural wonder, personal luxury, and easy access remained constant themes.[10]

Promoting the tourist landscape fit well with other efforts to shape the state's identity. Since at least the beginning of the twentieth century, North Carolinians viewed their state as distinct from and more progressive than other southern states. Pointing to commitments to education, public health, and other programs often found lacking elsewhere in Dixie, North Carolinians could celebrate their state while turning a blind eye to racial discrimination, lynching, persistent poverty, and other ills that plagued their society.[11] Tourism helped create this image and, to some degree, helped make it a reality. This progressive impulse spawned the good roads movement, which became crucial to tourism development as automobiles replaced railroads in the early twentieth century. Good roads meant better access, more tourists, and a more modern image for the state and its communities. Local good roads movements developed as early as 1899, and statewide efforts emerged by 1902. Progressive leaders like Harriett Morehead Berry and Governor Cameron Morrison pushed highway construction, and by the 1920s the state had become known as the "Good Roads State." These new roads enhanced the tourist landscape in many important ways. "A visit to Asheville in the 'Land of the Sky,'" one state-produced guide claimed, "formerly involved a tedious and expensive journey. Today the hard-surfaced roads carry the tourist between suns from Wilmington at the mouth of the Cape Fear to a view after dinner in Asheville of the towering peak of Mount Mitchell." The roads brought prosperity to the state as "constantly increasing throngs pass through our gateways." Governor Angus McLean told an audience at the Toe River Fair in Mitchell County that "Western North Carolina already rivals Florida as a resort section. Your mountains are alive with tourists and visitors, intrigued by good roads, claimed by beauty, invited in many instances to remain citizens to take advantages of wide-spread opportunity."[12]

As new roads brought new tourists in the early twentieth century, business and political leaders sought ways to preserve large natural attractions to keep them entertained. After a fishing trip near Sapphire Valley in 1899, Dr. Chase Ambler and Judge William P. Day convinced the Asheville Board of Trade to establish a Parks and Forestry Committee. Its mission was to lobby political leaders for an Appalachian National Park. Ambler's activism in this cause and his work with the Buncombe County Good Roads Association demonstrates a link between improved access and tourist attractions. By November 1899, the Appalachian National Park Association formed for the purpose of "the establishment of a national park somewhere in the Southern Appalachian Mountains" with headquarters in Asheville and a membership drawn from across the South. Senator Jeter C. Pritchard was an early supporter, as was George Vanderbilt until he realized much of his own land might be claimed for the proposed park. These efforts soon stalled due to landowner resistance, including the owners of several mountain resorts, but this campaign planted a seed that would soon bear fruit.[13] Other efforts saw greater success. In 1914 Governor Locke Craig signed a bill creating the first state park on the summit of Mount Mitchell, the highest peak east of the Rockies. At Mount Mitchell, visitors camped, hiked, and simply enjoyed its matchless views. By the 1940s and 1950s, tourist courts and other accommodations sprang up in nearby communities as locals capitalized on growing Mount Mitchell traffic.[14]

The Great Depression fueled the work of image making and enhancing the tourism landscape, a campaign Governor O. Max Gardner led personally. In an advertisement in a special travel edition of the *New York Evening Post*, he reminded readers of North Carolina's impressive tourist landscape. "Our resorts," he noted, "climatically are ideal for both winter and summer sojourns, with the lofty and majestic mountain peaks of Eastern America in the western section, a distinct pineland retreat in the center, and a balmy seacoast on the east." Visitors would find North Carolina "a prototype of the New South" and would "not be able to resist the temptation to prolong [their] stay." State officials also recognized that large federal public works projects would increase tourist traffic. As early as 1929, Gardner praised efforts to establish the Great Smoky Mountains National Park so "this wonder-land of our mountain region may be saved for the enjoyment of our own people and the nation." Collaboration, and sometimes clashes, with national park supporters in Tennessee led to the establishment of the Great Smoky Mountains National Park in 1934, and four years later Congress created the Cape Hatteras National Seashore. The Blue Ridge Parkway, also an important New Deal project, would eventually offer motorists breathtaking views, recreation, and cultural exhibits along a 469-mile route from Cherokee, North Carolina, to Virginia's Shenandoah National Park. These publicly owned scenic attractions, founded during the nation's severest economic crisis, bolstered the state's tourist appeal and protected important environments.[15]

The economic pressures of the Great Depression also generated public and private efforts to promote the tourist landscape. In 1934, North Carolina travel industry leaders L. B. Moore and Coleman W. Roberts formed The Carolinas, Inc., "to build tourist travel, to encourage additional industries, to attract farmers and capital, and to encourage the development of the natural resources" in both North Carolina and South Carolina. The organization served as a clearinghouse for visitor information and as a lobbying group for the tourism industry. According to members, tourism could bring over $50 million annually to North Carolina alone, a phenomenal boost to the state's economy during the 1930s. Coleman Roberts, head of the Carolina Motor Club, argued that "a large travel market ... will help every community whether it be a resort center or a sleepy rural village, and it will help every individual, whether it be a hotel proprietor or a store clerk." The organization viewed tourism as a component of a much needed comprehensive economic vision. By increasing "our portion of the [national] tourist business, now estimated to be worth five billion dollars a year," North Carolina would reap enormous important benefits. Tourism would "not only bring about greater local consumption of products and provide greater local employment" but also enhance the state's overall economic future as "the travelers themselves become residents, investors, [and] manufacturers." In short, the tourist landscape could be catalyst for all forms of economic development.[16]

These efforts convinced state officials that North Carolina should improve tourism advertising. Lobbying by governors Gardner and J. C. B. Ehringhaus, the Carolina Motor Club, and other travel-related groups convinced the legislature in 1937 to create a Division of State Advertising within the Department of Conservation and Development. Economic development advocates praised this move. R. Bruce Etheridge, director of the department, spoke for many when he noted that "this campaign, we believe, will be one of the soundest investments made by the state in some time." With a $125,000 appropriation, the division published a full-color tourist guide titled *North Carolina: Variety Vacationland* and specific brochures on golf, hunting, and fishing and took out advertising in leading national magazines and newspapers. Tobacco magnate R. J. Reynolds Jr. funded a documentary film to accompany the campaign. The Variety Vacationland campaign depicted the state's diverse natural environments and history, and it attempted regional balance among the coast, the Piedmont, and the mountains. It also presented the state as a prosperous, modern, and progressive bastion of hospitality in words, images, and even postcards. This campaign, which would remain the state's most enduring tourism catchphrase, marked a realization that creating and promoting the tourist landscape required aggressive and comprehensive marketing.[17]

If the Variety Vacationland was built on hospitality, the unspoken truth remained that not all tourists were welcome. Like the rest of Tar Heel society, North Carolina's tourism businesses were rigidly segregated. Hotels and motels, restaurants, and attractions followed the prevailing racial conventions. That does not mean that African Americans did not play important roles in the tourism industry. Across the state African Americans emerged as the chief labor force in the litany of service jobs tourism created. In some cases, African American entrepreneurs turned to tourism. Bishop Charles C. Pettey and his wife Sarah briefly owned All-Healing Springs around the turn of the twentieth century, an Alexander County resort that included a medicinal spring and an impressive two-story hotel. Not coincidentally, the resort was near where Bishop Pettey was held as a slave. Local folklore erased the Petteys' race, but not their ownership, from memories of the resort.[18]

The Petteys' experiment at All-Healing Springs—an African American–owned resort serving a white clientele—was very much the exception in the state's tourism economy. More often, African American businesses served travelers and tourists of their own race. Publications like *The Negro Motorist Green Book* provided black travelers with information about restaurants, hotels, and other accommodations along their routes, as well as advertising a few resorts that catered to African American tourists. The dictates of Jim Crow prevented white and black tourists from enjoying the trappings of leisure together. Official advertising would not include images of African Americans until the 1980s, and then such images remained rare. Near Wilmington, Robert Bruce Freeman, his descendants, and other business owners carved out an African American resort for visitors prevented by segregation from vacationing at other North Carolina beaches. Called Freeman Beach, it offered hotels, restaurants, music venues, and other trappings of coastal leisure until beach erosion and the Civil Rights Act spelled the end. Places like this demonstrate that the development of North Carolina tourism was far from an exclusively white enterprise.[19]

Creating the tourist landscape also generated controversies over land use, development strategies, and power. Grandfather Mountain's Hugh Morton and Little Switzerland owner Heriot Clarkson, both politically powerful businessmen, engaged in a bitter legal battle with Blue Ridge Parkway officials over the parkway route, access to private attractions, view sheds, and ultimately, control over the tourist landscape. Despite such conflicts, tourism development continued to grow in the late twentieth century, and that growth threatened the tourist landscape and the environmental foundations on which it rested. Although many resort communities felt these pressures, nowhere was this tension more pronounced than in the North Carolina mountains. A federal land use report noted in 1982 that "the very features and characteristics which have made the [North Carolina] mountains a very special place to live, and which also attract thousands of vacationers each year ... are being eroded away by unregulated, uncontrolled development."[20] The next year, the U.S. Capital Corporation began construction on a ten-story resort complex on Avery County's Little Sugar Mountain. Leveling the mountaintop to make room for the project, the developers raised the ire of local residents, who felt outside interests were exploiting their land. Although builders completed this project, state representatives took notice and passed the Mountain Ridge Protection Act that prevented the construction of buildings over forty feet high on ridgetops in twenty-four mountain counties. Local governments had the option of enacting more stringent regulations or adopting this state standard, an option pursued by eight affected counties. Some locals praised the bill as saving the region's scenery for the enjoyment of all, while developers and resort homeowners criticized it as proscribing profitable real estate development. This case captured the problems of unbridled development, but it also demonstrated the social and economic importance of North Carolina's tourist landscape.[21]

Successful tourism required more than facilities, imagery, and an attractive environment. North Carolina's history and culture emerged simultaneously with the tourist landscape as the second great theme in the state's tourism development. Diverse Native American experiences, a compelling colonial story, revolutionary and Civil War battlefields, and other manifestations of a rich past made Tar Heel history an essential tourist commodity for communities across the state. In some cases, a romantic, evocative narrative resonated with visitors who sought stories that reinforced their own sense of the past. As one historian has noted, "As southern tourism evolved, ... it increasingly became a commercially oriented celebration of the South's architecture, landscape and history." In rarer instances, attractions presented history and culture in ways that challenged and complicated visitors' understanding. Both approaches could prove profitable and controversial, and both public and private entities used history to draw visitors. The stories they elected to tell reveal fissures within North Carolina over history, memory, and identity.[22]

In 1937—the same year *The Variety Vacationland* campaign debuted— the Roanoke Island Historical Association approached Pulitzer Prize–winning playwright and Buies Creek native Paul Green. They wanted Green to write an outdoor drama centered on the mysterious disappearance of the Roanoke colony and the birth of Virginia Dare, the first English child born in North America. Green recalled that *Elizabeth City Independent* editor W. O. Saunders came to Chapel Hill where Green taught to convince him

FIGURE 12.1. To promote tourism on the Outer Banks, *The Lost Colony*, a symphonic drama by Paul Green, opened on Roanoke Island in 1937. It is still performed annually. Shown here (*left to right*) are President Franklin D. Roosevelt, Governor Clyde Hoey, and Congressman Lindsey Warren, who attended a performance of *The Lost Colony* that first summer. Photograph courtesy of the North Carolina State Archives.

to write a play that would be "the biggest thing ever to hit North Carolina." Intrigued by Saunders's proposal, Green agreed to come to Manteo and explore the possibilities. Convinced by his visit and his fascination with the Roanoke story, Green agreed. Soon, Saunders and Dare County state senator D. B. Fearing organized local efforts, including drafting men from a local Civilian Conservation Corps camp to build an outdoor theater near historic Fort Raleigh.[23]

As Green labored over his manuscript, Saunders and Fearing sought support for the drama. They solicited nearly $200,000 in pledges to defray expenses, but because of the economic circumstances of the lingering depression most were never collected. They were more successful in lobbying the Rockefeller Foundation for an organ and the University of North Carolina for production equipment and the services of director Samuel Seldon and several actors. An extensive publicity campaign, including a Virginia Dare commemorative stamp, bore fruit when twenty-five hundred people

Tourism and North Carolina History 299

watched the inaugural production of *The Lost Colony* on July 4, 1937. The play, which Green would revise several times until his death in 1981, told the story of the ill-fated colonists through the eyes of Eleanor and Ananias Dare as they experienced the hardships and uncertainties that accompanied the first serious attempt at English colonization. Armed with the barest of facts, drawn mostly from Eleanor Dare's father and absentee colonial governor John White, Green crafted a story of love, betrayal, and mystery that did not purport to be history. *New York Times* theater reviewer Brooks Atkinson described it as "a simply stated idealization of the adventurous impulse that founded this great nation in a restless image of Shakespeare's England." Regardless of its historical accuracy and its portrayal of Roanoke's native people, the romance and mystery that *The Lost Colony* evoked certainly resonated with visitors. The drama attracted 50,000 attendees that first year, including President Franklin Roosevelt, and nearly four million since that first season, proving that the state's past, real and imagined, had real economic value.[24]

The Lost Colony's success led other communities to pursue similar productions. After the Second World War, mountain tourism leaders recognized they might have a story to tell visitors through an outdoor drama. In 1947, members of the Western North Carolina Associated Communities organized the Cherokee Historical Association (CHA) to leverage the Cherokee historical experience for regional and tribal tourism development. Recalling earlier tribal efforts, the CHA began to raise funds to stage an outdoor drama based on the horrific "Trail of Tears," the forced removal of most Cherokee to Indian Territory in 1838. The CHA hoped to create a seasonal attraction built on Americans' fascination with Native American history and majestic mountain scenery that would entice more visitors and their dollars to the region.[25]

Although few Cherokee were members of the CHA, the pageant received strong support from Chief Jarrett Blythe, Bureau of Indian Affairs agent Joe Jennings, and several prominent tribal members. The CHA estimated that the drama initially required $65,000, including the construction of an amphitheater, the cast payroll, and advertising costs. Eleven mountain counties provided funds for the project, as well as the Catholic Diocese of Charlotte, several tourist-related businesses in Cherokee, and the Eastern Band of Cherokee Indians' Tribal Council. The North Carolina General Assembly provided a special $35,000 appropriation in 1949. CHA leaders even approached Paul Green to write the script, but he declined. Kermit Hunter, a University of North Carolina graduate student, agreed to write the drama titled *Unto These Hills* as his master's project. Reporting to the CHA and the tribal council, Hunter penned a compelling and romantic account of Cherokee removal emphasizing the sacrifice of Tsali, who in the play offers his life and those of his sons so the scattered remnants of the tribe could stay in their beloved mountains forming the Eastern Band. The title, a dual reference to the region's geography and the 121st Psalm, did cause tourism leaders a bit of consternation. They hoped the title would be "something that would be more likely to attract tourists directly," but Hunter stuck with it.[26]

On July 1, 1950, *Unto These Hills* premiered, and tourists responded enthusiastically. Hunter's script emphasized the nobility of the Cherokee people in the face of violence and betrayal and Tsali's Christ-like sacrifice for his people. In doing so, Hunter strayed far from the historical origins of the Eastern Band, but it made for compelling theater. The *Asheville Citizen* noted that "those who have seen this drama have come away with a deep feeling that [in] the sad history of the Cherokee Indians they have been given a remarkably grand and timely vision of the future of America and the world." Tourism business leaders, more interested in profits than history lessons, were satisfied with the initial season's attendance of more than 107,000 people from across the United States and several foreign countries. The CHA netted a $70,000 profit and established the region's single largest cultural tourist attraction. Despite this early success, the Eastern Band and the CHA later clashed over profits, historical accuracy, and other issues until the tribe took control of the CHA in 2004.[27]

The success of *Unto These Hills* led CHA and tribal officials to explore other tourism uses of the tribe's historical experience. The Oconaluftee Indian Village was another CHA-sponsored project that marketed Cherokee culture to tourists. While the drama presented a romantic historical interpretation, the village itself attempted to depict the everyday life of an eighteenth-century Cherokee village. Constructed in 1952, the village included a period home, gardens, and a tribal lodge. Cherokee crafters in period dress demonstrated basketry, stonework, canoe making, pottery, and other traditional crafts. while a trained docent placed the activities in historical context. As a reenactment of tribal social history, the village entertained and educated visitors while pumping much-needed revenue into the tribal economy. In fact, the same arrowheads and baskets produced at the village found their way to souvenir shops, where their provenance gave them perceived authenticity and a higher market value.[28]

Other communities used tourism to preserve their own history. Since their arrival in the Piedmont in the mid-eighteenth century, the Moravians—a Bohemian Protestant dissenter sect—made great contributions to North Carolina culture through their faith, folkways, and enterprises. Always a religious minority in the backcountry, settlements like the village of

Salem in Forsyth County became centers of Moravian life. Over time, growing populations and the eventual industrialization and urbanization of the region threatened to erase Salem from the urban landscape. In 1946, civic leaders and historic preservationists in Winston-Salem considered how to preserve, interpret, and disseminate the story what had come to be called Old Salem. Preserving Old Salem could create a lucrative attraction for the region, but more important, it would preserve an important touchstone of regional history and identity. By advocating a series of often controversial zoning decisions, leaders like *Winston-Salem Journal* editor William K. Hoyt, preservationist James A. Gray, and Moravian Bishop J. Kenneth Pfohl pushed for a historic district designation to prevent demolition, to govern development, and to preserve the village's historical aesthetics. In 1950 they formed a nonprofit corporation called Old Salem, Inc., to "acquire and, whether not having acquired, to preserve or restore historical monuments, buildings, sites, locations, and/or objects" in the former Moravian village.[29] The nonprofit raised nearly $500,000 by 1953 to support an ambitious restoration and interpretive program. Soon, costumed docents were leading visitors through the village and offering historical interpretations grounded in deep research in the Moravian archives. Christmas and Easter quickly became popular times to visit as Old Salem immersed visitors in the Moravian experience through candlelight love feasts, music, and sugar cakes and cookies from the Winkler Bakery. In addition to the buildings and the pageantry of craft demonstrations, the restoration work and archaeological excavations became attractions themselves. The city of Winston-Salem and the North Carolina General Assembly provided funds in the early 1960s to augment receipts and private donations to continue what would soon be hailed as a national model of historic preservation. Tourists were a way to pay the preservation bills, but Old Salem clearly captivated visitors. In 1961, novelist Wilma Dykeman remarked that "visitors who stroll along the streets of Old Salem today will be amazed by careful workmanship in the buildings and the unusual features of some of the houses," a compliment to both the Moravians and those who sought to preserve their village. By the 1980s, in the words of one travel writer, Old Salem had become "a clear reminder of a life worth remembering." That is exactly what the preservationists had in mind.[30]

As Old Salem sought to preserve a unique and compelling historical experience, other tourist sites saw conflicts over which stories to present to tourist audiences. In Washington County, Somerset Plantation had been one of the Upper South's largest plantations. Owned by the Collins family, by the Civil War Somerset had become a notable agricultural operation with more than 2,000 acres in cultivation worked by more than three hundred slaves.

The Collinses lived as planters of their station in an impressive frame house and enjoyed the comforts provided by extensive wealth, power, and unfree labor. The death of Josiah Collins III in 1863 and the end of slavery meant the demise of Somerset's antebellum grandeur. The family left the plantation before the end of Reconstruction. After decades of neglect, the state of North Carolina obtained a ninety-nine-year lease on the property and formed Pettigrew State Park in 1939. After purchasing the house, grounds, and a large tract of surrounding acreage in the 1940s, the North Carolina Division of Parks and Recreation began to restore the main house and some of the outbuildings with the goal of creating a historical attraction in rural northeastern North Carolina. Transferred to the North Carolina Division of Archives and History, this property became Somerset State Historic Site in 1969 and more focused restoration, archaeological, and historical work commenced.[31]

As they began to plan how they would present the site's history to visitors, state historians initially emphasized the experiences of the Collins family as representatives of the master class. This choice reflected what white tourists expected at this type of historic site, but it also reflected a historical interpretation of antebellum life that was being challenged by interest in the slave experience and the cultural empowerment of the civil rights movement. A descendent of Somerset slaves influenced by Alex's Haley's *Roots*, Dorothy Spruill Redford delved into her genealogy and began to push for a broader and deeper interpretation of slave life on the plantation. She realized that many African Americans felt a strong tie to their slave ancestors and the places they were held in bondage. After initially being rebuffed, Redford began to take part in the site's interpretive program. Soon, Redford planned for a homecoming of slave descendants at Somerset so that they too could reconnect with their lost histories. Held in 1986, the first Somerset Homecoming attracted thousands of African Americans with roots on the plantation, as well as Josiah Collins IV and Governor James G. Martin. Amid food, tears, and laughter, the homecoming clearly demonstrated the power of place for African American visitors. Redford recalled, "The need to belong. That's what this was about. Not just my need, but the need of our entire people." She continued to press for more extensive interpretation of slave life, including rebuilding the slave quarters, and would eventually serve as site manager for more than two decades. At Somerset, tourism became a mechanism for historical inclusion and a forum to debate how stories were told at a historical attraction.[32]

The Great Smoky Mountains National Park's use of history in its official interpretations offers another example of the conscious choices of inclusion and exclusion at work when the past becomes an attraction. For its first half century, the park emphasized nature over history, in part to help portray the landscape as remote and unspoiled. As one visitor wrote, "A park like this is a living museum, whose exhibits change with the altitude and the seasons."[33] When it did depict historical themes, the park chose a narrow view, basing its interpretive program on the popularly held image of Appalachians as isolated, often ignorant frontier dwellers who appeared out of touch with the main currents of American life. It also defined the region's history as almost exclusively that of white settlers, with the Cherokees assuming the role of the exotic, and often invisible, forebears to pioneer settlement. In 1961, U.S. Park Service naturalist Arthur Stupka noted that "the area we now know as Great Smoky Mountains National Park was virtually unknown." The Cherokee "came in occasionally to hunt or fish and a few hardy white settlers dwelt in simple cabins which they built from the forest trees." To reinforce this interpretation, cabins, frame houses, barns, smokehouses, corn cribs, and other outbuildings were often razed, and others were relocated, leaving visitors with artificial and often inaccurate perceptions about mountain life. The Park Service virtually ignored many compelling stories, especially the removal of families during the park's establishment and the expansive logging industry that had left much of the park land barren of trees at the time of its creation. Although more recent interpretive efforts have sought to convey a broader history, for most of its existence the park offered a single, myopic historical vision.[34]

Like North Carolina history, the state's material culture served as an important tourist attraction, and communities attempted to use crafts and folkways to carve out niches in the tourism marketplace. Frances Louisa Goodrich, destined to be one of the most important figures in the commercialization of mountain crafts, first encountered native handicrafts while serving as a Presbyterian missionary. In 1895, Goodrich began encouraging mountain women in her rural Buncombe County community to produce coverlets aimed toward a national market. Goodrich marketed their goods in Asheville and in several northern cities. In 1897, she founded a new mission at Allenstand in Madison County where she expanded production. Goodrich's advertising, the growing regional tourism industry, and a national fascination with traditional American crafts fueled the market for hand-woven goods. In 1908, in response to growing demand among seasonal visitors, she opened an Asheville showroom. Sales to tourists exceeded all expectations, and mountain homespun became so popular that Woodrow Wilson's White House bedroom was redecorated using largely Allenstand fabrics. In 1917, Goodrich formed Allenstand Cottage Industries, Inc., and continued to sell quilts, cloth, woodcarvings, and ironwork until 1931.[35]

North Carolina's material culture became a type of living history, but one that could sometimes sacrifice authenticity for the sake of marketability. In 1901, Edith Vanderbilt, wife of Biltmore Estate owner George Vanderbilt, became interested in indigenous weaving and woodcarving techniques. Attempting both to preserve these folk crafts and to produce goods for a wider market, Vanderbilt formed a school near her family's estate outside Asheville to teach mountaineers traditional techniques. Like Goodrich, Vanderbilt appreciated the aesthetics and heritage of mountain cloth but sought to "improve by modern methods on the old fashion [sic] homespun weaving of the mountain people of the Southern Appalachians." The school and sales shop, known as Biltmore Industries, attracted large numbers of tourist customers and boasted a significant mail order business. But after her husband's death in 1913, Edith Vanderbilt returned north. She sold the school and other related concerns to Fred Seely, son-in-law of E. W. Grove and a partner in the Grove Park Inn. Seely continued the business, and by 1947 Biltmore Industries was purportedly "the largest hand weaving establishment in the world." Seely modernized the processing of wool, but the cloth itself was "woven by hand on old-fashioned oak looms, built by our own men in our wood-carving shop." More than 48,000 tourists visited the shop in 1947, and as late as the 1960s Biltmore Industries was hailed as an opportunity for visitors to take a "trip into another century." Guides told tourists that the mountain craftsmen they observed learned weaving "from their parents at the same hand-looms and dye vats." In truth, the work of the Biltmore hand weavers bore only a slight resemblance to the Appalachian cottage weavers of the nineteenth century. Seely actually had to import hand weavers from Scotland and Ireland to teach their craft. Visitors left with the impression that they witnessed a historical reenactment when in reality Biltmore Industries created a myth in which culture became a commodity to be bought and sold. Like Frances Goodrich and other leaders of the craft revival, Biltmore Industries manufactured crafts and culture, successfully marketing both to mountain tourists.[36]

The same cultural forces that drew tourists to *Unto These Hills* made Cherokee crafts and culture tourist commodities, something that actually predated mass tourism on the Qualla Boundary, the Cherokee reservation. Demand for Cherokee goods led David Schenck, a prominent North Carolina judge and politician, to conclude in 1882 that there existed "a mania among Northern tourists in this region for collecting ancient relics of the Cherokee."[37] By 1900, a few tourists already made their way to the Qualla Boundary, and the market for native baskets, pottery, artifacts, and even blowguns grew quickly. Regional resorts like the Grove Park Inn purchased

Cherokee crafts to sell at hotel gift shops, and the number of Cherokee crafters offering their handiwork for sale increased. By 1910 at least ten regional shops sold Cherokee baskets, carvings, and other crafts to visitors. During the 1920s and 1930s the Cherokee saw a dramatic increase in tourist traffic as the good roads movement literally paved the way to the Qualla Boundary. As tourism grew more important, Cherokee crafters began to look at their traditional arts as a source of supplemental income. One early sociologist noted that, as a result of better roads and more tourists, the price for Cherokee baskets had doubled during the 1920s.[38]

In 1946, a group of native crafters working under the auspices of the Bureau of Indian Affairs organized the Cherokee Indian Crafts Co-op. Structured similarly to Asheville's renowned Southern Highland Handicraft Guild, the co-op was designed to help Cherokee crafters market their goods for a fair price. Unlike the guild, the co-op did not attempt to impose the aesthetic values of mainstream America on artisans but, rather, sought to protect and enhance the place of Cherokee crafts in the regional and national market. In the 1950s the organization became an independent nonprofit called the Qualla Arts and Crafts Mutual exclusively under the direction of tribal members and provided marketing, a retail outlet, and a training program led by accomplished artisans. The mutual successfully built a market based on the cultural authenticity of Cherokee crafts, proving that it was possible to profit from tourism without compromising cultural authenticity. It also provided much-needed income and helped preserve Cherokee culture. Craftsman Davy Arch noted that "without something like the tourism industry here a lot of the arts would've been lost." He also recalled that his grandmother, mother, and "most everybody in the family supplemented the income [sic] by selling something to the craft shops."[39]

As the mutual sought to preserve Cherokee culture, "chiefing" emerged as a more controversial aspect of cultural tourism on the Qualla Boundary. Beginning in the late 1930s, Cherokee men donned the elaborate headdresses of the Plains Indians and stood beside teepees strategically positioned near souvenir shops. They allowed tourists to have photographs taken with them, and most charged a fee and suggested that visitors also include a tip. Cherokee "chiefs" realized that their income was tied to their exotic appearance. Henry Lambert, a long-time "chief," understood the way stereotypes held by tourists could be manipulated for profit. "If you are going into show business," he declared, "dress for it." Lambert experimented with wearing the traditional Cherokee buckskins, only to find that tourists were more interested in seeing the familiar Native American images present in popular culture rather than a historically accurate portrayal of Cherokee dress. Lambert realized he was a businessman, not a reenactor. The "chiefing" trade was quite lucrative, and after twenty-five years Lambert hoped "to be doing this until I'm 99." Even though Lambert recognized that he was not depicting a historically accurate image when he posed for photographs, he often faced criticism from tourists who confronted him about the images he embodied during his work. "Local folks," he said, "don't do it anymore. I outgrowed that, they outgrowed that 30 years ago," a recognition of the sacrifices sometimes necessary to make a living in a tourist economy. "But it's all the tourists now that come through [and criticize his costume]," he noted, "especially the ones, the wannabes [people who want to claim some Native American heritage]." For their part, "chiefs" like Henry Lambert, Carl Standingdeer, and others separated cultural reality from tourist stereotypes, playing the role visitors expected of them to make a living.[40]

Still, cultural tourism could come with a price, and some Cherokees remained critical of cultural tourism and its implications. Tribal member R. F. Stamper, home on leave from the U.S. Navy, noted that his son had come to embrace the "chiefs" with their elaborate head dresses and teepees as the embodiment of Indian identity. When reminded that he was also an Indian, the boy replied, "Yes, but not that kind." Stamper lamented, "I guess when I get back home I will have to buy him an outfit so he can become that kind of Indian." Tourism did not force all Cherokees to become "that kind of Indian," but it led some to question the exploitation of Cherokee culture by white tourism entrepreneurs. Some tribal members resented the Cherokee Historical Association for using native culture to draw visitors while funneling profits off the reservation. Former vice-chief Fred Bauer noted that CHA projects like *Unto These Hills* had caused many Cherokees to embrace a counterfactual version of their own history and culture. "Little Indian children are in the cast, and a generation has grown up to adulthood impressed with the Drama as their history," he wrote. "The myth comes at the Indians from all sides; it has completely supplanted the history, and the true origin of the Eastern Band is not to be found." In these and countless other examples, tourism altered historical and cultural contexts and, in some cases, sacrificed accuracy in the pursuit of profit, all the while shaping how natives and visitors understood the state and its people.[41]

With all its complexities, tourism offers scholars of North Carolina a treasure trove of potential topics that will both broaden and deepen our understanding of our people and their histories. Future scholars should investigate how tourism shaped community identity in resort communities from the mountains to the coast, narratives that will likely yield important insights into the dynamics of economics, culture, and power. Workers in the state's mills and farms have had their stories told, but what about the voices of tourism workers? Using such lenses as race, gender, and demographic change will uncover fascinating and meaningful insights into the nature of tourism work and the scope and limits of tourism's economic benefits. Scholars know little more about the people these workers served. Some studies have treated the pilgrimages of the wealthy elite to Pinehurst, Asheville, and the coast, but what about those whose means bought less luxury? How did class shape where people went and what they did during their vacations? Tourism development has also reshaped patterns of land ownership, politics, and power in resort communities. In some areas, tourism promoters and industrial interests battled for local economic supremacy. Elsewhere, second-home communities have attracted new wealth and new tensions between locals and newcomers. The environmental effects of tourism development need additional scrutiny. The pursuit of tourism growth meant more automobiles, more hikers on trails, more boaters on rivers, and more motels by the beach. Understanding the environmental implications of Tar Heel tourism provides an opportunity to ask questions about humankind's relationship with nature, who controls the environment, and how nonindustrial development shapes demographic and cultural realities.

By creating the tourist landscape and transforming history and culture into lucrative commodities, North Carolina tourism developed into a powerful social and economic force, but one that did not remain static. Recent changes show how North Carolina tourism evolved in response to changing tastes and growing competition from resorts across the state and nation. Cherokee is still home to the village and *Unto These Hills*, but Harrah's Cherokee Casino has become one of the state's most popular tourist attractions as attendance at historical and cultural attractions has declined significantly. Gamblers, it seems, are not that interested in history. Amusement parks like Charlotte's Carowinds and outfitters like the Nantahala Outdoor Center cater to tourists seeking different types of thrills. Mayberry Days in Mount Airy brings fans to the Piedmont seeking a North Carolina that never really existed as they stroll past Floyd's barbershop or eat the fried pork chop sandwich at the Snappy Lunch. Second-home communities in places like Cashiers, Pinehurst, Nags Head, and Bald Head Island offer affluent tourists an opportunity to make their leisure experience permanent in the mountains, on the links, or beside the sea. Race fans flock to Charlotte's NASCAR Hall of Fame to connect with the history of a sport rooted in North Carolina red clay, and festivals in communities large and small tempt visitors to eat barbecue in Lexington, shag to beach music at Carolina Beach, or toss the caber at the Highland Games.[42]

However, these and countless other examples of contemporary tourism development simply represent new wine in old bottles. Tourism has long been a powerful catalyst in the Old North State, something historians have recognized but are only now truly exploring. Integrating it into the state's history offers fresh ways to examine and complicate our understanding of the state and its people. Tourism history shows how the landscape, history, culture, and image became commodities with profound social and economic effects in communities across the state. The history of North Carolina tourism also offers new ways to explore politics, economics, and identity by illuminating the processes that decided which places to sell, how to promote them, and whose history and culture could be transformed into attractions. In this way, tourism provides new perspectives on the state's past and innovative fields of inquiry to deepen, enrich, and reimagine the multiple narratives that make up the North Carolina experience.

NOTES

1. Hargrove Bowles, "American's Variety Vacationland," in *The Travel Industry in North Carolina: Proceedings of the Governor's Travel Information Conference, Oct. 28, 29, 30, 1964*, ed. James H. Bearden (Greenville, N.C.: East Carolina College Bureau of Business Research, 1964), 4–5. Portions of this essay are drawn from the author's *Creating the Land of the Sky: Tourism and Society in Western North Carolina* (Tuscaloosa: University of Alabama Press, 2005) and are used here by permission.

2. "Fast Facts: 2013 Impact of Visitor Spending," North Carolina Tourism Commerce, http://www.nccommerce.com/tourism/research/nc-fast-facts (accessed April 17, 2014).

3. The historical literature on American tourism is growing. The most influential for this essay include John F. Sears, *Sacred Places: American Tourist Attractions in the Nineteenth Century* (New York: Oxford University Press, 1989); Dona Brown, *Inventing New England: Regional Tourism in the Nineteenth Century* (Washington, D.C.: Smithsonian Institution Press, 1995); David M. Wrobel and Patrick T. Long, eds., *Seeing and Being Seen: Tourism in the American West* (Lawrence: University Press of Kansas, 2001); Hal K. Rothman, *Devil's Bargains: Tourism in the Twentieth-Century American West* (Lawrence: University Press of Kansas, 1998); Marguerite S. Shaffer, *See America First: Tourism and National Identity, 1880–1940* (Washington, D.C.: Smithsonian Institution Press, 2001); Catherine Cocks, *Doing the Town: The Rise of Urban Tourism in the United States, 1850–1915* (Berkeley: University of California Press, 2001); John Urry, *The Tourist Gaze*, 2nd ed. (London: Sage, 2002); John Jakle, *The Tourist in Twentieth Century America* (Lincoln: University of Nebraska Press, 1985); and Cindy S. Aron, *Working at Play: A History of Vacations in the United States* (New York: Oxford University Press, 1999). A partial list of recent works on southern tourism includes Karen L. Cox, ed., *Destination Dixie: Tourism and Southern History* (Gainesville: University Press of Florida, 2012); Stephanie E. Yuhl, *A Golden Haze of Memory: The Making of Historic Charleston* (Chapel Hill: University of North Carolina Press, 2005); Anne Mitchell Whisnant, *Super-Scenic Motorway: A Blue Ridge Parkway History* (Chapel Hill: University of North Carolina Press, 2006); Anthony J. Stanonis, *Creating the Big Easy: New*

Orleans and the Emergence of Modern Tourism, 1918-1945 (Athens: University of Georgia Press, 2006); Jonathan Mark Souther, *New Orleans on Parade: Tourism and the Transformation of the Crescent City* (Baton Rouge: Louisiana State University Press, 2006); Harvey K. Newman, *Southern Hospitality: Tourism and the Growth of Atlanta* (Tuscaloosa: University of Alabama Press, 1999); Anthony J. Stanonis, ed., *Dixie Emporium: Tourism, Foodways, and Consumer Culture in the American South* (Athens: University of Georgia Press, 2008); Richard D. Starnes, ed., *Southern Journeys: Tourism, History, and Culture in the Modern South* (Tuscaloosa: University of Alabama Press, 2003); Tracy J. Revel, *Sunshine Paradise: A History of Florida Tourism* (Gainesville: University Press of Florida, 2011); Bren Martin, *Tourism in the Mountain South: A Double-Edged Sword* (Knoxville: University of Tennessee Press, 2007); Rebecca Cawood McIntyre, *Souvenirs of the Old South: Northern Tourism and Southern Mythology* (Gainesville: University Press of Florida, 2011); and Harvey H. Jackson III, *The Rise and Fall of the Redneck Riviera: An Insider's History of the Florida-Alabama Coast* (Athens: University of Georgia Press, 2012). For an early call for research into southern tourism, see Rembert W. Patrick, "The Mobile Frontier," *Journal of Southern History* 29 (February 1963): 3-18.

4. Andrew Holden, *Tourism and the Environment* (New York: Routledge, 2000).

5. Lawrence Fay Brewster, *Summer Migrations and Resorts of South Carolina Low-Country Planters*, Historical Papers of the Trinity College Historical Society, ser. 26 (Durham, N.C.: Duke University Press, 1947), 53-73; John C. Inscoe, *Mountain Masters, Slavery, and the Sectional Crisis in Western North Carolina* (Knoxville: University of Tennessee Press, 1989), 44-52; Richard D. Starnes, *Creating the Land of the Sky: Tourism and Society in Western North Carolina* (Tuscaloosa: University of Alabama Press, 2005), 13-15; Ora Blackmun, *Western North Carolina: Its Mountains and Its People to 1880* (Boone, N.C.: Appalachian Consortium Press, 1977), 289-91.

6. Brewster, *Summer Migrations*, 74-108; Starnes, *Creating the Land of the Sky*, 17-19; Charles Lanman, *Letters from the Allegany Mountains* (New York: George P. Putnam, 1849), 117.

7. Aron, *Working at Play*, 45-68.

8. Christian Reid, *"The Land of the Sky"; or, Adventures in Mountain By-ways* (New York; D. Appleton and Co., 1875), 3-5.

9. Thomas H. Lindsey, *Lindsey's Guidebook to Western North Carolina* (Asheville, N.C.: Randolph-Kerr Printing Co., 1890), 1, 20-16. See also Frank Presbrey, *The Land of the Sky and Beyond* (New York: Frank Presbrey, c. 1896).

10. *The City of Wilmington, the Metropolis and Port of North Carolina: Its Advantages and Interests, Also a Series of Sketches of Representative Business Houses* (Wilmington, N.C.: Wilmington Chamber of Commerce, 1912), 22-25.

11. For more on the nature of North Carolina Progressivism, see William A. Link, *The Paradox of Southern Progressivism, 1880-1930* (Chapel Hill: University of North Carolina Press, 1997); and Paul D. Escott, *Many Excellent People: Power and Privilege in North Carolina, 1850-1900* (Chapel Hill: University of North Carolina Press, 1988).

12. Howard Lawrence Preston, *Dirt Roads to Dixie: Accessibility and Modernization in the South, 1885-1935* (Knoxville: University of Tennessee Press, 1991), 11-38; *Constitution and Report of Work Accomplished by the Good Roads Association of Asheville and Buncombe County* (n.p., 1912), North Carolina Collection, Pack Memorial Library, Asheville, N.C., 1-5;

Cecil K. Brown, *The State Highway System of North Carolina: Its Evolution and Present Status* (Chapel Hill: University of North Carolina Press, 1931), 34; *North Carolina: The Pacemaker in Industry, Agriculture, and Substantial Progress* (Raleigh, N.C.: Department of Conservation and Development, 1926), 11 (first quotation); "Potentialities of Western North Carolina," in *Public Papers and Letters of Angus Wilson McLean, Governor of North Carolina, 1925-1929*, ed. David Leroy Corbitt (Raleigh, N.C.: Council of State, 1931), 229-32 (second quotation on 231). For an excellent study of the Good Roads movement in North Carolina, see Harry Wilson McKown, "Roads and Reform: The Good Roads Movement in North Carolina, 1885-1921," M.A. thesis, University of North Carolina at Chapel Hill, 1972. For an important new interpretation of highway construction in the South, see Tammy Ingram, *The Dixie Highway: Road Building and the Making of the Modern South, 1900-1930* (Chapel Hill: University of North Carolina Press, 2014).

13. Chase P. Ambler, "Activities of the Appalachian National Forest Association," 1-3, Appalachian National Park Association Collection, North Carolina State Archives, Raleigh, N.C.; William R. Day to Chase Ambler, October 31, 1899, and Day to Ambler, November 10, 1899, Minute Book, Appalachian National Park Association, 3-8, Appalachian National Park Association Collection; Charles Dennis Smith, "The Appalachian National Park Movement, 1885-1901," *North Carolina Historical Review* 37 (January 1960), 39, 62-65. For an example of hostility toward this movement by resort owners, see James F. Hays to M. V. Richards, January 6, 1900; Richards to Hays, January 10, 1900; and Richards to Charles Ambler, January 13, 1900, Minute Book, Appalachian National Park Association Collection, 50-55.

14. Timothy Silver, *Mount Mitchell and the Black Mountains: An Environmental History of the Highest Peaks in Eastern America* (Chapel Hill: University of North Carolina Press, 2003), 177-85, 211-16.

15. Telegram from O. Max Gardner to George L. Lemmer, c. May 1931 (first quotation); telegram from *New York Evening Post* to Gardner, May 18, 1931; and radio broadcast transcript by Gardner, WMAQ-Chicago, May 18, 1929 (second quotation), Administrative Reports and Correspondence Files, 1926-35, North Carolina Department of Conservation and Development Records, North Carolina State Archives (hereafter NCDCD Records). The best treatments of the formation of the Great Smoky Mountains National Park are Daniel S. Pierce, *The Great Smokies: From Natural Habitat to National Park* (Knoxville: University of Tennessee Press, 2000); and Margaret Lynn Brown, *The Wild East: A Biography of the Great Smoky Mountains* (Gainesville: University Press of Florida, 2000).

16. Coleman W. Roberts to Members of The Carolinas, Inc., February 9, 1935, The Carolinas, Inc. File, Miscellaneous Subject Files, 1920-36 Administrative Reports and Correspondence File, 1936-41, NCDCD Records.

17. Semiannual report of R. Bruce Etheridge, Director, July 1, 1937 to January 1, 1938, July 1, 1937 to January 1, 1938, Administrative Reports and Correspondence File, 1936-41, NCDCD Records; *North Carolina: Variety Vacationland* (Raleigh, N.C.: Department of Conservation and Development, 1939); David Ogeron, "Nothing Could Be Finer: George Stoney's *Tar Heel Family* and the Tar Heel State on Film," *Moving Image* 9 (Spring 2009): 161-82.

18. Glenda Elizabeth Gilmore, *Gender and Jim Crow: Women and the Politics of White Supremacy in North Carolina, 1896-1920* (Chapel Hill: University of North Carolina Press, 1996), 29, 243; Starnes, *Creating the Land of the Sky*, 171-80.

19. Derek H. Alderman and E. Arnold Martin Jr., "Southern Hospitality and the Politics of African American Belonging: An Analysis of North Carolina Tourism Brochure Photographs," *Journal of Cultural Geography* 30 (February 2013), 6–31; Andrew W. Karhl, *The Land Was Ours: African American Beaches from Jim Crow to the Sunbelt South* (Cambridge, Mass.: Harvard University Press, 2012), 155–77. In 2000, the North Carolina Department of Commerce published a brochure designed especially to appeal to African American visitors, the first publication of its kind and recognition of the growing economic importance of African American visitors to the state. See *The Rich Heritage of African Americans in North Carolina* (Raleigh: North Carolina Division of Tourism, Film and Sports Development, Department of Commerce, 2000).

20. Whisnant, *Super-Scenic Motorway*, chaps. 4 and 7; Drew A. Swanson, "Marketing a Mountain: Changing Views of Environment and Landscape on Grandfather Mountain, North Carolina," *Appalachian Journal* 36 (Fall 2008–Winter 2009): 30–53; *Impacts and Influences on the Great Smoky Mountains National Park: An Annotated Bibliography with a Discussion and Review of Selected Findings, Recommendations, and Conclusions* (Atlanta, Ga.: National Park Service Southeast Regional Office, 1982), 39 (quotation).

21. Bruce Hobson, "Mountain Condo Generates Talk of Land Use Law," *Charlotte Observer*, January 23, 1983, 1D; "Election Returns," *Asheville Citizen*, May 10, 1984, 29; "Developers Say They Will Challenge New Restrictions," *Winston-Salem Journal*, January 1, 1984, 1A; Milton S. Heath Jr., "The North Carolina Mountain Ridge Protection Act," *North Carolina Law Review* 63 (November 1984): 183–96; Robert M. Kessler, "North Carolina's Ridge Law: No View from the Top," *North Carolina Law Review* 63 (November 1984): 197–221.

22. W. Fitzhugh Brundage, *The Southern Past: A Clash of Race and Memory* (Cambridge, Mass.: Belknap Press, 2005), 184. For a broader context, see James C. Cobb, *Away Down South: A History of Southern Identity* (New York: Oxford University Press, 2005).

23. Paul Green and Laurence G. Avery, *The Lost Colony: A Symphonic Drama of American History* (Chapel Hill: University of North Carolina Press, 2000), 149 and passim.

24. Green and Avery, *Lost Colony*, 203; William S. Powell, *Paradise Preserved: A History of the Roanoke Island Historical Association* (Chapel Hill: University of North Carolina Press, 1965), 131–69; Brooks Atkinson, "Founding Fathers: Paul Green's 'The Lost Colony' Performed on Roanoke Island," *New York Times*, August 15, 1937 (quotation); *The Lost Colony, Souvenir Program, 1937* (Manteo, N.C.: Roanoke Island Historical Association, 1937).

25. Wallace Randolph Umberger Jr., "A History of *Unto These Hills*, 1941 to 1968," Ph.D. diss., Tulane University, 1970, 1–2; Matthew D. Thompson, "Staging 'the Drama': The Continuing Importance of Cultural Tourism in the Gaming Era," Ph.D. diss., University of North Carolina at Chapel Hill, 2009, 45–49. The drama itself had deep roots. In 1934, Bureau of Indian Affairs official R. L. Spalsbury began to research the possibility of staging a pageant during the summer season based on the Cherokee historical experience. Harold Foght, Spalsbury's successor, led the creation of a drama called "Spirit of the Great Smoky Mountains," a celebration of the tribe's culture and history. Four successful performances convinced some tribal leaders of the viability and profitability of such a project. In 1937, with the help of the Knoxville-based Tsali Cherokee Foundation, the tribe produced a larger, more elaborate drama, drawing more than 5,000 attendees to six performances. See John Finger, *Cherokee Americans: The Eastern Band of Cherokees in the Twentieth Century* (Lincoln: University of

Nebraska Press, 1991), 99–104; and "Colorful Pageant Will Portray Tribal History of Cherokee Indians," *Asheville Citizen*, June 27, 1937, 8C, and "Crowd of 1,200 Attends Final Indian Pageant," August 16, 1937, 1.

26. "Report Made by Mrs. Doyle D. Alley, Secretary-Treasurer, at the Meeting of the Western North Carolina Associated Communities, Held on Monday, October 10, 1949," Western North Carolina Tourist Association Minutes, Western North Carolina Associated Communities Papers, Special Collections, Hunter Library, Western Carolina University, Cullowhee, N.C.; George L. Simpson, Harriet L. Herring, and Maurice B. Morrill, *Western North Carolina Associated Communities* (Cherokee, N.C.: Cherokee Historical Association, 1956), 24–31. Historian John Finger noted that Cherokees connected with tourism were more likely to support efforts such as *Unto These Hills*. See Finger, *Cherokee Americans*, 114–17. For more on Cherokee history and removal, see John R. Finger, *The Eastern Band of Cherokees, 1819–1900* (Knoxville: University of Tennessee Press, 1984).

27. "Photographers Get a Chance to 'Shoot' Cherokee Drama," *Asheville Citizen-Times*, July 10, 1950, 3; *Rocky Mount Evening Telegram*, July 15, 1950; *Unto These Hills Souvenir Program, 1950* (Cherokee, N.C.: Cherokee Historical Association, 1950), 1–7; Umberger, "A History of *Unto These Hills*," 72–80.

28. Nina Anderson, "A History of the Western North Carolina Associated Communities," 67–69, unpublished manuscript, Western North Carolina Associated Communities Papers; and Finger, *Cherokee Americans*, 137–38.

29. "Certificate of Incorporation of Old Salem, Incorporated," reprinted in Frances Griffin, *Old Salem: An Adventure in Historic Preservation* (Winston-Salem, N.C.: Old Salem, Inc., 1970), 70–71.

30. Griffin, *Old Salem*, 10–61; Charles Herrold Jr., "Restoring Old Moravian Salem," *New York Times*, October 31, 1953; Nora Brown, "Old Salem Is on Road to Restoration," *New York Times*, May 22, 1960; Wilma Dykeman, "Christmas in Old Salem," *New York Times*, December 10, 1961; Caryl Stern and Robert W. Stock, "The Past Lives on In Old Salem, N.C.," *New York Times*, August 5, 1979. For a similar story of the links between tourism and historic preservation, see Anders Greenspan, *Creating Colonial Williamsburg: The Restoration of Virginia's Eighteenth Century Capital* (Chapel Hill: University of North Carolina Press, 2002).

31. Alisa Y. Harrison, "'History as Tourist Bait': Inventing Somerset Place State Historic Site, 1939–1969," in Cox, *Destination Dixie*, 113–36.

32. Dorothy Spruill Redford, *Somerset Homecoming: Recovering Lost Heritage*, with Michael D'Orso (New York; Doubleday, 1988), 236 (quotation); Julie Ann Powers, "One Woman's Quest Made Somerset Place a Plantation that Presents History in All Its Shades," *News and Observer* (Raleigh, N.C.), August 25, 1994, E1. For a detailed critical examination, see Harrison, "Reconstructing Somerset Place: Slavery, Memory, and Historical Consciousness," Ph.D. diss., Duke University, 2008. For slavery depictions in public history sites, see James Oliver Horton and Lois E. Horton, eds., *Slavery and Public History: The Tough Stuff of American Memory* (Chapel Hill: University of North Carolina Press, 2006).

33. Paul Brooks, "The Great Smokies," *Atlantic Monthly* (May 1959), 63 (quotation); Pierce, *Great Smokies*, 177, 182–84; Richard D. Starnes, "Tourism, Landscape, and History in the Great Smoky Mountains National Park," in Cox, *Destination Dixie*, 267–80. See also Alex Tooman, "The Evolving Impact of Tourism on the Greater Smoky Mountain Region of East Tennessee and Western North Carolina," Ph.D. diss., University of Tennessee,

1995. For a study of similar dynamics on the Tennessee side of the park, see Terence Young, "False, Cheap, and Degraded: When History, Economy, and Environment Collided at Cades Cove, Great Smoky Mountains National Park," *Journal of Historical Geography* 32 (January 2006): 169–89.

34. Arthur Stupka, *Great Smoky Mountain National Park: North Carolina and Tennessee Natural History*, Handbook Series no. 5 (Washington, D.C.: U.S. Department of the Interior, 1961), 54–55. For further examples of this focus on nature over human experiences, see William Gillman, "Uncle Sam's Gift to Easterners," *Travel*, September 1937, 39; and John Kord Lageman, "You'll Be Comin' Round the Mountain," *Collier's*, May 15, 1948, 88.

35. Frances Louisa Goodrich to unknown recipient, November 9, 1890, Frances Louisa Goodrich Papers, Special Collections Library, Duke University, Durham, N.C.; Frances Goodrich, *Mountain Homespun* (New Haven, Conn.: Yale University Press, 1931), 21–23; Allen H. Eaton, "The Mountain Handicrafts: Their Importance to the Country and to the People in the Mountain Home," *Mountain Life and Work* 6 (July 1930): 22–30; Jane S. Becker, *Selling Tradition: Appalachia and the Construction on an American Folk, 1930–1940* (Chapel Hill University of North Carolina Press, 1998), 63–66; Henry D. Shapiro, *Appalachia on Our Mind: The Southern Mountains and Mountaineers in American Consciousness* (Chapel Hill: University of North Carolina Press, 1978), 221–24; Allen H. Eaton, *Handicrafts of the Southern Highlands* (New York: Russell Sage Foundation, 1937), 64–68. See also Davydd J. Greenwood, "Culture by the Pound: An Anthropological Perspective on Tourism as Cultural Commodification," in *Hosts and Guests: The Anthropology of Tourism*, ed. Valene Smith, 2nd ed. (Philadelphia: University of Pennsylvania Press, 1989), 171–86.

36. Bill Sharpe, "Biltmore Homespun," *State*, December 12, 1947, 6–9 (quotation); C. R. Sumner, "Biltmore Industries Has Unique Setting, Now Offers New Services," *Asheville Citizen*, April 17, 1949, A9; J. Gerald Cowan, "Industry, Tourists, and Agriculture Aid WNC Economy," [unidentified newspaper], January 25, 1959. For more on depictions of mountain culture in similar contexts, see David Whisnant, *All That Is Native and Fine: The Politics of Culture in an American Region* (Chapel Hill: University of North Carolina Press, 1983).

37. David Schenck, "The Cherokees in North Carolina," *At Home and Abroad* (February 1882): 329 (quotation); Sarah H. Hill, *Weaving New Worlds: Southeastern Cherokee Women and Their Basketry* (Chapel Hill: University of North Carolina Press, 1997), 224–25.

38. Finger, *Cherokee Americans*, 53–56; Ellen Englemann Black, "A Study of the Diffusion of Culture in a Relative Isolated Mountain County," M.A. thesis, University of Chicago, 1928, 14–18, 25–29; Charles J. Weeks, "The Eastern Cherokee and the New Deal," *North Carolina Historical Review* 43 (July 1976): 202–25.

39. Betty J. Duggan, "Tourism, Cultural Authenticity and the Native Crafts Cooperative: The Eastern Cherokee Experience," in *Tourism and Culture: An Applied Perspective*, ed. Erve Chambers (Albany: State University of New York Press, 1997), 31–57; *Cherokee One Feather*, December 3, 1975, 4; Davy Arch oral history, interviewed by William Mansfield, March 28, 1996, 1–2, Mountain Heritage Center, Western Carolina University (quotation).

40. Finger, *Cherokee Americans*, 161–63, 181; Henry Lambert oral history, interviewed by William Mansfield, 1–4, 13 (quotations), Mountain Heritage Center.

41. R. F. Stamper, "Letter to the Editor," c. June 1979, quoted in Pat Arnow, "Tourons in Wallyworld," *Now and Then* 8 (Spring 1991): 2. See also Larry R. Stucki, "Will the 'Real Indian' Survive? Tourism and Affluence at Cherokee, North Carolina," in *Affluence and Cul-*

tural Survival, ed. Richard F. Salisbury and Elizabeth Tooker (Washington, D.C.: American Ethnological Society, 1984); Fred Bauer, *The Land of the North Carolina Cherokee* (Brevard, N.C.: Buchanan Press, 1970), 55; and Christina Taylor Beard-Moose, *Public Indians, Private Cherokees: Tourism and Tradition on Tribal Ground* (Tuscaloosa: University of Alabama Press, 2009).

42. Derek H. Alderman, Stephanie K. Benjamin, and Paige Schneider, "Transforming Mount Airy into Mayberry: Film-Induced Tourism as Place-Making," *Southeastern Geographer* 52 (Summer 2012): 212–39; Rodger Lyle Brown, *Ghost Dancing on the Cracker Circuit: The Culture of Festivals in the American South* (Jackson: University Press of Mississippi, 1997), 179–92; Deepak Chhabra, Erin Sills, and Frederick W. Cubbage, "The Significance of Festivals to Rural Economies: Estimating the Economic Impacts of Scottish Highland Games in North Carolina," *Journal of Travel Research* 41 (May 2003): 421–27; Christopher Arris Oakley, "Indian Gaming and the Eastern Band of Cherokee Indians," *North Carolina Historical Review* 78 (April 2001): 133–55.

CHASING SMOKESTACKS
LESSONS AND LEGACIES

James C. Cobb

North Carolina's reputation as the most progressive state in the South may well make it seem somewhat atypical in certain respects, but the story of its post–World War II industrial development efforts and their results is in many important aspects both quintessentially southern and globally relevant as well. Like its southern neighbors, North Carolina had benefited handsomely from the massive monetary infusion served up by World War II, adding some 2,000 new factories between 1939 and 1947 alone. As Tyler Greene has noted, when Governor W. Kerr Scott took office in 1949, he became but one of a number of post–World War II southern governors who pledged themselves not simply to hold onto those gains but to build on them to offset the steady loss of jobs and people triggered by the accelerating shrinkage of the agricultural sector. By that point, every southern state had long promised relocating manufacturers cheap, "native-born," nonunion labor, low taxes, and government cooperation, but North Carolina was particularly well positioned to deliver on those promises.[1]

Building on its Progressive Era "good roads" initiatives, North Carolina had become known as the Good Roads State as far back as the 1920s, when it issued $50 million in bonds to improve its highway system. As an adjunct to his industrial development efforts, in 1949 Governor Scott upped the ante to $200 million for a program of further improvement and expansion of rural and secondary routes that, over the next four years, gave North Carolina an additional 12,000 miles of paved roads. A few years later, Governor Luther H. Hodges made it clear from the outset that he was all in for industrial development as well, and he, too, proved eager to invest in the state's highways as avenues to that end. The prevailing Cold War emphasis on industrial dispersion as a means of minimizing the damage of a potential nuclear attack clearly worked in favor of such efforts, as did the National Interstate and Defense Highways Act of 1956. Offered ostensibly as a means of assuring the speedy movement of troops across the national expanse, this initiative spawned a profusion of interstate highways throughout the South, five of which would eventually enswathe the North Carolina countryside. By the 1960s, North Carolina boasted more state-supported highway mileage than any other state, and its industrial-recruitment efforts were going so well that from the mid-1950s to the mid-1960s only California attracted more manufacturing jobs.[2]

North Carolina's industrial advance doubtless passed largely unnoticed by adherents of the traditional monolithic, urban-centric model of industrial development. Derived primarily from the example of England during the Industrial Revolution and the subsequent course of events in the northern manufacturing states, this model was of limited applicability to the industrial development pattern that unfolded in North Carolina and the other southern states. Instead of large manufacturing cities that drew hordes of workers of varying geographic and cultural origins into huge population concentrations, in North Carolina and the South at large, much of the late-developing industrial expansion accommodated itself to widely dispersed rural populations in a process wherein the jobs moved to the workers rather than vice versa. This shift was possible in no small part because federal programs like the Rural Electrification Administration and the Tennessee Valley Authority had dramatically increased locational options for manufacturers by making cheap electric power available throughout the rural countryside. Because the South remained predominantly rural, however, an extensive highway network was also critical to giving remote and formerly well-nigh inaccessible areas of states like North Carolina a realistic shot at landing a manufacturing payroll. Recognizing this opportunity, as Greene has pointed out, Governor Scott had consciously melded his road-building initiative with his industrial development efforts by assuring northern manufacturers eager to escape the higher wages and taxes more typical of large urban centers that his state's excellent road system allowed them to choose from a multitude of sites that he simply described as "distant from congested metropolitan sections."[3]

Overwhelmingly low wage and labor intensive, incoming industries could now fan out across a countryside ripe with eager, fresh-off-the-farm laborers likely to deem any wage better than none, not to mention grateful local officials offering free land and buildings and promising minimal taxation or interference with their community's new industrial benefactors. In short, the North Carolina highway network made every little crossroads hamlet a potentially alluring location for low-wage, labor-intensive manufacturing. Not the least of the advantages of this dispersal of relatively small plants across a vast rural expanse was that it forced union organizers to traipse from one end of the boondocks to the other, fending off all manner of threats and harassment from local officials, including law enforcement, as they tried to convince scattered workforces of one hundred or fewer to follow the urgings of a complete stranger over those of an employer all too recently hailed as a savior. Distant observers who posited that some sort of exotic indigenous folkways must have left southern white workers peculiarly ill-disposed toward unions failed to recognize that, in contrast to the experience of their northern counterparts, for a sizable segment of the post–World War II workforce the switch from farmer to factory hand had entailed no great change of physical or sociocultural scenery whatsoever. They might now work on an assembly line rather than behind the plow, but their social interactions at work, in churches and stores, and elsewhere still transpired with essentially the same cast of characters and within the same matrix of community mores, including, as before, a tendency to look askance at strangers, especially those bearing promises to change their lives for the better.

Accordingly, by the early 1960s, more new manufacturing jobs were popping up annually outside the South's metropolitan areas than within them. Between 1963 and 1965, four out of five new manufacturing jobs in Tennessee were created in rural counties, while in Virginia the figure was two out of three. By 1969 nearly 40 percent of the industrial plants in ten southern states were situated in rural or small-town settings. A survey by two University of North Carolina geographers showed that 61 percent of the manufacturing plants that came to North Carolina in the 1960s were located in rural counties. Thus it was that, while leading the nation with 41 percent of its nonagricultural labor force employed in manufacturing in 1969, North Carolina was effectively tied with Mississippi as the most rural state in the old Confederacy.[4]

The parallels with the Magnolia State did not end there, because the two states, which had shared the bottom rung in regional wage rankings in 1960, occupied the same relative positions ten years later. With state and local officials continuing their unremitting pursuit of labor-intensive industries, by 1980 North Carolina's manufacturing wage had actually managed to dip below Mississippi's, and for several years it enjoyed the dubious distinction of having the worst paid manufacturing workforce in the country. In a stark demonstration of the difficulties of untethering from an industrial economy anchored in cheap labor, over the next three decades of ballyhoo about the cutting-edge sexiness of the Research Triangle and Charlotte's emergence as a national banking colossus, the Tar Heel state languished in the bottom ten in state wage rankings until, with some assistance from declines elsewhere, it finally broke through in 2010 to claim the fortieth position.[5]

This wage stagnation has struck some scholars examining economic development in this and other southern states as a regional aberration traceable to the persistence of a powerful landed elite that kept the South from following what one called "the classic capitalist path that had been blazed by England ... and followed by the Northern states." Though still widely embraced, the idea of a single, unvarying "classic capitalist" path to modernity can be traced at least as far back as Karl Marx, whose narrow obsession with England as the "classic ground" of capitalist development led him to insist that "the country that is more developed industrially only shows to the less developed the image of its own future."[6]

The resulting one-size-fits-all development model ignored the possible effects of significant variations in historical, cultural, and geographic factors, not to mention, as we shall see, dramatic shifts in global conditions. It also overlooked the possibility that each nation's experience with modernization would influence and even potentially reshape those that came after. Needless to say, globalization has greatly facilitated this process, for as we have seen time and again by now, the innovations in technology, technique, and organization registered in more economically advanced "leader societies" can actually provide shortcuts for other "follower societies" that have lagged behind. The same is also true for the problems encountered by leader societies. By way of example, seeing that many labor-intensive industries could no longer operate as profitably as they would like in urban locations, North or South, Governor Scott had championed an aggressive road-building effort that went well beyond what the state's agricultural economy could justify at the time but paid off handsomely later in a large influx of new manufacturing plants. When he became governor, Luther Hodges continued to recruit low-wage industries for rural areas but also noted the emergence of a more remunerative, knowledge-intensive industrial sector elsewhere. Distinguished University of North Carolina sociologist Howard Odum had already suggested that the university join forces with North Carolina State College to create a research center committed to further development of southern resources. Hodges went Odum's idea one better, adding Duke University to the equation and noting that, with the state's three leading universities lying only roughly fifteen miles from a central location, their combined research resources and expertise might be harnessed collaboratively in support of a state initiative aimed at bringing in more knowledge-oriented industries employing highly educated workforces of scientists, engineers, and other specialists. Building on the triangular geographic configuration of the three schools, in 1957 Hodges pushed the idea of a "Research Triangle Park," designed to attract the research and technical facilities of the nation's cutting-edge corporations at a time when the state's industrial base remained overwhelmingly labor intensive. Twenty years later, RTP boasted twenty-two

FIGURE 13.1. Governor Luther H. Hodges, a successful businessman before he entered politics, expanded North Carolina's aggressive campaign to recruit new industry to the state. In this political cartoon by Hugh Haynie of the *Greensboro Daily News*, c. late 1950s, he appears as a flamboyant Confederate cavalryman leading "Hodges Raiders" in recruiting industries from the North and Midwest. © Greensboro News and Record. All rights reserved.

research facilities, with six more on the way. With a staff of thirty-three hundred, IBM was the largest employer among RTP's tenants, which included research operations for the U.S. Environmental Protection Agency and the National Center for Health Statistics.[7]

In essence, the idea behind the Research Triangle Park was that a developmentally laggard society need not complete every stage of institutional advance registered by its predecessors or necessarily invest resources in developing products and processes that have already been introduced in leader societies. Thus, the globe-trotting Mississippian David Cohn could observe in 1951 that even as its people struggled to sustain themselves on stale bread and Borscht, the Soviet Union had "performed the feat of jumping from the oxcart into the airplane in one generation." Forty years later, humorist Lewis Grizzard would ponder the other side of this paradox by asking how the Soviets could possibly manage to send a man to the moon but fail so miserably at producing toilet paper.[8]

Viewed in global perspective over time, societies with an appetite for economic modernization confront not a fixed menu but a cafeteria line. Although not all the offerings are adaptable to the tastes or budgets of all would-be diners, ironically, the later one arrives at the serving line, the greater the availability of development options. As a relative latecomer to the modernization buffet, the South encountered a variety of possibilities, but its severely limited capital resources ultimately dictated a fairly mundane set of selections that had actually been on the table for quite a while. The bargain-priced textile industry amounted to a genuine blue-plate special, for instance, and textile production was an entrée well suited for a region where cheap, eager labor was hungry for work. On the other hand, as David Carlton and Peter Coclanis point out, situated near the trailing edge of the American manufacturing economy, the textile industry's major technological and production advances were largely behind it by the turn of the early twentieth century, and hence, it was unlikely to generate the pressures for investments in education or inventive or experimental activities that might have paid off in terms of attracting more high-energy investment capital from outside the region.[9]

By the 1970s, however, North Carolina and the other southern states were able to circumvent, at least to some extent, the protracted and expensive process of developing a generally better-educated workforce. Thanks to the highly specialized nature of modern factory work and major advances in technology and training techniques, state-funded "start-up" training programs customized to fit the specific skill needs of each new employer could guarantee an up-to-speed labor force practically from the first day of operation. North Carolina's "New and Expanding Industry Training Program" is billed as the oldest customized state-supported training program in the United States, and an estimated $5 million for workforce training was bundled in with the standard tax breaks and other concessions offered Dell Computer in 2004 before they agreed to locate a plant in the Piedmont Triad area, consisting of Winston-Salem, Greensboro, and High Point. The promise of a similar training program doubtless helped to allay BMW's concerns about the educational deficiencies of South Carolina workers in 1993. Elsewhere, despite Alabama's consistent last or near-last standing in national educational rankings, only a threatened lawsuit by a teachers group prevented Governor Fob James from raiding the state's public school fund in 1995 to pay off the remainder of its subsidy pledge to Mercedes, whose entire workforce at its Alabama facility had also been custom trained at state expense. Meanwhile in the neighboring hotbed of educational fervor, Mississippi, when state officials promised $80 million to train 4,000 workers for a new Nissan production facility, the cost per worker was more than four times its annual per-pupil expenditures in grades K–12.[10]

BMW, Mercedes, and Nissan were but three of the foreign businesses drawn to the United States in the 1990s, more than half of which settled in the South. By 2002, one of eight southern manufacturing workers was already employed by a company headquartered in another country, and in 2011, six of the ten states registering the largest increases in jobs related to foreign direct investment were in the South. The most aggressive and effective early pursuit of foreign manufacturers came from South Carolina, whose promoters could boast by the end of the 1970s that, in addition to plant investments from England, Italy, the Netherlands, Austria, Belgium, and France, there was more West German industrial capital in their state than anywhere in the world except West Germany itself. As the southern states plunged into a highly competitive courtship of European industrial capital, the objects of their affection were nudged into the open arms of their suitors in no small measure by concerns about inflation, tighter labor markets, a resurgence of leftist politics, and tighter government regulation in their own backyards. In the latter category, tightening pollution restrictions in Europe enhanced the appeal of more environmentally lax southern states like North Carolina, where in 1967 an ambitious statute promising more aggressive efforts to curtail air pollution was not even discussed in the legislature until a copy had been circulated among key industrialists and state development officials. The upshot was a hastily revised bill in which "maintenance of a proper environment in which people may live and work" had given way to providing only such regulation as would be consistent with achieving and maintaining "maximum employment and full industrial development of the state."[11]

It certainly did not hurt, of course, that these ultra-accommodating Southerners who promised an escape from such headaches also showed up with huge goody bags bulging with financial and other enticements. Another incentive for European industrial investment in the South came in 1971 when the Nixon administration took steps to reverse a massive U.S. trade deficit by devaluing the dollar and simultaneously imposing a 10 percent surcharge on imported manufactures. At that point, industrial investments in the United States became all but irresistible. It was, exulted a jubilant British banker, "like getting Harrods's at half price."[12]

Both the favorable exchange rate and the prospect of dealing with more "hands-off" state and local governments were clearly appealing, but it soon became apparent that the real bottom line for foreign employers eyeing southern locations was little different from that of their domestic predecessors. Many observers seemed to assume that European or other foreign manufacturers opening plants in the South would simply bring along the labor practices they had maintained back home. Yet although they consistently offered wages noticeably higher than the local average, none of the South's new foreign employers showed much inclination to lug along the extensive benefits and worker perks that constituted what one German executive called "the social baggage we have back home." In reality, a dependably virulent anti-unionism struck most foreign employers as one of the most appealing aspects of locating a plant in the South. A consistent ranking as the nation's least unionized state stood North Carolina in good stead in this category. Indeed, North Carolina's local industrial development leaders sometimes seemed more committed to keeping out unions than to bringing in new industry. In 1977 the Person County Economic Development Commission voted to welcome a Brockway glass company beer bottle plant to Roxboro only if the workforce would not be unionized. The plant, which would eventually be built in Danville, Virginia, would have brought three hundred new jobs with starting salaries well above the local average into the Roxboro area, but as a local banker explained, "a lot of people around here have jobs who wouldn't have them if a strong union came in here and drove those other industries out."[13]

That such an attitude was actually music to the ears of many of the South's recently arrived foreign employers became apparent in 1977 when the French tire maker Michelin, which had been drawn to the Greenville, South Carolina, area three years earlier by the prospect of a union-free operating environment, joined forces with local development leaders in an effort to keep a large, relatively high-wage but likely to be unionized Phillip Morris plant out of the area. Thirty years later, South Carolina developers were still promising Japanese industrialists "a cost-effective workforce" not only because "like Japan, South Carolina emphasizes a strong work ethic and pride in workmanship" but also because the state's "unionization rate" was "one of the lowest in the nation" and its manufacturing wage was "among the lowest in the country."[14]

States known for chronic underinvestment in public education have been warned repeatedly that they would simply fall further behind in the new "knowledge-based" global economy. Yet striking testimony to the ability of Southern states to use their customized worker-training programs to leapfrog many of their more educationally advanced Northern neighbors in attracting international industrial investment came when a 2014 ranking of states' perceived capacities to participate in the global economy showed that (in terms of percentage employment by foreign firms and production for export) the South accounted for four of the nation's twelve most economically globalized states. South Carolina boasted the second highest percentage of workers employed by foreign companies, and North Carolina stood seventh, with Kentucky, and Tennessee also placing in the top twelve in this category. In outright defiance of the assumptions behind the survey itself, however, for all their success in attracting foreign direct investment, these four were also among the Southern states holding down ten of the bottom thirteen spots in rankings of the overall educational preparedness of their workforces. Delighted at the dramatic savings in the expense of putting plants into production afforded by the fully funded and staffed training programs in these and other southern states, incoming foreign employers showed little more concern than their domestic counterparts about whether their new tailor-made, union-free work forces had ever taken calculus, much less written an essay or read a sonnet.[15]

Such incentives typically came as part of larger subsidy packages, of which, as the twenty-first century unfolds, there seems as yet no end in sight. After losing out to Alabama in the multistate scramble to win the hearts of Mercedes executives, who ultimately succumbed to a seduction package valued at roughly three times North Carolina's approximately $110 million offer, a spurned Governor James B. Hunt Jr. and other Tar Heel development leaders acted as if such a whopping payoff was beneath them and their state. Chapel Hill economic development expert George Autry huffily declared, "We're better off than Kentucky, Mississippi and Alabama—the states who have given away their tax base for every Yankee industrialist flirt that comes by." As Autry saw it, Alabama officials had seen landing the Mercedes plant "as a way to put themselves on the map.... This is going to raise their profile. North Carolina doesn't need that kind of recognition." Needless to say, that prideful spin quickly rang hollow as the jobs continued to flow out of their state. "If we had known in '93 how bad it would get across our economy," one development official admitted, "we may have been willing to put $200,000,000 on the table." Suitably chastened, North Carolina's industrial recruiters soon rejoined the fray and, thanks to some aggressive new legislation, with checkbooks at the ready. This much became clear in 1998 when the state offered roughly $115 million to land a FedEx hub, where it was understood at the outset that as many as two-thirds of the jobs might be part time. Close on the heels of that transaction came a $166 million concession to steelmaker Nucor, which reportedly included a twenty-five-year exemption from state income taxes.[16]

This trend led ultimately to what proved to be one of the most controversial subsidy arrangements consummated in any southern state, Dell Computer's 2004 agreement with North Carolina to build a $110 million assembly plant and distribution center that would employ fifteen hundred people somewhere in the Triad. In return, Dell would receive not only incentives valued at $250 million (roughly 2.5 times its initial investment) from the state but also the opportunity to wring additional payoffs from competing locations within the Triad itself. The predictable bidding war reportedly yielded an additional $37.5 million subsidy for Dell, courtesy of Winston-Salem and Forsyth County. The legislation approving this deal had been rushed through the legislature a few days after the 2004 election, and the arrangement drew immediate criticism from those concerned with the escalating price tags, especially the massive tax credits that came with enticing new industries to the state. Needless to say, the furor did not abate in the wake of revelations that Dell's principal negotiator had made a reference to the "2,000 jobs" the company would bring and asked the state's commerce secretary point-blank, "Shouldn't you be happy with no [tax] revenue?" If North Carolina officials had been a bit taken aback by Dell's aggressive and abrasive negotiating style, they were nothing short of livid when the company announced in October 2009 that it would soon be closing down its Winston-Salem facility and laying off in excess of nine hundred workers.[17]

Subsequent reports that most of these jobs would likely be outsourced to Mexico were both frustrating and ironic because the pressure to offer bigger and bigger subsidies had arisen in great measure from a desperation born of the massive job losses already inflicted on North Carolina at that point by industrial out-migration to cheaper labor markets such as Mexico. In fact, this fiasco offered a classic reminder that while economic globalization has clearly benefited some parts of the South, it has also helped to devastate others, frequently those least able to absorb the loss. Implemented in 1994, the North American Free Trade Agreement (NAFTA) lowered trade barriers with Mexico and opened its pool of cheap labor to American garment and textile operations concentrated in the South. As the pace of industrial out-migration quickened in response, between 1996 and 2006 alone North Carolina lost some 153,000 textile and apparel jobs and bade farewell to nearly 60 percent of a total of 434,000 manufacturing jobs that disappeared between 1989 and 2011. This amounted to some 41,000 more manufacturing jobs than were lost over the same period in South Carolina and Georgia combined. Because the state's housing sector was not particularly overbuilt, the Great Recession of 2007 hit North Carolina less severely than some states, but to say the least, it did nothing to reverse the ongoing exodus of manufacturing jobs in a state where manufacturing accounted for nearly 22 percent of all economic output, compared with a national average of 13 percent. Although job losses appeared to bottom out a bit at the end of 2010, a recent analysis shows that as of mid-2012 the number of payroll jobs available in North Carolina represented but a 0.3 percent increase over the same figure for 2000, despite a more than 20 percent increase in the working-age population over the same period.[18]

Needless to say, owing to the rural locational pattern of so much labor-intensive manufacturing activity, some of the worst suffering inflicted by the industrial exodus fell on communities with little economic resiliency. Some areas hit hard by plant closings managed to attract new employers, but rarely were they even as generous as their tight-fisted predecessors. In many cases, however, having kept taxes low to appease their new industrial guests, southern communities with a history of chronic underinvestment in their schools lacked the educated workforce or physical infrastructure to compete for more dynamic, better-paying industries.

Billed as "a global epicenter of technological innovation," North Carolina's sprawling 7,000-acre Research Triangle Park is currently home to more than 170 companies (including, in addition to IBM, such giants as RTI International, Cisco, and GlaxoSmithKline), with nearly 40,000 full-time employees. Regardless of their actual physical proximity, however, RTP may as well have been on the moon as far as many rural North Carolinians were concerned. Rural counties had traditionally registered the state's highest rates of dependence on manufacturing, which still accounted for an average of more than 14 percent of their total employment in 2012, compared with 9 percent in urban counties. Rural counties also showed the state's lowest levels of educational attainment, with 28 percent of their adult population lacking high school diplomas in 2000 compared with 17 percent in metropolitan counties, and 14 percent holding college degrees compared with 30 percent in metro areas.[19]

However they may have stacked up wage-wise nationally, the vanished manufacturing jobs were sorely missed in nonmetropolitan counties. The average rural manufacturing worker in North Carolina earned a little over $42,000 in 2012, which was about 35 percent less than his or her urban counterpart, but still 30 percent more than the average for rural jobs outside the manufacturing sector. Such jobs as remained represented a paycheck but, frequently, not much of one. Some of the laid-off workers managed to find service jobs, but where a sewing machine operator in North Carolina might earn a little over $21,000 in 2012, a typical clerk or hotel maid would likely make some $3,000 less.[20]

To make matters worse, when the state scrambled to prepare laid-off, middle-aged, and modestly educated manufacturing workers to compete for new and better jobs, the results were less than impressive. North Carolina's biotechnology retraining program had benefited unemployed textile workers hardly at all, according to one self-described "displaced worker in his mid-forties" who had managed "after much effort" to land only "two temp jobs" before he finally "gave up looking in biotech." Aggregate statistics showed that scarcely half of such workers who did find new jobs were earning as much as 80 percent of their former wages. Commenting on the plight of unemployed North Carolina workers whose jobs in the furniture industry had fled to China, practically en masse, a state employment official noted that, although "the people in the think tanks say we are going to become—what's the term?—an 'information and services' economy . . . that doesn't seem to be working out too good."[21]

Although North Carolina's state and local officials had done admirably well in holding the line against granting subsidies to incoming employers likely to pay less than the local average, by 2010 soaring unemployment rates had taken their toll, and a number of firms offering decidedly subpar wages received state assistance. Decimated by unrelenting losses in the furniture industry over a number of years, Caldwell County had seen its jobless rate creep above 16 percent before state and local officials granted a $147,000 subsidy to a company slated to pay employees less than $20,000 a year, which fell nearly $10,000 short of the local average. Similar economic distress led to two companies receiving subsidies to locate in Rockingham County, where their pay scales were expected to fall some $8,000 shy of the prevailing wage. While it might be argued that desperate times call for desperate measures, given the well-documented "drag effect" on pay scales that results from adding a significant number of lower-than-average-wage positions to the local employment mix, such measures amount to rekindling job growth at the expense of hard-won gains in job quality.[22]

Since so much of the competition for new payrolls has effectively gone global, it is, if anything, more difficult than ever for southern states to abandon the promises of cheap labor, low or no taxes, and other concessions that gave the region the nation's balmiest business climate but deprived many of its communities of the educational and other institutional resources needed to make themselves attractive to better-paying, more socially conscious employers. The failure of the South's promising post–World War II flurry of industrial expansion to provide a more effective springboard to greater economic and institutional progress was not ascribable simply to the burdensome legacy of a politically persistent, ultraconservative agricultural elite. The region's social and institutional sectors have remained recognizably "southern" in no small measure because its leaders found no effective means of jettisoning their traditional development strategies before the rapid rise and expansion of an intensely competitive global manufacturing economy actually began to encourage, if not necessitate, their continued emphasis on cheap labor, low taxes, and deal-sweetening subsidies.

Dramatic and still accelerating increases in industrial mobility and equally rapid and remarkable improvements in communications and production technology have not only eliminated many of the low-skill positions that were once a regional mainstay but also facilitated the transfer of well over a million southern jobs to distant concentrations of labor, cheaper even, perhaps, than any the South could have offered a century ago. When sewing machine operators in Bangladesh earn roughly $0.22 per hour while working sixty hours or more a week, a similar worker in rural North Carolina making $10 per hour becomes an outright extravagance, especially in the intensively competitive apparel industry. As the case of the North Carolina worker illustrates, the South's manufacturing labor costs may remain relatively low by U.S. standards, but in the broader global context the region has become at least a moderately high-wage zone. Moreover, all too many of the southern communities that once mortgaged their futures to employers who then skipped town now lack the kind of labor force or supportive infrastructure likely to attract new industries that pay even as well as those recently departed. Surely no state is home to more communities trapped in this ironic predicament than North Carolina.

The pain of such a sudden and severe downturn in their circumstances and prospects may seem deeply personal to residents of these areas. Yet each of these individual dramas is actually playing out on a global stage, where corporate actors no longer concern themselves with political boundaries, and the identities and fortunes of nations or regions are but temporal expressions of where they may stand relative to their economic competitors at any given instant. In the 1990s when Mexico was hungrily lapping up a NAFTA-induced flood of textile and apparel jobs pouring over the border from the southern states, a German worker noted glumly that, with BMW and Mercedes preparing to open plants in two of those states, the American South was fast becoming "our Mexico." Twenty years later, hourly manufacturing wages 20 percent lower than China's, plus an enticing tax structure and freewheeling regulatory climate, have led some to dub Mexico "the China of the West." In addition to its cheap labor and business-friendly reputation, multiple free-trade agreements, including those with the United States and Canada, as well as the European Union, have also helped Mexico to quietly claim as much as 40 percent of the auto industry jobs in North America and positioned it as a formidable threat to further expansion of the foreign automaker footprint in the South.[23]

Based on recent and rumored decisions by the likes of Audi, BMW, Volkswagen, and Nissan to begin or expand operations in Mexico, contemporary allusions to an "automotive building spree in Mexico" call to mind excited references to the "Southern Auto Corridor," which have been around since the 1990s. There is certainly no denying the economic benefits derived from the South's nineteen auto assembly plants (eleven foreign and eight domestic), whose aggregate annual payrolls alone now average approximately $5.8 billion. By the same token, however, neither should we ignore the chilling reminder of the impermanence of it all offered by Markus Schaefer, CEO of Mercedes-Benz U.S. International, at a 2013 meeting of the Alabama Automotive Manufacturers Association. After crowing about $8 billion sales figures that made 2012 his organization's "best year ever," Schaefer proceeded in practically the same breath to demonstrate what two decades' worth of Alabama's warmest hospitality meant to his company by warning that "our business is not guaranteed forever here." Lest he be misunderstood, Schaefer added frostily that state officials should definitely interpret Volkswagen's recent decision to open an engine plant in Mexico as "a wake-up call." Though doubtless sobering to Alabama officials, on their face, certainly, Schaefer's comments likely seemed most encouraging to their Mexican competitors. Yet, this exuberance south of the border might be difficult to sustain over the long haul, for, as hundreds of thousands of laid-off workers in North Carolina and across the South already know from bitter experience, lurking between the lines of Schaefer's remarks lay the none-too-subtle implication that, even now, a search for the place destined to become "Mexico's Mexico" may be well under way.[24]

NOTES

1. Tyler G. Greene, "'Accessible Isolation': Highway Building, Long-Haul Trucking, and the Geography of Industrialization in North Carolina, 1945-1990," Ph.D. diss. proposal, Department of History, Temple University, typescript in possession of the author.

2. Ibid.; Bruce J. Schulman, *From Cotton Belt to Sunbelt: Federal Policy, Economic Development, and the Transformation of the South* (New York: Oxford University Press, 1991), 124, 131.

3. Greene, "'Accessible Isolation'" (Scott quote); Schulman, *From Cotton Belt to Sunbelt*, 158.

4. Richard E. Lonsdale and Clyde E. Browning, "Rural-Urban Locational Preferences of Southern Manufacturers," *Annals of the American Association of Geographers* 61 (June 1971): 262–63.

5. U.S. Bureau of the Census, *Statistical Abstract of the United States: 1972* (Washington, D.C.: Government Printing Office, 1973), 12, 18, 235; U.S. Bureau of the Census, *Statistical Abstract of the United States: 1988* (Washington, D.C.: Government Printing Office, 1989), 393; U.S. Bureau of the Census, *Statistical Abstract of the United States: 2012* (Washington, D.C.: Government Printing Office, 2013), 640.

6. Jonathan Wiener, "Class Structure and Economic Development in the American South," *American Historical Review* 84 (October 1979): 985. Marx is quoted in Reinhard Bendix, "Tradition and Modernity Reconsidered," *Comparative Studies in Society and History* 9 (1967): 292–346 (quotation on 308). My broader analysis in the pages that follow is heavily indebted to Bendix's essay.

7. James C. Cobb, *The Selling of the South: The Southern Crusade for Industrial Development, 1936–1990*, 2nd ed. (Urbana: University of Illinois Press, 1993), 171–75.

8. David L. Cohn, "The American Temperament," *Atlantic Monthly*, September 1951, 65.

9. David L. Carlton and Peter A. Coclanis, "The Uninventive South? A Quantitative Look at Region and American Inventiveness," *Technology and Culture* 36 (April 1995): 220–44.

10. Greg LeRoy, *The Great American Jobs Scam* (San Francisco: Berrett-Koehler, 2005), 35–37.

11. Cobb, *Selling of the South*, 230–31; James C. Cobb, *The South and America since World War II* (New York: Oxford University Press, 2010), 208.

12. James C. Cobb, "Beyond the 'Y'all Wall': The American South Goes Global," in *Globalization and the American South*, ed. James C. Cobb and William W. Stueck (Athens: University of Georgia Press 2005), 2; Marko Maunula, "Another Southern Paradox: The Arrival of Foreign Corporations, Change and Continuity in Spartanburg, South Carolina," in Cobb and Stueck, *Globalization and the American South*, 173–74 (quotation on 174).

13. Cobb, *Selling of the South*, 255.

14. "Opportunities for Japanese Manufacturers in South Carolina," South Carolina Department of Commerce, March 2006, quoted in Cobb, *The South and America*, 206. See also ibid., 340n10; and Cobb, *Selling of the South*, 255, 189.

15. Cobb, *The South and America*, 208.

16. Paul Nowell, "Officials of North Carolina Second-Guessing Themselves," *Tuscaloosa News*, October 10, 1993, http://news.google.com/newspapers?nid=1817&dat=19931010&id=Ej4dAAAAIBAJ&sjid=N6YEAAAAIBAJ&pg=6674,3175953 (accessed June 18, 2012) (Autry quote); "'Might Have Been,' Saddest of All Words," *Birmingham News*, June 16,

2002, http://nl.newsbank.com/nl-search/we/Archives/?p_action=keyword&s_search_type =keyword&p_product=NewsLibrary&p_theme=newslibrary2&d_sources=location&d _place=BI&p_nbid=& (accessed June 12, 2012) (N.C. developer quote); LeRoy, *Great American Jobs Scam*, 35.

17. LeRoy, *Great American Jobs Scam*, 37, 223n91; Paul Johnson and David Nivens, "Repaying Incentives: Governor Wants to Get Back 'Every Red Cent' from Dell," *High Point Enterprise*, October 9, 2009, http://issuu.com/hpenterprise/docs/hpe10092009/1.

18. "Dell to Outsource N.C. Jobs to Mexico," *Austin Business Chronicle*, October 16, 2009, http://www.bizjournals.com/austin/stories/2009/10/12/daily34.html; Cobb, *The South and America*, 209; "Key Industries: Textiles and Apparel," Learn North Carolina, http://www.learnnc.org/lp/editions/nchist-recent/6259 (accessed June 8, 2012); Daniel P. Gitterman, Peter A. Coclanis, and John Quinterno, "Recession and Recovery in North Carolina: A Data Snapshot, 2007–12," Global Research Institute, University of North Carolina, August 2012, http://gri.unc.edu/files/2012/08/GRI-Data-Snapshot-August-2012.pdf.

19. Research Triangle Park, "RTP Companies," http://www.rtp.org/about-rtp/rtp-companies (accessed July 6, 2012). See also Rick Weddle, "The Research Triangle Park: A Legacy of Economic Transformation . . . Lessons for Regional Economies," PowerPoint presentation, November 15, 2007, http://doi.wayne.edu/pdf/rick_weddle_presentationleaders _without_bordersnov_2007.pdf; and Cobb, *The South and America*, 210 (statistics).

20. Cobb, *The South and America*, 209–10, 341n17; North Carolina Rural Economic Development Center, "Our Manufacturing Future, Part 1: Findings" (2013), 5, http://www.ncindian.com/docs/NC%20Manufacturing%20Future%202013.pdf (accessed July 6, 2012).

21. Peter A. Coclanis and Louis M. Kyriakoudes, "Selling Which South: Economic Change in Rural and Small-Town North Carolina in an Era of Globalization, 1940–2007," *Southern Cultures* 13 (Winter 2007): 97; Peter Whoriskey, "Globalization Brings a World of Hurt to One Corner of North Carolina," *Washington Post*, November 10, 2009, http://www.washingtonpost.com/wp-dyn/content/article/2009/11/09/AR2009110903705.html ?sid=ST2009110903766 (accessed June 8, 2012) (employment official quote.).

22. David Bracken, "State Settles for Low-Wage Jobs," *News and Observer* (Raleigh, N.C.), September 19, 2010.

23. Kris Kromm, "Southerners Should Remember Seattle, State of the South," Institute for Southern Studies, http://www.southernstudies.org/records/seattle.html (accessed June 8, 2012); Dean Barber, "The China of the West: Why Mexico Is in the Driver's Seat," BarberBiz, October 27, 2013, http://deanbarber.wordpress.com/2013/10/27/the-china-of-the-west-why-mexico-is-in-the-drivers-seat/; see also "INSIGHT-RPT-Mexico Drives North American Auto Investment, Challenges China," Reuters, October 21, 2013, http://www.reuters.com/article/2013/10/21/autos-mexico-investment-idUSL1N0I81ZM20131021.

24. Mike Randle, "The Southern Auto Corridor: The Past, Present, and Future of the Center of North America's Automotive Universe," *Randle Report*, http://www.randlereport.com/Home/tabid/39/Article/82220/the-southern-auto-corridor-the-past-present-and-future-of-the-center-of-north-a.aspx (accessed July 15, 2012); Nedra Bloom, "Record Sales, Great Workers—but Maybe Not Forever," *Business Alabama*, March 2013, http://www.businessalabama.com/Business-Alabama/March-2013/Record-Sales-Great-Workers-But-Maybe-Not-Forever/ (accessed July 15, 2012) (Schaefer quote).

Lessons and Legacies 331

FAILING TO EXCITE

THE DIXIE DYNAMO IN THE GLOBAL ECONOMY

Peter A. Coclanis

The motivation for this essay—and the reason for placing it at the end of this collection—is presumably related to the fact that we are currently living in an uncertain period wherein North Carolina's principal economic problems, challenges, and opportunities have global dimensions or, at the very least, global connections.[1] This being the case, someone perforce had to take on North Carolina's engagement with the world over the last few decades, a period of rapid globalization, and speculate a bit about the future—about the direction of the state's "new voyages," in other words. Fair enough, I'll get to such matters by and by, but not right away. Let me take a moment to explain why.

From my perspective, North Carolina in many ways should be seen as a global region from the start, despite several periods of decelerating globalization or even deglobalization. This is so throughout its history, both when one conceives of globalization in a narrow economistic sense as a relative increase of transnational economic flows—products, capital, labor, and the like—over a sustained period of time and, even more emphatically, when one conceives of economic globalization more broadly as a process wherein the behavior and actions of economic actors are substantively affected, if not decisively shaped, by transnational processes, events, opportunities, and challenges.[2]

Viewed so, North Carolina was global even during its so-called Rip Van Winkle period in the nineteenth century—indeed, even before the first permanent settlement of Europeans and Africans in the Albemarle area in the 1650s and 1660s. And the ways in which the groups of elites that historically have controlled North Carolina engaged and responded to the problems, challenges, and opportunities attending globalization have had profound long-term consequences, shaping the state's developmental trajectory and imposing sharp limits on its options in subsequent periods. Economists like to use the concept of path dependence or path influence to capture this idea, which essentially means history matters, and in the case of North Carolina's development, history matters a lot.³

At this point, a rough periodization scheme for globalization is perhaps needed in order to structure North Carolina's historical policy responses, whether explicit or implicit. Although they often use different nomenclature and vary a bit on dating schemes, most global economic historians follow more or less the same basic periodization and conceptual scheme for globalization during the modern era, by which we basically mean the period between roughly 1450 or 1500 CE and the present. This scheme can be criticized for being somewhat Eurocentric—its fit with the West is better than with Asia—but because we are most interested in North Carolina's place in things, let us proceed. The first phase in modern globalization schemes generally runs from 1450 or 1500 until 1750 or 1800. The phase corresponds closely with the outward economic expansion of certain nation-states or other geopolitical entities in Europe to other parts of the world. Some writers break down this lengthy period into subperiods, with a period of slower expansion and growth in the seventeenth century (long or short). But, considered in toto, this was a period of economic dynamism in much of the West, the principal results of which were the beginnings of what could for the first time be called a real "world" economy, the relative economic rise of Europe or at least of parts thereof in the order of things, and the onset of a fundamental rerouting or reorientation of world economic power from East to West.⁴ As part of this process of economic restructuring, we see a global reallocation of labor and capital in a relative sense, perhaps most notably to what Kenneth Pomeranz has famously referred to as the "ghost acres" of the Americas. It was there that these factors of production were combined with American "land" (natural resources) to generate greater economic output, a preponderance of which output redounded over time to the advantage of European and Euro-American individuals and collectivities of one sort of another, for the processes of production and accumulation were initiated and led by the same.⁵ North Carolina's early development can be viewed as one very, very minor part of this global economic shift.

Abstracting a bit, in the area constituting what is now North Carolina the period between roughly 1650 and 1750 can be viewed as one of primitive extraction and accumulation, marked, as it was, by the enslavement and sale of Indians, piracy, lumbering, extractive forest industries—tar, pitch, turpentine, resin, and the like—and the beginnings of plantation agriculture in parts of the region, particularly in the area around Cape Fear in the southeast. Whatever else occurred in North Carolina during this murky period—

sources are much less complete than they are for neighboring South Carolina, which developed more rapidly—we can be sure that there was plenty of the "barbarism" that Marx associated with primitive accumulation and about which Bernard Bailyn has recently written so eloquently.[6] And by the end of the period, c. 1750, roughly 20 percent of the population of North Carolina was enslaved, a stark illustration at that time of social asymmetry and economic inequality and a harbinger of further asymmetries and inequalities to come.[7]

Most writers on the history of globalization argue that this early phase of globalization was followed by a second, more emphatic and fully realized phase running from the middle to late eighteenth century until around the time of the First World War. These writers employ slightly different chronologies; Eric J. Hobsbawm, for example, employs the concept of the "long" nineteenth century (1789-1914) to encapsulate this period, while Immanuel Wallerstein sometimes begins a bit earlier—c. 1750—but also sees this period ending in 1914, while C. A. Bayly, more recently, uses the dates 1780-1914.[8] Such small differences in chronology notwithstanding, what all three of these writers, and many others, see happening in this period is at once an acceleration and intensification in the process of global economic integration that the world had experienced in the period beginning in c. 1450-1500 CE.

During this period, the U.S. South, already an important source of staple commodities for the Western world—tobacco and rice, most notably—became the entire world's leading exporter of cotton, linking the region's fortunes closely to those of rapidly industrializing parts of what some refer to as the core and others the metropolis and still others, less grandiosely, Lancashire and New England. Indeed, such was the importance of cotton from the U.S. South to both globalization and industrialization during the long nineteenth century that Hobsbawm, who coined that term, has argued that the true importance of the American Civil War in world historical terms was "the transfer of the South from the informal empire of Britain (to whose cotton industry it was the economic pendant) into the new major industrial economy of the United States, which economy was dominated, of course, by the victorious North." Hobsbawm goes on to argue, moreover, that this transfer "might be regarded as an early if giant step on the road which was in the twentieth century to turn all the Americas from a British to an American economic dependency."[9] But enough about the twentieth century—we are getting ahead of ourselves.

What of North Carolina during this long period? The state increasingly found its niche as a provider of raw materials and agricultural staples (cotton, tobacco) for world markets and, after c. 1880, as a provider of relatively rudimentary processed manufactured goods (textiles, tobacco products, and later furniture) as well. The Old North State was hardly one of the South's agricultural leaders in the nineteenth century, but it did partake in the principal developmental patterns informing the region, and it did pick up its economic pace a bit in a relative sense in the latter part of the century. It was the ninth largest cotton-producing state in 1860, for example, and the eighth largest in 1900. It was the fifth largest tobacco producer in 1860 but rose to second in 1900, although it still remained far behind Kentucky in overall production.[10]

What about manufacturing production? The general public—and, alas, more historians than one would think—believe that North Carolina had become one of the South's manufacturing leaders by the end of the nineteenth century. The state may not have been one of the principal plantation states of the South, this line goes, but because of the rise of the cotton-textiles industry, it had become one of the region's manufacturing bellwethers by 1900. Well, not really. Measured in terms of the total value of manufacturing product, North Carolina's relative position in the region actually slipped from sixth in 1860 to eighth in 1900, in the latter year trailing behind Maryland, Kentucky, Virginia, Louisiana, Texas, Georgia, and Tennessee. Even if we define the South more narrowly and exclude Maryland and Kentucky, North Carolina only rises to sixth. Interestingly, North Carolina's relative decline in manufacturing between 1860 and 1900 becomes even greater if one uses this narrower definition of the South. By excluding Maryland and Kentucky, North Carolina moves up to number four in manufacturing output in the South in 1860, trailing only Virginia, Tennessee, and Georgia, which means that Texas and Louisiana had leapfrogged the Tar Heel State in the late nineteenth century.[11] To be sure, the textiles complex that emerged in North Carolina after 1880 would later prove instrumental to the state's rising economic fortunes, but that sector was not yet large enough in 1900 to move the needle significantly.

Interestingly, the role of tobacco in nineteenth-century North Carolina is similarly misunderstood today. While the relative importance did in fact grow dramatically in North Carolina in the late nineteenth century with the rise of "bright" tobacco, the industry was not yet sufficiently powerful to lift the agricultural sector, much less the state as a whole, out of the economic doldrums. Even though North Carolina had risen to number two in tobacco production in the United States by 1900, the state still produced only about

40 percent of the amount of tobacco (primarily burley) produced in Kentucky. It was not until much later in the twentieth century that North Carolina came to dominate tobacco production in the United States.[12]

Whether we focus on agriculture or manufacturing, we find that throughout the "long" nineteenth century in North Carolina most production occurred under conditions of tight controls over labor, whether slave or free, agricultural or industrial. Remember that roughly one-third of the state's population was enslaved in 1860, and even after the end of slavery, agricultural labor, however free in a titular sense, often worked under tight constraints of one sort or another.[13] Industrial labor, too, was subjected to considerable regimentation, whether in lumber camps, turpentine orchards, or cotton-textile mills.[14] Not surprisingly, there were social and political concomitants of such a labor regime. We find little state investment in human capital of any form, for example, and but for a few exceptional—and brief—periods (Congressional Reconstruction, Fusionism in the 1890s), very tight political control by a narrow and narrow-minded white elite.

The upshot of elite control over the state, from a developmental perspective, was a thin and attenuated economic base in North Carolina, characterized by many structural weaknesses. Briefly put, North Carolina's economy was characterized throughout the nineteenth century by a large primary sector and a relatively rudimentary secondary sector; a thin, disarticulate internal market; a linear, conveyor-belt transportation system; low levels of support for education, public health, and other public goods; and highly unequal distributions of income and wealth. In other words, the economy in many parts of North Carolina very much resembled those of other plantation-based states in the South.[15] If the state did not have plantation districts such as those in the South Carolina–Georgia Low Country, the Natchez area of Mississippi, or southeastern Louisiana, or even such as that emerging in the Mississippi-Arkansas Delta, it nonetheless was home to many large plantations, particularly in the eastern part of the state, and shared many of the characteristics and, alas, socioeconomic pathologies of these other, better-known plantation districts.[16] In this regard, keep in mind the name Halifax County, a plantation district in the eastern part of the state, for it will reappear later in this essay.

In any case, circa 1900, as William Link has pointed out, the state, which never reaped the same level of benefits that had accrued from plantation agriculture in these other areas, was known for its poverty, illiteracy, and underdevelopment—even in a southern context—as much as anything else.[17] Indeed, North Carolina was still known for these things as late as the middle of the twentieth century and had the dubious distinction of being one of the poorest states in the South, the poorest region in the United States—ahead of only Mississippi and Arkansas—as late as 1952.[18]

Back to 1900, though: At the turn of the last century, North Carolina was in trouble, and as a result, during the so-called Progressive Era momentum began to build among political and economic elites to invest somewhat more in infrastructure, public education, and human capital. Such investments were in fact made, impacting the state's development in a positive way on balance, despite the fact that most of these investments were made in ways that continued to discriminate explicitly or implicitly on the basis of race and class. Moreover, the policy preferences and patterns established during the early twentieth century continued during the next phase of the global economy during the 1920s and 1930s. It was during these interwar decades, for example, that the University of North Carolina was transformed from irrelevancy into a force for social betterment not only in North Carolina but also in the South as a whole.[19]

Before moving on to this next phase in the global economy, a few words are in order about the accuracy of a label North Carolina has worn for some time with respect to the nineteenth century: the Rip Van Winkle State. Although various commentators disagree about the label's origins and even its meaning, most of those who employ the label use it in some way to suggest that the state was "asleep," if not dormant, during much of the century, that not much "was going on anywhere" in the state for parts of the century, and that the state was little interested in economic development.[20]

There are a number of problems with this formulation, especially if we are speaking of the state's economy. For starters, North Carolina, as we have seen, was already well integrated into extraregional, indeed, transatlantic factor and product markets even during the colonial period, and such integration only intensified in the nineteenth century with the spread of cotton and tobacco cultivation in the state and the rise of the cotton-textiles industry in the 1880s and 1890s. Charges of state-level torpor and somnolence notwithstanding, North Carolina and North Carolinians were very much "awake," interested in economic development of a limited sort, and part of the wider world during that century. Two anecdotes involving African/African Americans attest improbably but amply to this last point: an African Muslim slave living in the Wilmington area wrote an autobiography in Arabic in 1831, and a Hindi-speaking African American from the state was one of the builders in 1899–1900 of the Gokteik Viaduct, a world-famous railroad trestle in the remote Shan State of Burma.[21] Who would have thunk it?

There is clear evidence of international attachments, then—and many more examples can be referenced. But one must nonetheless always keep in mind that the degree of global consciousness and level of global engagement in evidence in North Carolina were clearly shaped and structured—and ultimately delimited—by the state's political economy. In developmental terms, North Carolina got precisely what the elites who controlled the state wished for in the nineteenth century: an "extractive" economic and institutional framework, based upon arbitrary power, a narrow political base, rigged markets, and a capricious legal system, all of which redounded to the advantage of small groups of insiders. Poverty and underdevelopment may have been the result for the masses, but that mattered little to the ever watchful elite, which was able to garner a disproportionate share of power and resources while keeping the masses, but for brief outbursts, in a position of political repose. In many ways, then, nineteenth-century North Carolina comports well with the "extractive" state template developed recently by Daron Acemoglu and James Robinson in *Why Nations Fail: The Origins of Power, Prosperity, and Poverty*.[22]

During the second decade of the twentieth century the world entered into another economic phase, this one quite unexpected. For a variety of reasons—two monumental wars, a great depression, political upheavals, and an economic and sociopolitical backlash against globalization—the world deglobalized between 1914 and 1945, a period some refer to as that of "the Second Thirty Years' War." Economic trends and patterns long in evidence—robust transnational flows of capital, trade, and labor—were all reversed during this period, as the world suffered through three decades of severe economic stresses, myriad political and social woes, and truly cataclysmic military conflicts.[23]

Not surprisingly, North Carolina's economy, which had shown a bit of spark early in the twentieth century, was adversely affected by these changes, finding itself in a dizzying downward spiral by the early 1930s, from an already pinched and parlous economic position. Per capita income in North Carolina in 1929, for example, was but 47.4 percent of the national average, while living costs in the state, as represented by the Consumer Price Index, were 71 percent of the national average.[24] And, in an absolute sense, at least, things only got worse. The agricultural economy, which had been rebuilt in a retrograde manner after the demise of slavery, completely collapsed during the 1930s, and the state's textiles industry, scissored by overproduction and underconsumption and buffeted by competition, found itself in crisis as well.

North Carolina's political leaders attempted to respond, extending the "Progressive" framework established in the decades before the First World War, with continued investment in infrastructure (especially roads), education, and public health, but the approach to development was still narrow, top down, and subject to many class/racial constraints. If "Progressivism" was "for whites only," as C. Vann Woodward put it, the interwar years meant more of the same. The "progressive plutocracy" that V. O. Key Jr. talked about after the Second World War was already busy promoting and protecting its programs and initiatives—and prerogatives—albeit at the same time attempting to beat back even more retrograde political forces at home, forces represented by Josiah Bailey and anti–New Deal pols of his ilk, not to mention business interests represented by reactionaries such as David Clark of the *Southern Textile Bulletin*.[25] In any case, understanding and interpreting "Progressivism" is a trickier proposition than it might appear to be on the surface, laden, as the concept is, with ambiguity. To be sure, the adjective "progressive" can connote improvement and amelioration, but it can also merely mean moving to another phase or stage, or even getting worse or advancing in severity, as in a progressive disease. Progressivism as made manifest in North Carolina can fit comfortably under any of these definitions, depending on what one chooses to emphasize, what one chooses to see.

However one chooses to interpret "progressive plutocratic" policies in postwar North Carolina, the broader economic landscape wherein they were hatched was a far cry from that of the interwar years. Beginning in 1945 the entire world economy entered another phase of globalization, one that, despite some short reversals, we are still living through today. Although most scholars view the entire period since 1945 as one of globalization, many break the epoch into two subperiods, the first lasting from 1945 to the 1970s, and the second beginning c. 1980. Both subperiods were marked by robust transnational economic flows over sustained periods of time, but the intensity of such flows accelerated and intensified in the latter subperiod. For the world as a whole, the surge in globalization was on balance extremely positive, especially for less developed countries, but in a relative sense much of the population of the United States—and certainly much of the population of North Carolina—clearly benefited more in a relative sense at least during the first subperiod than they have in the second.[26]

In terms of public policy in North Carolina, the main takeaway, I believe, is that the business-oriented, pro-development governmental responses in both subperiods were often on balance pretty sound—and in some cases prescient, inspired, and even admirable—within the confines of what Key called plutocratic progressivism and what others have subsequently (perhaps more charitably) referred to as business progressivism.[27] That said, governmental responses were much more successful in the first subperiod, and in my view they will have to change going forward if they are to achieve such success again. Why? Because of the path-dependent nature of the state's history or, in other words, because of the legacies of the implicit economic development strategy that has characterized much of North Carolina's history virtually from the start.

The key to North Carolina's growth strategy in the postwar decades—indeed, to the strategy of the Sunbelt considered as a whole—was the removal of a huge number of marginalized workers out of a backward, dreadfully inefficient, low-skill, undercapitalized agricultural sector and into sectors where even unskilled labor such as theirs could be employed more efficiently. Where? For the most part in low-skill, low-value-added manufacturing industries (particularly those of an assembly or processing rather than fabricating nature).[28] While such industries (textiles and apparel, furniture, tobacco products, light assembly, food processing, etc.) aren't great, by adding capital to human labor they significantly increased productivity, allowing for rising wages, income, and living standards for increasing proportions of the state's population. In this, the state (and the region as a whole) was following (or at least repeating) a tried-and-true, time-tested development strategy that most other areas of the developed world had already experienced: the move from agriculture to light industry. To be sure, new industries were beginning to emerge in the period, and obviously there was the growing importance of banking and finance and the (slow) rise to prominence of the Research Triangle Park, but the big story, developmentally speaking, was getting people off the farms—not into investment houses or labs but into factories, mills, and plants. It was this process, more than anything else, that allowed North Carolina and the South to grow. In terms of per capita income, for example, the mean figure for the South was only 60 percent of that of the United States in 1940 and a little over 70 percent in 1950, but the rise of manufacturing in the 1950s, 1960s, and 1970s brought this figure up to the 87 or 88 percent of national norms by the late 1970s.[29]

By the 1980s, however, this very successful strategy began to play itself out. As technological change reduced labor requirements in southern manufacturing and jobs were increasingly lost to other lower-cost parts of the world due to globalization, the Sunbelt's convergence upon national economic norms slowed before coming entirely to a stop in the early 1990s. Southern per capital income—with the "South" defined as the states comprising the Confederate States of America plus West Virginia and Kentucky—has been stuck at about 90 percent of the national average since then and would likely be trending lower without the outlier Texas, whose energy-based economy has been doing fairly well in recent years.[30]

Even before the end of convergence, the "lead story" of the so-called Sunbelt was misleading—or at least incomplete. As the North Carolina–based policy center MDC, Inc., put it in a seminal report in 1986, there were, even then, many "shadows" in the Sunbelt, particularly in rural and nonmetropolitan parts of the region. And once the decline of light industry accelerated in the 1990s and the first decade of the twenty-first century, these areas have often become economic basket cases, forlorn if not hopeless places, beset by every imaginable social pathology, places where the best economic development strategy is often "a ham sandwich and a one-way bus ticket out."[31]

To be sure, the trajectory of better-situated parts of the region—metro areas (particularly financial centers and information and communication technology hubs populated in large part by what Richard Florida calls the "creative class"), tourist areas, affluent retirement communities, energy-rich areas, and areas around major universities, military bases, government centers—have done better economically, increasingly pulling away from the rural and nonmetropolitan South. But even the dynamism of such areas has not been able to lift the economic fortunes of all of the residents living therein—all of the major metropolitan areas of both North Carolina and other parts of the South include zones of terrifically high poverty—much less of the region as a whole.[32]

In many ways, what we are seeing in the South looks a lot like what many development economists call a "middle-income trap," wherein economies stagnate after reaching a certain "middle" level, usually because their manufacturing and labor-cost structures no longer allow them to compete with lower-cost producers, but their labor forces aren't skilled enough to compete higher up the value chain.[33] Once so ensnared, it has proven hard historically for nations to escape this condition. Indeed, in international context, the motto of southern workers—including North Carolina workers—reads "I'm pretty expensive and not very skilled." And there doesn't seem to be much in the way of political will to change things, at least in North Carolina, a state some people for some reason still see as different from other parts of the South. As my friend Ferrel Guillory noted long ago, though, "the farther you get from North Carolina, the more progressive it looks."[34] That is to say, once you're here, you know the truth.

For some sobering context about both North Carolina and the South more generally, let's think globally, as the cliché goes. In Bangladesh, even after a state-mandated 77 percent increase in November 2013—effective December 1—the minimum wage for textile workers was roughly $68.00 a month. The absolute minimum workweek there is fifty hours per week or two hundred hours per month—which means wages of 34 cents an hour. Many of these workers have access to the same technology as do Southern

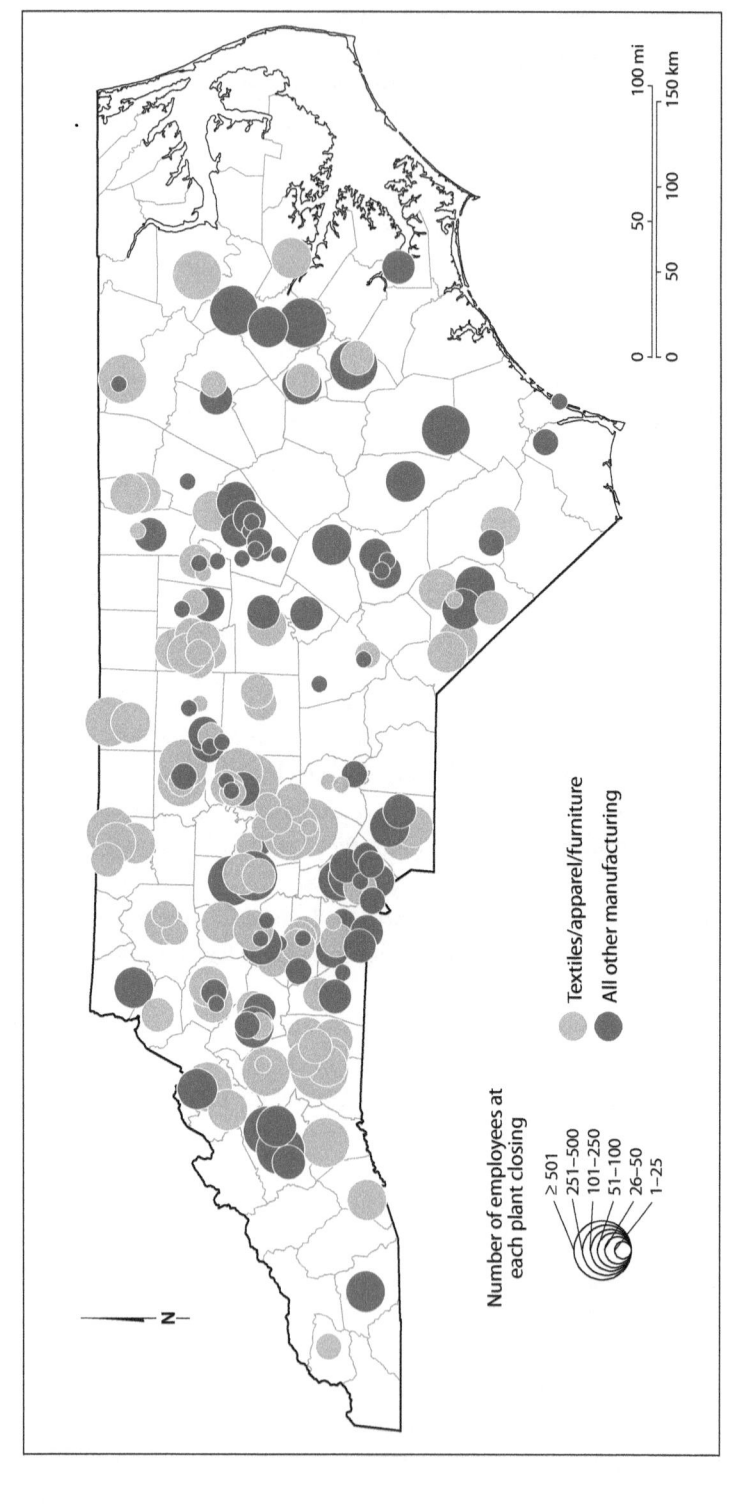

workers—one major reason that Bangladesh is a major supplier for Tommy Hilfiger, the Gap, Calvin Klein, H&M, and so forth.[35] David Carlton and I wrote a piece in 2005 called "Southern Textiles in Global Context," which emphasized this same point but focused on earlier periods in the industry's history.[36] Then as now, the South, a low-cost manufacturer in a United States or even North American context, is a very high-cost manufacturer when viewed in a global context. Tens of thousands of displaced textile and apparel workers in North Carolina know this all too well. And such displacement did not begin or end with the much-mentioned closure of the Pillowtex facility in Kannapolis in July 2003, the largest plant closure in North Carolina history, which led to the termination of almost 5,000 workers in one fell swoop (see fig. 14.1).[37]

With these points in mind, it shouldn't surprise anyone that the South in general and the state of North Carolina in particular were hit so hard by the recession of 2007–9. North Carolina's unemployment rate was one of the highest in the nation from the onset of the recession until well into 2013, and even in January 2014—four and a half years after the end of the recession—it was still 6.7 percent, higher than the national average. Moreover, despite the fact that the unemployment rate fell sharply in 2013, there were still 71,000 fewer payroll positions in North Carolina in January 2014 than in December 2007—in a state growing rapidly in population.[38] In fact, the structural factors just discussed, combined with the problems in Charlotte's financial sector (with Wachovia/Wells Fargo and Bank of America), the state's heavy concentration on manufacturing, the collapse of the construction industry, and continuing robust in-migration, mean that the state's labor market has been really stressed, especially since it never really recovered from the recession of 2000–2001. In net terms, North Carolina in 2011 had only 0.3 percent more jobs than it had in 2000—despite the fact that the population of the state grew by 18.5 percent between 2000 and 2010.[39] Very distressing data indeed.

Income data tell much the same tale. Median household income in the state from 2008 through 2012 was $46,450—about 87.6 percent of the national average. A just-released study has found that the gap between median household income in the state and the national average in 2013 was the greatest it has been since 1984 and that, in real terms, median household in-

(*opposite*) FIGURE 14.1. This map charts a sudden wave of manufacturing-plant closings in North Carolina during 2003 and 2004, undermining the state's long-standing appeal as an industrial haven with a lower-wage workforce. There were 185 manufacturing plant closings involving 26,609 employees. Data from Employment Security Commission of North Carolina.

come in North Carolina had not grown since 1984. Figures for per capita income are similar: in 2012 the figure for North Carolina ($37,910) was about 87 percent of that of the United States as a whole, placing the state thirty-ninth in the nation. The cost-of-living index for North Carolina is about 96 percent of the national average, so the income figures can't be explained away, as they sometimes are, by claiming that low income is more than made up for by low living costs.[40]

And what about poverty levels in the state? One result of North Carolina's protracted economic difficulties, not surprisingly, has been a significant rise in poverty and near poverty in the state during the last decade: the poverty rate in the state in 2012 was about 18 percent, well above the rate (16 percent) in the United States as a whole.[41] As many economists and business analysts have recently pointed out, we have slowly come out of the recession—North Carolina tends to lag national recoveries—but what are we coming out to?[42]

Unemployment and poverty will likely go down as the economy gathers momentum, but the state's stock of human capital is still relatively low, and the current administration isn't likely to improve it much. And even if it does improve, what are the prospects for much of the North Carolina's labor force—indeed, much of the U.S. labor force—to get good jobs in the years ahead? Seven of the ten occupations predicted to grow fastest in North Carolina by 2018 demand less than a high-school diploma: home health aides, food preparation and serving workers, retail salespersons, cashiers, waiters and waitresses, personal and home care aides, and landscaping and groundskeeping workers.[43] Only one—accountants and auditors—demands a bachelor's degree. Moreover, if scholars such as Erik Brynjolfsson and Andrew McAfee are correct, that's not the half of it. In two well-regarded books, *Race against the Machine* (2011) and *The Second Machine Age* (2014), the authors argue that, whereas until now technological change has always added jobs in a net sense, this may no longer be the case.[44] The fact that Foxconn—the biggest assembler of electronics, including the iPhone, in China, where it employs over one million workers—is increasingly replacing its workers with what it calls its "robot army" is enough to give one pause. That the company hopes to be employing only technicians and engineers in China a few years from now should be enough to stop us in our tracks. If Foxconn succeeds in so doing, it will provide evidence in support of Brynjolfsson and McAfee's provocative point that "offshoring is often only a way station on the road to automation."[45]

But back to the South, where a huge number of jobs have already been offshored. Although overstated, Michael Lind's controversial 2013 piece in

Salon, titled "Southern Poverty Pimps: The 'Original Sin' of the Southern Political Class Is Cheap, Powerless Labor," contains more than an element of truth.[46] The fact that in 2013 North Carolina still had the lowest rate of unionization of any state—3.0 percent—is only the beginning.[47] Many of the poorest parts of the South today—the most plantation-intensive areas— were once the richest. In North Carolina, for example, forlorn Halifax County—home of the late lamented Randy Parton Dinner Theater and not much else—is one of the poorest counties. It once was among the wealthiest. A few years ago, a team of economic development specialists at the University of North Carolina at Chapel Hill was engaged to create a growth plan for the town of Enfield in that county. After a lot of work, the authors produced a lengthy study, the principal conclusion of which was that the future of the town, which had once flourished, was extremely precarious, maybe even hopeless. Some recommendations were made at the margin, but little of substance could be done.[48] Why? To invoke the memorable title of Linda Flowers's well-known book, another place in eastern North Carolina had been "throwed away" by history.[49] And there are plenty of Enfields all over the state.

North Carolina, going in and coming out of the Great Recession, is essentially two states—one with some future possibilities, one burdened unduly by developmental strategies of the past. To be sure, economic development can be viewed as being about places or about people, and this distinction matters. Fifty years ago Beaufort County, South Carolina, was desperately poor; now it is the richest county in South Carolina, ranking first in personal per capita income. Was it because the people living in Beaufort in 1960 and their descendants somehow acquired vast new stocks of human capital and saw their fortunes change dramatically as a result? Hardly. It was because the development of Hilton Head and other rich beachfront resort communities drove out the old, largely African American population and imported affluent outsiders from other parts of South Carolina, the South, and the United States to take their place.[50]

Clearly, some people and some places in North Carolina are well positioned to benefit from technological change and globalization. Others are not. Cary and Morrisville, *sí*, Lumberton, Roanoke Rapids, and Forest City, *no*.[51] And I've written an entire article on the problems splayed before us up and down Highway 52.[52] It is up to us to try to come up with sufficiently creative public-sector and private-sector initiatives to bring greater equity and justice to these vast forces, or the economic future of North Carolina, playing off of Faulkner, is both gone and past.

The developmental successes we have achieved over time in North Carolina have been real but built on too narrow a base, with the state's middle class, however much expanded, still far too narrow to transform the state. The North Carolina development strategy historically has been ameliorist at best, with elites never willing *really* to share control. Too often they have acted as an old boy (and, more recently, old boy and girl) network, opting for rather conservative, begrudging approaches to development, akin in spirit and effect to that implied in the young Sicilian aristocrat Tancredi's famous quote in Giuseppe Tomasi di Lampedusa's great novel *The Leopard*: "If we want things to stay as they are, things will have to change."[53] And this is the kind of conservative approach to development—one minimizing structural change—that North Carolina has generally done well. Plutocratic progressivisim, business progressivism, call it what you will. Unfortunately, whatever it is called, it will no longer do in the increasingly borderless, ruthlessly competitive global world in which we live today. Going forward we'll need higher aspirations and broader empathies than those evident in our historic developmental strategies to date if we are to break the yoke of history, the prison of path dependency, and move ahead. If not, the economic outlook for much of the population of North Carolina is bleak, and for most of the rest, uncertain.

NOTES

1. In 1962 an article on North Carolina appeared in *National Geographic* titled "North Carolina: Dixie Dynamo." The piece garnered a lot of attention and was adopted by many politicians, economic development apparatchiks, and members of the business community as the unofficial nickname of the state. Some people still recognize the nickname even today. See Malcolm Ross, "North Carolina: Dixie Dynamo," *National Geographic* 121 (February 1962): 141–83. This chapter grew out of a paper prepared for a conference in Greensboro in March 2013. The paper was part of a session titled "Dixie Dynamo," hence its title.

2. The literature on globalization is vast, and definitions of the concept and globalization periodization schemes many. For a narrower economic view, focusing on the relative increase of transnational economic flows, see, e.g., Paul Krugman, *The Accidental Theorist and Other Dispatches from the Dismal Science* (New York: Norton, 1998), 73. Note, though, that other economists privilege different measurable phenomena to gauge globalization—price convergence, for example. See Kevin H. O'Rourke and Jeffrey G. Williamson, "When Did Globalisation Begin?," *European Review of Economic History* 6 (April 2002): 23–50; and O'Rourke and Williamson, "Once More: When Did Globalisation Begin?," *European Review of Economic History* 8 (April 2004): 109–17. By focusing narrowly on measurable, quantitative variables, most economists tend to see globalization as a relatively recent historical process, commencing in the nineteenth century. For broader socioeconomic approaches emphasizing qualitative changes, see Thomas L. Friedman, *The Lexus and the Olive Tree: Understanding Globalization* (New York: Farrar, Straus, and Giroux, 1999), esp. 59; David Harvey,

The Condition of Postmodernity: An Enquiry into the Origins of Cultural Change (Oxford: Blackwell, 1990), 173–88; Manuel Castells, "European Cities, the Informational Society, and the Global Economy," *New Left Review* 204 (March/April 1994): 18–32, esp. 21; and David Harvey, *Spaces of Hope* (Berkeley: University of California Press, 2000), 59. For a good, succinct history of globalization, see Jürgen Osterhammel and Niels P. Peterssen, *Globalization: A Short History* (Princeton, N.J.: Princeton University Press, 2005). On the welter of periodization schemes, see, e.g., Jan Nederveen Pieterse, "Periodizing Globalization: Histories of Globalization," *New Global Studies* 6 (July 2012): 1–24.

3. More formally, "path dependence" can be defined as a causal sequence in which the eventual outcome is virtually predetermined by antecedent factors or events. These factors or events may be proximate or remote in temporal terms and either circumstantial or structural in nature. "Path influence" relaxes the determinism somewhat while retaining the implication that numerous outcomes are excluded because of antecedent factors or events. For an excellent introduction to the concept, see Douglas Puffert, "Path Dependence," *EH.Net Encyclopedia*, ed. Robert Whaples, February 10, 2008, http://eh.net/encyclopedia/path-dependence/.

4. On the many scholars employing such periodization schemes, see, e.g., Pieterse, "Periodizing Globalization."

5. "Ghost acres" is a term coined in the 1960s denoting external, often underpopulated lands that can be utilized by a given area or country for additional "carrying capacity," thereby easing "land" (natural-resource) constraints and allowing for additional economic production, surplus extraction, etc. Some scholars in recent years have argued that the Americas after 1492 served such a function for Europe. For one inspired attempt to employ the concept in such a way, see Kenneth Pomeranz, *The Great Divergence: China, Europe, and the Making of the Modern World Economy* (Princeton, N.J.: Princeton University Press, 2000), 264–97.

6. Karl Marx, *Capital*, ed. Frederick Engels, trans. Samuel Moore and Edward Aveling, 3 vols. (New York: International Publishers, 1967; originally published in German, 1867–1894), 1:713–74; Bernard Bailyn, *The Barbarous Years: The Peopling of British North America: The Conflict of Civilizations, 1600-1675* (New York: Knopf, 2012).

7. For estimates of the enslaved population of North Carolina c. 1750–1770, see A. Roger Ekirch, *"Poor Carolina": Politics and Society in Colonial North Carolina, 1729-1776* (Chapel Hill: University of North Carolina Press, 1981), 11; and Marvin L. Michael Kay and Lorin Lee Cary, *Slavery in North Carolina, 1748-1775* (Chapel Hill: University of North Carolina Press, 1995), 226–27, table 1.2.

8. See Eric J. Hobsbawm's trilogy on the "long nineteenth century": *The Age of Revolution: 1789-1848* (New York: New American Library, 1962), *The Age of Capital: 1848-1875* (New York: Charles Scribner's Sons, 1975), and *The Age of Empire: 1875-1914* (New York: Pantheon, 1987); Immanuel Wallerstein, *The Modern World-System*, 4 vols. (New York: Academic Press, 1974–89; repr., Berkeley: University of California Press, 2011); and C. A. Bayly, *The Birth of the Modern World 1780-1914: Global Connections and Comparisons* (Oxford: Blackwell, 2004).

9. Hobsbawm, *The Age of Capital: 1848-1875*, 82. On the role of U.S. cotton in the world economy in the nineteenth century, see especially Sven Beckert, *Empire of Cotton: A Global History* (New York: Knopf, 2014).

10. Rankings drawn from U.S. census data brought together in Donald B. Dodd and Wynelle S. Dodd, comps., *Historical Statistics of the South 1790-1970* (University: University of Alabama Press, 1973).

11. Rankings drawn from U.S. census data brought together in ibid.

12. Rankings and figures for tobacco production are based on U.S. census data brought together in ibid. Note, however, that bright tobacco, which predominated in North Carolina, generally sold at much higher prices than did burley tobacco, which dominated in Kentucky.

13. See U.S. Department of Commerce, Bureau of the Census, *Eighth Census of the United States, 1860: Population* (Washington, D.C.: Government Printing Office, 1864), 348–57. North Carolina's total population in 1860 was 992,622, broken down in the following way: whites, 629,942; free colored, 30,463; slaves, 331,059; Indians, 1,158. The percentage enslaved was 33.4 percent.

14. On the tight, coercive labor regimen in North Carolina, see, e.g., Philip J. Wood, *Southern Capitalism: The Political Economy of North Carolina 1880-1980* (Durham, N.C.: Duke University Press, 1986). On the tight labor controls in the North Carolina lumber industry and labor's efforts to loosen them, see William P. Jones, *The Tribe of Black Ulysses: African American Lumber Workers in the Jim Crow South* (Urbana: University of Illinois Press, 2005). Note that one of Jones's cases centers on Elizabethtown, N.C.

15. See, e.g., Wood, *Southern Capitalism*; Dwight B. Billings Jr., *Planters and the Making of a "New South": Class, Politics, and Development in North Carolina, 1865-1900* (Chapel Hill: University of North Carolina Press, 1979). Note that both Wood and Billings tend to downplay some of the real changes that were in fact beginning to occur in parts of North Carolina (particularly in the Piedmont) in the late nineteenth century. On these changes, see David L. Carlton, "The Revolution from Above: The National Market and the Beginnings of Industrialization in North Carolina," *Journal of American History* 77 (September 1990): 445–75; and David L. Carlton and Peter A. Coclanis, "Capital Mobilization and Southern Industry, 1880-1905: The Case of the Carolina Piedmont," *Journal of Economic History* 49 (March 1989): 73–94. For an extreme example of the economic structure to which most plantation areas of the South tended, see Peter A. Coclanis, *The Shadow of a Dream: Economic Life and Death in the South Carolina Low Country, 1670-1920* (New York: Oxford University Press, 1989).

16. There are few modern general studies of slavery or even of agriculture in nineteenth-century North Carolina, though there are some excellent local and regional studies. See, e.g., Edward W. Phifer, "Slavery in Microcosm: Burke County, North Carolina," *Journal of Southern History* 28 (May 1962): 137–65; and John C. Inscoe, *Mountain Masters, Slavery, and the Sectional Crisis in Western North Carolina* (Knoxville: University of Tennessee Press, 1989). On agriculture in antebellum North Carolina, see two studies by Cornelius O. Cathey: *Agricultural Developments in North Carolina, 1783-1860*, James Sprunt Series in History and Political Science, vol. 38 (Chapel Hill: University of North Carolina Press, 1956); and *Agriculture in North Carolina before the Civil War* (Raleigh, N.C.: Division of Archives and History, 1966).

17. William A. Link, *North Carolina: Change and Tradition in a Southern State* (Wheeling, Ill.: Harlan Davidson, 2009), 289.

18. Ibid., 376.

19. On southern progressivism, see, e.g., C. Vann Woodward, *Origins of the New South*,

1877-1913 (Baton Rouge: Louisiana State University Press, 1951), 369-95; George B. Tindall, *The Emergence of the New South, 1913-1945* (Baton Rouge: Louisiana State University Press, 1967), 219-53; Dewey W. Grantham, *Southern Progressivism: The Reconciliation of Progress and Tradition* (Knoxville: University of Tennessee Press, 1983); and William A. Link, *The Paradox of Southern Progressivism, 1880-1930* (Chapel Hill: University of North Carolina Press, 1992). On some of the effects of progressive reform on education in North Carolina specifically, see J. Morgan Kousser, "Progressivism—for Middle-Class Whites Only: North Carolina, 1880-1910," *Journal of Southern History* 46 (May 1980): 169-94; James L. Leloudis, *Schooling the New South: Pedagogy, Self, and Society in North Carolina, 1880-1920* (Chapel Hill: University of North Carolina Press, 1996), 143-228; and Rob Christensen, *The Paradox of Tar Heel Politics: The Personalities, Elections, and Events That Shaped Modern North Carolina* (Chapel Hill: University of North Carolina Press, 2008), 39-45. On the rise to prominence in the 1920s and 1930s of the University of North Carolina, see Michael O'Brien, *The Idea of the American South, 1920-1941* (Baltimore: Johns Hopkins University Press, 1979), 3-27, 213-27; and Daniel Joseph Singal, *The War Within: From Victorian to Modernist Thought in the South, 1919-1945* (Chapel Hill: University of North Carolina Press, 1982), 115-52, 265-338.

20. On the varying ways in which the label is employed in general histories of North Carolina, see, e.g., William S. Powell, *North Carolina through Four Centuries* (Chapel Hill: University of North Carolina Press, 1989), 245; Link, *North Carolina*, 151-52; and Milton Ready, *The Tar Heel State: A History of North Carolina* (Columbia: University of South Carolina Press, 2005), 13, 360-61.

21. See Omar Ibn Said, *A Muslim American Slave: The Life of Omar Ibn Said*, trans. and ed. Ala Alryyes (Madison: University of Wisconsin Press, 2011); and J. C. Turk, "Building an American Bridge in Burma," *World's Work* 2 (September 1901): 1148-67, esp. 1166.

22. See Daron Acemoglu and James A. Robinson, *Why Nations Fail: The Origins of Power, Prosperity, and Poverty* (New York: Crown Business, 2012).

23. See, e.g., Harold James, *The End of Globalization: Lessons from the Great Depression* (Cambridge, Mass.: Harvard University Press, 2001); and Jari Eloranta and Mark Harrison, "War and Disintegration, 1914-1945," in *The Cambridge Economic History of Modern Europe*, ed. Stephen Broadberry and Kevin H. O'Rourke, 2 vols. (Cambridge: Cambridge University Press, 2010), 2:133-55.

24. See U.S. Department of Commerce, Census Bureau, *Statistical Abstract of the United States: The National Data Book* (Washington, D.C.: U.S. Department of Commerce, 2004), 66-67, https://www.census.gov/statab/hist/HS-35.pdf (accessed March 3, 2014). The data are from the U.S. Bureau of Economic Analysis, *Survey of Current Business* (May 2002), and from the bureau's unpublished data. On the Consumer Price Index in North Carolina in 1929, see Abner Hurwitz and Carlyle P. Stallings, "Interregional Differentials in Per Capita Real Income Change," in *Regional Income*, Studies in Income and Wealth, vol. 21, National Bureau of Economic Research, Conference on Research in Income and Wealth (Princeton, N.J.: Princeton University Press, 1957), 195-270, esp. 226, table A-2. Note that Hurwitz and Stallings actually put per capita income in North Carolina as a percentage of the U.S. average at 46.6 percent, a bit lower than the figure used in the text. See ibid., 252, table A-7.

25. Woodward, *Origins of the New South*, 369-95; Tindall, *Emergence of the New South*, 219-84; V. O. Key Jr., *Southern Politics in State and Nation*, with Alexander Heard (New

York: Knopf, 1949), 205–28; Christensen, *Paradox of Tar Heel Politics*, 35–108; David L. Carlton and Peter A. Coclanis, "Another 'Great Migration': From Region to Race in Southern Liberalism, 1938–1945," *Southern Cultures* 4 (Winter 1997): 437–62; Bart Dredge, "Defending White Supremacy: David Clark and the *Southern Textile Bulletin*, 1911–1955," *North Carolina Historical Review* 89 (January 2012): 59–91. On road building and highway infrastructure, which were high developmental priorities in North Carolina during this period, see Tammy Ingram, *Dixie Highway: Road Building and the Making of the Modern South, 1900–1930* (Chapel Hill: University of North Carolina Press, 2014).

26. On the basic periodization, see, e.g., Osterhammel and Peterssen, *Globalization: A Short History*, 113–52; Ronald Findlay and Kevin H. O'Rourke, "Commodity Market Integration, 1500–2000," in *Globalization in Historical Perspective*, ed. Michael D. Bordo, Alan M. Taylor, and Jeffrey G. Williamson, National Bureau of Economic Research Conference Report (Chicago: University of Chicago Press, 2003), 13–62; and Jeffrey A. Frieden, *Global Capitalism: Its Fall and Rise in the Twentieth Century* (New York: Norton, 2006), 253–476. On the South's place in this scheme, Alfred E. Eckes Jr., "The South and Economic Globalization, 1950 to the Future," in *Globalization and the American South*, ed. James C. Cobb and William Stueck (Athens: University of Georgia Press, 2005), 36–65.

27. See, e.g., George B. Tindall, "Business Progressivism: Southern Politics in the 1920s," *South Atlantic Quarterly* 62 (Winter 1963): 92–106; Tindall, *Emergence of the New South, 1913–1945*, 219–84; and James C. Cobb, *Industrialization and Southern Society, 1877–1984* (Lexington: University Press of Kentucky, 1984), 27–50. Note that Tindall argues that the "business progressive" approach established in the 1920s continued strong in southern politics in subsequent decades. Most analysts of politics in twentieth-century North Carolina have accepted Tindall's point, although they have not always used the same terminology. Paul Luebke, for example, prefers the term "modernizers." Writers including V. O. Key Jr., Rob Christensen, and Tom Eamon, however, have all identified and written about a tradition similar to the one Tindall referred to as "business progressive." See Key, *Southern Politics in State and Nation*, 205–28; Paul Luebke, *Tar Heel Politics: Myths and Realities* (Chapel Hill: University of North Carolina Press, 1990); Christensen, *Paradox of Tar Heel Politics*; Rob Christensen, "Which Wing Will Prevail?," *News and Observer* (Raleigh, N.C.), January 30, 2011; and Tom Eamon, *The Making of a Southern Democracy: North Carolina Politics from Kerr Scott to Pat McCrory* (Chapel Hill: University of North Carolina Press, 2014), 369n32 and passim. Note, too, that Jack Bass and Walter De Vries, writing in the mid-1970s, accept the nomenclature but view North Carolina as anything but "progressive" politically at the time. See Bass and De Vries, *The Transformation of Southern Politics: Social Change and Political Consequence since 1945* (New York: Basic Books, 1976), 218–47.

28. See Cobb, *Industrialization and Southern Society*, 51–120; Gavin Wright, *Old South, New South: Revolutions in the Southern Economy since the Civil War* (New York: Basic Books, 1986), 239–74; Bruce J. Schulman, *From Cotton Belt to Sunbelt: Federal Policy, Economic Development, and the Transformation of the South, 1938–1980* (New York: Oxford University Press, 1991), 63–173; and David L. Carlton, "Smokestack-Chasing and Its Discontents: Southern Development Strategy in the Twentieth Century," in *The American South in the Twentieth Century*, ed. Craig S. Pascoe, Karen Trahan Leathem, and Andy Ambrose (Athens: University of Georgia Press, 2005), 106–26.

29. Peter A. Coclanis and Louis M. Kyriakoudes, "Selling Which South? Economic

Change in Rural and Small-Town North Carolina in an Era of Globalization, 1940–2007," *Southern Cultures* 13 (Winter 2007): 86–102; Robert Lewis, "World War II Manufacturing and the Postwar Southern Economy," *Journal of Southern History* 73 (November 2007): 837–66; Peter A. Coclanis and David L. Carlton, "Southern Economic Commentary in Historical Perspective," in *A Way Forward: Building a Globally Competitive South*, ed. Daniel P. Gitterman and Peter A. Coclanis (Chapel Hill: Global Research Institute, University of North Carolina at Chapel Hill in association with the University of North Carolina Press, 2011), 12–16; Peter A. Coclanis and Louis M. Kyriakoudes, "The Rural South and the Burden of the Past," in Gitterman and Coclanis, *A Way Forward*, 17–25; Mac McCorkle, "History and the 'New Economy' Narrative: The Case of Research Triangle Park and North Carolina's Economic Development," *Journal of the Historical Society* 12 (December 2012): 479–525.

30. See Coclanis and Carlton, "Southern Economic Commentary," 14; David L. Carlton, unpublished database, Southern PCI, 1929–2012. This database tracks per capita income in the South against per capita income in the United States as a whole. Carlton generously made this database available to the author.

31. See MDC, Inc., *Shadows in the Sunbelt: Developing the Rural South in an Era of Economic Change* (Chapel Hill, N.C.: MDC, Inc., 1986). Another very important report, expressing many similar themes, was published in the same year by the Southern Growth Policies Board: *Halfway Home and a Long Way to Go: The Report of the 1986 Commission on the Future of the South* (Research Triangle Park, N.C.: Southern Growth Policies Board, 1986). Also see Schulman, *From Cotton Belt to Sunbelt*, 178–205; and Coclanis and Kyriakoudes, "Selling Which South?"

32. See Richard Florida, *The Rise of the Creative Class* (New York: Basic Books, 2002); and Florida, *The Flight of the Creative Class: The New Global Competition for Talent* (New York: HarperBusiness, 2005). On the way in which these factors played out in North Carolina, see Michael L. Walden, *North Carolina in the Connected Age: Challenges and Opportunities in a Globalizing Economy* (Chapel Hill: University of North Carolina Press, 2008); and Coclanis and Kyriakoudes, "Rural South and the Burden of the Past." On high poverty rates within thriving metropolitan areas of North Carolina, see Allen Serkin and Stephen Whitlow, *The State of North Carolina Urban Distressed Communities* (Chapel Hill: Center for Urban and Regional Studies, University of North Carolina at Chapel Hill, February 2005); Gene Nichol, "In Urban North Carolina, Deep Pockets of Misery Are Masked," *News and Observer* (Raleigh, N.C.), September 29, 2013, http://www.newsobserver.com/2013/09/29/3239177/in-urban-north-carolina-deep-pockets.html; Jim Wise, "Poverty Persists While Durham Prospers," *Durham News*, December 31, 2013; and William High and Todd Owen, *North Carolina's Distressed Urban Tracts: A View of the State's Economically Disadvantaged Communities*, CURS Report no. 2014-01 (Chapel Hill: Center for Urban and Regional Studies, University of North Carolina at Chapel Hill, February 2014), https://curs.unc.edu/files/2014/02/NC-Distress-Update-final.pdf.

33. On the middle-income trap, see, e.g., Homi Kharas and Harinder Kohli, "What Is the Middle Income Trap, Why Do Countries Fall into It, and How Can It Be Avoided?," *Global Journal of Emerging Market Economies* 3 (September 2011): 281–89, http://eme.sagepub.com/content/3/3/281.full.pdf+html. For some important new empirical work on the same, see Barry Eichengreen, Donghyun Park, and Kwanho Shin, "Growth Slowdowns Redux: New Evidence on the Middle-Income Trap," NBER working paper 18673, National Bureau of

Economic Research, Cambridge, Mass., January 2013, http://www.nber.org/papers/w18673. On the possibility of such a trap in the South, see Peter A. Coclanis, "Chasing the Shadows from Today's Sunbelt," *Wall Street Journal*, September 14, 2012, http://online.wsj.com/news/articles/SB10000872396390444709004577649552864075244.

34. Quoted in Bass and De Vries, *Transformation of Southern Politics*, 218–19.

35. See, e.g., Jim Yardley, "Bangladesh Takes Steps to Raise $38 a Month Minimum Wage," *New York Times*, November 5, 2013; and Jason Burke, "Bangladesh Garment Workers Set for 77% Pay Increase," *Guardian*, November 14, 2013, http://www.theguardian.com/world/2013/nov/14/bangladesh-garment-workers-pay-rise.

36. David L. Carlton and Peter A. Coclanis, "Southern Textiles in Global Context," in *Global Perspectives on Industrial Transformation in the American South*, ed. Susanna Delfino and Michele Gillespie (Columbia: University of Missouri Press, 2005), 151–74.

37. See "Pillowtex Closing 16 Plants, Laying Off 6,450," *USA Today*, July 30, 2003, http://usatoday30.usatoday.com/money/industries/manufacturing/2003-07-30-pillowtex_x.htm; and Tim Reaves, "10 Years after the Fall, Dream Endures for 'New Kannapolis,'" *Hickory (N.C.) Daily Record*, July 29, 2013. For a scholarly case study of the closing, see Timothy J. Minchin, "'It Knocked This City to Its Knees': The Closure of Pillowtex Mills in Kannapolis, North Carolina and the Decline of the US Textile Industry," *Labor History* 50 (August 2009): 287–311.

38. Daniel P. Gitterman, Peter A. Coclanis, and John Quinterno, "Recession and Recovery in North Carolina: A Data Snapshot, 2007–12," Global Research Institute, University of North Carolina, August 2012, http://gri.unc.edu/files/2012/08/GRI-Data-Snapshot-August-2012.pdf; David Bracken, "NC Jobless Rate Dips to 6.7% in January," *News and Observer* (Raleigh, N.C.), March 17, 2014.

39. Gitterman et al., *Recession and Recovery in North Carolina*, 5.

40. The figures on median household income and per capita income in North Carolina in 2012 are from U.S. Department of Commerce, Bureau of the Census, "QuickFacts, North Carolina, Median Household Income, 2008–12," http://quickfacts.census.gov/qfd/states/37000.html (accessed March 3, 2014); U.S. Bureau of Economic Analysis, Regional Economic Accounts, "BEARFACTS, North Carolina, Per Capita Personal Income, 2012," http://www.bea.gov/regional/bearfacts/action.cfm (accessed March 3, 2014). The comparative data on median household income in 1984 and 2013 are from South by North Strategies, Ltd., "A Comeback Short of the Mark: Income Trends in North Carolina in the Wake of the Great Recession," prepared for Think NC First, April 2015, http://files.www.thinkncfirst.org/news/new-report-finds-nc-household-income-missing-from-a-carolina-comeback/Trends_Report.pdf. The cost-of-living index for North Carolina is from Missouri Department of Economic Development, Missouri Economic Research and Information Center, "Cost of Living Data Series: Third Quarter 2016," http://www.missourieconomy.org/indicators/cost_of_living/index.stm (accessed March 3, 2014).

41. Alemayehu Bishaw, "Poverty: 2000 to 2012, American Community Survey Briefs," doc. ACSBR/12-1, U.S. Department of Commerce, Economics and Statistics Administration, U.S. Census Bureau, September 2013, http://www.census.gov/prod/2013pubs/acsbr12-01.pdf, p. 5, table 2.

42. Michael L. Walden, "Has North Carolina Lost Its Mojo?," *News and Observer* (Raleigh, N.C.), September 21, 2012.

43. Daniel P. Gitterman and Peter A. Coclanis, "Moving beyond Plato versus Plumbing: Individualized Education and Career Passways for All North Carolinians," Global Research Institute, University of North Carolina, September 2012, 10–12, http://www.sbnstrategies.com/wp-content/uploads/2012/09/GRI-Plato_vs_Plumbing-Sept-2012.pdf.

44. Erik Brynjolfsson and Andrew McAfee, *Race against the Machine* (Lexington, Mass.: Digital Frontier Press, 2011), esp. 28–52; Brynjolfsson and McAfee, *The Second Machine Age: Work, Progress, and Prosperity in a Time of Brilliant Technology* (New York: Norton, 2014), esp. 163–85.

45. Michael Kan, "Foxconn to Speed Up 'Robot Army' Deployment," *PCWorld*, June 26, 2013, http://www.pcworld.com/article/2043026/foxconn-to-speed-up-robot-army-deployment-20000-robots-already-in-its-factories.html; Jason Dorrier, "Foxconn's Pivot to America: Reverse Outsourcing with Robots," SingularityHUB, February 23, 2014, http://singularityhub.com/2014/02/23/foxconns-pivot-to-america-reverse-outsourcing-with-robots/; Brynjolfsson and McAfee, *Second Machine Age*, 142, 184–85.

46. Michael Lind, "Southern Poverty Pimps: The 'Original Sin' of the Southern Political Class Is Cheap, Powerless Labor," *Salon*, February 19, 2013, http://www.salon.com/2013/02/19/southern_poverty_pimps/.

47. U.S. Bureau of Labor Statistics, "Union Members Summary," January 24, 2014, http://www.bls.gov/news.release/union2.nro.htm.

48. G. Jason Jolley, E. Brent Lane, and Aaron Nousaine, "Enfield Economic Development Master Plan," prepared for Enfield Partnership for Tomorrow, UNC Center for Competitive Economies, August 2011, http://www.kenan-flagler.unc.edu/~/media/Files/kenaninstitute/C3E/Enfield_EconomicDevelopment_Plan.pdf.

49. Linda Flowers, *Throwed Away: Failures of Progress in Eastern North Carolina* (Knoxville: University of Tennessee Press, 1990).

50. On Beaufort County's economic position in South Carolina over the centuries up until the 1980s, see Coclanis, *Shadow of a Dream*, 299–300 and passim. On personal per capita income in Beaufort County today, see South Carolina Association of Counties, *County Profiles* (Columbia: South Carolina Association of Counties, June 2012), 7.

51. Three "areas" in North Carolina—Forest City (no. 9), Roanoke Rapids (no. 3), and Lumberton (no. 1)—were recently ranked by credit.com as being among the ten poorest in the United States in terms of median household income. The ranking scheme was based on data from the U.S. Census Bureau's 2012 American Community Survey. Note that the units were not the cities themselves but the micropolitan and metropolitan statistical areas of which the cities were part. See Christine DiGangi, "The Poorest Areas in America," credit.com, September 24, 2013, http://blog.credit.com/2013/09/poorest-cities-in-america/.

52. Peter A. Coclanis, "Down Highway 52: Globalization, Higher Education, and the Economic Future of the American South," *Journal of the Historical Society* 5 (Fall 2005): 331–45.

53. Giuseppe Tomasi di Lampedusa, *The Leopard*, trans. Archibald Colquhoun (New York: Pantheon, 1960; originally published in Italian in 1958), 40.

A NEW DESCRIPTION OF
NORTH CAROLINA

Larry E. Tise and Jeffrey J. Crow

The essays in this volume were inspired in part, as we said at the outset, by John Lawson's classic book *A New Voyage to Carolina* (1709). Looking back over the preceding pages, we are reminded of Lawson's long journey and the skillful narratives of early North Carolina that resulted from his voyage. Lawson explored the Carolina realm in company with nine other adventurers with whom he chewed over what he saw and heard before he set about compiling his notes into a book. He listened to their perspectives as they encountered the complicated terrains, the rolling waters, and the native inhabitants of Carolina. He and his companions also heard many native voices, offering their own explanations through unskilled interpreters on how and why things were the way they were in their homeland. Lawson thus experienced in the field a virtual litany of Indian names and European terms for the hundreds of plants, animals, birds, rocks, and fossils they observed, as well as stories about what they meant. Upon the completion of his long journey, Lawson transcribed his notes into three basic documents: (1) a daily journal of his travels; (2) a classification of the vegetables, beasts, insects, birds, and fish encountered, which he called "the natural history of Carolina"; and (3) a magnificent essay on the natives he met titled "An Account of the Indians of North Carolina." Each of these established a baseline analysis of North Carolina history, its natural environment, and its native culture that has had an imprint on virtually every book about the state written since 1709. The same can be said for two briefer summary portrayals of North Carolina, one of which he titled "A Description of North Carolina" and the other "The Present State of Carolina."[1]

As editors of this volume, we traversed North Carolina on our own long journey in 2012 and 2013, visiting five campuses of the University of North Carolina system, listening to many voices about the history and "present" state of North Carolina, and subsequently working with authors to generate the essays contained here. As an outgrowth of this rich and rewarding experience, we, reminiscent of Lawson's adventures, are inspired and prepared to present the thread lines for a new narrative of North Carolina's history. In doing so, we have articulated and sought to be mindful of several broad themes that we believe need to infuse any informed new narrative of the state's history.

Five guiding ideas emerged from the hundreds of conversations leading up to this present work, and those fundamental motifs manifested as these essays came into focus. First, one must understand that North Carolina's land, its abundant waters, and its distinctive terrain from mountains to sea form a geological and natural configuration that has changed over time but also remains fundamentally beyond abilities of any generation to modify. Second, many human populations have resided on this land for thousands of years, and they all have considered it to be their home. Third, the unique configuration of North Carolina's natural and geological environment from a sandy barrier coast to tall mountains has defined and constrained the economic opportunities of its inhabitants. These delimiting factors remained dominant until the technological infrastructures of the late twentieth century rendered the geographic location of residents less determinative. Fourth, North Carolina has long been inhabited by some people who have worked the land for subsistence and others who have exploited its resources for commercial advantage. Both of these social arrangements require labor and an assignment of laboring responsibilities. Finally, whoever has ever inhabited these lands has had to choose, organize, or submit to some form of governance. The struggle to control and shape that governance has persisted from earliest human settlement to the present.

In addition to these basic characteristics prescribing and delimiting the state's history, we are also attentive to other variables that have given character and meaning to certain eras of North Carolina's development. These are ever-changing factors that give luster, fiber, and depth to the experiences of those who have inhabited this land. For hundreds and even thousands of years, North Carolina has been the scene of frequent migrations and expulsions that have changed the character of the place. The ethnic or racial composition of North Carolina's population has, through these processes, changed dramatically over time. Through oral traditions and the archaeological record we have only glimpses of the indigenous populations who originally inhabited these lands. We know more about the four centuries of recorded history when those people lived in tension with newly arriving Europeans and Africans. More recently, but still sometimes inscrutable, is our rich but also conflict-ridden era when a community of global immigrants live side by side—some who live as "native" North Carolinians and some who have arrived far more recently.

Against this backdrop, a variety of quite particular issues have consistently challenged and perplexed every government that has prevailed in the land from Indian nations to successive colonial, state, or national authorities. Citizenship itself is one such issue. Until the American Revolution, European immigrants and dependent Indian nations were subjects of the king of England. After the Revolution and to the present the definition of citizenship in the United States has been a topic of continuous discussion and debate within both states and the nation.

Religion is another matter of consistent importance. Indigenous peoples practiced their own forms of religion until Christian missionaries and colonial governance sedulously lured them into European forms of worship. Africans too brought their own practices of worship, some of which persisted into the nineteenth century. Since the colonial era North Carolina's inhabitants have seen wave after wave of religious enthusiasms under the general guise of Protestant Christianity. While these have often modified the religious landscape, they have not altered the fundamental religious outlook of the state's residents.

Education is a third concern. Despite constitutional mandates for state and local governments to provide a basic education for all its children, North Carolina's methods of support for education have shifted regularly over three centuries, often leaving its public education system near the bottom among all states.

Finally, we look to the richness of culture in all its diverse forms. The pursuit of literature, music, art, dance, and other forms of cultural expression or appreciation has been supremely local in North Carolina from the time of Indian habitations through European settlement to the present. Whether taught formally through schools and cultural organizations or not at all, North Carolina's peoples—Indian, African, European, Latino, and Asian—have made the land a rich and varied seedbed for cultural expression, and often for spellbound participation by engaged audiences.

With this quilt-work tapestry of diverse heritages in mind, we began *New Voyages to Carolina* with an eye toward articulating a new narrative for North Carolina's history. We thought, in the beginning, that we needed to update, expand, redefine, or even replace an existing narrative. But we soon concluded that we would have to reimagine the type of narrative needed to explain the state's history. We do not believe that a traditional chronological or political narrative will any longer suffice in telling North Carolina's story. We also believe the state's narrative history must move beyond older story lines that have tried to explain its character and relative greatness compared with presumably better-endowed neighboring states. Nor should a new narrative gloss over the evidence that many of North Carolina's legal and political choices have sometimes contained distressingly negative antidemocratic and discriminatory consequences for large segments of its citizens.

But we also believe that, wherever this new narrative might take us, we see no reason to apologize for what North Carolina has been and is. We like to think that we as historians have an obligation to help North Carolinians recognize both our strengths and our failings as a state. We have much to embrace and joyously commemorate about our past and present. There are honors and achievements to be recognized. But there are blemishes as well. Our new narrative must be able to encompass both success and failure—warts and all—but with as much accuracy and objectivity as we can muster.

THE GENESIS STORY

The purpose of a genesis story is to describe both the beginnings and the fundamental purpose for the existence of the state or nation or institution being depicted. Along the way, that founding story can also serve as a symbolic account of origins that can guide the resolve and moral purposes of those who hear and read the genesis story. A tool both for teaching and for preaching, in a religious context the genesis story is often the most fundamental portion of the narrative.

When we begin looking for a North Carolina genesis story that articulates the reason for the state's existence, we run into an immediate problem. While many other states have enjoyed the emergence of both genesis and purpose stories for their realms, no basic creation narrative has appeared in North Carolina that explains its core reason for being. There are no pilgrims, no proud survivors of Jamestown, no William Penns or Lord Baltimores or Roger Williamses or Thomas Hookers. Not even a James Oglethorpe or Ethan Allen or Benjamin Franklin. No Dutch merchants, Puritans, or Cavaliers making solemn business, religious, or political pacts.

There are many reasons for the absence of a central genesis story for North Carolina. Europeans displaced the principal Indian inhabitants of the North Carolina realm and for centuries erased both their stories of creation and most of the Indian nations as well. Meanwhile, the European-fed North Carolina colony authorized by an English monarch in payment of royal debts had no purposeful founding that grew into a permanent estate. Sir Walter Raleigh's efforts at settlement on Roanoke Island were dismal failures, as were those of earlier Spanish explorers who penetrated to the Catawba River region. North Carolina had instead many foundings at separate points along its coast and in multiple backcountries as diverse and complicated as its geophysical terrain. Furthermore, unlike almost every other English colony, for some of the same reasons that North Carolina never had a single landmark port city, it also never established and has never had a cultural center where gentlemen philosophers and a literati could gestate and spin the type of narrative that germinated and took shape in other colony-states.

When North Carolina created a permanent capital in Raleigh, the wilderness capital had just about the same cultural relevance to the state as a whole as did Albany in New York, Harrisburg in Pennsylvania, or Columbia in South Carolina. When the state put its public university in the woods of Chapel Hill, the school could not match for cultural relevance to North Carolina such virtual state universities as Harvard in Massachusetts, Yale in Connecticut, Penn in Pennsylvania, William and Mary in Virginia, or even the College of Charleston in South Carolina. While North Carolina and Georgia tussle for the right to claim the oldest state universities, these two states have been the most deprived of all the original thirteen states when it comes to having had true and vibrant cultural centers throughout their histories.

It is perhaps thus not surprising that authors who were not really of the land—and not even very long in the colony or state—wrote many of the state's earliest histories. Hugh Williamson, author of the state's first *History of North Carolina* (1812), was more associated with Philadelphia, London, and New York than with North Carolina. Although he represented North Carolina at the Constitutional Convention in Philadelphia in 1787, he had little connection with North Carolina from that time until he published his history. His work covered North Carolina's colonial and revolutionary era but provided no memorable narrative for the origins of the colony or state. François Xavier Martin, author of the second history, *The History of North Carolina, from the Earliest Period* (1829), had even less connection with North Carolina. A native of France, Martin spent barely a decade in North Carolina as a printer and newspaper editor in New Bern before he pushed on to New Orleans for the rest of his life, bearing a large trunk of North Carolina records and transcripts that he used many years later to write his history.

While Archibald DeBow Murphey had aspirations to write a state history as well as to build canals across North Carolina, he never completed his book. Nor did Joseph Seawell ("Shocco") Jones. John Hill Wheeler accessed and collected many state and private records in the 1840s and successfully published in 1851 a book titled *Historical Sketches of North Carolina, from 1584 to 1851*. While the book was chock full of rich data and biographical sketches of numerous North Carolina leaders, it contained no unified narrative. The Episcopal clergyman Francis Lister Hawks, although born in North

Carolina, was another expatriate who compiled thousands of documents for a state history and actually completed two volumes of his projected much larger *History of North Carolina* (1858). He resided at the time in New York City, and the Civil War intervened to quash any further volumes.

When North Carolina pledged its loyalty to the newly established Confederate States of America and declared its independence from the United States on May 20, 1861, its would-be historians had failed to provide a narrative for anything that could serve as a founding story for the state. Still bereft of a historically useful and nurturing story of its origins and rise as a unique land, the state's political leaders had long since turned to the spurious Mecklenburg Declaration of Independence of May 20, 1775, as the launching pad for a brave new future. While the experiment of the Confederacy would prove after four years of bloodshed to be a colossal mistake, the fictitious "Mec Dec" would survive to find a permanent place on North Carolina's state seal and flag well into the twenty-first century. Although North Carolina would go forward to assemble the most complete and accessible state archives of perhaps any state in America, the formulation of a legitimating genesis story seems to have eluded the legions of historians who have labored over the state's rich heritage.

But that is not to say that North Carolina has failed to elicit some important and enduring pronouncements about its meaning and purpose. The distinguished jurist William J. Gaston penned probably the best-known expression of North Carolina's attitude in the constellation of American states. Shortly following the 1835 state constitutional convention, where as chief justice of the North Carolina Supreme Court he played a pivotal role, Gaston sat down to describe his state in a poem that he titled "The Old North State." Having listened to a month of debates about North Carolina's limits and opportunities, he distilled in this one brief poem his understanding of what he understood to be the identity and spirit of North Carolina. While he no doubt poured his heart and soul into the poem, he could not know that it would survive to become in 1927 the official state song of North Carolina or that it would remain a warm refrain on the lips of North Carolinians into the twenty-first century.

If future North Carolinians would stumble a bit in singing the main stanzas, none have faltered in the song's rousing refrain: "Hurrah! Hurrah! The Old North State forever! / Hurrah! Hurrah! The good Old North State!" This classic drinking song ending to each stanza obscured Gaston's cowering glances toward "the scorner [who] may sneer at and witlings defame her [North Carolina]." Gaston apologized that though "plain and artless her sons," at least "let all those who love us, love the land we live in." Thus, not even the state's official anthem—sung for generations across the land—helps Carolinians celebrate a shared notion of laudable beginnings.

Despite its legions of poets, lyricists, novelists, journalists, and nonfiction writers, none seems to have captured an image of North Carolina that conveys a more uplifting and positive identity of the state or its peoples. Many important historians have pored over the state's history as well, and they have written among the most detailed and descriptive histories that can be claimed by any state. And yet, despite all of the valiant efforts, none has moved much beyond explaining North Carolina's past in the same episodic manner as most national histories—moving from war to war with interregnums of peace presided over by governors reflecting Federalist, Jeffersonian, Jacksonian, Whig, Democratic, Republican, or Progressive policies. These histories are more political chronicles than living and breathing human sagas.

FUNDAMENTAL PERIODS OF NORTH CAROLINA HISTORY

Whereas we traditionally have thought about North Carolina's history in much the manner of English and European precursors—as the reign of kings or governors or of intervals between wars and periods of peace—we have heretofore often neglected other transformative shifts within society. If we allow ourselves to move beyond those traditional constraints in thinking about the past, a new and vibrant understanding of North Carolina's story emerges. Rather than segmenting our past into worn-out and musty chronological periods, much longer patterns of persistence and change appear. History becomes less a march toward progress than an uneven struggle to tame dual natures—the environment and the human.

From this perspective, North Carolina's history has actually fallen into quite long periods during which the people living on the land have sought answers to such basic questions as the nature of human society and its governance. These questions in turn have revolved around such matters as who possesses the land, who rules the land, what kind of community the people envision, and whether that vision has been realized. These are the kinds of questions that sometimes rise above mere politics, economics, and social habits to reveal the soul of North Carolina.

Possessing the Land, Prehistory to 1713

The central driving force, the guiding purpose of nearly all peoples who passed onto or occupied the lands that came to comprise North Carolina was that of possession. In the case of the territory that became North Carolina, native Indians possessed the land for thousands of years. Unlike Europeans, however, the Indians held the land in common with other members of their nation, not as individuals. Despite the intrusion of Europeans beginning in the 1560s, Indians continued to occupy and use the land until the opening years of the eighteenth century. Then suddenly, in the space of a few short years between 1711 and 1713—the years of the Tuscarora War, one of the most consequential military events of colonial America—virtually all of what is now coastal North Carolina was wrested from Indian possession and taken over by a cast of conquistadors who have remained virtually unknown and nameless in the annals of North Carolina history.

It is not that we do not know the names of the perpetrators of this conquest—we have the names of the whole cast of characters. It is rather that they have not been characterized for who they were and the role they played in making North Carolina what it is today. In the case of New England, historians long sanctified the conquest of those northeastern lands by saying that the Pilgrims were seeking freedom from oppression and that the Puritans were planning to build a "City on a Hill." William Penn's venture in Pennsylvania has been long described as a "Holy Experiment." Lord Baltimore created in Maryland another haven for religious freedom—for Roman Catholics. Georgia was an asylum for another holy experiment to provide English convicts one-way "transportation" from England to another land. Even Virginia and South Carolina were havens for self-proclaimed Cavaliers and for some West Indian planters who wanted to transfer the cash crop culture of the Caribbean to mainland North America.

The closest traditional narrative with allusions of great moral purpose for what happened in North Carolina is perhaps the "conquest of Canaan."[2] That biblical image of the people of Israel departing Egypt to take the land of Canaan from the worshipers of Baal befits in certain respects what happened in North Carolina. Both Spanish and English explorers thought that they had arrived in a land of heathen peoples when they penetrated North Carolina in the sixteenth century. The other Europeans who followed them believed the same thing, and they thus treated Indian natives who had possessed the Carolina territory for a thousand years in much the same manner as the people of Israel treated the peoples who had occupied Canaan for perhaps thousands of years.

But what's missing from the story is the idea that the territory between the Albemarle Sound and the Cape Fear River was a "promised land." Virtually no one involved with the European conquest of North Carolina looked upon the territory as a sacredly promised land. Instead, they viewed it as a land of promise and opportunity. It offered new beginnings for many people who had perhaps failed elsewhere; who may have been divested of a portion to any estate in England; who had no cash to invest—just their strong hands and hopefully quick wits; and, at least in the case of a number of Quakers, a large company of Moravians, a goodly number of German Palatines and French Huguenots, some Swiss, and many more Scots, it was a land of freedom from religious oppression. Thus, if the transfer of the land that became North Carolina from native Indians to a diverse contingent of many Europeans in the century and half from 1565 to 1713 was not the conquest of a sacral promised land, it was at least the transfer of a land of promise to a vast number of people who were seeking a place for new beginnings.

Interestingly, many of the native people who occupied North Carolina also viewed the place as a land of promise. Deep in the genesis and exodus story of the Tuscarora was the belief that they were always a "people moving about" and that they had originally migrated from the lands of the Great Lakes to North Carolina eons in the past. Even to the present the Tuscarora word for North Carolina means "pine in water." For the thousand years they occupied the Carolina realm they sought to live in quiet possession of those portions of the land that would permit a level of fishing, hunting, and agriculture that would sustain their nation. They wanted to maintain access to trading routes and to trading paths for the purpose of bartering their goods for materials brought to them by Indian traders. They aspired to live in peaceful coexistence with other nations—especially those with whom they were related by ancestry or language. But this was not a paradise, as there were other Indian peoples who might from time to time have looked covetously upon their neighbors' fields and harvests.

The earliest European explorers—Spanish and English—were at first less interested in occupying territories than in gaining access to precious metals; in finding plants, spices, woods, and organic materials for producing dyes for use in printing and coloring textiles or other plants and herbs for use in treating or curing European diseases; and in identifying locations for military fortifications to defend a potential New World empire. Thus, both Thomas Harriot and John Lawson, a century apart, provided lengthy catalogs of plants, organic materials, animals, trees, potential dyes, and medicines that might be made available through trade or harvest in North Carolina. When their explorations evolved into efforts of permanent settlement, both Spanish and English leaders sadly miscalculated the complications of creating viable living places among North Carolina's native Indians. While the Indian nations were eager to pursue trade and commerce with the Europeans, they could not provide a sufficiency of food to support both themselves and the newcomers. Nor were they willing to give up their valuable lands to threatening outsiders without a fight.

When the Europeans eventually established permanent settlements on the North American coast, North Carolina immediately fell far short of the lively trading activities radiating out from the adjacent port towns located near the mouths of the Chesapeake River in Virginia and at the confluence of the Ashley and Cooper Rivers in South Carolina. These vibrant commercial centers drained most of the merchantable goods from North Carolina. A wave of European brokers from these places established trading networks with Indian nations living in the backcountry of North Carolina. The Indian traders opened pathways for a second wave of Europeans more interested in securing rich lands for occupation and the pursuit of both subsistence and commercial agriculture.

With the establishment of the Carolina proprietary in 1663, even more Europeans appeared in North Carolina—agents and emissaries of one or more of the eight proprietors who held title to the entire Carolina territory. This influx consisted of a new variety of adventurers who were on the make—looking for ways to enrich themselves or to secure a productive foothold in some portion of the land—especially in the Albemarle region near the Chesapeake market. Because many of these individuals had no money to invest in lands or the development of a business or a farm, they had to live by their wits and look for opportunities to serve as middlemen or as agents either of the proprietors or of Virginia governors and business operatives who viewed the Albemarle region as but an extension of Virginia.

Yet amid this surge of adventurers there was another cohesive group of people who also chose the Albemarle region for settlement and provided a leaven to the financial opportunists. Quakers repaired to the Albemarle for the same reasons that others of their number went almost simultaneously to William Penn's great "holy experiment" in Pennsylvania. They infected other upright settlers already there with the spirit of Quakerism. Unlike the many moneyless squatters who came to North Carolina at the same time, these Quakers brought money to invest. They wanted to live in peace and in the unfettered pursuit of their religion while they too built fortunes as commercial farmers and merchants.

In the absence of any effective European governing authority in the Albemarle region or elsewhere in the territory that would become North Carolina, agents of the proprietors and individuals pretending to have the ear and favor of the proprietors engaged in constant conflicts with one another for authority and power in northeastern North Carolina. With the only real authority still held by the mainly absentee proprietors in England, the Albemarle region of North Carolina more resembled a lawless territory of later American frontiers than an orderly extension of English civility and order.

Audacious opportunists willing to intimidate both Indians and Quakers thwarted the authority of the proprietors. Their excessive use of deceit and intimidation undermined any possibility of a peaceful coexistence between native Indians and newly arriving English settlers. These practices included cruel and uncivil treatment of Indian leaders, capture and sale of Indians into slavery, flooding the Indian market with spirituous liquors, destruction of Indian crops of corn, and the taking of Indian lands with neither treaty nor compensation. The principal individuals engaged in these dangerous activities were Indian traders, unsupervised agents and surveyors in the employ of the proprietors, and landowners either from England or from the West Indies with visions of replicating in North Carolina one of the great estates they had known in England or one of the rich plantations they had observed on West Indian islands.

The culmination of this long era of turmoil was the Tuscarora War between 1711 and 1713. The Tuscarora nation was caught between two spheres of influence radiating out of Virginia and South Carolina. Virginia's policy was to convert Indian nations into tributary status that made them part of an interior trading network. South Carolina's goal was to eliminate Indian nations from the land through conquest, relocation, and enslavement. Given the proclivities of the largely unsupervised operatives living and working in North Carolina in 1711, the South Carolina alternative seemed to them by far the most desirable. When the ire of Tuscarora leaders was driven to a fever pitch by the intrusive activities of the provincial surveyor and land speculator John Lawson, North Carolina's impotent and inept leaders authorized South Carolina's Indian warriors to subdue the Tuscarora nation by military conquest and removal.

When the blood stopped flowing at Fort Neoheroka in March 1713, the largest and most powerful Indian nation that had survived until that time among the coastal English colonies from New England to Florida had been effectively displaced. With the defeat of the Tuscarora, European immigrants, unopposed, spread into the newly opened coastal plain. The possession of the land that would be North Carolina had been transferred forever from the hands of native Indians to those of European immigrants. Although the English proprietors of Carolina had never set foot on the soil, a largely unguided campaign by unruly opportunists had wrested possession of the land into the hands of ambitious newcomers. The first era of North Carolina's complicated history, the taking of a land of promise, had thus come to an end.

Choosing the Rulers, 1713–1835

To the victors went the spoils. Among the small contingent of Europeans who planned and prosecuted the Tuscarora War were the people who derived the greatest benefits from the conquest and scattering of the Tuscarora and their allied Indian nations. Acting governor Thomas Pollock was able to secure the lands beyond his already large plantation at the head of the Albemarle Sound. Edward Moseley, one of the greatest land speculators and operatives North Carolina has known, replaced John Lawson as provincial surveyor and succeeded over the next four decades in both keeping his own head and amassing vast landholdings in northeastern North Carolina as well as along the Cape Fear River. Moseley's closest allies in what became one of the largest land grabs in North Carolina history were the South Carolina Indian fighters James Moore Jr. and his younger brother Maurice Moore. James was the commander of the South Carolina force that leveled the Tuscarora towns and fortifications in 1713. Maurice was one of his chief lieutenants in the campaign. And both went into partnership with Moseley soon after the war to build rich plantations on the Cape Fear River and its tributaries in southeastern North Carolina.

While Pollock, Moseley, and the Moores carved up the newly conquered lands into hugely profitable estates, North Carolina entered into a new phase of defining its basic character as a geopolitical entity. Whereas the bloody war resulted in the transfer of thousands of square miles of lands from the Tuscarora Nation to an ambitious group of English speculators, it did not help clarify who would rule over the emerging northern province of the Carolina colony. That process—so crucial to the ultimate shape of North Carolina—would require a full century to unfold across its changing status from a proprietary land to a royal colony and ultimately to one of the thirteen founding states of a new American nation. Although its governing authority changed three times, the peoples who occupied the land would ultimately choose its rulers.

The Tuscarora War coincided with a recognition on the part of the proprietors that a governor was needed in the northern half of the Carolina proprietary. When the ill-fated Edward Hyde assumed responsibility in 1712 as the first of North Carolina's many colonial governors—he died from yellow fever only a year after his appointment—he inaugurated another era of nearly indistinguishable, undistinguished, and ineffective governors that continued from 1712 until the northern half of Carolina became a "royal" colony in 1729. Until William Tryon's governorship from 1765 to 1771—during which he made a valiant effort to regularize the administration of North Carolina to some semblance of a royal colony—the colony, if not ungoverned and ungovernable, lacked strong leadership. Royal governors clashed with the assembly. Within the assembly regional conflicts between the Albemarle, which was overrepresented, and the rest of the colony, especially the lower Cape Fear, hobbled governance. Although some of the characters who were appointed proprietary and royal governors were distinguished individuals, none of them succeeded in managing the virtually unregulated exchanges of land and the issuance of questionable titles to land within the colony. Governors such as George Burrington contributed to the confusion by issuing blank patents to be filled in by claimants and speculators themselves. Gabriel Johnston then tried to attract some of his fellow countrymen from Scotland to settle in the colony with promises of land and the suspension of taxes. In the end, however, it took the War of the Regulation (1766–71) to bring to a head the irregularities surrounding land titles and the frequently corrupt practices of colonial administrators.

North Carolina became a royal colony when the crown reclaimed the title to Carolina in 1729 by buying out the rights of seven of the eight original proprietors. Since the eighth proprietor, John Carteret, Lord Granville, was awarded title to roughly one-half of North Carolina, the colony took on an extraordinary character not replicated in England's other American colonies. Because North Carolina's royal governors from 1729 until 1776 had no authority over the sale and thus essentially the exchange of property in half of its territory known as the Granville District, unregulated land exchanges and irregular court proceedings were perpetuated until the American Revolution.

After 1712, when governors began to be appointed to oversee a separate North Carolina, the rulers of these settled portions of the colony were those who could rely upon individually appointed governors to secure favorable treatment or to form a collaborative partnership in business or land ventures. Failing that, a minority faction could almost always be created to operate quite comfortably in opposition to any governor and his following.

With the presence (or most often absentee ownership) of Lord Granville in the northern half of colonial North Carolina, an aggressive clan of entrepreneurial plantation owners aligned with South Carolina interests settled in the Cape Fear region. A second group of planters with vested interests evolved in the New Bern region and were further emboldened when Governor Tryon moved North Carolina's colonial capital from Brunswick Town to New Bern. Thus, rival factions in three geographically separated seats competed with one another to serve as the principal rulers of North Carolina. In the absence of either rivers or roads that connected these regions to the central and western sections of North Carolina, the competition for control of the whole colony remained mainly among leaders in these three coastal regions.

Neither the War of the Regulation nor the American Revolution had a major impact upon this coastal competition for a controlling dominance of North Carolina. The vicissitudes of security during the American Revolution required that the meeting places of provincial congresses and subsequently of the state's General Assembly be moved to interior locations such as Hillsborough, Fayetteville, and Halifax, but the essential struggles for control of North Carolina remained an intramural coastal matter. The selection of Raleigh as the site of the state's permanent capital and of Chapel Hill as the location of the state's first public university was less a concession to the demands of the interior population of North Carolina than it was to follow the common practice of the time of moving capitals (as in the case of Washington, D.C., as the nation's capital—designated in 1790) to neutral locations beyond the realm of coastal factionalism. When North Carolina chose a basically unknown but more central location in 1792, it followed precedents of other states (Delaware: Dover, 1777; Virginia: Richmond, 1780; New Jersey: Trenton, 1784; South Carolina: Columbia, 1786; and Georgia: Augusta, 1786). Other states, including Pennsylvania, New York, and Connecticut, later followed this same immediate postwar custom.

While the War of the Regulation highlighted the irregularities of landholding and land titles, especially in the Granville District of North Carolina, the matter of securing effective titles to land was not resolved until the American Revolution. In the midst of the war North Carolina's revolutionary General Assembly authorized the confiscation of the landholdings of loyalists, those owned by anyone who did not support the Revolution, and most notably those held by any nonresident owner of lands. This meant that the millions of acres of unsold land still owned by Lord Granville and even those lands held in trust by the London-based bookseller James Hutton for the Moravians in western North Carolina were subject to confiscation by the new state of North Carolina (see fig. 15.1). By quick maneuvering the Moravians were able to regain title to half of their lands, but the other half went the way of other confiscated lands in North Carolina. Amidst all of the revolutionary fervor, North Carolina's nascent state government opened a claims office and began selling lands to virtually anyone who filed claims for the confiscated lands (including those lands that had been owned by the Moravians in Wilkes County). These wartime actions opened up the largest land grab in North Carolina since the Tuscarora War. Just as the lands of the Tuscarora had been seized without effective compensation from North Caro-

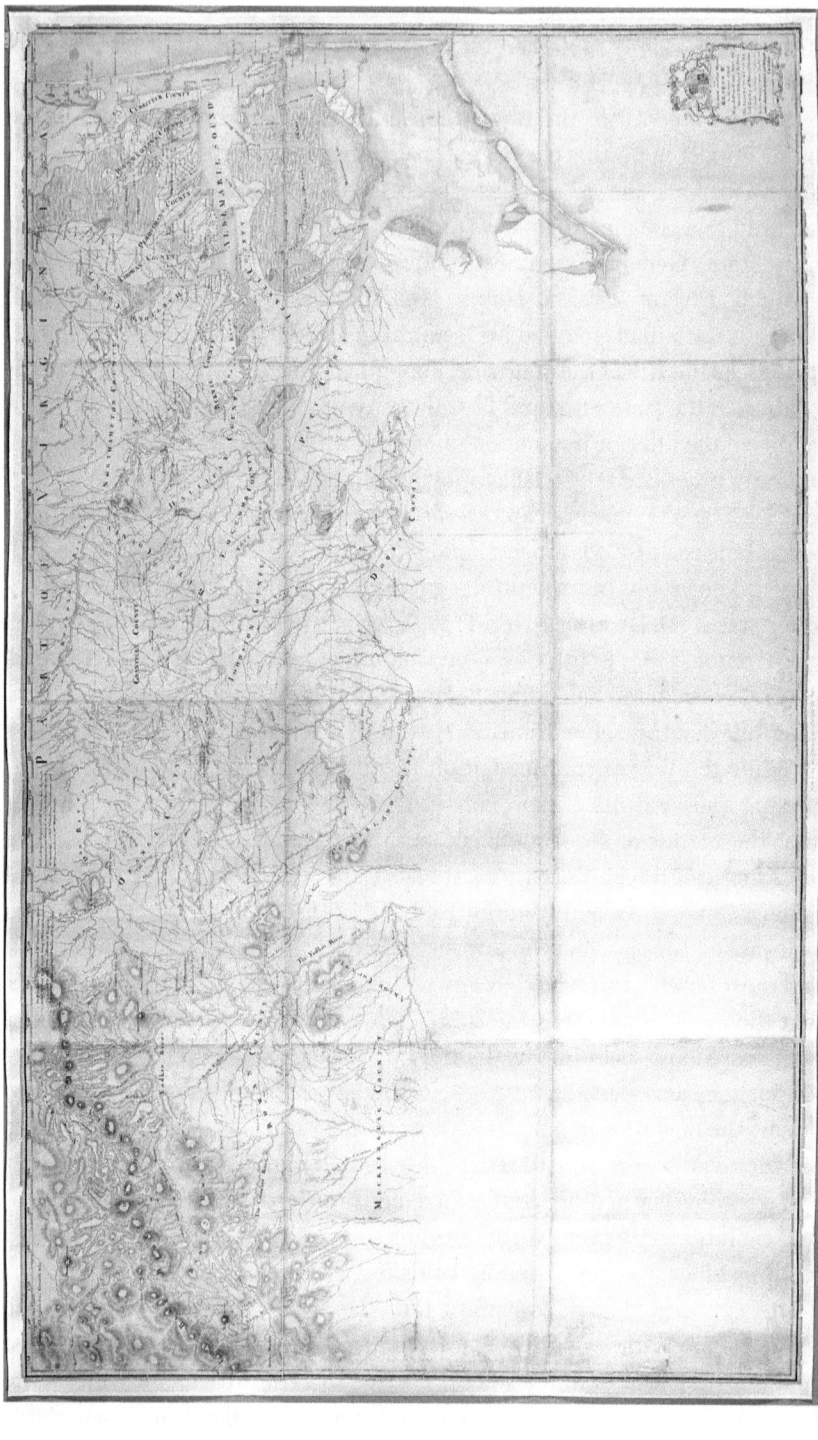

lina, so were those of a large minority of Americans in North Carolina who did not support the Revolution.

Nor did the American Revolution define who would be the rulers of North Carolina. Again in the midst of the war, North Carolina's revolutionary General Assembly wrote a constitution for the new state. Although the Fourth Provincial Congress meeting at Halifax adopted a set of resolves on April 12, 1776, authorizing the colony's delegates in Philadelphia to vote for independence from Britain, North Carolina was one of the last colonies to write and ratify a state constitution. Before the Continental Congress adopted the Declaration of Independence on July 4, 1776, New Hampshire, New Jersey, Virginia, and South Carolina had already adopted state constitutions.

When North Carolina eventually ratified its own constitution on December 18, 1776, it thus had quite a few models to draw upon. Like a few other states in the heat of revolution, North Carolina's constitution makers declared "That all political Power is vested in and derived from the People only." And they specified that the term "people" meant "Freemen of the Age of twenty-one Years." These were the people who could vote in the new state—if they additionally owned land and/or paid taxes. No further definition of "freemen" was given in the constitution, nor were specifications made with regard to either gender or race. As of December 1776, therefore, North Carolina's rulers (i.e., voter participants) in the new state were to be "freemen."

While the patriots in North Carolina may have known precisely what they meant by "freemen" at the time of the Revolution, it would take the leaders of North Carolina almost six decades—until 1835—to decide exactly what that term would mean in actuality in the state. While some of its neighbors (Virginia and South Carolina) determined almost from the outset that in their states freemen meant white male persons specifically, the question remained open in North Carolina. While it does not appear that women in North Carolina exercised the vote generally, as they did in New Jersey until 1807, many free blacks did. Perhaps because this somewhat open-ended meaning of the status of freemen continued so long, North Carolina developed a large and

---

(*opposite*) FIGURE 15.1. William Churton (fl. 1749–67) was the handpicked surveyor of Lord Granville, who retained title to more than half of North Carolina until the American Revolution. Churton's meticulous map of the Granville District shown here carefully delineated the vast holdings of the absentee proprietor. Granville's confused land dealings became major factors in both North Carolina's War of the Regulation and the American Revolution. Churton's 1768 map, with virtually no modification, also formed the basis for John Collet's North Carolina map of 1770 and Henry Mouzon's map of 1775—both of which thereby left the southern part of North Carolina largely blank. © British Library Board, Map K.Top.122.52.

active population of free blacks who participated in the society and commerce of the state. There were artisans, barbers, craftsmen, builders, river pilots, teachers, farmers, planters—even slaveholders—among the free black population of the state until 1835. But whenever scares of slave revolts arose (especially in Virginia and South Carolina), North Carolina's entirely white male bodies of legislators began whittling away the rights and freedoms of free blacks until by constitutional amendment in 1835 any person of African ancestry to the fourth generation was excluded from the ranks of rulers. While the 1835 revised North Carolina constitution did not exclude Indians specifically from the ranks of rulers, the state's white leaders, jurists, and citizens at large believed that Indians were also eliminated from both participation and rights.

The exclusion of free blacks from citizen participation was never as much a deliberate as a gradual process. The rights of free blacks were whittled away bit by bit until it became clear in 1835 that in North Carolina, as in other states North and South, the only people who could be citizens of either state or nation were white males. Pennsylvania followed North Carolina's example in its own constitutional convention two years later, making the exclusion of free blacks from citizenship unanimous among all American states outside of New England. Because the U.S. Constitution had not defined citizenship for all those people who lived in America at the end of the Revolution, all of the states, except a few in New England, agreed by 1837 that the rulers of the United States would be white males only.

In many respects the United States was an experimental nation until the 1830s. And North Carolina was thus also an experimental state. By 1783 the American Revolution secured independence for the thirteen colony-states. The U.S. Constitution of 1787 established a workable union of the original states and provided for the management of territories to the west until they became states. It also provided for the creation of a central government, a central system of managing foreign policy (including dealing with Indian nations), and—at least initially—a national bank for controlling the economy. But the fledgling United States suffered an almost fatal blow during the War of 1812. By cleaving to the notion that the nation should not have a standing army or a permanent military or naval establishment, the country nearly foundered when its ships became the objects of seizure by the British navy, and it was nearly defenseless to protect its ports and national capital at Washington. The dismal war became a clarion call for the nation to develop its coastal defenses, build an internal infrastructure of roads and canals, and establish an even more expansive system of banking to finance these and other improvements. Despite some periods of financial calamity, the United

States built a system of canals and river improvements that enabled many of the states to engage in a developing global market economy.

During much of this experimental period, North Carolina remained an undeveloped provincial land much as it had existed during the colonial era. Having a little, but not a lot, in common with either Virginia or South Carolina, the state government made modest contributions to locally generated volunteer groups and citizen-driven corporations to tackle some of the state's needs for infrastructure. Initiatives by individuals and citizen groups for building roads, bridges, canals, ferries, and ports arose locally and sought state licensure for the exclusive right to operate these transportation services at given locations or on defined routes. Operating in this laissez-faire, unplanned manner, North Carolina fell far behind other states in developing an infrastructure to support its commerce. As it had in the past, Virginia ports drained the commercial potential of northeastern North Carolina, and South Carolina did the same downriver from central North Carolina.

But during the War of 1812 volunteer soldiers and sailors from North Carolina traveled across many other states and returned to their homes in 1815 jealous of the internal improvements they saw in those places. Tapping into this soldier awakening, Archibald DeBow Murphey organized a campaign to undertake a statewide program of internal improvements that would put North Carolina on a par with other states. Murphey persuaded the General Assembly to invest seed funds in a new program of state-supported but privately controlled projects to build canals, widen rivers, and remove obstructions to navigation on most of the state's rivers and estuarine waterways. But whereas many other states were able to complete and open river and highway channels to their coastal ports during the 1820s, North Carolina's financial engagement with similar internal efforts was insufficient for them to be completed. Until the 1830s North Carolina remained almost the only one of the original thirteen states still without either a viable port city or an internal system of travel and transportation. Despite the efforts of Murphey and other dedicated leaders, North Carolina lacked a will, a governmental structure, or a pool of leadership to move programs that would benefit the state as a whole. By the 1830s the state had determined that its rulers would be white males, but it had not yet decided what the state itself would ultimately be or how the state's governance and resources could be organized to get to that end.

Defining the Realm, 1835–1900

Until 1835 neither the people of North Carolina nor its leadership had come together to create a statewide system of governance or to begin the difficult process of defining what North Carolina ought to be. There had been no mythic stories that its founders were building a city on a hill, a holy experiment, a state of yeoman farmers, a plantation society, or any other symbolically ideal state or society. North Carolina's origins had been so unplanned and happenstance, its evolution so ragged and uneven, its geography and landscape so complicated that there was, in essence, until the 1830s no general idea of from whence it came or where it was going. The first issue, once the land had been transferred from Indians to Europeans, was to determine who would rule the land. By 1835 in the state's revised constitution, that question had been resolved to be white males. The next major challenge was to define what this realm would be among the rapidly growing number of states in the expanding American union.

The need for a symbolic beginning of North Carolina was solved in part during the 1820s when a few aging Carolinians recalled (as it turned out somewhat incorrectly) that a group of discontented people had gathered in Charlotte on May 20, 1775, and had adopted America's first defiant declaration of independence from England. To be known from the 1820s forward as the Mecklenburg Declaration of Independence (often by its detractors as the "Mec Dec"), this proud founding story proved to be so persuasive that its date was placed upon both the North Carolina state flag and its permanent seal of state. And there the date has remained into the twenty-first century. Although Thomas Jefferson and most historians in and outside North Carolina have always doubted the veracity of the supposed declaration and its reconstructed language, this mythical founding story has weathered many storms. It was so much believed by North Carolinians at the time of the Civil War that the state's secessionists selected May 20, 1861, as the date for North Carolina to formalize its secession from the Union. Their aim was to bless the state's resignation from the Union by honoring the brave Mecklenburg patriots who, it was said, pioneered North Carolina's secession from the British Empire.

But the fixing of a state genesis story in this manner was merely incidental to a much larger revolution that was about to occur in both the nation and North Carolina. During the 1830s both underwent a sudden and monumental transformation. During that decade President Andrew Jackson abolished the national banking system. His election to the presidency ushered in a second-party system and a more democratic way of choosing presidents. At Jackson's ruthless urging, remaining groups of Indian nations living on state lands in the Southeast were removed to the West. The system of slavery as an institution came under attack. Free blacks saw controls over their lives and liberties tightened. And the national economy failed spectacularly in the Panic of 1837. The United States had to find a new way to operate virtually all of its institutions. With the powers of the central government under attack, the states sprang back into bold action, operating once again as separate entities much as they had under the Articles of Confederation between 1781 and 1789.

North Carolina's need for self-identity and to define what it was going to be as a state coalesced during the state's constitutional convention of 1835. As the delegates to the convention gathered in Raleigh's First Presbyterian Church to revise the constitution of 1776, they had both tangible and symbolic reminders of what they were attempting to do every morning as they entered the doors of the church. The state's first capitol lay in ashes, having burned to the ground in 1831. But a new and permanent State Capitol was rising in its place. It would be a grand Greek Revival structure as sleek and imposing at the time as any state capitol building in the nation. And its huge building blocks of stone were being delivered to the site every day the delegates met, on the tracks of an experimental railroad—a revolutionary mode of transporting goods and people across the land that did not require navigable waters.

At the 1835 North Carolina Constitutional Convention there was a long postponed reckoning between the power brokers of eastern North Carolina and a rising cadre of ambitious political voices from the Piedmont section of the state. Westerners conceded to the wishes of eastern leaders to eliminate free blacks from voting and thereby from the rights of citizenship. Easterners conceded to the desires of westerners to build a railroad linking the west to the Carolina coast. Both sections agreed on a system of representation that would enable the ends of the state to work on problems of statewide interest—such as common schools for white children and other railroads that would link North Carolina farmers and planters to the global market economy. A huge portion of the convention was devoted to bickering over whether someone who was not a Protestant should be allowed to hold office. Unlike their peers in Virginia and Tennessee, no portion of the convention was devoted to a discussion of whether slavery should be abolished.

The substantive outcomes of the 1835 state constitutional convention were a virtual cascade of causes and effects, one flowing from another and with ever-wider implications for the character of the state as a whole. These results gave a cast to North Carolina that nudged it ever closer to the slaveholding colossi that lay north and south of its borders. First and foremost, North Carolina would remain a slave state for the foreseeable future, and its principal labor force would consist of slaves. The state's workforce would continue to be bound, and with the disappearance of a system of indentured white servants, African Americans and their descendants would be held in slavery in perpetuity. The implications for persons of African (and Indian) descent that were not slaves turned out to be just as ominous and decisive. With the exclusion of persons of African descent to the fourth generation from voting and with most of their other rights of citizenship excised, the convention defined North Carolina for the foreseeable future as a "white" state where white males would constitute a ruling race.

But the 1835 constitution also provided a new system whereby the white male ruling race could govern the entire state. By breaking the stranglehold of the eastern counties and towns over the state's General Assembly, the new constitution balanced representation and political power in the legislature between eastern and western counties, making it necessary and thus possible to enact state laws and policies that addressed the needs of all sections of the state. Where Archibald D. Murphey sought an internal improvements plan that offered something concrete for virtually every segment of the state—complete with local capital projects—it was suddenly possible for North Carolina to move aggressively to build a North Carolina railroad through the center of the state. By consolidating economic power in the General Assembly, it also became possible to adopt laws and subsidies to reward virtually every special interest in the state—grist and lumber mill owners, ferry operators, inn and tavern keepers, toll road builders, speculators in lands vacated by Cherokee Indians removed to the West, wagon builders, slaveholders whose slaves were executed for criminal behavior, fishermen seeking exclusive rights to waters rich in fish or shellfish or turtles, harvesters of turpentine and pine tree products, hunting rights for fowl and game, and thousands of other ways in which the bounty of North Carolina's lands could be carved and sliced among people with special interests.

By making so many monumental decisions in one dramatic gathering in 1835, the fundamentally different character for North Carolina began to unfold over the decades that followed. North Carolina would be a "free" state built on classic republican principles (especially those of Greece and Rome) where its true citizens (white males) would be educated to rule and would be chosen by an electorate of their peers. This principle was underscored by another provision of the 1835 constitution that permitted these true citizens to elect their governor directly for the first time. As an antidote for excluding an underclass of slaves, free blacks, and Indians from its society, North Carolina's educated republican rulers would send wise delegates to the General Assembly to devise laws to care for all members of society in a paternalistic manner.

By focusing attention on those white children who would succeed their parents as the state's rulers, North Carolina would develop a system of education that would train its white children to participate as citizens and voters in the republic. It would build a state university where a selected few could attend and be prepared as fully educated men to take over the reins of government. With this enlightened polity North Carolina and its republican leaders would be ready to undertake the building of roads, bridges, aqueducts, impressive public buildings, and any other great work for the good of the republic (such as a much vaunted railroad) while minimizing the tax burden.

This vision of an enlightened slaveholding republic (also shared with other southern states) defined the state through the Civil War. The state's genesis story was in place—North Carolina had been the place where the first group of Americans (it was thought) had declared their independence from the brutal oppressions of England. With that independence came freedom from the enslavement of white Americans to a tyrannical British monarch and the right to build an interconnected American republic of many states where North Carolina would be a coequal member. Those potential internal enemies who were in any case not worthy to be a part of the republic (blacks, mulattoes, Indians) had been firmly bound legally into statuses where they belonged. The resulting republic would build houses, homes, highways, schools, halls of government, and even a university worthy of a great state. It should be noted that, as a consequence of all of this fighting for liberty, the prototype for what would eventually emerge as a "progressive" state was thus put into place well before the American Civil War.

This vision of North Carolina as a virtuous republican state emerged slowly, not quickly as in some other southern states, but by the 1850s the idea was firmly in place. The conception of the state as a well-managed republic was an important and fundamental accretion to the North Carolina narrative. Once the idea had been established, it was there to stay. Neither winds nor storms nor famine nor great wars could shake the basic foundations of this republic. As vicious and destructive as the Civil War was, that great conflict neither shattered nor essentially modified the basic North Carolina story that it was and always would be a virtuous and moderate republic. The state that seceded from the Union on May 20, 1861, to avert enslavement to an oppressive national government headed by a new and dangerous tyrant (Abraham Lincoln) was a benevolent and enlightened republic led by virtuous statesmen. Despite the destruction of the Confederacy to which North Carolina provided more soldiers than any other state (it was said), and whose troops got farthest to the front at Gettysburg (further elements in the traditional North Carolina story), its white leaders—victors and vanquished—never altered their conviction that North Carolina was a "white man's country."

Reconstruction was a bitter pill for white leaders. Seeing blacks emerge from generations of bondage with white Republican (not republican) sponsors was a further insult. Black citizenship, black suffrage, and new economic and labor systems, however, only reinforced the belief in white rule. Rather than accept such revolutionary changes meekly, whites responded with violence and terror. Although Reconstruction was a time of promise and challenge for emancipated blacks and black leaders who thrived briefly as a free people, the promise eventually slipped away. North Carolina's white leaders soon found common cause with their counterparts in most northern states. In those states free blacks had also been marginalized prior to the Civil War. As Reconstruction faded in southern states, resulting in a new effort to exclude blacks from the political process, there was a similar diminution in the rights of blacks in the North. When North Carolina's white leaders coalesced again in the 1890s to expunge black elected officials, to crush fusion government, to enact Jim Crow laws, and to deny voting rights to blacks and illiterate whites, North Carolina's basic vision of a white republic was restored to the status it had held before the Civil War.

The process of restoring North Carolina to a white-governed republic was not entirely separate from the other great hallmark of the republic: that state government could be an essential tool in its economic development. Building the North Carolina Railroad in the 1840s and 1850s had shown the potential. The white political leaders who found the North Carolina General Assembly a congenial place after 1835 to secure economic and political support for their business pursuits never lost faith that with their restoration to power they could again win favorable laws, tax policies, and pork barrel legislation to support their particular business ambitions. Just as statehouses and Congress in the rest of the nation after the Civil War became the scenes of favoritism toward the barons of railroads, industry, and trade, the state government of North Carolina, its governors, and its General Assembly kept taxes low on large business and agricultural ventures. Indeed, the election of leaders to the General Assembly and even to the governorship after the Civil War was as likely as not part of a business decision to secure money, tax concessions, or development rights as to provide enlightened leadership to the state.

During this long period of political recovery of a supposedly virtuous republic to be operated by enlightened whites, a further corollary was added to the basic credo of North Carolina's vision of its proper realm. Because the Confederacy had been defeated by what was perceived to be a northern industrial giant, the new North Carolina and the New South needed to industrialize so that it would never again be exposed to such a foreign power (i.e., the industrial North) with a superior ability to produce guns, boats, boots, and bullets. Bringing industry to North Carolina, as to the South, was redefined from a commitment of money and land and the risk of contaminated waters or skies to one of the most virtuous things one could do in this enlightened republic. When the Dukes, the Reynolds, the Holts, the Cannons, and the Jordans wanted lands, rivers, and undisputed rights to build railroads, dams, and belching smokestacks, efforts to support their aims were not viewed as a sacrifice of the bounty of nature by North Carolina (see fig. 15.2). Granting special privileges to these visionary industrialists was, instead, one of the greatest contributions of virtue and goodness to the people of North Carolina. Indeed, the process of adding jobs, smokestacks, and mill villages to North Carolina became one of the greatest acts of civic virtue by any member of the white ruling populace of the state. A further benefit to an orderly society was that, instead of opening these industries to waves of foreign immigrants, North Carolina's workforce would come from its marginally productive farms.

By the 1890s the fundamental definition of what North Carolina should be and would be had been firmly put into place. The basic vision was that of a virtuous republic controlled by a white electorate and governed by a class of leaders who had the education and calling to shape the republic for the good of all residents in the realm—farmer, cabinetmaker, white, black, factory worker, and elected official. This vision, first propounded in the antebellum South, lived through the Civil War and was augmented with the idea that the most virtuous leader in the society was the entrepreneur who got roads, railroads, dams, and factories built to advance economic development without respect to their impact on the state's natural environment, its communities, or its fundamental society.

Pursuing "Progress," 1900–1980

The fundamental idea of transforming North Carolina into a virtuous republic in the post–Civil War, post-Reconstruction world was lodged firmly in place by 1900. The only thing missing was a proper term to describe it. Somehow the idea of a virtuous republic did not fit in an era of American history during which the United States became the industrial workshop of the world. Although North Carolina had become a bastion of Protestantism during the nineteenth century, and its industrialists were in the process of building company towns filled with churches, no public terminology that smacked of the religious would work to characterize the secular state.

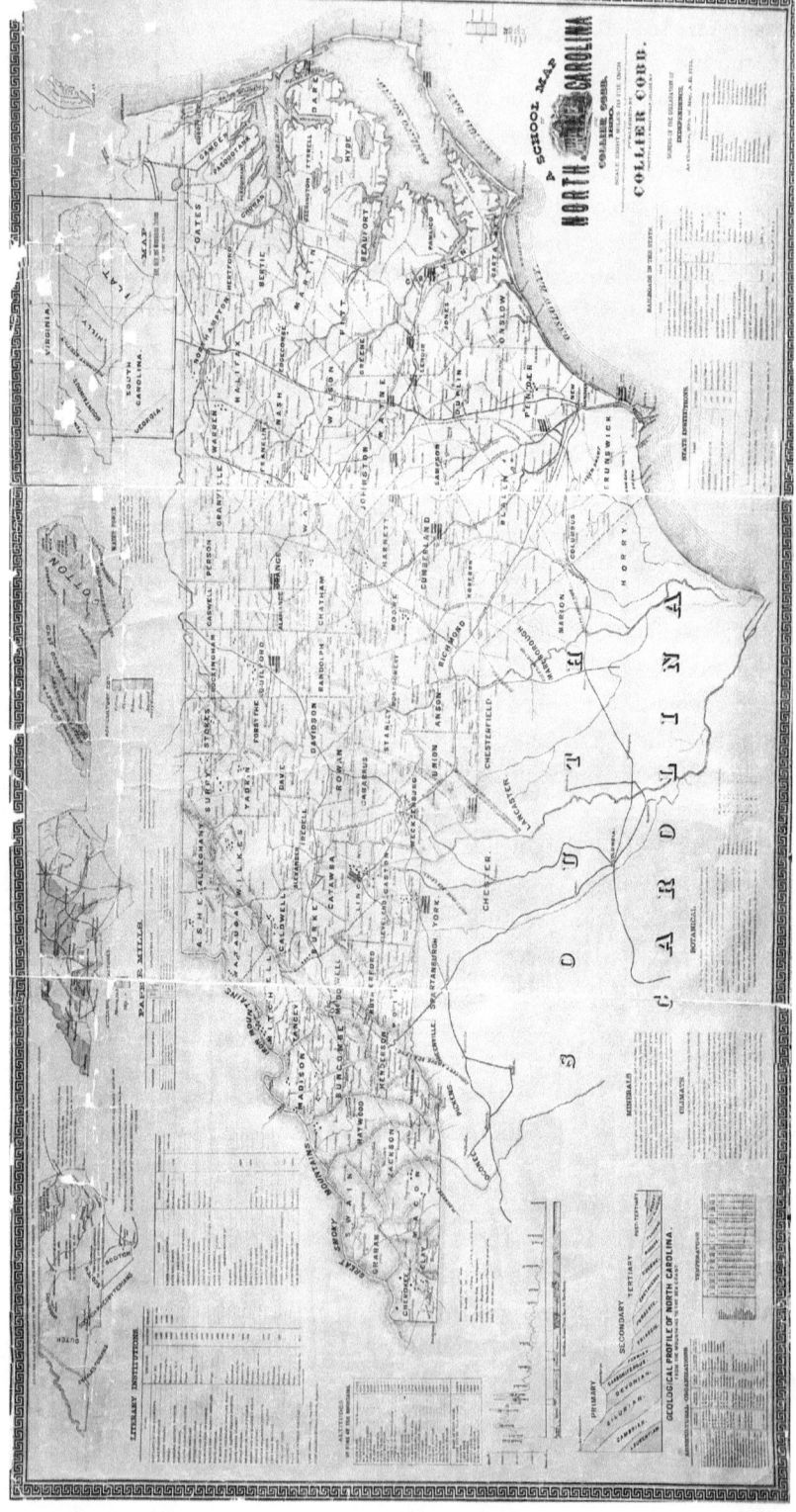

Although North Carolina was a land that was very friendly to business and entrepreneurs—especially budding industrialists—any term that might associate North Carolina with the black and sooty smoke of iron, coal, and steel industries was also too dark to imagine. North Carolina's self-image hinged on a radically undemocratic idea that only white males could rule properly and, moreover, should rule due to the purported dull incapacities of blacks. Even though pronouncements of "white supremacy" undeniably contradicted America's democratic ideals, governance by enlightened white leaders was essential to sustain a program of economic development.

To cloak such contradictions, a widening group of preachers, pedagogues, politicians, promoters, developers, speculators, and even historians latched onto the idea of "progress" as a term that seemed synonymous with America's special destiny in history. From the first arrival of the Puritans on Massachusetts Bay, America's story was one of endless progress. Coming from worn-out Europe was progress. Building farms and towns in North America was progress. Moving to new frontiers was progress. Securing independence from England was progress. Writing and ratifying the U.S. Constitution was progress. Building roads, canals, and railroads was progress. "Universal manhood suffrage" (but no women or blacks, of course) was progress. Moving Indians west of the Mississippi was progress. Building an industrial America was progress. There were economic setbacks, recessions, and depressions, even a Civil War among the states, but those were mere pauses in America's inexorable march toward progress.

"Progress" was such a captivating concept and idea that it became the secular version of religious beliefs, the positive spin on industrial development, the bright banner at ribbon cuttings for factories that employed children to operate spinning machines for twelve hours a day, the songs of praise for North Carolina–based business tycoons who created national business monopolies or who were awarded the rights to dam the state's rivers with little concern for environmental or social consequences. The term became even more appealing when it attached the notion that industry and jobs would inevitably lead to social progress as well: schools, health care, playgrounds, churches, auditoriums for music, libraries for every community, and schools for every race.

North Carolina at the turn of the twentieth century bought the idea of

(*opposite*) FIGURE 15.2. This rare 1880 Collier Cobb map on linen shows North Carolina on the cusp of industrialization. Smaller maps at the top denote ethnic settlement patterns, major agricultural areas, and waterpower sites. "Literary" institutions are also listed. Reproduction courtesy of the North Carolina State Archives.

progress. It became a shibboleth for the whole body of belief that has defined the state's image of itself ever since. Yet, the pursuit of progress can be used to mask many machinations of the human spirit. It can be employed smoothly and easily to divert attention from a variety of harsh realities in society and the body politic. If the state's political leaders could keep the public focus on "progress" as a positive outcome of hardworking human endeavor, they could explain away many habits and instincts that, according to other measures, might seem entirely unprogressive.

Progressive ideology carried within it a deep irony. Retrogressive policies became defined as progressive. Progressive politicians had to remove "inept" elected black leaders by vote or by force to substitute supposedly capable white politicians. The enactment of Jim Crow laws and "grandfather" clauses in voting laws helped to eliminate a black "menace" that undermined good government and a smoothly operating progressive society. The establishment of "separate but equal" schools not only had a blessing from the U.S. Supreme Court but also enabled North Carolina to justify schools commensurate with the supposed limited capabilities of an alleged inferior race. The creation of factories that employed men, women, and children for most of the hours of their waking life was a blessing to them because it gave them jobs and kept them from spending unproductive lives on subsistence farms.

It was, moreover, progressive to support the good works of successful businessmen. The election of business leaders, factory owners, and prominent lawyers to local and state offices placed some of society's best minds, most successful entrepreneurs, and dedicated civic leaders in positions where they could benefit society as a whole. Luring factories to a business-friendly, nonunion-labor environment in North Carolina from the North's industrial heartland, with union-dominated cities, would benefit the welfare of the people of the state. This would result in a larger and richer class of business leaders. Besides, North Carolina benefited from having a large number of millionaires and magnates of industry in state. They could proudly pour some of their wealth into building schools, hospitals, churches, and the culture of the state.

The idea of progress in North Carolina led to another corollary: the best solution for any threat or crisis that threatened progress was to develop a carefully planned strategy of diversion. The education of black children has been a constant focus for this strategy in North Carolina's pursuit of progress during the twentieth century and beyond. From the moment the U.S. Supreme Court ruled in its dramatic *Plessy v. Ferguson* (1896) decision to uphold state laws that separated races in public accommodations and schools, North Carolina's jubilant white leaders set about attempting to demonstrate that at least their state could abide by both the letter and the spirit of the new ruling. Almost from the outset in this new era, North Carolina's black leaders pouring out of St. Augustine's College in Raleigh, Livingstone College in Salisbury, Slater Institute in Winston-Salem, and the State Normal Colored School in Fayetteville monitored the progress of public schools for black children. Booker T. Washington extended a helping hand from his Tuskegee Institute in Alabama to advise and assist in working with black communities to build good-quality training schools for black children. With the financial assistance of the generous Julius Rosenwald Fund, North Carolina participated in the construction of more than a thousand schools for black students. With such assistance, by the 1940s North Carolina's progressive politicians could claim that the state was doing more to educate its black children than any other state in the South.

North Carolina's progressive leaders were so pleased with the state's achievements under the *Plessy v. Ferguson* dispensation that the reversal of course represented by *Brown v. Board of Education* (1954) was a shocking challenge to what they perceived had become an ideal peaceable kingdom. The *Brown* decision was characterized by North Carolina's leaders not as about race or civil rights but as an assault on a land of enlightened governance and social order. But still favoring peace over war—especially the kinds of bloody confrontations they observed in places like Alabama, Arkansas, and Mississippi—North Carolina's progressive intelligentsia devised a clever strategy to transfer all decisions about the integration of schools from the state to the local level. This particular diversion, which was extolled by leaders and even historians as a sound and wise progressive policy, enabled North Carolina to generally sidestep the issue of school integration in most of its counties for another twenty years or longer. And then, with the passage of another twenty or thirty years, another state-authorized local option initiative—the creation of charter schools—established a new route whereby parents who objected to having white and black schoolchildren together in public schools could enroll their children in a charter school of their choice, with the full financial assistance of state and local school districts.

The careful management of public schools has been but one method whereby practices classified as progressive became an accepted and laudable norm of public and private policy in North Carolina. In addition to creating self-contained mill towns surrounding textile, tobacco, and metal processing plants with all of the comforts of an ideal community, North Carolina's progressive leaders proudly proclaimed the state to be a haven for manufacturers seeking a low-wage, nonunion workforce. Despite the rise and fall of unionizing campaigns across the textile industry nationally, of tobacco workers in other states, and of communications and transport workers especially in the North, the state's manufacturers have waged mainly successful campaigns to resist union-organizing efforts, mounting employee loyalty programs through employee profit sharing and organizing company athletic programs to put their men's and women's teams in competition with those of other companies. Nor have the state's manufacturers been averse to characterizing some union promoters as secret agents or "outside agitators" of socialist, communist, or radical organizations seeking to subvert the American way of life.

One of the unanticipated outcomes of North Carolina's emphasis on boosting manufacturing jobs through the twentieth century is that the state could not maintain its manufacturing workforce in a global market. Despite the state's competitive low wages in the context of the United States, its manufacturers and workers eventually could not compete in a world filled with much-lower-wage workers in places like Japan, China, India, Indonesia, Mexico, and other third-world nations around the Pacific Rim and in Central and South America. Thus, in the closing decades of the twentieth century going forward, North Carolina found itself in the position of seeing the manufacturers it had lured to the state over the period of a century departing for other nations, or at least conducting its manufacturing off-shore. Textiles, furniture, electronics, and even tobacco manufacturing—bedrocks of the state's economy—could be performed elsewhere at a fraction of the cost in a North Carolina factory.

The greatest need for North Carolina in these years was to find ways to diversify its economy and to establish incentives for encouraging and nurturing small businesses—or at least businesses whose main revenues did not derive from manufacturing. Beginning in the 1930s and increasing dramatically into the twenty-first century, savvy promoters on the coast and in the mountains of North Carolina boosted tourism as core economies for those regions of the state. And, beginning in the 1950s, North Carolina's embattled progressive governors—both Democrats and Republicans—wisely also saw dollar value in developing the engineering and research potential that existed within the state's major universities. First with Governor Luther Hodges and then for all of his successors, the nurturing of the Research Triangle Park became a clear demonstration that North Carolina—even within the limitations of a progressive emphasis on basic manufacturing—could find an important role in a complicated world economy. Some of these same leaders also gloried in the promotion of North Carolina as a busy center for both college and professional sports. College basketball, golfing, NFL football, NBA basketball, and NASCAR racing (the latter three concentrated primarily the state's bustling border commercial hub, Charlotte) have found comfortable and economically productive places in North Carolina's geophysical and social environment.

However one might assess the ulterior motives of progressive politicians and those who endeavored to seek progressive ends in North Carolina throughout the twentieth century and into the early decades of the twenty-first, there is no doubt that progressivism was and has been a powerful and generally positive animating force in North Carolina. In a state not endowed with the tropical climes of Florida or Hawaii, the coal and iron of Pennsylvania, the vast plantation lands of South Carolina or Mississippi, the oil of Texas or Oklahoma, the metropolises of New York or Illinois or California, the fruited plains of Iowa or Kansas, or the river deltas of Virginia or Louisiana, North Carolina has had to devise a strategy for preaching and catalyzing its development. The idea of pursuing progress—despite all of its foibles, diversions, and sleights of hand—has been a richly rewarding organizing principle. Into the early years of the twenty-first century, no one in the North Carolina firmament has put forth a viable or meaningful alternative organizing principle for the state.

Turf Wars and Bragging Rights, 1980–Present

One of the oldest and most persistent habits of human beings has been valorizing the ownership of places and using those places to promote one's ideas and interests. Whether one looks at the control of a piece of land, the possession of a symbol won in battle, or a lofty perch from which to preach, battles for turf and the winning of bragging rights animate human society. And such struggles for power are the kinds of competitions that give birth to partisan rivalries.

For example, take the case of a favored historic natural crossing on the Yadkin River just northeast of Salisbury, North Carolina, known historically as the Trading Ford. When the Spanish explorer Juan Pardo came to the place in 1566, he called it Guatari and found that a community of powerful women ruled over a few hundred men who did the bidding of their female leaders. These Indians were on the eastern fringes of a vast network of mound builders that lived mainly in the Mississippi River valley. A century later in 1670 the German explorer John Lederer found that the Trading Ford site was controlled by a band of Saura Indians from the Dan River region of North Carolina. These Indians were using the place to trade the cinnabar (red pigment) and salt that they mined in the Saura Mountains. Thirty years after that the English explorer John Lawson (1701) found the place occupied by Saponi Indians who used the spot as a center to handle trade up and down the Yadkin River and on the heavily traveled Great Trading Path extending from Virginia across the North Carolina Piedmont into South Carolina. A century after John Lederer came to the place, the armies of Nathanael Greene used the shallow river crossing to elude the pursuing forces of British general Lord Cornwallis in the midst of the American Revolution. Another thirty years later farmer-merchants—mainly of the large Richmond Pearson clan—depended on the spot to conduct trade from the upper Yadkin River down the Peedee River to the South Carolina port at Georgetown on the Atlantic coast. In yet another thirty years, this spot was found to be an ideal location for laying the tracks for the North Carolina Railroad. And another century later, by the 1920s going forward to the twenty-first century, Alcoa, the mighty aluminum company from Pittsburgh, negotiated its own "treaty" with the state of North Carolina. Under the terms of its agreement, Alcoa acquired exclusive use of the place (by then inundated by High Rock Lake to feed a hydroelectric dam) for the production and trade of aluminum products.

All of these occupants of the Trading Ford site on the Yadkin River had to win this crucial geographic spot in North Carolina by war, negotiation, intimidation, the payment of tribute, or a combination of these methods for gaining valuable turf. In the case of every successive occupant, it was necessary to determine that the site was worthy of being possessed, capable of being obtained, and a suitable place from which the new occupant could trade, sell, barter, or manufacture valuable goods. The goods could be cinnabar, tools, corn, tobacco, aluminum, or perhaps even religious teachings or political arguments. But whatever the goods or the ideas, Trading Ford has been a strategic North Carolina location from the earliest times of recorded history.

The North Carolina State Capitol built on a square of vacant land in the created capital of Raleigh became symbolically a place similar to Trading Ford in 1792. Since that time there have been countless turf wars between political parties and factions. With the exception of the Civil War, there has been more continuity than disruption, more evolution than revolution since the United States won its independence. Although the founding fathers hoped that they had perfected a system of government that would rise above the rancor and bitterness of partisan wrangling, they knew even before the last states (North Carolina and Rhode Island) had ratified the Constitution that they had failed. Like it or not, the United States emerged in such a manner that its political parties came to serve as instruments for choosing candidates for office and not, as in many other nations, mirrors for expressing potentially disruptive ideological cleavages in the body politic. Unlike other nations where ideological points of view can be the causes of revolution, the rise of tyrants, or the beheading of an entire ruling class, American parties have generally served as blunt instruments for beating back or watering down dangerous ideological upheavals.

While political historians and political scientists analyze the changes in political parties, the scope of voting bases, and the habits of voters in a great many elections, the American political system and that of North Carolina have been scenes of battles for turf almost from the outset of colonial settlement to the present. Factions or parties fought for possession of the office of the governor and for sufficient numbers in the governor's council and in both houses of the colonial or state assembly to exercise control. In a state where governors had neither the power of veto nor the option of succession until late in the twentieth century, it was the governor's powers of appointment, of conferring titles to land, and of serving as the head of the party in power that made the governor's seat such a prized possession. It was the taxing power and the control of spending—the power of the purse—that has made the North Carolina General Assembly such a powerful body on the state level. By the same token, the assembly's perennial strong control over county and local governments within the state has made it a controlling colossus above subject counties and towns. By controlling the assembly the party in power in North Carolina has always been able to pass favorable session laws to support its favored interests and make subtle modifications in the state's General Statutes to permit or annul developments believed to be important or detrimental to the state and its current rulers. Session laws in North Carolina—as opposed to the state's constitution and its General Statutes—have been used from the creation of the revolutionary state in 1777 to the present as powerful edicts to enforce partisan ideologies and interests.

From factions to political parties, from voting by the landed to voting by white males to voting by white and black males to voting by all males and females over twenty-one years of age and then eighteen, from the selection of leaders in party caucuses to party conventions to party primaries, the process of choosing rulers in North Carolina has indeed expanded over the centuries. Campaigning has become more complicated over time and much more expensive. But the nation and North Carolina's political party apparatuses have grown to meet the needs and, except in a few complicated situations, succeeded in transferring power peacefully from one elected official to another and one political party to another. That is, as long as the party contending for power can characterize its mission as being devoted to the progressive goals of the state's perennial ruling elite.

While politicians in both state and nation would have citizens believe that the forthcoming election is the most important election in which they will ever have the privilege of voting, except in rare instances those candidates available for election and the issues on which they have run are well within the panoply of North Carolina's long trajectory as a geophysical political entity. A majority of the candidates for office remain committed to leading a state always wishing to better itself. While succession in office without term limits is a troublesome aspect of American politics, it is at least a feature that is shared across nearly all states. While longevity of tenure in office on the state and national level is often rewarded with more power and influence, few reformers have attempted to change the basic system.

In recognizing these verities as some of the basic characteristics of America's political system, we see that it has always been inevitable that there would be shifts and modifications in the political parties in power in North Carolina. For most of the twentieth century, from a rocky but triumphant beginning around 1900, North Carolina was controlled and dominated by a white supremacist Democratic Party. The party cast itself as the state's progressive party and its goals as progressive from 1900 forward. This meant that many decisions about the governorship and control of the General Assembly could be made in Democratic Party caucuses and primaries. That is, until 1954, when the multiplying effects of the *Brown v. Board of Education* decision forced the Democratic Party to begin a long period of introspection about what its commitment to progressive values really meant. That self-examination continued until around 1980, when cleavages within the party and beyond the party made it clear that North Carolina was going to have a true two-party state for the first time in the twentieth century.

A mild-mannered and genial Republican, James Holshouser, won election in 1972 as the state's first Republican governor in the twentieth century. His tenure fell well within the parameters of the moderate progressive Democratic governors who preceded him. The most unexpected political victory of that same year—for both North Carolina Democrats and North Carolinians as a whole—was the election of the outspoken television commentator Jesse Helms, who had recently switched to the Republican Party, to the U.S. Senate over a beloved moderate congressman Nick Galifianakis. With a well-crafted campaign of television ads, Helms defeated his opponent by portraying him as more Greek than American and as too liberal for North Carolina.

Many observers considered Helms's election a fluke, a brief interregnum in the "progressive" tradition of North Carolina. But Helms proved by his reelection in 1978 and three further times that the 1972 election was not a brief sidestep in a historically progressive state. Vaulting himself into the center of controversial national issues and inserting his homegrown campaign machinery in the national presidential elections of 1976 and 1980, Helms became a power broker on the national level as well. Winning recognition as the Republican Party's leading conservative, he eagerly wrote some provisions of the Republican Party platform and played a major role in the electoral process that brought Ronald Reagan to the White House in 1981. At the same time he helped engineer an unexpected transition of the U.S. Senate from a Democratic to a Republican majority. From 1980 until 2003, when he concluded three uninterrupted decades in the Senate, Helms continued to be among the most consequential politicians in the United States and the symbolic head of the American conservative movement.

Almost single-handedly Helms made it respectable for America's most important elected elite, as represented by the U.S. Senate, to pursue seemingly contrarian positions on many issues. From America's foreign policies in Latin America and Africa to the operations of its intelligence agencies, from reforming agricultural policies to assisting disabled veterans, and from assistance programs for HIV and AIDS to a virtual control on the appointment of U.S. ambassadors, Helms bent policies in directions that would have been unimaginable before he arrived on the scene. In a world that seemed to nudge politicians and political parties into a posture of moderation, Helms inspired prickly questions about the nature and correctness of mainstream politics.

While Helms declined suggestions that he seek election as North Carolina's governor in 1984 and thus avoid a head-on political collision with a powerful Governor James B. Hunt Jr. in the senatorial race, he stuck to his guns. Having finished two terms—the first governor in North Carolina permitted to succeed himself—Hunt was one of the most successful and influential Democratic politicians the state had ever produced. But in what was popularly billed at the time as the most expensive senatorial election in American history, Helms once again proved that he had come to resemble more than anyone else in the last decades of the twentieth century the essence or the core values of North Carolina's political system. The popular Hunt later returned for another eight years as North Carolina's governor and again proved his continuing power as a skillful politician by securing the veto power for North Carolina's governors for the first time in history. Two more Democratic governors would follow Hunt. But even Hunt to some extent and his two successors in retrospect appeared as lame duck governors at the end of the Democratic Party's long dynasty. The state's political majority was already becoming Republican. Finally in 2010 Republicans gained a majority in both houses of the General Assembly. In 2012, North Carolina completed the circle by electing its third Republican governor since the beginning of the twentieth century.

But while control of the principal offices of state government were occupied by Republicans by 2012 and both houses of the General Assembly saw the election of Republican majorities, the policies that were being pursued by Republicans were far from outside the tradition of North Carolina's hallmark progressive past. Revisions to voting rights looked much like those pursued by progressive Democrats throughout most of the twentieth century. Revisions to the state's educational system by granting special funding to charter schools much resembled the efforts of Democratic progressives in the Pearsall Plan to avoid integration of the state's schools. The intrusion of Republican-controlled houses of the General Assembly into the business of women's rights to have abortions or to protect the life of the unborn had eerie similarities to North Carolina's establishment of a eugenics board during progressive Democratic rule in 1929. This expansion of the power of an already preponderant General Assembly by 2016 into laws regulating the activities of individuals of transforming gender identity looked very much like the use of state power in past ages to identify all persons to the fourth generation (mixed race) as all of one race or another.

The intervention of the Republican General Assembly into matters of free speech at the University of North Carolina at Chapel Hill echoed the Democratic General Assembly's enactment of a Speaker Ban Law in 1963 forbidding the appearance of known communists for speaking engagements on that campus. Nor was that the first time North Carolina's progressive Democrats had attempted to silence freedom of speech on college campuses in the state. When Trinity College (later Duke University) historian John Spencer Bassett uttered in print the opinion that "Booker T. Washington [is] the greatest man, save General Lee, born in the South in a hundred years," the state's most outspoken Democrat, Raleigh editor Josephus Daniels, demanded that Bassett be fired. When the Democratic-controlled House of Representatives threatened in 1925 to outlaw the teaching of Darwinism in North Carolina, Wake Forest College (later University) president and biologist William Louis Poteat steadfastly refused. Thanks to the trustees of both Trinity and Wake Forest, in the midst of those politically trying moments the rights of both Bassett and Poteat to speak their minds were upheld.

■ As these many representative examples suggest, North Carolina's proud reputation as a progressive state will most likely not be permanently tarnished by the proceedings of either a liberal or a conservative governor or General Assembly. Its reputation as a land of progressive thought and action will be better understood by students of the state's history if we expand our understanding of what has fallen in the last century under the banner of progressivism. Many North Carolinians have worried that a conservative General Assembly will lead the state away from a grand tradition of liberalism, inclusion, and providing a good basic education for every child—no matter race, gender, class, or background. But those good and worthy goals are not and never have been at the core of North Carolina's political and social agendas. Those ideals are just as close to the fringe of North Carolina's historic progressivism as are some of the aims of North Carolina's twenty-first-century leaders to keep the state firmly on its traditions of social conservatism, exclusion, and providing every child with among the most modest basic educations among the nation's states—no matter race, gender, class, or background.

To do things much differently would actually be more of a radical departure from North Carolina's past. North Carolina has always been something of a middling state—a lot of people, a lot of diversity, a complicated geophysical landscape, moderate aspirations, low taxes and low salaries, a lot of agriculture, tourist lures at both ends of the state, some talented and renowned expatriates, a good state university and many outstanding private colleges, and barely adequate schools. A horticulturist might prune some unruly and unmanageable branches from a flowering plant, but in the end the conservative roots will prevail in securing the political bragging rights for control of the state. Those controlling the state, whoever they may be, will continue to claim that they are leading and advancing one of the most "progressive" states in the nation, that they are doing it better than the wrong-headed people they replaced, and they will thus exercise all of the bragging rights that goes with being in power.

NOTES

1. John Lawson, *A New Voyage to Carolina*, ed. Hugh Talmage Lefler (Chapel Hill: University of North Carolina Press, 1967).

2. In addition to the biblical account of the conquest of Canaan by Hebrew exiles from Egypt under the command of Joshua, the idea of inspired conquest by Christianity pervaded Spanish, French, and English voyages of conquest into North and South America. Through the pen of the Congregational minister and educator Timothy Dwight, a formal American codicil was in the 1785 epic poem titled "The Conquest of Canaan," describing how American revolutionaries wrested the territory of Connecticut from British rulers. See Timothy Dwight, *The Conquest of Canaan* (Hartford, 1785).

About the Editors and Contributors

EDITORS

Jeffrey J. Crow is the former director of the Office of Archives and History and deputy secretary of the North Carolina Department of Cultural Resources. He received his Ph.D. from Duke University, where he was elected to Phi Beta Kappa. He is the author or editor of numerous publications on North Carolina and southern history. His scholarship has concentrated on the American Revolution and the New South. His 1980 article "Slave Rebelliousness and Social Disorder in North Carolina, 1775–1802" won the Daughters of the American Wars Award for the best article in the *William and Mary Quarterly*. He was the historical consultant on the emmy Award–winning documentary *Birth of a Colony* (WUNC-TV).

Larry E. Tise is a native of Winston-Salem, N.C., with A.B. and M.Div. degrees from Duke University and a Ph.D. from UNC–Chapel Hill. He is former executive director of the North Carolina Division of Archives and History (1975–81), the Pennsylvania Historical and Museum Commission (1981–87), the American Association for State and Local History (1987–89), and the Benjamin Franklin National Memorial (1989–97). Since 1997 he has been president of the International Congress of Distinguished Awards and a private practice historian located in Philadelphia. Since 2000 he has been a Wilbur & Orville Distinguished Professor at East Carolina University. In 2011 he and his successors at Archives and History, William S. Price and Jeffrey J. Crow, launched a statewide multidisciplinary effort to formulate a new narrative for North Carolina that resulted in *New Voyages to Carolina*.

CONTRIBUTORS

Dorothea V. Ames is a research associate in the Department of Geological Sciences at East Carolina University. She has a B.S. in zoology and chemistry from McGill University, and a B.S. in science education and an M.S. in geology from East Carolina University. She has worked on the origin and evolution of the North Carolina coastal system and its relationship to human history since 1988 and has taught numerous college earth science courses and science, technology, engineering, and math (STEM) teacher education programs.

Karl E. Campbell is an associate professor of history at Appalachian State University, where he teaches North Carolina and recent U.S. history. He is the author of *Senator Sam Ervin, Last of the Founding Fathers* and is working on a biography of Governor Luther H. Hodges.

James C. Cobb is Spalding Distinguished Professor of History, Emeritus, at the University of Georgia. A former president of the Southern Historical Association, he has written widely on the economy, politics, and culture of the American South.

Peter A. Coclanis is Albert R. Newsome Distinguished Professor of History and director of the Global Research Institute at the University of North Carolina at Chapel Hill. He came there in 1984 after taking his Ph.D. at Columbia University in the same year. He is an economic historian who works primarily on the U.S. South and on Southeast Asia and has published widely on these areas.

Stephen Feeley is an associate professor of history at McDaniel College. He earned his Ph.D. from the College of William and Mary. His chapter is part of a larger project examining the Tuscaroras, their experiences during the Tuscarora War, and their flight and subsequent integration as the sixth nation of the Haudenosaunee (Iroquois) Confederacy.

Jerry Gershenborn is professor of history at North Carolina Central University. He is the author of *Melville J. Herskovits and the Racial Politics of Knowledge*. He is currently working on a book titled *Louis Austin and the Carolina Times: A Life in the Long Black Freedom Struggle*.

Glenda Elizabeth Gilmore is the Peter V. and C. Vann Woodward Professor of History at Yale University and earned her Ph.D. from the University of North Carolina at Chapel Hill. Her most recent book is *These United States: A Nation in the Making, 1890 to the Present*, coauthored with Thomas Sugrue.

Patrick J. Huber is professor of history and political science at the Missouri University of Science and Technology. He received his Ph.D. from the University of North Carolina at Chapel Hill. He is the author of *Linthead Stomp: The Creation of Country Music in the Piedmont South*.

Charles F. Irons is professor of history and chair of the Department of History and Geography at Elon University. He is the author of *The Origins of Proslavery Christianity: White and Black Evangelicals in Colonial and Antebellum Virginia*.

David Moore teaches archaeology at Warren Wilson College in Asheville, North Carolina. He received his M.A. and Ph.D. degrees from the University of North Carolina at Chapel Hill. He is the author of *Catawba Valley Mississippian: Ceramics, Chronology, and Catawba Indians* and co-author of *Fort San Juan and the Limits of Empire*.

Michael Leroy Oberg is Distinguished Professor of History at the State University of New York, College at Geneseo. He is the author of seven books, including most recently *Professional Indian: The American Odyssey of Eleazer Williams*.

Stanley R. Riggs is the Distinguished Professor of the College of Arts and Sciences and Distinguished Research Professor of East Carolina University. He is a coastal-marine geologist who has researched ancient and modern coastal systems since 1964 and has been on the faculty of East Carolina University since 1967. His recent research focuses on the interrelationship of environmental dynamics with development of human civilization. He is founder and director of the nonprofit organization North Carolina Land of Water (NC LOW).

Richard D. Starnes teaches history and serves as dean of the College of Arts and Sciences at Western Carolina University. His books include *Creating the Land of the Sky: Tourism and Society in Western North Carolina* and the edited collection *Southern Journeys: Tourism, History, and Culture in the Modern South*.

Carole Watterson Troxler, professor emerita at Elon University, studies the impacts of the American Revolution in the Southern backcountry, maritime Canada, and the Bahamas. Twenty-plus articles feature white and black "loyalist" persons, settlements, and themes. Her latest book is *Farming Dissenters: The Regulator Movement in North Carolina*.

Bradford J. Wood is professor of history at Eastern Kentucky University, where he has taught since 2000. He is the author of *This Remote Part of the World: Regional Formation in Lower Cape Fear, North Carolina, 1725-1775*, and coeditor, with Michelle LeMaster, of *Creating and Contesting Carolina*.

Karin Zipf is professor of history at East Carolina University and is author of *Bad Girls at Samarcand: Sexuality and Sterilization in a Juvenile Reformatory* (2016 winner of the Ragan Old North State Award Cup for Non-Fiction) and *Labor of Innocents: Forced Apprenticeship in North Carolina, 1715-1919*.

Index

Page numbers in italics refer to illustrations.

Acemoglu, Daron: *Why Nations Fail: The Origins of Power, Prosperity, and Poverty*, 338
Acuff, Roy, 231
Adams, John, 125
African Americans: disfranchised, 6, 202–3, 243–44; financial independence of women, 9; African colonization, 101, 103; and religion, 145, 151, 156, 160–61; and national black denominations, 160–61; census of church memberships, 161; refugees flee to New Bern, 168; views of property, 175–79; delegates to 1868 Constitutional Convention, 188–89; demand better education, 196–98; women, become teachers, 200–201; forced to fund own schools, 203–4; seek more-equal schools, 204, 206–7; attack Jim Crow, 249; paternalistic attitudes toward, 249; begin to shift allegiances, 250; denied place in politics, 256; and impact of Pearsall Plan, 258; fight to desegregate schools, 269–84 passim; and segregated tourism, 297; and *The Negro Motorist Green Book*, 297; story of, at Somerset Plantation, 302–3; Hindu-speaking slave in North Carolina, 337
African Methodist Episcopal Church, 160
African Methodist Episcopal Zion Church, 160
African Muslim slave in North Carolina, 337
Africans: enslavement of, 5, 8; in Albemarle region, 87–88, 90–91; in Cape Fear region, 91–92
Alamance County, 135; erects marker to Battle of Alamance, 115

Albemarle Sound region: plantation system in, 87–90; Quakers and slavery in, 93–95; always part of a global economy, 332–33; connection to Chesapeake market, 363; rivalry with Cape Fear region, 366
Alcoa Aluminum Company, 384
Alexander, Benjamin (land agent), 121
Alexander, Kelly: heads state NAACP, 272, 275
Alexander, Moses (land agent), 121
Alexander County: African American resort in, 297
Algonquians, 49; admire English technology, 50
Allenstand Cottage Industries, Inc., 303
Allenstand crafts center, 303
Allen v. State Board of Education of North Carolina, 208
All-Healing Springs (African American resort), 297
Alvord, John, 199
Amadas, Philip, 49, 50
Ambler, Chase, 294–95
American Colonization Society: role of blacks in, 156
American Freedmen's Union Commission, 182
American Missionary Association, 183; establishes schools for blacks, 199–200
American Revolution: and rights of free blacks and Indians, 94, 97–98, 104; and links to Regulation, 113–17 passim, 124–37 passim; as one of largest land grabs in North Carolina history, 367
Ames, Dorothea V., 7
Anna T. Jeanes Fund, 203
Anson County, 118, 120, 121

Appalachian culture: interpreted at Great Smoky Mountains National Park, 303
Appalachian National Park, 294, 295
Arch, Davy, 306
Artis, Fannie, 179
Artis, John Edward, 179
Ashe, Samuel A., 2
Asheville: as tourist mecca, 292–93; Board of Trade, 294
Asheville Citizen, 301
Ashley, S. S., 198
Atkins, Jasper Alston (civil rights lawyer), 206; sues to desegregate schools, 207–9
Atkins, Simon Green (black educator), 199–201; establishes Winston-Salem State Teachers College, 204
Atlantic Ocean, 14, 15, 17–18
Austin, Louis, 275, 283
Autry, George, 324
Avery County: construction of Little Sugar Mountain in, 298
Aycock, Charles B., 261; leads white supremacy campaign, 202; promotes "universal education," 202–3, 212–13, 244, 247, 255; election of, 242–43
Ayllón, Lucas Vázquez de, 41

Backcountry: settlement of, 111
Bacon's Rebellion (1676), 60, 63, 64
Bailey, Josiah, 250, 339
Bailyn, Bernard, 55, 334
Banks, Emeline, 183
Baptists, 6, 9; expansion of, 145, 147–48, 153–54, 156–59; black, 160–61
Baptist State Convention of North Carolina: established, 154
Barlowe, Arthur, 49, 50
Barnwell, John: Indian allies of, 71; leads expedition into North Carolina, 71–73
Bassett, John Spencer: writes about Regulators, 116; in Trinity College academic freedom case, 388
Bateman, Parmelia, 173
Bath, N.C., 27
Battle of Alamance (1771), 113, 136, 137

Batts, Nathaniel, 144
Baucom, Luke, 231
Bayly, C. A., 334
Bay River Indians, 64
Beaufort County, 282
Beck, Robin, 48
Berry, Harriett Morehead, 294
Berry site: excavation of, 46–47
Beyle, Thad, 241
Biblical Recorder, 154; and slavery debate, 159
Bickett, Thomas: progressive policies of, 247–49
Biltmore Estate, 305
Biltmore Industries, 305
Bird, Valentine: slaves in estate of, 90
Black Codes: limit freedmen's rights, 170–71
Blount, Tom: remains neutral in Tuscarora War, 67–69, 77–78
Blue Ridge Parkway, 295
Blythe, Jarrett (Cherokee chief), 300
Board of Trade: sets fees, 123
Boomer v. Beaufort County Board of Education (1968), 282
Bound labor: as imported indentures, 88–89
Bounty money: for Union troops, 172, 173
Bowles, Hargrove "Skipper," 290–91
Bowles, James, 133–34
Boyd, Josephine, 277–79
Boyd, William K., 2
Branchhead Boys, 252, 255
Briarhoppers (string band), 224, 225
Broughton, J. Melville, 254
Broughton High School (Raleigh), 276
Brown, Susan, 185
Brown v. Board of Education (1954), 241, 256, 261, 381, 386; and desegregation of schools, 269–84 passim
Brynjolfsson, Erik, 344
Bullock, Marva, 281
Burke, Thomas, 132–33
Burma, 213
Burnside, Ambrose, 29; organizes Union regiments, 168

Burrington, George: issues blank patents, 131, 366
Business progressivism: defined, 246–47; implemented, 249, 255, 256, 261–62; repudiated by Republicans, 263. *See also* Progressivism
Busing, 10; achieves desegregation, 208–9
Butler, John, 134

Cabarrus County, 119
Caldwell, David, 149
Caldwell, Joseph, 153
Calvinism, 111
Campbell, Alexander: and Campbellites, 158
Campbell, Karl E., 10
Cape Fear region: rise of plantation system in, 91–92; rivalry with Albemarle region, 366
Cape Hatteras National Seashore, 295
Caribbean plantation system: and North Carolina's pursuit of, 86, 87
Carlton, David, 321, 343
Carolina Motor Club: and tourism, 296
Carolinas, Inc.: promotes tourist travel, 296
Carolina Tar Heel String Band, 217
Carowinds theme park, 308
Carr, Julian Shakespeare, 115
Carr Junior High School (Durham), 279
Carter, James (deputy land agent), 121
Carteret, Peter (Colleton Island planter), 89
Cary Rebellion (1709–11): contributes to Tuscarora War, 75, 77
Catawba River: area of early Spanish settlements, 357
Catechna Alliance, 61, 63, 69, 72, 74–77; allies (Tuscaroras, Corees, Neuses, Bear Rivers), 61
Catechna Town, 61, 66–67
Caveats: entered against land claims, 129
Cecelski, David: *Along Freedom Road: Hyde County, North Carolina, and the Fate of Black Schools in the South*, 270
Chafe, William: *Civilities and Civil Rights: Greensboro, North Carolina, and the Black Struggle for Freedom*, 270
Chambers, Julius, 212, 282–83
Chapel Hill: as location for public university, 358, 367
Chapman, Robert, 153
Charles II (king of England), 118–19
Charlotte, N.C.: and rise of banking, 11; and desegregation of schools, 194, 209, 212, 270; as center of southern Piedmont, 217; and Carowinds, 308; impact of 2007–9 recession on, 343; as banking and sports center, 383
Charlotte and Mecklenburg County Parents Committee, 276
Charlotte-Mecklenburg School System, 212, 270
Charlotte Second Ward School, 204
Charter schools: growth of, 212–13
Chatham, Thurmond, 274
Cherokee Historical Association, 300–301, 306–7
Cherokee Indian Crafts Co-op, 307
Cherokee Indians: role of, in Tuscarora War, 70, 73; and removal, 99–100; and development of *Unto These Hills*, 300–301; and story of, in Great Smoky Mountains National Park, 304; and revival of crafts, 305–7; and Qualla Boundary, 306–7; and cultural tourism, 307; and Harrah's Casino, 308; and removal after 1831, 374
Chesnutt, Charles Waddell, 199
Childs, Thomas (land agent), 121
Chisca Indians, 45
Chowan Indians, 64
Christensen, Rob, 249
Christian Connection, 145
Church of England, 111, 119, 146; disestablished, 150–51
Citizenship: as persistent theme in North Carolina history, 5; as a debated issue, 356
Civil rights: demonstrators, 5; movement, 10, 255, 261; lawsuits to desegregate

Index 397

schools, 208; sit-ins begin, 260, 269; and opposition to Pearsall Plan, 269
Civil Rights Act: 1866, 188; 1964, 270, 281
Civil War: caused little change in North Carolina, 375
Clark, David, 339
Clarkson, Heriot (Little Switzerland owner), 297
Class tensions: provoke Regulators, 111, 123
Climate change, 20–22; defined, 15
Coastal storms: and effect on ecosystems, 22–24
Coats, Andrew, 172
Coats, Annie, 173
Cobb, James C., 11–12
Coclanis, Peter A., 11–12, 321; "Southern Textiles in Global Context," 343
Cohn, David, 321
Cole, Gatsey (legatee), 166, 176
Colleton Island: Peter Carteret plantation on, 89
Collins family: and Somerset Plantation, 302–3
Collins, Josiah, III, 303
Collins, Josiah, IV, 303
Colonial Records of North Carolina, 116
Columbia (record producer), 226
Commons House of Assembly, 122
Confederate bonds: worthlessness of, 169
Confederate States of America: compared to Regulation, 116; and North Carolina secession vote, 372
Confiscation: of loyalist property, 127, 134
Congress of Racial Equality, 281
Connor, Abram, 185
Connor, Charlotte, 185
Connor, Robert D. W., 2, 113; endorses white supremacy, 3
"Conquest of Canaan": as most suitable genesis story for North Carolina, 361–62
Cooper, Anna Julia (black educator), 199
Cooperative Sewing Society, 184–85
Corbin, Francis (land agent), 121
Core Tom, 76
Cornwallis, Charles Lord, 133, 136

"Cotton Mill Blues" (Wilmer Watts and the Lonely Eagles), 227
"Cotton Mill Colic" (McCarn): depicts mill conditions, 227–31
Counts, Dorothy, 278
Courthouse rings, 118, 130
Coverture, 176; reversed by 1868 constitution, 188–89
Craig, Locke, 245–46; signs bill for Mt. Mitchell State Park, 295
Crazy Mountaineers (string band), 225
Croatan Normal School: for Lumbees, 201
Croom, Simon, 178
Cullowhee Normal School: coeducational, 201
Culture: as persistent issue in North Carolina history, 356

Daniels, Josephus: leads white supremacy campaign, 202, 244; as political operative, 246
Dare, Eleanor, 300
Dare, Virginia, 300
Davidson County, 119
Davie Country, 120
Davis, Archie K., 257
Day, John: leads migration to Liberia, 156
Day, Thomas (c. 1801–61): as free black cabinetmaker, 95, 97, 156
Day, William P., 294
de Bry, Theodor: 1590 map, 26, 50
de la Bandera, Juan, 44, 48
Dell Computer Co.: and recruitment efforts by Winston-Salem, 322, 325–26
Democratic Party, 386–88; and white supremacy campaigns, 243–44; dominates North Carolina politics, 244–63 passim, 271; factions in, 245
Depression (Great): as tourism catalyst, 295–96
Dewey, Thomas, 253
Dickey, James, 126
di Lampedusa, Giuseppe Tomasi: *Leopard*, 346
Diseases: impact on Indians, 52
Disfranchisement, 202, 243–45, 271, 275
Dismal Swamp, 87, 94

Dismal Swamp Canal: construction of, 27, 29
Disosway and Guion (bank), 170
Divorces: granted by 1868 Constitutional Convention, 188–89
Dixon, Dorsey, 219; composes work songs, 227, 233; as Christian fundamentalist, 230–33
Dixon, Howard, 230–33
Doctor Bennett's Mountain Boomers (string band), 225
Douglas, Davison: *Reading, Writing, and Race: The Desegregation of the Charlotte Schools*, 270, 277
Drake, Sir Francis, 53
Dromgoole, Edward, 151
Dudley, Elias, 174
Dudley, Margaret, 174
Duke University: and development of Research Triangle Park, 319–20
Dunkers (German and Swiss Baptists): land of, confiscated, 128–29
Dunlap, Eula Wellmon, 200
Durham, N.C.: and desegregation of schools, 272; and growth of NAACP membership, 276
Durham City School Board, 279
Durham Committee on Negro Affairs, 276, 279
Durham High School, 279
Dykeman, Wilma: on Old Salem, 302

Eastern Band of Cherokee Indians, 300–301. *See also* Cherokee Indians
Economic development: effect on North Carolina coastal system, 33–37; effect of World War II on North Carolina, 316; and globalization of economies, 332–39 passim; and North Carolina's "middle-income trap," 341; and human capital versus "robot armies," 344
Edenton, N.C., 27
Edenton district court, 122
Edmondson, William, 93
Education: religious influences on, 6–7, 152–54; as human capital, 9–10; and desegregation, 10–11, 207–9, 212, 269–83 passim; and history of public schools, 194–213; North Carolina's public schools rank last, 201; and white supremacy campaigns, 202–3; addition of twelfth grade, 204, 207; and increased funding for black schools, 206–7; resegregation, 212–13; school construction, 244; and debate on Darwin, 245; to combat illiteracy, 247; and *Brown* decision, 256, 258–59; start-up and retraining programs to lure industry, 321, 324–25; chronic underinvestment in, 322, 324; persistent issue in North Carolina history, 356
Educational capital, 194–95
Educators, black: lose positions with desegregation, 283
Edwards, Jane, 186–87
Eisenhower, Dwight, 279
Ekirch, Roger, 125
Elementary and Secondary Education Act (1965), 281
Elizabeth City Independent, 298–99
Elizabeth City Normal School, 201
Ellis, Thomas: opposes integration, 259
English colonization, 7; fails at Roanoke Island, 55; in backcountry, 111; and relations with Indians, 362–63
Entries: for land, 127, 128, 129
Environmental protection: relaxed to attract industry, 322–23
Episcopalians, 156
Ervin, Samuel J., Jr., 263
Estis, John, 135
Etheridge, R. Bruce: and tourism, 296
Evangelical religion, 8; dominates North Carolina, 144–45; geography of, 144–61 passim; defends slavery, 151; supports prohibition, 246

Fanning, Edmund: target of Regulators and revolutionaries, 127, 131, 134
Fayetteville Normal School: as first for blacks, 200–201. *See also* State Normal Colored School
Fearing, D. B., 299

Feeley, Stephen, 8
Fees: set by Board of Trade, 123
Ferguson, James, 282
First National Bank of New Bern, 170
Fisher, Fred, 232
Fitch, William Edwards: writes about Regulators, 116–17
Forbush, James, 126
Foreign investment: competition for specific companies (BMW, Mercedes, Michelin, Nissan), 322–25; recruitment of foreign companies to North Carolina, 322–25
Fort Bragg: desegregates schools, 272
Fort Christanna: Virginia refuge for Saponis, Nottaways, Tuscaroras, and Meherrins, 67
Fort Neoheroka: in Tuscarora War, 364. *See also* Neoheroka
Fort San Juan, 7, 44, 45–47
Foster, Gwin, 219
Fowle, Nellie, 185
Fox, George, 93; North Carolina itinerary of, 144, 146
Foxx, Anthony: supports integrated schools, 194–95, 196, 209
Foy, Julia Ann, 178
Foy, Samuel, 174
Franklin, John Hope: *The Free Negro in North Carolina, 1790–1860*, 103; on free blacks in North Carolina, 103–4
Free blacks: disfranchised, 6; erosion of rights, 97–104; as "persons of color," 100–103, 373–75; and orchestra at Sulphur Spring Hotel, 292; in North Carolina to 1835, 370; excluded by 1835 constitution, 370, 375; excluded after Reconstruction, 376–77
Freedman's Savings and Trust Co., 9; established for freedmen, 166–89 passim
Freedmen's Bureau, 168; defends Civil Right Act (1866), 170–71; works with bank officials, 172; agents of, enforce gender roles, 187; establishes schools for blacks, 199
Freedmen's Convention (1865), 198

Freedom of choice plan, 282
Free labor, 170, 171; as Reconstruction goal for freedmen, 168
Free market, 170; as Reconstruction goal for freedmen, 168
"Freemen": as used in North Carolina constitution (1776), 369; in 1835 constitution, 370
French: settle backcountry, 111
French Huguenots, 362
Frinks, Golden, 281
Frohock, John (land agent), 121–22
Frohock, Thomas (land agent), 121–22
Fundamental Constitutions (1669), 146
Furniture industry, 11, 262

Galifianakis, Nick, 386
Gallay, Allan, 7
Galloway, Abraham (delegate to 1868 Constitutional Convention), 189
Gardner, O. Max, 261; defeated in primary, 249; governorship of, 250–51; appoints Kerr Scott agriculture commissioner, 252; opposes racist rhetoric, 255; restructures government, 256; promotes tourism, 295, 296
Gaston, William J., 157; as author of state song "The Old North State," 359–60
Gastonia, N.C., 251
Gavin, Robert, 260
General Education Board (Rockefeller Foundation), 203
Genesis story: North Carolina lacks one, 357; and failure of Spanish and English colonization, 357–58; and Mecklenburg Declaration as a spurious story, 359; other states' genesis stories, 361; and "conquest of Canaan" as best traditional genesis story, 361–62
Geology: defined, 14; coastal plain systems, 14–37 passim; North Carolina as land of water, 87; as fundamental influence on North Carolina history, 355
George II (king of England), 120
German Palatines, 362
German Reformed church, 145

Germans: settle backcountry, 111, 120, 136
Gershenhorn, Jerry, 10–11
Gillespie Park School (Greensboro), 277
Gilmore, Glenda Elizabeth, 9–10
Global economy, 11; as persistent theme, 5; and history of globalization, 332–39; in new narrative, 382
Glorious Revolution of 1688–89. *See* Revolution of 1688–89
Glymph, Thavolia, 181–82, 193n40
Goal displacement, 209, 212
Godding, Becky, 177–78
Godding, Sally, 178
Goodrich, Frances Louisa, 304
"Good Roads State," 249, 294, 316–17
Governance: as fundamental motif of North Carolina history, 355
Graham, Frank Porter, 206, 246, 261; appointed to U.S. Senate, 252; and 1950 U.S. Senate primary, 254–55
Graham, William A.: writes about Regulators, 114
Grandfather clause, 202, 247, 271
Grandfather Mountain: as tourist attraction, 290, 297
Grandy, Moses, 175
Granganimeo, 49, 50, 55
Grant, Roy "Whitey," 224
Granville, Lord (John Carteret), 120, 121, 366
Granville County, 118
Granville District: and land disputes, 120, 121, 125, 126, 130, 136, 366, 367, 369
Gray, James A., 302
Great Recession: impact of, on North Carolina, 345
Great Smoky Mountains National Park, 295, 303–4
Great Trading Path, 135, 384
Green, Paul: *The Lost Colony*, 298–300
Greenberg, Jack, 280
Greene, Christina, 276
Greene, Nathanael, 384
Greene, Tyler, 316, 317
Greene Monument Association, 114–15
Greensboro, N.C.: and beginning of sit-ins, 260, 270; and harassment of black students and parents, 276; ordered to desegregate schools, 282–83
Greensboro Senior High School, 201, 277
Green v. County School Board (1968), 282
Gregory, Thomas D.: writes about Regulators, 116
Grenville, Sir Richard, 53
Grizzard, Lewis, 321
Grove, E. W., 305
Grove Park Inn resort, 305–6
Grovey v. Townsend (1935), 206
Guatari (Indian town), 383
Guilford Battleground, 115
Guilford County, 129, 130

Haley, Alex: *Roots*, 303
Halifax district court, 122, 134
Hall, Jacquelyn Dowd: *Like a Family: The Making of a Southern Cotton Mill World*, 234
Hamilton, J. G. de Roulhac, 2; prejudice against blacks, 3
Hanes, Frank Borden, 257
Hanes, Robert M., 266n35
Hanes, Robert M., Mrs., 257
Harding High School (Charlotte), 278
Harrah's Cherokee Casino, 308
Harriet-Henderson mills, 257
Harriot, Thomas, 26, 49, 362; scientific studies of, 7, 41
Harris, James Henry, 188–89
Hart, Thomas, 131–32
Harvey, Roy, 224
Haskett, Triphemia, 173
Hawfields: land disputes in, 131–37 passim
Hawks, Francis L.: writes about Regulators, 114; *History of North Carolina* (1858), 358–59
Helms, Senator Jesse, 252, 263, 386–87; supports Willis Smith, 254–56; opposes integration, 259; as national power broker, 387
Henderson, Archibald, 3
Hendersonville, N.C.: as early resort town, 292
Highland Games, 308

Index 401

Highlands, N.C.: as early resort town, 292
High Rock Lake, 384
Hillbilly music: among textile workers, 6; rise of, 10; origins of, 217–35 passim; urban-industrial origins of, 218, 224; shaped by mass culture, 222, 233; offers response to modern South, 230, 234; critiques moral decline, 230–33; national popularity of, 234
Hillsborough district court, 122; disrupted by Regulators, 110–11; orders new survey, 133
Hinderaker, Eric, 63
Historians: creating new paradigm, 3–4
Historical Sketches of North Carolina, 114
Hix, Robert (Virginia trader), 71
Hobsbawm, Eric J., 334
Hodges, Luther H., *257*; becomes governor, 256; recruitment of low-wage industries, 257, 275, 316, 319; and development of Research Triangle Park, 257, 319–20, 321; promotes Pearsall Plan, 258–59, 271–72, 274, 280; and end of Shelby Dynasty, 261; political cartoons of, 273, 320; tries to suppress NAACP, 275–76
Hoey, Clyde R., *299*; makes concessions to black education, 206–7
Holden, William Woods, 116, 198
Holmes, Preston, 275
Holshouser, James E., 262, 386
Holt, Edwin Michael (governor), 137–38
Holt, Elwyna, 276
Holt, Joseph, Jr., 276
Holt, Joseph, Sr., 276
Holt, Michael: and disputed lands, 135–38
Holt, Thomas, 171
Home schooling: growth of, 212–13
Honolulu Strollers (string band), 225
Hood, James Walker: as missionary, 160; as delegate to 1868 Constitutional Convention, 188–89; as educator, 198–200
Hoover, Herbert, 250
Horton, George Moses (1797–1884) (slave poet), 97
Hot Springs Hotel, Madison County, 292

Howard Johnson's restaurant: efforts to integrate in Durham, 281
"How Can I Keep My Mind on Driving" (Three Tobacco Tags) 231–32
Howe, George, 53
Howe, Harold H., II, 282
Hoyt, William K., 302
Huber, Patrick, 10
Hudson, Charles, 45
Hunt, James B., Jr., 255, 263, 324, 387
Hunter, Kermit: *Unto These Hills*, 300–301
Hunter, W. H. (Union chaplain), 160
Husband, Herman: as Regulator spokesman, 115, 120, 127, 150; supports Revolution, 125; as evangelical, 149
Hutton, James (trustee for Wachovia), 367
Hyde, Edward: ill-fated governorship of, 365
Hyde County, N.C., 270, 283

IBM: lured to Research Triangle Park, 321
"I Didn't Hear Anybody Pray" (Dorsey Dixon): and hillbilly religion, 231–32
Immigration: of English, Scots, Scots-Irish, Germans, Swiss, and Africans, 5; as persistent theme, 5; and settlement of backcountry, 111; as fundamental motif of North Carolina history, 355
Indentured servitude, 8; William Tryon on bound labor in North Carolina, 85; in North Carolina, 86, 88
Indians: enduring presence of, 5; as enslaved labor, 5, 8, 70–72, 89–90, 91, 333–34, 364; disfranchised, 6; defined as "persons of color," 97–100; removal of, 99–100; residual Indian populations (Chowans, Meherrins, Enos, Sauras, Occaneechis, Waccamaws, Catawbas, and Indians of Robeson County), 100; and John Lawson's account, 354; relations of, with Spanish and English explorers, 362–63; and Indian traders, 364. *See also* Native Americans
Industrial recruitment, 257
Industrial welfare: in mill villages, 225–26

Integration, token, 258–59, 277. *See also* Civil rights
Internal improvements, 6
Iredell County, 119
Ireland, John, 174
Irons, Charles F., 9
Iroquoia: confederacy of, 61, 63, 71, 77; and intervention in Tuscarora War, 78–79n2

Jackson, Andrew: abolishes national bank, 372; and Indian removal, 372
James, Horace: organizes relief for freedmen, 168
James City, 179, 182; founding of, 168; bank depositors from, 185–87
Jarrett, Devereaux, 152
Jefferson, Thomas, 372
Jenkins, Alonzo T. (bank president), 169–70
Jennings, Joe, 300
Jews, 6, 151; and conversion to Christianity, 156
Jim Crow: segregation laws, 244, 376, 380–81; attacked, 249; defended, 255. *See also* Civil rights
Joara (Indian town), 44, 45, 46, 55
Johns, Noble, 184
Johnson, Lyndon B., 260
Johnston, Gabriel, 119, 120
Johnston, John, 127
Johnston County, 118
Jolson, Al, 222
Jones, H. G., 114
Jones, Jacqueline, 183, 193n40
Jones, Joseph Seawell "Shocco," 358
Jones, Lucy Mae, 278
Jordan, B. Everett, 266n35
Jourdan, Mary, 185
Joyner, William T., 277
Julius T. Rosenwald Fund, 204, 381. *See also* Rosenwald schools
Justices of the peace, 122, 123, 129

Kannapolis, N.C.: Pillowtex factory closing in, 343
Kehoe, Emeline, 173

Kelley Harrell and the Virginia String Band, 217–18
Kennedy, John F., 260
Ker, David, 153
Key, V. O., Jr., 10, 261; on North Carolina's progressive plutocracy, 241–42, 246, 251, 338–40
King, Mitchell: summers at Flat Rock, 292
King Hancock, 68
King Philip's War, 60
Kitchin, W. W., 245–47
Ku Klux Klan, 277–78
Kyi, Aung San Suu: decries decline of school system in Burma, 213

Labor: systems of, 5; sharecropping, 5, 10; tenancy, 5, 10; "unfree," 8; strikes, 251, 257; right-to-work law, 253; fresh-off-the-farm labor supply, 317–18; retraining programs, 321–22; start-up training for new industry, 321–22; "New and Expanding Industry Training Program," 322
Lake, I. Beverly, Sr.: opposes integration, 259; runs for governor, 259–60, 280
Lamas, Alexander, 262
Lambert, Henry, 306, 307
Land: as persistent theme, 4; as Regulator grievance, 9, 117–38 passim; and American Revolution as major land grab, 367
Lane, Ralph, 26; attacks Roanoke Indians, 53
Lanman, Charles (early travel writer), 292–93
Larkins, John, 259–60
Lathbury, George, 134
Laundering, 183
Lawson, John, 7, 362, 383; publishes *New Voyages to Carolina*, 1; identifies Indian groups, 44; collaboration and capture of, 61, 76; and search for Weyanoke Creek, 65; journey across Carolina, 354; in Tuscarora War, 364, 365
Lazarus, Henry, 156

Lazarus, Rebecca, 156
Lederer, John, 383
Lefler, Hugh T., 3
Lehman, Harriet, 173
Le Jau, Francis, 71–72
Leloudis, James, 202
Lincoln, Abraham, 375
Lincoln County, 127–29
Lind, Michael: *Salon* article on North Carolina's "poverty pimps," 345
Lindsey, Thomas (photographer), 293
Link, William A., 3, 336; *North Carolina: Change and Tradition in a Southern State*, 270
Lipsitz, George, 228
Literacy test, 197, 202, 243, 247, 271
Little Sugar Mountain resort, 298
Little Switzerland resort, 297
Livingstone College, 200; produces black leaders, 381
Locke, Francis, 127
Lords proprietors, 119
Lost Colony, 7; development of outdoor drama on, 298–300
Lost Colony, The (Paul Green), 298–300
Loyalists: as dissenters, 5; lands of, confiscated in Revolution, 367–68
Luebke, Paul, 262
Lumbee Indians: normal school for, 201
Luna y Arellano, Tristán de, 41
Lutherans, 145
Lyons, Elijah, 126

Macon, Nathaniel, 5
Madison County, 304
Mainer, J. E., 219, 225
Mainer, Wade, 219
Major, Nick: interrogated by John Lawson, 66
Malone, Bill C., 218–19, 236n4
Manteo (Indian): visits England, 50–51
Manumission: Quaker attempts at, 93–95; and abolition of manumission system, 94–95
March on Washington (1963), 281
Marion, N.C., 251

Marketable goods (rice, tobacco, indigo), 85
Marshall, Daniel, 147–48
Marshall, Martha Stearns, 149–50
Marshall, Thurgood, 276
Martin, François Xavier: *History of North Carolina from the Earliest Period* (1829), 358
Martin, James G.: and Somerset Plantation, 303
Martin, Josiah, 124
Marx, Karl, 319, 334
Mattamuskeet Indians, 64
Maxwell, Charlotte, 185
Mayberry Days, 308
McAden, Hugh, 149
McAfee, Andrew, 344
McCarn, David, 219; composes work songs, 227–31, 233
McCrory, Pat, 263
McCulloh, Henry Eustace (land speculator), 119–22, 127, 135, 136–37
McDonald, Ralph, 246, 251
McKissick, Andree, 278
McKissick, Evelyn, 279
McKissick, Floyd, 279
McKissick, Joycelyn, 278, 281
McKissick-Melton, Charmaine, 279
McLean, Angus: and tourism, 294
McMillan, Bill, 209, 212
McMillan, James B., 209
Mebane, Alexander, Jr., 133
Mecklenburg County, 118, 119, 120, 129; asks black parents to pay for schools, 204
"Mecklenburg Declaration of Independence," 114; date of, observed with North Carolina secession from Union, 359; nicknamed "Mec Dec," 359; mythical North Carolina founding story, 359, 372
Meherrin Indians: border status of, 66–68
Menéndez de Avilés, Pedro: and Juan Pardo, 42, 45
Meredith, Thomas, 154
Merrell, James, 63

Methodists, 6, 9; expansion of, 145, 151–52, 156, 157–58, 159–60; itinerants, 151–52; and slavery, 152, 159; and creation of Methodist Episcopal Church South, 159
Methodist Youth Fellowship, 279
Mexico: outsourcing of North Carolina jobs to, 325–26; comparison of North Carolina to, 329
Mico ("great lords,") 44
Migration: as fundamental motif of North Carolina history, 355
Militia service, 123
Mill hands: as musicians, 219, 222; working conditions of, 221; consumers of mass culture, 221–22, 233, 234; dominate hillbilly music, 223; as transients, 227, 238n18
Mill villages: as outgrowth of textile industry, 221; musical culture of, 222; industrial welfare in, 225–26
Mississippi: similarities with North Carolina, 318–19
Missouri ex rel. Gaines v. Canada (1938): impact on education in North Carolina, 206
Mitchell, Elisha, 153
Modernity: reflected in hillbilly music, 228
Modernizers: as political faction, 262
Montgomery County, 119; and harassment of black students and parents, 276
Montoac (Indian term for magic), 50, 52–53
Moore, David, 7
Moore, James: leads expedition into North Carolina, 73–74; Indian allies of (Yamasees, Waxhaws, Essaws, Catawbas), 74; becomes North Carolina land speculator, 365
Moore, John W.: writes about Regulators, 115
Moore, L. B.: and tourism, 296
Moore, Maurice: as North Carolina land speculator, 365
Moore, Stephen, 181; describes freedmen, 171

Moravians, 6, 362; as dissenters, 5; as slaveholders, 91; settle backcountry, 111; and confiscation of land, 129, 367; friends to German settlers, 136; Wachovia settlement of, 146–47; develop Old Salem, 301–2
Mordecai, Ellen, 156
Morrison, Cameron: and good roads movement, 249, 294
Morton, Hugh: as tourism promoter, 290–91; owns Grandfather Mountain, 297
Moseley, Edward: as slaveholding planter, 88; vast landholdings of, 131, 365; and Tuscarora War, 365
Moses Cone Hospital (Greensboro), 281
Mountain Ridge Protection Act, 298
Mount Mitchell (first state park), 295
Moyano de Morales, Hernando, 45, 48
Mulattos: and mixed race people in North Carolina, 100–102
Murphey, Archibald DeBow, 6; aspirations to write a state history, 358; as proponent of internal improvements, 371
Murray, James: as Cape Fear planter, 92; imports slaves from Africa, 92
Murray, Pauli: sues for admittance to University of North Carolina, 206–7
Music. *See* Hillbilly music
Musical culture: in southern Piedmont, 226–27

Nantahala Outdoor Center, 308
Narrative: new needed for North Carolina history, 354–57; new for North Carolina history, 357–89 passim
Narváez, Pánfilo de, 41
NASCAR: Hall of Fame, 308; as economic engine, 382–83
Nash, Francis, 131–32
National Association of Colored People (NAACP): successful lawsuits of, 270; North Carolina branch, 272; efforts to suppress, 275–76, 280; and growth of membership, 276; leads protests to integrate schools, 281
National Basketball Association, 382

Index 405

National Center for Health Statistics (U.S. Environmental Protection Agency): at Research Triangle Park, 321

National Football League, 382

National Industrial Recovery Act (1933), 221

National Interstate and Defense Highways Act (1956), 316–17

National Park Service, 303, 304

Native Americans: encountered by John Lawson, 1; impede settlement, 7; prehistory eras, 15–16, 24–26, 43; language groups, 44; impact of early European colonization, 56. *See also* Indians

Natural environment: as fundamental motif of North Carolina history, 355

Neal, Phyllis, 183

Negro Motorist Green Book, The, 297

Nelson, Charles A. (bank cashier), 171–72, 182

Nelson, Emma, 173

Nelson, Jane C., 173

Neoheroka: fort and battle, 61, 73, 74

New Bern, N.C.: becomes colonial capital, 27, 366–67; in Tuscarora War, 61, 75, 76; and Freedman's Savings and Trust Co., 166–89 passim; bank closures in, 169–70

New Bern district court, 122

Newby, Jane, 172

New Hanover County, 131

New narrative for North Carolina history, 357–89 passim

Newsome, Albert Ray, 3

New Voyage to Carolina, A (1709), 1; and "A Description of North Carolina" as evocation for a new narrative of North Carolina history, 354; features John Lawson's essays on Indians and present state of Carolina, 354; as inspiration and guide for *New Voyages to Carolina*, 354–55

New Voyages to Carolina (2017): persistent themes in, 4–7, 355; uses John Lawson's journeys to produce a new narrative of North Carolina history, 354–57; and genesis story, 357–60; offers new narrative of North Carolina history, 357–89 passim; examines fundamental periods of North Carolina history, 360–89 passim

Nineteenth Amendment, 249

Norris, Emma, 185

North American Free Trade Agreement (NAFTA): effect on jobs in North Carolina, 326, 328–29

North Carolina: history of, 1–2; new interpretations of, 1–2; historical literature of, 2–4; character of, 3–4; old and new paradigms of, 3–4; cultural legacy of, 4; progressive reputation of, 4, 9, 241, 247, 269, 280, 316–18, 377–83; dissenting tradition in, 5; religious traditions of, 6; as "land of water," 7; and absence of genesis story, 7, 357–60; anti-authoritarian tradition of, 8; slaveholders in, 8; efforts to attract industry, 11; geology and coastal system of, 14–37 passim; draining of wetlands, 31; colonial studies of, 60–61; Indian policy of, 63–65; disputes with Virginia over land and Indians, 66–69; invites South Carolina's intervention, 69–70; internal divisions on Tuscarora War, 75–76; impact of Tuscarora War on Indians, 77–78; William Tryon's view of bound labor in North Carolina, 85; colonial slave population, 85–86; copies Virginia and South Carolina plantation models, 87–88, 99–100; enslaved Indians in, 88–89, 90; slave code, 90; and transition to slave labor, 89–90; "takes up" manumitted slaves, 93–95; and slavery as an imperative in North Carolina, 93–104; restricts rights of free blacks, 97–104; defines persons of color, 100–102; becomes separate colony, 119; compared to Pennsylvania, 120; women in Reconstruction, 166–89; debates on public education, 194–213 passim;

406 *Index*

and illiteracy rates, 201, 203; attack on schools decried, 213; education in, ranks near bottom, 275; new plant investment in, 275; and tourist industry, 290–309 passim; as "Good Roads State," 294; Variety Vacationland campaign, 296–97; devotion to nonunion manufacturing, 316–29 passim; low manufacturing wages of, 318–19; similarities to Mississippi, 318–19; manufacturing recruitment efforts of, 319–29 passim; competition of, with South Carolina for manufacturers, 322–24; tax subsidy programs for new industry, 322–25, 327–29; loss of jobs to Mexico and China, 326–29; likened to Mexico for cheap labor for foreign investors, 327–29; as always global economically, 332–36; in global economy, 332–46 passim; profile of, in nineteenth century, 334–35; decline in manufacturing rank begins in 1860, 335; plantations as economic base throughout nineteenth century, 336; economic decline begins in 1930s, 338–40; post-World War II recruitment of low-skill manufacturing jobs, 340–41; relation of, to Sunbelt economies, 340–41, 343; wages in, compared with Bangladesh, 341, 343; impact of 2007–9 recession on employment and wages, 343–44; economic development policy of, 345–46; and fundamental motifs of North Carolina's history, 355; persistent issues in North Carolina's history, 355; and formulating a new narrative for North Carolina's history, 356–57; absence of cultural center or central public university, 357–58; new narrative for North Carolina history, 357–89 passim; earliest state histories of, 358–59; importance of Tuscarora War in history, 361; as land of promise, not a "promised" land, 361–62; limited early trade capacities, 363; North Carolina proprietors, 363–69; as royal colony, 366–67; as experimental state, 370–71; as state ruled by whites only, 371–75; limited impact of Civil War, 375–76; as enlightened slaveholding republic, 375–77; Reconstruction, 376; and turf wars for political power, 384–89; as perpetual middling state, 389

North Carolina Agricultural and Technical College, 206; sit-ins by students from, 260

North Carolina Constitution (1776), 125, 129; and use of term "freemen," 369

North Carolina Constitutional Convention (1835), 369; disfranchises free blacks, 6, 370; defines persons of color, 101–2; religious debate in, 157; reshapes North Carolina as white-governed, Protestant, slave state, 373–75

North Carolina Constitutional Convention (1868): institutes reforms, 188–89

North Carolina Department of Commerce, 291

North Carolina Department of Conservation and Development, 290; Division of State Advertising, 296

North Carolina General Assembly: more powerful than governor, 129; resolves land dispute, 133; establishes public schools, 198; appropriates money for black normal schools, 200–201; passes grandfather clause, 202; threatens to implement prorated taxes, 202; appropriates more money for white schools, 203; enacts pupil assignment law, 269, 271–72; and tourism, 300, 302; and movements in colonial and revolutionary periods, 366–67; supports internal improvements, 370; consolidates powers in 1835 constitution, 374, 376; supports business from 1835 forward, 376; and power over local government, 385

North Carolina "Land of Water," 7, 16, 18, 33, 35

North Carolina Railroad, 6, 376, 384

North Carolina Ramblers, *223*

North Carolina Reader, The (Wiley), 113
North Carolina School for Negroes: secures professional schools, 206
North Carolina State Capitol building(s), 373, 384–85
North Carolina State University: in conception of Research Triangle Park, 319
North Carolina Supreme Court: permits slaves to own hogs, 176; rules against prorating taxes, 199
North Carolina Teachers Association: demands integration of schools, 272, 274; urges retention of black educators, 283
North Carolina: The History of a Southern State (Lefler and Newsome), 3
North Carolina through Four Centuries (Powell), 3
North Carolina: Variety Vacationland (tourist guide), 296

Oath of allegiance: to revolutionary government, 127–28
Oberg, Michael Leroy, 7
Oconaluftee Indian Village, 301
Oden, Allen, 185
Odum, Howard, 319
OKeh (record producer), 218, 226
O'Kelly, James: and Methodist Protestant church, 158
Olde Time Fiddlin' Tunes (catalog), 218
"The Old North State": as state song, 359; as apology for North Carolina's character, 359–60
Old Salem, Inc., 302
Old Salem historic village: development of, 301–2
O'Neal, William, 136
Orange County: as site of land grievances, 117–38 passim
Oratas ("lesser lords"), 44
Orfield, Gary, 281–82

Palmer, E. B., 283
Pangaea, 14, 17
Paramount (record producer), 218
Pardo, Juan, 42, 383; leads expedition, 42–48

Parker, John J., 274
Pattillo, Henry, 152–53; *Plain Planter's Assistant*, 152–53
Pearsall, Thomas, 258, 274, 277
Pearsall Plan, 10, 207, 269; North Carolina's response to *Brown v. Board of Education* (1954), 258–59, 274–77, 280, 283, 381, 388; leads to end of Shelby Dynasty, 261
Pearson, Conrad: files civil rights lawsuits, 279–80, 282
Peer, Ralph S., 217
Pemisapan. *See* Wingina
Penn, William: "holy experiment" in Pennsylvania, 361, 363
Penningroth, Dylan C., 175
Pensions: for Union troops, 172, 174
"Persons of color": as developed in North Carolina, 100–103
Pettey, Charles C. (black bishop): develops African American resort, 297
Pettey, Sarah, 297
Pettigrew State Park, 303
Pfohl, J. Kenneth (Moravian bishop), 302
Philanthropists: and support for black education, 203–4
Phillips, James, 153
Piedmont (southern): center of textile industry, 217, 219, 221; musical culture of, 223–28, 237n12; political power of, 262
Piedmont Middle School (Charlotte), 209
Pillowtex (Kannapolis): largest plant closing in North Carolina history, 343
Pittman, Mary F., 173
Plantation culture: in industrial villages, 5; and colonial pursuit of plantations, 85–92; "plantation system," 86–87, 92; plantation agriculture, 333–35, 337
Planters: rise of, in North Carolina, 87–88
Plessy v. Ferguson (1896), 269, 380, 381
Political realignment: defined, 242–43; after white supremacy campaigns, 244
Politics: as persistent theme in North Carolina history, 5
Polk family: as land agents, 121
Pollock, Thomas: on cause of Tuscarora

War, 61; follows Virginia's policies, 68–69; on South Carolina's assistance, 74–75; as planter and slaveholder, 88, 90–91; and new lands from Tuscarora War, 365
Poll tax, 243, 271
Pomeranz, Kenneth, 333
Ponce de Léon, Juan, 41
Poole, Charlie, 219, *223*; musical influences on, 222–23
Populists: as dissenters, 5; defeated in white supremacy campaigns, 243–44
Poteat, William Louis: and Darwinian controversy, 388
Potter, Robert (U.S. district judge): overturns busing, 212
Potwin, Marjorie: *Cotton Mill People of the Piedmont: A Study in Social Change*, 222
Powell, William S., 3
Powhatan, 54
Poythress, Francis, 151
Presbyterians, 6, 9; expansion of, 148–49, 152–53, 156, 157, 158; influence of, on University of North Carolina, 153
Pritchard, Jeter C., 295
"Progress": as secular term with religious vision, defined, 377, 379; encompasses industrial development, 379, 381–82; encompasses Jim Crow laws, 380; supports separate schools for black children, 380–81
Progressive plutocracy, 10, 350n27; economic foundations of, 11; described in political and historical literature, 241–63 passim; economic policies of, 338–40
Progressive state: North Carolina's reputation for, 316–18, 338–40; and infrastructure for global economy, 337; vision of, defined before Civil War, 375; as virtuous republic, 377–83 passim
Progressivism: for whites only, 9, 338; perpetuates racial and class discrimination, 337; defined as secular vision for North Carolina, 379–81; disguises many sins, 380–82; supports nonunion labor, 381–82; as major animating force for North Carolina, 383. *See also* Business progressivism
Prohibition, 245, 246
Proprietors: as absentee landlords, 363–64; control colony, 363–69; Granville District, 366
Provincial Congress: Third, pardons Regulators, 125; Fifth, approves constitution, 130
Provincial surveyors: John Lawson as, 364; power of, 364, 365; Edward Moseley as, 365
Public schools. *See* Education
Pugh, Daniel: kidnaps Tuscaroras, 66
Pupil assignment law, 269, 271–72, 275, 277, 280

Quakers, 6, 362, 363; antislavery beliefs of, 5, 8, 93, 149; as dissenters, 5, 146; and Tuscarora War, 65, 75, 77; attempt manumissions, 93–95, 104; lands of, confiscated, 129; global network of, 144–45
Qualla Arts and Crafts Mutual, 306
Qualla Boundary (Cherokee reservation), 305–6

Racism: perpetuated by progressivism, 246, 337
Radio stations: broadcast hillbilly music, 224–25
Ragsdale, G. N., 174
Railroads: and tourism, 293
Raleigh, N.C.: and harassment of black students and parents, 276; not North Carolina's cultural center, 358; as permanent capital city, 358, 367; scene of 1835 Constitutional Convention, 373
Raleigh, Sir Walter: expeditions of, 26, 41, 54, 55; failed settlements of, 357
Ramsey, William, 74
Randolph County, 128
Raymond Lindsey's Combinators (string band), 225
RCA Victor (record producer), 228, 231. *See also* Victor Talking Machine

Index 409

Ready, Milton, 3; *Tar Heel State: A History of North Carolina*, 270
Reagan, Ronald, 387
Reconstruction: women in, 166–89; and public schools, 198–99
Redford, Dorothy Spruill, 303
Red Patterson's Piedmont Log Rollers, 218
Regulators: as dissenters, 5, 8–9; disrupt Hillsborough district court, 110–11; as interpreted by historians, 113–17; grievances of, 118–24; pardoned by revolutionaries, 125
Religion, 6; evangelical geographies of, 9; and dominance of evangelicalism, 144–51; and education, 152–54; and blacks, 156, 160–61; and slavery, 158–60; in hillbilly music, 230–33; and black churches' support of integration, 279; as a persistent issue in North Carolina history, 356; North Carolina as land of religious freedom, 362. *See also* Evangelical religion
Republican Party, 252, 386–88; defeated in white supremacy campaigns, 243–44; embraces white supremacy, 246; realignment of, 255; growing strength of, 261, 263; not far from progressive traditions, 388
Research Triangle Park, 257, 317, 319, 321, 326, 340; as "global epicenter of technological innovation," 326–27; as bipartisan engine of economy, 382
Revolutionaries: use land policies to enforce allegiances, 125–37 passim
Revolutionary History of North Carolina (Hawks, Graham, and Swain), 114
Revolution of 1688–89, 111, 119
Reynolds, R. J., Jr.: promotes tourism, 296
Reynolds, Robert "Our Bob," 246
R. H. Rountree and Co., 170
Riggs, Stanley R., 7
Rip Van Winkle State: North Carolina's reputation as, 332, 337
Road building: connects southern Piedmont, 225. *See also* "Good Roads State"
Road work: as form of taxation, 123

Roanoke Island, 7; failed English settlement of, 49, 50, 357
Roanoke Island Historical Association: produces *The Lost Colony*, 298–300
Roberts, Coleman W.: and tourism, 296
Robinson, James: *Why Nations Fail: The Origins of Power, Prosperity, and Poverty*, 338
Rockefeller Foundation, 299
Roman Catholics, 6, 151
Roosevelt, Franklin D., 251, *299*; election of, 242, 250; and civil rights, 255
Rorey, Posey, *223*
Rosenwald schools: support education of African Americans, 204, 207, 381; architectural plans for, 205, 210–11
Rowan County, 118, 119, 120, 126, 127, 128, 129
Rural development: and commitment to rural infrastructure, 317–18; and rural industrialization, 317–18, 327–28
Rural Electrification Administration, 317
Rutherford, Griffith, 128

Saint Augustine, Fla.: founding of, 42
Saint Augustine's College, 199–200; produces black leaders, 381
Saint Joseph's AME Church (Durham), 279
Salisbury district court, 122
Salter, Margaret, 186
San Domingue (Haiti): slave revolt in, 94
Sandy Creek Baptist Association, 147–48, 150
Sanford, Terry, 255, 275; supports Pearsall Plan, 259; runs for governor, 259–61, 280; and meeting on North Carolina tourism, 290–91
Santa Elena, S.C.: founding of, 42, 46
Saponi Indians, 383
Saunders, W. O. (newspaper editor), 298–99
Saura Indians, 383–84
Schaefer, Markus, 329
Scots-Irish: settle backcountry, 111, 120, 136

410   *Index*

Scott, Eliza, 178
Scott, W. Kerr, 246, 261; progressive policies of, 252–54; promotes road-building, 253, 319; elected to U.S. Senate, 255; supports Pearsall Plan, 259; commitment to nonunion manufacturing, 316; commitment to rural electrification, 317
Scottish: settle backcountry, 111
Scruggs, Earl, 235
Seawell, Malcolm, 260
Seely, Fred, 305
Segregation, 244, 258. *See also* Jim Crow
Segregationists: bolt Democratic Party, 253; defend Jim Crow, 255; oppose *Brown* decision, 256, 269–70, 272; harass black students and parents, 276–79
Selden, Samuel, 299
Sharp, Susie, 253
Shelby Dynasty, 251–52, 255, 256, 257, 258, 261
Shepard, James E.: seeks professional schools for blacks, 206
Sheriffs, 122
Sherrill, Homer "Pappy," 225
Sherwood Forest school (Winston-Salem), 207
Shuford, George A., 274
Simkins, George, Jr., 280–81, 283
Simmons, Celia, 174
Simmons, Furnifold M.: leads white supremacy campaigns, 202, 243–44; political machine of, 245–46; defeated, 250; and racist rhetoric, 255
Simmons, Nicholas, 174
Simon G. Atkins High School (Winston-Salem), 209; architectural drawings of, 210–11
Sit-ins: begin in Greensboro, 260, 269, 280, 281
Skinner, Charles, 154
Slater Industrial and State Normal School, 201; produces black leaders, 381. *See also* Winston-Salem State Teachers College

Slaveholders: dominate antebellum politics, 6
Slavery: and Africans, 5; and Indians, 5, 70–72, 88–89, 90, 364; William Tryon on slaves in North Carolina, 85; rise of, in North Carolina, 85–93; slave code, 90; Evangelicals' defense of, 151; and church debates, 158–60; families in, sold away, 178–79; interpreted at Somerset Plantation, 303; and North Carolina's slave economy, 333–34
Slaves: as insurgents, 5
Slover, Charles (bank president), 169–70
Smith, Al, 250
Smith, Benjamin L., 274
Smith, Norman B., 208
Smith, Theodore Clark: writes about Regulators, 117
Smith, Willis, 254
Soelle, George, 149
Somerset Plantation, 302–3; as state historic site, 303; homecoming, 303
Sothell, Seth: as slaveholder, 88
Soto, Hernando de, 41–42
South Carolina: Indian strategy of, 61, 63, 69, 364–65; Indian slave trade system of, 70–72; and Barnwell expedition, 71–73, 77; and Moore expedition, 73–74; North Carolina copies plantation culture of, 87–88
Southern Christian Leadership Conference, 281
Southern Politics in State and Nation (Key), 241
Spangenberg, August, 146–47, 149
Spanish colonization, 7, 41, 55; failed settlements, 357, 362
Sports: as economic engine for North Carolina, 382–83
Spotswood, Alexander: courts Upper Towns, 67; Indian strategy of, 67–69, 72
Stamper, R. F., 307
Standingdeer, Carl, 307
Stanly, John Carruthers (1774–1846), 95
Stanly County, 119

Index 411

Stanton, Eliza, 176–78
Staple crop economy, 85–87, 91–92
Starnes, Richard D., 11
State Normal Colored School (Fayetteville): produces black leaders, 381. *See also* Fayetteville Normal School
Stearns, Shubal, 147–48, 149–50
S. T. Jones and Co., 170
String bands: formation of, 224
Strudwick, Samuel: and disputed land, 131–35
Stupka, Arthur, 304
Stutts, George D.: *Picked Up Here and There*, 227
Suffrage: property limitation on, 6. *See also* Voting; Woman's suffrage
Summey, Reid, 231
Summonses: in land transactions, 128
Surry County, 129
Swain, David L.: writes about Regulators, 114
Swann, Samuel: as slaveholding planter, 88
Swann v. Charlotte-Mecklenburg Board of Education (1971), 209, 283
Swiss: settle backcountry, 111; settle at New Bern, 362

"Taking up": of slaves and free blacks as a North Carolina practice, 93–95, 98–99
Tatum, Isham, 151
Tax lists: used to identify voters, 130
Teachers: salaries between whites and blacks equalized, 207. *See also* Education; Educators, black
Tennessee Valley Authority, 317
Textile companies: sponsor music education, 226
Textile industry, 262; rise of, 10; decline of, 11, 235, 321–22; centered in southern Piedmont, 219; strikes in, 251, 257; growth of, after 1880, 338
Thomas, Rachel, 182–83
Three Tobacco Tags (string band), 231–33
Thuesen, Sarah, 197; *Greater Than Equal: The African American Struggle for Schools and Citizenship in North Carolina, 1919-1965*, 197
Thurman, Strom, 253
Tiernan, Frances (pseud. Christian Reid), 293
Tindall, George, 246–47
Tise, Larry E., 8
Tobacco industry, 11, 262; rise of, in twentieth century, 335–36
Tourism, 11; impact on ecosystems, 32–33; history and strategies, 290–309 passim; and focus on landscape and attractions, 291–96; impact of Great Depression on, 295–96; as catalyst for economic development, 296; segregation in, 297; and cultural attractions, 307–9; and environmental concerns, 307–9; as core economy for North Carolina, 382
Trading Ford (Yadkin River): as strategic place of power, 383–84
Traditionalists: as political faction, 262
Trent, Judy Scales, 209
Trinity College (later Duke University): upholds academic freedom, 388
Troxler, Carole Watterson, 8–9
Truman, Harry, 251, 253, 255
Tryon, William, 150; moves capital to New Bern, 27; on bound labor in North Carolina, 85; role in suppressing Regulation, 114, 115, 124, 131–32; governorship of, 365–66
Tryon County, 120, 129
Tsali (Cherokee hero), 301
Tubize Royal Hawaiian Orchestra, 226
Tullos, Allen, 225
Tuscarora Indians, 7; and role of Upper Towns in war, 67–69, 77–78; migrate to Pennsylvania and New York, 71, 78; possess land for a thousand years, 361; and stories of genesis and exodus from North Carolina, 362; call North Carolina "pine in water," 362; suffer major land grab, 365, 367. *See also* Catechna Alliance
Tuscarora Nation, 364, 365
Tuscarora War (1711-13), 8, 16; history of,

60–78; dries up Indian slave market, 91; as consequential event in North Carolina history, 361, 364–65
Tuskegee Institute, 381

Umstead, William B., 255, 256, 271
Union Baptist Church (Durham), 279
Unionists: as dissenters, 5; in New Bern, 168
Unions, labor: opposition to, 5; North Carolina as least unionized state, 316–24 passim, 345. *See also* Labor
Union troops: family beneficiaries of, 172–74
United States: as experimental nation, 370–71
U.S. Commission on Civil Rights, 280
U.S. Department of Health, Education, and Welfare (HEW), 282
U.S. Fourth Circuit Court of Appeals, 208
U.S. Justice Department, 270
U.S. Route 29: as spine of southern Piedmont, 225
U.S. Supreme Court, 270; overturns grandfather clause, 202; rules in *Brown* decision, 256, 269, 272; strikes down freedom of choice plan, 282
University of North Carolina, Chapel Hill: Presbyterian faculty of, 153; denies admission to black students, 206; assists outdoor drama, 299–300; as force for social betterment, 337; develops growth plan for Enfield, 345; inability to serve as North Carolina's "state" university, 358; and Speaker Ban Law (1963), 388
Unto These Hills (outdoor drama) (Hunter), 300–301, 307, 308

Vance, Rupert, 221
Vanderbilt, Edith, 305
Vanderbilt, George, 295, 305
Van Eps, Fred, 222
Variety Vacationland campaign, 296–99
Victor Talking Machine, 217. *See also* RCA Victor
Virginia: "tributary" Indians in, 63–64; Indian policies of, 63–66; and dividing line issue, 65–66; and Alexander Spotswood's Indian strategy, 67–69, 72; North Carolina copies plantation culture of, 87–88; and control of Albemarle region, 363–64
Vocalion (record producer), 218
Von Graffenried, Christoph, 61, 76
Voting: efforts to limit, 6; qualifications for, 129–30; disfranchisement, 202, 243–45; drops, 245; black, increases, 271; black, crucial in Winston-Salem, 275. *See also* Suffrage; Woman's suffrage

Wachovia, 146–47; and types of settlement, 147; as commercial center, 149
Wade, George, 231
Wake Forest College: established, 154; Darwinism controversy, 388
Wallace, Henry, 253
Wallerstein, Immanuel, 334
Wanchese (Indian), 50–51; destroys English settlement, 53
War of 1812, 370, 371
War of the Regulation (1766–71), 8, 367. *See also* Battle of Alamance; Regulators
Warren, Lindsey, *299*
Washington, Booker T.: supports Rosenwald schools program, 381; lauded by John Spencer Bassett, 388
Washington County, 302
Water: as fundamental motif of North Carolina history, 355
Watson, Alan, 138n4
WBT (radio station), 10; broadcasts hillbilly music, 224–25, 232
"Weave Room Blues" (Dixon): depicts mill conditions, 227
West, I. Edwin, 173
West Charlotte High School, 194, 209, 212
Weyanoke Creek, 65
Wheeler, John H. (Durham banker and attorney): opposes pupil assignment act, 272; resists Pearsall Plan, 274–75

Index 413

Wheeler, John Hill: writes about Regulators, 114; *Historical Sketches of North Carolina, from 1854 to 1851* (1851), 358
White, John: drawings, 7, 41; map, 26; weakness as leader, 53–54
White, Richard, 63
White Citizens' Council (Charlotte), 278
Whitefield, George, 146
White supremacy: as dominant force in politics, 196–97, 201–3, 243–46, 256, 258, 379, 386
Whitfield, Wright, 178
Whittlesey, Eliphalet: attacks Black Codes, 170–71
Wiley, Calvin H.: writes about Regulators, 113–14
Williams, Gatsey (bank depositor), 166, 167, 176
Williams, James, 135
Williams, Mary J., 185
Williams, Robert, 271
Williams, Sharper, 167
Williamson, Hugh: *History of North Carolina* (1812), 358
Willie, Charles, 209
Willis, Mrs. Meade, 257
Wilmer Watts and the Lonely Eagles (string band), 227
Wilmington, N.C.: race riot of 1898, 242–43
Wilmington district court, 122
Wingina, 49, 50; attempts to control English, 51–52, 55; assassinated by English, 52–53
Winston-Salem, N.C.: sued to desegregate schools, 207–9; black vote in, crucial, 275; and courtship of Dell Computer Co., 322, 325
Winston-Salem Journal, 302
Winston-Salem State Teachers College, 204. *See also* Slater Industrial and State Normal School
Woman's College (Greensboro), 201
Woman's suffrage, 6; efforts to secure, 189, 245, 248
Womble, William F., Sr., 208
Women, 167; and banking, 9; as bank depositors, 167; roles of, 171; receive veteran benefits, 172–74; African American, dominate markets, 175–76; occupations of, 182–85; cooperatives of, 184–85; married, and bank accounts, 187; seek reforms in 1868 Constitutional Convention, 188–89; become teachers, 201
Wood, Bradford J., 8
Woodward, C. Vann, 9, 339
World War II: effects of, on industrialization in North Carolina, 316
Worth, Jonathan, 198
"Wreck on the Highway (Acuff)." *See* "I Didn't Hear Anybody Pray"
Wrightsville Beach: early tourist destination, 293–94
Writing North Carolina History (Crow and Tise): generates new research, 2

Yamasee Indians: war against, 60, 74; ally with South Carolina, 69, 71, 73, 74, 76
Yamasee War: curtails Indian slave market, 91
Youth March on Washington for Integrated Schools, 279

Zipf, Karin, 9

www.ingramcontent.com/pod-product-compliance
Lightning Source LLC
Chambersburg PA
CBHW051203300426
44116CB00006B/421